Thinking Strategically About Anti-Corruption Reforms

Sean Fitzpatrick

THINKING STRATEGICALLY ABOUT ANTI-CORRUPTION REFORMS

ADDRESSING FACTORS THAT INCREASE THE LIKELIHOOD AND MAINTENANCE OF CORRUPT EXCHANGES

PETER LANG

Frankfurt am Main · Berlin · Bern · Bruxelles · New York · Oxford · Wien

Bibliographic Information published by Die Deutsche Bibliothek
Die Deutsche Bibliothek lists this publication in the Deutsche Nationalbibliografie; detailed bibliographic data is available in the internet at <http://dnb.ddb.de>.

Zugl.: Hamburg, Univ., Diss., 2003

Cover Design:
Ariel Blanga - Haifa, Israel.

D 18
ISBN 3-631-51393-3
US-ISBN 0-8204-6483-X

© Peter Lang GmbH
Europäischer Verlag der Wissenschaften
Frankfurt am Main 2003
All rights reserved.

Printed in Germany 1 2 3 4 5 7

www.peterlang.de

To Limori

ללימורי,
שעיצבה אותי,
ובזכותה הדבר אפשרי.

ACKNOWLEDGEMENT

This work with cosmetic revisions was prepared as a PhD dissertation within the German Research Foundation (DFG) sponsored "Graduate College in Law and Economics" (Graduiertenkolleg für Recht und Ökonomik), Institute for Law and Economics at Hamburg University. The persons that assisted me in the completion of my undertaking are too numerous to mention. I would, however, like to take this opportunity to thank those who assisted me most in my efforts. In particular, I would like to extend my sincere thanks to Prof. Hans-Bernd Schäfer at Hamburg University for both his faith in me and for giving me the opportunity to participate in this unique program which provided an ideal environment conducive to academic research. I would also like to express my gratitude to other participants and guest professors in the aforementioned program for their comments and contributions in both one-to-one discussion and within a series of formal and informal presentations. In this context, I would like to thank Prof. Roger Bowles at the University of York for comments on a preliminary draft of this work

Prof. Robert Cooter at the University of California, Berkeley deserves special thanks for his approachability and for comments he made on early notions of my work. I would also like to express my appreciation to him for giving me the opportunity to partake in his weekly seminars on law and economics at Berkeley, which provided me with insight on the state-of-the-art of current research. This is also an occasion to recognize the assistance provided to me by Prof. Ugo Mattei at the University of California, Hastings, who invited me as a visiting scholar to the aforementioned law school in the summer of 2001. I would also like to give thanks to Prof. Rainer Tetzlaff from the Department of Political Science at Hamburg University for agreeing to co-supervise my work and for being so benevolent and approachable.

On a more personal level, I would like to thank Angel Castro, a PhD student at Hamburg University, who provided me with much needed assistance in issues related to legal structures in Latin America, and moral support for which I am especially grateful. Moreover, I would like to express my heartfelt gratitude to Victor Castro, formally of the State Comptroller's Office in Peru, for useful tips and information, and especially for sharing some of his intuition and experiences with me. My parents deserve special mention for their warmth and continuous encouragement and support. I would also like to take this opportunity to thank the entire Riza family in Haifa, Israel for their affability and hospitality. Toda Raba! Most of all I would like to thank Limor Riza, to whom I dedicate this work, for her thoughts, support, love and sacrifices.

TABLE OF CONTENTS

FOREWORD

There is a near unanimous position today strongly underscored by statistical evidence among economists, policy analysts and others who have seriously looked at the issue of corruption and development, that corruption, particularly long-term corruption, has an adverse effect on investment and growth. The setting has changed substantially from earlier years when corruption was accredited almost solely to developing countries, where corruption was perceived to be enmeshed intangibly in cultural factors, perhaps even serving a functional role in economic development. These rationalizations have thankfully been dismissed and the ball is now very much in the court of those authors wishing to evince otherwise. Corruption is common to all countries. It tends, however, to inflict greater damage to poor countries, primarily by distorting the allocation of important talent unfavorably from productive activities towards unproductive rent seeking activities, and by substantially weakening incentives to invest, property rights and the rule of law.

As later discussion will explicate, curbing corruption has taken on an increasingly important role in social consciousness, policy debate and reform initiatives. Domestic measures in many countries are reshaping the legal and institutional environment in which government officials operate, as are recent multilateral initiatives by governments, private professional organizations and nonprofit organizations alike. Newspapers commonly bombard us with two types of stories of corruption: One class manifests itself around accusations of improbity and misuse of public office or position by a government official or group of officials, the other takes the shape of political, business and social leaders condemning corruption as a vice that bedevils the nation. Commonly implicit in both groups of stories are strong moral undertones, and it is not difficult to guess that every party wishes to be on the side of the morally righteous. As a game theorist may put it, verbally lashing out at corruption per se is the dominant strategy of not just those persons averse to corruption but also those that actively partake in corrupt transactions. This simple observation makes most of this discussion purely horatory, as are unfortunately many of the reform initiatives undertaken.

Grounded in basic insights largely from game theory and economic theory, this work is policy-oriented. Given, however, the encompassing nature and complexity of the issue, I have taken onboard insights and material from a broad range of disciplines which in a policy-oriented work on curbing corruption of this size can only scarcely and injudiciously afford to be ignored. Influenced primarily by writings on corruption in the law and economics tradition, the approach and framework developed to understand corruption and develop anti-corruption strategies, however, is novel and a significant contribution to the literature.

15

Though from a policy perspective, our work is of primary interest to those interested in reforming governmental institutions and curbing corruption in less developed countries, much of the discussion and mechanisms involved can similarly be considered, sometimes more appropriately, by developed countries.

Chapter I of the dissertation offers a reexamination and critique of the issues. Whilst the literature is vast and diverse and has been studied within a wide range of disciplines, I concentrate primarily on the dominant paradigm in corruption research in the social sciences today, based primarily on micro-economics and new institutional economics, which has made its way into most recent analytical work on corruption well beyond the perimeters of the initial discipline. An aim of this chapter is to offer the reader insight *inter alia* into: early discussion on the concept of corruption and its understanding within the developmental discussion; understanding the costs of corruption with simple economic tools; basic structures and types of corrupt systems; sources of information and efforts at measuring corruption; the development of measures to curb corruption. A corollary aim of this chapter is to place my efforts in context.

Corruption is a form of reciprocal, cooperative behavior. The fact that corruption is a form of cooperative behavior is normally overlooked in the literature or mentioned *en passant* and has never been given systematic attention in developing reform proposals. Even when corruption has been identified as cooperative behavior, central factors that potentially increase the likelihood and maintenance of cooperation have never been analyzed in the context of corruption. This is the main focus of Chapter II. Illustrated later in greater detail, the fact that corruption is a form of cooperative behavior is a mixed blessing. On the one hand, parties need to be able to search for and identify one another, agree on the terms of an agreement and enforce the provisions of the deal without being detected which leaves parties exposed to detection. One can see that in each of these steps, parties must incur substantial risks and there is a significant degree of uncertainty and trust involved. On the other hand, corruption must be understood within the broader perspective of reciprocal rewards and sanctions, often firmly entrenched within regular (legal) social and economic transactions. This factor makes corruption particularly difficult to curb. To cope with this, there is a need to think in terms of systems. Within this web of reciprocities and punishments, there are key conditions that make corruption more likely to manifest itself. This chapter is suggestive of those areas where corruption is most likely to occur and how it is likely to be maintained by the parties involved, as well as developing means to expose these aforementioned vulnerabilities and invert corruption. I argue that it is the reformers task to identify those factors that are most conducive to corruption and to eliminate as many of them as possible, which I deal with in ensuing chapters. Crucial to subsequent chapters, I identify using factors and conditions set out here some of the areas where we can expect corruption to flourish and develop several possible mechanisms that can be used to invert corrupt exchanges.

16

In Chapter III, I concentrate on and develop means for removing incentives and opportunities to engage in corruption. We turn our attention to some potential institutional and structural reforms that shape government activity, alluded to in chapter II as important in reshaping both the desirability and stability of corrupt exchanges. Discussion and proposals are generally put in context with recent developments in public administration and the changing province of governmental activities, highlighting important lessons and shortcomings.

To remove incentives and opportunities for corruption effectively, however, there is a need to understand how corrupt systems operate. To successfully curb corruption as developed in chapter II, there are several barriers to introducing effective instruments. For example, reforms may be ineffective in targeting the source of the problem, or more ominously, reforms may sometimes increase rather than decrease the stability of patterns of corrupt exchanges. In Chapter IV, I develop further a notion adumbrated in Chapter II that there is need to think systems and not individuals in order to successfully curb corruption and implement reforms. Faced with policing institutions that are unsatisfactory in uncovering and/or pursuing criminal violations, due to organizational inefficiency, capture or worse still corruption, I suggest that a society may concentrate on decentralizing monitoring and enforcement. This entails generally seeking the reporting, monitoring and sanctioning efforts of the public. Information is fundamental. Arising from this, the suggestion is made that there is a need to get inside a corrupt organization in order to understand the inner-workings of the systems, including the patterns of payoffs, the mechanisms of exchange- including the ability of the parties to sanction- as well as the role and identity of the various actors involved. To receive this information, we need to recruit the assistance of parties with knowledge of corruption, These parties may be best understood as falling within a series of concentric circles. On the outside, we have those persons that do not actively engage in corruption but may have some knowledge of the location and types of corruption. As we move closer inside, we progress towards those parties that come into contact with corruption but do not necessarily engage in corrupt exchanges. They enjoy, however, a certain amount of insider knowledge through their proximity to corrupt transactions. At the very inside are those actors that actively engage in corrupt exchanges. They are privy to extensive knowledge of the running of the system and the actors involved. The varied means and incentives required to procure this assistance is developed in this chapter.

There are significant social barriers to developing and implementing effective and sustainable anti-corruption reforms which are the subject of our discussion in chapter V. Some of these obstacles are apparent in well-established democracies and less developed countries alike, but these obstacles are especially significant where there has been a long term failure of governments to respect and secure property rights, as well as ensure parties honor contractual obligations. Shared problems include: a low willingness to pay or support for reforms or laws, making them effectively obsolete; a high cost of enforcing norms against corruption, because of the fear of retaliation, but particularly because of the sparse number of other persons willing to follow suit. In a similar vein, there may be a collective action problem, where efforts made by one party may be subject to the familiar problem of free-riding, or apathy generally. These obstacles are especially significant where there has been a long term failure of governments to either respect and secure property rights as well as require parties to honor contractual obligations. I address here five major obstacles to reform, which are themselves not mutually exclusive. First, the willingness to pay or support reforms is too low to meet the necessary costs of effectively shifting corruption from a high level to a low level equilibrium. Second, citizens no longer trust government and reforms in this context are not considered as either credible or feasible so they fail to receive widespread support. Third, there may be a vacuum of interpersonal or reciprocal trust among citizens, in particular as a result of the continued absence of legal and institutional safeguards to economic transactions. This has the consequence that citizens forgo mutually beneficial legal exchanges making illegal exchanges relatively more profitable. Fourth, in order to combat these societies may have developed interpersonal trust relations with members of their own group, clan etc. which make relations between strangers less likely to evolve. Societies have developed alternative ways of "getting things done" that have led to the establishment of relations which hinder or sabotage reform efforts. Fifth, these divisions can be very large which can make measures traditional measures aimed at good governance redundant. Public trust in government is not forthcoming as a result of more fundamental cleavages in society.

In Chapter VI, I address common legal barriers to reform and the need to clarify duties and close off conduits to curb self-dealing. This is a subject matter of some complexity. It is not uncommon for societies to develop quite different solutions to the nature of reciprocal exchanges considered as legal or illegal over either time or geographical expanse. Subtle cultural differences and preferences do exist, but some societies have been much better at delineating clear lines of conduct important to suppressing undesirable self-interested behavior. Most countries have laws in some form or another prescribing bribery of public officials, which causes some commentators to disclaim the use of changes in the law to curb corruption. This is a very hasty and in my opinion unwise decision. The fact that practically every country has some law or another against bribery says nothing, for example, about such important factors as the scope and inclusion of such laws, or the exceptions that accompany them. Several important questions of clarification need to be addressed in multifarious areas and niches of governmental activity to close off conduits of undesirable influence and harmful quid pro quo agreements.

Chapter VII addresses structural and institutional barriers to reform and effective oversight. I address here some of the central components necessary for successful supervision by external bodies, imperative for the control of corruption (particularly high level corruption) lessons learned from previous reforms, and the strengths and weaknesses of these institutions. Instead of concentrating here on the familiar "*locus classicus*" of external or inter-branch oversight in the form of the separation of powers among judicial, legislative and executive bodies, I concentrate on select aspects of those institutions currently salient in the debate on corruption and reform, and those, in addition, which deserve greater attention in both the literature and surrounding debate.

Chapter VIII offers a note on political will and the political incentives to adopt reforms. It is slightly different from the preceding chapters in that instead of focusing on designing and addressing the incentive effects of anti-corruption reform measures, it offers provisional comments on the incentives to adopt the incentives. Though particularly dependent on local conditions and the nature and scope of reforms, I offer some tentative arguments and observations on those structural factors and dilemmas facing politicians and would-be reformers to sustainable reform efforts, and assess conditions that make reform more or less likely.

In addition to restating the general conclusions and recommendations, I close off the work with concluding comments on the role of anti-corruption efforts within the broader notion of governance and economic development, and highlight some of the intricacies inherent in separating the notion of corruption control from public sector reform and performance in general.

CHAPTER I

REEXAMINATION OF THE ISSUES

I. Introduction

Curbing corruption is now taking on an increasingly important role in policy debate and reform around the world. There are a multiplicity of reasons why the anti-corruption debate has managed to push itself to the fore. Explanations range from suggestions that corruption has increased to a general lack of tolerance of the phenomenon today, perhaps traceable to the democratic and economic reforms common throughout the nineties. It is also suggested that corruption is at the forefront of the developmental debate today as a result of political liberalization that granted new freedoms of the press and a greater flow of information and documentation (Klitgaard, MacLean-Abaroa, and Parris 2000: 8-9). Undoubtedly, the fact that successful organizations such as Transparency International, established in Berlin in 1993 with the intention of being for corruption what Amnesty International is for human rights transgressions, and the perceived importance and prioritization of governance issues at the OECD and World Bank, but to name a few, has had a significant impact on shaping the debate. Moreover, the fact that academics and policy reformers have highlighted how detrimental corruption can actually be for economic performance and economic growth must also be considered an important constituent related to why corruption has attained greater cogitation in many governments throughout the world.

The literature is vast and disparate, and has been studied within a wide range of disciplines. For the purposes of this chapter, I have concentrated primarily on the dominant paradigm in corruption research in the social sciences today, based primarily on micro-economics and new institutional economics, which has crept into most recent analytical work on corruption, well beyond the boundaries of the initial discipline.

II. Corruption: A Misnomer?

Commentators on corruption commonly bemoan the lack of attention that is given to the definition of corruption by those working on the subject (*see e.g.*, Philp (1997), Williams (1999)). Despite these criticisms, entire papers have been produced just on the definition (*see e.g.*, Johnston 1986). Truth is, however, there is no accepted definition, and definitions seem to be *soi-disant*, chosen for the purposes of an individual author's inquiry. For example, the understanding of corruption over the course of history has greatly changed its character. The

21

classics in political philosophy understood corruption to refer less to the actions of individuals than to the moral health of whole societies (Johnston 1996: 321). "It meant the perversion of a political system in its entirety" (Bouckaert 1997). Corruption was not perceived "so much as a class of illegal practices as a kind of complete subversion to which states and civilisations were vulnerable" (Bowles 1999: 462).

From the perspective of development studies, the definition and indeed nature of corruption was enflamed from early on in didactic debate, typified by the positions held by what became known as the "moralists", "culturalists" and the "functionalists." The moralists viewed corruption as a weak act of an individual, which deviates from the societal norm and has as its consequences the decline of morals and customs in a society. Corruption is viewed as a deviant type of behavior (Williams 1976: 43). The culturalists on the other hand explained corruption under the setting of cultural factors and referred to the traditional mentality of the giving and receiving of presents. The functionalist position which was at odds with this type of approach to corruption, wielded significant sway in early social science research on corruption. It was argued by economists at the time that corruption could function as a means to further economic development (Leff 1964).[1] Accordingly, corruption was far less a subversive or illicit activity but rather as an alternative more efficient method for using the machinery of government (Williams 1976: 44-45). Corruption therefore was mainly perceived as a temporary transition in developing countries which would be overcome with eventual modernization; a notion which influenced development planning greatly in the 1960's and 1970's, but has for the greater part been abandoned today (Pritzl and Schneider 1997). Indeed, all three of these approaches have been largely discredited in the dominant strands of the literature and are unpursued in current writing.[2]

Public opinion or cultural standards are also advanced as a means to assess what is actually considered as corruption, why it is considered as such and what is its relevance to a specific group, population, or population segment (Johnston 1996: 322). Opinion-based definitions of corruption suggest that what comprises corrupt behavior can really only be measured according to personal perceptions of what constitutes corrupt behavior. Here authors point to a divergence between what constitutes corrupt behavior in the letter of the law, and what are the public or personal definitions of corruption. These definitions offer an alternative

---

[1]   According to the anthropological version of functionalism, attempts to eradicate corruption can "threaten to destroy the delicate social fabric of traditional societies which are already undergoing the stresses of rapid social and economic change" (Williams 1976: 44).

[2]   That is not to say that, for example, fine cultural distinctions do not exist and that practices in one region may be considered corrupt but in another perfectly acceptable. The argument and the evidence suggest, however, that these distinctions are commonly overdrawn (Rose-Ackerman 1999: chp. 6; Sen 1999).

benchmark for analysis of corruption as opposed to any legal terminology.[3] Accordingly, Definitions are therefore always in a state of flux. In particular cultural or subgroup perceptions of corruption have been the focus of studies in recent years. Mancuso (1993), for example, conducted a survey of the ethical attitudes of British MP's and found some that politicians could often be divided up into subgroups with very distinctive beliefs on what constitutes unethical behavior. Similar studies have been conducted by Gorta and Forell (1995) who surveyed over 1300 public servants in New South Wales related to their perception of what corruption is and their willingness to take action based on this perception. What these studies offer is a different focus than comparing how private roles conflict with public duties, documenting the attitudes of those that are involved in daily operations and serve as a potential to understand organizational norms, as well as the informal barriers to overcoming undesirable behavior.

These studies suffer from the same weaknesses as other perception-related studies, such as bias and honesty in response. They are often based on a brief description of a multiplicity of scenarios in order to attain the opinion or potential response of individuals. In addition to the aforementioned difficulty of acquiring honest, unbiased responses, opinion-based definitions of corruption are problematic from a scientific point of view, because they aggravate problems of comparative research.

Other authors have attempted to reach an understanding of what actually entails corruption through a process of elimination, *i.e.*, that which remains, the author considers as corrupt. First we may try to distinguish between private sector and public sector corruption. As Bardhan (1997) points out that there are many everyday acts of corruption in the private sector, such as using connections to get a job, or tipping a bouncer for entry into a night club, which may be considered private sector corruption.[4] A particularly problematic form of private sector corruption is naturally insider trading, where an agent or agents (accountant, employee, lawyer) hold(s) information that when published will affect the share price of firm. The agent(s) may act on this information themselves or sell this

---

[3] This observation is particularly important where there may be a conflict between what is considered a social custom or norm on one hand and what may be the black letter of the law on the other (*see* Bowles 1999: 462).

[4] Within the private sector, there are examples of illegal activities that clearly violate the will of the principal and can thus be considered as private sector corruption. For example, a doctor and patient may both collude to defraud an insurance company, or a valuer of some good or service may collude with a seller to intentionally over-price a product. Alternatively, other activities that are not illegal, but are tolerated and even sometimes expected, may be considered with the language of principal-agent-theory as services performed by an agent for a client in return for remuneration to the agent solely. For example, a hairdresser, will frequently expect a tip for services performed and an even bigger tip for efforts made beyond the normal that may or may not be in the interest of the owner (Bowles 1999: 461).

information to a third party prior to the publication of this information to acquire illicit gains. Another distinction can be drawn between acts which are illegal and acts, which are corrupt. For example, consider donations to political parties by lobbyists, or perhaps the acquisition of benefits offered to bureaucrats as part of recreational or retirement policies by firms that they are supposed to regulate (*ibid.*: 1321). Some of these activities may be legal in a given jurisdiction but may well qualify as corrupt. Hence, not all acts which are corrupt are viewed as illegal and not all acts which are legal can be viewed as corrupt.

Another distinction must be drawn between acts which are immoral and act which are corrupt. The moral aspect of corruption leaps into the minds of most people when they hear the term mentioned, which makes policy discussions problematic (Klittgard 1988: 190), but an act may be seen as corrupt but not immoral. It is largely based on the intent and ends of the bribe. Take the example of an entrepreneur, who facing extremely perverse regulation (which may have been, deliberately imposed to facilitate the extraction of bribes), offers money to receive that which he would have been entitled to under less restrictive conditions; or alternatively an individual bribing a police officer in order not to torture a suspect (Bardhan 1997).[5]

A further distinction is sometimes raised between bureaucratic and political corruption. Bardhan (1997) gets around this narrow line by referring to the former as economic corruption. He admits, however the distinction can be easily blurred: "Does striving for private gain include policies that are primarily orientated to increasing the chances for remaining in office?" (Bardhan 1997: 1321). Economics has often traditionally separated the two, choosing to consider the political behavior of the politician above under the category of rent seeking as opposed to corruption. To wit, the very fact that corruption is a form of reciprocity, engenders difficulty in pinpointing the precise nature of those quid pro quo acts that may be considered corrupt. Lowenstein (1985) considers corruption within a series of concentric circles, the closer we get to the center the more likely we are to consider behavior or reciprocities as corrupt.[6] Campaign promises that are made in order to get elected and are later delivered upon are clear a form of quid pro quo but must surely find themselves located on the outer-most layer of the series of concentric circles, far from the center which would unequivocally be considered as hard-core bribery.[7]

---

[5] Moreover, as Osterfeld (1992: 204) submits, "the Marcoses, Duvaliers, and Noriegas of this world can be distinguished from the humble street vendors both in the effect of their corruption on the economy and society as a whole, and in the morality of their actions."

[6] For example, at the core one would find such acts as offering a public official a substantial cash sum for personal use, in exchange for a benefit to which the private person is not reasonably entitled.

[7] Moreover, any definition in order to be complete would have to contain both sides of the corrupt equation, I including both officials and private sector individuals (*see* World

Given the complexity of finding an all-encompassing definition which satisfies everyone, others have sought to simplify the matter somewhat by looking at corruption within a theoretical framework, thereby bypassing some of the complexities. Within theoretical frameworks, one attempts to examine the typology or the nature of corrupt relationships and actions - the most common of which is the principal-agent or principal-client agent framework. Here the agent is said to be acting corruptly when he pursues his own interest as opposed to those of the principal. The client is the person with whom the agent transacts. The principal-agent-client framework as Johnston puts it "places both officials and citizens in more realistic surroundings and complex incentive schemes than do most behavioral-classifying definitions. It thus shifts the focus of the analysis from individual standards to the significance of officials and clients' conduct within an institutional and political setting" (Johnston 1996: 326). Authors differ as to whether illegality under this framework is a necessary component of corruption.[8] Applying this type of definition allows for application to issues of optimal incentive schemes and a broad range of issues in organization theory in general.[9]

Other extensions of a typology-based definition of corruption include dividing corruption further into different categories, such as:

- **Individual level corruption (incidental corruption)**, considered as corruption which occurs randomly at an individual level only without institutional support.
- **Institutionalized corruption**, considered as corruption within any particular government institution, often organized with principals and agents, *e.g.*, police corruption.
- **Endemic or entrenched corruption**, considered where corruption has manifested itself as a regular form of doing business with government officials in an economy, or the only way of getting things done.[10]

Clearly different policy measures are imperative depending on the nature of corrupt transactions. There is for example a notable difference between the nature of corrupt transactions that occur at an individual level, specifically between a few individuals and institutional corruption that develops into a network with

---

Development Report 1997). Most authors working on the subject today, however, seem to settle for the definition of corruption somewhere along the lines of abuse (or misuse) of public office for private gain (Klitgaard 1988, Rose-Ackerman 1999).

[8] Compare Rose-Ackerman (1978) with Klitgaard (1991).

[9] *See* further Chapter III, Section V, Subsection D.

[10] *See* Kaufman (1998a) for a more detailed description of types of corruption as used for statistical analysis by the World Bank, which includes factors such as grand and petty corruption, organized and disorganized corruption and high versus low incidence corruption.

hierarchical structures. Institutional corruption commonly manifests itself where opportunities for corruption, coupled with weak controls, are more evident in one ministerial department relative to others (Robinson 1998: 3). Endemic or entrenched corruption occurs when corruption has manifested itself as a norm of doing business. This type of corruption, as Robinson (1998: 4) notes, occurs generally in a society with "low political competition, low and uneven economic growth, a weak civil society, and the absence of institutional mechanisms to deal with corruption...the form which corruption assumes in different contexts also depends on whether politicians or bureaucrats take the lead, and whether key interest groups in civil society are actively involved through patronage and clientelism."[11]

A final observation on the nature of corruption is in order here. Corrupt transactions distinguish themselves from many other crimes in that they involve more than one person, thereby implying a degree of illicit cooperation between at least two parties.[12] As we shall develop in later discussion, the fact that corruption is a form of cooperative behavior potentially makes parties significantly more vulnerable than other forms of malfeasance. For example, parties must find a like-minded partner, negotiate and form an agreement, and deliver on their arrangements. All three stages involve substantial risks, which can be exploited in any anti-corruption policy. This argument is substantially developed later.[13] For the purpose of our inquiry, in line with other more recent commentaries on the subject, I shall take corruption to represent the misuse of public power for private gain.[14]

III. Effects on Investment and Growth

There is a near unanimous position today among economists, strongly underscored by econometric evidence, some of which I present below, that corruption has an adverse effect on investment and growth; the ball is now very much in the court of those authors wishing to argue otherwise. The precise degree of damage incurred and how it affects growth levels is unclear and depends on several factors including the nature, scope and timing of corruption as well as other local and institutional factors. The famed argument testifying that corruption is not necessarily bad for development was generally held up to the performance of some countries considered to have high levels of corruption but maintaining

---

[11] For a more complete typology compiled by the World Bank used for diagnostic tools, see Kaufmann (1998a).
[12] Corruption has been distinguished from fraud, embezzlement and extortion because it in principle relates to two or more parties colluding together at the expense of a third (Bowles 1998).
[13] See further, Chapter II.
[14] See, for example, Rose-Ackerman 1999: 91.

relatively good economic performance, such as South Korea. These countries were compared to others that ranked consistently lower in corruption indexes but enjoyed lower levels of economic performance. Although offering food for thought, the general explanation for this must rest with the patterns, nature and efficiency of corrupt systems rather than on the size or amount of corruption per se. Traditional systems in Asia where corruption was/is an integral part of many forms of business, but nevertheless that performed well were/are generally more centralized and more efficient than other systems where corruption occurs within decentralized structures (Khan 1998).[15]

Mauro (1995) was one of the first to conduct systematic empirical work on the effects of corruption on economic performance and growth. Using corruption-ranking data taken from the Business International correspondents stationed in about 70 countries, the purpose of his paper was "to identify the channels through which corruption and other institutional factors affect economic growth and to quantify the magnitude of theses effects" (*ibid.*: 682). He has shown that the efficiency of the judiciary system, the political stability and the level of corruption all effect the level of growth in the economy. He, furthermore, showed that countries with higher rates of corruption have a lower ratio of private sector and overall investment to income. Ades and Di Tella (1996) have confirmed the general finding that corruption adversely affects investment. Similarly, Wei (1997) has tackled the issue of how taxing corruption is on foreign direct investment (FDI). An increase in the level of corruption for a country that is relatively clean such as Singapore to the level of a country where corruption is rather common such as Mexico, he finds would be like increasing the tax rate in a country by 20 percent. One of the most ambitious recent econometric studies was that conducted by Evans and Rauch (2000). Taking the opinions of experts on 35 developing nations they showed that growth level are strongly associated with a Weberian State bureaucracy, based primarily on meritocracy.

In particular, corruption can affect the supply of entrepreneurs in directly productive activities, which can negatively affect growth levels, investment and economic performance more generally. Recent figures from a Business Environment and Enterprise Performance Survey conducted on 3,000 East European companies have shown that corruption in these regions mostly effects small companies.[16] Forty percent of the small businesses surveyed submitted that they pay bribes frequently. This has the effect of increasing the costs of vital young companies getting established in Eastern Europe. Similarly, findings from the rent-seeking literature have shown that talented people when they start firms innovate and increase growth, but when they become rent seekers they only

---

[15] Compare for example the economic performance of India in the 1990s, where corruption is considered to be decentralized and inefficient with South Korea that operates under a centralized, more efficient structure.

[16] See "Bribery fills East European Commerce," *The Wall Street Journal*, Nov. 9, 1999.

redistribute wealth and reduce growth (Murphy, Shleifer and Vishny 1991, 1993). They, furthermore, suggest that the occupational choice (of talented people) depends on returns to ability and scale, market size and compensation contracts. Where rent seeking rewards talents more than entrepreneurship this can cause stagnation in the economy. Moreover, Murphy, Shleifer and Vishny have argued where there are increasing returns to rent seeking and that in times of market recession the returns to rent seeking relative to entrepreneurship increase. Hence, if in the first instance, society rewards rent seeking behavior better than productive behavior those involved in production will shift to rent seeking, and if there are increasing returns to rent seeking it may become more profitable for those persons to stay in these activities, which has the effect of stagnating the economy.

IV. Nature and Costs of Payoffs

"Everywhere rules are bent in return for payoffs. The loci of payoffs are remarkably similar throughout the world considering the large differences in culture, economic conditions, and political organization" (Rose-Ackerman 1999: 18).

States control the allocation and distribution of scarce and valuable resources through officials possessing discretionary power working within an institutional set up. This fact affords officials potential for illicit gains. As Rose-Ackerman (1999: 9) observes: "Institutions designed to govern the interrelationships between the citizen and the state are used instead for personal enrichment and the provision of benefits to the corrupt." Payoffs are naturally paid for a range of services.[17] Common services and their loci of payoffs include:

- Evading regulations, fines and taxes and both evading and acquiring licenses, permits and signatures;
- Acquiring monopoly power (through, for example the creation of entry barriers for competitors, to the framing of over-specific regulations and the denial of licenses to harassment);

---

[17] A survey of Transparency International conducted in 1995 suggests that corruption in the public sector in manifold countries occurs in the same areas. They note:
"The areas of government activity most vulnerable to corruption were: public procurement; rezoning of land; revenue collection; government appointments; and local government; The methodologies, too, were remarkably similar, including: cronyism, connection, family members and relatives; political corruption, through donations to political campaigns, etc.; kickbacks on government contracts (and subcontracting consultancies); and fraud of all kinds." *See*, http://www.transperancy.de/documents/ source-book/a/Chapter_2/index.htm.

- Access to public infrastructure and assets, including the illegal award of public procurement and services contracts;
- Access to the use of public physical assets, or their outright stripping and appropriation, for example privatization of state-owned enterprises;
- Access to preferential financial assets (credit and subsidies);
- Appointments to administrative, judicial and state-owned or state-controlled enterprises;
- Turning a blind eye to other criminal activity, particularly the selling and production of drugs, black market operations and money laundering;
- Access to insider information on planning and zoning projects and information on financial sector and competitors activities;
- Influencing administrative and legislative policy (for example budgetary decisions on percentage spent on military);
- Influencing prosecutorial and judicial decisions.

Adapted in part from Kaufman (1998a: 148-49).

Not surprisingly, the costs of corrupt payoffs differ greatly depending on several factors.[18] We can distinguish between at least four different scenarios: (1) Those circumstances where the supply of qualified candidates exceeds the demand; (2) the situation where the public official can alter the quantity and quality of the resource or service, such as a monopolist; (3) whether corruption is centralized or decentralized; (4) whether corrupt payoffs serve as a means to speed up access to a commonly held entitlement (greasing the wheels), or simply a means of procuring something to which one is not and should not entitled.

Looking first at the most innocuous case where the supply of overqualified candidates exceeds the demand (not artificially but as a result of competition), one may argue that bribes here simply use the willingness to pay of the different suppliers to allocate scarce benefits. Rose-Ackerman (1999) identifies several problems with this contention. She suggests that illegality causes participants to waste resources keeping the transactions secret, which has the knock on effect of reducing information about the prices, thus making prices 'sticky'. Furthermore, certain members of society with moral constraints may be excluded from transacting and other members of society, such as friends may receive special treatment. She concludes, therefore, that a corrupt market can never, even under the above-mentioned conditions, be efficient. It will always be more uncertain than the legal market and may jeopardize wider policy goals.

Under variable supply, as is the case in the second scenario, the situation is, as one may expect, exacerbated. Where the public official(s) have the power to

---

[18] In this section, I borrow extensively from the analysis presented in Rose-Ackerman (1999: 9-23).

alter the quantity or the quality of a scarce resource they may function as discriminating monopolists.[19] Further to the costs already identified under fixed supply, under the first scenario above, it can be expected that an unqualified party of equal financial means has a higher willingness to pay than a qualified party. This is the case given that they may have no other means of procuring the goods or service. When the situation is particularly pronounced, those that are qualified may also be forced to pay depending on the amount of discretion available to the bureaucrat and the chances of successful legal recourse.[20] Uncertain standards supply the bureaucrat with additional protection. To further understand these costs, it is useful to distinguish two types of corruption: namely, corruption with theft and corruption without theft (Shleifer and Vishny 1993). Corruption with theft implies that the government receives no part of the costs of a permit license etc., while corruption without theft implies that an additional price is added to the cost of the license by an official. The latter is achieved by creating a shortage and letting the market clear at the monopoly prices.

Corruption with theft is more detrimental to society. In this case, the government receives none of the income accrued by payment for a good or service, as this is put into the pocket of the official. Moreover, the demand for corrupt services may increase, given that when there is corruption with theft the official has incentive to charge below the price set by the government for a good or service, giving those that purchase the product through corruptive means an unfair advantage over those that purchase the product legally at a higher price.

As a third point, I emphasized that one should also distinguish between centralized and decentralized corruption, in order to assess the economic impact of corruption. To understand this, Shleifer and Vishny (1993) compared the situation of two independent monopolists to that of a joint monopolist, producing complementary goods. The general model on joint monopoly shows us that if a joint monopolist wants to maximize her profits for both goods then she will do so if she sets the price for good one at which $MC_1 = MR_1 + MR_2(dX_2/dX_1)$, where MC denotes marginal costs, MR_1 and MR_2 the marginal revenue from goods one and two respectively, and X_1 and X_2 the quantities of the goods one and two sold respectively. This implies that the monopolist charges less for good 1 in order to increase the demand for good 2.[21] In the case of two single monopolists they will, however, try individually to maximize their profits on both goods, setting $MC_1 =$

---

[19] Examples include: the misallocation of subsidies, city contracts going to undeserving firms, permits and licenses being purchases outside for a bribe instead of according to merit, violation of health and safety standards, and so forth.

[20] As an aside, it should be noted that a subtle form of establishing monopoly power is through the use of vague or uncertain standards. *See* Chapter III, Section IV.

[21] As Shleifer and Vishny (*ibid.*: 606) suggest, when the goods are complements, as is the case for government permits for the same project, then $dX_2/dX_1 > 0$ and, therefore, at the optimum $MR_1 < MC_1$.

MR_1. If we identify good 1 and good 2 as being the services in return for bribes, and MR as being the (per unit revenue from a) bribe then we may say that in the case of independent agencies the per unit bribe is higher and output is lower than in the case of joint monopolists, as is the aggregate level of bribes received. The independent agencies damage one another as well as social welfare, a factor seriously aggravated by free entry into the procurement of bribes (*ibid.*: 606).

In a similar vein, Bardhan (1997: 1324) argues that a centralized system of corruption will internalize some of its adverse effects. If corruption is not centralized, then the citizen does not know what he has purchased. For example, the sudden intervention of the necessity for complementary licensees by agencies wishing to maximize their bribe intake is a feature of decentralized corruption, which causes great inefficiencies. Centralization of corruption has been offered as a reason for the better economic performance of Indonesia over India in the 1980's, although corruption levels may have been even higher in the former than in the latter over this period (Bardhan 1997: 1325; and Mauro 1995). Moreover, in South Korea where corruption was centralized, it took the form of lump-sum contributions which government officials consistently had the ability to honor- a factor high level officials in many developing countries generally do not possess (Bardhan 1997).

Recent work in the public choice literature has yielded some interesting explanations on the size of the bribe relative to the rents. In particular it suggests that there is a possible coordination failure among politicians (Rasmusen and Ramseyer 1994). Apparently, politicians in democratic countries often receive very small bribes relative to the favors they perform. If politicians could centralize their bribery and enforce agreements among themselves, they would be able to reap the full benefits of the statutes they pass. The essential problem is that each democratic legislator imposes externalities on other legislators when collusive agreements cannot be honored. Rasmusen and Ramseyer also offered the same reason for politicians' position regarding making the acceptance of types of payments illegal. Wherever this coordination problem can be reduced then it would appear that the expected benefits of accepting bribes may converge to the expected costs of acceptance. Such problems do not exist in some developing countries which helps to explain why it may cost more to buy a politician.

To conclude this discussion, I shall refer to the forth distinction drawn above in the context of corrupt payoffs, namely those that speed up access to a commonly held entitlement (greasing the wheels). This was the subject of much early debate but rarely raises it head now in policy circles. A commonly presented arguments was that in the context of extensive over-regulation, corruption instead of being costly may improve efficiency and help growth (Leff 1964, Huntington 1968). These authors put forward the position that corrupt practices such as speed money may "grease the wheels of squeaky administration" (Leff 1964: 11), suggesting that allowing officials to ask for bribes would encourage them to work harder because of an increase in their potential returns.

Viewed from a static perspective, bribes as an incentive to work may well have the effect of motivating a public official to increase his effort. There are, however, serious flaws with this argument from a more dynamic perspective, as officials have incentives to create backlogs and other opportunities to extract bribes (*see* Rose Ackerman 1999: 16-17; Bardhan 1997: 1322). Furthermore, the showing of impartiality towards corruption encourages its expanse, effects how public support the government, holds back state reform and increases the uncertainty of doing business (Rose-Ackerman 1999: 16-17). The problem is not a static one, but very dynamic with repercussions far beyond the simple context of any individual transaction.

V. Corrupt Systems

Corruption in hierarchies is largely of two kinds. There is the bottom up model where low level bureaucrats collect the bribes and share the pickings with top-level bureaucrats (*see* Cadot 1987; Basu and Mishra 1992). "Initially, payoffs to superiors may be a means of buying their silence, but if payment are institutionalised, they become a condition of employment, organized by superiors for their own gain" (Rose-Ackerman 1999: 82). The "bottom-up" model works where low level officials are usually the ones to transact with the public.[22] The top down model on the other hand transpires when most major decisions are made at the top and the money in turn trickles down to those below as they supply the inputs, and are tolerated when they enter into their own petty crime. Many models argue that a means to mitigate corruption is to limit the amount of information the official has on the identity of the persons with whom he transacts. Incomplete information has been shown to increase the effort level of a police agent and thus decrease the level of crime within society (*see* Marjit, Rajeev, and Mukherjee 1997). The result thereof is a theoretical basis for supporting the regular transfer of public officials. If, however, corruption operates at a 'top-down' level, this policy may well support the top-level public officials by giving them extra power. It may also have the effect of encouraging officials to treat transferal as an "end-game - situation." Additionally, it may have the effect of reducing accountability, as it becomes more difficult to trace what decisions were made by which public officials.

In the literature it is often argued that the best way to control corruption is to take away the monopolistic hold of the bureaucrat by introducing other

---

[22] Klitgaard, MacLean-Abaroa, and Parris (2000: 17-18) cite an interesting example of bottom up corruption in Hong Kong in the 1970s where the police were involved with drug traffickers, gambling and prostitution rings and organized themselves into syndicates which managed a very evolved scheme of redistribution among members, passing payments up the chain to superiors for closing their eyes.

bureaucrats which may administer the same license, permit etc. Competitive bribing rates by the officials should theoretically cause the bribe amount to fall to zero (see, for example, Shleifer and Vishny 1993). This only seems to work if there is a higher authority that can supervise the bureaucrats. If not, the bureaucrats may collude which may actually help entrench corruption. This problem becomes most serious when corruption becomes systematized and when organized crime begins to make inroads into legal business. The longer this is allowed to prevail the more likely it is that organized crime and systematic corruption become inseparable from politics (Rose-Ackerman 1999: 25).

Above I outlined analytically different types of corrupt transactions that may occur including corruption with theft and without theft, from the top-down and the bottom up and through other hybrid forms. One other particularly problematic aspect of (systematic and endemic) corruption manifests itself when the general activities conducted by public officials, are shifted to those where they can receive greatest rents. As we have seen, public agencies can enlarge their income by functioning cooperatively as discriminating monopolists and designating cooperatively market-clearing-rates for services and goods they offer. They can do this within both the traditional and developmental function of administration (Jagannathan 1986, 1988). Because existing administrations face excess demand, they even have discretion on the provision of "free" public services, which creates rent seeking opportunities and opportunities for corruption. Rent seeking activities are omnipresent in public institutions in less developed countries. Under the traditional functions of administration, rent-seeking opportunities arise largely because of ineffectual enforcement of property rights. Many citizens' complaints may go unheard because of the inability of the officials to cope with such a large number of people. In India for example, an average civil court has jurisdiction over 800,000 persons and a police station has 100,000 persons under its responsibility (Jagannathan 1986: 128).

Rent seeking possibilities arise in developmental functions of administrations that are supposed to promote economic development because buyers believe benefits from the services offered by the public bodies will increase their personal wealth. The personal wealth of demanders of services within the developmental functions of the administrations may be increased if they receive a greater allocation of newly created common property, example, irrigation water, or control access to vital economic goods (Wade 1985). An important point worth observing is that there has been a near institutionalization of rents. Often when someone from one office is transferred to another he may immediately begin collecting his bribes (Jagannathan 1986: 128). Such "sick institutions seem to have evolved into complex and sophisticated corruption machines, with a shape, size and modus operandi and also the statutory legitimacy "fit" for corruption" (MacLean-Aboroa, Mayor of La Paz cited in Klitgaard, MacLean-Abaroa, and Parris 2000: 33).

A further feature of less developed countries is that of systematic fraud, *i.e.*, endemic to governmental activities. This occurs more in developing rather than traditional functions of administrations (Jagannathan 1986). Systematic fraud is, however, not just a phenomenon of developing countries: it has been argued that the Sicilian Mafia earns most of its money now by defrauding local, national and European Community schemes of subsidization (Fiorentini and Peltzman 1995: 16). Technically complicated projects cause huge information asymmetries, which enable fraud to flourish in areas of complexity. Furthermore, unlike in the traditional functions of public office, the developmental functions of public office are not area specific. Because of this, there is more room for opportunism and cunning. Among the many implications of such systematic defrauding is the ineffectiveness of development and stabilization's programs in less developed countries. Furthermore, if defrauding is systematic it increases the chances of informal contracts being enforced. Informal contracts may be enforced through regional networks, the threat of transfers by higher official for noncompliance, by personal involvement in the granting of contract by officials and in rare cases the threat of physical violence. The enforcement of informal contracts on the side of the bureaucracy is further strengthened by the fact that positions themselves were often acquired through purchases (Jagannathan 1986, 1988). These purchases are seen as an investment and legitimize corrupt transactions in the eyes of officials and their families, treated similarly to a legitimately acquired property right. An unfortunate feature thereof, is that the longer corruption is allowed to remain institutionalized, the greater the potential that legitimacy is awarded to particular practices and the more likely that a system of stable well-designed informal, transferable property rights will develop.

VI. Measuring Corruption

As with other areas of social science, the true test of theory or policy proposals lays in consistence with observations. For this reason, the empirics of corruption should be and indeed has begun to be an explicit and key objective of researchers aiming to at understand the phenomenon and policy advisors wanting to pass on reliable information. Attempts to measure corruption are, however, a relatively new endeavor. First dominated by professional agencies interested primarily in compiling information on the riskiness of investment in particular countries sold to investors, later academics concentrated on cross-country analyses and most recently on surveys and diagnostic studies. There are several problems particular to corruption, when one wishes to conduct empirical research. First, as with all empirical research the initial question that must generally be asked is what do we want to measure. In the case of corruption, as earlier discussion identified, this is not an easy question to answer given that there is no clear definition of what corruption actually is. Second, there is frequently no reliable empirical basis for research. Corruption is secretive, involves complex transactions, oftentimes with the use of intermediaries; payoffs often result after substantial time delays and causation is rarely verifiable, which is indicative of the low level of prosecutions for corruption. To develop an understanding of the operations and dynamics of corruption, researchers are like investigators often needing to rely on rumors and other bits and pieces of information. In the next section, our brief discussion will concentrate on key empirical foundations of current corruption research. Rather than presenting a survey of existing empirical models of corruption research and the areas of their application, I concentrate instead on basic approaches and sources of information.

One source of information commonly used is the courts. Fisman and Gatti (1999), for example, use the number of public officials that were convicted for abuse of office as an indicator of the level of corruption.[23] Looking closer at the operations of the courts, jurimetric data on such factors as the number of cases and processing times may be collected to provide an indication of the level of efficiency of the corruption in the judiciary (Buscaglia 1999; Buscaglia, Dakolias and Ratliff 1995).[24] In addition to hard data that can be collected by the courts, legal records provide important information on the mechanisms of a corrupt system, that are frequently absent from specific questionnaires and other sources of information designed for comparative analysis. Legal records and transcripts are especially important because they frequently provide an insiders view.[25] This information becomes more reliable when there is a cooperative defendant who is willing to divulge the inner- workings of the corrupt system in return for a more lenient sentence. Another internal avenue to corrupt systems is provided by undercover agents who infiltrated a corrupt system. This avenue to information is often erroneously ignored in the social science literature.[26]

One of the problems with court cases and transcripts is that they are very few in number compared to the actual extent of corruption and are subject to judicial and prosecutorial bias. In some circumstances, they may be more revealing of priorities of politicians and public prosecutors or the efficacy of the judiciary than of the underlying problem of corruption (Andvig 2001: 9). Other potential sources of hard information are provided by the police, who among other things file complaints; nonprofits, who may similarly file complaints and conduct their own surveys, and other investigative units such as the customs and tax

---

[23] Comparative information on corruption has been collected by the Crime Prevention and Criminal Justice Division of the United Nations Office at Vienna.

[24] One of the key deficiencies in these studies is that it is difficult to distinguish between inefficiency and corruption. Indeed as we shall see later, there are several problems in determining corrupt behavior. One such problem is that we often cannot distinguish between malfeasance, nonfeasance, poor policy and corruption.

[25] See further, Chapter IV.

[26] One notable exception is Della Porta and Vannucci (1999).

authorities, who frequently offer estimates of the degree of evasion on corporate, VAT, income and excise taxes. (Such information must however not be exaggerated in its usefulness. For example, as with court cases it is only a selective cross section of available information. The number of complaints may result from an increase in the number of nonprofit or investigative units that exist, thus improving accessibility, or alternatively may be a result of changes in the methods of filing complaints, for example where complaints can be filed anonymously, one must expect an increase in the number of complaints.)

Other sources of information that are potentially relevant may be provided non investigative agencies such as governmental financial institutions and international financial institutions that record procurement data that frequently allow for a comparison of unit costs for standard items (Kaufman 1998a: 154).

Another source of information is provided by investigative journalists and newspaper articles. The public exposure of journalists allows them to build up informal connections and a large supply of informants (Andvig 2001: 9). Political scandals in particular, as we shall see later, are particularly important in bringing about reform, but color the public perception on the relative degree of corruption across time. Obviously, the nature, type and scope of the stories that reach public ears are dependent on not only the supply of such stories, but the incentives and capacity of the media to pursue such stories, the freedom of the press and the degree of media competition. The widespread reporting of corruption scandals in the domestic media are more a representation that democracy is at work than that corruption levels have risen.

More recently, social scientists have begun using data from commercial organizations. These commercial organizations provide subjective indexes on the amount of corruption in a particular country, region or sector. One older source is the Business International Index, a publication of the Economist Intelligence Unit, composed of surveys of a large number of commercial and political risk factors, including corruption, based on an international network of correspondents that included journalists, country specialists and international businessmen. Correspondents were asked to rank the degree of corruption or questionable payments on a scale between 0 and 10, where efforts were made to keep the correspondents answers consistent (Mauro 1995). Other well-known sources of comparative data based on the opinion of experts continuous over time include *inter alia* the Political and Economic Risk Consultancy, Asian Intelligence Issue and the Economist Intelligence Unit.[27] The main problem with these surveys is despite their broad coverage, there are often merely a few experts devoted to each country involved.

The best known index on corruption is undoubtedly Transparency International's Corruption Perceptions Index (CPI), reproduced in the chapter

---

[27] *See* http://asiarisk.com and http://eiu.com, respectively.

appendix for the year 2001. Prepared under Johann Lambsdorff of Göttingen University, it is a "composite poll of polls", developed from the weighted average of 14 different indexes prepared by 7 different organizations.[28] According to Lambsdorff (2001: 2) the strength of the index is "based on the concept that a combination of data sources combined into a single index increases the reliability of each individual figure. The idea of combining data is that the nonperformance of one source can be balanced by the inclusion of at least two other sources."[29]

A senior economist and leading author on corruption at the World Bank, Daniel Kaufman has criticized the index as not being very accurate, chiefly because it is not comparable over time and that the country rankings for any particular year are subject to large margins of error. He does, however, concede that the index provides an indication of whether "perceptions are that the country is very corrupt, relatively corrupt, somewhat corrupt, or relatively free of corruption" and that it has provided a "useful flag" and raised "awareness about corruption generally" (Kaufman 1998b: 152-53; see also Kaufman 1998a; Kaufman Kraay, and Zoido-Lobaton 1999; Andvig 2001). Nevertheless, the CPI is used extensively in econometric work (Galtung and Pope 2001). Perhaps, however, the most significant aspect of the CPI index is that it has provided for a large impetuous to discussion on corruption well outside of academic circles. Governments have been forced by media attention to react to the index, and it has even provided the impetus to the launching of anti-corruption campaigns (*ibid.*: 275-277).

Another approach that has been developed more recently in particular by the World Bank, is that of detailed questionnaires addressed not to country specific experts, but to the business community. Commonly enterprises are asked about how large the share of their expenditures are that are paid out on bribes as well as the purpose thereof (*e.g.*, Brunetti, Kisunko and Weder 1997).[30] These surveys concentrate in large part on the institutional obstacles to doing business and on the experiences of firms paying bribes.

Other work attempts to measure corruption by concentrating on the experiences of public service users -rating the performance generally of the delivery of services- and on single-agency diagnostic surveys (Kaufman 1998a, 1998b). Current practices frequently involve surveying public sector agents themselves to develop an understanding of the institutional obstacles to corruption and more generally the perception of public sector employees with regard to corruption (Gorta and Forell 1995). The shortcomings of this approach were adumbrated above.

---

[28] Figures valid for the year 2001. *See* http://www.transparency.org/cpi/2001/cpi2001.html.

[29] Transparency International has also prepared a second index known as the Bribe Payer's Index, which attempts to provide a ranking among leading exporters of their willingness to pay bribes in international business. *See* http://www.transparency.org.

[30] Available at http://worldbank.home.by/wbi/governance/pdf/wps1759.pdf.

VII. Accounting for Different Incidences of Corruption

> "Obviously, subtle differences in culture and basic values exist across the world. But there is one human motivator that is universal and central to explaining the divergent experiences of different countries. That motivator is self interest, including an interest in the well-being of one's family and peer group. ..Endemic corruption suggests a pervasive failure of tap self-interest for productive purposes" (Rose-Ackerman 1999: 2).

There is of course no simple answer that accounts for the different levels of corruption in various countries. The number of variables that conceivably play a significant role are mind-boggling. Though ideology undoubtedly seems to drive many of the commentaries, it would appear, however, to be unanimously accepted in the literature that three factors influence greatly the level of corruption in a society, namely: The level of government intervention in the economy (this assigns the public official with a monopoly right); the discretion officials actually have in performing their job, and their level of accountability. In developing countries there is commonly a high rate of government intervention, a high level of official discretion and a low level of official accountability. These create avenues for corrupt activities, where regularly the perceived expected payoffs of entering into corrupt transactions are greater than the perceived expected costs. Thus one may argue with confidence that there are various degrees of corruption in different countries because there are different opportunities available to the self-interested individual. This leads us to a more fundamental quandary: why are there different opportunities for corruption available in different countries?

The first approach taken to explaining this was that of the culturalists (outlined above), who argued that different levels of corruption in society are a result of social norms. This has, however, been dispelled with at both a theoretical and practical level, in all but marginal circumstances (Rose-Ackerman 1999: ch. 6). While subtle differences on what constitutes corruption most definitely exist, they should not be overplayed. Another explanation came from the liberalist camp, who argued that widespread corruption is the result of government intervention in the economy, and the only way to curb corruption is to scale back government (Becker 1994).[31] Whilst government intervention in the economy is clearly of primary importance in explaining the prevalence of corruption in society, it presents by no means a complete picture and has shown itself to be limited in its general application from a policy perspective in curbing corruption, as later discussion will highlight.

---

[31] *See* Becker, Gary S., "To Root Out Corruption, Boot out Big Government," *Business Week* (31 January 1994).

Another perspective put forward for corruption and the persistent failure of certain institutions, is that indigenous institutions in those countries with a colonialist past were not taken into the legal framework; arising therefrom citizens and officials alike felt disconnected from the law on the books (Dia 1996). The degree with which a colonial past is responsible for corruption in specific countries is moot. What is particularly important, however, as work on political science has emphasized, is that corruption is a function of the lack of durable, resilient political institutions and political competition, as well as an insufficiently involved and under-developed civil society (*see* Robinson 1998: 4). Fortunately both reforms and discussion now seem to be concentrating their efforts on these elements.

Figure 1: Increasing Marginal Returns to Corruption

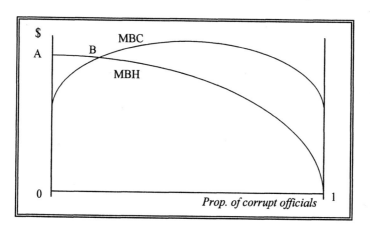

Recent work has concentrated on explaining disparate levels of corruption by concentrating on multiple equilibria models. Multiple equilibria models have shown that motivated by beliefs on the number of other corrupt persons in society, two cities or countries with the exact same parameters (for example economic conditions) can end up at two very different levels of corruption equilibria (Sah 1991; Andvig and Moene 1990; Murphy, Shleifer and Vishny 1993; Rasmusen 1996). This is likely to happen if the profitability of corruption increases as the number of corrupt agents increases. Put differently, a rise in the aggregate level of corruption decreases the incentives of any individual to remain honest. This scenario becomes more serious if one considers that the high equilibrium level of corruption has the capacity to become more stable with the evolution of informal property rights with the passage of time. In a similar vein, stigma and social disapproval within one's peer group tend to reduce as the number of others participating in criminal activity (within the same group) increases (Rasmusen 1996).

The basic idea of multiple equilibria can be shown in what is known as a Shelling diagram, depicted in Figure 1.[32] As one moves out horizontally, the proportion of corrupt officials (or transactions) ranges between 0 and 1. There are two curves, the MBC curve and the MBH curve, which represent the marginal benefits of engaging in corruption and the marginal benefits of not engaging in corruption for a dishonest and an honest person respectively, for a given proportion of honest/dishonest officials.

As one can see, according to the curves, the marginal benefits of engaging in corruption (MBC) increase relative to the marginal costs of honesty (MBH) depending on the proportion of corrupt officials. There are three different equilibria. At point A, the proportion of officials that engage in corruption is 0, no official engages in corruption as the relative gains for doing so are less that the losses. This is an example of a stable equilibrium. At point B, however, an official is indifferent between being honest and being dishonest, for a given proportion of honest/dishonest officials. This is an example of an unstable equilibrium. At point B, it only takes one additional official to decide to engage in corruption to shift the situation to one where all officials are corrupt, which is again a stable equilibrium, denoted by point C. Note that the payoffs for corruption at point C are lower for the officials than at either A or B. As one can see, the gains from corruption initially increase and then decrease at a certain point. This is not an implausible scenario. It commonly takes a certain number of officials to get around basic administrative safeguards and to perform corrupt tasks, but after a point, through competition among officials or inefficiencies that can accompany size, the returns to corruption per individual decrease.

Initial positions are, therefore, important. If an economy or institution begins with high level corruption, it is relatively stable. A very large shock is needed to affect the (perceived) returns to corruption to a sufficient proportion of officials to shift the equilibrium from high to low level corruption (as the curves are drawn here, the proportion of corruption is all or nothing). Depending on the initial starting point, anti-corruption efforts can either have no impact or a fundamental one, depending on the starting point. The above is useful to understand frequency dependent equilibria, but as Bardhan (1997: 1332) notes: "The problem with such simple diagrams is that the mechanisms through which an economy reaches one or the other equilibrium are not fully spelled out."

A final recent explanation for differential levels of corruption worthy of mention is based on the belief that corruption is "a function of the process of accumulation and evolution of property rights over time" (Khan 1998; *see* also

---

[32] A simple Shelling diagram is quite popular to use in explaining multiple equilibria models, *see* also Andvig (1991) and Bardhan (1997).

Robinson 1998: 7). Khan (1998) argues that economic explanations have failed to take into account the differences in the political power of groups that compete for benefits allocated by the state. He contends rather persuasively that one reason that effects the efficient allocation of resources is that strictly legal ways are often perceived to be illegitimate. Economic development entails processes fostering the emergence of new "wealth-owning" classes, perceived frequently to be illegitimate, and because of which the allocation of critical rights may be forced to go outside of legal channels because transparent allocation may be impossible to agree upon (Khan 1998: 16). The political power of contending groups of clients, each demanding benefits from state patrons is fundamental to understanding the problem of corruption, which can have long run and the "inter-genererational" repercussions for allocating rights and resources to the emerging capital classes. The state often is forced to allocate property rights and benefits to those which have the greatest potential to cause political problems rather than those with the greatest willingness to pay (*ibid.*).

VIII. Early Approaches to Curbing Corruption

> "Yet it surely follows from basic economic principle that when some people wish to behave in a certain way very much, as measured by the amount they gain from it or would be willing to pay rather than forgo it, they will pursue that wish until it becomes too expensive for their purse and tastes" (Becker and Stigler 1974: 2).

The economics of crime has its roots in early work published by Bentham and Beccaria. An application of the theory of demand, it proposes that crime rates may be influenced by altering the risks and benefits of criminal behavior (Garoupa 1997). According to the economics of crime "everybody may become a criminal if placed in the appropriate situation: it is opportunity that makes the thief" (Panther 1995: 366). Becker (1968) and Stigler (1970) provided the initial approach necessary to tackle the economics of crime. It was based on deterrence theories, which presumed that potential law-breakers know the fines and punishments associated with various crimes as well as the probabilities of enforcement. They provided the framework for much of the following work which targeted individual agents allocative choice between activities which are legal and those which are illegal, when they are constrained by different deterrence systems and different opportunity costs.

An individual chooses to engage in a corrupt act if his expected benefits outweigh his expected costs. Becker (1968) in his original framework denoted the expected utility for an individual of engaging in criminal activity as follows[33]:

---

[33] From Becker (1968: 177, fn. 16).

$$EU_j = p_j U_j(Y_j - f_j) + (1 - p_j) U_j(Y_j)$$

Where the expected utility of committing an offense for person j is denoted by EU_j, p_j denotes the probability of detection that individual j faces, U_j represents his utility function, Y_j is his income, both monetary and psychic from engaging in offense, f_j the monetary equivalent of his punishment upon detection. Simply stated, the expected benefits from an offense are the probability of not being detected times the utility derived from engaging in the offense. The expected costs are the probability of detection times the cost of detection.

An individual shall engage in crime as long as the marginal utility from doing so is positive.[34] Put differently, there is no reason for him not to engage in corruption as long as the benefits he believes he will receive from doing so exceed his expected punishment. From a policy perspective the application of these models is commonly applied to the selection of an optimal level of resources to be put into the detection of corruption as well as the determination of an optimal fine level.[35] The general conclusion of these models is that high fines are desirable, as they deter criminal activity and permit society to reduce the level of resources utilized for enforcement- similarly it can compensate a low probability of detection which is itself desirable in order to conserve costly resources trying to discover transgressions. Another advantage put forward is that in contrast to altering the probability of detection, fines are transfer payments that are not costly to impose. This argumentation becomes more important when we consider that the amount of resources commonly needed to unveil corruption are costly, because of the secretive nature of corrupt exchanges (Bowles 1999: 467). Bribery reduces the deterrence effect of criminal sanctions, particularly when bribes are significantly less than the (monetary) equivalent of the sanction (Becker and Stigler 1974). These models, however, only depicted one party in a criminal transaction, but corruption, generally consists of an action of two or more parties acting at the expense of a third; hence, there are additional basic strategic considerations that must be considered. In corruption both players have to consent to an action and usually agree not to reveal this information to third parties. The income one receives from corrupt behavior as well as the probability of detection are a function of the behavior of additional parties with whom one could potentially transact. It is this potential to make additional income contingent on the behavior of others that provides both incentives to collude in the first place as well as makes corruption inherently risky.[36]

---

[34] Arising from this, one can easily derive $\Delta EU_j / \Delta p_j = U_j(Y_j - f_j) - U_j(Y_j) < 0$ and $\Delta EU_j / \Delta f_j = p_j U'_j(Y_j - f_j) < 0$. This suggests that as long as the marginal utility of income is positive, we can expect transgression to occur.

[35] *See* Garoupa (1997) and Polinsky and Shavell (1999) for a concise treatment and summary of the economics of optimal law enforcement.

[36] *See* further, Chapter II.

Empirical evidence seems to indicate that increasing punishment by altering the level of sanctions, the probability of being apprehended and the associated level of enforcement may deter crime, but the evidence is spread fitfully over different policies and different types of crime (*see* Cameron 1988). The potential of increasing wages to deter malfeasance was already recognized by Becker and Stigler (1974). An increase in the wages of the bureaucrat will increase his opportunity costs of entering into a corrupt transaction; hence, if there is no relative increase in the expected benefits for the bureaucrat, he would be less likely to engage in a corrupt exchanges. This is indeed the recommendation of several studies on corruption. For instance, Cadot (1987) in his model of corruption as a gamble showed us that the level of corruption is linked to the wages of the government officials. The World Development Report (1997) recommends that the wages of bureaucrats be raised in the fight against corruption. Poor wages have led to a near incentive crisis in the public sectors in many developing countries. The incentive problem can largely be divided into two parts. First, wages have dropped so low that the necessary talent required for public bodies is unavailable as these people are going to the private sector. The second incentive problem, which arises, is that there is no reasonable linkage between wages and performance for those working as public officials- this has been called incentive myopia in the literature (Klitgaard 1988). Moreover, low wages can potentially justify the receipt of bribes in the publics eyes, thus fostering a climate conducive to endemic corruption.

There are a few cautionary observations one should make regarding reliance on the aforementioned approach in policy reforms. First, increasing the fine for one criminal activity may actually just displace criminals who may then pursue other means to acquire illicit gains. Any approach must, therefore, be systematic. Second, enforcement officials may themselves be corrupt and use higher fines to blackmail parties into paying them bribes. The higher the fine, the larger the bribe law enforcement officials can demand. Third, higher fines may lead to a reduction in the number of persons that participate in criminal activity, but this does not necessarily reduce the amount of criminality per se. When criminals specialize in certain markets (as we see with organized crime), there may be fewer participants which can actually increase the level of corruption given that parties enter into more frequent repeat dealings. Fourth, potential criminals are neither aware of the (precise) fines nor the probability of punishment (Opp 1989). Publicizing that sizable fines are in place may increase the level of deterrence. People may be more "boundedly rational" than economists would sometimes like to admit.[37] Fifth, decisions to engage in transgressions are actually

---

[37] Not particularly relevant for corruption, but an important criticism against the aforementioned approach nonetheless salient to other types of crime, comes from the sociologist and criminologist camp, who contend that a high fine level may just lead to increases in the rate of recidivism. At stage one there may be a modest change in the level of criminality, but at stage

social. The decision of any individual to break the law depends on his or her perception of the number of other persons willing to do likewise. The desirability of engaging in an activity depends on the number of others engaging in the same activity. A final notion that should also be mentioned but can scarcely be captured in the above approach is the fact that much compliance is actually the result of the internalization of values or norms, as well as social sanctions. In the case of the former, individuals voluntarily do not engage in certain behavior- a type of voluntary compliance or endogenous preference. For example, feelings of guilt prevent many people from engaging in socially undesirable behavior, and conversely prevent many people from not engaging in socially desirable behavior. In the case of the latter, it should be recognized that most activity is regulated by social as opposed to legal sanctions; as discussed in later sections any reform package against corruption must foster an environment conducive to such social sanctions.

Of the cautionary observations I have just presented, I would like to draw attention to the need to understand strategic factors in reform, and for this reason I deal at greater length with this below.[38]

A. Strategic Factors

Crime, like many other activities, is strategic and is not the result of a stable portfolio allocation by an individual in one particular activity independent of the activities of others. Accordingly, Tsebelis (1990, 1993) argues that certain decisions such as whether I take an umbrella to work fall within the realm of decision theory, whereas other decisions such as whether or not I speed depend on the behavior of an opponent (*e.g.*, an enforcement official) and are therefore strategic. Essentially he argues that when a game has no pure strategies modifying the size of the penalty does not affect the frequency of the criminal activity at the equilibrium, but rather the frequency of law enforcement.

Let us cast our attention to Figure 2. In Figure 2, a_1 represents the utility a motorist receives from speeding when the enforcement official enforces; b_1 denotes the utility a motorist receives from speeding when the enforcement official doesn't enforce; c_1 depicts the utility a motorist receives from not speeding when the enforcement official enforces, and d_2 denotes the utility a motorist acquires from not speeding when the enforcement official doesn't enforce.

---

two there may be a more dramatic increase because criminals have fewer opportunities, and hence a lower opportunity cost.

[38] Note, I are not suggesting that the economics of crime ignores these factors, but rather stress their important in policy proposals.

Figure 2: Enforcement Game

	Enforce	Don't Enforce
Speed	a_1, a_2	b_1, b_2
Don't Speed	c_1, c_2	d_1, d_2

Where $c_1 > a_1$ and $b_1 > d_1$ for the violator
And $a_2 > b_2$ and $d_2 > c_2$ for the enforcer

a_2 denotes the utility the enforcement official receives from enforcing when the motorist speeds, c_2 depicts the utility the official derives from controlling when the motorist doesn't speed, b_2 depicts the utility the official derives from not controlling when the motorist speeds, and d_2 indicates the utility the enforcement official acquires from not controlling when the motorist doesn't speed. We make the following assumptions: $c_1 > a_1$ and $b_1 > d_1$ for the violator and $a_2 > b_2$ and $d_2 > c_2$ for the enforcer. Given the structure of the game we can easily see that there is no Nash Equilibrium (for pure strategies).[39] Player 1 has no one best response independent of what choice Player 2 makes, for example if Player 2 decides not to enforce it is in his interest to speed, if however Player 2 decides to enforce, it is in his best interest not to speed. Similarly, Player 2 has no one best response. Tsebelis argues that parties, given the fact that there are no pure strategies will then play mixed strategies.[40] Mixed strategies for both players may be computed as shown.

The probability that the motorist will speed, $p*$ is derived as follows

$pa_2 + (1-p)c_2 = pb_2 + (1-p)d_2$
$$p* = \frac{d_2 - c_2}{a_2 - b_2 - c_2 + d_2}$$

Similarly, the probability that the enforcer will enforce is derived as follows

$q* = qa_1 + (1-q)b_1 = qc_1 + (1-q)d_1$

---

[39] A Nash equilibrium may be best considered "as a strategy profile in which each player's part is as good a response to what the others are meant to do as any other strategy available to that player" (Kreps 1990: 404).

[40] Players can mix their strategies so that neither the motorist nor the enforcer will gain a higher expected payoff by choosing an alternative strategy given the strategy pursued by the other player. *See,* Dixit and Nalebuff (1993) for a nontechnical introduction.

$$q^* = \frac{d_1 - b_1}{a_1 - b_1 - c_1 + d_1}$$

According to mixed strategies, a change in the fine has no impact on the behavior of the violator as he chooses his best strategy according to the payoffs of the enforcer, *i.e.*, a change in a_1 has no affect on the equilibrium strategy chosen by the violator. A mixed strategy Nash Equilibrium shows the situation where when both players can learn from one another, they have no incentive to deviate. This is an obscure and counterintuitive result, but it is subject to a series of assumptions. First of all it assumes that the players are playing mixed strategies, which is only one possible strategy that the parties can choose (for other strategies, *see* Holler 1993; Fudenberg and Tirole 1996). Furthermore, playing mixed strategies effectively assumes a vast knowledge of the opponents payoffs, that can be realistically only be acquired by playing repeatedly with the same opponent. It is highly unlikely, however, that parties shall interact a sufficient number of times to acquire such knowledge, as in the example above. Moreover it is assumed that the players' payoffs were not interdependent, which may not be plausible. For example the payoff to the enforcer may be tied to the amount of revenue (fines) he collects (indeed, in order to maximize the effort level of the enforcer, his gains should be tied to the revenue attained through his own effort level, as we learn from principal agent theory). Moreover, he may receive different types of payoffs such as praise etc. that ensure he does not reduce his effort level substantially.

An important contribution of authors like Tsebelis is, however, to highlight the need to assess criminal behavior in lieu of strategic factors. For example, it highlights the fact that a drop in crime may have an adverse effect on the behavior of the police, given that they now have greater incentive to shirk. Furthermore, it begins to highlight some of the complications that occur in analysis when we do not take a look at the shift in opportunities that may occur with policy changes. I shall incorporate some of these changes into later analysis, emphasizing that one needs to look at strategic opportunities as implications of policy. A simple example may help illustrate the importance of taking strategic factors into account. Consider again the same situation as above, a police officer that controls for speed. If we set the fine at $100 for any violation of the speed limit, the citizen well-versed in Becker-like reasoning will take into account the probability of detection and multiply this by the fine before transgressing. A police officer who is responsible for enforcing this fine may solicit a maximum bribe of up to $100 (or slightly more if there are additional costs for the violator). If we now increase the fine to $1000, there may be a corresponding increase in deterrence for the citizen, but there is also a corresponding increase in incentives for the police officer to solicit a bribe. The police officer, being himself well-versed in Becker-like reasoning, shall now compute his own expected gains and expected costs of corruption. Given that he may now solicit a bribe of $1000, all other things equal, he has greater incentives to engage in corruption. Furthermore, the police officer now has greater incentives to harass the citizen and falsify accusations to extract a bribe. Summing up, we may argue that an increase in the fine level may lead to greater deterrence from the point of view of the citizen from breaking the law, but there is a corresponding negative effect that it increases the gains from corruption for the enforcement officer. Furthermore, the newfound potential for bribing also dilutes the deterrent effect.[41]

Furthermore, increasing the fine may lead to increases in the effort levels of parties to get around the fine, as well as opportunities for others to assist in the process. A very banal example of how this works is the following. In Hamburg. Germany, the fine for traveling by public transport without a ticket is 30 Euros. As in the above example, increasing the fine may result in increasing the probability of collusion between a control and a patron. In order to get around this (in addition to security and possibly efficiency purposes), controllers may travel, as indeed they do in groups. This results in the fact that it becomes difficult for any one controller to solicit a bribe (note, he may get around this if the group can collude and can enforce their agreement). An additional strategic problem is, however, also at work if we take third parties into account. Assume it is possible that third parties may print false tickets. Increasing the fine suggests that the demand for the services of third parties may increase and forgers can now change a higher price, at least temporarily for their tickets. Moreover, the shift in demand itself may encourage others to enter into the forging business as long as the original counterfeiters are achieving above cost prices. The overall result can be more as opposed to less transgressions.

IX. Recent Developments in Curbing Corruption

The general character of economics-based policy proposals to curb corruption still take as their basis the reduction of gains from paying and receiving bribes relative to costs but have moved away from simple deterrence models. While the nature of the measures are dependent on the models involved, there are certain controls that are regularly put forward as helpful which I sketch out comprehensively though concisely below, some of which I touched on in earlier discussion.

Explicitly or implicitly, work in the area generally takes a principal-agent type framework, where corruption can manifest itself as long as there is a principal, an agent, and a third party, whose welfare depends on the actions of the agent.[42] The principal is normally considered to be the government, but can

---

[41] *See* Polinsksy and Shavel (1999) for an analysis of how corruption of law enforcement agents affect the optimal fine level. Paper available at http://www.nber.org/papers/w6945.

[42] *See* Banfield (1975), Rose-Ackerman (1975, 1978), Lui (1986), Klitgaard (1988), Tirole (1986, 1992) Cadot (1987) Bac (1996ab, 1998). The list of authors is long and distinguished, and the above is only representative of some important work using this approach.

sometimes be considered broadly as the population in general; the agent is a public official (elected or appointed is of little importance); the citizen refers to an outside party willing to enter into a corrupt or collusive transaction at the expense of the principal. The bribe-receiver has acquired a position of power, because of either market imperfections or an institutional position which divests onto him discretionary authority (Rose-Ackerman 1975: 187).[43] Principal-agent models have two characteristics: principals and agents follow different goals; and secondly, there is uncertainty or incomplete information. Uncertainty can manifest itself in two forms depending on whether principals are influenced by either the "hidden actions" of agents or by "hidden information" to which they are privy. Associated with these two types of uncertainty are the actions known as moral hazard and adverse selection respectively (Breton 1995: 419).

One means of preventing corruption is through preempting it and designing pay structures (through the use of contracts) that make engaging in corruption undesirable.[44] As adumbrated earlier, one method for doing this is to set wages above that which can be received elsewhere (Becker and Stigler 1974; Klitgaard 1988). Another is to set pensions conditional to "good behavior", where all is lost if malfeasance is discovered (Becker and Stigler 1974). These can be considered as bonds paid by officials that are forfeited in case of corruption. Other uses of bonds are also important. For example, in the case of public contracts performance bonds can be used whereby payment is (partially) a result of the achievement of well-specified goals.[45]

Alternatively, additional layers within or external to an organization may be developed whose aim is to control malfeasance. The internal affairs department common in the United States is one example of an internal device to control police impropriety, as it falls within the control of the police department itself. Similarly, internal auditors within public organizations provide an additional supervisory layer. Whilst such mechanisms are important, they are subject to two major criticisms. First, the same problem may still occur within an organization just one step removed. Second, it is a form of self-policing where the incentives to uncover and disclose malfeasance are limited as there are a reputational costs for an entire agency or department.[46] Alternatively, such policing devices may as suggested above, be external. Examples of these include external auditors,

---

[43] The economic approach to the principal agent relationship focused originally on issues related to sharecropping, insurance and physician-client relations. This models grew with the increased interest in the role of the delegation of decision making authority and the development of models of imperfect monitoring and imperfect information (Breton 1995: 418). From a theoretical point of view the principal agent model views bureaucracies no different to any other firms, namely as a nexus of contracts (Coase 1937).

[44] This has been advanced in the literature by mechanism design proponents, see Laffont and Tirole (1993) for an introduction to this literature.

[45] See further, Chapter III, Section VII.

[46] See further, Chapter III, Section V, Subsection D.

ombudsmen, inspectorates etc. As we shall see later, the ability of these parties to uncover and disclose widespread corruption is often limited by such factors as partiality, budgetary deficiencies and political steering and control (particularly through budget allocation) and the fact that they generally provide ex post as opposed to ex ante supervision.

A further means of controlling corruption, is based on the control of hidden information or adverse selection mentioned above. Frequently, it is important both for performance and as an anti-corruption measure to adequately screen (potential) employees. This should already occur at the recruitment stage, as corrupt systems frequently find it in their interests to plant one of their people within an organization. Adequate means need to be developed in order to weed out this practice; this should begin with the elimination of appointments based on patronage.

An additional means of designing institutions preemptively against corruption is the "selling the store solution". Such measures may include privatization and contracting out certain services.[47] More controversially, it has included in the past selling the rights to collect taxes, as was practiced at one stage in the Roman Empire (MacMullen 1988). These measures may be useful against corruption but can also open up a whole new loci of payoffs.

Moreover, the government might consider introducing competition both within and among agencies as described briefly above. This is particularly important in order to reduce the monopoly hold that any person may have within an organization or the monopoly hold that an organization may have itself on the supply of a particular public good (Rose-Ackerman 1978; Shleifer and Vishny 1993; Bardhan 1997).

Finally, the government might try instigating competition among firms in their domestic market. This generally involves deregulation and opening the economy up to competition from outside, in order to reduce the monopoly power of a domestic producer. These measures should also be accompanied by suitable anti-trust laws.[48]

---

[47] *See* further, Chapter III, Section VIII.
[48] On this last point, *see* Ades and Di Tella (1995) and Della Porta and Vannucci (1999).

X. Appendix

Table 1: Corruption Perceptions Index 2001[49]

Country Rank	Country	2001 CPI Score	Surveys Used	Standard Deviation	High-Low Range
1	Finland	9.9	7	0.6	9.2 - 10.6
2	Denmark	9.5	7	0.7	8.8 - 10.6
3	New Zealand	9.4	7	0.6	8.6 - 10.2
4	Iceland	9.2	6	1.1	7.4 - 10.1
5	Singapore	9.2	12	0.5	8.5 - 9.9
6	Sweden	9.0	8	0.5	8.2 - 9.7
7	Canada	8.9	8	0.5	8.2 - 9.7
8	Netherlands	8.8	7	0.3	8.4 - 9.2
9	Luxembourg	8.7	6	0.5	8.1 - 9.5
10	Norway	8.6	7	0.8	7.4 - 9.6
11	Australia	8.5	9	0.9	6.8 - 9.4
12	Switzerland	8.4	7	0.5	7.4 - 9.2
13	United Kingdom	8.3	9	0.5	7.4 - 8.8
14	Hong Kong	7.9	11	0.5	7.2 - 8.7
15	Austria	7.8	7	0.5	7.2 - 8.7
16	Israel	7.6	8	0.3	7.3 - 8.1
17	USA	7.6	11	0.7	6.1 - 9.0
18	Chile	7.5	9	0.6	6.5 - 8.5
19	Ireland	7.5	7	0.3	6.8 - 7.9
20	Germany	7.4	8	0.8	5.8 - 8.6
21	Japan	7.1	11	0.9	5.6 - 8.4
22	Spain	7.0	8	0.7	5.8 - 8.1
23	France	6.7	8	0.8	5.6 - 7.8
24	Belgium	6.6	7	0.7	5.7 - 7.6
25	Portugal	6.3	8	0.8	5.3 - 7.4
26	Botswana	6.0	3	0.5	5.6 - 6.6
27	Taiwan	5.9	11	1.0	4.6 - 7.3
28	Estonia	5.6	5	0.3	5.0 - 6.0
29	Italy	5.5	9	1.0	4.0 - 6.9
30	Namibia	5.4	3	1.4	3.8 - 6.7
31	Hungary	5.3	10	0.8	4.0 - 6.2

---

[49] Source: http//www.transparency.org/cpi/2001/cpi2001.htm.

32	Trinidad & Tobago	5.3	3	1.5	3.8 - 6.9
33	Tunisia	5.3	3	1.3	3.8 - 6.5
34	Slovenia	5.2	7	1.0	4.1 - 7.1
35	Uruguay	5.1	4	0.7	4.4 - 5.8
36	Malaysia	5.0	11	0.7	3.8 - 5.9
37	Jordan	4.9	4	0.8	3.8 - 5.7
38	Lithuania	4.8	5	1.5	3.8 - 7.5
39	South Africa	4.8	10	0.7	3.8 - 5.6
40	Costa Rica	4.5	5	0.7	3.7 - 5.6
41	Mauritius	4.5	5	0.7	3.9 - 5.6
42	Greece	4.2	8	0.6	3.6 - 5.6
43	South Korea	4.2	11	0.7	3.4 - 5.6
44	Peru	4.1	6	1.1	2.0 - 5.3
45	Poland	4.1	10	0.9	2.9 - 5.6
46	Brazil	4.0	9	0.3	3.5 - 4.5
47	Bulgaria	3.9	6	0.6	3.2 - 5.0
48	Croatia	3.9	3	0.6	3.4 - 4.6
49	Czech Republic	3.9	10	0.9	2.6 - 5.6
50	Colombia	3.8	9	0.6	3.0 - 4.5
51	Mexico	3.7	9	0.6	2.5 - 5.0
52	Panama	3.7	3	0.4	3.1 - 4.0
53	Slovak Republic	3.7	7	0.9	2.1 - 4.9
54	Egypt	3.6	7	1.5	1.2 - 6.2
55	El Salvador	3.6	5	0.9	2.0 - 4.3
56	Turkey	3.6	9	0.8	2.0 - 4.5
57	Argentina	3.5	9	0.6	2.9 - 4.4
58	China	3.5	10	0.4	2.7 - 3.9
59	Ghana	3.4	3	0.5	2.9 - 3.8
60	Latvia	3.4	3	1.2	2.0 - 4.3
61	Malawi	3.2	3	1.0	2.0 - 3.9
62	Thailand	3.2	12	0.9	0.6 - 4.0
63	Dominican Rep	3.1	3	0.9	2.0 - 3.9
64	Moldova	3.1	3	0.9	2.1 - 3.8
65	Guatemala	2.9	4	0.9	2.0 - 4.2
66	Philippines	2.9	11	0.9	1.6 - 4.8
67	Senegal	2.9	3	0.8	2.2 - 3.8
68	Zimbabwe	2.9	6	1.1	1.6 - 4.7
69	Romania	2.8	5	0.5	2.0 - 3.4
70	Venezuela	2.8	9	0.4	2.0 - 3.6

71	Honduras	2.7	3	1.1	2.0 - 4.0
72	India	2.7	12	0.5	2.1 - 3.8
73	Kazakhstan	2.7	3	1.3	1.8 - 4.3
74	Uzbekistan	2.7	3	1.1	2.0 - 4.0
75	Vietnam	2.6	7	0.7	1.5 - 3.8
76	Zambia	2.6	3	0.5	2.0 - 3.0
77	Cote d´Ivoire	2.4	3	1.0	1.5 - 3.6
78	Nicaragua	2.4	3	0.8	1.9 - 3.4
79	Ecuador	2.3	6	0.3	1.8 - 2.6
80	Pakistan	2.3	3	1.7	0.8 - 4.2
81	Russia	2.3	10	1.2	0.3 - 4.2
82	Tanzania	2.2	3	0.6	1.6 - 2.9
83	Ukraine	2.1	6	1.1	1.0 - 4.3
84	Azerbaijan	2.0	3	0.2	1.8 - 2.2
85	Bolivia	2.0	5	0.6	1.5 - 3.0
86	Cameroon	2.0	3	0.8	1.2 - 2.9
87	Kenya	2.0	4	0.7	0.9 - 2.6
88	Indonesia	1.9	12	0.8	0.2 - 3.1
89	Uganda	1.9	3	0.6	1.3 - 2.4
90	Nigeria	1.0	4	0.9	-0.1 - 2.0
91	Bangladesh	0.4	3	2.9	-1.7 - 3.8

Note on the Bangladesh score:

Data for this country in 2001 was available from only three independent survey sources, and each of these yielded very different results. While the composite score is 0.4, the range of individual survey results is from -1.7 to +3.8. This is a greater range than for any other country. TI stresses, therefore, that this result needs to be viewed with caution.

Explanatory Notes

1. A more detailed description of the CPI methodology is available at www.gwdg.de/~uwvw/ 2001.htm.
2. **2001 CPI Score** relates to perceptions of the degree of corruption as seen by business people, academics and risk analysts, and ranges between 10 (highly clean) and 0 (highly corrupt).
3. **Surveys Used** refers to the number of surveys that assessed a country's performance. A total of 14 surveys were used, and at least three surveys were required for a country to be included in the CPI.
4. **Standard Deviation** indicates differences in the values of the sources: the greater the standard deviation, the greater the differences of perceptions of a country among the sources.
5. **High-Low Range** provides the highest and lowest values of the sources. Since each individual source has its own scaling system, scores are standardised around a common mean

52

for the subset of countries featuring in the individual survey. As a result, it is possible in rare cases that the highest value exceeds 10.0 and the lowest can be lower than 0.0. Only the aggregate final country scores are restricted to the reported range between 0 and 10.

CHAPTER II

THE EVOLUTION AND MAINTENANCE OF CORRUPTION

"Think systems not individuals" (Klitgaard 1996: 43).

I. Introduction

To comprehend the problem of controlling corruption a useful endeavor is to conjure up a climate where corruption is most likely to evolve; one, so consummate to malfeasance that even an honest person would be find himself enticed to enter into corrupt exchanges.[1] Among the more salient factors that induce this likelihood are a large bribe, a low probability of detection, and a high probability that others in a similar situation would also do the same, in order to lower the psychological and social costs of engaging in such undertakings. As Klitgaard is suggests: "Corruption is a crime of calculation, not of passion. People tend to engage in corruption when the risks are low, the penalties mild and the rewards great" (Klitgaard, MacLean-Abaroa and Parris 2000: 27). The ability of the official to receive a bribe in the first place is contingent upon government involvement in the regulation or allocation of valuable activities. In turn, the size of the bribe is contingent on the allocation of discretionary and monopolistic authority of governmental decisions enjoyed by the official, *i.e.*, whether he or she must act alone or whether the decision is made by more than one person, thus reducing the size of the bribe and increasing the risk and the difficulties of maintaining collusive agreements.

In such an environment, to avoid detection, the official's decision must be so lacking in standards as not to draw suspicion or alternatively, unobservable or nontransparent, hidden within and indistinguishable from other actions. Actions would be secretive. Moreover, he would be familiar with those with whom he transacts and their interests would be largely aligned. To reduce the pangs of conscience and the threat of social sanction (such as ostracism), the individual would operate in an environment where corrupt as opposed to noncorrupt transactions are considered the norm, and where failure to participate was subject to derision and ridicule, if not sanctions of their own. Moreover, loyalty to the public that the official is supposed to service would be foregone, perhaps in favor of some other group.

---

[1] As logical as this suggestion may seem, it has to my knowledge only once before been presented in the literature (*see* Heymann 1996).

Those are some of the key conditions that make corruption more likely to evolve - the reformers task is clearly to limit as many of them as possible. Corruption can be fought at several levels, some of which I introduced in our reexamination of the issues in chapter I. Parties to corruption generally wish to keep the transactions secret, which leaves them vulnerable. My emphasis here is on both the secrecy and accompanying vulnerabilities aspect of corrupt transactions, in particular searching for, agreeing and delivering on corrupt deals, as well as those factors that allow the evolution and maintenance of such corrupt exchanges.

Corrupt transactions distinguish themselves from many other illicit activities in that they involve cooperation from at least two people, *i.e.,* bribe-giver and bribe-receiver. The fact that corruption is a form of cooperative behavior has often been overlooked in the literature.[2] This lacuna is the main focus of this chapter. Even when corruption has been identified as cooperative behavior, central factors that increase the likelihood and maintenance of cooperation have never been analyzed in the context of corruption. The fact that corruption is a form of cooperative behavior is a mixed blessing. One the one hand it must be understood within the broader perspective of reciprocal rewards and sanctions, often firmly entrenched within regular (legal) social and economic transactions, a factor which makes corruption particularly difficult to curb. To cope with this, it will be argued there is a need to think in terms of corrupt systems. On the other hand, given that corruption is a form of cooperative behavior, parties need to be able to search for and identify one another, agree on the terms of an agreement and enforce the provisions of the deal without being detected leaves parties exposed to detection. One can see that in each of these steps, parties must incur substantial risks and there is a significant degree of uncertainty and trust involved (*see* Heymann 1996: 332).[3] The following is suggestive of those areas where corruption is most likely to occur and how it is likely to be maintained as well as means to expose these aforementioned vulnerabilities and invert corruption.

---

[2] Of course many works have identified but not developed this fact. Notable exceptions include the work of Tirole (1986, 1992), Rose-Ackerman (1986) and Bac (1996a, 1996b). These authors, however, did not look at the factors which may lead to the evolution or maintenance of corruption, but frequently on the impact of collusion on organizational design, or designing incentive packages.

[3] As we shall see below, however, the fact that corruption is a form of reciprocity is a mixed blessing in for reformers. There are several reasons for this, including: Life is full of reciprocity and reciprocity is often considered a virtue in itself. Secondly, illegal as well as legal exchanges are likely to be enmeshed together. Third, patterns of reciprocity may be based on ascribed trust, *e.g.*, based on ones ethnic group, making them more difficult to break.

II. Corrupt Exchanges

Adumbrated above, the road to corrupt exchanges may be froth with dangers. Officials and private parties must perceive each other as potential corrupt partners, find a way of reaching an agreement and then deliver as agreed without being detected. All of these steps potentially make corruption exposable to detection. Corruption, as suggested, unlike many other illegal acts such as plain theft, is a form of cooperative behavior.

Parties willing to engage in corruption should find themselves in a kind of a prisoner's dilemma situation. This is depicted in Figure 1.

Figure 1: Prisoner's Dilemma

	Cooperate	Defect
Cooperate	5, 5	-10, 10
Defect	10, -10	0, 0

For convenience I have given numerical examples. As a player you may rank the four possible outcomes as follows: The best to is for you to defect on the opposing player and have him cooperate. Next best is for you to cooperate and have the opposing player also cooperate. The third best outcome for outcome you can have is for you to defect and the other player also to defect. The worst possible outcome is for you to cooperate and other player to defect. Here given the structure of the payoffs the gains from trade are not necessarily exploited because the dominant strategy for both parties is unconditional defection. Put differently defection by Player 1 strictly dominates cooperation as a strategy, as does defection by Player 2 strictly dominate cooperation. The solution, therefore, as a result of strict dominance in a one-shot game is for both parties to defect, which implies that potential gains from transacting for both parties are not realized. Note Parties cannot force one another to cooperate, given weak monitoring systems. As with all illegal transactions they are not enforceable in court so parties need to find other means to promulgate cooperation and enforce agreements. They need ways to resolve the prisoner's dilemma. Viewed from this perspective, the prisoner's dilemma may be looked upon as an accurate model to depict both mutual trust or distrust. In the case of mutual trust the game at each round is merely part of a long sequence of exchanges between the parties, allowing for some variation in the payoffs at each exchange. In the case of distrust, the game is commonly one shot or at an end-game situation (Hardin 2001).

Alternatively many corrupt transactions may be looked upon as a "game of trust" depicted in Figure 2, which shares almost identical properties to the prisoner's dilemma, but is of a sequential nature. It is sometimes referred to as one-way trust, because it is only Player 1 that has to trust Player 2 to honor his agreement and Player 1 can never cheat on Player 2. Again for simplicity I have taken numerical examples.

Figure 2: Game of Trust

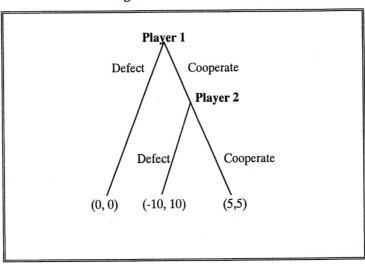

The above game begins at the point where Player 1 decides whether or not to cooperate, *i.e.*, pass on a bribe or a favor to Player 2 in return for a quid pro quo at a later stage. Among the many examples one can think of to visualize such a situation, consider the decision of an individual to bribe a bureaucrat in order to receive a license. Should Player 1 decide not to cooperate then the game is over. Should Player 1 decide to cooperate, then Player 2 has two options, he may either reciprocate, or he may not reciprocate (defect). Player 1's decision to take the first move is sometimes referred to as preemptive commitment; Player 2's decision pledge to honor player 1's move in a specified contingent way is sometimes referred to as reactive commitment (Hirschleifer 2000). As Player 1 you may rank your outcomes. The best possible outcome for you occurs when you cooperate and Player 2 also cooperates. The second best outcome for you is when you decide not to bribe (defect) and Player 2 is never called into action. The worst possible outcome for you is for you to cooperate by investing and for Player 2 to defect and expropriate the investment. Given the above payoffs, we can see that Player 2 would prefer to cooperate rather than get nothing at all, but his preferred strategy is to defect, which yields him the greatest payoff. Player 1 is aware of the fact that Player 2 maximizes his payoff by defecting, so he therefore does not invest in the first place. This decision is reached by backward induction.[4] The only possible solution to the game is for player 1 not to invest, which from the perspective of the parties is not efficient as both would prefer cooperation to no transaction at all.

A. Resolving the One-Shot Game

The above are examples of one shot games, which are not characteristic of many of the forms of corruption that we are interested in addressing which occur beyond the incidental level. There are, nevertheless, of course, many real life situations that fit this description. Take, for example, the case of a police official that gives someone a ticket for speeding (I shall show, nevertheless, that even here, one needs to consider corruption as part of a repeated game). How can the parties here come to a corrupt transaction? There are four key means to overcome the dilemma in such a situation.

First, the parties here may cooperate if the officer can signal his type without incriminating himself, for example by giving a well established sign (*see* Hirschleifer 2000).[5] The citizen may take up this signal if he is aware of this sign (again, we can argue that this is a norm that has established itself among certain elements of society and that although these persons may meet only once, the game is played repeatedly). Furthermore, even if the citizen is aware of this sign and is unwilling, there is a verification problem, and it is difficult for the citizen to show that the policeman solicited a bribe. *Second,* cooperation may occur when a person gives his word of honor and abides by a commitment, considering abiding by his word to be a goal or virtue in itself. *Third,* perhaps the most straightforward reason for cooperation in this situation is based on the fact that one party may be worried that the other will be upset and seek revenge (Tirole 1996). Whether or not a player would be willing to seek revenge is not important, it is the probability and the uncertainty surrounding this that is consequential. For example, in a world of two types of players, Clint and Barbie, the policeman may give the impression that he is a Clint and will seek revenge on the motorist if he does not pay him a bribe. He may do this even if he is a Barbie and fearful of seeking revenge, provided the psychological costs of doing so are not to high. Because, it is a one-shot game, the motorist may not willing to take the risk if he cannot distinguish which class of person the policeman actually belongs to.

---

[4] As Güth, Ockenfels and Wendel (1997: 17) note, unwillingness to cooperate is the only strategy vector " surviving repeated elimination of dominated strategies and also the only subgame perfect equilibrium point...".

[5] This is equivalent to what a game theorist may term clues, *see* Hirschleifer (2000).

Fourth, another reason for cooperation, that is normally overlooked in the literature, is that there is a certain amount of uncertainty as to whether or not the parties will meet again in the future. Where there is a certain probability that the parties will meet again in the future, the parties may be willing to cooperate, the parties being unsure as to whether or not it is a repeated game. Alternatively, one can readily perceive a situation where neither party wants to see each other again, because of shame, the risk of blackmail etc.- where it is unlikely that the parties will meet again, parties may be more willing to bend the law. It should be noted, for example, that in this particular example with the police officer and the motorist there is no victim, so when the bribe that is solicited is below the fine, as must be the case (unless we also include the possibility of the police officer fabricating the severity of the offense), both parties have incentives to remain quiet and their interests are aligned.

III. Inverting Corruption

With an aim to inverting illicit cooperation, in what follows I shall analyze the development and maintenance of corruption, a form of cooperative behavior. Whilst, it is possible to think of iterated one-way trust games of the type described above as fitting this description, they are probably rather unusual in the general body of all trust or cooperative relationships. Indeed, one can expect "the more stable and compelling trust relationships to be mutual and ongoing" (Hardin 2001: 12). The prisoner's dilemma as opposed to the game of trust which I use for the greater part as the basis of our discussion approximates more accurately most ongoing relationships, which form the greater part of our discussion, as they are, as mentioned above, an example of a model of mutual trust, where the game at each round is merely part of a long sequence of exchanges between the parties, with perhaps some variation in the payoffs at each exchange (Fudenberg and Tirole 1996; Hardin 2001: 12-13).

As suggested above, it is the reformers task to identify those factors that are most conducive to corruption and to eliminate as many of them as possible. By controlling the opportunities for parties to reciprocate illicit behavior, we shall reduce the level of corruption. The fact that corruption is a form of reciprocal behavior is a mixed blessing. On the one hand, it permits a policy-maker to exploit those weakness associated with the many steps of corruption outlined earlier, such as finding a partner, negotiating a deal and delivering what one has promised without being detected, as well as the enforcement problem faced by the parties involved in corrupt exchanges. On the other hand, however, the fact that corruption is a form of reciprocal behavior may make curbing it all the more difficult. There are several reasons for this. First, illicit transactions of reciprocity are frequently intertwined with perfectly legal transactions, making them appear more legitimate and more difficult to detect. Second, reciprocity may be an aim in itself. People are motivated by both social acceptance as well as by economic gain (Harsanyi 1969). Where trust, for example, is ascribed, *i.e.*, related to members of ones one clan or group, it is highly stable and difficult to overcome. Reciprocity can become an ends in itself, where actors desire to reciprocate because they generate positive feelings from doing so, and negative feelings from not doing so. A similar point was raised by Noonan (1984: xiii) who suggested: "Bribes are a species of reciprocity. Human life is full of reciprocities." Reciprocities may become a motivational factor by and of themselves.

One key factor that I wish to get across is that reform measures are commonly not good per se. It depends very much on the nature and patterns of reciprocity that have developed and may simply reallocate discretion to corrupt parties for their own purpose. Understanding the mechanisms that are used to maintain cooperation and understanding their vulnerabilities assists us in assessing the importance of a mechanism in fighting corruption. To identify the values of particular reforms, given that reforms may shift the balance of power to those that are themselves corrupt, it may be necessary to identify the corrupt organization itself in order to ascertain the running of the system as well as its means of self enforcement.

To reiterate, the central aim of this chapter is to highlight some of the vulnerabilities of corrupt exchanges and the factors that assist or are used by corrupt actors in overcoming basic dilemmas. Moreover, though there are a multitude of reasons for cooperation evolving, I submit that the factors highlighted here are of great importance to understanding factors that influence both the evolution and maintenance of corruption. Of course, there is no easy way to identify when illicit cooperation will occur. For example, findings of Axelrod and others that followed suggest that "cooperation can get started even in a world of unconditional defection...(that) strategies based on reciprocity can thrive in a world where many different kinds of strategies are being tried (and that) cooperation, once established on the basis of reciprocity, can protect itself from invasion by less cooperative strategies" (Axelrod 1984: 21). [6] Axelrod has been criticized as being too optimistic about the evolution of cooperation (*see* Binmore 1997; Geddes 1994).[7,8] But what the results of Axelrod and others do identify is that cooperation can evolve under a multitude of circumstances. We cannot

---

[6] Axelrod identified the following factors that increase the level of cooperation derived from a two-person prisoner's dilemma: Enlarge the shadow of the future, change the payoffs, teach people to care about each other, teach reciprocity, and improve recognition abilities.

[7] In our case of course the evolution of illicit cooperation is undesirable.

[8] As Roth (1995: 29), a renowned experimental game theorist, puts it: "Computer simulations are useful for creating and exploring theoretical models, while experiments are useful for observing behavior... Computer tournaments thus suggest that behavior will eventually converge to cooperation. This conclusion is at odds with experimental results... I suspect that the difference in results has a great deal to do with the learning that goes on with experience with the game and with the behavior of the rest of the subject pool."

eliminate all of those circumstances, but we can identify and eliminate many of them.

A. Repetition and Reciprocity

Russel Hardin in a recent article on trust told the following story taken from Dostoyevsky's The Brother Karamzov:

> "In *The Brothers Karamozov*, Dmitry Karamazov tells the story of a lieutenant-colonel who, as commander of a unit far from Moscow, managed substantial sums of money on behalf of the army. Immediately after each periodic audit of his books, he took the available funds to the merchant Trifonov, who soon returned them with interest and a gift. In effect, both the Lt. Colonel and Trifonov benefited from the funds that would otherwise have lain idle, producing no benefit for anyone. Because it was highly irregular, theirs was a secret exchange that depended wholly on personal trustworthiness not backed by the law of contracts. When the day came that the Lt. Colonel was abruptly to be replaced in his command, he asked Trimonov to return the last sum, 4,500 rubles, loaned to him. Trifonov replied, "I've never received any money from you, and couldn't possibly have received any"" (Dostoyevky 1982: 129).[9]

As Hardin noted: "Trifonov's "couldn't possibly" was an elegant touch because it drove home in a subtle way that the entire series of transactions was criminal. The Lt. Colonel could not have wanted any of it to become public- not even at the cost of the final 4500 rubles to keep it secret" (Hardin 2001: 1).

The aforementioned captures much of what we shall look at in this section. It shows how repetition can bring about illicit cooperation. It captures nicely how an end in the game (or series of transaction) can easily lead to one party not honoring its agreement when there is the expectation of no future gains, and moreover shows the inherent dangers of illegal transactions. We shall later see that had the relationship of the Lt. Colonel and Trifonov been embedded in other social relations or involved other parties the problem may not have occurred, an observation that Hardin also does not fail to make.

Repetition is perhaps the most essential factor that may lead to cooperation, given that it increases opportunities and returns from reciprocity.[10] In order to understand why parties reciprocate cooperative behavior, it is necessary to look at repeated games. Repeated games as Fudenberg and Tirole (1996: 145) suggest are a "good approximation of some long-term relationships in economics

---

[9] Retold in Hardin (2001: 1).
[10] As Becker and Stigler (1974) suggested: "The quality of enforcement depends, ... on the temporal pattern of violations. It is difficult to bribe or even intimidate the enforcers who would be involved in a nonrepetitive violation."

and political science- particularly where "trust" and "social pressure" are important, such as when informal agreements are used to enforce mutually beneficial trades without legally enforced contracts." It is easy to see how the expectation of mutually profitable arrangements between repetitive violators and enforcement officials can lead to cooperation and are particularly difficult to restrict.[11]

We must expect players to have a plethora of strategies that may still lead to an equilibrium, as opposed to the impression commonly perceived that only one strategy, namely tit for tat, can maintain an equilibrium in the long run.[12] Binmore (1997) suggests Axelrod (1984) emphasized what has been apparent in the economic literature for some time, namely that cooperation among knaves may develop similarly to cooperation among the morally righteous. To wit, the folk theorem in game theory indicates that if players are patient enough cooperation will occur.[13] Institutional design must therefore take account of possibilities for opportunistic behavior (Williamson 1985).

There is an apparent anomaly, however, in the argument that many stages of repetition can lead to cooperation as demonstrated in what is known as the "chain store paradox". When the parties are aware that there is a fixed and understood duration of time, the dominant strategy of defection should occur in the last stage. Adopting backward induction, player 1 shall anticipate that player 2 will defect in the last round and shall therefore try to preempt his defection by defecting before him.. This logic can then continue until the very first round. There is only one Nash equilibrium and that is where both players defect.[14] Economists began to get around this problem by making small perturbations in the game. Kreps, Milgrom, Roberts and Wilson (1982) in a landmark article for game theoretic analysis formally showed how an irrational player may cooperate in the first round and continue playing tit for tat and how player 2, not wanting to reveal that he is rational, also cooperates. The result of this game is that parties may achieve high levels of cooperation until they approach the final rounds of the

---

[11] In this context, Becker and Stigler (1974: 4) propound: "The expectation of mutually profitable contracts between repetitive violators and enforcers is part of the logic behind the widely held view that prostitution or the regular sale of consumer goods cannot be successfully prohibited. It also helps explain the development of organized crime: an organization is engaged more continually in violations than its individual members are, and can, therefore, make arrangements with judges or police that would not be feasible for these members". (note: contracts should not be interpreted in a strict sense as enforceable in court, and is perhaps better substituted with arrangements).

[12] See Binmore (1997) for a critique of Axelrod's "Evolution of Cooperation (1984) and subsequent work by Axelrod on the Prisoner's Dilemma.

[13] More accurately, "[folk theorems] describe the equilibria when players are either completely patient or almost so" (Fudenberg and Tirole 1996: 146).

[14] Recall a Nash equilibrium refers to a situation where no individual has incentive to deviate from his strategy given that it is a best response to the strategies of the other players.

game. In general high levels of cooperation may be achieved if players perceive others not to be fully rational (maximize expected utility), even if they are convinced of their own rationality, and change their strategies accordingly.

Experimental results and casual observation however convince us that there are a myriad of factors and motivations behind the level of and maintenance of cooperation. There is a great deal more cooperation than one would expect according to the above reasoning of backward induction. In a famous article Selten and Stöcker (1989) highlight a commonly observed phenomenon in experimental games that there is cooperation normally in the initial stages, followed by initial defection and then a period of noncooperation for the remainder of the game. Players having learned to cooperate, start to defect at earlier stages in subsequent games, *i.e.*, further from the end.

Highlighted above, an outcome of the "folk theorem" is that if players are patient enough then they will cooperate. This outcome lends itself to the notion that mechanisms that affect the degree of patience of the players (the degree of repetition) may curb the level of undesired cooperation. Affecting the "patience" of the players is to alter a repeated or on-going relationship, by shortening the time-horizon of players transactions. When players are in a long term relationship, they commonly cooperate because they fear that defection will lead to forgoing all future gains that can be accrued from the relationship. The future values of a relationship according to self-interested calculation are approximately, albeit haphazardly, discounted to present values by parties when they start or continue a relationship. Parties are interested in the accumulated sum of future transactions. Thinking of corruption in this manner, one can easily see how corruption is more likely when a particular individual or political group retain there stranglehold on power for a lengthy period of time, thus rendering repeated transactions more worthwhile.[15] There is a certain dynamic involved here, given that those groups that manage to retain power may become more popular for clientelisitic privileges relative to other groups, which can itself further assist them in retaining power. Similarly, one can understand the important role of the bureaucrat in political corruption given that she is generally in the administration for lengthy periods of time, and can therefore amass greater information and contacts and makes corrupt relations more significant because of a lengthy time horizon of relationships.

There are two basic ways for increasing the future value of continuing a relationship, also known as enlarging the shadow of the future: One means is by making interactions more durable, the other by making them more frequent (Axelrod 1984: 129). Durability is increased by prolonging the length (and consequence) of the interaction. When parties meet more frequently the gains from interaction discounted to the present rate are greater. One can increase frequency of interaction by increasing the amount of specialization in positions or

---

[15] For this reason political competition is so important.

transactions in a bureaucracy (*ibid.*: 1984: 130-132), which entails interaction with a chosen few. Furthermore, breaking down interactions into small pieces or stages has the same effect as specialization. It should be noted that the benefits of repeated play depend not just on the value of the future discounted payoffs, but also on other factors such as the ability to detect when someone has defected, the opportunity costs of continuing the game and the degree with which parties discount the payoffs.[16] Inverting the aforementioned factors: durability, frequency, specialization, stages etc. can reduce undesired cooperation by affecting the degree or necessity of repetition.

Further measures related to repetition include rotating officials that have been in sensitive positions for lengthy periods of time to other positions.[17] For this to work, it is important that the rotation of supervisors (and not just agents) serve as an alternative or complementary mechanism, given that the same factors that increase cooperation among supervisors also increase cooperation among line-level officials.[18]

An additional instrument that may be used is the use of random supervisors or random inspectors, similar to the above, but here supervisors are rotated and officials are not given information on who shall supervise them. This device is particularly useful when employed for spot inspections (unanticipated once-off inspections).[19] It works best when supervisors are taken from a pool of unknown composition to agents, so as to preserve anonymity for as long as possible. Furthermore, enforcers may try to put the parties involved in corrupt transactions into end game scenarios. They can do this by setting up reward

---

[16] *See* further, Section III, Subsection D.

[17] This measure is widely practiced. *See*, for example, Wade (1985) for the Indian context. Discourse in Germany has also led to similar conclusions on the use of rotating personel in sensitive positions. The Bundesministerium des Innern (Federal Ministry of the Interior) in Germany, in a recent OECD report entitled: Public Sector Corruption: An International Survey of Preventative Measures, suggested, "[i]n areas particularly exposed to corruption and their supervisory bodies, personnel rotation is considered to be an indespensible element of personnel management" (OECD 1999: 41).

[18] In the case of Germany, this policy of rotating supervisors is also pursued.

[19] The idea of not revealing supervisors to agents as a means to control their behavior is naturally very close to the idea of random inspections, as carried out by internal accounting controls and audits, in that there is an element of surprise (randomness) and uncertainty. Random audits and controls should be an inherent part of fraud and corruption control within government. In Germany, for example, a policy is pursued whereby, "[d]epending on the size and tasks of the administration, an organisational unit should be assigned for carrying out *internal auditing controls and audits*. This unit should, in particular, make random checks on matters currently processed, and on decisions taken on the placement of orders, appropriations or the granting of permissions and licenses. In case of complaints, it develops recommendations on how deficiencies can be made up" (OECD 1999: 41). One notable difference, however, is the fact that random supervisors, if not taken from a known pool, are unknown to agents. The aforementioned audits may be random, the auditors, on the other hand, well known.

systems for coming forward, such as amnesties and financial remuneration, by leaking information and sending out signals that parties have already began to talk. These are discussed in below.

One should note that when corruption is systematic, the aforementioned may actually become part of the sanctioning mechanism employed by corrupt officials themselves, as was reported by Wade (1985) in India. In order for such a device to work, there need to be clear rules and procedures set out in advance in order to limit capture of the system by certain officials. One means to limit discretion is to make rotation of all officials mandatory. Naturally, as always the device is only as good as those that supervise it.

B. Changing Payoffs

> "Bribes come openly or covertly, disguised as an interest in a business, as a lawyer's fee, or, very often, as a loan. Bribes come directly, paid into the waiting hands of the bribee or, more commonly, indirectly to the subordinate or friend performing the nearly indispensable office of bagman. Bribes come in all shapes as sex, commodities, appointments, and most often, cash" (Noonan 1984: xxi).

As identified above, parties to corrupt exchanges need to find one another, negotiate a bargain and find a means to deliver and ensure the other party delivers without being detected by third parties. This exposes many risks. Altering both the desirability and the willingness of parties to make payoffs is fundamental to curbing corruption. There are several means that the government has at its disposal to alter payoffs, many of which are discussed in later sections of the work. Similarly, there are many means that parties have at their disposal to modify or disguise payoffs in their own favor. This discussion is furthered in later chapters, based on our analysis here. The following is a very much a synopsis of points in later discussion. I begin our discussion by identifying some means with which parties may modify or disguise payoffs.

Recall first, that in order to successfully subvert cooperation, the law needs to make defection by one or more of the parties the unconditionally preferred strategy, *i.e.*, the law needs to create a prisoner's dilemma. I refer the reader back to Figure 1: the prisoner's dilemma. Contrarily, parties in corrupt transactions are looking for means to get out of such dilemmas. Where corruption occurs, parties no longer find themselves in a prisoner's dilemma, or they have found a solution to the dilemma that effectively has the same result.

There are several means for parties to change the payoffs.[20] Among the more interesting we consider to be the following: *First*, parties can bargain around

---

[20] *Ibid.*

the rules of the game and in the process shift the payoff structures in order to ensure that all sides comply with their agreement. An example of which is to delay payment until delivery or to place payment with a trusted intermediary. An alternative to this is to pay in steps. Note this may also be achieved by using a central authority to "put his reputation on the line" and vouch for the transaction.

Second, but relatedly, parties may prescribe the nature of the payoffs and resources exchanged in order to make them less determinable by authorities, which increase the expected returns from cooperation by decreasing the chances of getting caught. As adumbrated above the resources exchanged can be manifold, ranging from money to sex, from utilities to services - moreover, the transfer of which can be simultaneous of sequenced and divided into parts to avoid detection. Similarly, corruption may come in the form of employment and patronage, where clients supplied by the politician are passed onto private business, increasing influence in the private sector, and permitting clientelism and corruption to feed off one another (Della Porta and Vannucci 1999: 52).

All of these factors make corrupt payoffs particularly difficult to detect, and the payoffs to corruption therefore increase. Parties may disguise bribes as gifts not just to avoid detection and possible administrative or penal sanction, but also to reduce pangs of conscience (*ibid.*: 50-51). Della Porta and Vannucci (*ibid.*: 50-51), for example, describe a supplier of the Milanese Municipal Transport Company whose conscience disturbed him because he had to go to the company offices with an envelop full of money. He decided instead to pay in gold sterling, relieving himself of guilt.

Figure 3: Third Party Enforcement

	Cooperate	Defect
Cooperate	5, 5	-10, 10-Δ
Defect	10-Δ, -10	0, 0

A *third* means of changing the payoffs is for third party enforcement. One obvious means of this through the Mafia who that can credible commit to punishing any defector for following his own self interest. This is depicted in Figure 3 above. We assume that where both parties defect, it does not come to any transaction. Here we let Δ denote the punishment dished out by a third party when one party defects on an agreement. When $\Delta > 5$, the Nash equilibrium in the game is cooperate/cooperate. When, however, $\Delta < 5$, then the Nash equilibrium remains defect/defect and third party enforcement is ineffectual. Note, for simplicity, I have assumed symmetry in payoffs.

But, there are many other mechanisms to increase enforcement, discussed below, particularly where economic and social relations are embedded. Similarly, games, as we shall see below, normally involve more than two persons and sanctions may be handed out by other parties than the immediate players.

Of course, concentrating on just the payoffs alone is not a complete picture of the problems associated with parties willing to engage in corruption exchanges. I have identified the fact that parties must be able to locate one another agree on different tasks, make payments go unnoticed and enforce these agreements. So in addition to the prisoner's dilemma that parties may find themselves in, they may previously find themselves in a coordination dilemma, whereby partners may not be able to locate one another. In order to solve this coordination dilemma, parties will realistically find one another within the cover of an alternative (preferably legal) institution, which can also function as a means of ensuring that agreements are honored.[21] Among the most common are consulting companies, clubs and bogus research institutes. Hidden from much formal regulation, the aforementioned provide both a coordinating role and a retreat from unwanted supervision, in addition to a supervisory role for corrupt transactions ensuring that complaints are heard and agreements honored. In Italy, masonic lodges developed that helped aid secrecy and provide a co-ordinating role and solidarity among members. They were "sites of covert power (that) offer the possibility of across-class connections" (ibid.: 167). They helped coordinate activities in such areas as economic and social institutions such as banks as well as the local authorities, the press and different state institutions. In the case of the masonic lodge of what became known as Propaganda 2, or P2, the membership boasted "three government ministers, thirty members of parliament, more than fifty generals (including the highest ranks of the secret services), high level functionaries, diplomats, journalists, financiers, and industrialists" (ibid.: 168). It presented "a confidential arena in which entrepreneurs, members of the liberal professions, intermediaries, functionaries, and politicians could meet, get to know each other, propose business deals, negotiate, and work out agreements and guarantees. Indeed, secret masonic lodges generally represent a market for individuals disposed to and interested in making clandestine contacts, legal or otherwise" (ibid.).

The government has several means at its disposal to alter the payoffs available to corruption. The *first* means the government has of altering the payoff available is to remove the government activity in its entirety. This can be done through the removal of both inefficient regulations and corruption-ridden programs.[22] Similarly, the government may privatize the previously state-owned body, removing it from state-owned control.[23]

---

[21] *See* further this chapter, Section III, Subsection F.
[22] *See* further, Chapter III, Section II.
[23] *See* further, Chapter III, Section VIII.

A *second* means that government has of reducing the payoffs is to introduce both competition among public agents -which potentially decreases the size of the bribe available due to officials bidding each other down with the result that it may not be worthwhile to take the risk- and between both public and private firms, in the provision of goods and services; factors which largely affect any agent's or organizations monopoly power. Similarly, the government may deregulate a market, instituting and observing anti-trust laws, which reduce the gains the private sector business can acquire by making payoffs. Relatedly, monopoly power within an organization can be decreased by providing for hierarchical review of decisions. Monopoly power at an institutional level can be decreased by a separation of functions among sub-units, and at a constitutional level by a separation of functions among different institutions.

A *third* important means of reducing payoffs is by redrawing rules, organizational aims, and procedures more clearly and more open to public observation, and, in particular clarifying the legal and organizational responsibilities with respect to self-dealing and what is forbidden.[24] Difficult questions need to be addressed including the distinction between a gift and a bribe, or a bribe and a campaign contribution, and clearly drafted conflict of interests laws need to be imposed to reduce both the appearance and likelihood of quid pro quo agreements and payoffs.[25] Such factors target discretion and make the deliverance of payoffs more transparent and open to scrutiny, thus making the activity more risky.

A *fourth* important means of affecting the payoffs is by aligning the interests of the agents with those of the principal.[26] For example, making pay conditional on performance and not seniority, and increasing salaries to reduce the need for corrupt payoffs, and the increase the costs of losing ones job.[27] Note, in general reforms that increase administrative efficiency also decrease corruption. Administrative inefficiency creates red tape and provides a further reason for corrupt payoffs, particularly in the form of grease payments. Increasing performance by increasing administrative efficiency reduces the opportunities for corruption.

A *fifth* means of reducing payoffs is by selecting and screening officials. Recall that the provision of a corrupt service is largely dependent on parties being able to search for and identify one another, form an agreement and deliver on promises. Where an agent is recruited via nepotism or patronage, it is likely that these costs are substantially lower than in the case of an official that has been selected according to merit, and must locate partners from scratch.

---

[24] *See* further, Chapter III, Section IV.
[25] *See* further, Chapter VI.
[26] *See* further, Chapter III, Section V, Subsection D.
[27] *Ibid.*

A *sixth* means of attacking payoffs is by solving what is known as the bribers' dilemma. International companies among other frequently contend that if they do not bribe then they cannot win a contract because the competition will do so, and thus assume a competitive advantage. Given this threat, and where these expectations are shared, all actors will willingly offer bribes. The government to curtail such payoffs, may, of course, follow other instruments sketched here, but in particular it must design a mechanism to guarantee companies that others will not bribe. One means developed by Transparency International is an anti-bribery clause. Here parties sign an agreement that they will not engage in corruption.[28] Alternative mechanisms would be to have the parties post bonds that would be forfeited upon detection, or even better have the companies monitor one another. The notion, however, that companies always find themselves in a bribers' dilemma is disingenuous. There are obvious returns to economic rents and companies accrue benefits from collusion that they are unwilling to give up and let to the forces of the competitive market. Barriers to entry and the monopoly rents that come with them are often only unwillingly foregone.[29]

A *seventh* means of curbing corruption is by concentrating on deterrence.[30] Increasing the probability of detection by beefing up on monitoring as well increasing size of the punishment to the point where the expected punishment exceeds expected gains should deter rational persons from entering into corrupt exchanges.[31] As we have seen, in previous discussion, deterrence has some limitations, particularly given that it can be a relatively costly undertaking and the punishments that need to be imposed may be considered too severe. Moreover, high punishments themselves may open up new opportunities for corruption.[32] Reliance on deterrence as a successful mechanism against corruption tends to assume relatively honest law enforcement. To increase the efficiency of law enforcement, new anti- corruption agencies may be necessary. Other potential candidates for re-inspection include the office of ombudsman, internal and external auditing bodies, in particular, the supreme audit institutions (SAI's) etc.[33]

Eighth, an important factor to increase the risk of taking payoffs, is to encourage the assistance of the public and those with insider knowledge.[34] The natural difficulty of this is that those persons with the knowledge of the running of corrupt systems are frequently those involved in the exchanges themselves.

---

[28] *See* further, Chapter III, Section VII.
[29] *See* further, (*ibid.*).
[30] I refer the reader to Chapter I, Sections VIII & IX.
[31] For a survey of the issues surrounding optimal law enforcement, *see* Polinsky and Shavell (1999) and Garoupa (1997). *See* also Chapter I, Section VIII.
[32] *See* above Chapter I, Section VIII.
[33] *See* further, Chapter VII.
[34] *See* further, Chapter IV.

A *ninth* mechanism is related to reforming reward structures. There are several means of changing reward structures, such as instituting an amnesty for those that come forward, or plea bargaining and offering reduced charges and reduced sentences to cooperative defendants.[35] For other persons that derive utility from merely performing their civil duties, a more permissive for of public action litigation may also be considered as reforming reward structure, as could the admission of anonymous complaints, which reduce the risk of retaliation for those that come forward. Some of these means, such as plea bargaining and amnesties can induce distrust among corrupt actors. Offering a reward such as a bounty or returns from a qui tam suit may also reform information structures, granting special incentives to with insider knowledge to come forward, which is particularly helpful given the secretive nature of corruption. This notion is developed further below.[36] One problems, however, is that those at the core of corrupt transactions with the greatest amount of information are frequently those that partake in corrupt transactions themselves. Therefore, the government may provide an amnesty and a bounty to any corrupt party that comes forward and secures the conviction of another party (Cooter and Garoupa 2000). This is depicted in Figure 4.

Figure 4: Amnesty and Bounty

	Cooperate	Defect
Cooperate	5, 5	-10, 10-Δ+ $p.f$
Defect	10-Δ+$p.f$, -10	0, 0

Assuming once again for simplicity a symmetry of payoffs, and that where both parties defect it doesn't come to any transaction, let Δ again denote the sanction handed out by a third party for defection, f the fine that the government imposes on a convicted party and p the fraction of the fine an individual receives upon his coming forward and reporting another individual. Given the way the payoffs are structured, I also assume that an individual that defects (when the other party cooperates, thus bringing about a transaction in the first place) will come forward and always report the other party, because $p.f$ is always positive, or at least cannot be below 0. In order for the government to have Defect/Defect as the only Nash Equilibrium, $p.f > \Delta + 5$ must hold. Where $p.f < \Delta + 5$, the Nash Equilibrium remains Cooperate/Cooperate.

---

[35] This is developed further below. *See* further Chapter IV.
[36] *See* further Chapter IV, Section II, Subsection F.

It should be noted that when the government offers such a reward system, it is enough to offer a reward that is attractive for just one party (*i.e.*, where payoffs are not symmetric is the case in the above example), because the party who does not benefit from the reward will reason that defection is the dominant or unconditionally preferred strategy of the other player and therefore be deterred from entering into a corrupt transaction. Furthermore, when we consider the game to be iterated, small changes in the payoffs may be enough where parties heavily discount future income (*see* Axelrod 1984: 131-132). By applying such a system, the government can set up races among corrupt officials (Cooter and Garoupa 2000).

I would like to close off this section with some provision comments on how to set up of races. *First,* a tactic pursued in Italy in the "Mani Pulite" (Clean Hands) investigations, when parties expect that others are willing to talk or have already, they fear for their own neck and may rush forward. Here the authorities being about end game situations. Sending out signals that others are about to, by leaking reports to the media, releasing them early from detention etc., can be an effective means to get parties to come forward.[37] When parties perceive that their expected chances of detection have increased ceteris paribus, they will be more willing to accept a deal with the authorities. Where corruption resembled more extortion than corruption, *i.e.*, where one side threatened to withhold a legal entitlement from the other, or blackmailed the other party, amnesties can be a useful reward system to get the "victimized" party to come forward and report an incident. This was recently proposed in a draft bill before the Sejm, the Polish Parliament to induce those parties that are victim to extortion-like corruption to come forward.[38] Understanding the ability to break out of such relationships requires an understanding of hostages.[39]

1. Choosing When to Quit: Lock in and Hostages

The degree, or ease with which one party can leave a relationship is particularly important in the case of corruption. In the case of criminal organizations, there is a great degree of lock in. This suggests that interestingly the degree of lock in and the potential to damage another party should act as a deterrent to entry, but also that once entry has occurred then it may be stable. Once a commitment has been made, it greatly influences ones bargaining position. It greatly increases the ability of the criminal organization, and a central authority, to blackmail, among other

---

[37] *See* further, Chapter IV, Section II, Subsection C.
[38] *See* further, Chapter VI, Section I.
[39] One could include a tenth mechanism, which concentrates on long-term results, namely through have parties internalize certain norms of honesty, at a social level though from instance education and social marketing strategies, and at the level of the administration through internal training, workshops etc.

things. This has the effect of increasing the desirability following the wishes of the organization.[40] An interesting example of lock in is cited in Klitgaard et al (2000). It is part of a report commissioned by the Governor of Hong Kong.

"It is said that Police corruption is, for the most part, "syndicated" and that corruption on an individual basis is frowned upon by the organizers of these "syndicates"- indeed anyone operating on his own is liable to be "fixed." The organizers are good psychologists. New arrivals in the force are tested to see how strong is their sense of duty. The testing may take various forms -sums of money placed on their desks, etc. If an officer fails to report the first overture of this sort he is really "hooked" for the rest of his service, and is afraid to report any corrupt activities which may thereafter come to his notice..."[41]

Furthermore, hostages may be taken involuntarily, *i.e.*, where persons are framed for something they didn't do, or out of necessity, evidence in both cases may be used against further noncompliance. In Somalia, because their wages in the 1990s were so low, civil servants had to transgress the law in order to survive. As a result of this, allegiance to President Barre's kleptocratic regime could be preserved, given the danger of prosecution (Coolidge and Rose-Ackerman 1997: 28). Discussed earlier corrupt organizations may use legal devices to sanction, where they control this devices and institutions. In a similar manner, they may also use legal devices as hostages. One such device common to political corruption is the withholding of a budget destined for an agency in order to force it into compliance. For examples of how this works in Russia, *see* Levin and Satarov (2000). One can easily see in this context how compromising information on willing or unwilling partners in corrupt exchanges permits persons to weave a massive rod in their hands, to be used to keep dissidents in line. For this reason the secret service becomes an important instrument in the corrupt system (Della Porta and Vannucci 1999: 56). It also permits those, outside of the political or administrative arena to continue their influence long after they are no longer in power.[42]

---

[40] In many developing countries the degree of lock in is a result of the fact that the government do not provide legal alternatives, and that continuing the relationship is the only means of getting things done. Where legal recourse is not available, parties may have little choice. Providing legal recourse may therefore be a prerequisite to reform.

[41] Excerpts from "Second Report of the Commission of Enquiry under Sir Allistair Blair-Kerr," (Hong Kong, 1973) in Klitgaard, MacLean-Abaroa and Parris (2000: 18-19).

[42] For example, dossiers from the Italian intelligence agency were located in the luggage sent from Italy to former the prime minister Bettino Craxi's hideout at Hamamet (Della Porta and Vannucci 1999: 56).

The future costs of the illegality of corrupt transactions may feature highly in the decision to stay in a relationship. Hence legal recourse for parties that wish to escape such a relationship may be desirable. Parties use hostages to insure long term cooperation.[43] "In general the greater the symmetry between the losses suffered by the briber and the bribee from exposure, the less credible the threat to destroy the other's reputation Rose-Ackerman" (1999: 102). This suggests that introducing asymmetry of punishments may be a way to decrease the level of corruption, but as emphasized from the outset the affect of such a measure is complicated and depends on the type of corruption that has already established itself.

Parties wishing to leave a corrupt system may find themselves in a kind of a "hostages' dilemma". A hostages' dilemma is characterized by the fact that it is better for all to move, but not for any particular person. Communication and coordination is difficult, and intentionally so. Reliance on the hostages dilemma may be a cheaper alternative to providing material or spiritual rewards (Dixit and Nalebuff 1993: 17). The hostages dilemma is vividly described in the following:

> "Khrushchev first denounced Stalin's purges at the Soviet Communist Party's 20th Congress. After the dramatic speech, someone in the audience shouted out, asking what Khrushchev had been doing at that time. Khrushchev responded by asking the questioner to please stand up and identify himself. The audience remained silent. Khrushchev replied: That is what I did, too."

Both history and experience teach us, that the hostages dilemma can sustain itself for lengthy periods of time. An alternative to reliance on whistleblowing is getting employees involved through workshops and participatory diagnosis.[44] Given that officials and clients understand how corrupt systems work, they can be motivated to share their knowledge in the form of anonymous written comments discussed at workshops. Further, given that these workshops may be facilitated by outsiders such as foreign experts fear of reprisal is not as likely. Moreover, setting up well-functioning systems where whistleblowers receive rewards is only workable when the whistleblower does not fear reprisal, and institutional safeguards are in place, which is not the case in many developing countries.

---

[43] Vladimiro Montesinos, the former spy chief in Peru, understood this perfectly. He made numerous videos which he used and continues to use as hostages. Facing dozens of criminal charges, he professed to have recorded up to 30,000 secret videos, which he threatened to hand over. *See*, "Yes, He's Back," *The Economist*, June 30, 2001.

[44] See further, Chapter IV, Section E.

2. To Understand Payoffs Think Systems

The methods for carrying out corrupt deals depend on the specific area of governmental activity. The techniques will clearly differ in different forms of corruption, such as police corruption, the sale of legislation, the sale of tax and regulatory exemptions, judicial corruption, procurement, grease payments etc. (*see* Heymann 1996: 333). These differences naturally suggest that different techniques are required to curb corruption in the different areas. What is important, however, to recognize is that the where there is systematic corruption, the areas of governmental activity may provide a type of coordinating role for parties in corrupt exchanges, as well as commitment devices. For example, a police officer who regularly patrols one area is likely to collect payments from persons during his patrol. Parties interested in procuring favorable treatment know where to find him (coordinate) and the fact that he will be back again regularly is a form of commitment device. Similar examples, could be given for any area of corruption. The point is this, organizational structures and guidelines provide the loci of payoffs, and that where corruption is systematic, it is not implausible to expect that in some instances legal procedure are used as disciplinary device to supplement informal devices to insure that parties fulfill their side of the bargain. When this is the case, it is not improbable that whistleblowers that wish to report a corrupt organization may find themselves accused of corruption (Manion 1996). Another example is described by Wade (1985) of India where corrupt officials captured the appointment and rotating procedures; those officials that are least compliant or complicit are sent to the least attractive areas (*see* also hostages above). Where officials have captured the disciplinary mechanisms, it is not difficult for them to disguise their actions as legitimate and they are thus less vulnerable to detection.

Where corruption is institution or endemic, there is a need to understand the mechanisms of corrupt exchange in every given case, otherwise those means that are supposed to curb corruption may actually increase the strength of corrupt systems, or merely shift the bargaining positions of all actors involved, simply redefining the opportunities for corrupt behavior.

3. Interdependence: Where to Look

> "Hey Willie, why did you rob the banks?"
> "Because that's where money is."
> (Attributed to Willie Sutton, bankrobber)

I make two key suggestions here: First, parties will seek out those officials that are in a position to "get things done", and second, reform measures are generally not good per se, but must be seen as shifting the bargaining powers of actors, and shifting the patterns of corrupt transactions necessary to realize a gain- what I refer to as interdependence.

Delegations of power, be they administrative, constitutional or otherwise, set out the positions that are themselves most valuable. Allocations of discretion over resources are fundamental to understanding the loci of corruption. I have identified above several reforms related to corrupt payments including dispersing organizational and institutional power into the hands of many, providing for hierarchical supervision. Under such conditions, a party willing to engage in corruption needs to know the number of agents involved in the decision-making process and the scale of distribution of information and authority among the authorities involved. "In order to know who should be bribed and how much, the corrupter must eliminate the influence each individual has on the public choice and the risk of being denounced to the magistracy" (Della Porta and Vannucci 1999: 41).

But persons cannot perform corrupt transactions or operate corrupt systems on their own; the function of which is interdependent on others. We have seen in the review of the issues in chapter 1, that corrupt agents are often part of networks, which commonly are of the top down or bottom up kind. In the former decisions are made at the top, but the fulfillment of these agreements require compliance among lower ranking officials. Payments therefore flow down the chain. This is particularly the case in "grand corruption", i.e., corruption among high ranking officials. In the bottom up model, payments are received by low ranking officials and transferred up the ladder. One salient example of such corruption is among police officials, where lower ranking officials come in contact with citizens and are therefore in a better position to solicit bribes. The operation of a corrupt network depends greatly on the functions of officials and on the distribution of officials that allocate scarce resources. Summing up, illicit agreements cannot be conducted on their own but often require a chain of officials, what I term interdependence. Officials that enjoy discretion are in a position to get things done and are targeted.

One can readily envisage a scenario in which government officials and private citizens search for strategies as a means for acquiring rents, that they are not entitled to. Corruption may, therefore, be seen as one pathway among many, including political lobbying and other legitimate activities. To achieve a particular goal, such as acquire monopoly power, receive a permit, contract etc., a citizen can either pursue the legitimate pathway determined by law, or an illegitimate pathway, determined by chains of interdependence shaped by the allocative decision-making process; this is depicted in Figure 5. For illustrative purposes Figure 5 is divided into three scenarios. In scenario 1, a citizen, denoted by C, can pursue a legitimate pathway to achieve a particular goal, a good or service denoted by X. Alternatively, the citizen can go through an agent, denoted by a, to receive X illegitimately. In scenario 2, the citizen can similarly pursue a legitimate or an illegitimate pathway to procure a good or service. Instead of having one agent to deal with, there are numerous agents within the one agency responsible for decision making, denoted by $a_1 ... a_n$. The agent needs to go through these in order to procure good X illegitimately. In scenario 3, the citizen may similarly pursue either a legitimate and an illegitimate pathway to procure a good or service. In addition to having to pass through numerous agents within one agency to procure a service illegitimately, there are agents within a second agency that play an oversight role, denoted by $b_1 ... b_n$. One would expect corruption and collusive behavior, generally, to be least likely in the third scenario and most likely in the first. Where such chains of interdependence exist, an anti-corruption strategy can redefine the allocative decision making process itself, or concentrate on perturbing individual links in the chains.

Figure 5: Legitimate and Illegitimate Pathways to Receive a Good or Service

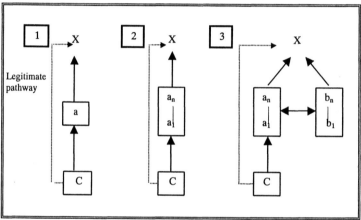

In this context, it might be helpful to look at a corrupt system as a grand coalition made up of several actors that can form sub-coalitions. Actors will decide to enter into such a coalition if it is individually rational for them to do so and for the group to allow them in (given that it becomes more difficult to maintain secrecy and prevent free-riding as the group increases in size). For any individual, the choice is between acting alone and legitimately, acting alone and corruptly, and acting within different coalitions to get something done. We can consider reforms generally to change both the desirability of acting alone and the optimal composition of various coalitions, including the returns from the grand coalition. Moreover, individuals may not just try to maximize their individual payoffs, but coalitions will also try to do so. As a result of this, we can expect coalitions, subject to constraints, to change their composition depending on what reforms are passed.[45,46]

Summing up, reforms may actually strengthen or weaken corruption levels depending on the composition of a corrupt network.[47] They shift the allocation of decisions to various actors or institutions, and thus affect chains of interdependence necessary to "get things done". Changes in government that are often also considered as anti-corruption measures open up new opportunities for payoffs. Our reading of the evidence from transition economies highlights this phenomenon, best exemplified in our discussion on privatization.[48]

C. Behaviorial Factors: Going Along With It

> "One of the most general things that experiments demonstrate is that subjects adjust their behavior as they gain experience and learn about the game they are playing and the behavior of other subjects" (Roth 1995: 327).

Evolutionary game theory has emphasized that the benefits attained by playing a certain strategy as well as the likeliness of continuing to play that strategy (fitness), depend to a large extent on the strategies others are playing in a

---

[45] Another means of looking at interdependence is to loosely borrow from cooperative game theory the idea of the core. The core is a solution concept in cooperative game theory in characteristic function form. To understand the concept consider an n-person (transferable utility) game, where transferable utility means that the players can transfer the payoffs of the game among themselves. The characteristic function of the game assigns to each possible coalition S of s players the value v(S). This value function may be seen as the amount that each coalition S can secure itself. Let N = {1,2,...,n} be the grand coalition of n players. Consider some allocation $X = \{x_1, x_2, ..., x_n\}$. This allocation is in the core if and only if (1) for each coalition S contained in N, it satisfies the constraint

$$\sum_{j \in S} x_j \geq v(S) \text{ and } (2) \sum_{j \in N} x_j = v(N)$$

What these constraints suggest is that in order to satisfy the core solution concept, no subgroup of individuals would have done better had they gone it alone and secondly that the grand coalition do as good as it would have done had the members gone alone (see Kornhauser 1998).

[46] Noncooperative models like the ones we are looking at here specify the sets of actions available to each individual. Coalitional models, by contrast, start from the payoff vectors that each group of individuals can jointly achieve. Each of them capture different types of strategic considerations.

[47] Decisions for example to increase the fine level offer greater bargaining power to law enforcers, and should not, as one may interprete from some law and economics proposal be interpreted as good per se.

[48] See further, Chapter III, Section VIII.

population.[49] Put simply, what others do, how they do it, and who does it matter greatly at the level of individual decision making.[50] Results have shown that no strategy is evolutionary stable in the iterated prisoner's dilemma (Binmore 1997). People change their behavior depending on the behavior of others as well as their environment.[51]

A key point I wish to get across is this: Reform efforts may be seriously distorted when one considers corruption only within the light of explicit agreements. To wit, collusive transactions and particularly corruption are prone to legal sanction all over the world. A factor usually overlooked however is that violations of the law may not just be the result of formally agreed upon behavior but actually the result of action as part of reciprocation of patterns of behavior, or implicit collusion.[52] Employees generally reciprocate the conduct, or rules of behavior of their colleagues, particularly, senior coworkers. This is particularly important at the recruitment stage, when employees are being initiated into organizational practices and the "rules of the game".[53] Everyday activities that may be condoned within an organization include making long distance phone calls for personal use, taking extended coffee breaks, taking lengthy vacations etc.[54] Such behavior represents an implicit contract and clearly violate the alignment of preferences between the principal and agents.[55]

By implicit collusion I mean parties go along with well-established practices, and do not reach any formal or informal agreement on those practices. They follow discernible patterns of behavior. People not just accept this behavior but also learn to imitate it. Parties do not need to explicitly have any dealings with one another. Behavior may not just be the result of apathy, but may enjoy wide support. In some instances it may be desirable to legalize already widely practiced acts, but in other instances, this is undesirable. Raising the level of consciousness and organizational attitudes in particular towards self-dealing may be important.

Where illicit cooperation is a result not of explicit agreements, but rather of parties going along with well-established practices, any shift in these particular

---

[49] For the classic reference on evolutionary models in law and economics, see Hirschleifer (1982).

[50] More accurately the above would state that our *perceptions* of what others do, how they do it, and who does it, and the perception of parties to convey their *type* matter.

[51] This is naturally not dependent on a person being rational. Even persons that are irrational will generally learn by doing and adapt their behavior.

[52] In a similar vein, a central thesis of Huber (1984) derived from Axelrod (1984) is that anti-trust law is seriously limited in its application because parties do not have to enter into explicit agreements, such as price fixing, but just follow "meaningful patterns of behavior" (p. 1160).

[53] Moreover, new recruits may consider that they owe their position to senior members, and feel obliged to follow practices.

[54] This is best captured by attitudinal studies, see for example Gorta and Forell (1995).

[55] This does not rule out the notion that some of these activities may be considered as a perk, or a nonmonetary payment for services.

type of corrupt practices should be preceded by teaching the costs of corrupt practices and raising them to the awareness of people.[56] Social marketing devices in order to persuade individuals that the rules of the game have changed are an important tool to raise the costs of corruption to the awareness of the individuals. Similarly, social marketing strategies should be targeted at changing expectations.[57]

Summing up, cooperation thus may be a form of apathy (unconsciousness) or systematization of behavior, which naturally gives additional stability to corrupt systems, where behavior is not even considered corrupt.

D. Clear Strategies and Clear Signals

Fundamental to good performance is the ability to provide clear signals of strategy and intent, to be able to discern cooperators from noncooperators, and to be able to distinguish erroneous signals and actions from accurate ones. Put simply, where parties cannot identify the actions of others, cooperation becomes unstable. Where actions are unclear a game theorist speaks of "noise". In the case of noise, strategies such as tit for tat that worked well in one scenario may not work well in other scenarios.[58] Controlling the information structure of actors is a useful means of curbing corruption.

Relationships that are based on corruption are characterized by the fact that they are more immobile than others, and tend therefore to be long-term. One reason for this is that, persons need to acquire as much information on the other as possible in order to continue dealings because of the high risk that is involved. The longer the parties know each other the greater the level of trust, and trust may grow with use (Dasgupta 1988). Being able to clarify what a player has done in the past is beneficial to recognizing what actions a player may take in the future; it may help identify what strategy a player is playing, or in evolutionary game theoretical terms the type of player a person is. Uncertainty about past behavior may decrease cooperation.[59]

An important means of curbing corruption is a policy of interjecting honest officials to pose as dishonest officials to increase uncertainty of player type, and therefore the risk of detection.[60] Adumbrated above and in later sections,

---

[56] *See* further, Chapter IV, Section II, Subsection C.

[57] *See* further, *ibid.*

[58] Take for example two players playing tit for tat. One mistake and the tit for tat strategy leads to both parties punishing one another infinitely.

[59] Furthermore in the presence of noise, reciprocity may still work but it depends on how forgiving a player is. In some environments, players are not so forgiving. Gambetta (1993) notes, for example, that luck is not looked upon highly in Sicily.

[60] The dangers as we shall see of undercover tactics include the fact that they often require secrecy themselves and that when used widespread "conformity may increase as candor,

the role of undercover reporting and policing is far more important that this, as it gives us insight into the workings of a corrupt system, the courses of transaction, members involved etc. This is most manifest in undercover policing, but as discussed later, is a far wider instrument than this. As with other instruments there are compromises involved. For example, the original decision to opt for a uniformed police force in the United States was for "a moral separation of police from criminals and a visual separation of police from everyone else" (Marx 1988: 21). This trade-off is universal. A uniformed police officer can offer a deterrent to crime occurring in this vicinity, but this uniform also provides a red flag to criminals of his whereabouts. Like other resources, policing is scarce and the (potential) criminal is advantaged by this additional information that comes with the uniform, which serves *inter alia* the aforementioned purposes of moral separation and also functions to increase accountability and protect civil liberty (*ibid.*).[61]

Corrupt systems can go to great pains to increase their information on player type, made easier by such factors as embeddedness in exchanges etc. sketched below.[62] For instance, the Mafia as reported in Gambetta (1993) is interested in finding out all it can about the parties with whom it transacts. It attempts to discover all it can about the other side including, creditworthiness, private life, and whether the party is protected. The Mafia, Gambetta suggests is like a bank that needs information on where to acquire the assets. In Italy, for example, he reports that many of the people that one perceives as hanging about idly, are actually gathering information. Related are also the role of gossip, curiosity and the exchange of gifts. Collecting information on player type depends on many factors such as memory, an aptitude for gathering information and the number of other persons involved (*ibid.*; Axelrod 1984). Spying becomes more complicated the greater the number of people involved, the more complex the market and the greater the size of the territory to be covered.

Finding out information on player type is only one side of the informational activities engaged in by organizations. Criminal organizations also try to control the information structure of its members both among themselves and also from outsiders, most commonly by enforcing secrecy. The most vivid example is again provided by the Mafia. This is exemplified in the following passage:

"Omertá, although etymologically related to being a man, to being strong, has come to mean the capacity for silence and secrecy even under compelling conditions. More precisely, the meaning spread by scholars and

---

spontaneity, innovation, and risk-taking decline" (Marx 1995: 232). Fears that discussions will be monitored and integrity tests prevalent, may lead to passivity and less reciprocity, generally.
[61] *See* further, Chapter IV, Section II, Subsection D.
[62] *See* further, this chapter Section III, Subsection G2.

journalists refers to the silence that a large section of Sicilians would be capable of maintaining when facing public enquiries concerning crime, and, more generically, their reluctance to talk to even vaguely threatening strangers. The mafia represents the quintessential embodiment of the code of secrecy, having an almost mythical capacity for it, which, together with the capacity for violence, is usually set at the top of their list of its specific attributes" (Gambetta 1988: 135-36).

Note, to enforce secrecy they can use the same structures that they use to enforce illegal transactions. Here the size of the sanction for failing to behave is often the maximum one, as there may be fewer social hesitancies than in the case of the legal fine, where the legal fine is not set at the level of maximum deterrence for moral reasons, among others. When parties cannot overcome noise, they cannot detect who is responsible for defecting, thus increasing the chances of free-riding and appropriation. Two mechanisms commonly used by criminal organizations are to either sanction an innocent party to facilitate a chain of sanctions leading to the defector, or to sanction a whole group when the actions of one or more persons are not easily recognizable.[63]

There are several mechanisms that reformers can use to curb corruption related to information structure. *First*, they can increase the number and range of anonymous transactions. Game theoretical experiments have consistently shown that the decision with whom to play can be just as important as how to play, *i.e.*, what strategy to play (Yamagishi 1992).[64] When people can choose with whom they must transact, this discretion can lead to higher levels of cooperation.[65] Tullock (1999) warns against the usual conditions used in experiments in prisoner's dilemma experiments. He says that contestants are usually pre-selected, communication is usually prevented, and partners are not allowed to be changed. He reversed all of these in an experiment of his own and found a great deal more cooperation. Interesting from a policy perspective is that this argument somewhat goes against the notion of competitive bureaucracy, whereby having two or more officials providing the same service should encourage the reduction in the bribe attainable as a result of competitive pressure and therefore decrease the desirability of corrupt relations (*see* Rose-Ackerman 1978; and Shleifer and

---

[63] For a theoretical discussion of the ability of sustaining high levels of cooperation by punishing the innocent *see* Binmore 1997.

[64] In an experiment conducted by Yamagishi (1992), players were allowed to choose their partners and to exit the game freely. The strategy that achieved the highest payoff was the out of tat strategy.

[65] Hence removing this discretion can sometimes be fortuitous. An obvious example of this is political appointees to state owned organizations. If parties are allowed to choose between actors, they are more likely to find someone to cooperate with, than if they are given no choice between actors, e.g. the appointment decision is outside of their control.

Vishny 1993). Providing additional means to procure a service may actually enable a corrupt citizen to find someone he considers most trustworthy.

A potentially important tool the government can use to curb corruption is to increase the number of anonymous transactions, especially by keeping officials anonymous. Many transactions with government are anonymous, or more accurately there is one-sided anonymity, where the official knows the identity of the citizen but the citizen is unaware of the identity of the official. When I file my tax returns, I am not aware of the identity of the person that processes my returns, and verifies this information.[66] But there are many instances that I can indeed find out the identity of decisionmakers, for example, if I wish to receive planning permission, I may make enquiries in most instances at little expense to find out the name of the person, names in a committee of a few members, that are responsible for my application.[67]

Second, reformers may design organizational functions so as to make it more difficult for outside observers to recognize who decisionmakers actually are, a type of anonymity of functions. When functions are anonymous, it makes it difficult for (potentially) corrupt officials to send clear signals of past, present and future strategies, thus making signals noisy.

A *third* means of controlling the information also related to anonymity, is by preventing the parties from identifying whether someone has complied with an agreement. There are several examples of this. For example, before voting was conducted in secrecy and votes were observable, electoral corruption was a common phenomenon. Candidates or their supporters could bribe voters for their support and check whether the agreement was complied with by simply observing how the bribe-receiver voted. When voting was conducted in privacy, bribers could no longer detect whether agreements were complied with, hence corrupt agreements became unverifiable and corrupt deals intangible.[68] A similar suggestion to limit lobbying activities would be to have the votes of members of assemblies and committees conducted anonymously. Another example, is by

---

[66] In most cases, we know that information in tax returns is not even controlled but judt processed, but this should not distract from the basis of my argument (*See,* for example, Frey 1992).

[67] Withholding this information may sometimes come at a cost. It can be argued that in some cases, there is a loss in accountability particularly where a citizen serves to monitor the behavior of those officials that process his applications. This should, however, not infringe upon my basic suggestion, however, that a re-examination of the circumstances where anonymity is preferable to citizen verifiability may be useful in curbing certain types of corruption. There are tradeoffs involved. The citizen has an incentive to monitor the official and see to it that he is not treated unfairly. The costs of permitting the citizen to monitor the official most often than not outweigh the benefit. Furthermore, the aforementioned mechanism does not affect the ability of other internal accountability mechanisms and governmental bodies to control officials.

[68] *See* further, Chapter VII, Section VI.

making supervisor's reports anonymous, so that the agent cannot verify whether or not the supervisor complied with agreement. For similar reasons auctions are also sealed bid. Looking for similar scenarios can be a particularly successful tool against corruption.

A *fourth* but related means of injecting noise is by withholding information on officials from other officials. For example, in law and consulting offices, salaries and promotion agreements are frequently withheld from fellow employees as a means to prevent jealousy and collusion among agents.[69] Agreements need to be reached under asymmetric information.

A *fifth* method is to separate the monitor from the monitored. Aggressive actions are more likely to be administered by outsiders. In New York City, after an official has worked in Internal Affairs he or she can generally not work elsewhere in the department (Marx 1995: 218). To further control the information structure, the building is separate as are its officials "even to the point of being promoted in secret so other members of the department won't know their identity" (*ibid*.: 218). Mixed with anonymity and undercover work, this method can provide a potent instrument to inject distrust in the market for corruption. These arguments are related to those developed under repetition above.[70]

E. The Number of Other Players

Obviously most forms of cooperation in the real world involve more than two players. Experiments have consistently shown that as the number of players involved in an agreement increase, the more difficult it becomes to enforce an agreement (*see* van Lange et al. 1992). Of course, this was realized by constitutional engineers already over two centuries ago. The traditional separation of powers doctrine makes it more difficult not just for one power to gain control of the entire machinery of government, but makes it also more difficult to sustain such agreements.[71] Today, agencies usually combine functions of adjudication, rulemaking, and investigation, particularly at the top level, which can be troubling. To counteract this possibility, the American Procedures Act (APA) mandates a precise separation of staff functions in an agency's investigative and adjudicatory position below the top of an agency or commission directly. Similarly, administrative law judges are insulated from the direct influence of agency heads and commissioners, particularly in matters concerning salary and

---

[69] For example, when an official does not know who is in line for promotion, he must take greater care in recruiting persons for transgressions.

[70] There are a few chief criticisms against anonymity and secrecy as a tool. First, it can lead to false accusations. Second, it can cause distrust in legitimate as well as legitimate transactions. Third, it can make reporting and monitors themselves less accountable.

[71] Indeed, work on anti-trust theory suggests that in parties of 4 and above it becomes very difficult to maintain a cartel (Cooter 2000).

tenure (Aman and Mayton 1992: 200). Indeed, several of the mechanisms I discussed against corruption under altering the payoffs are related to increasing the number of players. For example, anti-trust laws increase the number of firms operating in a region making cartels more difficult to sustain. Having several officials or organizations provide the same service is another means directly related to using size to reduce the changes of illicit agreements.

When we move from a situation where the game is no longer a two-person dilemma to an n-person dilemma, we must expect corrupt systems to suffer from collective action problems. There are several explanations offered for this. *First*, the greater the number of players, the more difficult it becomes to recognize the actions of other players (Ostrom 1998). *Second* and related to this, it is easier for parties to make an anonymous choice, thus not facing the same chances of retribution for their actions. *Third*, players no longer perceive their contribution as being important to the general game. *Fourth*, in addition players no longer feel responsible for others as causation becomes weaker. *Fifth*, players can no longer easily shape others' behavior with their own strategy. Discussed below, it is well documented, for example, that the Mafia intentionally keeps the number of people it protects to a low number in order to maintain control of its own house.[72]

As aforementioned, experimental results have shown that it is far easier to sustain cooperation in a two person prisoner's dilemma than in an N person dilemma. Experiments have, however, also indicated that the impact of increasing the number of players becomes smaller when the groups are already relatively large. In particular there are few differences between groups of seven or twenty persons (Lange et al. 1992: 18). Many corrupt systems often consist of relatively large numbers and are still remarkably stable. The following description illustrated in Della Porta and Vannucci (1999: 33, 129) is illustrative of this phenomenon:

"Between the mid 1970s and the end of the following decade a system of corruption existed within the ATM, Milan's public transport company, so extensive and well-rooted (the magistrates were able to document over two thousand illegal transactions) that not a single denunciation or internal controversy disturbed its functioning (*ibid.*:129)..."In the whole fifteen years not a single denunciation or hint of internal controversy had disturbed the well-oiled machinery of corrupt exchange. Those bureaucrats whose position meant that they would inevitably become aware of the corruption of others were gradually brought within the system. A careful and precise division of the proceeds of corruption existed, "each person being due a predetermined percentage.... Calculations were precise to a ridiculous extent. Even a handful of lira would be paid out" (TAM:82) (*ibid.*:33).'"...The politicians who managed the ATM transferred some of the money they received in

---

[72] *See* further, Chapter V, Section IV, Subsection B.

bribes to their parties or, as the price protection of their careers, to the political bossed who could influence nominations to the offices they held."

The factors that are identified elsewhere in the chapter such as norms of reciprocity, hostages, behavioral factors etc. are fundamental to understanding how cooperation can still be maintained and how additional members may not have a large impact on stability, but there are also other factors strictly related to the sanctioning ability in N -person transactions that are at work and help explain this apparent anomaly.

First, the stability of cooperation in an N-person dilemma depends not just on the ability of one person to detect and punish a defector as in a 2 person transaction, but on the ability of the group as a whole (or members of the group) to detect the defector. What this effectively means is that in a single interaction between two or more parties, other members are willing to sanction nonconformists; the game, therefore, is no longer a single interaction but again a repeated game, composed of the many transactions that occur within the group. Parties sanction in this manner as they assume it will influence their own future payoffs. A result of this is that even when a weak player plays against a strong player and has no way of effectively sanctioning the strong player, the stronger player may still need to cooperate. A second conclusion of this is that players need only meet each other once in order for cooperation to be stable. Naturally the ability of the other members to sanction itself depends on their own strength and their ability to recognize deviant behavior.

This can be understood in a very simple overlapping generations model discussed in Binmore (1997). Consider a society where there are only two persons alive at any particular time, a mother and a daughter. At the end of each period, the daughter becomes old after having a child of her own. When young she can produce 200 loaves of bread. She would ideally eat half the bread now and put away the other half for later in life but this is not possible, because the bread cannot hold. One possible equilibrium of the game would be for each mother to eat all of the 200 loaves of bread in her youth and die in misery in her old age. Another equilibrium (the Pareto efficient equilibrium) is for the daughter to eat half of the bread and give the other half to the mother. How can this strategy hold? Let us call the daughter that gives the bread to the mother a conformist (non-defector). Consider now a strategy whereby a conformist daughter only has to give the 100 loaves of bread to the mother if her mother was a conformist in her youth. The daughter now has every incentive to support her mother, because failing to do so would mean that she would not be supported herself in her old age. This model shows that the weaker members of a society or a group will not necessarily be neglected even if nobody cares for their welfare and they are not in a position to punish defectors or nonconformists themselves.[73]

A second key element that makes the group stable is what has been termed in the literature as meta-norms (see, for example, Axelrod 1986) or second-order dilemmas (Ostrom 1998), namely the ability or process of sanctioning those that fail to sanction. Should player 1 fail to sanction, he may himself be sanctioned by player 2 or player 3 etc. Punishing those that do not support a norm, may dramatically change the payoffs of the game. Meta-norms may also involve punishing those who although compliant in their own behavior, are not willing to sanction others for noncompliance.

Note, meta-norms also lead to the result that parties that were before unwilling to cooperate originally now find themselves being punished for not playing the game in the first place. For example, they will be punished for not participating, by numerous group members, who themselves fear being punished for not doing so. It becomes especially problematic where there is no exit option for a player in a game. This is a rampant means of recruiting new persons into corrupt practices. In such circumstances, one can hardly speak of a prisoner's dilemma anymore as one party such as the citizen may have to cooperate irrespective of what the other party does.

Consider the scenario where a bribe is solicited at boarder crossings to let players pass. In the case of institutionalized corruption, where the official himself shall be punished or ridiculed for not soliciting a bribe, and he enjoys the protection of his colleagues, it also being in their interest to continue the practice, corruption may start to resemble extortion.[74]

In some former communist countries when the authorities accused someone of an impropriety, others were expected to denounce the accused (Axelrod 1986). Metanorms offer part of an explanation for the continuance of inefficient norms. This is a rapid means of establishing the dominance of one norm or practice over another.

There are several other reasons, beyond those looked at elsewhere in this chapter, why corrupt systems as they grow in size may not necessarily become more unstable. *First*, the larger the system, the more costly it can be to break it, as it may have links to high level officials. *Second*, in the case of corruption with a great number of players, there is a substantial reduction in the psychological costs of engagement. Unlike other N-person dilemmas, where, as stated above, increases in the number of players normally increase the risk of noncooperation, given the countervailing reduction in psychological costs, increases in numbers engaged in corruption may make the group more stable. *Third*, the temptation to

---

[73] Note, to be included in the group in the first place the mother had something to trade in the first place.

[74] It should also be noted that metanorms may also be imposed not to support systematic cooperation but systematic defection as when one plays with outsiders or perceived rivals.

defect is also reduced by the fact that the greater the number of persons that are corrupt, the lower may be the probability of detection, especially when officials belonging to the same organization control one another.[75] *Fourth*, there may also be positive benefits from belonging to a group, such as status etc. *Fifth*, where there is kinship involved (interdependence of utility functions), the increase in size of the collective action problem is only very marginal. A *sixth* consideration why increases in the number of parties involved in corruption do not necessarily make the group more unstable is that interests may be better aligned than is suggested in the prisoner's dilemma. Frequently, for example, the interests of the parties are largely, though not perfectly, aligned, thus mitigating the need for trust and other mechanisms to ensure compliance. Members of an alliance, for example, may both have a common interest in realizing a specific goal but in doing so, they may disagree as to the best means to do so. The greatest problem now is to coordinate their activities. This is best depicted by the payoff structure in the "Battle of the Sexes" game common to choices arrived at by alliances.

Figure 6: Battle of the Sexes

	C_1	C_2
R_1	2, 1	0, 0
R_2	0, 0	1, 2

In the original story, a husband and wife are going out for the evening. Although, they both have a strong desire to be together, the woman prefers to go to the opera, whereas the man prefers to go see a boxing match. Of the two mutually beneficial patterns, strategy pair $[R_1, C_1]$ marginally favors Row, whereas, $[R_2, C_2]$ marginally favors column. It is in the interests of both to coordinate their activities. There are several examples, that one could conjure up related to corruption. Imagine two policemen that pull over a motorist for speeding. Both policemen desire the solicitation of a bribe from the motorist for the violation (as they know that there is little or no chance of them being punished for doing so), but they disagree on which one of them should do it, because of say possible unforeseen events that could arise, feelings of guilt or shame, or inconvenience.[76] The payoff structure for the two policemen replicates that of the "battle of the sexes" game described above. There are several other illustrations possible. Two

---

[75] Additionally, the greater the proportion of corrupt officials the lower the search costs citizens incur to find them.

[76] In Russia for example, it has been reported that over 90% of all motorists have admitted to bribing police officers for traffic violations (Levin and Satarov 2000).

officials wish to grant a license in return for a bribe, but one of the officials needs to write a lengthy, burdensome, procedural report stating why the license was given. Similarly, it is in both of their interests to coordinate their activities. Note, there are several foreseeable patterns that may emerge. For example, the officials may rotate between their mutually preferred strategies, or they may just focus on just one strategy (so called focal point), for example $[R_i,C_i]$.[77] This is particularly likely if there is an asymmetry in the relations between the players, *e.g.*, supervisor-agent relationship. The important point to note is that where interests are strongly aligned, the need for trust diminishes.

F. Central Authority

The ability of a corrupt system to organize itself and effectively administer sanctions is affected by a plurality of factors ranging from leadership ability of the head and the size of the organization to the management of the resources at its command. A central authority has the ability to solve an N-person dilemma.[78] A leader may serve as a central authority or an intermediary with a co-ordinating role (*see* Gambetta 1988).[79]

A key characteristic of a central authority is that it has the advantage of being able to *discipline (potential) defectors for non-cooperation*. Where corruption is systematic there is most likely a central authority or a series of authorities that can sanction uncooperative parties. Where a central authority, such as a politician has acquired a reputation for being powerful, he can cut back on the "production costs" of the services he offers (Della Porta and Vannucci 1999: 58). A key aspect of a central authority is that it has the ability to credibly sanction at a minimal cost, *i.e.*, the costs of sanctioning are not necessarily born by the sanctioning party, or the immediately affected party.

---

[77] "An equilibrium is focal because a group of people have come to believe that members of this group will expect play consistent with this equilibrium. When an equilibrium is known to be focal then it becomes "rational" for each player to expect that all other players will expect play consistent with this equilibrium and to act on that expectation" (Ochs 1995: 195).

[78] Note: We have seen in the literature review that it is possible that more than one corrupt organization or central authority develop within an agency. When there is only one central authority, this may be termed centralised corruption, when there are several corrupt units that work separately, this is termed decentralised corruption. The consequences of the later being more devastating for society (Shleifer and Vishny 1993).

[79] It is also possible that central authorities come from outside an agency in the form of organised business interests. There are many possibilities for such arrangements which are influenced by bargaining power among other things (*see* Rose- Ackerman 1999). The shape or constitution of the network depend on its goals, *e.g.*, it may be orchestrated by a political leader in order to remain in power and rewards be given in the form of patronism, or by a business leader who seeks a monopoly position in a market. There is however no strict dichotomy, and one can think of many possibilities.

Another key function is that it also has the affect of offering *a place of redress and dispute resolution*. Yet another role is that of a management function. Within the corrupt organization, the leader may have to take self- initiative in order to align the actions and preferences of the agents with the greater group. For example, one such tactic, no different from other types of management, is to try to get people to identify with the aims of the group. This is a type of preference manipulation, which has the affect described above of increasing cooperation by aligning preferences. The central authority through preference manipulation may encourage such factors as in-group bias, which encourages parties to value interaction with their own above that of outsiders. Knowing the intermediary may be enough to break the chain, it may, however, exist without him. (*see* also embeddedness).

Another important player is the middleman. In corrupt markets given the fact that transactions are illegal, the chances of being offered a lemon are quite high. In any market where goods are sold honestly or dishonestly, the purchaser's quandary is to identify this quality. Where inferior goods can be provided either unnoticed or unpunished, those people in the market that are willing to offer inferior goods can drive the market out of existence- the bad drive the good out (Akerloff 1970). For corrupt dealings, this is a significant problem as those that are willing to defect can drive those willing to honor agreements out of the market. Bribe-givers, again where they cannot distinguish the quality of the service themselves, or where an adequate sanctioning mechanism that suits their purposes does not exist, will assume that only dishonest dealers are left in the "market". The costs of defection are not just that individual agreements will not be honored but that they can drive cooperators out of the market (*ibid.*: 495). This would suggest that efforts to inject endemic distrust among participants in corrupt exchanges would lead to low levels of corruption. The problem, however, is that middlemen may assist in overcoming this difficulty, in a similar manner to a central authority. The middleman reduces the need for parties to trust one another. He also reduces the aforementioned coordination costs of searching for and identifying corrupt partners, the costs of bargaining and agreement, and the costs associated with enforcing agreements. He increases the level of secrecy. Moreover, the middleman is an entrepreneur who can reduce the vulnerabilities associated with detection and compromising information inherent in each of the above stages as well as identify the quality of a buyer and a seller for corrupt exchanges. The key point I am trying to make here is this: A middleman can seriously reduce the capacity of many of the aforementioned mechanisms that endeavor to prevent corrupt transactions, not just because he mitigates the aforementioned vulnerabilities and uncertainties, but also because he is a player that engages in repeated transactions. He is an entrepreneur who offers skills in getting around existing laws and regulations. In corrupt transactions, that are normally by definition illegal, regular institutions such as brand name, that overcome the "lemons problem" do not exist nor can they arise, making the role of the entrepreneur and the reputation he brings with him all the more significant. Mechanisms that aim to inject distrust and push the parties into a prisoner's dilemma can be largely mitigated by an unchecked middleman.

G. Personalized Relationships

> "People's behavior can largely be explained in terms of two dominant interests: economic gain and social acceptance" John Harsanyi (1969).

Where governmental activities are based on personal and social relationships, and in particular on traditional exchange, corruption can be very stable, penetrating domains that should be governed by "hand-off" relations.

1. Kinship and Shared Utility

> "Every man feels his own pleasures and his own pains more sensibly than those of other people... After himself, the members of his own family, those who usually live in the same house with him, his parents, his children, his brothers and sisters, are naturally the objects of his warmest affections. They are naturally and usually the persons upon whose happiness or misery his conduct must have the greatest influence". (Smith 1853: 321 in Becker 1981: 1).

According to Adam Smith persons are selfish in market transactions, but altruism is common in family relations (Becker 1981: 10). Whether or not one shares this strict dichotomy is one thing, the fact that kinship increases the level of corruption is a separate matter entirely. It can be argued that kinship, similar to hands on relations, where social interactions encroach upon economic interactions, has the effect of increasing the number of plays in a game, as well as the range of sanctions and benefits Corrupt transactions can, therefore, only be understood when viewed from a broad perspective of reciprocity. The result of which is that members of the same group are on average more likely to engage in corrupt behavior than other unrelated persons. Furthermore, where kinship is at hand, persons shall also have relations outside the workplace. Agents have near perfect information on player type and actions. Nonconformity (defection) results in the fact that sanctions are higher, being both social sanctions within the workplace and outside of the workplace, and the shadow of the future (discussed below) is also greater, *i.e.*, the gains from future transactions, both legal and illegal. This is dealt with below in the discussion on hands on relationships. This naturally suggests that a fundamental first move in the reduction of corruption, particularly in the administration, is the introduction of a meritocratic system of employment relations. Finally, not just the fact that parties derive some utility from the well-being of their family (or alternatively, derive disutility from their suffering), or the fact that they have many other interactions outside of the economic sphere increase the level of secrecy and bonding between family members, another feature of kinship is that if there is a reputation loss for one party, then there is a loss for the other. For example, if one of my kin develop a reputation for not being cooperative, then I also suffer a reputation loss, having the same name. This increases what economists call the level of lock- in.

2. Hands-On Relations or Economic Embeddedness

Hands-on relations have the characteristic that economic actions are embedded in social actions. Hands-on relations effectively increase the number of repetitions that occur in a game as well as the possible payoffs and sanctions, effectively increasing the returns from and opportunities for reciprocity.[80] These are common to closed-knit communities or sub-communities. Hardin (2001) refers to these as thick relationships. Furthermore, in developing countries hands-off relationships (separation from economic and social life) are less common than in more developed nations (Tanzi 1995, 2000) and with the passage of time have often become convention. Embeddedness of social and business life may offer a corrupt system a solution to the N person prisoner's dilemma. To wit, many developing countries are characterized by behavioral norms of reciprocal obligations. Where organizations or societies have developed strong norms of obligations, there may be a long list of IOU's or favors kept on a mental balance sheet (Tanzi 1995). Moreover in such a world there may be a blur between what may be considered as gifts and what may be considered as bribes Rose-Ackerman (1999: 103-104).

A characteristic of reciprocal obligations identified in the sociological literature is that one means of continuing a relationship is to repay a favor with more than what was necessary to further the relationship, by creating new obligations and therefore new opportunities (Coleman 1990: 179). Paying back someone more than is necessary in order to create a new obligation in the future in an example of one such development.[81] The important characteristic of reciprocal obligations is that they may be self-sustaining, with the direct affect of making them more costly to break, given their long term nature. Expectations can also be self-enforcing. For example, a public administrator may view his appointment as a reward for party loyalty and as a means for returning a favor. Such expectations

---

[80] In the language of transaction cost economics, there are more relationship specific assets between the parties.
[81] Carmichael and Macleod (1997) present an evolutionary model of gift giving where they illustrate how the custom of gift giving by imposing costs at the onset of a relationship may support cooperation even where cheaters are never detected.

may generate feelings of obligation. In Japan, the use of *giri*, the traditional obligation to secure an equilibrium between gifts made and received, contributes to the diffusion of bribes, and to clientelistic voting, as has the tradition of offering a gift to a person that is responsible for a dossier (Della Porta and Vanucci 1999: 90). However, one should also note that reciprocation, based on obligations and expectations has the characteristic that it may wither away with time if left unused. Reform measures may be very costly at the onset and must be sustained over a certain period of time, but there may be a long term sustainable shift in behavioral patterns, which may itself be sustainable.

A key factor in controlling the degree of embeddedness are conflict of interest laws. Embeddedness has four key affects. *First*, the sanctioning mechanism is far more stable. Parties no longer need to sanction individually but can rely on others to sanction on their behalf. The problem of meta norms or the second order dilemma has been solved. *Second*, reputation becomes an even more powerful instrument. Having a reputation to cooperate increases the likelihood of finding someone else that is willing to cooperate as the information is more widespread. Inversely, a loss of reputation is more quickly disseminated. *Third*, when there is great degree of embeddedness a party has to consider the losses occurred by others as a result of his transactions. This suggests that when actions are interrelated then there is a greater degree of reliance (and possible utility). This is similar to the argument with kinship, where parties share the utility of another. *Fourth*, information on criminal behavior cannot, as a result of the inherent need within criminal action for secrecy, be purchased on the market. In those societies where closed-knit relations are pervasive, one can plausibly expect a quicker dissemination of information on player type, information related to those that are willing to engage in corrupt exchanges and those that are less so. Furthermore the concept of embeddedness gives us insight into how parties may align after reforms. Where corruption is based on ascriptive factors such as ethnicity, etc., exchanges are stable and can only be destabilized by substantive reforms.

H. Cognitive Factors

Cognitive factors are sometimes a euphemism for anomalies that authors find difficult to classify. One may, however, consider some concrete well-documented phenomenon.

1. Bias

As argued earlier frequent social exchange results in an increase in trust among parties (Dasgupta 1988). What is, however, also important about frequent social exchange as experimental evidence suggests is that it can lead to "(1) positive emotions that solidify and strengthen the person-to-group bond and (2) uncertainty reduction that renders the focal group more salient in relation to others. These two mechanisms produce a sense of psychological group formation and ultimately increase observable acts of commitment" (Lawler, Thye and Yoon 2000: 616). These factors support what may be termed in-group bias. In- group bias refers to the belief that ones own group is superior to another resulting in persons acting in favor of their own group over another (Ridgeway and Erickson 2000). Hence, repeated interaction may also lead to a certain degree of interdependence and the formation of the group as a focal point. Experimental evidence also shows that a further example of such bias occurs in the formulation and maintenance of status beliefs (*ibid.*). Social construction theory argues that repeated interaction between persons can lead to the reinforcement of false beliefs. Furthermore, these players can teach their status beliefs to others through their own actions which may lead to consensus within groups (*ibid.*). Bias may similarly be enforced through repeated play. Most drivers claim that they drive better than the average, although this is statistically impossible. This claim is reinforced through biased selection of external occurrences in order to reinforce ones personal stand point.

2. Preferences and Ideology

Preferences and ideology share many of the characteristics of kinship. Where parties have similar preferences, or a common ideology, they are more likely to agree.[82] Indeed what is important is that parties may identify the group or the success of an ideology as a goal in itself (Lawler, Thye and Yoon 2000), or as mentioned earlier in our example of cooperation in a one shot game, people may feel that cooperation is a goal in itself worth honoring.

As a concrete example, consider the following: From a rationality perspective, it seems unthinkable for soldiers to take upon himself many of the undue risks of battle and lay down their lives for their country. As Dixit and Nalebuff (1993: 161) point out, there is no reason why beds should be made in a particular way or that socks should be folded except that it is to increase the obedience of the soldier, so that when later called upon for more important matters he shall remain obedient. Such is a means to acquire an automatic reaction and overcome individual rational calculation for strategic rationality.

Alluded to above, cognitive factors that affect preferences may be manipulated by a central authority. This occurs for three reasons. *Firstly*, common preferences allow agreement on the value of a certain action. For example where ideology is involved, there may be a common disliking for a government policy

---

[82] Here we refer to agreement in general and not just agreements to behave illegally. In the case of preferences for non-corrupt behavior, then the parties should find it easier to enforce this norm. One can see that similar preferences increase group cohesion.

which encourages the parties to go around the law. The *second* effect of preferences and ideology is that where parties believe in a certain action, then they have less psychological (moral) costs of pursuing the action. Take for example the belief that one's own kin should always receive preferential treatment. A third and most important aspect of preferences and ideology is that it is a good indicator of with whom parties are most likely to collude, *i.e.*, when a new reform is introduced it opens up new opportunities for corruption, parties may need to shift their alliances to maintain the running of the old system. Collusion is more likely where there are similar goals, preferences and ideologies

It has been widely documented that bargaining and coming to agreements are seen as an interactive process, with inferences not just on the size of the payoffs available but also about the psychological characteristic of proposals. Decisions to cooperate or not to cooperate are often a reflection of cognitive and motivational processes. There are biases and limitations that necessarily do not arise out of self interest. Parties may overvalue the opinion or decision of a leader for instance. Contrary to this, is the well documented phenomenon in conflict resolution of "reactive devaluation" whereby a proposal is rated less positively if it comes from an adversary rather than from someone who is considered a neutral or beneficial party (*see* Ross 1995). The message is clear here: parties may have a cognitive tendency to underestimate appeals and information presented by the government and cognitive bias to follow certain persons or keep the status quo.[83] Where government is not regarded highly, as a result of consecutive failures or otherwise, there may be a cognitive bias against any reform measures that are proposed. This in turn leads to citizens and officials alike to be biased towards non-legal forms of cooperation.

Indeed, in order for reform measures to have a greater chance of success, *i.e.*, increase the credibility of reform proposals, cognitive factors must be taken into consideration, particularly after a series of failures. This is important in general in overcoming problems of dysfunctional institutions.[84]

Cognitive factors may not be easily overcome and require a fundamental shift in attitude and preferences. Where corruption is a result of a long period of socialization, changes in behavior can only be achieved through long-term sustainable reforms. In such cases, freezing out old officials to let in the new might be imperative.

---

[83] One should again note that trust is likely to increase over the passage of time. This means that where a relationship, or a network, has been exchanging for a longer period of time, there is likely to be greater levels of trust among the members. This means that less resources need to be spent on monitoring, which makes exchange even more attractive.

[84] *See* further, Chapter V.

I. Unstable Environment

Where the income accrued by entering into a corrupt transaction is uncertain, parties may change the discount rate they associate with future relations, thus refusing to enter into a deal. However, the same logic may be reversed in many developing countries, where it is the legal environment that is unstable. When wages are uncertain (or permanently low) parties may be lead to change the discount rate they give to corrupt transactions and enter into deals. This is expounded on greater detail below.[85] Moreover, when officials feel that there job is threatened, or private sector individuals suffer from market uncertainty, they may be in an "end game situation" and try to appropriate as much as they can, given that the perceived future gains to honesty are low. These problems are clearly aggravated when there is is the lack of trust in government.[86]

IV. Reciprocity as goal onto itself?

> "There is no duty more indispensible than that of returning a kindness. All men distrust one forgetful of a benefit" (Cicero).[87]

Adumbrated above, it is sometimes argued that reciprocity can become an ends in itself, where actors desire to reciprocate because they generate positive feelings from doing so, and negative feelings from not doing so. Cicero seemed to place great emphasis on the norm of reciprocity. Corruption and bribes per se are a form of reciprocity, and socio-economic life is full of reciprocities (*see* Noonan 1984: xiii). Corruption, once perceived as implanted within web of reciprocity becomes difficult to untangle.

There is, of course, a sound distinction to be made between notions of fairness or altruism and notions of pure self-interest behind reciprocity. The shared utility that one has from another persons benefits may be considered terminologically a general definition of altruism. People do not always operate according to personal interests but as part of complex altruistic motivations. Although difficult to show empirically, recent game theoretic experimental

---

[85] See further, Chapter III, Section V, Subsection D.

[86] As we will see in Chapter V, there are broadly two kinds of trust. One refers to trust within the corrupt system and is counterproductive to reform. The other aspect of trust that is productive to reform is trust in government (*see* Braithwaite and Levi 1998, and Putnam 1995). The importance of trust to effective reform and governance is not perfectly clear. Good governance may be either the cause or the affect of social trust. Winning back trust should be a part of any reform measures, and the effect on trust part of any institutional restructuring.

[87] Taken from Alvin W. Gouldner (1960) cited in Putnam (1993: 172).

literature, based largely on the Dictator Game and the Ultimatum game seem to provide a priori conclusive evidence of altruism and notions of fairness.[88]

In a dictator game, an individual decides on the division of a fixed sum of money between himself and an anonymous player. There is no contact between the players. From a game theoretic perspective there is only one equilibrium in the game. The dictator decides to keep everything for himself. In the ultimatum game, one party proposes a certain division of a fixed sum and the other party has the discretion of accepting this division or having both players go home empty handed. Similar to the last game, the only solution to the game is that player 1 offers the smallest possible divisible of the amount at stake. Both games have shown parties to have been more generous that one would expect and have led to a divergence between what standard game theory predicts and what actually happens.

Another important lesson from games such as the ultimatum game, is that they teach us not only that people often reciprocate, when it is not "rational" to do so, making reciprocity an end in itself, but they also are willing to reject positive offers, if they are considered to be uneven, although rejection is itself costly for them (Gueth Schmittberger and Schwarze 1982). Another important result of these experiments is that even in the case of anonymous interactions, reciprocity is often generated. Furthermore, reciprocity has even been documented where it is common knowledge that nobody can observe individual choices, but only aggregate choices (Bolton and Zwick 1995). Moreover, the ultimatum game has been conducted in high stakes conditions, where the payoffs to the players involved are significant relative to income levels. For example, Cameron (1995) conducted a one-shot ultimatum game in Indonesia in which the bargaining pie was the equivalent of three months on income. She observed similar results in this high stakes game relative to other low stakes games.[89]

This evidence is, however, not conclusive. In a much-cited summary of the experimental bargaining literature, Roth (1995: 328), a forerunner in the field, concluded: "Further evidence, however, made clear that whatever the extent to which notions of fairness may play a role in determining the outcome of bargaining, it is not the case that bargainers are primarily trying to be fair." It would appear that notions of fairness are unsettled and are still subject to strategic considerations.

---

[88] The results of many of these experiments are well documented in Roth (1995) and more recently in Ockenfels (1999).

[89] Cited in Fehr and Gächter (1998: 847).

97

V. Concluding Comments

> "Once the subtle nature of the web of reciprocal rewards and punishments has been appreciated, it becomes easier to understand why it is so hard to reform corrupt societies in which criminality has become socially acceptable" (Binmore 1997: 270).

I would embrace the above statement by Binmore wholeheartedly and it is a point that goes amiss in many policy reforms and commentaries. Reform measures, like corruption per se, do not act unilaterally. Corruption, embedded in a web of reciprocities, is onerous to untangle. There are many reasons for the maintenance of undesired cooperation in the form of corruption, and the patterns of exchanges may be maintained by a plurality of factors, as we have seen above. Nevertheless, within this web of reciprocities and punishments, there are key conditions that make corruption more likely to evolve. It is the reformers task to identify those factors that are most conducive to corruption and to eliminate as many of them as possible. The mechanisms of corrupt exchange and the factors that tie them together will vary from context to context. The more salient measures, however, that may be considered are dealt with in the following chapters. The factors and conditions set out here are indicative of some of the areas where we can expect corruption to flourish and possible mechanisms that can be used to invert corrupt exchanges. I first concentrate on removing incentives and opportunities to engage in corruption.

CHAPTER III

REMOVING INCENTIVES AND OPPORTUNITIES FOR CORRUPTION

I. Introduction

As suggested, it is a useful exercise to visualize a backdrop where corruption is most likely to evolve; one that is so consummate to malfeasance that any regular individual would be find himself or herself enticed to enter into corrupt exchanges. A central notion behind the former chapter was that by understanding those factors most conducive to the evolution and maintenance of corruption and the different steps and vulnerabilities that accompany them, the reformer may try to remove as many conditions as possible that lead to corrupt exchanges.[1] I highlighted several reform measures that may be applicable based on the framework developed, some of which are law enforcement or managerial strategies, others, however, may require needed administrative, legal, social or political initiatives. Here, we turn our attention to some noteworthy reforms shaping government administration important in mitigating the conditions conducive to corruption and reshaping both the desirability and stability of corrupt exchanges. This chapter concentrates on those factors essentially targeting the province, range and nature of administrative activity. The desirability of each measure is naturally subject to several local conditions, and in particular the nature and patterns of illicit reciprocity that have developed. Though each measure developed here may be and essentially must be adjudicated according to its own individual merits within a given context, the seven different sections I discuss may also be considered as seven different steps in a chain of possible reforms.

II. Revoking Inefficient Laws and Programs

Where corruption is rampant, a first step by a rational reformer to prevent or curb corrupt transactions is to look at the possibility of removing the area of government activity in it entirety. At its most basic, this idea manifests itself in the notion of reducing both the level of government interference and government regulation in the market. This position is exemplified by such notables as Nobel laureate Gary Becker, who suggested that "the only way to reduce corruption permanently is to drastically cut back government's role in the economy" Becker

---

[1] *See* also Heymann (1996: 331).

(1994: 10).[2] However, most economic liberalists would agree, that this does not call for a flat all-encompassing swoop of all governmental economic activity per se, but rather that certain activities, programs, regulations etc. are less efficient than others, some of which should be repealed (Rose-Ackerman 1992).

In less developed countries, more so than developed countries, it is a fair generalization that the government's role in the economy tends more frequently and more egregiously to transcend spending and taxing activities into a wider setting of extensive authorizations, regulations, and other quasi-fiscal activities. Formulations of factors conducive to corruption must take into account the level of governmental activity or interference. Klitgaard (1988, 1996) has formulated corruption heuristically as monopoly power + discretion - accountability (C= M +D-A). This is a useful rule-of-thumb, but it does not take into consideration that a precursor to corruption is generally government activity in the market or government regulation of certain behavior. If there were no government activity or no regulation, there could be no governmental corruption, C = 0. This does not suggest that scaling back government activity necessarily reduces the level of corruption. Indeed, from a policy perspective this is an unnecessarily simplistic and rushed conclusion. Closing down one avenue to corruption, or loci of payoffs, has the potential of shifting corruption to other areas, not dissimilar in many respects analytically from the effect of turning on the light outside one's house, with the resulting effect that burglars simply look beyond your house (if they cannot prevent you from turning on the light in the first place) and go to the next.[3]

Put succinctly, my point is this: scaling back unnecessary or inefficient governmental activities or interference (including among them programs, subsidies, regulations, laws, and authorizations) is a good starting point to curbing corruption. Consider inefficient laws for example. Recall the impact of Prohibition in the United States, which led to widespread transgression and provided incentives for the rise of organized crime. Alternatively, consider the impact of gambling restrictions which have been reversed in many countries and jurisdictions throughout the world (Rose-Ackerman 1999: 40). Indeed, this argument is often extended to other consensual crimes, such as prostitution and drugs. It is so difficult to curb these transgressions because they are consensual, demand generates its own supply. Putting a law or regulation in place offers potential for collusion between law enforcement and transgressors.

To wit, many regulations and authorization serve primarily as a means of increasing incomes for some government officials. The desire of these officials

---

[2] From Becker Gary, S., "To Root Out Corruption, Boot out Big Government," *Business Week* (31 January 1994).

[3] Of course, analytically, one notable difference is that corruption is normally a form of cooperative behavior, and it is very unlikely that two burglars will attempt to rob the same house at the same time and unify their efforts. They do not need to because there is no interdependence between them to accomplish the task.

often to maintain the status quo is self-evident, but the costs of doing so, as we have seen, can be devastating for a country.[4] Eliminating unnecessary laws, regulations, and inefficient government programs and subsidies is not always easy, and it can be problematic to identify those areas that are primarily for rent-seeking or corruption purposes, and those that are merely inefficient.

Looking at poor results per se does not necessarily teach us much. Bad results may be the result of nonfeasance (inaction), malfeasance (corruption), ethical lassitude (poor work ethic) or bad policy. This should not, however, obfuscate anti-corruption reforms, because those same factors that increase performance are generally the same factors that reduce corruption: there is, thus, a fruitful symbiosis to be had between the efforts at curbing corruption and efforts and increasing performance more generally.[5]

To reiterate reducing unnecessary or ineffective governmental activities commonly in the shape of public or social welfare programs, subsidies, regulations and procedural requirements is an important means to mitigate corruption. In addition to the difficulties that a reform-minded government may face in introducing these measures (because of *inter alia* the embedded nature of special interests and there ability to effectively veto reforms), there are well recognized prima facie difficulties in measuring performance. Unlike a private corporation whose only goal is profit maximization, government is characterized by a multiplicity of goals. The mandate is multidimensional, and the very reason for governmental activity is commonly based on a presupposed market failure, or alternatively that profits are not the main goal of a particular program (Banfield

---

[4]   The reader will recall the most common costs of corruption include: Increasing the costs of doing businesses in a country through increasing risk, the cost of inputs, the costs of formalism etc.; higher prices and lower quality of services and products, which ominously in some instances endanger life and limb (as in construction, health care and product liability); an inefficient allocation of resources, whereby those that value the resources the most do not acquire them; an efficient allocation of talent, whereby talented persons engage in rent-seeking activity and corruption outright, because the gains of doing so outweigh alternative choices. Moreover, the costs of corruption include increased secrecy, which excludes many from the market and increases distrust of government and government officials; an increase in the level of gray-market and black-market activities, which are not taxes and can lead to an increase in the level of organized crime and other entities that can in extreme cases challenge the legitimacy of government itself; the fact that corruption can bread corruption, by decreasing both the social and psychological costs of engaging in the activity as the greater proportion of the population that engages in a similar activity increases. Similarly there may be increasing gains to corruption relative to the gains of not engaging in corruption as the proportion of corrupt persons in a society increases (recall the Shelling diagram in Chapter 1, Figure 2). Corruption, in addition, widens the fiscal deficit and reduces the amount of tax revenue available for public expenditure.

[5]   This naturally presupposes that anti-corruption efforts take the (marginal) gains from anti-corruption measures into consideration weighed against the (marginal) costs of doing so, and do not attempt to reduce corruption to a level of 0 on a type of moral quest.

1975; Tirole 1994). As Tirole (*ibid.*:4-5) notes, for example: "A regulator of a natural monopoly is supposed to ensure 'reasonable' prices, but even an econometrician may have a hard time measuring the regulator's contribution to the net consumer surplus." Weights need to be assigned to the multiplicity of goals and, where government agencies enjoy a monopoly position, there is a general inability to compare performance accurately.[6]

Nevertheless, program elimination and program evaluation are prerequisites to curbing corruption in many instances, and constitute a fundamental part of any system of administrative accountability. We shall take a brief look at this in the next section, not offering an expansive treatment of the issue, but outlining some fundamental considerations and provisional remarks.

III. Program Evaluation and Elimination

In New York City, a priest and a taxicab driver died and went to heaven. Saint Peter first showed the priest his new eternal home - a slum dwelling. Saint Peter then turned to the cab driver and guided him to his new home - a mansion.

The priest was angry and asked Saint Peter, "Why the difference? I have led a humble life, was true to your guidelines and your rules."

Saint Peter succinctly replied, "When you preach, people sleep. When riders get into his cab, they pray!"[7]

For performance measurement it is results that count.

Argued above, certain programs are sometimes retained primarily because they offer opportunities for rent-seeking and corruption. In these cases, it is imperative that reformers take a hard look at the merits of the program, to weigh its desirability or usefulness against the general costs of its elimination.[8] Sometimes, program elimination outright is important, but in other cases, programs can be redefined to include both procedural constraints and oversight mechanisms. I shall not address these procedural constraints and oversight mechanisms here; the

---

[6] This does not of course distract from the fact that government agencies and state-owned bodies often compete with the private sector, allowing for comparison. Additionally, comparison can be drawn by, government organizations that compete against one another and more generally from the performance of other foreign governmental organizations and agencies (Tirole 1994: 4-5).

[7] Joke adapted from Hatry (1999).

[8] This discussion is clearly related to later discussion on corruption in procurement, given that a common source of corruption in the aforementioned projects and programs involves the promotion of unnecessary and unproductive spending, which can take the form of overpaying for goods and service or making payments to persons not entitled to payments such as ghost workers etc.

reason they are raised here, is that it is important in measuring program evaluation and performance to recognize that the reasons for poor results may not be a result of a poor project per se, but poorly designed oversight mechanisms.

Tracking expenditures and the physical outputs programs and agencies produce has been a common feature of government for decades and is an essential feature of good governance (*see* Hatry 1999). It provides a basic amount of information to program personnel and perhaps a broad indication of outputs, but generally little information outcome of program outcomes, nor individual inputs. Outcomes are defined as the effect of a program on the community. Output refers to the goods and services produced (Bale and Dale 1998: 107).[9] What is needed, however, is regular tracking of outcomes and performance.

It is an unfortunate reality that in too many countries one is often hard challenged to find governments that effectively ascertain the performance of their public administrations in accordance with key policy and program objectives, and in turn apply the knowledge and information garnered regularly to better performance and policy and program design.[10] Establishing quantifiable targets and measuring impact may, as Hauge (2001: 1) puts it, "help bridge the gap between bureaucratic action on the one hand and the tracking of progress with long-term developmental goals on the other".

Program evaluation and performance measurement are two means to determine whether program and policy objectives are being met.[11] Performance measurement may be regarded as a field of program evaluation. Program evaluation, nevertheless, routinely refers to in-depth, special studies examining in addition to a program's outcomes questions related to how and to what extent programs actually occasioned the outcomes (Hatry 1999).[12] Although performance measurement systems and in-depth program evaluations are interrelated activities, it is time and cost constraints naturally that form the basis of why in-depth program evaluations are conducted less frequently and particularly only for selected programs (*ibid.*). Fundamental to good governance and reforming government is the importance of information, for which performance measurement is crucial.

Except for the most blatant cases of disastrous performance, performance measurement is a complex multi-faceted phenomenon. Performance audits, are

---

[9]   As Reid suggests: "Output measures can be used to assess whether or not resources are being efficiently managed to deliver non-contingent results or products. In contrast, outcome measures focus on underlying policy objectives; they enable an evaluation of whether the outputs produced are actually achieving underlying goals" *See* Reid, World Bank, Administrative and Civil Service Reform available at http://www.worldbank.org/publicsector/ civilservice/service.htm.

[10] *Ibid.*

[11] *Ibid.*

[12] As McKinney and Howard (1998: 389) propose: "Program evaluation aims to obtain valid verifiable data on the structures, processes, outputs and impacts of programs."

becoming more frequent and are commonly conducted by auditors or an inspector general. They are frequently random studies similar to in depth program evaluations. As mentioned, in the private sector performance is easier to measure as it based generally on profits. In the public sector government activity is characterized by a multiplicity of goals. Costs of inputs and expenses on their own are not very revealing. Two related factors of particular salience exist that make performance measurement more important in public bodies than private bodies and particularly government business enterprises.[13] First, the fact that government business enterprises habitually operate in a noncompetitive market environment thus enjoying a monopoly position in service delivery, and second, when other socio-political objectives exist (which is the normal justification for the continued existence of government enterprises) additional information should be provided on whether these objectives are being met.[14] Competitive pressures that may curbing inefficiency and improbity may be lacking.

Performance measurement is difficult to define but may be considered as some measure of quantitative and qualitative results against specified benchmarks. The use of performance measurement is twofold. On the one hand, performance measurement is an internal tool important in assisting managers supervise and regulate activities on a regular basis.[15] On the other hand, it is a tool for external parties to hold officials accountable.[16] Indeed, in many developed economies such as the UK and the US, there has been a trend towards removing traditional central constraints to afford high level (and in some cases line level) officials greater responsiveness to market demands. Accordingly, there is less reliance on a command and control type of accountability system; government enterprises and

---

[13] Energy utilities, national railways, communication services are but a few examples of these enterprises.

[14] As a rule government business enterprises should provide financial statements in line with International Accounting Standards and follow national accounting standards and requirements applicable to other businesses (see IFAC Public Sector Committee, International Public Sector Guideline 1, "Financial Reporting by Government Business Enterprises"). But reporting on service performance and delivery requires widespread dissemination of information to stakeholders. The provision of information provided about an enterprises performance is supplementary to financial statements.

[15] As noted in a recent report by the IFAC: "Comparison with budgeted performance provides a good basis for evaluating actual performance because users can use it to assess whether resources were obtained and expended as planned, and whether stated goals and objectives were achieved" (IFAC, Performance Reporting by Government Business Enterprises: para. 44).

[16] The aforementioned classification is an oversimplification. The principal users of performance reports include the legislative and other governing bodies, the public, investors and creditors, ratings agencies, other governments, international agencies and resource providers. Some of these rely almost solely on general purpose financial reports for their information on government. Others have access to special reports (see IFAC Public Sector Committee, Government Financial Reporting: Accounting Issues and Practices (2000).

bodies are held answerable more by performance and not on each step of "production." This is particularly the case for the countries that have followed the new public management model of government and service delivery,[17] but other countries are increasingly relying on performance mechanisms as a tool to hold government bodies accountable.[18]

The basic building blocks of a framework of performance measurement comprise:

- Numbers (quantification),
- Comparability (yardsticks),
- Relationships (input to output/outcomes and impacts).

(IFAC, Performance Reporting by Government Business Enterprises: para. 30).

Performance indicators and measures in former years concentrated primarily on financial targets and cash limits, but there has been a movement towards non-financial factors.[19] At least two technical challenges must be met: deciding what to measure (*e.g.*, outputs or outcomes) and how to measure them (agency and program records, user surveys, technical instruments, expert ratings etc.), the latter is made more difficult by the fact that policy objectives are often very vague and therefore very difficult to measure.[20] A well-formulated performance monitoring strategy will support both the development and monitoring of a diversified portfolio of outcome and output indicators.[21] Outputs as one would expect are more controllable than outcomes by agencies and are therefore their preferred tool (Bale and Dale 1998: 107). A rich body of tests have been

---

[17] *See* further, Section V, Subsection F1.

[18] The United States passed the Government Performance and Results Act of 1993 (GPRA) which obligates federal agencies (including Government Business Enterprises) to develop, strategic plans covering a period of at least 5 years that cover the agency's mission statement, identify the agencies goals, and outlines how the agency expects. Strategic plans are a basis for agencies to set goals for programs and measure the performance of these programs in accomplishing these goals. It also requires agencies to deliver annual program performance plans. (IFAC, Performance Reporting by Government Business Enterprises: 30). As with NPM reforms, there was a small movement to waive certain administrative nonstatutory requirements, in return for holding agencies accountable for achieving better performance. The factors that can be relinquished are only related to budgeting and spending within agencies (*ibid.*).

[19] For example, the Citizens Charter, the product of a government White Paper in the United Kingdom in July 1991 placed great emphasis on the quality of public services and the importance of value for money for service users. Similar initiatives are being followed in Canada with the Public Service 2000 programme. (IFAC, Performance Reporting by Government Business Enterprises: para. 126).

[20] *See* Reid, *supra* note 9.

[21] *Ibid.*

developed.[22] Outcomes are more important from a policy perspective as they shift the emphasis from organizational maximization to social welfare maximization, subject to well-designed objectives.

Government should provide information for each discrete part of the business for which it is likely that there are users who require the information for decision making and accountability purposes (IFAC, Performance Reporting by Government Business Enterprises: para. 91).[23] To improve transparency, opinions should be collected on the outcome or impact of a service from the users themselves. As one would expect, there are significant implementation problems. Supervisory and line- level officials often are not presented with proper incentives to provide the requisite information. Basic factors of incentive incompatibility may need to be addressed. Among the more salient are the following:

- Agencies are not interested in assisting the monitoring of their own performance.[24]
- Different groups will care about different aspects of performance.
- Agencies, being aware that what they produce will be monitored, are more likely to report only what is justifiable (Verheijen 1998).

In order to assist compliance, certain strategies should be considered, the most important of which are compiled below.
- Involving stakeholders in developing performance indicators. If they promote their policy objectives, there is greater likelihood that they will be complied with.

---

[22] A diverse body of tests common to evaluating public programs have been advanced. Just the tip of the iceberg of this rich body of tests would include: Program impact indicators both directly expressed or implied in program objects; output efficiency, which ascertain the level of economic performance in which resource inputs such as skills, materials and money are survey and directly compared with resource outputs (benefits) achieved; factor analysis which assess options before any decision is made about undertaking a new program; operation indicators that quantify output activities, commonly expressed in nonfinancial terms, such as the miles of highway built or the number of permits issued over a given period etc. For a comprehensive listing of these concepts and tests, see McKinney and Howard (1998: 391-92).

[23] Traditional reasons for non-widespread dissemination of information included the physical problem of accessibility as well as technical complexity (IFAC, Performance Reporting by Government Business Enterprises: para. 105). In addition, one could argue that there are additional costs for each amount of information that has to be disseminated, particularly if a general purpose financial report has to account for service delivery interests of all users. The internet, however, greatly reduces the physical problem of accessibility as well as some of the above cost factors, e.g., marginal cost of additional user utilizing the information is approaching 0. Furthermore, technical complexity may be exaggerated and should not be a factor in the publication of information on the internet.

[24] Ibid.

- Noncompliance should not result immediately in high sanctions, but there should be levels of sanctions, *i.e.*, failure to comply could result first in a clarification of the performance standards expected, the second stage could result in a warning etc.[25]
- Make information on services standards available and ensure that customers know whom to complain when these services are not performed. Create expectations![26]
- Make evidence on service delivery performance a focal point of the annual budget formation process. Including performance measures in general purpose financial statements is one means of increasing the effectiveness of performance measures. Another is to bring these measures within the scope of the auditor's report, when possible.[27]
- Assign group and individual bonuses.
- In the case of contracting out, tie contract payments to achieving performance targets, similar to performance bonds.[28]

IV. Rules

"Misera est servitus ubi jus est vagum aut incertum"[29]

Discretion in an environment where rules or precise standards are lacking can greatly facilitate corrupt exchanges. It does so firstly by putting officials in a position to allocate scarce resources according to their own volition, and secondly by allowing safety from detection once decisions have been made. Here I dissertate the usefulness and application of rules as a tool to mitigate discretion and corruption. Long a topic of administrative lawyers,[30] rules and discretion have recently been studied by economists, most notably in the form of the rules versus standards discussion (Kaplow 1992), and also in the related discussion on the

---

[25] *See* Ayres and Braithwaite (1992).

[26] The Citizens Charter in the United Kingdom provides an excellent model of this. It tries to ensure that service users, particularly the public, have a right to know the standards being used by an agency and that avenues of complaint are available for grievances.

[27] Naturally, there are certain constraints involved in extending auditor reports to include a list of performance indicators, such as expertise of the auditor to assess a diverse range of factors, and perhaps awarding an auditor too much discretion over difficult to measure factors.

[28] Measuring performance in contracting out is assisted when performance of different enterprises can be compared. Especially important after contracting out, there must be a valid basis of comparison or yardstick such as: standard targets or norms; inter-service comparators; alternative suppliers; inter-organization comparators; and time (IFAC, Performance Reporting by Government Business Enterprises: para. 54). *See* also below, Section VII on procurement.

[29] "It is a miserable slavery where the law is vague or uncertain." Black's Law Dictionary (1999, 7th ed.) p. 1658.

[30] *See*, for example, Kenneth C. Davis (1969).

optimal precision of administrative rules (Ehrlich and Posner 1974; Diver 1983) Lately the desirability of rules over standards has been introduced into the development debate (Posner 1998, Schäfer 2000). Given the recentness of the application of the discussion to development, valuable insights from the economics and legal literature have as yet not been *a priori* tested for their usefulness or application to developing countries and countries in transition. Furthermore, recent developments in the literature in the United States have argued for more as opposed to less discretion for government officials, managers and inspectors, which are worth looking at.

The discussion of rules in the economics literature has, as suggested, been largely confined to the discussion of the usefulness of rules versus standards and the related discussion on the optimal precision of administrative rules. Looking at the discussion of rules only within the confines of the rules versus standards debate is unnecessarily myopic.[31] Rules must be understood as just one of a set of many important tools of government. Too often, knee-jerk reactions to corruption can simply lead to the promulgation of simply more rules. But unwanted discretion may be curbed by a host of other political, economic, social and organizational forces, many of which are examined below, that may be a more appropriate tool of governance. Indeed, the proper role of rules as a means of curbing discretion is very much unclear after decades of debate in the public law literature.[32] To wit, recent reforms in Anglo-Saxon countries seem to be taking the approach that rules and strict procedural requirements may not be the best way forward. The changing shape of government in recent years has led countries to reexamine the tools applied to controlling the behavior of government officials in many governmental functions, beyond the regulatory debate. For example, recent developments in the delivery of government services in the United Kingdom in the form of Next Steps agencies, and their counterparts in Australia, New Zealand, and Sweden have emphasized that rules and strict procedures were not the best tools for government performance and that discretion could be limited by emphasis on results and performance against well agreed upon performance targets, as opposed to controlling closely the factors that lead to these results.

---

[31] As suggested by Becker and Stigler (1974), "rules [don't] provide any guidance or incentive to their enforcement: on the contrary, rules usually provide neither the slightest hint of where to look for violations nor the incentive to convict violators. Nothing in the Sherman Act tells us where to look for collusion; nothing in the motor vehicle laws tells us who will be a speeder; nothing in a pure food law tells us who will be an adjudicator. Moreover, ... often there is little incentive to convict the colluder, speeder, or adulterator."

[32] As Wade and Forsyth (1999: 345) submit: "It used to be thought to be classical constitutional doctrine that wide discretionary power was incompatible with the rule of law. But this dogma cannot be taken seriously today, and indeed it never contained much truth. What the rule of law demands is not that wide discretionary power should be eliminated, but that the law should be able to control its exercise."

These factors highlight a tendencially important shift towards alternative mechanisms to control discretion.

A. Defining Characteristics of Rules

The distinguishing property of a rule is that it attempts to specify outcomes before a particular case arises (Kaplow 1992, 1999; Sunstein 1995). Convictions to a system of rules refer to advances in the law that try to make most or nearly all legal (or administrative) decisions under the governing provision prior to actual cases (Sunstein 1995: 961). A list specifying hazardous substances that may not be released into the water would be constituted as a rule, a standard may only prohibit the discharge of hazardous substances, leaving the determination of what constitutes hazardous to officials and adjudication (Kaplow 1999: 508). A law that states that no one should drive his car above the speed of 100 kilometers per hour is a rule. A law that states the one should drive at a reasonable speed is a standard. Rules are more costly than standards to create given that the institution responsible (for example the legislature or government agency) must research and gather enough information before making it law, whereas standards are more costly than rules to interpret for individuals and to apply for adjudicators (Kaplow 1992). Furthermore, arguments on whether a law is a rule or a standard frequently emphasize whether or not the law is given content ex ante or ex post.

Designing a rule for every eventuality is wasteful. The desirability of a rule over a standard depends on the frequency with which a certain decision occurs. Contingencies that frequently arise, such as should persons over the age of 60 be permitted to pilot commercial airplanes are best decided by rules. These rules may not be considered along the terms of binary decisions but may be complex (Diver 1983; Kaplow 1992).[33] Compare, as Diver (ibid.) suggests the following two rules (Diver 1983):

A. No person may pilot a commercial plane after her sixtieth birthday.

B. No person may pilot a commercial airplane if they fall within one of the following categories - high blood pressure, high prescription on corrective lenses etc.

Both of the above are rules. The first is a general rule, the latter more precise. The advantage of the latter is that it allows for greater inclusiveness, *i.e.*, a more accurate picture of actual persons that are still able to pilot a plane. The greater the degree of precision, however, the greater the costs of formulating legal commands

---

[33] The Internal Revenue Code in the United States is an example of just how complex rules can become. As Baldwin suggests, when rules become so complex, agencies are once again afforded discretion (Baldwin 1995: 23).

(Kaplow 1999: 503). In addition to greater formulation costs there are also greater costs of implementation (enforcement and adjudication costs) and greater accessibility costs, *i.e.*, the law becomes more difficult for citizens to understand and to comply. There are, therefore, important trade-offs between general and complex rules.[34] A standard may be converted into a rule through use of precedent (Ott and Schäfer 1997; Kaplow 1992: 564), or through constant agency practice (Sunstein 1995). Precedent, however, bares similarities to capital stock that depreciates over time, indicating that when not in use it becomes less rule-like (Kaplow 1999: 512).

B. Benefits of Rules

Rules have many potential benefits as a tool to mitigate corruption. the more salient of which I trace next. For simplicity of exposition, I present these in bulleted format.

- Deciding factors ex ante in the form of rules as opposed to standards limits the discretion of enforcers and adjudicative bodies, therefore minimizing abuses of power and corruption (Kaplow 1992; Sunstein 1995; Schäfer 2000).[35]
- Standards decentralize the decisionmaking process, delegating discretion to sublevels of the legal system and government, granting low level officials discretion (Posner 1998; Schäfer 2000). Where decisionmakers have incommensurate information or skill to make complex decisions, delegation is imprudent.
- The legislature and/or agencies may be better rigged to draw on technical expertise than courts and may have specialized knowledge.[36]
- Rules may provide for a specific course of action to be followed providing for procedural fairness,[37] allowing criteria that are important not to be forgotten,

---

[34] The term accessibility is related to what Kaplow calls private interpretation costs. Other points of interest on private interpretation costs identified by Kaplow is that parties only incur these if they wish to find out about the law, and that precise commands better differentiate behavior allowing for activities that are more harmful to be subject to a higher sanction than less harmful activities therefore mitigating the problem of overdeterrence (Kaplow 2000: 504).

[35] For example, in the case cited earlier of hazardous materials, it is far easier to detect when an official has ignored the use of a hazardous blacklisted substance, than when the substance is not blacklisted but generally considered toxic (*see* also Schäfer 2000: 2). *Available at* http://www.dse.de/ef/instn/schaefer.htm.

[36] This does not suggest that courts cannot also develop specific knowledge. Furthermore, expertise may also come from the use of private sector models, for *e.g.*, in the United States nonobservance of the auditing rules of the ASC (Accounting Standard Committee) establishes a *prima facie* proof of negligence in court (Schäfer 2000: 2).

[37] Rules can provide for procedural fairness, where "people have a right to be told about prevailing requirements and a correlative right to test whether those requirements have been

as is the case with administrative procedure, and permit complicated processes to be done by persons with little training.[38]

- Rules can advance the perceived legitimacy of decisions, allowing the citing of a rule as a justification (Baldwin 1995: 13). Legitimacy can be increased when the application of the rules is visible and there are clear lines of responsibility by those that apply the law. Similarly, rules can increase trust in government and protect against bias and personal attack.[39]

- Rules prevent things from having to be justified at each instance. They also establish frameworks within which decisions can be made.

- Rules may reduce human error caused by confusion and ignorance.

- Rules allow monitoring of compliance by public turning citizens into right holders (Sunstein 1995: 977).[40]

- Rules can help cope with pluralism in a heterogeneous society (ibid.: 969). Similarly, standards may require a cultural understanding of the underlying policy, an infrequent feature in many emerging markets (Schäfer 2000: 2).

- Where norms are slow to manifest themselves into established conventions, for example in the case of a tragedy of the commons, rules may be able to establish such conventions overcoming collective action dilemma.[41]

- Given that rules make actions more observable, they may also function as a precommitment strategy of government, thus promoting deterrence of unwanted behavior.

---

violated." An alternative more "particularistic conception of procedural fairness" suggests that "people are entitled to argue that they are relevantly different from those that have come before, and that if their case is investigated in all its particularity, it will be shown that special treatment is warranted" (Sunstein 1995: 958). People who are affected by the rule can be enabled to participate in the creation of the very rule to be applied to their case.

[38] Relatedly, they can encourage consistency and equality of treatment, particularly when noncompliance with the rules is verifiable and avenues of complaint are available. For an example of this in use, see 5 U.S.C. § 553.

[39] Legitimacy can also be increased through citizen participation in the promulgation of a rule. This is the case in the United States falling under the American Procedures Act. See, 5 U.S.C § 702. On the American Procedures Act generally, see 5 U.S.C. §§ 551-559, 701-706. This can be particularly important in developing countries and countries in transition where government is not trusted.

[40] Where rules are clearly defined, as previously suggested, they grant a well-defined right in addition to obligations. Moreover, rules may serve to embolden certain functionaries such as judges to enforce a command even when particular stakes are high, such as a political cost (Sunstein 1995).

[41] This argument can easily be extended to emerging markets where certain business practices are new and only being introduced. While it is to be expected that many practices will depend on already established norms and conventions, it is likely that well defined rules can fill a vacuum, until such norms mature.

C. Costs of Rules

Rules have also potential costs as a tool to mitigating corruption. Among the more important for consideration by the reformer are the following.

- Rules may be published by governments so as to give the impression of taking some action. In reality, the rule may be a poor one, inaccurate and not enforced (*see* Baldwin 1995: 14). Indeed, one must ask, what are the incentives of primary and secondary legislative authorities to formulate accurate rules? Are their incentives really aligned with the common good? One inherent problem with rules is that they serve a signaling quality. They give the impression that the legislator is working hard to solve a problem, or that an agency is working hard to tackle a particular issue.
- Given time constraints inherent in government, it is commonplace that suboptimal rules are chosen, rules that are either over- or under-inclusive.[42]
- Rules may serve as a vehicle to extend the life of both good and bad policy.[43]
- Rules may be a mechanism that bureaucrats exercise in "diverting individual or collective entreaties" (*ibid.*).[44] In cases where there are irrational results, it is obvious that there is a needed avenue to re-examine these irrational results first hand.
- Given the signaling affect of rules, rules may be used at the expense of alternatives. There is a need to view rules not just as an alternative to standards but more generally as an alternative to other tools of government.[45]

---

[42] In developing countries, often identified by greater social unrest and conflict, where drafting skills are normally not as forthcoming, it is far more likely that ill-researched, poorly drafted rules will be made law. Rules become both manipulative and conciliatory tools of government to signal policy and intent. Where time constraints are a serious problem, developing countries should enact general rules that are not complex or precise (as discussed above). These rules are not necessarily the best fit (under- or over-inclusive) but they reduce the complexity of the law making it more interpretable for private citizens and reduce the discretion of those agents enforcing these laws.

[43] A rule may "serve quite readily as a cover for unflinching policy beliefs" (Baldwin 1995: 14). Similarly, Spence (2001: 928) notes: "By memorializing policy choices in formal rules, current policymakers can ensure that any future policymakers who are hostile to the status quo will be unable to make a policy change quickly or easily."

[44] This problem is partially remedied in the United Kingdom where "[i]t is a fundamental rule for the exercise of discretionary power that discretion must be brought to bare on every case: each one must be considered on its own merits and decided as the public interest requires at the time (Wade and Forsyth 1999: 328)." There is a duty to use discretion, and failure to do so is unlawful!

[45] Baldwin (1995: 16) captures this nicely, suggesting: "Using governmental rules is one way of controlling or executing governmental functions but it is by no means the only one. Alternative controls include accountability to variously constituted bodies scrutiny, complaints, and inspections systems; arrangements to insure openness (such as requirements to publish

The important point I am making is here is that inefficient rules with signaling properties can oftentimes be promulgated very inexpensively. This point cannot be overstated and may help explain some of the regulator.

- There may be adverse effects in imposing formal rules where informal rules and relationships once governed (Cooter 1996a, 1996b). Moreover, rule-makers can sometimes not anticipate the circumstances to which their rules will be applied (Sunstein 1995: 957).
- Rules may be more difficult to reverse. The ability to update a rule is largely determined by the type of written rule.[46]. It is, therefore, important to know about the character of the institutions that will give rise to rules in the first instance or apply them after the fact" (*ibid.* : 959).[47]
- Rules may drive discretion underground. When a rule does not reflect the wishes of regulators, people in a position of authority may just ignore them.[48]
- When rules are not practical or efficient, or a poor fit for a given circumstance, discretion may be an important tool to overcome this problem. A key point is this: Strict rules governing the realm outside of which a transgression occurs are not and should not be interpreted as strict rules of enforcement or prosecution. The problem with much current discussion, as it relates to the corruption debate, is that discretion is often considered necessarily as corruption per se, or as a factor that necessitates corruption. This perspective fails to take into account the possibility that regulators and regulated firms sometimes agree to ignore or bend formal commands because full compliance may result in great efficiency losses, particularly in the case of inefficient

---

indicators and statistics) and schemes for giving effect to consumer's views. Alternative executive devices include arbitrations, managerial decisions, inquiries, adjudications, contracts, and negotiations".

[46] There are a host of rule types. "Apart from primary legislation.....; secondary legislation; delegated legislation; sub-delegated legislation; quasi- legislation, administrative rules; codes of practice; approved codes of practice; guidance; guidance notes; policy guidance; guidelines; circulars; framework documents; outline schemes, and statements of advice" (Baldwin 1995: 7).

[47] For example, as identified above, formally promulgated rules in the United States are subjected to a process set out in the Administrative Procedures Act, where publication of the proposed rule and a period of comment before publication are necessary. These are lengthy courses of action that are designed to protect, *inter alia*, against regulatory capture, prevent bias and ensure consistency. They, however, also greatly affect the flexibility of the rule-making process, making it subject to judicial review and making rules generally less adaptable to the changes in information. Similar problems may also be present in the legislature, *see* Sunstein (1995: 1005-06).

[48] Sunstein (*ibid.*: 995) suggests, for example, that the Clean Air Act in the United States, as a result of harsh penalties for listed pollutants "operating in rule-like fashion", the Environmental Protection Agency stopped listing pollutants in the first place. This can lead to a void in enforcement, transferring substantial costs onto society.

rules or stochastic factors not previously taken into consideration.[49] Indeed, law enforcement frequently exercises what Landes and Posner (1975) have termed "discretionary nonenforcement".[50]

Over-inclusive laws are the result of many factors, the most important of which include: The pervasive costs of drafting precise rules; the desire to close out loopholes to particular groups that are the target of the law, e.g., organized crime; unforeseen circumstances when drafting the law, and changes in the regulatory environment. Discretionary nonenforcement itself must, of course, be constrained and reserved for only compelling circumstances.[51] One means of doing so is to permit regulated parties that are subject to rules to object to others receiving different treatment. An alternative means is to permit citizen suits in cases of noncompliance, or private prosecution.[52]

D. Concluding Comments

I have highlighted the many uses and misuses of rules. There are a few important additional comments I should make before concluding the discussion.

Stiffening the judicial and administrative spine by relying primarily on rules to mitigate discretion is undesirable, for reasoned outlined above. Moreover, whilst there are obvious gains to be had from mitigating discretion through increasing the use of rules in an environment where corruption is rampant, even at the cost of over-inclusion, under-inclusion or fairness, it should not be forgotten that noncompliance is frequently the result of bodies of regulation over-extending themselves, and becoming unnecessarily complex. When rules become to complex, they may challenge the capacity of even the most informed individuals, thus reducing the deterrent effect of laws, but more importantly perhaps the level

---

[49] The costs incurred of undertaking to draft a "complete" agreement *ex ante* or redraft a contract *ex post* to take into consideration new contingencies frequently drive parties to depend on adjustment mechanisms which do not entail formal amendments to written covenants (*see* Kovacic 1998a: 148). Just as these formal features are sometimes sidestepped for efficiency purposes so too can and does discretion serve as a necessary tool of regulators and law enforcement officers. Customs or understandings that permit parties to respond to contingencies that laws fail to address govern day-to-day dealings (*ibid.*).

[50] Discretionary nonenforcement they note is a technique "by which the costs of overinclusion can be reduced without a corresponding increase in underinclusion (loopholes) The police overlook infractions of the traffic code; building inspectors ignore violations of building code provisions that, if enforced, would prevent the construction of new buildings in urban areas; air traffic controllers permit the airlines to violate overly stringent safety regulations involving the spacing of aircraft landing at or taking off from airports" (Landes and Posner 1975: 38).

[51] This is indeed part of the more serious problem of favoritism, cronyism, bias and corruption outright. *See* further, Chapter VII, Section III.

[52] *See* further, Chapter VII, Section III

of voluntary compliance, which must be seen as the long-term goal of any regulation. There are also important questions of political economy and political feasibility that cannot be ignored. In certain developing countries, there may indeed be strong incentive on the part of the regulators or administrators to keep rules inefficient or standards unnecessarily vague in order to promote noncompliance and facilitate corruption. Indeed recent empirical work seems to reconfirm the use of vague standards as opposed to rules in developing countries, which adversely affects economic development (Buscaglia 2001). In extreme cases, rules or standards may be selected primarily not according to their merits but according to their capacity to increase the fruits of rent-seeking and corruption. Hence, there can be strong opposition even to what may appear as modest reforms.

Another factor which hinders the use of rules as a device to mitigate official discretion is the number of people that remain unaware of the law. Even in highly developed countries, it has been noted that small businesses will frequently do what a leaflet says irrespective of its status, not being able to distinguish it from the law. Only larger, more sophisticated ones may comprehend the difference (Baldwin 1995: 150-51). The potential to bluff private citizens and small firms in developing countries is more often than not increased as a result of unfamiliarity with the law and higher personal costs of accessing the law. Small employers are unable to distinguish between leaflets, oral communications and the law (rules) itself. Agencies and inspectors may continue to take advantage of this. An accompanying instrument to rules would, therefore, be factors that make them more accessible. A government that is interested in furthering compliance with the law should extend widespread efforts to make the law known to its citizens.

V. Administrative Reforms

It is undisputed that civil service performance has shown itself to be of fundamental importance to the economic welfare of both industrialized and developing countries alike, and for this reason has been a central part of the development agenda for the past decade. The World Bank alone has had an extensive civil service reform portfolio with about 169 operations in 80 countries between 1987, when lending for civil service reforms commenced, and 1998 (Nunberg 1999). The problem for less developed countries is as follows: They wrestle with the unwieldy dilemma of cutting the overall public sector wage bill whilst attempting to better remuneration to attract or retrain able staff.[53] Of primary importance to the task of civil service reform is the restructuring of government pay and employment practices that have become gravely

---

[53] *See* World Bank, Administrative and Civil Service Reform, *available at* http://www1.worldbank.org/publicservice/establishment.htm.

dysfunctional in recent decades (Lindauer and Nunberg 1994: 2). Lindauer and Nunberg (*ibid.*: 2) capture the dilemma as follows:

"[T]he basic outline of the problem involves surplus employees, eroded wages, compressed salary structures and aggregate wage bills commanding an increasing share of public revenues. The consequences for civil service performance have been disastrous: low morale, high absenteeism and moonlighting, difficulties in attracting and retaining skilled professionals, a breakdown in supervision and discipline, and the unavailability of complementary inputs to carry out routine tasks."

It is not difficult to understand that the opportunities for corruption and the evolution of corrupt practices in such an environment are great. Once again, the reader should note the overlap between improving performance and curbing corruption is clearly discernible.

Where the civil service, as is generally the case in many developing countries, has become too large and as a result of this spending relative to GDP unsustainable, wages tend to crowd out other government activity. It is not a stretch to understand that in such conditions, civil servant salaries have often dilapidated and wage compression scales do not reflect qualifications or provide incentives for further education or betterment. Nonmonetary benefits are oftentimes very high as a percentage of total compensation in developing countries and official remuneration is given through the likes of housing allowances and other nonwage mechanisms (Nunberg and Nellis 1995: 25). Clearly, such factors are undesirable from the perspective of corruption control. Nonwage mechanisms or benefits are commonly non-transparent and subject less regulation and hence greater official discretion. It is clear that "disentangling the enormously intricate webs of benefit structures" is a mammoth task, notoriously cumbersome, and a fertile ground for corruption- there is, therefore, a need to overhaul it with a monetary-based wage and incentive structure (*ibid.*). Hence, in many instances, cost containment measures may be seen as a prerequisite to corruption control.

Table 1

Ranking continuum for the most politically sensitive reform measures
1. Removal of ghost employees 2. Elimination of officially sanctioned post that are currently not filled 3. Retrenchment of temporary and seasonal workers 4. Enforcement of retirement age 5. Freezing of recruitment 6. Elimination of guaranteed entry to the civil service from the educational or training system 7. Suspension of automatic advancement 8. "Voluntary" incentive induced retirement of surplus workers. 9. Containment of wages (restraints or freezes) 10. Dismissal of serving civil servants Source: Nunberg (1994: 128); Nellis and Nunberg (1995: 9)

A. Downsizing

The use of downsizing as a means to curb corruption is well documented (*see* Klitgaard 1988; Klitgaard, MacLean-Abaroa and Parris 2000).[54] As we can see in Table 1, efforts to reduce government expenditure, pay reform and employment strategies are multifaceted extending from the removal of "ghost" workers (based on a census of workers and basic payroll fraud controls), to the halting of recruitment and the enforcement of mandatory retirement ages, all which differ in political feasability or practical effect. In addition, reform programs have increasingly been addressing specific pay conditions for civil servants in an attempt to remove demotivating distortions in government remuneration structures. A number of reform programs have been aimed at improving pay conditions, rationalizing the overall system of remuneration, and building institutional capacity in the government to formulate and implement sound salary policies (Nunberg and Nellis 1995, Nunberg 1994). The ranking continuum

---

[54] Roe (1998) claims that policy conclusions reached by law and economics are not appropriate for developing countries given that these countries are characterized by conflict which makes first best policy conclusions inappropriate. Conflict can be treated, however, as another constraint on optimizing behavior, and recommendations can still be reached. One area where there is potential for conflict in developing countries is when it comes to downsizing the civil service. This does not suggest, however, that theoretical work is a substitute for political realities.

illustrated in Table 1 provides an excellent guideline for what must surely be the most critical issue in downsizing the civil service- the political sensitivity of the measures- a result of best practices in several countries. Such measures should be supported by measures presented in earlier discussion, such as revoking inefficient programs, as well as by functional reviews.[55] Important functional reviews include:

- Job inspections, which assess both structure and staffing of agencies, and the appropriateness and the ability to reach desired functions. They also look at "whether the staffing numbers, grades and levels of responsibility are appropriate to the needs of the work; and whether some degree of consistency is maintained across agencies."
- Organization and method studies, which appraise the efficiency of a service to ascertain performance weaknesses and to locate bottlenecks, and particularly addressing means to simplify procedures.
- Budgetary analysis, which *inter alia* examines the areas in which manpower is being inefficiently employed to reach certain budgetary savings. Here for example they may look at the spending patterns of certain organizations and try to assess in which areas cutbacks can be made, and where there have been significant deviations from identified goals.
- Ratio analysis, which involves looking at the precise ratio of staff to functions, which are then reviewed against government targets. (Nunberg and Nellis 1995.: 22)

Governments are naturally concerned about the socio-political effects of laying off large numbers of civil servants. Not surprisingly experiences differ. Primary concerns are centered around increasing the number of unemployed, as well as on the possible backlash or conflict that may occur as well as political repercussions. Given such factors, as well as the important role of the balance of patron-client relations and reward structures, it not surprising that governments have been reluctant to push through reforms. Reports differ, however, on the level of political disruption accompanying reforms. Gregory reports, for example, that there was little evidence that redeployment lead to a substantial increase in the level of unemployment in Ghana (Gregory 1994).[56] Alderman, Canagarajah and Younger (1994: 232) report that the majority of civil servants who were redeployed found work relatively quickly because they remained in occupations

---

[55] Functional reviews "are essentially an organizational audit of the functions of component agencies of government, and the number and type of staff presently carrying them out, in an attempt to determine the optimal staffing arrangements for basic government tasks" (Nunberg and Nellis 1995: 21-22).

[56] For the Ugandan case, where broad based structural reforms were undertaken, *see* Langseth (1995).

undertaken on the side whilst working for the government. On a less positive note, Lindauer and Nunberg (1994: 241) suggest that the reason for the relative lack of political disruption may be as a result of the shallowness of the reforms taken thus far.

Lessons from the private sector and labor economics would suggest compensating officials forced to leave the civil service, a measure that may be prohibitive for most developing countries. Downsizing, as can be seen above, importantly does not necessarily involve the use of compensation, or widespread dismissal of legitimate workers. The removal of ghost workers, the enforcement of retirement ages and the freezing of recruitment, for example, do not involve compensation packages. One may distinguish between voluntary and involuntary compensation. Voluntary compensation packages may be easier to compute than involuntary packages, but are subject to a hold up problem.[57] Furthermore, officials that leave the public sector voluntarily are potentially the more skilled, *i.e.*, those that can find work most readily in the private sector, thus separating themselves from less productive personnel.[58] The determination of compensation as a result of retrenching- the involuntary or direct dismissal of civil servants- should be based on a number of factors such as the political sensitivity of removal and the ability of the labor market to absorb employees. Private sector promotion policies and deregulation can help advance this prospect (MacGregor Peterson and Schuftan 1998: 73). Savings from downsizing may then be used to increase the wages of remaining officials along meritocratic lines, or to provide semi-annual bonuses based on performance (*ibid.*). Experience with the welfare state particularly in Western Europe, but also in the United States, has shown us, as Haggard and Kaufman (2001: 4) note, that "public programs that cushion individuals against the dislocation of the market have contributed to the political and social stability necessary for capital economy to function effectively."

I would like to make two closing comments before closing our discussion on downsizing. Downsizing as defined above may be a precursor to reforming corrupt administrations. It is important to note, however, that subscribing technical, administrative fixes is not an instrument for overhauling substantial problems of political economy. Clearly, governments will be more willing to utilize those instruments that are least politically sensitive. Whilst reform measures generally require a scapel as opposed to a meat-ax, experience with civil service reforms in many transition economies and developing countries seems to indicate the opposite and have generally not produced the desired results, in large

---

[57] The hold up problem refers to a situation where implementation of an agreement or reform is contingent on many persons agreeing to that reform. Those individuals upon whom the implementation of a certain proposal is contingent have incentive to delay their decisions for as long as possible in order to acquire as much of the gains from the proposal in its entirety as possible (*i.e.*, the social welfare surplus).

[58] *See* also discussion on market for lemons in Akerlof (1970).

part because what was needed was not the minor surgery adopted. Second, despite the fact that civil service reforms, as sketched above, have not had in many cases the destabilizing effect feared by many governments, this should not distract from basic economics, and give the go-ahead to ignore basic productivity considerations. Merely shifting workers from low productive employment to unemployment does not of itself increase productivity- productivity is actually reduced, and some productivity most be considered better to none at all (Stiglitz 1999a: 6). Governments should not hope for the scenario that a large supply of inactive workers will create demand." Reforms entailing movement into unemployment stand on sound footing only after the government has deliberated the possibilities of transferring workers directly from low productivity to higher productivity employment (*ibid.*).

B. Selecting and Screening Agents

Touched on in chapter II, one means of reducing the level of corruption and corrupt payoffs is through selecting and screening officials. It is imperative for governments serious about reform that they address safeguards related to selecting and screening agents. Recall that the facilitation of corrupt exchange is largely dependent on the fulfillment of several steps: Parties must be able to search for and identify one another, come to an agreement and then deliver on promises, as agreed, undetected. Where agents are recruited by nepotism or patronage, it is likely that these costs are substantially lower at each of the above stages than in the case of an official that has been selected according to merit, and must locate partners from scratch. Similarly, where selection is according to nepotism or patronage, those individuals that are selected may be based not according to productivity, but rather on their ability to facilitate corrupt transactions and their willingness to engage in corruption.

A well functioning civil service with high standards of professionalism and performance is subject to many contingencies, some of which such as the education level of the labor market cannot be remolded in the short term, other such as personnel management arrangements are more tractable to change.[59] In general, there is a great degree of disparity with regard to hiring practices in developed countries. In particular, recent changes in administration have redefined the province of government and reshaped the boundaries of the core civil service. In developed countries, recruitment systems generally break down to two prevalent models with many countries falling somewhere between them on

---

[59] *See* World Bank, Administrative and Civil Service Reform *available at* http://www1.worldbank.org/publicsector/civilservice/personnel.htm.

the continuum.[60] The first model is that of a "closed entry, rigid hierarchical systems with limited inter-class (and often inter-departmental) mobility and highly selective entry requirements," the second is representative of "more open systems with lateral entry, greater vertical and sometimes horizontal mobility, and more flexible entry mechanisms" (Nunberg 1995: 21).

Nunberg catalogues Japan, Korea, Singapore, Germany, the Netherlands, and France as all approximating the first category, with Australia, New Zealand, and Sweden, as well as the UK and the US to a certain extent, as falling into the second category. In particular the latter are subjecting recruitment to market considerations.

The closed systems model in industrialized countries, also referred to as a Mandarin or career systems model relies heavily on initial recruitment into the civil service, based primarily on university degrees and entrance examinations, and supplemented *inter alia* by intensive interviews and assessment centers. Competitive recruitment herein is centralized and recruits are commonly selected through single "feeder" institutions of higher education or training.[61] Such a system serves to lock individuals into a closed system, where admission to the civil service is only generally possible at entry level. Employees can easily be rotated between positions, and elite cadres are generalists and not hired for a specific job. The two countries that embody this tradition the most are Japan and France (*ibid.*: 21-22).

The more open, or position-based model, is aimed at "flexible, decentralized, sometimes market-oriented practices" (*ibid.*: 23). Civil service recruitment is aimed at finding the appropriate candidate, either externally through open recruitment procedures, *i.e.*, from outside of the civil service, or internally through active mobility of administrators inside agencies. In particular, recent trends have pushed towards a decentralization of personnel management, particularly at lower levels, and in the case of the United States to in certain cases noncompetitive examinations for certain positions. Emphasis in this model is continuing to shift from high security careers, shaped by length of service and seniority, towards shorter term employment contracts and achievement-oriented promotion, with the aim of supporting a new cadre of "responsive" managers (Kaul 1997).

---

[60] I draw in this review on the dichotomy of recruitment and employment models developed by Nunberg, in particular Nunberg (1995). Note, it is intractable for the discussion here to separate between recruitment and promotion.

[61] In France, entrance to high positions in the civil service are determined by successful admission into either the Ecole National d'Administration (ENA) or other specialized grand 'coles. In Japan, Tokyo University provides a similar function. Competitive entrance examinations to these higher institutions must thus be regarded as competitive examinations one step removed from entrance to the civil service.

Of course, from the perspective of corruption it is impossible to suggest which system is *de facto* more favorable. It depends in large part on the dominant behavior within an organization. Within the closed system, cadres particularly elite cadres may undergo a more extensive period of socialization to internalize the core values inherent in the civil service. Dependent on what those core values actually are, one can say whether such an institution is more or less conducive to corruption. When the core values, are ones of honest and hands-off economic relations, can one expect corruption to be low. However, where those core values involve favoritism or bias and the closed system invokes a strong period of socialization to adopt these values, corruption can be rampant. In such a system, one can experience a greater degree of lock-in and asset-specific investment related to officials. There appear to be obvious efficiency gains to be accrued from allowing open recruitment procedures (*i.e.,* including applications from outside the administration), particularly for senior positions, as they insure posts are filled by those with skills and proficiency for a particular job, dispelling the notion of a public service as a safe bet with semi-automatic promotion upon recognition of time served (Kaul 1997: 19).

Either way, the most important factor in recruitment is that it is based upon merit; the appointment of the best person, or group of persons for any given job. A public service based around patronage appointments is not accordant with a democracy where parties alternate in power (Rose-Ackerman 1999: 69). Where appointments are based around patronage, civil servants most probably do not enjoy protection, increasing the potential for those who expect to lose their positions to put money aside for the future (*ibid.*: 70). This is akin to the end game scenario, outlined in chapter II, the results of which are known to us from earlier discussion.[62]

C. Costs and Benefits of Merit and Patronage Appointments for Anti-Corruption Reforms

As adumbrated, the introduction of an apolitical recruitment process is an important feature of a well-functioning democracy and still remains a challenge for many countries today. Here, I wish to sketch some of the primary considerations from the perspective of anti-corruption reforms. Recruitment is, but one factor in the merit system. The objectives of the merit system in recruitment should include:

- Adequate publicity of job openings
- Genuine opportunity for interested parties to apply
- Realistic and fairly applied standards

---

[62] Recall, an endgame situation refers to a situation where as a result of parties anticipating the end of a relationship, cooperation begins to unravel (*see* Kreps and Wilson 1982).

- Ranking of candidates based on relevant qualifications.
- Public knowledge of the results of the process
- An improvement of the publics image of the civil servant

Source: McKinney and Howard (1998: 321).

Essentially, each one of the above six characteristics can potentially reduce the level of corruption. At the heart of merit criteria is the idea that they are both specified and contestable, where failure to select any given candidate can be appealed and reexamined against guidelines for the position.[63] The above-listed criteria are generally precursors to making recruitment more transparent. Corruption can enter into any step of the recruitment phase. For example, specifications may be tailor-made for a particular applicant, where even if there is a competitive process, there are inherent advantages for one candidate. Indeed, many of the complexities we see and opportunities for corruption in recruitment are reiterated in government tenders and procurement contracts.[64] Furthermore, in general allowing for lateral entry where administrators are permitted to move from one department to another seems advantageous, as it potentially increases the level of competition among officials for positions and can those reduce the gains from corruption, as discussed in chapter II. Moreover, this can be supplemented by authorizing competition for positions with outside persons from the market; with selection based according to meritocratic principles.

1. Difficulties with Recruitment by Merit

There are significant differences of opinion as to the quantification of merit, or, more generally, how one identifies one candidate as better than another.[65]

Intuitively, one can make a case that standard competitive examinations are suited to general positions, where recruits receive on-the-job training and skills after recruitment. Accordingly, the more specific the requirement, the more specific the examination should be. There is, therefore, a strong argument for decentralizing recruitment decisions to experienced agency officials away from centralized examinations the specific the position becomes. Indeed, more flexible recruitment has made inroads in recent years.[66]

Selecting agents according to meritocracy is considered to be the selection of the most qualified person for a particular job. However, there may be an

---

[63] *See* World Bank, *supra* note 59.

[64] *See* further, this chapter, Section VII.

[65] Of course, positions may also have other objectives such as increasing the degree of representativeness of a given class, sex or ethnic group.

[66] New Zealand and Sweden serve as two examples where recruitment is relatively decentralized.

inherent assumption behind the correct use of the meritocratic system. Caiden (1981) identifies, "[i]n the quest to replace the evils of the spoils system with the virtues of the merit system, it was assumed too readily that clever people would also be moral people."[67] Tradeoffs may be necessary in order to mitigate corruption. As Klitgaard (1988: 74) recommends, in order to curb corruption, "the principal may be willing to give up something in technical capability to get more of what might be called "honesty" or "dependability"". The government needs to screen out honest agents by surveying past records, tests and other predictors of honesty (Klitgaard 1988; Klitgaard, MacLean-Abaroa and Parris 2000). The potential problem with this mechanism is that it may be viewed as awarding more discretion to an examiner and shifting attention away from qualifications.[68]

2. Virtues and Vices of Patronage Appointments

Highlighted in earlier discussion, the facilitation of corrupt transactions depends on parties being able to search for and identify each other, come to an understanding and then deliver on promises undetected. Each one of these stages opens up several vulnerabilities. Recruitment by nepotism or patronage, is likely to reduce these costs substantially lower than would is the case for an official selected according to merit, who if interested in pursing corruption would have to from scratch orchestrate exchanges and account for the vulnerabilities of such exchanges at each individual step.

The powers of patronage appointments within the overall scheme of corruption are easily understood. In Italy in the seventies and eighties entrance to the domain of the public administration was performed in 60 percent of the cases through temporary contracts and assignment of tenured positions as opposed to a competitive basis (Della Porta and Vannucci 1999: 130). Furthermore, payments for quid pro quos included employment of clients supplied by the politician. In this manner, "corrupt politicians extend their influence into the private sector as well, giving rise to a triangular exchange permitting the allocation of public goods to be transformed directly into political support" providing a system that is "mutually reinforcing" (*ibid.*: 52). Disguising corrupt payoffs in this form makes them difficult to recognize, and payoffs carry with them the same moral undertone that accompanies say monetary payoffs; hence, these payoffs may even be

---

[67] Gerald E. Caiden. 1981. "Ethics in the Public Service: Codification Misses the Real Target," *Public Personnel Management* 10:145-52 cited in Klitgaard 1988: 74.

[68] It is important that recruitment procedures take account of the problem of hidden information on the part of the agents, leading to a problem of as adverse selection. It is essential that adequate proxies and tests are set that indicate the "type" of individual a person actually is. When this is not possible, there may be an argument for patronage appointments, where agents selected are considered more trustworthy by their principals. The regularity of this failure may naturally be exaggerated by government officials that wish to reward loyal supporters or other cronies.

perceived as legitimate and non-risky by the parties involved. The symbiotic relationship of corruption and patronage further manifests itself where bribes and other IOU's awarded extend the scope of a politician or political machine to a broader electoral clientele, because these resources can be use to facilitate more effectual political machines and corrupt systems. Moreover, recruitment along patronage lines facilitates the gradual introduction of semi-legal and illegal ideas to persons who have themselves been "introduced" semi-legally or non-transparently to practices of malfeasance and corruption and are themselves then beholden or hostage to their benefactors.[69] Therewith, lies a gradual socialization of practices.

Though not as disturbing as the Italian case, in Britain, Members of Parliament, ministers, civil servants, local government officials, National Health Service official, and universities employees have all come in for strong criticism in recent years in part related to appointments to public bodies and hybrid governmental bodies, such as non-departmental public bodies, quasi autonomous non-governmental organizations and semi-public organizations (Oliver 1997: 540). The response of the government was to set up a Commissioner for Public Appointments.[70] What is also particularly worrisome about such practices is that, given that civil servants tend to have longer time horizons than politicians, they may be in a position to obtain sustainable links between corrupt players and coordinate these with party affiliates.

As the reach of government expands *ceteris paribus*, clearly so do the opportunities for patronage. Government reach, however, may not be the problem, but that of political parties, as seems to be the case in Germany. As von Arnim (1993:202), a leading commentator on party finance in Germany, notes: "Contrary to the intention of the founders of the Basic Law, the parties have emerged as the ruling organizations of the entire sphere of public life. By use of patronage they penetrate the public service, the radio and television networks, the courts, the universities, and other institutions that were conceived by the Basic Law as independent and nonpartisan."

Despite this, to varying degrees, patronage still exists in several industrialized economies. Although in the US, for example, 94 percent of all federal employees are recruited through the merit system, recruitment along patronage lines occurs at all levels of executive positions, including department heads, commissioners, judges and prosecuting attorneys.[71] Indeed, professional

---

[69] *See* Della Porta and Vannucci (1999: 103 *et seq.*) for the development and discussion of a similar argument applied to the Italian context.

[70] *See* First Report on the Committee of Standards in Public Life, Cm 2850 (1995). *See* also, Second Report of the Committee on Standards in Public Life, Local Public Spending Bodies, Cm 3270 (1996).

[71] By way of contrast, great emphasis is place in the United Kindgom that the civil service contain no political appointees. Excluding the ministers themselves, "who come and go with

jobs such as physicians and accountants are often based on political recommendation, as are jobs at the lowest level, such as part-time summer jobs (McKinney and Howard 1998: 321; 323). There are more than 2500 presidential appointees, in comparison with an average of slightly more than 100 in most well-established democracies such as Germany and Britain (*ibid*.: 323).[72]

It may be argued that patronage appointments can sometimes provide *outside assurances and prevent against fragmentation*. An excellent starting point is provided by the United States Supreme Court, which in recent verdicts, concerned in large part with the constitutionality of patronage appointment, has taken a "hard look" at the virtues of patronage and patronage appointments. What is remarkable about the plurality verdicts is the sheer dissensus among the justices as to the virtues and vices of patronage.[73] Relevant to our discussion here, is how patronage has been extolled as part of the American political make-up, and its role in strengthening political parties against fragmentation.[74] It has been argued that candidates for local offices derive their support from "cadres of friends and political associates who hope to benefit if their "man" is elected,"[75] and that it is consistent with the "vigorous ideological competition in the political "marketplace"".[76]

Justice Scalia of the Supreme Court has further argued that patronage serves to mitigate the role of interest groups, given that candidates can rely on the former to provide sufficient resources in political campaigning, and submits that in the United States, the decline in patronage has contributed to the rise in interest groups.[77] He does, however, concede that it can facilitate "financial corruption, such as salary kickbacks and partisan political activity on government-paid time" and "reduce the efficiency of government because it creates incentives to hire more and less qualified workers and because highly paid workers are reluctant to

---

fluctuating tides of politics", government departments are comprised of career officials, apart from temporary staff who are appointed for specific purposes and non-political motivations (Wade and Forsyth 1999: 55). Ministers may retain a few personal advisers, who do not acquire civil servant status and leave their departments when their ministers leave (*ibid*.).

[72] These positions have been divided up into three separate categories or schedules. Schedule A positions are those for which examinations are impractical because of the complexity involved and discretion that must be exercised. Schedule B employees are often appointed on the basis of noncompetitive examination. For example, tax specialists for Treasury Department positions are given such an examination to determine if they are qualified. The Schedule C appointments are of a policymaking or confidential character, such as upper-ranking staff assistants or secretaries to policymaking officials" (*ibid*.: 323-324).

[73] *Compare*, Elrod v. Burns, 427 U.S., 347 (1976) (Powell, J., dissenting); Branti v. Finkel, 445 U.S. 507 (1980): Rutan v. Republican Party of Illinois, 497 U.S. 62 (Scalia, J., dissenting).

[74] Elrod v. Burns, 427 U.S., 377-79, 382-83 (1976) (Powell, J., dissenting).

[75] *Ibid*., at 384.

[76] *Ibid*., at 388.

[77] Rutan v. Republican Party of Illinois, 497 U.S. 107 (Scalia, J., dissenting).

accept jobs that may last only until the next election."[78] Traces of these arguments applied to corruption reform can be found in Klitgaard (1988), who suggests that a spoils system,[79] where appointments are awarded according to family, clan or tribe, can, despite the obvious disadvantages, have a "virtue". He suggests that "such a system may be able to invoke outside guarantees of the agent's dependability" (ibid.: 76). Networks can be used in order to gain information on the honesty of an individual, as well as punish an individual for dishonest behavior, thus overcoming the principal agent problem (ibid.). Klitgaard notes, however, two main problems for the principal in using the spoils system. First, the principal may be left with individuals that are technically relatively unfit and relatively dishonest. Secondly, the connection of clan and tribe may further the position of the agent relative to the principal (ibid.).

Again referring to chapter II, this should be obvious to us. The profitability of corruption increases the greater the amount of information one has on the partner with whom one colludes. The same extra-legal structures that empower the principal to sanction the agent also empower the agent to sanction other agents. There are several other considerations including the hostage or blackmailing power of the agent relative to the principal. If the principal does not tolerate the agents behavior, he can cry disloyalty, a factor that may greatly affect the group standing of the principal. Further, when kinship is involved there may be a hierarchy of preferences, or an expectation of a hierarchy of preferences. Most problematic with looking at the spoils system as a potential factor that may curb corruption is that one assumes the principal to be acting bona fide, which is most likely not the case.[80] There may, however, be other outside assurances that can be sought after- e.g., the nomination of agents from other departments or from international agencies, whereby honesty may be determined by previous results (ibid.). Recruiting persons from high profile agencies or those with standing in a

---

[78] Ibid., at 108-109.

[79] A factor most definitely not just confined to developing countries. For example, as we have seen political appointments at both lower-level as well as higher-level local and state government in the United States are still commonplace. "In the Commonwealth of Pennsylvania, 30 percent to 40 percent of the jobs are not in a merit system but are handled through the governor's patronage secretary" (McKinney and Howard 1998: 324).

[80] Heady (1996: 216-225), for example, classifies the qualities required for recruitment into the civil service along a continuum based on the impact bureaucrats themselves can have on their own qualification requirements.
Patrimony→ Party Loyalty→ Party Patronage→ Professional Performance→ Bureaucratic Determination
As one moves from left to right, one departs from situations where decisions are determined by the whim of a ruler, as in pure kleptocracy, to other criteria. The principal agent model described above is not useful here for policy recommendations (see Chapter VIII, Section II). Heady suggests that most civil services in parliamentary and presidentialist democracies can be placed in this category and gives examples of countries at each level in the continuum.

society, who incur a potentially significant reputation loss as a result of any transgression (or alleged transgression) whilst in office may be a useful means of selective appointment. In the case of a member of an international organization, unearthing venality bears not just a reputation loss for the individual, but also for the organization. The organization has, therefore, incentive itself to screen out honest employees, given this potential reputation loss, and perhaps even to monitor the actions and progress of its (former) employee(s). In the case of an individual with standing in a society, unveiling corrupt behavior leads potentially to a very high social sanction, itself a deterrent to corruption.

Another argument that may be made in favor of political appointment is that of *responsiveness*. There does seem to be obvious advantages to political appointments, particularly for high level positions, when officials must be responsive to policy and are, therefore, better able to carry out an electoral mandate. This can be particularly important where an official enjoys enough discretion that he can go against the will of the politician. Furthermore, it can reduce resistance and the potential to block reforms within the administration. Similarly, *flexibility* may be put forward as a consideration in support of patronage appointments. Managers and officials within an agency are often in the best position to determine their needs. Examinations may be too general and not tailored towards specific requirements. The absence of explicit examinations can sometimes be viewed as a rational response to the difficulties of measuring and verifying the merits of an individual in a multitask environment. Furthermore, competitive examinations involve costs for those partaking, often sunk costs for unsuccessful candidates, resulting in a dead-weight loss for society.[81] Where employment is short term and remuneration, therefore, of limited size, a competitive exam actually prevents candidates from coming forward. For such reasons and in such circumstances, a good case could be made for altering the nature of competitive exams relative to the remuneration.

Overcoming high levels of resistance or formal barriers may be considered as positive factors in political appointments. Public sectors are frequently highly unionized and employment is often de facto subject to the bargaining demands within union and labor management relations. Where open recruitment procedures that encourage managers to come from the private sector for senior positions are explicitly discouraged either as a point of law or as result of a high level of unionism, patronage appointments may be an efficiency enhancing means for overcoming this. this is, however, a temporary solution.

A final word should also be given to hybrid appointments, which entail both hiring by merit, *i.e.*, appointees (or a pool of appointees) meet certain criteria, and selection according to the subjective judgments of ministers and

---

[81] Deadweight loss can be understood as the fall in total surplus that results from a market distortion.

governmental officials- generally for positions at upper management level.[82] These appointees generally do not enjoy the security of comparable civil servants and may be more easily dismissed, a factor identified as possibly discouraging qualified applicants. A common solution is a pool system, which places the candidate in a pool upon satisfying relevant merit criteria. In the case of Germany, for example, the approximately 140 most senior positions are all hybrid appointments effectively managed under a pool system. Appointments to these senior positions automatically lapse on a change of government, with an option for the incoming government to reappoint them. Civil servants who are removed from a hybrid position are then retained in the pool in a position known as "Ruhestand" (resting). They acquire an allowance but not a pension given that they may be appointed at any time.[83]

From the perspective of curbing corruption, such hybrid systems are multifaceted. On the one hand allowing politicians to select civil servants always awards a certain amount of discretion, a factor that can be easily used to install loyal supporters to high ranking positions. On the other hand, however, having certain standards that need to be met, reduces this discretion substantially. The degree with which it reduces this discretion is a function of the specification of the standards; vague standards providing politicians with more discretion. Another factor which decreases the payoffs for loyalty and indirectly reduces the level of corruption is the fact that tenure is itself not usually offered to officials recruited through such systems.[84] A perfectly functioning recruitment procedure is ineffectual if it still doesn't attract qualified candidates. Of primary importance to attracting "the best and the brightest" are naturally wages.

D. Wages And Remuneration

> "...The civil servant had either to survive by lowering his standard of ethics, performance and dutifulness or remain upright and perish. He chose to survive."[85]

The deterrent effect of increasing wages has been recognized in the economics literature for some time (*see*, Becker and Stigler 1974). The underlying rational is as follows: Salaries should be raised above what enforcers could receive

---

[82] *See* World Bank, *supra* note 59.
[83] *Ibid.*
[84] As it arguably should not be offered, given that the senior justification for political appointments is responsiveness to government policies.
[85] 1982 Ugandan publication, "Report of the Public Services Salaries Review Commission" cited in Lindauer (1994: 27).

129

elsewhere so as to increase the costs of malfeasance.[86] Moreover, higher salaries can engender more trustworthy employees. As Becker and Stigler (*ibid.*:12) propose: "Trust calls for a salary premium not necessarily because better quality persons are thereby attracted, but because higher salaries impose a cost on violations of trust".[87] Furthermore, in addition to the deterrence effect of increasing wages above the market rate in order to attract better quality persons, there is evidence that increasing wages above the market rate may increase the intrinsic motivation of an employee, as a result of feelings of loyalty, appreciation etc. (Frey 1992; Kreps 1997).

Most developing countries, however, are a far cry from the ideal described above. Salaries for government officials are often so low that officials cannot have even a basic standard of living, without illicit incomes (Klitgaard 1988, Klitgaard, MacLean-Abaroa and Parris 2000; Rose-Ackerman 1999; Lindauer and Nunberg 1994; World Development Report 1997).[88] Indeed, poor wages have led to a near incentive crisis in the public sectors of many developing countries (World Bank 1997). The incentive problem can be divided into two parts. First, wages have dropped so low that the necessary talent required for public bodies is unavailable as more qualified persons are going to the private sector. Second, there is no reasonable linkage between wages and performance for those working as public officials; a factor referred to as incentive myopia in the literature. Wages in many circumstances must be raised in the fight against corruption. In this section I address the importance of packaging incentives and raising salaries beyond a minimum level, and particularly the importance of tying pay, promotion and other monetary rewards to performance as a means of overcoming corruption and increasing public sector performance.[89]

---

[86] The empirical evidence on that corruption is fostered by low wages is surprisingly sparse. Van Rijkeghem and Weder (1997) for example do suggest that there is a negative relationship between corruption and wages in developing countries. See also sources cited therein.

[87] According to Becker and Stigler (*ibid.*: 6), salaries should be raised above what officials receive elsewhere "by an amount inversely related to the probability of detection and directly related to the size of the bribes and other benefits from malfeasance."

[88] There are not just substantial differences in wages levels, as one would expect, between developed and less developed countries, but rather between the public-private wage differential. Whereas OECD and high-growth Asian countries like Singapore and Hong Kong offer there officials salaries that are relative to their private sector equivalent, African and Latin American counterparts generally receive wages that are substantially lower than private sector equivalent.

[89] An important caveat is in order here. The economic analysis of crime á la Becker and Stigler, introduced in chapter 1 suggests that increasing wages should decrease the profitability of corruption, given higher expected losses. More recent advances in economic modeling that fit our discussion here include what is known as a satisficing model of behavior. Accordingly, when workers do not receive a fair wage, they reduce their effort. In this sense, government officials punish unfair principals. Fair is determined by many factors, such as standard of living, status, wages of peers, etc. Van Rijkeghem and Weder (1997) test the impact of the

Table 2: Packaging Incentives

		Contractually-provided		Non-contractual/ intangible
		Monetary	*in-kind*	
Current rewards	*base rewards*	1. base wage/salary	2. health insurance	3. job security, prestige, social privileges
	allowances	4. transportation, housing, meals, telephone, travel, cost-of-living	5. transportation, housing, meals, travel	6. trips abroad, training
	future expectations	7. pension	8. housing, land, etc.	9. reputation, re-employment after retirement

Source: World Bank, Administrative & Civil Service Reform. Available at: http://www1.worldbank.org/publicsector/civilservice/agency.htm

In order to understand rewards and incentives, it may is helpful to look at things from the perspective of the civil servant. We can see that the reward and incentive structure facing a civil servant is multifacited and contains both contractually-provided rewards and allowances and non-contractually provided allowances. When we speak of an incentive crisis, we do not just mean low wages but rather the general failure to structure incentives within the civil service to increase efficacy and efficiency. Indeed from an incentive perspective one cannot separate selection and screening processes from the reward structure within the civil service in general. From earlier discussion, it should be apparent that redesigning the appropriate pay structure can be beneficial to curb corruption and more importantly increase overall performance and welfare. Reform strategies within the public sector frequently look at the private sector for inspiration - one need only look at the impact of New Public Management, outlined below as an example. Common to the discussion of employee incentives is to look at them within the familiar principal-agent framework.[90]

---

satisficing model of wages for the level of corruption. They find that fair wages would be unattainable as a rule in developing countries.

[90] The economic approach to the principal-agent relationship, where the agent is employed to perform tasks in the interest of the principal was initially focused on issues such as insurance, sharecropping, physician- client relations and the delegation of decision making authority grew with the formulation of models of imperfect monitoring and imperfect information. For a brief

Recall, this term comes from economics and refers to situations where one individual (agent) acts on behalf of another (principal) with furtherance of the principal's goals as the basis of the relationship. A moral hazard problem here occurs because the agent and the principal have different goals and the latter has difficulty in distinguishing whether the agent is acting according to his own best interests or those of the principal.[91] We can see that taking the principal-agent relationship as the basis for understanding corrupt behavior incorporates behavior in a broader sense, encompassing factors that affect performance and alignment of interests generally and not just corruption. Milgrom and Roberts (1992: 185) identify three conditions for a moral hazard problem to hold. There must be divergence of interest, *i.e.*, interests are not aligned. Secondly, the parties must be in an arrangement that allows these divergent interests to take place. Thirdly, there must be difficulties in monitoring actions as information is costly to obtain, or in enforcing violations before third parties (*ibid.*). Solutions to these problems may be attained through increasing expenditure in monitoring and information gathering, through explicit incentive contracts, through taking hostages (bonding) of the agent, or through redefining the manner or parties in a relationship.

Monitoring is of course the most obvious means to further the prospects that the agent acts as the principal desires. It does not merely entail punishing deviant behavior but rather also rewarding the positive. It takes many forms and can be both internal or external to an organization. On a day-to-day level, however, internal systems of monitoring and accountability are fundamental to good governance, and form part of the managerial approach to solving corruption (Heymann 1996).

Internal systems of accountability are crucial to curbing corruption. Although they are often discredited in many transition countries, given their communist legacy, and may be viewed upon warily by the citizenry, internal mechanisms of monitoring and accountability are essential to the day-to-day running of governmental bodies. There are strong arguments in favor of giving agencies and governmental bodies a first chance to solve something, in light of the fact that they best understand their own policies and the fact that it is generally inexpensive.[92] Internal appeal structures range from the primary decision to a

---

review see Breton (1995: 418). From a theoretical point of view the principal agent model views bureaucracies no different to any other firms, namely as a nexus of contracts (Coase 1937).

[91] Moral hazard is a term commonly associated with insurance markets. It may be defined as the risk that an insured party will destroy value or allow it to be destroyed in order to receive the benefits associated therewith. It is a very common phenomenon to all principal-agent relationships extending beyond the confines of corruption.

[92] As Aman and Mayton (1993: 404-405) note of external challenges to actions: "Litigation costs and judicial intervention may so stifle a new and unfolding agency program that its fruition (the time when the program's merits and demerits can probably most usefully be assessed) is defeated."

superior or other body within the organization. These appeals can work in conjunction with other instruments, such as more extensive complaints procedures like the Citizen's Charter in the United Kingdom, introduced in the 1990's, that required all public bodies involved in service delivery to enumerate standards of service accompanied by suitable mechanisms for complaint where this is not adhered to.

There are some general advantages of internal disciplinary and accountability mechanisms including that they are informal, speedy and inexpensive. Additionally, they are not confined just to matters of law, but to matters of general nonalignment with the aims of the principal (government, citizenry). Moreover, issues can be handled by those persons that have direct and specialized knowledge of the particular body, thus reducing information costs and costs of erroneous decisions based on technicalities. Furthermore, internal measures may not damage organizational capital, where involvement of outsiders in disciplinary measures can easily jeopardize a working climate.

There are, naturally, also limitations of internal accountability mechanisms. In particular, at an individual level, feelings of collegiality can interfere adversely with disciplinary measures. Moreover, it can be difficult to differentiate between the layers of the organization, in particular the supervisory (appeals) body or investigator and the decisionmaker. Another problem associated with internal disciplinary measures is that it can be of low standards, because the primary functions of the supervisor within the organization may lie elsewhere. A further serious limitation of internal mechanisms is that because high exposure of malfeasance or impropriety can be damaging to an agency, the agencies incentives are not aligned with optimal deterrence. This occurs for a few reasons. When an agency exposes improbity, it suffers a collective reputation loss and may even suffer budget cuts. It has, therefore, incentive to keep such transgressions secret and simply dismiss agents that have engaged in improprieties. When agents know this before hand, there can only be sub-optimal deterrence, as the maximum sanction agents most likely face is dismissal. Agents will tend to engage in activities when the expected gains from doing so, are higher than the expected losses. Here the expected gains refers to the probability of not being detected times the gains from transgression, and the expected losses denotes the probability of detection times the expected sanction. Putting a cap on the expected sanction, makes it worthwhile to engage in all those activities where the expected gains exceed the expected losses. Marginal gains from transgression may not be taken into consideration.

A similar reason for sub-optimal deterrence resulting from internal mechanisms is likely even when agencies are obligated to turn over proven transgressors to external bodies. This occurs because agencies incur costs mentioned above (collective reputation costs and perhaps budget cuts) when they turn over the transgressor. Obligating them to do so, and thereby incurring said costs, can give the agency great disincentives to monitor their own agents in the firsts place, and disincentives to initiate investigations when improbity is revealed.

Perhaps, however, the greatest problem with such mechanism is that they are often intransparent, and are conducted within the confines of secrecy. Where this is the case, there are obvious dangers, in addition to a low level of workmanship and expertise, including the danger that internal mechanisms are used as a means of constraining and aligning official behavior with other norms and objectives than those of the principal, ranging on a spectrum from collegiality and collective reputation to participation in corruptive systems. A final important limitation with internal mechanisms is that in those regions and countries where there is generally a high level of official corruption, levels of trust in government officials is most likely low. Internal accountability mechanisms will only have a very limited effect in changing beliefs among the citizenry that a governmental body is more accountable, and are, therefore, unlikely to help shift corrupt exchanges from a high level to a low level equilibrium.

Monitoring should, however, form only part of a system of carrots and sticks. One factor often overlooked is the role that *loyalty* can play in principal agent relationships. Where officials are generally loyal to the goal of public service, monitoring costs can be reduced substantially. What has begun recently to receive attention in the literature is the fact that monitoring can reduce intrinsic motivation to comply with certain goals, because it may be a symbol of distrust. Extensive monitoring can thus "crowd out" initiative and loyalty, or intrinsic motivation (see Frey 1992; Kreps 1997). I shall address later those external organs of particular interest in monitoring malfeasance in government.

Another common means for tackling the principal agent problem is through the use of *incentive or performance based contracts*. Here one should note that "the firm is not paying directly for what the employees are supplying but instead uses a proxy for it" (Milgrom and Roberts 1992: 179). Government agencies like firms may use bonds. Bonding generally refers to a sum of money that an employee would have to pay upon violation of a contractual agreement. There are cases where such a mechanism is practical, *e.g.*, where an employee cannot leave employment without returning a fixed sum similar to that which has been invested into training the employee. This practice is common where there has been on-the-job training. It is often written into contracts that an employee cannot leave the firm for a certain number of years. From an economic perspective, this is, however, not always practical as the punishment is not necessarily tied to marginal gains and can therefore lead to over- or under-deterrence. In order to fix a suitable bond, one would need to tie marginal gains to marginal benefits, so the bond may have to be extremely large, which can be impractical for two reasons. First, the employee may not have sufficient capital to cover such a bond, and second it may be reputation damaging, or in the case of the bureaucracy, politically sensitive.

An explicit incentive contract that is conscious of malfeasance (corruption), may in addition to posting either entrance or performance bonds, explicitly structure the contract to discourage corruption. One problem that needs to be overcome is that agencies may voluntarily tie their own hands related to sanctioning malfeasance. A common result of discovery of corruption is mere dismissal of an employee for three major reasons. First, where there is an additional reputation cost for a private company or government agency when an employee is discovered to have engaged in corruption, they will be reluctant to reveal this information to outside sources. Secondly, this may transpire because an agency has the power to keep this information secret, thus preventing public outcry as a result of a scandal that demands prosecution. Third, where the evidence is clear-cut that the agent engaged in corruption, he may be content to be let go without prosecution. In a similar vein, as a further means to discourage malfeasance, the government can offer a salary premium in each year of employment greater than what the employee would get elsewhere, which has the effect of delaying the rewards from employment. A further measure would be to offer a sizeable pension, which would be forfeited as a result of impropriety.[93]

There are naturally some problems with the above-mentioned mechanisms in their application to controlling bureaucratic corruption. *First*, performance mechanisms are themselves naturally subject to collusion. *Second*, in the case of institutionalized or systematic corruption, tying wages to performance may result in an official being able to demand a higher bribe to compensate his own loss. This is particularly damaging when his services are relatively inelastic and where he enjoys monopoly power.[94] *Third*, incentive based contract generally award the manager more discretion in order to make decisions making more responsive. This may be a particular result of a poorly designed contract. Additionally, the designing of the contract *per se* awards great discretion, that itself must be transparent and monitored. Again where corruption is also pervasive among parties drawing up the contracts, they are then likely to be intentionally defined so as to increase the revenue of its own members. *Fourth*, drawing up such contracts and redesigning the principal agent relationship is politically sensitive in nature. It may be a source of conflict in itself and lead to an environment of distrust. Furthermore, it may also lead in certain circumstances to employees actually exerting low effort, so as to avoid the so called ratchet effect, which describes how performance standards increase after a period of good performance, thereby

---

[93] Support for these suggestions is already found in Becker and Stigler (1974: 10) who suggest, "enforcers post a bond equal to the temptation of malfeasance, receive the income on the bond as long as they are employed, and have the bond returned if they behave themselves until retirement."

[94] Elasticity (the opposite of Inelasticity) can be understood as measurement of the percentage change in one variable that results from a 1% change in another variable. An elasticity less than 1 is considered relatively inelastic. An elasticity precisely equal to 1 is termed unit elastic.

demanding an increase in performance by employees if they want to attain the same gains (Milgrom and Roberts 1992: 233). *Fifth*, it may require a higher degree of human capital in order to be successfully implemented.

It should be noted that monitoring can be beneficial not just to the principal but also to the risk averse agent who is part of a team.[95] Given that the effort level of the agent is not observable, the principal is forced to shift risk to the agent. Could the principal measure the effort level of the agent (or alternately, measure the impact of randomness on the outcome), the outcome may indeed be better for both parties (than in the case of a suboptimal incentive based contract). Similarly, the risk averse agent is worried about the performance of other agents and the chances of them free-riding on his own efforts, which can be reduced by increasing the level of monitoring.

E. Revenue Collection: A Good Place to Begin

The institutions active in public expenditure management systems, such as budget, treasury, tax etc., are fundamental to government and economic development.[96] The costs of malfeasance or maladministration in these areas are exorbitant, so they would appear to be a good place to start for any government interested in reforming its institutions to mitigate corruption. Below, I focus on revenue collection but I wish to emphasize the importance of standards and reform, if needed, in all areas and operations of public expenditure management.[97] Tax evasion has been widely studied in the economics literature; corruption in tax administration less so, although there are widely documented studies of collusion between tax officials and taxpayers. The costs of corruption in tax collection were already understood in the days of the Greek and Roman empires. Given that corruption was pervasive, in a practice known as tax farming, it was considered advantageous to 'privatize' tax collection by auctioning rights to collect taxes (MacMullen 1988). Just how pervasive corruption in revenue collection can be was identified by Chu (1990), who reported the results of a survey conducted in Taipei in which 94 percent of the taxpayers polled admitted to paying off tax officials as part of collusive practices and/or tax evasion.

---

[95] A risk-averse person favors having a smaller constant payment to an uncertain payment, on average of higher value.

[96] *See* Premchand (1993) for a review of these systems.

[97] In Russia, Levin and Satarov (2000) report that both execution and distribution of budget founds is an area of rampant corruption, with negligible levels of discipline and almost a complete absence of reaction to audits. Federal budget factors which foster corruption include: the receipt of taxes; the receipt of foreign credits; the means of allocation and financial assistance to regions with delays and hold up commonplace. It is guessed that around half of all decisions related to state credits or the distribution of state budgetary resources are with the presence of bribes. Regional budgets are frequently only allocated when bribes are paid.

Table 3: Common Forms of Corruption in Revenue Collection

Tax administration.

- The provision of tax exemption certificates to nonqualified persons
- The deletion or removal of a taxpayer's records from the tax administration's registration, filing and accounting systems
- The provision of confidential tax return information to a taxpayer's business competitors
- The creation of multiple false taxpayer identifications to facilitate tax fraud
- Writing-off a tax debt without justification
- Closing a tax audit without any adjustment being made or penalties being imposed for an evade liability
- The manipulation of audit selection, etc.

Customs administration

- Facilitating the smuggling of goods across a national border to avoid tax and duty payments
- Facilitating the avoidance or understatement of a tax or duty liability through acceptance of an undervaluation or misclassification of goods in the processing of a customs entry
- Permitting goods held in a bonded warehouse to be released for consumption in the domestic market without payment of a duty or tax
- Facilitating false tax and duty refund claims through certification of the export of goods that have been consumed in the domestic market or that have not been produced at all, etc.

Source: Tanzi (1998: 114)

A corrupt tax system can be woefully crippling to an economy. Where governmental institutions collapse, parties in order to maintain a level of income may attempt to serve themselves. When tax officials begin to do this, the result is a startling decline in revenue collection, which has a knock-on effect for other government institutions. Officials who man these institutions see their budget and their wages dwindle and cities no longer see their services provided.[98]

---

[98] For an excellent depiction of this problem, *see* MacLean-Abaroa's description of the state of affairs in tax and revenue collection when he took on the job as mayor in La Paz, Bolivia in 1985 in Klitgaard, MacLean-Abaroa and Parris (2000: 6-7).

An important step is to scale back unnecessary or burdensome tax obligations which are be highly counterproductive. They frequently serve to raise inconsequential amounts of revenue, foster tax evasion and corruption, create a climate of noncompliance (in particular encouraging businesses to hide their profits and accounts even beyond that which may be taxable according to the initial regulation), and drive some companies and businesses either underground or out of business entirely.[99] In Russia, recent authorities on the subject have declared tax as perhaps "the single most important regulatory obstacle to earning an honest profit", declaring that absolute "tax rates can easily exceed 100% of profits" with companies operate in an environment of "vague and constantly changing rules and administrative interpretations" (Black, Kraakman and Tarassova 2000: 1748). Moreover, they point out that tax officials "have broad discretion to seize a company's bank accounts and other assets to pay whatever taxes the inspector claims are due" and companies who appeal "will be out of business long before the appeal is heard (*ibid.*)." One can readily understand how in such surroundings, tax audits manifest themselves as "a potent political weapon, deployed by the government against businesses that don't support the incumbents (*ibid.*)." Transactions are pushed underground, outside of the judicial system, firms out of business. Barter and nontransparent exchanges are encouraged and capital markets stunted, because companies hide income from their own creditors and shareholders in addition to the tax authorities.

Simplifying taxes in order to reduce both official discretion and the ability to hide or misrepresent taxes is important. But, clearly even the best-designed tax system is insufficient and can be made ineffective when the tax administration itself is poorly functioning. If government is to increase its revenues in addition to addressing questions of the appropriate tax rate and tax base, steps must be taken to reform institutions and the administrative mechanisms used in the tax-collection process, as well as improve the incentive structure facing both taxpayers and tax collectors.

Several additional steps can be taken. *First*, definitions of the institutional role and objectives of agencies must be clearly defined, responsibilities for steps in the tax administrative process clearly delineated to individuals agencies, and legal mandates and authority unambiguously stated.[100] *Second*, procedural steps

---

[99] For example, Black, Kraakman and Tarassova (2000: 1789) note that in Russia, enterprise-level income taxes on small businesses are still levied, a practice which has been of little success in wealthy countries and was even dropped recently in the United States. As they put forward, it is unlikely that Russia, a country with one of the highest levels of noncompliance with tax laws in the world can have greater success that these developed economies.

[100] For example, Tanzi (2001) notes that in Russia, one of the most serious problems facing reform of the tax administration is that institutional responsibilities are vague, overlapping and ill-defined, and legal mandates unclear.

can be simplified to reduce delays and increase transparency.[101] *Third*, functional assessments can be used to assess the productivity of different operative levels to see whether the authorities are under- or over-staffed in particular areas. *Fourth*, vulnerability tests can be used in order to assess the potential weaknesses for malfeasance in each operational area and step. *Fifth*, the overall incentive structure facing tax officials needs to be addressed. In particular, processes of selecting and screening, as discussed above need to be reviewed, as does the overall incentive structure of rewards and benefits facing officials and the structure of oversight mechanisms. *Sixth*, independence needs to be guaranteed, given the specially potent use of tax auditing and tax collection in political targeting as well as the potentially deleterious effect of political interference in softening tax obligations.[102] *Seventh*, the incentive facing taxpayers need to be redressed. According to Tanzi (2001: 58), high taxes common to industrialized countries can only be levied when three conditions are met: (i.) Taxpayers must be able to relate the benefits they receive from public spending with the taxes they pay; (ii.) the tax burden must be extended equitably among the population; and (iii.) an effectual tax administration must be constructed. *Eight*, administrative efficiency and transparency can be improved by the extended use of computerization and modern information and tracking systems.

Summing up, the costs of corruption and maladministration in revenue collection can be especially deleterious, making revenue collection a good area in which to begin reforms. In some environments, nothing short of a thorough overhaul of administration is necessary. Reformers need to concentrate on the incentives facing both sides of the equation, namely tax collectors and taxpayers.

F. Recent Trends in Civil Service Reform: A Cautionary Note for Developing Countries

The same deregulatory rhetoric that accompanied many reform measures for more than the last decade also made in-roads into the public sector. Many OECD countries have moved beyond the traditional model to improve efficiency and effectiveness of government and have adopted a more managerialist approach to personnel management. According to traditional models a central personnel office or comparable organ was the decision-maker of both how many and who should be employed, which removes discretion from unit managers and prevents them

---

[101] This policy, for example, was introduce at Mexico City Airport in the customs service, where the number of steps in the customs processes was decreased from sixteen to three, in addition to reducing the number of employees and increasing the wages of those who stayed (Rose-Ackerman 1999: 45).

[102] Regarding Russia, Tanzi (2001: 62) reports that high level political official frequently infer with administration, with the Prime Minister even entangled in the resolution of individual tax cases.

from hiring skills as they see necessary for a particular job. Similarly, the model is one of administration and not of management and the resources managers are supposed to manage are rigidly controlled.[103] Some have moved to a devolved "running cost" control system, whereby managers are allowed to chose their own combination of staff and other resources to deliver programs efficiently. A key objective of these changes is to allow managers to put in place the skills they deem necessary to carry out the job, without the aforementioned rigidities created by a central authority. Such steps should not be taken lightly and are accompanied by considerable risks. In those countries where decentralization of personnel management functions has been undertaken, and in particular where it has been taken farthest, it is being conducted under the oversight and protection of, as Nunberg (1995: 17) suggests, "elaborate, technologically sophisticated systems of information and financial management, utilizing complex and expensive computer software and hardware in order to maintain tight rains on running costs."

1. The State-of-the-Art of Reforms: The Rise of New Public Management

Touched on above, several trends in civil service reform have emerged in developed countries largely as a result of the two-pronged quest to "reduce civil service expenditures and at the same time to improve performance standards in government"(Nunberg 1995: 4). Many of these reform measures have be classified under the rubric of "new public management". A synopsis of these is given in Table 4. The first reform phase consisted largely of downsizing exercises, with "recruitment slowdowns and freezes, natural attrition, early retirement, reorganization and/or privatization of government activities" (*ibid.*: 11). A second stage of reforms emphasized the "cost-efficient management of "inputs" in the provision of services (*ibid.*). This period of reforms witnessed an expansive increase in the development of performance indicators. It was accompanied by a devolution of authority to top level departments. A third stage of reforms involved "increasing flexibility and devolving still more responsibility and accountability to lower management levels" (*ibid.*: 12). Departments increasingly exercised a more "hands-off" control over executive agencies (Carter and Greer 1993: 407).

---

[103] *See* World Bank, *supra* note 53.

140

Table 4: New Public Management

	Doctrine	Meaning	Typical Justification
1	Hands-on Professional management of public organization	Visible managers at the top, free to manage by discretionary power	Accountability requires clear assignment of responsibility, not diffusion of power
2	Explicit standards and measures of performance	Goals and targets defined and measureable as indicators of success	Accountability means clearly stated aims; efficiency needs "hard look" at goals
3	Greater emphasis on output controls	Resource allocation and rewards linked to performance	Need to stress results rather than procedures
4	Shift to disaggregation of units in the public sector	Unbundle public sector into corporatized units organized by products, with devolved budgets and dealing at arm's length with each other	Make units manageable; split provision and production, use contracts or franchises inside as well as outside the public sector
5	Shift to greater competition in public sector	Move to term contracts and public tendering procedures	Rivalry as the key to lower costs and better standards
6	Stress on private sector styles of management practice	Move away from military style public service ethic to more flexible pay, hiring, rules, PR, etc.	Need to apply "proven" private sector management tools in the public sector
7	Stress on greater discipline and parsimony in public sector resource use	Cutting direct costs, raising labor discipline, limiting compliance costs to business	Need to check resource demands of public sector and do more with less

Source: Hood (1996)

The UK approximates these phases of reform and currently finds itself in the third phase. Following a civil service report to the Prime Minister, entitled "Improving Management in Government: the Next Steps", as part of the third phase of reforms, a series of so-called "Next Steps" Agencies were established. Next Steps agencies remain part of civil service, answerable to their Minister, who in turn is answerable to Parliament (Mountfield 1997: 71-72). The Next Steps program has no statutory foundation and is entirely a matter of operational delegation within a Department (*ibid.*: 72). These executive agencies do not have a separate legal existence from their parent departments (Wade and Forsyth 1999: 48). The general notion of these agencies remains the "delegation to a Chief Executive of responsibility to achieve stated, usually quantified, targets of performance, with delegations of powers to match, in such areas as organization, recruitment, pay and grading and so on" (Mountfield 1997: 72).[104]

The "Next Steps programme" ceded a mass of centrally organized decision making to 'independent agencies' which were to perform under framework documents- essentially agreements between the chief executive and the responsible minister- but were to be given the 'freedom to manage' (Baldwin 1995: 30; Wade and Forsyth 1999: 49).[105] As Nunberg (1995: 12) puts it: "Too large and unwieldy to be managed as one organization, government as envisaged by Next Steps architects and other agency reform proponents is instead a collection of interrelated but separately functioning businesses." Fundamental to understanding these reforms is the belief in the difference between management in the provision of services and policy derived by government departments. The distinction has, however, not been as smooth as one might hope and a central issue of accountability that has been raised with respect to the agencies is that minister ministers are no longer willing to accept responsibility to Parliament for management and operation, just policy. In a system of executive accountability based on ministerial responsibility and ministerial accountability, it is not difficult to understand that this development is subject to much unease.

In addition to extending the practice of devolution of managerial discretion, key emphasis should also be given to the increasing role of performance indicators in the monitoring and control system. Discretion was afforded on the basis of achieving certain "formalized performance targets which were built into Agency business plans" (Carter and Greer 1993: 409). Consequently, the business plans may be perceived as the Agencies' 'contracts' according to which they consent to deliver a specified performance with a given level of resources, making use of Treasury predictions regarding uncertainties such as growth, inflation, and unemployment (ibid.). More than just being a tool to improve managerial competence, performance indicators present additional opportunities to a wide range of interested parties that can monitor government agencies. Performance indicators can be used by parliamentary committees and politicians as well as by professional and consumer groups to hold government responsible for service delivery in both the political and social arena (ibid.). The latter is enabled in the United Kingdom by the Citizens Charter initiative, whereby service organizations must publicly disclose details of individual branch

---

[104] The chief executive is a professional manager, frequently recruited from outside the civil service.
[105] According to the Civil Service (Management Functions) Act, management functions, including pay and conditions of service, may be delegated to the chief executive- which is indeed normally the case (Wade and Forsyth 1999: 49 n.17).

or unit performance against specified goals (*ibid.*; Wade and Forsyth 1999). The effectiveness of performance standards as a tool to monitor government is a function of *inter alia* their visibility, their specification, and the ability of external monitors to observe them. Increasing each one of these factors can potentially reduce the level of maladministration as well as the level of corruption.

The New Zealand model of government administration put the continence and province of government under substantial surgery, unseen in any other country. Government commercial enterprises, such as the banking, postal and telecommunication services, were "corporatized". Enterprises were set up under normal company legislation, common to all countries (Bale and Dale 1998: 104).[106] Analogously, deregulation usually occurred and companies were left to their own devices. Emphasized above, the model of reform in the United Kingdom made use of the notion of contracts with government administration; the New Zealand model of the core public sector, clearly influenced by "New Institutional Economics" and particularly "Transaction Cost Economics", has been termed government by contract- adopting what has been termed "hard edge contractualism" (*see* Schick 1998: 123-4).[107] Department heads, renamed chief executives, lost their tenure and were nominated to fixed terms not exceeding five years (Bale and Dale 1998: 106). They work according to specific performance based contracts that are negotiated with the responsible minister (*ibid.*: 106). Conditions of a private corporation were simulated, and public sector employees were placed under the same rules and regulations as the private sector (*ibid.*). Chief executives were also made generally responsible for all input decisions, including capital investment decisions (*ibid.*: 109). Whilst the department head or chief executive retains responsibility for outputs (goods and services produced), responsibility for outcomes (effect on community) remains with the ministers (*ibid.*: 107), a factor frequently criticized as in the United Kingdom. Most revolutionary in the New Zealand model is that ministers actually purchase resources from their departments and hundreds of contracts are formally bargained over every year (Schick 1998: 124). The government is obligated to purchase goods and services at the lowest possible price; in order to do so, ministers are free to purchase on the market, *i.e.*, outside of departmental sources, if they find the product for cheaper. Appropriations take into consideration private sector taxation in order to level the playing field (Bale and Dale 1998: 108; Schick 1998: 125).

One advantage of "new public management" reforms (not just common to New Zealand) from the perspective of corruption deserves additional mention. The general distinction between service purchaser and service provider permits, to

---

[106] Shares were not initially publicly traded but held by ministers, a practice later abandoned (Bale and Dale 1998: 104)

[107] For an illuminating discussion of New Institutional Economics, *see* North (1990). For an authoritative treatment of Transaction Cost Economics, *see* Williamson (1985).

a certain extent, institutions which have separate interests and separate incentives to reduce the discretion of the other. Setting out rights via "contract" has the affect of clarifying obligations, rules and duties in a fashion which mimics a modern version of the separation of powers doctrine; each party involved has an interest in mitigating the discretion of the other, but instead of delineating according to the confines of executive, legislative, and judicial functions the separation is according to the role of service provider and service purchaser. The fact that the government is both owner and client to their own departments can cause, however, conflict of interests. These are overcome by either using market prices, or coming up with alternative benchmarks. Furthermore, despite attempts to separate policy making functions and service delivery, ministers are free to turn to the market for either (Verheijen 1998: 259; Schick 1998: 125).

Developing countries with limited resources may benefit more by pursuing a model of centralized control allowing a finite degree of deconcentration, as exemplified by many Asian countries and other countries such as France, Germany and the Netherlands. Widely deconcentrated and decentralized structures are generally beyond both the technological and human resource capacity of developing countries. This is not to suggest that selective features of the approach cannot be adapted by particular countries, dependent on their individual positions- in fact quite the opposite- but rather that the basic safeguards that accompany such well-established democracies in which these reforms have been undertaken are not available. Similarly, the sophisticated institutional and technical systems, particularly of information and financial management are not available or implementable. In such an environment, the possibilities to obfuscate reforms, accompanied by poor control systems, would permit the spreading of malfeasance, and reduce the vulnerabilities of detection.

VI. Contracting Out

In recent years (as seen above), reformers have rediscovered the merits of contract as a means of dividing administration from politics (*see* Rose-Ackerman 1999: 84).[108] Though prevalent in those countries adumbrated above that embraced "new public management" reforms, the advantages of contract have been extolled globally. Common to these developments is frequently the belief that the state delivers many services and performs many functions inefficiently, that it has taken too much upon itself and that the private sector - driven by competition - can often outperform the state in the delivering of these services (Wade and Forsyth 1999: 50). Whilst it is difficult to escape a certain degree of ideology behind such

---

[108] One repercussion of reforms, such as "the contracting state" and hybrid organizations, is that it has become increasingly difficult to differentiate governmental from non-governmental functions. We do not make address this important discussion here, given that we are focusing more on mechanisms as opposed to areas of application.

movements, this should not distract the reformer from possible efficiency advantages.

From the perspective of corruption contracting out for services is really quite ambiguous: on the one hand, it can subject the delivery of services to market pressures, but on the other hand it shifts the loci of payoffs to the award of contracts, which have often traditionally been awarded along patronage lines or according to payoffs. The advantages of competitive pressures accrued by contracting out are only prevalent when there is more than one provider for a service (Rose-Ackerman 1999: 85). Clearly, where there is only one provider, there is a real danger of monopoly power being simply transferred to the private body, which would not be as well regulated as a public body in a similar position. Moreover, there are also other factors that need to be considered, such as the ability of these private bodies when they enjoy monopoly power to hold the government or service users hostage (Williamson 1985). In such circumstances, it is wiser for the government not to contract out and produce the service itself, even if there is an apparent efficiency loss. Similarly, contracting out is only desirable when performance can be measured; otherwise providers enjoy too much discretion and cannot be held accountable.

One should distinguish between competitive tendering and contracting out. According to competitive tendering, a governmental body which provides an activity 'in-house' invites outside offers for work in competition against it; the outside contractor can either be a private or a public body. In the United Kindgom, wide-spread competitive tendering for in-house services has been popularized in such fields as defense, the national health services (NHS), the support services of central government and multiple local authority services (Harden 1992). This principle was most advanced at the local level, where there was a compulsive competitive tendering before work was undertaken by a local authority for a wide list of categories, or before work was undertaken on behalf of another authority (*ibid.*: 18).[109] This principle was, of course, in line with the aforementioned reforms under the "Next Steps Programme", which entailed *inter alia* a separation of policy and delivery functions, *i.e.* of both purchaser and provider functions. Such forms of competitive tendering seem to be a marginally preferable means from the perspective of curbing corruption, given that it necessarily invokes competition, at least between the governmental body and one contractor; on the other hand a public body could in theory simply contract out a service to a sole provider without even this competitive element.

Of course, the nature of such contractual relationships described above are only the tip of the (recent) contractual-iceberg. Of the many types of arrangements possible, the common thread running through the contractual forms is perhaps merely that the government elects and enters into a contractual relationship with a

---

[109] This practice has since been revoked.

145

private contractor for a particular service. Such relations have reshaped substantially the boundaries of administrative and public law, a factor that troubles many legal scholars (*see* Vincent-Jones 1999) . Under such a framework, services previously delivered by a government agency or other public organ that were subject to judicial review and other administrative safeguards are now delivered by a private company, via a contract, to which the ordinary service recipient is commonly not a party (Wade and Forsyth 1999: 50). In short, contractualization from the perspective of accountability, opens up a variety of legal, economic and administrative dimensions that must be taken into account when assessing both the desirability of taking such steps, pertinent to evaluating the governance of public services.

VII. Procurement and Government Contracts

Transaction cost theory teaches us that when an organization desires a good, it can either produce it itself or it can go to the market for the good. Many forms of corruption occur when for example a city provides a good itself, *e.g.*, licensing, zoning, regulating, etc. Procurement contracts open up a new set of opportunities for corruption. To wit, many factors that can be used to curb corruption in the aforementioned areas are also valid when government decides to look to the market to buy a good, however, there are distinct features that arise when the government decides to procure such a range of goods, as well as particular measures to fight collusion and corruption in these relationships. Moreover, corruption in these areas is no doubt also pushed on by the massive sums involved.[110] Procurement is probably the area of both local and national government in terms of monetary value where corruption occurs to its fullest extent. It is these features and particularities I shall examine here.

A. Types of Collusion

There are unsurprisingly many possible systems that a cartel can introduce in order to disguise collusion. Indeed, it is the fitful nature and range of collusive and corrupt arrangements that make them so difficult to detect. For example, it may adopt a pure bid rotation scheme where members take turns in submitting bids in various auctions. Alternatively, members may, in addition to the intended winner, proffer trivial bids in order to create the impression of competition (Porter and

---

[110] Take for example, the numbers of a large city such as New York. According to Anerchiarico and Jacobs (1996: 123), for a given year in New York "agencies enter into approximately 40,000 contracts worth almost $8 billion, approximately one-fourth of the cities budget. These contracts cover everything from pencils to legal services for indigent criminal defendants, from methadone treatment for heroin addicts to architectural consultants, from external auditing to billion-dollar tender."

Zona 1993: 519). Despite the expansive literature already available on auctions and procurement contracts, sophisticated economic and econometric analysis that allow detection of collision in government contracting and procurement is surprisingly incomplete (Klemperer 1999).[111] The question that economists particularly try to investigate is namely, "can we distinguish between collusive and Nash, or relatively competitive, equilibrium behavior, given available data" (Hendricks and Porter 1989: 218). Put differently, "[a]s in most tests for the exercise of market power, the idea is to identify differences between the observable implications of collusive and competitive behavior. The difficulty is that both competitive and collusive equilibria depend, to a great extent, on the economic environment, such as the auction rules and the nature of the good being traded" (Porter and Zona 1993: 519). In general there is no single test that can be used to detect bid rigging. As Porter and Zona suggest, "[i]f a broadly applicable test to detect collusion could be devised, a cartel with full participation should be able to choose complementary bids so that the overall bid pattern passed the test" (*ibid.*: 520). Intuitively, therefore, one may infer that a broad range of (econometric) tests should be applied to any data set before one can draw preliminary conclusions. Furthermore, tests are further complicated by the fact that production costs are frequently correlated across jobs, which offers an obvious explanation to the fact that bidders may appear to be submitting clustered or similar bids. One clearly cannot deduce collusion per se from this phenomenon. Nor can one deduce collusion and patterns of bid rotation when there may be increasing average costs to accepting a second or third contract as a result of tied up machinery and backlogs etc. (decreasing economies to scale), so companies may legitimately forfeit the option of tendering for another public contract. A further problem in detecting collusion or corrupt procurement operations is the familiar quandary of distinguishing poor results that are the result of nonfeasance or malfeasance from plain erroneous decisions.

Despite the difficulties in detecting improbity, one can identify at a general level principal forms of collusion and corruption in procurement. Borrowing from

Klitgaard, MacLean-Abaroa and Parris (2000: 46) these include:

1. Collusion among bidders, leading to higher prices for the city which may or may not be shared with corrupt officials;
2. Kickbacks by firms to city officials in order to "fix" procurement competition; and
3. Bribes to city officials that regulate the winning contractor's behavior. The existence of this sort of corruption may encourage abnormally low bids, which

---

[111] *See* Klemperer (1999) for a comprehensive literature review of auction theory. On optimal auction design specifically, *see* the reviews by Milgrom (1985), (1987) (1989), and McAfee and McMillan (1987).

being below estimated costs win the contract but then are "rectified" in the corrupt contractor's calculation by the subsequent cost overruns and lucrative changes in contract specifications that the bribe-taking regulator permits.

B. Collusion and Procurement Form

As we shall see below, it is common for procurement auctions to facilitate high levels of collusion, given that they often supply the factors for cartel members to form and monitor in the first place. The emergence and characteristics of collusive mechanisms depend in large part on the nature of the object being auctioned, the market conditions for that object and on the auction rules in place (*see* Hendricks and Porter 1989: 218). Whilst corruption may often be the result, as argued in chapter II, not of explicit agreements but rather reciprocation of well pronounced patterns of behavior, making it particularly stable, this is unlikely to be the case for procurement contracts, where parties need to agree, coordinate and enforce several factors in order to "make things work". For example, a cartel is facing many problems if it wants to remain stable (or form in the first place). Many of the problems should be familiar to us now after chapter II including:

- Agreeing on the designation of a winner for each job and dividing the pie
- Keeping out outsiders and keeping the number of parties small and identifiable
- Knowing what objects to bid on
- The ability to monitor members properly to see that they stick to agreements
- Sanctioning members that do not fall in line

In what follows, I shall look at a stylized version of procurement procedures and highlight salient features of collusion and corruption at different stages of the procurement process, based on procedures in the United States, which although generally quite formal and different from agency to agency, normally have common characteristics. Corruption can naturally already occur in the determination of what an agency or governmental body wishes to procure. Once a decision has been made on what to purchase federal contracts are awarded on the basis of either sealed bidding or negotiation. In a sealed-bid procurement in the United States, the solicitations document is an invitation for submitting a bid. Selection is based solely on the lowest price submitted by a qualified supplier (Worthington and Goldsman 1998: 5).[112] Generally for each contract, a business

---

[112] *See* generally Federal Acquisition Regulation (FAR) Part 14 governing sealed bidding for federal procurement in the United States. For negotiations, *see* generally Federal Acquisitions Regulation (FAR) Part 15. Note, we are not examining military contracts here. For sealed bidding in military contracts, *see* generally Defense Federal Acquisitions Regulation Supplement, Part 214-Sealed Bidding, Airforce FAR Supplement Part 14-Sealed Bidding,

observes the bid and the identity of each firm tendering a bid, and the specifications of each job. Additionally, a government engineer frequently gives a cost estimate prior to the solicitation of the bids, sometimes announced publicly.[113] In a negotiated procurement, on the other hand, the solicitation document can be either a entreaty for a proposal or a request for quotation. Accordingly, the contract is given based on price and other additional technical considerations (Worthington and Goldsman 1998: 5). Here I shall be looking at sealed bid procurement.[114]

C. Curbing Corruption at Different Stages in Procurement Process

1. Stage I: The Specification of Procurement Contracts

Mentioned above, corruption can already occur in the determination of what an agency or governmental body wishes to procure. A government can reduce the level of corruption in the specification process by directing requirements to standardized products (Rose-Ackerman 1999: 65-66). Competitive pressures are a result of the market and not the bidding process itself and although competitive bidding from the perspective of corruption seems to be particularly positive, in a truly competitive market bidding is a redundant process; market prices are the result of the multiple transactions of several buyers and sellers (*ibid.*: 63;65). An auction process is, therefore, employed because the buyer is not cognizant of the precise costs of the sellers and the good is not readily subject to the aforementioned market prices (*see* Porter and Zona 1993: 520). It should be noted, that corrupt systems harbor not only bad procurement processes but may also entail procurement of the wrong goods and services generally (Rose-Ackerman 1999: 65).[115]

Army FAR Supplement, Part 14- Sealed Bidding, Navy Acquisition Procedures Supplement, Part 14- Sealed Bidding, Defense Logistics Acquisition Regulation, Part 5214-Sealed Bidding.

[113] Although often kept secret, in some instances, the government also publicly announces a reservation price for a job, designating the maximum amount it is willing to pay (Hendricks and Porter 1989: 219).

[114] Recent proposals in the US have seen attention shift from competitive bidding to negotiated sole source contracts whereby the government and a firm haggle on the price and other factors (Kelman 1990, 1994). But as Rose-Ackerman (1999: 60) observes: "...a sealed bidding process under International Competitive Bidding (ICB) principles is the accepted standard of fairness and economic efficiency. It is required by the World Bank under its infrastructure loans and has influenced the development of procurement codes worldwide."

[115] In a worst case scenario, as in the case of kleptocracy, a government will always procure those products that maximize its intake of bribes or creaming off from its budget irrespective of the impact of an acquisition on social welfare. Where the procurement process is even only partially transparent, however, more sophisticated types of collusion and corruption are likely to develop.

Types of corruption that occur at the selection stage include over-specification and lock-out specification resulting in procurement orders being prescribed to reduce the number of potential firms (Klitgaard, MacLean-Abaroa and Parris 2000: 119; Rose Ackerman 1999: 64). Over-specification refers to a situation where a contract is too specific, resulting in the exclusion of vendors attributed to product differentiation or "the weight and breadth of requirements". Lock-out specification refers to a tailor made contract that excludes all but one contractor (Klitgaard, MacLean-Abaroa and Parris 2000: 119). A potential contractor may try to influence a statement by having specifications tailor made for his firm.[116] This is potentially most serious when the selection of a contractor is dependent on the technical characteristics of a product as opposed to an output- or goal-oriented set of specifications (Rose-Ackerman 1999: 64-65). Furthermore, over-specification or lock-out may not be the problem, but rather vague specifications. As we have seen in our discussion of rules as a mechanism to curb malfeasance, vague specifications award an official discretion which may be exercised in order to further corruption.[117] Over-specification may itself not be the result of malice or corruption, but where it occurs unintentionally may be a factor that increases the stability of a cartel that has agreed to collude in order to suppress competition and increase profits. A letting that is too specific, has the impact of decreasing the number of potential bidders and, therefore, allowing the numbers in the cartel to remain small. Over-specification may also be the result of firms lobbying agencies to exaggerate the importance of specific characteristics shared by cartel members.

Particular factors that may influence the level of corruption include permitting contractors to play a role in determining the specifications of a potential contract. In the US for example, this is consistent with the revised version of part 15 of the Federal Acquisitions Regulation related to negotiated government procurements (Rose-Ackerman 1999: 62). Restrictions are, however, still in place for competitive procurements (*ibid.*). There are obvious efficiency trade-offs to be had here. For example, a company through being involved in determining an agency's requirements or by exerting influence in the process itself is able to make more efficient investments in its own research and development, equipment and marketing strategies by anticipating agency needs (Worthington and Goldsman 1998: 5). These factors that may lead to great *ex ante* cost savings. The practice may, however, also lead to favoritism and cronyism or other similar types of abuse (Rose-Ackerman 1999: 62).

Over-specification is a means that effectively debars firms from the competitive process. One might, therefore, suggest that under-specification would

---

[116] *See* Anechiarico and Jacobs (1996: 124) for an example of specification manipulation in practice.

[117] Alternatively, very tight specifications may actually increase the monopoly power of contractors.

stimulate greater competition by allowing more firms to compete for a contract. This, nonetheless, increases the discretion afforded to officials and opens up new opportunities for corruption. An alternative means of increasing competition would be to divide large projects into smaller ones which should have the affect of increasing the number vendors. This mechanism may be particularly useful for acquisitions large in volume or where the costs and quality of the products are relatively straightforward (Klitgaard, MacLean-Abaroa and Parris 2000: 129). The danger, one suspects, of applying such a measure is twofold: *First*, when division is done poorly it may not increase the number of suppliers but rather increase the monopoly power and potential hold-up problems associated with contracting; and *secondly*, it may help solve the division of the spoils problem facing companies that collude, as companies that were involved in bid-rotation schemes needed to wait for future bids in order to see if companies would honor their agreements.

Prequalification is a system used to screen contractors that would then form a pool from which potential contractors would be chosen (Rose-Ackerman 1999: 61). It allows for a more thorough screening of potential contractors at one particular stage rather than relying purely on screening upon contract submission. Prequalification can be accompanied by other measures such as "blacklisting" contractors, as was pursued in New York by the School Construction Authority (SCA).[118] The SCA debarred over fifty construction firms for a period of up to 5 years, nearly half of which were "based on suspected mob ties or criminality, not on poor contract performance" (Anechiarico and Jacobs 1996: 129). Blacklisting is dangerous for at least four reasons: *First*, selection may be according to moral criteria as opposed to economic criteria, leaving room for moral crusading. For example, under the Procurement Policy Board Rules in New York, "an agency's chief contracting officer and chief administrator [have] to determine whether a contractor or vendor is financially, operationally, and *morally* responsible" (*ibid.*: 126). Evidence of any a list of improprieties by principals, officials, directors and managers will likely lead to disqualifying.[119] *Second*, there is potential for abuse by high level officials with contacts to cartels or organized crime, that wish to suppress competition. *Third*, there may be significant economic cost as a result of blacklisting companies from doing business with the government. It may not offer a sound system of marginal deterrence, but might lead to over-deterrence and companies investing too many resources in self-monitoring. This is discussed later

---

[118] Would-be contractors had to answer a thirty page questionnaire which asked such questions as: "In the past ten years has the applicant firm, or any of its current or past key people or affiliate firms... taken the Fifth Amendment in testimony regarding a business related crime?...given or offered to give money or any other benefit to a labor official or public servant with intent to influence that labor official or public servant with respect to any of his or her official acts, duties or decisions as a labor official...[or] agreed with another to bid below the market rate." Source: Anechiarico and Jacobs 1996: 129.

[119] For a list of these improprieties, *see* Anechiarico and Jacobs (1996: 127).

under deterrence and corporate corruption.[120] Moreover, companies may have made capital specific investments for contracting with the government, which may now be forfeited. *Fourth*, in some industries, such as the construction industry in New York, it is likely that a firm in order to survive long-term has had encounters with "corrupt business inspectors, incompetent site supervisors, mob-dominated labor unions, and in some cases dangerous, crime-ridden neighborhoods Anechiarico and Jacobs" (1996: 124). As we learned in chapter II there are various means that can be used by a party to get another to comply, many of which are extortionary, *i.e.*, threats, hostages etc., where compliance is done almost out of necessity. Construction companies to operate may have become victims of such extortionary practices. An alternative policy would be to permit parties to declare themselves victims of extortion, which may generate evidence of bribe-taking and assist criminal law investigations.

An alternative system to screening firms for criminal behavior and punishing those that have criminal links by blacklisting, may be to encourage parties to signal their type.[121] Government procurement, although decided most often on a case by case basis, involves firms that are in a repeated game with government, a fact easily observable by looking at bidding and selection listing. Imagine a society where there are just good types and bad types. A bad type is one that is willing to deceive the government in its bidding, by launching a dishonest bid. In game theoretical terms, he has a higher discount rate for future transactions (Axelrod 1984, E. Posner 2000: 18). To distinguish good types from bad types, the government should encourage good contractors to send out signals. One signal that can be sent out is for all parties to incur large costs before the beginning of a relationship (*see* E. Posner 2000: 18). Such a policy induces contractors to incur costs that only a person that is in it for the long run (legitimate) can incur.[122] Ideally, in equilibrium all the good types send the signal, the bad types do not send the signal and are identifiable.[123] There are several conceivable signals that a firm can use. One is to invest in research and development, which itself only pays off in the long term. Even better, the firm can make capital specific investments in research and development that signal a firm's intention to contract with the government in future.[124] In areas where investment in research and development is

---

[120] *See* further, Chapter VI, Section VI.

[121] For a discussion of signaling models, *see* generally E. Posner (2000), Kreps (1990).

[122] I am working with the assumption that the government is interested in reducing corruption and gaining best value for money.

[123] Economists will recognize this as an example of a separating equilibrium.

[124] Recall signaling is a device to indicate ones type. One of the problems with research and development as a signaling device is that although it can signal type at stage 1, it can be easily copied by competitors and bad types in stage 2. A solution to this is, however, that research and development be continuous and not discrete, *e.g.*, a firm continuously invests in research and development and not just on a project by project basis, again signaling long term intentions, and making it more costly for imitators.

not so important, the firm may make other investments that only pay out in the long term, or better still invest in other capital specific investments, such as equipment or location.

Another mechanism for curbing malfeasance at this stage is related to controlling the information structure of companies involved. Particularly conducive to collusion is the common practice of publishing plan buyer lists, which allow the set of bidders to be ex ante common knowledge (*see* Porter and Zona 1993: 522). One means of disrupting (potential) collusion would be to abolish the publishing of such lists, thereby inducing a degree of randomness and insecurity into the cartel. The effectiveness of the two above measures can naturally be undermined when an official can be bribed and provide this information to the parties or where the number of possible suppliers is so small that their identity is common knowledge.

Another, more straightforward, means of destabilizing the cartel is to increase the size of the plan buyer lists in an attempt to introduce more players, which is counter to cooperation as discussed earlier; this could be guaranteed by regulations that make it mandatory to open procurement to non-local firms supported by anti-trust laws.

2. Stage II: The Bidding Process

In the bidding process contractors are invited to make offers according to the needs of the government as specified. Publicizing the invitation for bids is a *sine qua non* to affecting corruption levels, as it is increases competition, broadens participation (including smaller, less established firms) and furthers transparency. This can consist of *inter alia* the use of well publicized commercial journals, the mailing of bidding lists, and, generally, postings in public places. To increase transparency, this should also be done electronically over the internet.

Adumbrated above, common to US federal contracts under sealed bidding and with similar criteria in other states and international procurement contracts - such as, for example, the International Competitive Bidding (ICB) principles as required by the World Bank - selection is based on the lowest price submitted by a bidder meeting some criteria of responsibility. Generally for each contract, a business observes the bid and the identity of each firm tendering a bid, and the specifications of each job.

Types of collusion schemes common at this stage include:[125]

- Cover biddings (phantom bids)
- Bid suppression
- Bid rotation
- Market division

(Source: Klitgaard, MacLean-Abaroa and Parris 2000: 121)

Cover biddings or phantom bids refer to bids submitted in order to give the appearance of competition (Hendricks and Porter 1989: 221). Bid suppression refers to a situation where firms forgo bidding or drop out of a race in order to facilitate the winning of a contract by a designated firm. Bid rotation, as its name suggests, is a situation where "firms rotate winning bids among themselves, and, through side payments, ensure each receives a "fair" share of business over time" (Klitgaard, MacLean-Abaroa and Parris 2000: 121). Market division refers to a situation where firms agree not to enter into a particular market or division of a market according to well defined criteria in order to suppress competition against one another. The aforementioned characteristics are not mutually exclusive nor are they complete. Overlapping occurs as cartels decide which system is best for them.

2.1. Factors that Facilitate Collusion

There are many factors that facilitate bid-rigging.[126] The ability to monitor the actions of other players I have previously identified as being conducive, if indeed necessary to cooperation. Reversing the practice of publicly announcing bids as well as the identity of bidders may reverse the stability of the practice. This allows undercutting to be easily observable. Nondisclosure of this information is a means of destabilizing a cartel as it can make monitoring of individual actions more arduous. Do firms compete only on price or also on quality and whether product differentiation is allowed. When for example the quality is held constant, the only variable may be the price, which increase the cartel stability (Porter and Zona 1993; Klitgaard, MacLean-Abaroa and Parris 2000: 124). Another important

---

[125] As Klitgaard, MacLean-Abaroa and Parris (2000: 121) note: "Collusion may not involve bribing a government official. It may be a form of cartel behavior or anti-competitive activity that is illegal, but not, strictly speaking, corrupt. On the other hand, bid-rigging rings often do have the resources and sometimes the force to bribe or threaten officials who would expose them."

[126] In the US the measure of damages for bid-rigging is "the difference between what the government actually paid on the fraudulent claim and what it would have paid had there been fair, open and competitive bidding" (United States v. Killough, 848 F.2d 1523, 1532 (1988)).

factor is whether or not demand for a good inelastic.[127] When demand is inelastic, bids are still awarded to the lowest bidder irrespective of the cost estimates of engineers thus pushing up the profits associated with collusion (Porter and Zona 1993). Bare in mind from chapter II, that a person is more willing to cooperate if the expected future payoffs of an ongoing relationship are higher and predictable. Put differently, the higher the discount rate of future income, as a result of risk aversion, uncertainty or some other factor, the less likely he is willing to cooperate. When, therefore, future payoffs are easily identifiable and computable, collusion is more likely to occur.[128] Collusive agreements prefer a stable environment. Furthermore, engineers' estimates are frequently the result of previous costs of lettings. When a cartel has been established for some time, it may collectively group bids in order to push up engineers' estimates. In order to avoid collusion between engineers and cartels, it would be wise to rotate engineers frequently or to bring in outsiders. Are the number of firms bidding on a contract small or large? The smaller the number of firms, the more likely the level of cooperation (on average). Furthermore, are there same number of small companies bidding all the time, or are outsider coming into the bidding process? Has a particular pattern developed?.

If the answer to the above factors was generally yes, then one must address whether there were barriers to entry into the market? This entails inevitably looking beyond the procurement process to view the specifics of the industry and the labor and capital inputs involved. For example, is the reason that there are only a small number of bidders for a contract a result of such factors as large transportation costs, or are there more stealth reasons? Is there control of necessary factors of production or labor by local factories or companies that are used as hostages? When this is the case, the government may facilitate competition by decreasing the monopoly hold enjoyed by these companies. Further, recall that the ability of parties to cooperate is greatly increased when there is a central authority that can sanction members for upholding promises. Union officials, for example, are a notoriously ominous presence in holding hostages and controlling factors of production, who can tacitly or explicitly declare future union trouble if contracts go to outside bidders (*see* Zona and Porter 1993).[129] Furthermore, to overcome the coordination problem discussed in chapter

---

[127] Recall, elasticity can be understood as measurement of the percentage change in one variable resulting from a 1% change in another variable. An elasticity of less than 1 is considered relatively inelastic.

[128] If demand is elastic, it may shift discretion over to the official. He needs to specify precisely the reasons for not awarding a contract.

[129] As Anechiarico and Jacobs (1996: 136) note of the New York construction industry: "Historically, mob-dominated construction unions have established and enforced employer cartels which can allocate contracts and determine prices. A company which challenges the system finds itself without workers or threatened with sabotage."

II, a cartel may have many central authorities or institutions to regulate and monitor behavior, often in the confines of local trade associations that facilitate communication.

Of further importance is whether there is a particular time frame for letting contracts? Regularity in the timing of government lettings may increase and make more discernible, the future value of continued collusion relative to deviation (Porter and Zona 1993: 524). Introducing a degree of randomness may destabilize agreements, but the costs of doing so, in the form of delayed projects etc. may be prohibitive. By affecting the timing of lettings, i.e., distancing or randomizing the letting of large jobs, one can affect the returns from defection for any one of the parties that do not honor agreements (*ibid.*: 524). A similar result could be achieved by concentrating many contracts at one stage, thereby increasing the payoffs from defection.

Are the costs for the firms homogenous, or is one firm more productive than others? Do firms purchase their inputs on the same market and pay the same factor prices? Not surprisingly, where firms have homogenous costs we expect more collusion (Hendricks and Porter 1989). Where this is not the case, one firm can always underprice others. It is, however, difficult to assess the costs of firms involved in bidding. Another indication that collusion may occur is related to the stability of market shares, "the idea being that a cartel will seek to maintain stability in an effort to keep participants happy" (Porter and Zona 1993: 527). Quantifying market shares is, however, precarious as lessons from anti-trust law and economics suggest.[130] A final consideration is that when businesses have interests in many areas, it may be easy for them to switch from collusion in one market to another.

3. Stage III: Selection

The selection and evaluation stage opens up new opportunities for corruption. As Klitgaard, MacLean-Abaroa and Parris (2000: 122) propose: "The evaluation process, ... may give rise to bribes and kickbacks, in return for favorable consideration of a vendor's bid, and to "pork-barrel" politics, in which politicians support bids that favor their constituencies or contributors." Many events can signal corruption, including the awarding of a contract to a party that failed to offer the lowest bid, awarding a contract to a firm with no experience in an area or that has a poor record of performance, bestowing a contract through a rebid, or when the firm is considered the sole source, passing it off as the result of detailed negotiation or otherwise (*ibid.*: 125). One means to control corruption in the selection process is to assess the price of a similar product on the global market. As Rose-Ackerman (1999: 65) notes, "[b]ench marking may be relatively easy for

---

[130] Problems already manifest themselves at the stage of defining what precisely constitutes a market. On these and other empirical problems, *see* Rubinfeld and Baker (1999).

those countries and subnational governments that are small relative to the markets in which they operate. If they purchase standard products in the international market, market prices are excellent standards because the small government's own demand is unlikely to affect prices. One way to obtain a rough benchmark is through data on United States trade."

Screening companies for past performance may be a useful means in the selection process, but it may also lead to exclusionary practices and cronyism as we have seen earlier. There are, however, strong efficiency reasons why past performance should be taken into consideration. When contracts are effectively awarded according to the sole criteria of lowest cost and not according to performance, then even contractors that did a "shoddy job" will be awarded future contracts unless found to be "irresponsible" (Anechiarico and Jacobs 1996: 132). Recall that controlling corruption must be understood from the perspective of reducing corruption to an optimal level, i.e., where the marginal gains from reducing corruption are equal to the marginal costs. In other words, there is an optimal level of corruption, and curbing corruption must not be seen as the primary goal of contract selection.

Rotating officials that are responsible for the selection process, increasing the audits of the criteria applied in selection and the use of vulnerability tests and sting operations are important instruments that can be used to curb corruption in the selection process. Particularly suited to increasing accountability in the selection process is opening up the criteria of selection to public scrutiny and using external as opposed to internal auditors. It can be costly to use external auditors, so a process of randomizing their use is advisable, which when used properly can bring the same results. Furthermore, an outside expert of proven integrity can be brought in to select a winner. Another instrument that can be important is providing a platform for the grievances of unsuccessful or excluded bidders. Such platforms can take many descriptions. For example, in the United States an unsuccessful bidder for a federal contract may protest to the agency, the General Accounting Office, the United States Court of Federal Claims, or a federal district court. Furthermore, federal agencies have according to an executive order by President Clinton in late 1995, established alternative dispute resolution procedures for bid protests (*see* Federal Acquisition Regulation (FAR) 33.103). Perhaps more than in most other areas of corruption, conflict of interest laws governing the involvement of officials in financial decisions in which they have an interest (anticipation of future employment, as shareholder in organization etc.), as well as the regulation of gifts and honoraria are of particular importance.[131]

---

[131] In the United States for example "During the conduct of any federal agency procurement", no procurement official shall knowingly: Solicit, accept, or discuss future employment or business opportunity with any officer, employee, representative agent, or consultant of a competing contractor; solicit or receive any money, gratuity or any thing of value from any officer,

157

An important mechanism was developed by Transparency International in the early nineties, the main features of which are captured in Table 5 below. It is a pact (contract) among a government office and companies submitting a tender for a specific project with a specified set of sanctions written into the contract upon noncompliance. Constantly updated, it has been applied to several countries and regions globally with mixed results in an effort to mitigate corruption in public procurement. The explicit primary goals of the Integrity Pact are the following:

a. to enable companies to abstain from bribing by providing assurances to them that
   i. their competitors will also refrain from bribing, and
   ii. government procurement agencies will undertake to prevent corruption, including extortion, by their officials and to follow transparent procedures; and
b. to enable governments to reduce the high cost and the distortionary impact of corruption on public procurement, privatization and licensing programs (Transparency International 2002: 4).

A particularly attractive feature of the Integrity Pact system developed by Transparency International is, as they note, that "it will establish contractual rights and obligations of all the parties to a procurement contract and thus eliminate uncertainties as to the quality, applicability and enforcement of criminal and contractual legal provisions in a given country. This means that applying the IP concept can be done anywhere without the normally lengthy process of changing the local laws (*ibid.*)." The Integrity Pact is particularly attractive to economists, given that it makes use a of volitional, contractual solution to solve an economic and legal quandary. To wit, parties participating in the Integrity pact are encouraged to bargain around the terms of the pact in order voice their own fears and concerns. Legal obligations are, therefore, not imposed in a strict form from the top and are to a certain extent negotiable.

---

employee, representative, agent, or consultant of a competing contractor; or disclose any propriety or source selection information except as a contracting officer or agency head" (FAR 3.104-3(b)). Competing contractors or those acting for it may not knowingly: "engage in certain employment or business opportunity discussions with a procurement official; offer gratuities to a procurement official; or solicit or receive certain proprietary and source selection information from agency personnel" (FAR 3.104-3(c)). *See* also below, Chapter VI, Section IV on conflicts of interest.

Table 5: The Transparency International Integrity Pact

Main Features:
▪ A pact (contract) among a government office and companies submitting a tender for specific project;   ▪ An undertaking by the government authority that officials will not demand or accept bribes, gifts etc., with disciplinary or criminal sanctions in case of violation;   ▪ A statement by each bidder that it has not paid, and will not pay, any bribes to obtain or retain contract;   ▪ An undertaking by each bidder to disclose all payments made in connection with the contract in question to all parties including agents, middle men, family members of officials etc.;   ▪ Explicit acceptance by each bidder that the no-bribery commitment, disclosure obligation, and attendant sanctions remain in force until contract has been fully executed;   ▪ Undertakings on behalf of a bidding company are made with authorization of Chief Executive Officer;   ▪ Bidders are advised to have a company code of conduct and a compliance program for the implementation of the code of conduct;   ▪ The use of arbitration as a conflict resolution mechanism   ▪ A pre-announced set of sanctions for any violation, by a bidder, of its statements or undertakings, including some or all of the following: (i) denial or loss of contract, (ii) forfeiture of the bid security (iii) liability for damages to the principal and the competing bidders, (iv)debarment of the violator by the principal for an appropriate period of time.
Source: Transparency International (2002)[132]

Though the Integrity Pact is clearly an advance in curbing corruption in procurement, as well as licensing and privatization, it is weakened by the fact that it makes the assumption that firms all have an interest that others do not pay bribes and so may band together to regulate themselves and to ensure that penalties and a mechanism for investigation are in place.[133]

Firms it is argued are in a type of bribers dilemma, whereby a common and binding pact of honesty would allow parties to acquire an outcome that is more beneficial than what can be acquired under corruption There are, however, some problems with this. Assuming that firms do not desire corruption suggests that they are in a collective action dilemma where all would be better off if no one

---

[132] Available at: http://trasparency.org/building_coalitation/integrity_pact/I_pact.pdf.
[133] *See* Klitgaard, MacLean-Abaroa and Parris (2000: 60) who endorse this mechanism.

bribed. This is, however, often not the case as corruption may be both a means to divide up the pie in order to achieve above market profits and a means to suppress competition. When corruption takes this form, parties may be very content in this situation. Della Porta and Vannucci (1999: 207) make a similar point, suggesting:

"The model of corruption as a dilemma, leading to outcomes unsatisfactory for corrupters themselves, does not always appear convincing. It presupposes, among other things, that in reality no entry barriers to the corruption market exist; that any entrepreneur who seeks to corrupt a public functionary will be successful in doing so. But,..., open access to the market of political protection would be contrary to the interests of both corrupters and the corrupted, even if sometimes the functioning of market is not completely satisfactory."

How good an instrument is a system that asks companies and officials to sign codes of conduct? We learned earlier that one means for parties to align their preferences is the posting of a bond. This is particularly valuable when other mechanisms, such as reputation or expected legal sanction are insufficient. How good a bond is a code of conduct? A code of conduct can prove itself to be efficient only if it supplements the existing legal system by raising the expected costs of corruption equal to the expected gains, as is the case in the Integrity Pact put forward by Transparency International. This can be done in particular if it increases the reputation cost of a violation. The reputation costs from corruption are, however, already quite high and it is unlikely that such a mechanism will increase the sanction. So, can it affect the probability of detection? This can only be the case if an organization, through getting the parties to sign a code of conduct, also manages to facilitate the parties to come together to police themselves. This is highly unlikely.

Furthermore, having parties policing each other may also lead to collusion as they have more knowledge of the pricing behavior of their competitors as well as their competitors costs. We also learned in chapter II that collusion may not be the result of explicit agreements but also following well-established patterns of behavior (Axelrod 1984). Codes of conduct may be fortified when parties post monetary bonds, that would be forfeited if transgression occurred.[134]

---

[134] There may, however, be two uses for such a mechanism as a code of conduct. Ones rest on assumptions from behavior social science, that introducing a system may actually raise the level of awareness of the costs of corruption to the minds of the business engage therein, which may cause a business to change its assessment of the expected payoffs. A second justification manifests itself in the belief in the top down model of legal norms, which states that an authority may impose a norm of behavior on private parties and these parties may adopt this norm and change their behavior.

4. Stage IV: Delivery

There are also many abuses at the delivery stage of a contract. Signs include when a contract experiences unexpected overruns beyond inflation or altered market prices for input goods. Similarly contracts can also undergo many modifications and re-negotiations, or an award may be canceled receiving partial payment. Alternatively, products may not perform as specified, schedules of production or delivery are protracted or costs are significantly higher than international benchmarks. These factors can be affected greatly by the contract type selected by the government. When contracts are awarded solely according to criteria of the lowest cost, incentives for corruption are naturally shifted to the delivery stage. Contractors that have familiarized themselves with the system and manage to win contract according to the lowest bid may pile on costs through fraudulent change orders (Anechiarico and Jacobs 1996: 133).

In the US, for example, there are two broad categories of contract types awarded. One is fixed-price contracts, the other cost reimbursable contracts (flexibly priced). These pricing arrangements reflect the allocation of risk involved in the performance of a contract (Worthington and Goldsman 1998: 7). They are, however, also important in determining the opportunities for corruption that arise. They reflect the extent of government involvement with the contractor during contract performance (*ibid.*). Under the fixed price settlement, the contractor assumes all of the risk involved in performing the contract within the negotiated price. Under the flexibly priced settlement (cost reimbursement, incentive), the final price may be determined after work is completed or according to an interim phase (*ibid.*).[135] Furthermore, shifting some of the risk to the government may induce the problem of moral hazard. Naturally contracts that are fixed price in nature seem to be preferable from the point of view of reducing ex post corruption, but can entail serious economic costs that outweigh the benefits.[136]

Any cost reimbursement rule offers discretion to officials as well as to contractors. In the United States for example a contractor operating under a cost-reimbursement contract will generally be reimbursed for all acceptable costs incurred, determined by the government contract auditor, (after completion of the contract) (*ibid.*: 6). A government could experiment with different cost-sharing or cost reimbursement rules in order to balance efficiency concerns with corruption considerations. Furthermore, a government should take advantage of technological advances in areas such as high tech, computers and other fast changing industries, in order to safeguard against technological obsolescence and

---

[135] For a discussion of the major types of contract, *see* Worthington and Goldsman (1998: chapter 9).

[136] For example, fixed price contracts may adversely prevent efficient risk averse companies from entering into the bidding process.

abuse by contractors who otherwise would reap the gains connected to technological advances or the learning curve effect (Klitgaard, MacLean-Abaroa and Parris 2000: 139).

D. Closing Comments and a Final Possibility: Increasing Anonymity

An alternative means that the government could use, derived from the discussion in chapter II, would be to focus on anonymity.[137] One could distinguish between both official and function anonymity. Official anonymity, as its name suggests, involves withholding information on the identity of the individuals that are to decide on contracts; function anonymity refers to the situation where the identity of the officials are known to the private parties, but the precise functions are not.

As we can see from the above, the range of government contracts that are awarded is far-reaching. Many of these transactions could be provided for anonymously. There is, of course, a basic need to collect information, but the function of collecting the information and deciding on the information could easily be separated. Additionally, there is little reason for the identity of the decisionmaker to be shared with the private party. Alternatively, but perhaps less effectively, these two functions may be provided for within one organization, with a bright-line division between those that collect information and perhaps negotiate from those that process this information and decide. The latter group may be prohibited from engaging itself in any form of professional relationship with the private party.

The above has the affect not just of a separation of powers type arrangement but also that the identification and the meeting of these players (potential corrupt agents) is not permitted, which may prevent the evolution of cooperation and where identity is disclosed increase the vulnerabilities and barriers to corrupt exchanges. Where information is withheld on the identity of officials (as above) or on the functions of different officials (the officials themselves are common knowledge), parties find it difficult to identify those with whom they need to transact in order to "get things done" corruptly (interdependence is not identifiable). In the case of function anonymity, parties may be able to identify who works in a specific institution, but certain precise functions can be withheld. This information can also be withheld from many low-level officials. Officials may naturally try to leak out this information in order to put themselves again up for bribes. To counter this, conscious dissemination of

---

[137] Anonymity is sometimes erroneously understood to represent unaccountability. This is however not the case, as the official can still be held accountable to internal and external supervisory mechanisms, and the information could be retrieved upon formal request. Naturally, the best way to ensure anonymity is to focus purely on competitive market transactions, where prices are by definition independent of identity.

this information must be sanctionable, supplemented by the rotation of persons in vulnerable positions.

VIII. Privatization

In chapter II I identified a key means government has of altering the payoffs available to corruption is to remove the government activity in its entirety. This can be done through the removal of both inefficient regulations and corruption-ridden programs as discussed above, or alternatively the government may privatize previously state-owned bodies, removing them from state-owned control. As we shall see privatization is, however, both a reform measure against corruption as well as a potential reservoir for illicit gains (Rose-Ackerman 1999: 42). It may actually increase or lessen the level of corruption depending on the composition of corrupt structures. Changes in government regarded as anti-corruption measures open up new opportunities for payoffs.

The widespread use of privatization, unlike perhaps some other reforms, is not necessarily indicative of its success; after all it is easy to strip state assets or hand them over to friends and supporters in return for something in return. A brief perusal of the literature and journalistic reporting on privatization will quickly identify that there is some confusion as to its precise meaning. The following, for example, cannot be considered as privatization. Restructuring measures such as changing the legal form of a public enterprise, from perhaps a departmental agency or public corporation to a state company subject to regular company law; changing the management of a government enterprise; reducing the size of a large public enterprise to several smaller ones, or using incentive contracts for management and workers cannot be considered as privatization measures (Bös 1993: 368-69). Nor do I consider privatization as it is frequently referred to in the United States as a choice between in-house provision of goods and services by (state and local) administrative employees and the contracting out of that production or service to private firms to be privatization (Megginson and Netter 2001: 18). Whilst these may be considered as alternatives to privatization, they cannot be considered as privatization per se. The essence of privatization is "the deliberate sale by a government of state-owned enterprises (SOEs) or assets to private economic agents" (*ibid.*: 1). In the case of privatization the residual rights associated with an asset rest with private parties; in the case of restructuring measures, residual rights remain with the state, and government bureaucrats (Bös 1993).[138] Indeed the extent of privatization reforms are monumental. [139] What were once considered as peripheral measures have now become global orthodoxy

---

[138] Residual rights include everything that has not been decided by contract (Bös 1993).

[139] As Nellis (1999: 1) notes: "Every country including India, Russia, China, Vietnam, Cambodia and Laos, that still trains a significant number of publicly-owned firms, is privatizing some or most of them (save for Cuba and Democratic People's Republic of Korea)".

and a worldwide phenomenon, practiced by governments in more than 100 countries.[140]

A. The Importance of Institutional Reforms

Privatization is an anti-corruption measure because it transfers certain assets from state control and can transform discretionary official behavior into private, market-orientated choices (Rose-Ackerman 1999: 35). For example, urban land in many areas in Russia urban areas continues to remain non-privatized. This presents a significant problem given that starting a new business or expanding an existing one requires land, and hence furnishes great opportunities for corruption where *de facto* "[o]btaining land requires bribing government officials, who can then collect taxes from you, tell their Mafia buddies about you, and revoke your land rights if you don't pay enough taxes or bribes. Moreover, insecure land rights mean that businesses won't invest much in immovable buildings or equipment, and thus won't grow very large or employ many people" (Black, Kraakman, Tarassova 2000: 1761). Despite widespread privatization, property rights, the bread and butter of economic growth, are still lacking.

Privatization is, however, also a potential reservoir for illicit gains, as the process of transferring assets provides ample opportunities for corruption (Rose-Ackerman 1999: 42). The seriousness of the failed privatization and the opportunities for illicit gains presented therewith are highlighted by recent experiences in Central and Eastern Europe, which teach us that they failed privatization can have serious long term consequences for institutional and economic development. For this reason, in what follows, I pay particular attention to privatization in transition and developing economies, as this has most to teach

---

[140] It must be emphasized that although we focus on privatization as both a reform measure against corruption as well as a potential reservoir for illicit gains, it must be recognized that privatization per se is a major component of the continuing global heterodoxy of increasing the use of markets in the allocation of scarce resources. Moreover, from an analytic perspective, the economic theory of privatization must be considered a subset of the economics of ownership and more generally the role of government ownership and regulation of productive resources in the economy- a discourse that entails analysis of the proper role of government in economic affairs, which we cannot commit ourselves to here. Discussion of which goods and services should be produced publicly and which are better produced privately has a long history among economists. Accordingly, as Sappinton and Stiglitz (1987: 567) note: "The recent trend towards privatization suggests that previous assignments were incorrect and are better carried out within the private sector." From an economic perspective support for state ownership or control is based on some (perceived) market failure. Privatization, inversely, is a response to the shortcomings of state ownership. There is naturally a continuum of ownership structures between these two positions. On these points, *see* Megginson and Netter (2001) and Laffont and Tirole (1993).

us.[141] Furthermore, I argue that lessons from the whole privatization experience provide valuable insights into theories of institutional reform, that are of fundamental importance to curbing corruption in the long-term. For this reason, it warrants extended attention. I provide a nonexhaustive account and analysis tied to our special concerns here.

Given the diversity of ways that property and ownership have been divided as well as the broad expanse of assets and political climates, a great body of methods of privatization have developed with varied degrees of success.[142] Countries divide themselves, not just by method of privatization, but also by speed (gradual or rapid), sequencing (the nature of the industry or enterprise it first privatized), whether legal and institutional reforms preceded, accompanied or were considered unimportant for privatization, the willingness to allow foreign investment in the privatization process, and deregulation of the market in which the privatized firms operate.[143] The results of rapid, mass privatization have been poor to put it mildly. Citizens commonly acquired the poorest of assets, whereas the gems came under inside control.[144] Rapid privatization provided a shelter and

---

[141] As Stiglitz (1999) notes in the abstract to his paper discussing ten years of transition: "The varied experiences of the countries going through the process of transition represents one of the most important set of economic an social experiments ever conducted, and should provide a rich opportunity for researchers to understand the process of reform and to gain insights into workings of economies. The limited success in some many of the countries means that their remain many opportunities for applying the lessons of such studies."

[142] Borrowing from the taxonomy provided from Brada (1996), the *first* category refers to privatization through restitution. Rarely observed outside of Eastern Europe, it refers to the restitution of land or other easily identifiable property by the state that was expropriated in former years and can be returned to either the original owner or his or her heirs. A *second* method of privatization is through the sale of state property. This is a standard approach to privatization that was used in the United Kingdom and throughout Western Europe, as well as in Asia, Latin America and Hungary (Boycko, Schleifer and Vishny 1994: 251). The *third* category in Brada's typology is mass or voucher privatization, where eligible citizens use vouchers that are issued free or at nominal cost to bid for shares in state-owned enterprises or other property up for privatization. This method was used in Czechoslovakia, Lithuania, Mongolia, Poland and Russia (*ibid.*). A *fourth* method is privatization from below, which refers to the emergence of new businesses by local and foreign entrepreneurs.

[143]The fastest privatization of a former socialist economy unsurprisingly took place in Eastern Germany, where 35 per cent of the key-sector enterprises were fully privatized within twenty-one months of German unification (Bös 1993: 371). In Eastern Germany key sector enterprises were not sold by auction, but on the basis of negotiation between TWA (Treuhandanstalt) and bidders who are willing to take over the enterprise. In Poland and Hungary, privatization was more gradual and neither country embraced the mass privatization approach common to Russia or the Czech Republic.

[144] Miller Grodeland, and Koshechkina (1998) for example in extensive interviews conducted in the Czech Republic, Slovakia, Bulgaria and the Ukraine between November 1997 and February 1998 found that only about 13 percent of all respondents viewed themselves to have benefited in any manner in the restitution process. Furthermore, in the Czech Republic and

means for corrupt practices.[145] To wit, influential economic and legal scholars advocated mass and rapid privatization as an important factor, indeed even a necessity to the entire privatization process.[146] This is best captured by Sachs(1992: 71) who suggested:

"The need to accelerate privatization is the paramount economic policy facing Eastern Europe. If there is no breakthrough in the privatization of large enterprises in the future, the entire process could be stalled for years to come. Privatization is urgent and politically vulnerable...Because most of the effort in the next few years will involve industrial firms that are already subject to domestic or international competition, privatization should precede restructuring- at least for these enterprises" (Sachs 1992: 71).

Indeed, the existence of a weak legal and institutional framework was not even disputed by privatizers. "But writing good laws can take years and building good institutions takes decades. The privatizers weren't willing to wait" (Black, Kraakman and Tarassova 2000: 1753). The aim was to privatize as quickly as possible and the rules and institutions would follow. It was also hoped that private ownership would "create a constituency for strengthening and enforcing these laws" (*ibid.*: 1753). As we know in retrospect, particularly of Russia, this did not happen. Insiders didn't want strong rules and institutions that would jeopardize their self-dealing, and worse still they were frequently uninterested in increasing the companies value. Black, Kraakman, Tarassova (ibid.: 1736) describe the fundamental error of these policy suggestions as follows:

"Left unnoticed was that the new owners had two means of making money-increase the companies value, or steal what value already existed. The first was difficult, perhaps beyond their ability, and uncertain in outcome. The second was easy; they were expert at it; and it was sure to produce a handsome profit that could be tucked away overseas, beyond the reach of the

---

Slovakia approximately half considered the main beneficiaries of privatization to have been politicians and officials, one-fifth the nomenklatura and another fifth the Mafia in some shape or form.

[145] Similarly in Latin America, the need for rapid privatization appeared often an excuse to disguise illegal practices. Insufficient transparency occasioned frequent allegations of wrongdoing, "ranging from the state of privileged information to outright bribes, which failed to be investigated simply because of the heavy government influence in the judiciary, particularly in Argentina and Peru" (Manzetti 1999: 327).

[146] The list of scholars is long. For illustrative examples of the dominant thoughts at the time, *see* for example, Boycko, Shleifer and Vishny (1995), Black and Kraakman (1996). *See* in particular Black, Kraakman, Tarassova (2000) who cite a more thorough listing of the authors that supported this position, including themselves; they readily admit their mistakes and offer a comprehensive and illuminating analysis of the failures of reform.

future Russian government. Most of the kleptocrats [as they were labeled in the Russian press] choose the second, easy approach."[147]

Indeed, privatization in Central and Eastern Europe provides the strongest evidence to date in my opinion that institutions matter, and that these institutions must precede more ambitious reform measures, including more ambitious anti-corruption reform measures. It offers *prima facie* evidence in support of bottom up measures that are important for sustainable development and sustainable reform measures. This does not refute top-down measures per se, but rather highlights the fact that we cannot rely on market forces to do the job of institutions.

Evidence is abundant that insider control of privatized forms has been by far the most important impediment to effective reform.[148] Too often, citizens in countries such as Russia and the Czech Republic have in large part become owners of the poorest performing privatized assets, whereas the "crown jewels" have been seize via insider control (Megginson and Netter 2001: 23). Indeed, some commentators suggest, for instance, that the promise inherent in voucher privatization conducted through investment funds of, for example, speedy economic transformation and the establishment of a "people's capitalism," have been "illusory" (*see* Stiglitz 1999a). Today, for example, in the Czech Republic, the essence of the problem is that poorly regulated privatized investment funds ended up enjoying the position of either owning large or controlling stakes in many firms privatized by vouchers, as a result of citizens eagerness to diversify their risks by investing their coupons into their funds. Moreover, most of the large funds were owned by the major domestic banks; banks in which the Czech state preserved a controlling or even majority stake (Nellis 1999: 11). The opportunities for malfeasance and ill-gotten gains were elevated by the comparative difference gains that could be expropriated illegally relative to those that could be gotten legally. Not just were the benevolent benefits that could be accrued by these companies meager, but the opportunities for malfeasance and corruption were

---

[147] As Black, Kraakman, Tarassov (2000: 1750) contend, "by self-dealing enough to extract all of the firm's free cash flow, the controller can appropriate the payments that would otherwise go to the government as income taxes and to minority shareholders as dividends. By self-dealing beyond this point, the controller can skim revenues that would otherwise go to pay the firm's suppliers."

[148] Frydman, Hessel and Rapaczynski (1999), for example, compared the performance of privatized and state-owned firms in Central Europe and found that privatization works only when the firm is controlled by outside owners. Weiss and Nikitin (1998) looked at the performance of Czech firms during 1993-1995 and found that ownership concentration in the hands of a large shareholder other than an investment fund or company is associated with betterment of performance. For a detailed account of these phenomena, see Shleifer and Vishny (1998).

scarcely impeded by feeble institutional (particularly regulatory) and legal frameworks.

An institutional economist must shudder at the manner with which Russia conducted its privatization 'reforms'; indeed, from this perspective, it was a predictable disaster. Stiglitz an important critic not just of the manner in which reforms were conducted, but also of the policy advice given by western counsel submits: "What is remarkable about this episode is that economists, who should have known better, had a hand in helping create these interests, believing somehow- in spite of the long history to the contrary- that Coasian forces would lead to efficient social outcomes" (Stiglitz 1999a: 21).

Russia at the dawn of the fitful privatization era, was fully devoid of any institutional infrastructure to control self-dealing by managers of would-be private firms. Basic agents of the judiciary, such as prosecutors, judges, and lawyers, had not the wherewithal to unscramble corporate transactions nor an understanding of the dexterous, indirect methods with which company insiders can bleed out company profits. Notions of fiduciary duty and workable proscriptions against self-dealing didn't exist. There was no securities commission until 1994 and business lawyers and accountants, non-expendable features of a developed capitalist economy that govern transactions, insure financial accountability and oversee managers shareholders relations were similarly wanting, as was even the most basic commercial and capital market laws when voucher privatization was concluded (*see* Black and Kraakman 1996; Black, Kraakman, Tarassova 2000).[149] Add to this the fact that communism had essentially attacked trust within both social and business relations, creating an environment where deceit and evasion where more the rule than the exception, an environment where social norms were perfectly conducive to the evolution and maintenance of corruption, where those that actually obeyed the law were and are ridiculed by peer. These skills based on deceit and deception were particularly conducive to the new assignment of self-dealing and asset stripping (*see* Black, Kraakman, Tarassova 2000: 1753).

The resulting damage for economic development (particularly the problems associated with the creation of new enterprises) and the veritable political and economic inertia that is a result of the manner of privatization, has allowed Russia to firmly nest itself in a low-level corruption equilibrium that is endemic of practically every institution responsible for governance and supervising economic welfare.[150]

---

[149] Black, Kraakman, Tarassova (2000: 1753) note that "accounting rules were designed to meet the needs of central planners, not investors" and that the Finance Ministry "often develops rules to determine how much tax a company owes rather than to help investors understand company's cash flows."

[150] As Stiglitz (1999a: 21) notes, "... the resulting program of transferring assets to the private sector without regulatory safeguards ("depoliticization") has only succeeded in putting the "grabbing hand" into the "velvet glove" of privatization".

Just how insiders can capture an entire privatization process is exemplified in the loans-for-shares scandals. Insider banks were awarded shares in the country's top enterprises as collateral for loans they gave to the government, as Sakwa suggests (2000: 129), "it was understood by all sides that the government would default on the loans and the oligarchs would get the companies for a song." The government auctioned its shares in major oil, metal and telephone companies, giving the shares as collateral to whatever party would loan it the most money. Responsible for the auctions were the same banks that proposed the loan fund in the first place.[151]

Take a look, for instance at the bidding for Sidanko oil company, which was organized by Oneksimbank. The minimum bid was set at $125 million. An affiliate of Oneksimbank won the 'bidding' with a bid of $130 million. A rival bid was disqualified for arriving twenty-four minutes late. At the time, a Western oil analyst calculated that Oneksimbank had paid the equivalent of two cents a barrel for Sidanko's reserves, when the international going rate was $4 to $5 a barrel.[152] Alternatively, consider the case of Yukos, Russia's second-largest oil company. Here, the bank, that itself had been selected to evaluate the 'bidding' process, Bank Menatep, decided to place a bid of its own and won, effectively garnering control of an estimated 2 percent of the world's oil reserves. It rejected another claim from a consortium of other banks on procedural grounds.[153] These are but two examples of many.[154]

---

[151] Summed up by Lieberman and Veimetra (1996: 738) the entire process was "non-transparent... [and] involved clear conflicts of interest; the bank, acting as the government's agent for the sale, won the bid as a general rule, usually through proxy companies...[and] created collusion; a consortium of four to five banks, supported by the government, won all the auctions."

[152] *See* Bivens and Bernstein (1999).

[153] *Ibid.*

[154] The privatization of Gazprom, the Russian natural gas monopoly, is perhaps the most symbolic example of how corrupt privatization in Russia actually was. With a conservative estimated wealth of $400 billion (a more likely figure is anywhere between $250 billion and $950 billion), its market value upon privatization could have secured $4000 (between $1,700 and $6,400 according to the alternative estimate) in value for each citizen (Black, Kraakman, Tarassova 2000: 1775; Bivens and Bernstein 1999). Taking these numbers, as Bivens and Bernstein (*ibid.*) suggest, and multiplying them by a family of three persons, working with the latter estimate would have resulted in a value between $5,100 and $19,200 in stock. Had the Russians privatized the other 'crown jewels' accordingly, it would have gone some way to creating a middle class, that may spurned on by their newly created wealth and welcoming of economic reform and capitalism in general. "Continued [well administered] state ownership would have let the government finance its payments to pensioners and employees, while permitting future privatization" (Black, Kraakman, Tarassova 2000: 1775). But Gazprom was privatized secretly, with managers receiving a huge slice of the company. The governments share as of the year 2000 was about 38 to 40 percent, while the managers stake was in the region of 35%, held by a small group with shares of between one to five percent each (*ibid.*; Bivens and Bernstein 1999). The other 25 percent is euphemistically speaking "unaccounted for."

B. Long Term Effects of Failed Privatization and Lessons Learned

Russia, in particular, provides evidence that insider privatization and concentrated managerial ownership structure will hamper economies for many years. Black, Kraakman, Tarassova (2000) suggest that there have been several fundamental results from privatization in Russia. A kleptocracy has emerged where a "small number of individuals, who mostly achieved initial wealth through favorable deals with or outright theft from the government, ended up controlling most of Russia's major firms and, to a nontrivial extent, the government itself" (*ibid.*: 1746-47). Additionally, it failed to increase productivity, largely as a result of insider dealing. Moreover, the citizens "came to associate privatization with corruption, increased crime, and fabulous wealth for a chosen few while workers and pensioners go unpaid" (*ibid.*: 1747). These kleptocrats in turn bought television stations, newspapers, and other media apparatus to promote the election of friendly politicians and dampen public faultfinding and scrutiny of their activities; they now govern most of the major TV stations and newspapers (*ibid.*: 1749; Sakwa 2000).

Another affect of the Russia's 'poor' record with privatization is that many smaller transition economies have been strongly discouraged by the Russian experience, mainly those that were formerly part of the Soviet Union, but also Albania and Mongolia (Nellis 1999: 12).[155] Its affect on capital markets is also discernible. As of 1999, the total capital stock of Russian corporations was exceptionally low; shares were almost "penny stocks" having a value of nearly zero. These values are suggestive of only a small fraction of the probable value of the underlying corporate assets under the control of Russian corporations (Fox and Heller 2000: 1721).

Another repercussion is associated with the difficulties for future firms in raising capital. As Black (2001: 782) notes: "[C]reating strong public securities markets is hard. That securities markets exist at all is magical, in way. Investors pay enormous amounts of money to strangers for completely intangible rights, whose value depends entirely on the quality of the information that the investors receive and on the sellers' honesty."[156] Firms that wish to raise capital by selling equity at a price worthwhile to its owners, need to be able to credibly commit

---

[155] Nellis further suggests that many aspects of these economies "are still under the influence if not the control of Russian supply, transport, energy and criminal networks" (Nellis 1999: 12).

[156] Black (2001: 783) suggests that for strong public securities markets, two essential prerequisites must be satisfied: "A country's laws and related institutions must give minority shareholders: (1) good information about the value of a company's business; and (2) confidence that the company's insiders (its managers and controlling shareholders) won't cheat investors out of most or all of the value of their investment through "self-dealing" transactions (transactions between a company and its insiders or another firms that the insiders control) or outright theft." He cites a comprehensive list of institutions important to achieving strong securities markets.

themselves to abide by basic principles of corporate governance that include undertaking to maximize future residuals and ensuring shareholders some reasonable proportion of these residuals as dividends or other payoffs. Outsiders will not be willing to provide cash in return for shares unless these criteria are fulfilled (Fox and Heller 2000: 1725).

Even a company that wishes to operate benevolently in such a market cannot often find investors as it has no means to signal its intentions and separate itself from bad companies. This is a similar problem to one where legal and institutional safeguards are not provided for investors in a country. Even where a company wishes to conduct its affairs above board, it often cannot credibly signal its type. There are some partial solutions to this such as individual companies that list their shares on a stock exchange in a foreign country with strong institutions and bind itself to adhering to the country's rules. This is, however, of limited use as the company still operates within a particular business and legal environment, and is still subject to the reputations of the other firms in this environment. A reputation undefended by local enforcement and supervision is still very unstable relative to similar firms in an alternative legal and business environment.[157] Furthermore, where a basic institutional and legal framework does not exist, it is highly improbable that reputational intermediaries will also effectively operate, for the simple reason that the same problems may arise just one step removed.[158]

As the reader will have gathered by now, there are, of course, many possible systems that a cartel or members of a corrupt system can introduce into the privatization process to facilitate illicit gains, oftentimes inventive to disguise their steps, but on other occasions flagrantly corrupt. Many of these factors are similar to those involved in procurement contracts, and I refer the reader to this section, where these factors are treated more thoroughly.[159] Members of a cartel may, for example, operate a pure bid rotation scheme where members take turns in submitting bids in various auctions. Members may designate an intended winner, and submit trivial bids in order to create the appearance of competition, or where the treat of potential legal sanction is so low, they may not even make the effort (as was sometimes the case in Russia). One obvious component of a credible, operable privatization process is the enactment of appropriate legislation. Former leaders like Menem of Argentina and Fujimori of Peru frequently

---

[157] On this point, see Black (2001). See also Tirole (1996) for discussion and analysis of collective reputations.

[158] "Among the most important institutions are reputational intermediaries- accounting firms, investment banking firms, law firms, and stock exchanges. These intermediaries can credibly vouch for the quality of particular securities because they are repeat players who will suffer a reputational loss, if they let a company falsify or unduly exaggerate its prospects, that exceeds their one-time gain from permitting the exaggeration. The intermediaries backbones are stiffened by liability to investors if they endorse faulty disclosure, and by possible government civil or criminal prosecution if they do so intentionally" (see Black 2001: 787).

[159] See above, this chapter, Section VII.

attempted and were often successful at pushing their reforms through in a manner that often bypassed the legislature, by means that were "far from truly democratic" (Manzetti 1999: 322). Indeed, bypassing the legislature on policy reforms was accompanied by the emasculation of the judiciary and other independent institutions that clearly lead to a loss of transparency and accountability (*ibid.*: 326).

Another factor of fundamental importance is the provision of adequate information about performance records for the valuation of assets for state-owned enterprises being sold (accounting data). This is made all the more important by the fact that large enterprises, unlike procurement goods, cannot normally be subjected to benchmark standards (prices of goods or services elsewhere). Information asymmetries offer those with insider knowledge an unfair advantage in the bidding process. Ex post evaluations by experts generally will try to distinguish between the price that would have been paid for the enterprise under competitive behavior and compare it to the price that was actually paid for it. This is naturally impeded by both auction rules and the nature of the asset being purchased. Ideally such calculations would occur ex ante and should be accompanied by vulnerability assessments for (potential) exposure to corruption.

Another fundamental requirement is the development of new regulatory structures and an appropriate tax regime under which the company will operate (if this does not exist already), and generally the development of an appropriate post-sale relationship between it and the government. As we have seen with procurement contracts, corruption may already occur in the decision as to what to privatize. Insiders are in a privileged decision to judge better than others the areas where illicit gains can best be attained and may push for the privatization of these assets accordingly. There are several potential information-related opportunities for corruption; these range from the aforementioned nondisclosure of accurate accounts that reveal the true value of a firm to withholding the information that the firm is going to be privatized until the last minute from other competitors (particularly international competitors). Other indicators that can signal corruption in the privatization process are the awarding of a firm to a party other than the highest bidder, or alternatively when investors are presented as the sole source (as a result of expertise or other criteria) and the award is passed off as the result of intense negotiation.

As with procurement contracts, procedural safeguards need to be in place to prevent a continuum of procedure-related swindles, ranging from the fabrication of procedural errors in the submission of bids for firms to, at the most extreme, privatization in outright secrecy as was the case of Gazprom in Russia, where accurate records of the division of assets among officials, insiders and their associates do not even exist.[160] Platforms for grievances are also important. In the

---

[160] *See* above this chapter, Section VIII, Subsection A.

institutional void in which much privatization took place in Latin America in the 1980s and Central and Eastern Europe in the 1990s, such platforms were not forthcoming. There are a multitude of opportunities for reciprocity that may occur. One lesson is that insider control of privatized forms has been by far the most important impediment to effective reform, and doesn't just discredit the privatization process and those involved in it, but has long term effects that can potentially stagnate economic and indeed in some cases political development. Conflict-of-interest laws that are so important are either fully absent or not enforced; the mere size of the sum involved and the potential to divide some of this surplus among so many offer great temptation, which itself is increased by weak regulatory and oversight mechanisms and impotent or missing procedural safeguards.

One other key lesson of the last ten years of privatization must surely be that inevitably one must look beyond the privatization procedure itself to organize a credible privatization process. One rationalization why few firms may participate in the privatization process is that it is actually unprofitable for them to win the firm (in addition to the fact that they may know before hand that someone else is designated to win, so they have little chance of actually prevailing). Insiders may be able to achieve subsidies or other assurances after being awarded a firm that may be taken into account when bidding. After privatization, they may also continue the monopoly hold the company has on the market provided by restrictive licensing regulations and other barriers to entry such as bureaucratic red tape. Worse still, as we have seen the new owners may not have any intention of continuing the operation of the firm in any form but stripping it of the assets it acquired at a pittance of their real value in conjunction with officials that are either involved in the supervision of such behavior or can procure the company benefits in the form of subsidies, taxes or tax evasion.

Privatization should be seen as one strategy among many to increase economic performance. Many other reform measures, some of which are documented here in this work must either be seen as complementary or substitutes to privatization. For example, deregulating a market, thereby allowing competition between several firms within the one market may actually be a more preferable strategy than privatization and works best when accompanied by anti-trust regulations.[161]

Indeed, the level of competition may be as important as ownership given that competition may drive the weaker performers out of the market. Even when

---

[161] As Manzetti (1999: 328) notes in the context of Latin America: "With anti-trust legislation either weak (Brazil) or simply nonexistent (Argentina and Peru), privatizing under monopolistic/oligopolistic conditions raised serious doubts about the establishment of a true market economy." He goes further and suggests that in the case of Argentina the lack of a clear regulatory scheme in many sectors was a deliberate government action as part of the incentive package to lure investors.

privatization is still the selected strategy, it must be preceded by deregulation in order to lessen the future monopoly hold that a firm has on the market and to reduce the potential payoffs of bribery, and the ex post potential new owners may enjoy in preventing deregulation and retarding entrepreneurship.[162] Incentive contracts as discussed elsewhere are another viable- if temporary - alternative to privatization.[163] China is one example of a country that has undergone widespread economic reform with minimal privatization through the use of these incentive contracts.

Additionally, in Central and Eastern Europe, profit incentives to restructure privatized businesses and create new ones are often swamped by the burden on business imposed by collective factors such as a punitive tax system, official corruption, organized crime and an unfriendly bureaucracy - all of which are factors that promote self-dealing and asset-stripping which can delegitimize long-term reforms, the privatization process and trust in government. Under these conditions, corruption is rife, as managers bribe tax and customs officials, cheat on their taxes and avoid cash transactions just to survive. Furthermore, when the government does not pay its own debts to companies that furnished it with goods and services, one can readily understand why these companies have an incentive less incentives to pay their own tax bills (Black, Kraakman, Tarassova 2000: 1754).

Finally, the most fundamental lesson that has come out of many of the mistakes of privatization, principally in transition economies, and more particularly in the former Soviet Union and the Czech republic, is the importance of establishing an institutional and regulatory framework that not just accompanies but precedes major reforms, otherwise the development of a dynamic private sector and a vibrant market economy, that must be regarded as the *sine qua non* of both the developmental and transitional process of structural change, is endangered.[164] Where this cannot be credibly established we need to focus on improving what Stiglitz (1999a) calls "the bottom-up approach to transformation."

---

[162] The Chinese experience indicates that a country can gain much from first focusing on competition and then on privatization. Decentralization, the process whereby economic decisionmaking is delegated to lower level of an organization, must also be considered as an alternative to privatization. This position is taken by Stiglitz (1999a) who, having suggested mass privatization to have been a foreseeable debacle, considers decentralization to be a more favorable alternative to privatization in many instances; in decentralization decisionmaking. In decentralization, he argues, decisionmaking is pushed down to a level where stakeholders can guard their interests without presuming extensive legal machinery, that itself will take a long time to evolve.

[163] *See* above, Section V, Subsection D.

[164] On structural changes for the development of a dynamic private sector, *see* Cook, Kirkpatrick and Nixson (1998).

IX. Conclusions

Having addressed means for removing incentives and opportunities to engage in corruption, particularly by highlighting the range of possible structural measures aimed at affecting the nature, scope and province of governmental activity purposeful in curbing corruption, I proceeded to discuss important lessons and shortcomings of each mechanism. For example, one means addressed was the removal of a government activity in its entirety, such as through the elimination of both inefficient regulations and corruption-ridden programs or through privatization. Another means I looked at included introducing competition among public agents, with the intended effect of having agents monitor one another, as well as removing the monopoly power agents enjoy and the gains that may be accrued therewith in the delivery of a service.[165] At an institutional level, monopoly power can be decreased by a separation of functions among sub-units, and at a constitutional level by a separation of functions among different institutions. Alternatively, government can induce competition between both public and private firms, in the provision of goods and services similarly affecting any agent's or agencies monopoly power. Moreover, government may increase competition between firms by deregulating a market and/or instituting and observing anti-trust laws, which reduce the gains private parties can acquire by making payoffs.

Other strategies I addressed for affecting the desirability and opportunity for corrupt payoffs included measures aimed at aligning the interests of agents with those of the principal, by such means as making pay conditional on performance and not seniority, or increasing salaries to reduce the need for corrupt payoffs and increase the costs of losing ones job. Similarly, an important means of targeting opportunities and incentives for corruption, is by focusing on the procedures of selection and screening. The provision of a corrupt service is largely dependent on parties being able to search for and identify one another, form an agreement and deliver on promises. Where an agent is, for example, recruited via nepotism or patronage, it is probable that these costs are substantially lower than in the case of an official that has been selected according to merit, and must locate partners from scratch.

One important lesson we learned was that in general reforms that increase administrative efficiency also decrease corruption. Given that administrative inefficiency may create red tape, it may provide reasons for corrupt payoffs. Moreover, it may make decisions and outcomes less observable, providing room

---

[165] Furthermore, monopoly power within an organization can be decreased by providing for hierarchical review of decisions. Similarly, an important means of reducing incentives and opportunities for corruption as discussed in chapter VI below is by redrawing rules, organizational aims, and procedures more clearly and by making them more open to public observation.

for actions that do not draw suspicion as they are indiscernible from other actions. Also we know that poor results may be the outcome of many factors, including malfeasance (*e.g.*, corruption and fraud), nonfeasance (shirking), ethical laxity or erroneous decisions generally. Increasing performance by increasing administrative efficiency reduces the opportunities for all of the above, including corruption.

A point of special significance reiterated throughout this work is that reform measures are generally not good per se, but depend very much on the nature and patterns of illicit reciprocity that have developed. They may simply reallocate discretion to corrupt parties for their own purposes. For this reason, it is imperative that reformers understand the mechanisms that are used to maintain cooperation and understand the vulnerabilities that accompany these factors, in order to assess the importance of a mechanism in fighting corruption in any particular context. The desirability of each measure is subject to several local conditions, and in particular the nature and patterns of illicit reciprocity within systems that have developed. In light of these considerations, I refer the reader to chapter IV, where I focus on means to acquire insider knowledge on the mechanisms of corrupt exchanges.

CHAPTER IV

THINKING SYSTEMS

I. Introduction

In chapter II I outlined the need to step back and think in terms of structures and not individuals. Arising from this, I suggest that there is a need to get inside a corrupt organization to understand the inner-workings of the systems, including: the patterns of payoffs, the mechanisms of exchange, the ability of the parties to sanction, as well as the role and identity of the various actors involved.[1] There are several potential vulnerabilities invoked by corrupt exchanges. Corruption thrives in secrecy, so parties to corruption generally wish to keep the transactions secret. Furthermore, there are particular vulnerabilities in each step taken by parties involved in searching for, agreeing and delivering corrupt deals. Key to curbing corruption, therefore, is information. There are several channels to information and several points of departure. It is helpful to consider parties with knowledge of corruption as falling within a series of concentric circles. On the outside, we have those persons that do not actively engage in corruption but may have some knowledge of the location and types of corruption. As we move closer inside, we progress towards those parties that come into contact with corruption but do not necessarily engage in corrupt exchanges. They enjoy, however, a certain amount of insider knowledge through their proximity to corrupt transactions. At the very inside are those actors that actively engage in corrupt exchanges. They are privy to extensive information on the running of the system and the actors involved. The following discussion is loosely aligned with collecting information from these three different (though non-discrete) layers.

II. Decentralizing monitoring and prosecution

Faced with policing institutions that are poor in uncovering and/or pursuing criminal violations, because of organizational inefficiency, capture or worse still corruption, I suggest a society may be tempted to look at other models of monitoring and enforcement. The most apparent means of doing so is what I term

---

[1] Furthermore, recall the suggestion that reform measures are not necessarily good per se, and that in order to properly understand them, we need to understand corrupt systems. Reforms may actually strengthen or weaken corruption depending on the composition of a corrupt system, a factor that usually goes unmentioned. They shift the allocation of decisions to various actors or institutions, and thus affect chains of interdependence necessary used by corrupt interests to "get things done".

decentralized monitoring and prosecution, which entails generally seeking the reporting, monitoring and sanctioning efforts of the public.

A. Introduction

One can make a general distinction between two contingencies: one where incentives are given to the public to report information to a policing body, *i.e.*, the public has a reporting function and incentives are given to the public to police; and another scenario where incentives are given for the public to go around the policing agency and seek legal recourse itself, *i.e.*, legislating suit provisions that allow third parties to take private action. I identify the former as the reporting function, the latter as the reporting and prosecutorial function. In order for these mechanisms to be successful one needs to provide incentives for the public to offer its services.

B. Reporting by Coercion

As we know, one of the greatest problems with corruption is that it thrives in secrecy. Parties to corrupt transactions naturally have little willingness to come forward and the willingness of private citizens to voluntarily come forward is often poor due to fear of reprisal, the cost involved etc. There are, however, various factors that can increase third parties willingness to come forward. I shall concentrate first on mechanisms that coerce third parties to come forward, before looking at voluntary mechanisms.

Third parties by law frequently do not need to come forward and report criminal activities in cases where they are mere observers. One means of giving incentives to report would be by making it a crime for persons that do not report specific crimes, or intentions of specific crimes.[2] For example, failure to report being witness to an act of bribery may result in criminal prosecution. In this case the law creates a general obligation of compliance with specific laws applicable to all third parties. Such a means that involuntarily forces parties to come forward may, however, be interpreted by the courts as an infringement of basic rights, where willingness to assist may be perceived as a moral issue, one of choice, and not a criminal issue, served by criminal law.

Another coercive means of creating an obligation to report (potentially) criminal activity would be by means of contract. Provisions included in a contract that obligate an employee to report (potentially) criminal activity associated with the firm to a superior (where failure to do so may lead to dismissal) would be permissible in most legal orders, given the voluntarily nature of contractual

---

[2] For example, Israel has a seldom used, controversial law referring to a general requirement of persons to come forward and report a felony before it happens, failure to do so may result in an offense of omission (§ 262 of Israeli Penal Law (1977)).

agreements. To further this mechanism, the law could see to it that such contractual provisions could be used as a defense against criminal liability by the firm.[3] Similar provisions could be drafted for government officials that obligate them to report criminal activity to superiors, as well as for members of sport associations, guilds and private sector organizations.[4]

A third coercive means would be to increase the range of specific positions that statutorily obligate persons to report (certain types of) criminal activity- or alternatively to create this obligation through common law.[5] For example, making it statutory law that members of a political party, aware of cases of laundering illegal funds, are obligated to report this to the authorities would be one such cost effective deterrent against corruption. This approach may also be expanded to professional organizations such as banks, making it mandatory that they inform on activities which they suspect to be criminal.[6]

Coercive rules and laws may have the advantage that by passing a law, they may create both obligations and expectations. The mere fact that something is law or contractually binding may be enough for some to follow their duties, particularly if they associate a value with following laws and codes of conduct above their own inconvenience. As Sunstein (1995: 971) suggests, "[p]eople can agree on rules being binding, or authoritative, without agreeing on a high theory of why it is binding, and without agreeing that the rule is good." Coercive rules, however, being that they are by definition forced upon parties are more often than not predictably unlikely to make a significant impact on reporting, when they do not enjoy widespread support. This point is often reiterated in the discussion of the "top-down" model of law. The core concept of the "top-down" model of the law is that laws may be introduced effectively into a society without them growing from the popular norms of that society. The "bottom-up" model of the law is its antithesis, suggesting that laws should have their roots in the norms of a

---

[3] *See* further, Chapter VI, Section VI.

[4] For example professional boxers in order to attain and maintain their licenses frequently have to adhere a regulation that if someone offers them a bribe, they must report it.

[5] For example, social workers, frequently by law need to report domestic violence (*see*, for example, § 368d of the Israeli Penal Law (1977), S.H. 236). Other common examples include doctors that need to report if pregnant mothers are drug users.

[6] Obligating banks and other commercial associations to report (potentially) criminal activity involves monitoring costs for these private organizations that need to be taken into account. It would be unwise to adopt a general obligation on banks to root out such activity given the potential costs for banks of screening every transaction. On the other hand, where the obligation refers to organizations being knowingly aware of such actions a potential moral hazard problem is created, where banks have no incentives to investigate possible offenders. A standard needs to be set between being knowingly aware of (potential) criminal behavior and a more costly general obligation to root out such behavior (given the moral hazard problem), such as perhaps a reasonableness standard.

society in order to enjoy a broad base of support, greater effectiveness and sustainability.

Pertinent to our discussion here, Galtung (1998) postulates that in order for rules to be effective and sustainable they need to be perceived as both credible, *i.e.*, as good rules enjoying widespread support, and feasible, *i.e.*, as being realizable or attainable. When a rule is not considered credible, it will not be supported and may have the opposite effect from that which was intended. When a rule is not feasible it does not enjoy widespread support, as parties believe the costs of supporting it to be exorbitant and the law to be ineffectual. I shall concentrate next on creating voluntary means for parties to come forward.

C. Reporting by Incentives: Giving Incentives to Peripheral Actors

In the introduction I suggested it helpful to consider parties with knowledge of corruption as falling within a series of concentric circles. On the outside, are those persons that do not actively engage in corruption but may have some information or desire to acquire such information on the location and types of malfeasance. Moving closer inside, we advance towards those parties that come into contact with corruption but are not necessarily engaged in corrupt exchanges; these persons enjoy a certain amount of insider knowledge through their proximity to corrupt exchanges. At the very core are those persons that actively engage in corrupt exchanges, who share extensive knowledge of the running of the system and the identity of the actors involved. In this section, I concentrate in large part on the incentives facing the outer most layer, which I term peripheral actors, *i.e.*, third parties who may possess information but are not actively engaged or connected with particular corrupt exchanges.

Parties are often unwilling to report corrupt activity, for several reasons. Specifically, these include:

- A belief that the action is not serious enough to be reported, i.e., the action is not wrong or sufficiently wrong.
- A fear of retaliation
- A belief that effective action will not follow
- A belief that evidence is not sufficient to warrant reporting the action
- A belief that the events have little impact on the observer (for example, she is not a supervisor and it is not her job to do something, so someone else should take care of it).

(Adapted from Gorta and Forell 1995: 321)

Where these concerns are not dealt with reforms may fail. This is particularly the case with regard to recruiting the assistance of the public and its knowledge in order to curb corruption. Hong Kong provides an example of how educating the public on the harms of corruption and enlisting its support can function in anti-corruption efforts. In particular, the Communities Relations Department in Hong Kong is an example of how information can be gathered on inefficiency and corruption from citizens and professional organizations (Klitgaard, MacLean-Abaroa and Parris 2000: 44). These activities were arranged as part of larger measures taken by and within the Independent Commission Against Corruption (ICAC) established by statute in 1974, whose stated purpose was to fight corruption in Hong Kong.[7]

Among the steps taken were the following:

- It set up a separate department in the Commission, the Community Relations Department
- It set up eight regional offices where the public had easy access to the commission and from which it could use as a base to work with community leaders and local organizations
- It set up monthly meetings in every regional office where members of the community could make its sentiment known, the results of which were analyzed at headquarters
- It set up target audiences in the community to pass on the message to other groups. In doing so it divided the community into distinct groups and concentrated its educational efforts on community teachers, managers and other leader who then passed on the message to their respective groups.
- It used many means of communication from enlisting the help of the press and in order to increase public exposure to face to face communication
- It set up a Citizen's Advisory Committee on Community Relations, chaired by the Commissioner and composed of figures from the media, public relations, pedagogues, legislative and municipal councils and the academia

(Adapted from de Speville 1997: 30)

1. Social Marketing Strategies

Citizens are an indispensable tool to curb corruption. They furnish information on transgressions, areas of weaknesses and in some instances offer an insider

---

[7] *See* further, Chapter VII, where we discuss the strategies adopted by the International Commission against Corruption (ICAC) in greater detail. By no means the only Independent Commission against Corruption, nor the eldest, it has shown itself to be among the most successful and most discussed models among reformers (*see* Klitgaard 1988; Klitgaard, MacLean-Abaroa and Parris 2000). Other countries and regions with similar models include New South Wales, Australia, Singapore and Malaysia; the latter two predate the Hong Kong initiative.

perspective on the functioning of corrupt systems. Another far more subtle, but particularly important role in curbing malfeasance manifests itself in the form of social sanctions and dividends that shape individual behavior delineating what is socially desirable or sanctionable- without which the costs of law enforcement would be exorbitant and unattainable. The government must tap into this resource and mobilize opinion against corrupt behavior, using norms to shape actions and making malfeasance socially reprehensible; put differently, it should mobilize the use of social approval and disapproval to overcome the collective action problem inherent in sanctioning.[8] Indeed, it is well-established in economic theory that reputation is a key factor in the maintenance of social customs (see Akerlof 1980). If a negative value is associated with approval or disapproval then changing the level of social approval or disapproval will offer incentives to change behavior.

By identifying behavior that is socially desirable such as not engaging in corruption and reproaching others that pursue corrupt exchanges, it should try to create expectations and obligations and market the belief that those that fail to do their part are free-riders. Moreover, it should tap into the notion of meta-norms discussed in chapter II- second order sanctions to support a norm or expectation- to stabilize these expectations. The powers of the forces of social approval and disapproval are captured wonderfully in the following taken from Gächter and Fehr (1999: 342).

> "During World War I an important tool of the British government to 'persuade' adult males to join the army were big posters. The posters made it clear that non-subscription constitutes free-riding and deserves the contempt of the British people. One poster showed, for example a father with his two children and the subtitle was: "Daddy, what did YOU do in the Great War?" Some posters exerted social pressure by appealing to the girl friends of potential soldiers: "If you don't want to marry a wimp, send him to the army." Another techniques to mobilise social disapproval was the free distribution of red badges. They could be attached to a free rider's front door saying that the person living there was a dodger. Such government activities obviously only make sense if one assumes that social (dis)approval affects the behavior of potential subscribers."

2. Retaliation and Anonymity

In order to abate third parties' fear of retaliation, the government can employ the use of hotlines and dropboxes. There are, however, virtues and vices of using hotlines and dropboxes, both stemming from the fact that they are low cost and anonymous means of reporting. The benefits of such a measure are naturally that given the low cost of reporting there are a larger number of complaints. The

---

[8] *See* further, Chapter V, Section II.

problems therewith are that given there is little or no cost of reporting in most cases, we can expect many false claims motivated by unflattering factors, such as jealousy, opportunism etc. Traditional game theoretical solutions that involve separating the good from the bad (separating equilibrium) may not work here. For example, one means of separating suggests that parties should incur a cost of reporting that is prohibitively high for the disingenuous leaving just bona fide reporters of information who have internalized a norm or value. Another means would be that informers provide enough information so specific or detailed that it is most likely the truth. These mechanisms probably cannot work here because anonymity may be compromised. A similar device for gathering information is through surveys.[9]

Hotlines and dropboxes are sources that enable the anonymous passage of information without retribution. Parties with valuable information can oftentimes select between anonymous and nonanonymous communication. Anonymity facilitates communication, whilst lowering the chances of retribution (We shall see in later sections how the gain associated with anonymity may also be combined with a reward structure). There are many everyday examples where anonymity is encouraged in order to ascertain information. For example, students frequently evaluate their teachers anonymously which encourages feedback, and businesses occasionally provide drop boxes for suggestions and complaints on their services and staff (Levmore 1996: 2193). This is a form of third party monitoring assisted by minimizing retaliation through emphasis on anonymity. There may be a tradeoff between reliability of the information on the one hand (increased through identification) and incentives to communicate information on the other (facilitated through being able to provide information anonymously) (ibid.: 2194-5). When we consider that allegations of corruption may warrant investigation and necessary costs for the investigated party, it is only natural that we want to increase the reliability of the information we receive, but still encourage informants to come forward. Information is, however, incremental, i.e., information may not be very valuable on its own but may be valuable when assembled with other pieces of information.[10] What we get from one source may not be enough to warrant a proper investigation, but the value of the information is important particularly when eminent danger can be averted.

---

[9] The approach taken in Hong Kong should form part of a much slower process to encourage reporting of and abstinence from criminal activity, through the creation and enforcement of norms that are conducive to civic behavior. For example, through the publication of information, such as education on the costs of crime and corruption and praise for persons that uphold the law, the government can encourage norms conducive to legal behavior (Posner and Rasmusen 1999). It can also foster guilt and shame. Guilt and shame are naturally especially difficult to create or to change. They are shaped by social conditioning, which is not quickly or easily altered by individuals or governments (ibid. : 379).

[10] Given that tips may lead to an invasion of privacy, information, when it is not reliable and there is no immediate cost must be used incrementally, in the sense described above.

An alternative system is the use of an intermediary by an informer to avoid confrontation, maintain anonymity and increase the reliability of the information (*see ibid.*: 2199-2236). In our case, there are a host of intermediaries that can provide this function. I shall concentrate on just one here- nonprofit organizations. Put differently, my central suggestion here is that one way to overcome the problem of reliability of information is for citizens to make claims to nonprofit organizations, who then pass on these claims to the government without revealing the identity of the persons that made the claims.

Citizen oversight can be increased by enlisting the help of nonprofits in reporting. Citizens may be less willing to disclose nonanonymously improprieties to government officials than to nonprofits, mainly because they perceive the fear of retaliation to be too high. However, as adumbrated above, anonymous information is less reliable than nonanonymous information. Nonprofits may provide a sort of filtering function, their presence an indication that the information is reliable (given the associated reputation cost of false information). Furthermore, citizens that report anonymously are likely not to reveal any specific information for fear of giving away their identity. Nonprofits can develop specialized capacities in determining which information compromises anonymity and which is most valuable. The government can take some fundamental steps in order to facilitate the workability of nonprofits that provide a reporting function: it can, for example, provide tax incentives for third parties that donate to these agencies, it can facilitate the setting up of charter, or it can provide both technical and financial support.

Note, the aforementioned intermediary function could also be provided by a highly respected member with standing in a community. His reputation serves as a bond for both the informant and for the government: For the government his reputation is an indication that the information is accurate; for the informant, his reputation serves as a bond against further nondisclosure of his identity. I concentrated here on the possible intermediary function of nonprofit organizations, alternative sources, however, include journalists, lawyers, priests and other members in a community with standing. Furthermore, in this section I only concentrated on the usefulness of nonprofits as intermediaries with the function of retaining informant anonymity whilst simultaneously making information more reliable. This should not, however, take away from the rich role of services provided by nonprofits in efforts to curb corruption.

D. Citizen Suits

An alternative mechanism to the above would be to more actively engage the citizen in enforcement and oversight.[11] Although this may *a priori* appear to be an immoderate position, upon closer inspection one can see that private enforcement is a prevalent characteristic of the existing social and economic system. It is commonly used to enforce areas of contract, tort and property law, where parties either go through the court, bargain in the shadow of the law, or use of more informal sanctions such as discontinuation of on-going relationships, thereby revoking future business from the violator.[12] Within firms, when a violation is discovered employers frequently sanction illegal behavior by dismissing employees. Similarly, within associations, criminal activity frequently leads to revocation of a license or ostracism. Expanding the use of private enforcement implies that enforcement is no longer strictly confined to public law or to public officials but is expanded to private parties and forces. This seems *a priori* to be an attractive model of monitoring and enforcement when policing institutions are deficient in uncovering and/or pursuing criminal violations, due to administrative inefficiency, capture or corruption. Here I focus on one special feature of decentralized monitoring, namely citizen suits. Not wishing to get too deep into the legal quagmire behind the issue of citizen suits, particularly relating to the right of standing, I make only provisional comments on the use of citizen suits as a decentralized monitoring tool with specific regard to corruption..

By citizen suits here, I refer to the granting of standing authority to private parties to sue both agencies on the one hand that fail to enforce laws and firms on the other that refuse to follow them. Where such suits are permitted, it is not uncommon for courts to be authorized to award injunctive relief or impose penalties. Though subject to multifarious legal and particularly constitutional differences, many legal orders provide for room such provisions.[13] For example,

---

[11] The reader may recognize this discussion touches upon early approaches in the law and economics literature on the optimal means of enforcement of the law and particularly the demarcation between public and private enforcement, as pioneered by Becker and Stigler (1974). According to the proposal put forward by Becker and Stigler (*ibid.*), a private enforcer would be entitled to investigate and redress violations. If successful, he could retain the entire proceeds of the suit or fine paid by the violator; if unsuccessful, he would have to reimburse the defendant her legal expenses. To my knowledge, however, outside of the discussion on private tax enforcement, this has not yet received attention in the corruption literature.

[12] On these points, *see* Landes and Posner (1975: 1).

[13] One notable exception is Germany, where German law virtually proscribes private parties from suing for the benefit of public interests. Even in the U.S. where citizen suits are widely implemented, the question of the constitutionality of such suits is commonly raised, based on the principal of standing and the transferal of executive powers to private parties. Such notables as Justice Scalia of the Supreme Court, in an article of the same name, have suggested

options are available for most environmental statutes in the U.S. that include an explicit provision permitting private plaintiffs to sue dischargers to require compliance with the law (Rose-Ackerman 1999: 169).[14] If the suit is successful the plaintiffs obtain discharge compliance with the rule but do not obtain damages; legal fees of successful or "substantially prevailing plaintiffs" are normally reimbursed (ibid.: 170).[15] In particular, experiments with environmental law in the United States, particularly, the Clean Water Act[16] and Clean Air Act[17] are one area where citizen suits have on the whole been successfully employed by peripheral parties.[18] Citizen suits may be used for two broad purposes: First, they may be used against the unlawfully inadequate enforcement of the law by agencies and administrations. Second, they are a mechanism aimed at pursuing substantive penalties against defendants who were inadequately monitored by government agencies and policing authorities.[19] They provide a mechanism with which to sanction monitoring institutions poor who failed to uncover and/or pursue transgressions, as well as a means to sanction those private sector companies that enjoyed weak oversight. From the perspective of corruption control, citizen suits have the following attributes that should be taken into consideration: *First,* they provide an additional oversight mechanism over the

---

that "the doctrine of standing is an essential element of the separation of powers doctrine (Scalia 1983)." Compare this, however, to Sunstein (1992).

[14] Perhaps recognizing potential advantages of decentralized monitoring and enforcement, private rights of action or citizen suit provisions are used extensively in the United States. These areas include: "important elements of antitrust [see 15 U.S.C. §§ 15, 26 (1994) creating private rights of action under federal antitrust laws], consumer protection [see ibid. § 2060(a) citizen-suit provision of the Consumer Product Safety Act], environmental policy [noteworthy examples include 33 U.S.C. § 1365 (1994) (citizen provision of Clean Water Act)]; 42 U.S.C. § 6972 (1994) (citizen-suit provision of Resource Conservation and Recovery Act); 42 U.S.C. § 9659 (1988) (citizen-suit provision of Comprehensive Environmental Response, Compensation and Liability Act)], equal employment opportunity [42 U.S.C. § 2000e-5(f)(1) (1988)], securities [See Insider Trading and Securities Fraud Act of 1988, Pub. L. No. 100-704, § 21A(e), 102 Stat. 4677, 4679], and taxation [See 26 C.F.R. § 301.7623-1 (1995) (allowing payment of bounties to individuals who provide information leading to recovery of underpaid taxes)]" (Kovacic 1996: 1809).

[15] Of course, such provisions are concentrated for use by those we termed above, peripheral actors (i.e., third parties outside of the illegal activity). In later sections, we concentrate on incentives for proximate actors or snitches (third parties somehow connected with the illegal activity). For yet more examples, see Sunstein (1992: 165 n.11).

[16] 33 U.S.C. §§ 1251-1376 (1994).

[17] 42 U.S.C. § 7604 (1994).

[18] As Sunstein (1992: 221) notes, "There is good reason to believe that the citizen suit has indeed helped bring about greater compliance with law."

[19] Indicative of this two-pronged enforcement associated with citizen suits are the early pattern of actions that emerged under the Clean Water Act (1982) where in the period between 1984 and 1988 there were 800 suits files and the government found itself as defendant in 165 of these cases (ibid.: 220).

administration to ensure that it works effectively, particularly in respect to enforcing established rules and laws, providing a possible check on malicious, invidious, and malfunctioning prosecutorial discretion generally (*see* Thompson 2000: 192). For example in the United States the Clean Air Act is, as Blomquist (1988: 383) puts it "in essence, a model of citizens as prodders of governmental enforcement of environmental rules, the citizen as 'gadfly for agency action.'" *Second*, they provide an additional oversight mechanism over third parties who potentially break the law.[20] *Third*, citizen suits potentially lessen the payoffs associated with bribing and capturing the administration, given that violations, such as ignoring environmental regulations or quality standards, will be more actively monitored by third parties. Similarly, they increase both the probability of detection as well as the probability of enforcement. This factor may be mitigated somewhat by the possibility of collusion between agencies and firms against citizen suits.[21] *Fourth*, they may increase the punishment handed out to violators, when third parties are also entitled to sue for civil penalties in addition to the penalties sought by government. *Fifth*, they provide a means for third parties of going around administrations and directly to the courts, instead of reporting to the administrations themselves, a factor that can be crucial in overcoming an negligent or corrupt administration. *Sixth*, they may lessen the administrative costs of enforcement incurred by society. *Seventh*, they may encourage participatory democracy and democratic values. Standing, as adumbrated above, potentially

---

[20] This is commonly of varying degrees and depends on the potential penalties and proceedings involved. For example, in the U.S. as noted by Blomquist (1988: 384), "[i]n contradistinction [to the Clean Air Act], The Clean Water act establishes a model of citizens as prosecutors where the penalty provisions threaten substantial liabilities, and proceedings to impose these charges assume many of the features of a criminal prosecution."

[21] The availability of citizen suits as a tool to monitor both non-complying firms and the administration can be affected through the use of collusion. The recent Supreme Court case Friends of the Earth, Inc. v. Laidlaw Environmental Services (TOC), Inc. highlights one particular case of collusion, based on the premise behind most environmental statutes that citizen suits are barred from proceeding if the government is diligently prosecuting the violations in question (Spence 2001: 940). The facts of Friends of the Earth, Inc. v. Laidlaw Environmental Services (TOC), Inc. are outlined by Spence below.
"Landlaw concerned a defendant who had repeatedly violated the terms of its Clean Water Act permit. After receiving notice that the plaintiff intended to bring a citizen suit against it, Laidlaw sought to bar the citizen suit by persuading the state agency to institute a sham enforcement action covering the permit violations. Laidlaw drafted the state agency's complaint, paid the filing fee, and settled the state enforcement action by agreeing to a relatively modest fine and vaguely promising to address the source of the violations. Laidlaw then argued that because the Clean Water Act bars citizen suits in the face of diligently prosecuted government enforcement actions, the plaintiffs' citizen suit ought to be dismissed. At the urging of the plaintiffs and the EPA, the District Court rejected that claim, stating that the state enforcement action was not the kind of "diligent prosecution" that could bar citizen suits under the statute (Spence 2001: 940-41). (Laidlaw's appeal to the Supreme Court did not challenge the District Court's conclusion" (*ibid.*: 941 n.92.).

allows citizens and organizations to make a legal claim or seek judicial enforcement of a duty or right. When someone is personally aggrieved by a wrongdoing, a simple right of standing may be enough to get parties to come forward and no monitory incentive tied to a fine imposed by the courts may be necessary. Affording parties a right of standing does however present some legal problems of its own and comes at a cost. As Wade and Forsyth (1999: 667) note: "It has always been an important limitation on the availability of remedies that they are awarded only to litigants who have sufficient *locus standi*, or standing. The law starts from the position that remedies are correlative with rights, and that only those whose rights are at stake are eligible to be awarded remedies."[22] Lenient standing may be seen in some quarters as infringing upon the rights of those who are subject to litigation. In some instances, it may even give the impression or opportunity for vigilante justice (Blomquist 1988). This argument is further bolstered by the fact that civil litigation may not guarantee the same level of procedural fairness (*ibid.*). Another argument commonly put forward against more lenient laws of standing is that it may 'open the floodgates' leaving the courts swamped with litigation.[23] In some cases, there may be no need to award the right of standing because interested parties would arguably already monitor and report information to the authorities. However, in the case of an inept agency that fails to follow up on violations, the willingness to monitor and report of the public is oftentimes reduced as they see that their complaints are not being pursued. When we offer standing, we give the private association an ability to take action and go around the institution.

For less developed countries where there are often enormous judicial backlogs and judicial inertia, the floodgate argument must be taken into consideration.[24] The usefulness of citizen suits may be diminished by the inertia of the judiciary, but these considerations themselves may be exaggerated. For example, India has had some success with affording citizens, affected by unlawful government action, the right to file "Public Interest Actions" that defend the collective rights of the public at large (Rose-Ackerman 1999: 170; Susman 1994).[25] These initiatives have played a role in motivating the courts to force the

---

[22] For a discussion of the historical development of the doctrine of standing in England and the United States *see* Sunstein (1992).

[23] In the United States, however, another fundamental concern has been voiced as to the constitutionality of standing by the Supreme Court, most notably perhaps in Lujan v. Defenders of Wildlife, 112 S.Ct. 2130 (1992). It was argued that granting lenient standing is a violation of executive powers and Article II of the Constitution and Article III of the Constitution.

[24] *See* further, Chapter VII, Section II.

[25] In the case of India, the court reversed completely common practice in both British-based and American common law system. The Supreme Court even obliged the petitioner "to have no personal, political or financial interest of any kind in the public interest litigation brought" (Susman 1994: 70). Susman (ibid.: 76) goes on to say that "it appears that the Indian Supreme

government to pursue allegations of corruption against senior officials (Rose-Ackerman 1999: 170.). Traditional concerns regarding the aforementioned floodgate argument do not seem to have manifested themselves (Susman 1994). Another aspect that should be mentioned in regard to citizen suits is the potential adverse reputation loss for firms that are exposed to them, thus acting as a deterrent against improbity, but also as a cost of doing business and a potential instrument for strategic use by competitors.[26]

Moreover, it is widely recognized that prosecutors do not always prosecute for noncompliance with rules and regulations.[27] As any reasonable person will readily admit, the reasons for non-compliance are multifaceted and are not necessarily suggestive of bribery or corruption. Much noncompliance may be a result of a complexity of factors, such as persons not being cognizant of a regulation or other stochastic contingencies.[28] As Thompson (2000: 190) notes: "A perfect compliance rate, of course, is unrealistic and even undesirable. Violations often result from stochastic human and equipment failures that are neither intentional nor negligent. Regulated entities cannot avoid failures of this sort or can avoid them only at exorbitant expense." Citizen suits may adversely affect enforcement and prosecutorial discretion. There are trade-offs to be made between those instances where noncompliance is the result of inadvertent factors, such as mistake or failure to understand regulations in their entirety and more insidious circumstances such as willful neglect.[29] The key point I wish to make is this: Citizen suits have the potential to limit both socially beneficial enforcement and prosecutorial discretion, as well as socially deleterious. The fact then that citizen suits may not take into account the complex motivations behind noncompliance, a factor implicit to the use of prosecutorial discretion, may be an inherent flaw. Nevertheless, although clear and obvious indications are not available that citizen suits may on the aggregate be beneficial, given that they are subject to a host of local and particularly legal considerations, they are a factor deserved of more attention and analysis in the literature on corruption control.

Court, appropriately, does not view the petitioners as the real parties in interests at all, but rather as public agents for those parties."

[26] See further, Chapter VI, Section VI discussing corporate liability.

[27] See above, Chapter III, Section VII on procurement.

[28] See above, Chapter III, Section IV.

[29] In a similar vein in the context of citizen suits in environmental law in the United States, Spence (2001 : 940) notes: "Citizen enforcement is ...plagued by a split, rooted in the debate over the rational polluter model, between the model's implication that citizen enforcement is a necessary check against capture on the one hand, and the need for flexibility and discretion in environmental enforcement implied by the complexity critique on the other. Light handed enforcement may be an appropriate response to inadvertent violations, it may also be an indication of regulatory capture."

E. Reporting by Incentives: Giving Incentives to Central Actors

Previously, I concentrated largely on the use of citizen suits, which are primarily a tool of peripheral actors, falling on the outside of the concentric circles of actors with knowledge of malfeasance. Moving in a level, I shall now focus on central actors, *i.e.*, those actors that are not necessarily a party to malfeasance, but come into contact with corruption, cognizant of a certain amount of insider knowledge through their proximity to corrupt exchanges.[30] One can conjure up at least three types of relations: collegial, contractual and competitive. The first category refers to colleagues and peers in a public or private organization, both principals and agents. The second refers to those persons that are in a contractual relationship with parties partaking in a corrupt system, such as accountants, lawyers and subcontractors. The third refers to those organizations that are in competition for government business such as private firms.

Previously reported, the most prevalent reasons for not reporting corruption or criminal action commonly include: A belief that the action is not serious enough to be reported, *i.e.*, the action is not wrong or sufficiently wrong; a fear of retaliation; a belief that effective action will not follow; a belief that evidence is not sufficient to warrant reporting the action; and a belief that the events have little impact on the observer (because of his or her position in the organization or otherwise). As one moves from peripheral to central actors, the disincentives for reporting are in most cases multiplied, in large part because of the inability to remain anonymous.[31] Perhaps the most important potential whistleblowers are collegial and it is here I address for the greater part in the following sections. Furthermore, I concentrate primarily on the experiences in the United States, where such provisions are most extensive and subject to important discussion, providing a yardstick for other countries interested in introducing similar provisions.

---

[30] The incentives facing the two groups are very different. For example, in the case of proximate actors, suits may be used for strategic purposes, particularly in the case of competitors.

[31] The obvious exception being that of competitors, who may be victims of the corrupt practices of others, which affect them directly, and may be very willing to come forward.

1. Whistleblower Protection

> "Unless you are in a position to retire or are independently wealthy, don't do it. Don't put your head up because it will be blown off."[32]

Largely the product of hearings concerning fears over the effectiveness and inadequacy of the Civil Service Reform Act's whistleblower protections,[33] Congress in 1989 passed the Whistleblower Protection Act of 1989.[34] The House's stated purpose for this act was to "strengthen and improve protections for the rights of Federal employees, to prevent reprisals, and to help eliminate wrongdoing within the government..."[35] It consisted largely of amendments to provisions enacted or amended in the Civil Service Reform Act just over a decade earlier.[36] Whistleblower protection statutes generally protect an employee from

---

[32] *See* Senate Hearings on S.508, Whistleblower Protection Act of 1987, Committee on Governmental Affairs, 100th Cong., 1st Sess., 20 and 31 July 1987 (statement of Senator Carl Levin). *Cited* in Anerchiarico and Jacobs 1996: 64-65.

[33] The transit towards offering greater protection to whistleblowers in the United States. was marked by the federal Civil Service Reform Act of 1978 (CSRA) which established three new organizations: the Office of Personnel Management (OPM), responsible for the general administration of the civil service system; the Merit System Protection Board (MSPB), empowered to hold hearings and appeals of federal employees' grievances; and the Office of Special Council (OSC), an external control agency responsible for investigating allegations of waste, fraud, and abuse and complaints of reprisal by federal employees. Anerchiarico and Jacobs (1996: 64).

[34] Whistleblower Protection Act of 1989, 5 U.S.C.§ 2302, Pub. L. No. 101-12, 103 Stat. 16 (1989). In addition to a deluge of local laws following the 1978 and 1989 Acts, there are continuous introductions and innovations at federal level in the United States. For example the 1994 Anticorruption Act introduced the fact that whistleblowers, who were previously obligated to report to a specific party allegations of wrongdoing, now faced no specific requirement of to whom offenses should be reported, as well as authorized treble backpay and imprisonment sentences of up to five years for retaliating officers (Anerchiarico and Jacobs 1996: 66).

[35] 5 U.S.C.A. § 1201.

[36] Anechiarico and Jacobs suggest that the Whistleblower Protection Act of 1989 reinforced the whistleblowing machinery in five ways.
1. It made the OSC (Office of Special Council) more independent of the MSPB (Merit System Protection Board) so that it would be an advocate for self-proclaimed whistleblowers, rather than a watchdog for the merit system.
2. It permitted whistleblowers the option of bypassing the OSC entirely and taking their complaints to the MSPB.
3. It lowered the standard of proof necessary to make out a case of protected whistleblowing. The employee must show that his or her disclosure of information was "a factor" (rather than the *predominant or motivating factor*) in the subsequent negative personnel action or inaction.

demotion, dismissal and reallocation, and may grant assurances against actions such as failure to promote as a result of a person coming forward with information. Their aim is to create an environment conducive to whisleblowing by reducing the costs thereof. Given that whistleblower protection is receiving increased attention by governments, in large part it must be added as a result of the recent climate of anti-corruption efforts, I have assembled a list of prerogative questions worthy of consideration in Table 1.

Table 1: Prerogative Questions When Drafting Whistleblower Protection Legislation: A Guideline

Contentious and salient issues in whistleblowing laws include:

- Who is covered by the statute? Does it include only government employees or also private parties? In the case that it covers only government employees, must the information be acquired during employment in order to receive protections and possible benefits afforded to a whistleblower? (*see*, for example, the United Kingdom Whistleblower Protection Bill 1995).
- Is there a certain chain of command that must be followed or can one go straight to the media and other sources? (*see*, for example, the Swedish solution where public servants can blow the whistle to anyone even the press and are protected against exposure).
- Similarly, should an independent agency to hear complaints be established (as was the case in the United States)?
- What resources should be granted to the whistleblower?
- Should he receive financial compensation or monetary allowances for costs that cover his expenses and inconvenience?
- When can the whistleblower remain anonymous?
- What are the penalties for erroneous, mischievous or strategic complaints?
- Against what type of personnel actions can an employee appeal (for example, can an employee appeal against reassignment as in the 1989 Whistleblower Protection Act in the United States)?
- Should an employee prove he was discriminated against or can the burden of proof be reversed where a senior official or department head needs to prove whistleblowing actions were not a factor in his decision making?

---

4. It provided that once an employee showed that the disclosure was a factor in the negative personnel action or inaction, the burden of proof shifted to the agency, which must prove that it would have taken the same personnel actions regardless of the disclosure.
5. It authorized lawyers' fees in the event that the whistleblower prevailed before the MSPB. (Anerchiarico and Jacobs 1996: 65).

1.1. Collegial Incentives

Although whistleblower protection laws are practically prerequisite for officials blowing the whistle on others within their own organization, these laws may, however, by themselves prove insufficient, as they present an employee with little incentive to come forward given that she receives no personal gain and incurs a probable loss. Consider the list of criteria that need to be satisfied in order for an official to report criminal or corrupt activity. An actor will generally only blow the whistle if a series of contingencies arise.[37] First of all, she must consider an action to have been unlawful. Second, she must consider this act to be sufficiently unlawful to warrant complaint and the consequences of complaint to approximate the punishment.[38] Third, she must feel that she is in a position to do something about this action. Fourth, reporting an act must bare consequence for the perpetrators. Fifth, she must assess his costs of taking the action (monetary, violence, ostracism, reputation loss, psychological etc.) and weigh them against her benefits (psychological factors, praise etc.). Sixth, she must decide that she is going to take action, thus overcoming the free rider problem (one factor which may play a role here is her seniority in the organization.). Failure to report may be the result of the nonfulfillment of any one of the above steps.

1.2. Competitive Relations

Already identified by Becker and Stigler (1974) three decades ago, the quality of enforcement is greatly affected by whether or not there is a victim, *i.e.*, an individual that bares much of the cost of the violation. As they suggest: "The customer of the numbers game or of the prostitute or of the marijuana peddler is not, in his opinion, a loser by these activities, as contrasted (say) to the person who is burglarized or charged more than the permissible rent" (*ibid.*: 4). Corruption is regularly perceived as a victimless crime, but this is oftentimes not the case. In the case of government procurement contracts, housing, or licensing (particularly with fixed supply), more often than not there is an aggrieved party. Enlisting the assistance of these parties can be an important factor in curbing corruption. Although there are obvious costs of providing platforms for complaint, they are especially important in unveiling corruption. Such platforms can take many descriptions. For example, in the case of procurement contracts in the United States, as we have seen earlier,[39] an aggrieved bidder for a federal contract may launch a protest to the agency, the General Accounting Office, the United States Court of Federal Claims, or a federal district court. Moreover, federal

---

[37] A similar list is provided by Dozier and Miceli (1985) cited in Gorta and Forell (1995: 321).

[38] When an official reports an offense, he no longer has control over the punishment. When he considers the punishment unfitting, he is unlikely to report the crime.

[39] *See* above, Chapter III, Section VII on procurement.

agencies have, according to an executive order in late 1995, established alternative dispute resolution procedures for bid protests (*See* Federal Acquisition Regulation, FAR 33.103). Given that bidders key means for defrauding the government in procurement contracts, oftentimes assisted by government officials, are as a result of information asymmetry (cost of supplies, quality of goods and services etc.) which effectively grants discretion to contractors, competitors must be considered as insiders sharing much of this knowledge. They can therefore be used as a tool to limit the discretion of both corrupt firms and agents, as well as a willing actor that may reveal the mechanisms of defrauding government.

In their comparative survey of the law applicable to bribery in thirteen jurisdictions,[40] in all but Japan, a state-owned party has the remedy of nonperformance of a contract, if it were acquired through bribery. In all the jurisdictions, the government, can under civil law seek pecuniary remedies from the bribe giver, and in almost half of the jurisdictions from the bribe receiver (Hepkema and Booysen 1997: 416). Practically all legal systems allow victims to recover for damages as a result of bribery. The losing party has normally a remedy against the bribe giver and in eight jurisdictions against the state-owned party. Remedies include actions for damages, but also injunctions and annulment of contract and restitution (*ibid.*: 416).

There are, however, reasons why firms do not seek tort damages. First, corruption is secretive and the evidentiary requirements are often prohibitive, although the standard of proof is normally lower in private actions than in criminal cases. Secondly, the legal system may be lethargic and ill-functioning. Thirdly, damages may be diffused, making it profitless to file a suit. Fourth, a firm may be subjected to harassment and threats. Threats may also be more subtle and come in the form of threats to withhold factors of production or even labor.[41] Fifth, there may be the threat of blackmail for previous improprieties conducted by the firm.

Victims have a stake in apprehending violators particularly when they receive restitution (Becker and Stigler 1974: 4). They may, therefore, sometimes do the enforcing themselves. Indeed, it may be optimal for society to let victims do the enforcing themselves. As I suggest below, offering a reward system in the form of qui tam suits has many of the characteristics of engaging the victim in private law enforcement.

---

[40] Australia (New South Wales), Belgium, Canada, Chile, Denmark, England, France, Germany, Italy, Japan, the Netherlands, Sweden, United States (New York State).

[41] *See* above, Chapter III, Section VII related to procurement.

Revealing information can be considered a breach of contract or a statutory offense. For example, in the United Kingdom the Official Secrets Act of 1989 creates extensive categories of protected information whose disclosure is commonly a criminal offense. In addition to security or intelligence information, these categories are defense, international relations and law enforcement (Wade and Forsyth 2000: 61). "There is no public interest defence- so the civil servant who makes an unauthorised disclosure in order to reveal serious wrongdoing is as guilty as one who acts in the interests of a foreign power" (*ibid.*). Statutory and contractual obligations are also extended to professionals that are privy to confidential disclosures and information. Let us briefly address, for example, in addition to the factors identified above, the particular incentives for a professional, such as a lawyer or accountant, for coming forward and reporting impropriety. An attorney is normally bound by attorney-client privilege where confidential communications between an attorney and a client in the course of the professional relationship cannot be disclosed without the consent of the client. There is "[a] strong tradition of loyalty attaches to the relationship of attorney and client, and this tradition would be outraged by routine examination of the lawyer as to the client's confidential disclosures regarding professional business."[42]

This, however, does not rule out the possibility that lawyers have a legitimate reporting role to play. In Hepkema and Booysen's comparative survey of the law on bribery in thirteen jurisdictions referred to above, it was found that whether or not, a bribe is paid within or outside of the relevant jurisdiction, the aiding of a client in the committal of a crime constitutes a contravention of the professional codes in all jurisdictions (bar Japan, where it is within the scope of criminal law) (Hepkema and Booysen 1997: 416). There is generally a right but not a duty to report a fellow lawyer's breach of the professional code, exceptions being the U.S., England and Chile where there is both a right and a duty, while neither a right nor a duty exists to report a client's committal of a crime if such report would breach the legal professional privilege or a duty of confidentiality. In American law, for example, the attorney-client privilege protects discussions of past crimes,[43] but it does not extend to the client's intended commission of future crimes.[44] The privilege is bestowed indefinitely, and is not terminated when the attorney/client relationship ends or when either party is deceased.[45] A lawyer may however reveal the intention of his client and the requisite information to avert the

---

[42] John W. Strong, McCormick in Evidence § 87, at 1221-22 (4th ed.1992) in Black's Law Dictionary (1999, 7th ed.) pp. 1214-1215.

[43] U.S. v. Valencia, 541 F.2d 618 (1976).

[44] Clark v. U.S. 289 U.S. 1,15. (1933).

[45] People v. Linden, 338 P.2d 397, 408 (1959); Moore v. Bray, 10 Pa. 519 (1849).

crime.[46] Because a client utilizes advice in a course of action that is criminal or fraudulent does not, on its own, make the lawyer party to the course of action. Nonetheless, "a lawyer may not knowingly assist a client in criminal or fraudulent conduct. There is a critical distinction between presenting an analysis of legal aspects of questionable conduct and recommending the means by which a crime or fraud might be committed with impunity... A lawyer may not continue assisting a client in conduct that the lawyer originally supposes is legally proper but then discovers is criminal or fraudulent."[47] Similarly, in the Unites States, the accountant-client privilege is a statutory privilege in about one-third of the states rendering confidential all communications to accountants.[48] If these communications are not done privately, they are not privileged.[49]

Contrasting the incentives facing a lawyer or accountant with that of a regular government official, we can see that given the specific nature of the duty attended, the possibility of retaining anonymity is lower. Moreover, there would seem to be a reputation cost for the professional greater than that of the government official, given his reliance on maintaining his current clients and attracting new clients in the future, which cannot be secured, as in the case of a civil servant, by government legislation.[50] Whilst whistleblower provisions offer protection against unfair dismissal and retaliatory action in general for a government employee and in some instances for employees in private firms,[51] a lawyer or accountant cannot obligate his clients to stay with him, nor can he seek compensation from the government for future losses. As adumbrated earlier, creating a coercive mandatory requirement to report specific legal actions may be the only effective means of getting these parties to come forward.

Suggestive of the hurdles and uncertainties many third parties face, they are likely to conclude that the risk to their careers is too immense to warrant reporting information on illegal activity (Thompson 2000: 228). It seems plausible then that monetary incentives be granted to third parties who have turned informant in addition to protection from retaliation. In order to animate them to disclose illegal and unethical activity, the size of these monetary incentives for whistleblowing should be at least commensurate to the expected losses for whistleblowers.

---

[46] ABA MODEL CODE OF PROFESSIONAL RESPONSIBILITY DR4-101(c)(3) (1969).
[47] ABA MODEL RULES OF PROFESSIONAL CONDUCT R.1.2 cmt. (1983).
[48] See Cleary (1984: 185).
[49] Fischer v. U.S., 425 U.S. 391, 409 (1976); U.S. v. Gurtner, 474 F.2d 297 (1973).
[50] Moreover, as a more practical consideration, the limited penalizing capacity of professional codes and the legal constraints of legal privilege and the duty of confidentiality, render them more as supplementary rather than substantive tools against corruption (see Hepkema and Booysen 1997: 416).
[51] See False Claims Act discussed below, which ensures protection, in addition to public sector officials, to private sector employees that disclose information.

F. Rewarding Enforcement: Assessing the False Claims Act as a Model

In 1986, Congress in the United States, stemming mostly from fears of defense procurement fraud, enacted the False Claims Amendment Act, broadening the availability and attractiveness of qui tam suits enormously in the US.[52] The False Claims Act creates civil liability for *inter alia* any person who: knowingly presents a false or fraudulent claim for payment or approval; knowingly makes, uses, or causes to be made or used, a false record or statement to get a false or fraudulent claim paid or approved by the government; conspires to defraud the government by making a fraudulent claim; knowingly purchases or receives as an obligation or debt, public property from an officer or employee who is not entitled to do so, or knowingly uses a false record or statement to decrease an obligation to pay money or property to the government.[53,54] A qui tam law statute generally authorizes a private citizen (known as relator) to file suit on behalf of the government for recovery of a statutory forfeiture.[55] The essence of the qui tam law suit is that it encourages private enforcement of laws often allowing nearly anyone to receive as compensation for enforcement part of the fine imposed on the violator.[56]

The relator (whistleblower) is required to submit a copy of the complaint to the Department of Justice. The Department of Justice then has sixty days to review the relator's allegations (this period may be extended)[57] -the defendant is not served with the complaint during this period- before deciding on whether or not it takes up the complaint and proceeds with the action.[58]

---

[52] 31 U.S.C. §§ 3729-3731.

[53] 31 U.S.C. §§ 3729(a).

[54] Knowingly refers to situations where a person (1) has actual knowledge of the information; (2) acts in deliberate ignorance of the truth or falsity of the information; or (3) acts in reckless disregard of the truth or falsity of the information, and no proof of specific intent is required (31 U.S.C. §§ 3729(b)). Claims refer to requests or demands for money or property where the government provides any portion of that money or property (31 U.S.C. §§ 3729(c)).

[55] The term qui tam is derived from the Latin "qui tam pro domino rege quam pro se ipso in hac parte sequitur "who as well for the king as for himself sues in this matter" Black's Law Dictionary (1999, 7th ed.) p. 1262.

[56] The permissiveness of the qui tam laws suits under the False Claims Act capture many of the features of a proposal made by Becker and Stigler in their seminal article, Law Enforcement, Malfeasance, and Compensation of Enforcers (1974), where they suggested: "The essence of victim enforcement is compensation of enforcers on performance, or by a "piece-rate" or a "bounty," instead of by a straight salary. Why not then generalize this system, and let *anyone*, enforce statutes and receive as compensation for performance the fines levied against convicted violators?" (Becker and Stigler 1974: 14). Becker and Stigler's proposal, however, may lead to a privatization of law enforcement, which is clearly not advocated neither in our analysis, nor in the False Claims Act.

[57] 31 U.S.C. §§ 3730(c)(3), 31 U.S.C. §§ 3730(b)(2).

[58] 31 U.S.C. §§ 3730(b).

If the Department of Justice does not proceed with the case, the relator may continue independently.[59] This condition is necessary if the relator is to function as a watchdog not just over the firm that has defrauded the government, but also over the policing agencies. To wit, the general advantages of citizen suits that have been addressed above are relevant here and do not need to be re-enumerated. If the government decides to proceed with the action it has primary responsibility for prosecuting the action and is not bound by the acts of the relator,[60] an important factor in preserving the independence of the Department of Justice. The government may move to strike the action following provided the relator has been given an opportunity to be heard before the courts,[61] a factor which serves to prevent frivolous cases, but may also lead to collusion between law enforcement agencies and the defendant. It may settle the action provided that the court agrees the settlement to be fair.[62] It may also move to have the participation of the relator restricted if the relator's actions would interfere or unduly delay prosecution of the case.[63]

1. The Award to the Qui Tam Plaintiff

A party found to have violated the False Claims Act is subject to a civil penalty of "not less than $5,000 dollars and not more than $10,000, plus 3 times the amount of damages which the Government sustains because of the act of that person,...".[64,65] If the government pursues the case the relator shall receive at least 15 percent and not more than 25 percent of the proceeds of the action or settlement, depending on the magnitude to which the person substantially contributed to the action, as well as reasonable expenses and fees incurred and reasonable attorney fees and costs.[66] If the government did not proceed with the action, the amount awarded to the relator ranges between 25 and 30 percent, plus reasonable attorney fees and other reasonable costs and expenses.[67] Rewarding the informant subject to damages approximates the notion of pay for performance.

---

[59] 31 U.S.C. §§ 3730(b) (4)(A), 31 U.S.C. §§ 3730(c)(3).
[60] 31 U.S.C. §§ 3730(c)(1).
[61] 31 U.S.C. §§ 3730(c)(2)(A).
[62] 31 U.S.C. §§ 3730(c)(2)(B).
[63] 31 U.S.C. §§ 3730(c)(2)(C).
[64] 31 U.S.C. §§ 3729(a)(7).
[65] If the party cooperates, this may be reduced. *See* 31 U.S.C. §§ 3729(a)(7)(A-C).
[66] 31 U.S.C. §§ 3730(d)(1).
[67] 31 U.S.C. §§ 3730(d)(2).

2. Protection against Frivolous, Vexatious and Uninformative Suits

Defendants may move to limit the participation of the relator during the course of the litigation if they can show that "unrestricted participation during the course of litigation...would be for purposes of harassment or would cause the defendent undue burden or unnecessary expense.[68] Alternatively, when the Department of Justice does not proceed with an action and the relator loses the case and his action is termed "frivolous, clearly vexatious, or primarily brought for purposes of harassment", the defendant may be awarded all reasonable attorney fees and expenses.[69] Kovacic (1996: 1821) notes that from the enactment of the False Claims Amendment Act in 1986 through September 1995, "there has been only a single reported instance in which a defendant has successfully invoked either one of these provisions."

In keeping in line with the broader aims of qui tam suits as monitoring devices that primarily increase the flow of information on fraudulent claims against the government, courts have refused jurisdiction over suits when the facts supporting the relator's complaint are already public and the relator lacks direct, independent knowledge of the information (*ibid.*: 1815).

3. Rewards for Parties to Fraudulent Activity

The False Claims Act reduces and sometimes withholds proceeds from relators who partake in conduct that supports the qui tam action. "...if the court finds that the action was brought by a person who planned and initiated the violation...then the court may, to the extent the court considers appropriate, reduce the share of the proceeds...If the person bringing the action is convicted of criminal conduct arising from his or her role in violation of section 3729, that person shall be dismissed from the civil action and shall not receive any share of the proceeds of the action."[70]

Indeed, the aforementioned is indicative of the notion that parties to criminal activities face different incentives to report than those outside of the corrupt system. Note, the False Claims Act does not rule out the idea of granting parties to corruption an amnesty and not threaten future criminal proceedings, so that these parties can also avail of whistleblower rewards and come forward. Amnesties per se are dangerous and are outlawed in some countries as they offer extensive prosecutorial discretion and great incentives for collusion. Incentives for parties to come forward are still restricted by many of the factors dissertated in chapter II, which I need not repeat here. Moralists and the public at large may find it difficult to justify parties that were part of a corrupt system being rewarded for

---

[68] 31 U.S.C. §§ 3730(c)(2)(D).
[69] 31 U.S.C. §§ 3730(d)(4).
[70] 31 U.S.C. §§ 3730(d)(3).

reporting their activities according to this device. There is, however, a reasonable justification for the measured use of such a mechanism even to parties that were engaged in corrupt exchanges themselves. Offering a reward to equal to or greater than the future costs of continuing the relationship makes noncooperation the unconditionally preferred strategy in a game by both parties (*see* Cooter and Garoupa 2000). Given that corrupt transactions require at least two parties, a government official and a citizen, it is even enough to offer rewards to just one party greater than or equal to the future gains from the relationship (and none to the other), *e.g.*, to the citizen and not to the bureaucrat. One problem with such reward systems is that they generally do not take into account the fact that corruption is a long-term activity. Rewards need to approximate the expected future gains of cooperation by an individual for the continuing duration of the relationship. Qui tam suits on the other hand offer a percentage of the money retrieved from defrauding the government, unrelated to the future payoffs involved. Similarly, allowing a government official who is party to corruption to receive an amnesty and a reward may promote such conduct in anticipation of a future amnesty. The counterside of this argument is that if private citizens anticipate that government officials will report, they may not engage in corruption in the first place.

In summing up some of the principal efficiency advantages of qui tam suits, we would have to consider as being their most fundamental the fact that they grant insight and enforcement powers to those closest to the information. Additionally, being a decentralized enforcement measure, they have the advantages listed above, including serving as an additional oversight mechanism over ill-functioning administrative bodies, as well as providing additional oversight over parties that (potentially) break the law. They lessen the attractiveness of bribery to circumvent the law as violations may still be discovered and punished and provide a means to bypass an agency (going directly to the prosecution and to court), in whose interest it naturally is that the violations remain unreproached. Further, they may lessen the amount of resources a society must expand in order to detect malfeasance because payment for performance reduces the benefits from malfeasance in the first place (Becker and Stigler 1974: 15). I emphasize again, however, that the overriding feature of corruption and corrupt systems is that they thrive in secrecy, and there are vulnerabilities at each step involved in corrupt exchanges. Having those closest to the information come forward can help initiate distrust and invert cooperation. Information asymmetries, as emphasized earlier, play a significant role in malfeasance in procurement contracts, allowing suppliers ample room for false statements suggesting that the government can recruit the assistance of rivals privy to similar information. However, these parties may not be so willing to come forward for reasons adumbrated above. To supplement this, traditional methods for overcoming asymmetries in procurement are employed, but they may themselves be insufficient or prohibitively expensive. As Kovacic (1996: 1822) notes: "Audits and inspections can be costly, ... and even arduous examination schemes may fail to equip external government observers with the same knowledge possessed by internal contractor employees. Due to greater familiarity with, and understanding of, the contractor's activities, contractor employees ordinarily can identify and assess relevant information at a lower cost than external government observers." Rumors, instructions and closeness to information all make employees, subcontractors and professional affiliates excellent watchdogs.

4. Some Controversies and Shortcomings of Qui Tam Suits and the False Claims Act

Several unresolved or unsatisfactory questions remain regarding the use of qui tam suits and particularly the False Claims Act as a device to curb malfeasance. It is to here we turn our attention below.

4.1. Standing

Prior to the 1986 amendment, whistleblower standing had been limited and the number of suits only a handful per year (Kovacic 1996: 1801). Since the amendment the number of suits has grown enormously. Standing has been relaxed to the extent that customarily "the statute's language, legislative history, and interpretation by federal judges appear to give standing to private citizens, employees of government contractors, employees of government agencies, and private companies" (*ibid.*: 1812). This effectively opens up opportunities and incentives for almost all parties to come forward to report fraudulent applications and corrupt activity. The court does not seem to entertain the idea that the 1986 reforms improperly purported to give to relators standing who do not meet the constitutional requirement of inquiry in fact and causation (*ibid.*: 1812).[71] The qui tam informer endures no traditional injury in fact before starting an action: the False Claims Act authorizes the informer to sue on the government's behalf without regard to whether she has suffered harm as a result of the defendant's conduct (Beck 2000: 544).[72]

---

[71] As Beck notes, "Private prosecution of government claims seems difficult to reconcile with Article II's command that "[t]he executive Power shall be vested in [the] President of the United States" and with the basic principles of Article III standing. By exercising prosecutorial powers, the informer appears to execute the laws without presidential appointment or supervision" (Beck 2000: 543). *Compare* Antonin Scalia (1983) with Cass R. Sunstein (1992) for two substantially different though authoritative perspectives on this issue.

[72] Kovacic (1996: 1801) notes: "The permissive qui tam standing requirements contrast with other decentralized schemes for monitoring compliance with federal laws."

A contentious area has been whether public employees can file a qui tam suit based on information they acquired during their employment. Although there are apparently significant problems with this, courts seem to allow it in most instances, as long as the information was not in the public domain when suit was filed (Kovacic 1996: 1816). But permitting government officials under certain circumstances to also file a qui tam suit is particularly important given that a watchdog agency may have been captured or its members bribed.[73]

Figure 1: Who will Guard the Guardians

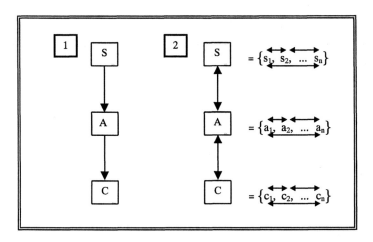

When one considers these factors collectively, the old problem of who will guard the guardians now is as depicted in Figure 1. Let S denote a supervising agency, A a government agency and C clients with whom the agency transacts. Traditional arrangements typically entail that the supervising agency monitors the actions of the government agency and the government agency, who transacts with citizens monitors its own affairs and actions of the citizens with whom it transacts. This is depicted by the direction of the arrows in Figure 1. By contrast, in Figure 1, Heading 2, when qui tam suits are permitted, the not just does the S monitor A and A supervise its own transactions with C, but C may also monitor A and A monitor S. Theoretically, C may also monitor S, but it is difficult to think of such

---

[73] The Department of Justice unsuccessfully argued that "permitting such lawsuits would trigger races to the courthouse in which government employees seek to file qui tam lawsuits based on information acquired in their official duties before the government can start a civil or criminal case in its own right" (Kovacic 1996: 1816-1817).

a scenario in reality. Moreover, with the possibility of qui tam suits, individual citizens, denoted by c_1, c_2... c_n, may monitor one another as well as the government agency. Similarly individual employees within the government agency, denoted by a_1, a_2...a_n, may also monitor one another and agency transactions, as may individual employees with the supervising agency, denoted by s_1, s_2... s_n, monitor other supervisors and agency transactions. Theoretically, at least, there is a solution to the old problem of who will guard the guardians.

4.2. The Remaining Problem of Anonymity

One problem with the False Claims Act is that it provides for financial rewards that encourage reporting of fraud only when parties actually come forward and identify themselves. In many ways these rewards must also be interpreted as a means of granting sufficient incentives for parties to come forward given their costs of reporting and more particularly the potential costs of retaliation (although the reward may be far larger than the costs incurred by the whistleblower). There are, however, many events in day-to-day life where financial rewards are offered and anonymity is still guaranteed. For example, someone who finds or who himself pilfered an item belonging to someone else can normally return the property anonymously. Although we may find its reprehensible that the theft occurred in the first place, or that someone failed to return what he or she found, we would still prefer to make arrangements for the item to be returned anonymously without any confession (Levmore 1996: 2203-04). Returning for example a wallet to promises of "no questions asked" may not be enough for the finder (thief) to come forward for fear of retaliation. The solution to the aforementioned is the use of an intermediary who is "beyond suspicion", "who can effect the exchange of missing property for reward" (ibid.: 2204).

The suggestion worth considering here is that a similar solution could also be provided in the case of whistleblowers that wish to be rewarded under a mechanism similar to the False Claims Act. As we have seen, anonymous tips and information are frequently used to start investigations of governmental and private sector misconduct. These tips could themselves be rewarded. More controversially, anonymity could be used in adjudication.[74] Although quite controversial, this would not be a first. In the United States for example,

---

[74] Levmore (1996: 2229) submits: "MODEL CODE OF PRE-ARRAIGNMENT PROCEDURE §290.4 (1975) [in the United States] provides that the identity of an undisclosed informant be revealed to the other party unless the judge determines that "there is substantial corroboration of the informant's existence and reliability" and the issue whether there existed reasonable cause to act based on an informant's tip "can be fairly determined without such disclosure." The judge may require the prosecution to disclose the informant's identity to the court for purpose of making the determination. The information if deemed to be confidential , must be under seal and transmitted to the appellate court in the event of an appeal."

informants identities are sometimes made available to a judge, who acts as an intermediary, and then put them under seal (Levmore 1996: 2229).[75]

4.3. General Dangers of Whistleblower Mechanisms

Where corruption is institutionalized or systematic, legal tools and instruments that work well in one context may perform dismally in another. Whistleblower protection is now offered in many countries, but with mixed results. Certain institutional safeguards need to be in place to protect against retaliation, as a first step to granting incentives for parties to report fraudulent and corrupt activity-factors which are wanting in most developing countries. As with other instruments designed to curb corruption, whistleblower protection may be used as a tool by a corrupt organization to regulate deviant behavior, where for example, an unwillingness to participate may result in whistleblowers themselves being accused of corruption (Rose-Ackerman 1999: 58).[76]

Another consideration is whether or not encouraging persons to come forward can actually encourage bribery and corruption itself given that the gains for the enforcer from coming forward are less than the offender's likely penalties (*see* Landes and Posner 1975: 24). Put differently, will the offender bribe the whistleblower? This is unlikely for the simple reason that agreements between the whistleblower and the offender are not enforceable, and the offender cannot guarantee that the whistleblower will keep to his word and not demand an additional bribe or turn him in anyway. Secondly, there is always a chance that a second whistleblower will come forward and a third, etc.

The False Claims Act in the United States is unsuitable as a blueprint for less developed countries for a plurality reasons. For one, private enforcement can

---

[75] Furthermore, whilst not fitting neatly into our framework of the judge or other government official as intermediary, the informant's privilege highlights the use of anonymity in criminal investigations. The informants privilege refers to: "The qualified privilege that a government can invoke to prevent disclosure of the identity and communications of its informants. In exercising its power to formulate evidentiary rules for federal criminal cases, the U.S. Supreme Court has consistently declined to hold that the government must disclose the identity of informants in a preliminary trial. McCray v. Illinois, 386 U.S. 3000, 312, 87 S.Ct. 1056, 1063 (1967). A party can usu. overcome the privilege if it can demonstrate that the need for information outweighs the public interest in maintaining the privilege" (Black's Law Dictionary (1999, 7th ed.) p. 1216).

[76] Landes and Posner (1975: 26) identify four means with which a private enforcer may increase his "catch" through enlarging the supply of offenders: "(1) He can fabricate an offense. (2) He can prosecute an innocent person for an offense that in fact occurred. (3) He can encourage an individual to commit an offense that he would not have committed without his encouragement, and then prosecute him for the offense; this is the practice known as "entrapment." (4) Knowing that an individual is about to attempt to commission a crime, the enforcer can wait until the crime has been committed and then prosecute him rather than apprehend him in the attempt stage and prosecute him for a criminal attempt."

itself be costly. Where several persons compete for a reward and only one can win, the efforts (resources) of the losing parties are often wasted.[77] Similarly, where there is an absence of property rights and there is free access to a resource, it is well known that the level of production will exceed the optimal level (where marginal social costs exceed marginal social benefits) (*ibid.*: 20). Experience in the United States has shown that it may generate high levels of litigation, a factor which could tie up judicial systems that more often than not function lethargically and ineffectually already.[78] Furthermore, many less developed countries are attempting to reform their civil service, often leaving behind a pool of aggrieved employees who may wish to take advantage of whistleblower protection laws and qui tam suits if available as a means of acting strategically to maintain their jobs and stagnating civil service reforms. Similarly where a whistleblower protection provision extends to the private sector, agents may also file suits in order to avoid being legitimately disciplined, and, similarly, competitors may act strategically in fragile markets by bringing suits and tying up rivals.

The greatest threat however, that can result in countries without basic institutional safeguards manifests itself in the form of blackmail and harassment that accompany any such reward structure, as well as the ability for collusion between law enforcement officials and whistleblowers, and particularly judicial corruption between the judge or judicial personnel and the relator. There is also great potential for such a mechanism to exasperate agency problems within organizations, where companies find themselves set up by employees wishing to extract financial gains. An additional agency problem may be the potential interference with internal compliance mechanisms as employees may aspire to file qui tam suits as opposed to report violations internally (Kovacic 1996). Moreover, given that agents now have incentives to monitor other agents as well as their principals, they have the added incentive of concentrating more of their efforts on monitoring as opposed to their regular activity in the course of their employment (*ibid.*). This can extend itself beyond the private sector to exasperate agency problems in the public sector. In particular, a potentially very pernicious problem would be the perverse incentive effects on law enforcement officials if they could file a qui tam suit against the companies they are supposed to be monitoring for an extensive array of offenses. They would then have incentives to withhold the information from their superiors in order to qualify themselves for a reward. Additionally, public inspectors may also blackmail for minor violations

---

[77] The same problem occurs in the following illustration. There is a competition for architects, with a first prize of $1000. There are ten architects that come into question. Each architect considers his chances of winning to be equal, *i.e.*, 10%. It is, therefore, in their interest to spend up to $100 each on designing models in order to win the prize. Only one firm can, however, win the prize, the investments of the others are, therefore, wasted unless they can be put to another use.

[78] *See* further Chapter VII, Section II.

and regulations may be deliberately complex in order to make compliance very costly to facilitate bribes or rewards.

An additional factor worthy of consideration is the potential deterrent affect for companies of doing business with the government given that potential suits in addition to other formalities serve as a barrier to conducting business as well as a potential source of bribes and lock in, where inconsistencies are discovered. In a similar vein, it can adversely effect international investment (*see* Kovacic 1998b).

Qui tam suits can limit discretion and flexibility. Contracts frequently possess relational features and, in the course of employment, agencies and contractors develop opinions on the specifications of a contract. The costs of drafting a complete contract ex ante are pervasive, as are the costs of redrafting an older contract according as each new unaccounted for contingency arises. Because of this, parties usually adopt adjustment mechanisms that do not involve formal changes to the terms of the contract (Kovacic 1998a: 148). "Customs or understandings that permit all parties to respond to contingencies that the written document either treats ambiguously or fails to address at all govern day-to-day dealings (*ibid.*)." Discretion, as I have argued is a necessary tool of regulators and law enforcement and any decision to remove it must be weighed carefully against the costs of doing so. Qui tam suits necessarily remove much of this discretion, given that discretionary actions may be interpreted as nonconformity with contractual terms.

One final problem which I refer to again in extended discussion below is related to norms against what is commonly known as snitching. Although snitching may be considered as an important avenue to information for law enforcement, it triggers a series of ambiguous norms on informing. Trust, like reciprocity, is often considered a value onto itself and indeed like reciprocity forms an important basis of social and business relations. Affecting trust levels can greatly affect the nature of such relationships, and in certain societies, especially those that have emerged from communism, all indications are that the level of trust is already very low. We shall disengage ourselves currently from the much broader implications of using morally ambiguous behavior to fight crime and corruption, referring the reader to later discussion.[79]

III. Internal Avenues to Corruption

A. Introduction

Qui tam suits capture only one type of a much larger market of internal avenues to information. Defendants who assist law enforcement are frequently rewarded for

---

[79] *See* below, this chapter, Section III, Subsection E.

assistance that is substantial to the investigation or prosecution of another individual. An alternative means to getting inside information is through use of confidential informants. Unlike cooperating defendants, confidential informants are not necessarily themselves the aim of an investigation or persons indicted on a particular charge who have agreed to inform in exchange for leniency; some may never testify in court but rather continue long term relationships with law enforcement officials (Schreiber 2001). A third means of getting inside information is going undercover, which itself frequently involves confidential informants. Indeed, corruption, given its defuse, often victimless characteristic lends itself particularly well to discovery via covert mechanisms (Marx 1995: 215). To wit, it is these characteristics of corruption that are the driving force behind the demand and need for an insider view.

B. Demand for an Insider View

> "Like drug trafficking, trafficking in corrupt political influence is extremely difficult to detect. In a bribery transaction, as with a drug sale, both participants are satisfied with the result. There is no victim, each side receives what is requested."[80]

As we know, the demand for cooperation is primarily a result of the fact that cooperators are endogenous to the corrupt system itself, and these very cooperators make it possible to find and prosecute violations that might otherwise go unpunished. Given that corruption thrives in secrecy, endogenous actors to corrupt systems provide insight into individual violations that are often victimless making them hard to detect. More importantly, however, they furnish insight into the workings of a corrupt system, which itself can be an extremely complex network of reciprocation, quid pro quos and overlapping complicity; aided by the fact that corrupt transactions are frequently conducted by intermediaries which makes it difficult to trace individual steps, illicit quid pro quos and causation.

Adumbrated later, there are several factors that make successful prosecution of corruption-related charges difficult.[81] Among the more striking features that account for the low level of cases that are prosecuted are the following. Corruption is a consensual or victimless crime, where both parties are generally happy with the outcome.[82] Corruption proceedings are notoriously resource-intense and highly costly which discourages many prosecutors from investigating and indicting parties on corruption-related charges. Another factor which discourages prosecutors and law enforcement officials is derived from the

---

[80] United States v. Myers, 527 F. Supp. 1206, 1236 (1981).
[81] *See* further Chapter VII, Section III related to prosecutorial discretion.
[82] This distinguishes corruption from extortion.

fact that there are oftentimes political sources involved, who actively seek to have the plugs pulled on investigations. Prosecutors and law enforcement officials must often be relatively certain of successful prosecution to proceed. When these factors are understood, then one can readily see how endogenous parties to a corrupt system provide evidence that would otherwise be inaccessible.

C. Cooperating Defendants

> "We have to introduce an incentive for the denunciation of the crime, foreseeing, within a very limited time span from the moment of the crime, a nonliability to punishment. With this 'premium' we introduce an asymmetry: we give those who confess an advantage over those who do not confess."[83]

It is encouraging to see that reformers are starting to take note of the possibility of destabilizing corruption by creating incentives for parties to the crime to cooperate with authorities. In this section I shall be focusing on cooperative defendants. [84]

The above quote is that of a leading judge in the "mani pulite" or "clean hands" investigations in Italy that began in the early 1990's, who recognized the advantages of bringing about an asymmetry in payoffs between those that cooperate and those that fail to cooperate to fight corruption, similar to a prisoner's dilemma.[85] Indeed, the *"mani pulite"* strategy took advantage of the sometimes fragile nature of cooperation oftentimes common to corrupt transactions. As Della Porta and Vannucci (1999: 267-8) submit on the strategy pursued:

---

[83] Judge Davigo was a judge within the largest ever investigation of corruption in Italy, the mani pulite investigations. Source: Davigo, P. "Tempo pre un nuovo inizio," Interview by C. Demattá. Economia & Management 2:9-17 cited in Della Porta and Vannucci (1999: 275 n. 19).

[84] Compensating defendants who assist law enforcement efforts is well entrenched in Anglo-American law. The ancient English common law practice of approvement, referred to "[t]he act of avoiding a capital conviction by accusing an accomplice; turning king's evidence (Black's Law Dictionary (1999, 7th ed.) p. 98). It effectively meant that an accused felon could implicate an accomplice and win a pardon upon the accomplices conviction (Richman 1995: 85). Weinstein (1999: 569) notes: "With the development of more systematic developments to crime control came the formal sanctioning and expansion of negotiated agreements. The traditional rewards of clemency or immunity have largely been replaced by pleas to less serious charges and other mechanisms for sentence mitigation."

[85] He made further suggestions that reflect the approach I am suggesting here such as increasing penalties, the confiscation of financial gains from corruption and importantly, "nonliability to punishment for those who, within three months after the corrupt exchange, confess their crimes and provide information on the others responsible" (Della Porta and Vannucci 1999: 275n19).

208

"The investigative strategy from the beginning of the inquiry confronted subjects with the pressing decision of whether to confess, sowing suspicions that others had already talked and raising the prospect of spending at least a period of preventative custody in prison in case of remaining silent or, vice versa, being released immediately in the case of a confession (a situation analogous to the archetypal of the famous "prisoner's dilemma")."

They also made use of bluffing, as suggested should be done earlier. Bluffing has several effects. First, it makes it difficult for parties to observe the present actions of other players. These actions can be both those of the authorities and those of the parties to corruption. The authorities can flood the market with false information, clouding signals between parties. Second, parties to a corrupt system may find it more difficult to show what action they actually choose. Thirdly, future actions are based on the perception of what happened at the last move, not what actually happened, hence bluffing can manipulate signals which as we know from chapter II are important for the establishment and maintenance of cooperation. Fourth, bluffing can cause a type of dynamic or domino affect. For example in the mani pulite investigations, even when persons under investigation had not talked, law enforcement gave the impression that they had talked by releasing them early from custody. They managed to create the general impression that nearly everyone was talking, thus increasing the willingness of others to come forward in a race to confess. Law enforcement succeeded in spreading the information that there was a chain of confessions and passed this erroneous information onto the courts and the press (*ibid.* :268).

In the U.S. cooperation occurs most frequently in narcotics cases.[86] Narcotics trafficking defendants ordinarily have the opportunity and a strong incentive to snitch, having information to offer on supplier customers or other drug dealers, as well as given the fact that they are facing harsh mandatory penalties upon conviction (Weinstein 1999: 580-81).[87] Fraud cases make up the next largest group of federally prosecuted crimes in the United States, but return a lower rate of cooperation than narcotics trafficking, possibly as a result of lower penalties, the fact that defendant's information may be less useful and the fact that they have other opportunities for mitigation (*ibid.*: 581-82).

The ability of prosecutors to enter into agreements with defendants varies

---

[86] Cooperative defendants turn on others in the hope of receiving a mitigating sentence. There are naturally other types of agreements that defendants and prosecutors (sometimes with judges) enter into, such as plea bargaining, where defendants normally wave their right to a trial in return for a guilty plea, and charge bargaining.

[87] It has been argued that in the United States, that tough laws have led to a substantial increase in cooperation, as wanting defendants try to furnish substantial information to have the charges or sentence against them reduced (Weinstein 1999: 563-64).

greatly among legal orders.[88] As one would expect, the prisoner's dilemma model that we are familiar with, which generally involves a situation where parties have equal power and equal access to information about everything but the others intentions and actions, is not very accurate. There are several factors that affect the structure of the game.

1. Bargaining in Prisoner's Dilemma-Type Situations

Noted above, the prisoner's dilemma model we are familiar with does not accurately depict scenarios between prosecution and defendant. In reality, the government frequently has broad discretion on the terms of the cooperation. The defendant may be aware that the government is willing to offer gains for cooperation, but is unaware just how much this is worth; even if he knows the governments willingness to pay, he cannot be sure that the government will keep to its agreement. Furthermore, he often has little means to enforce this agreement. The judge may, for example, offer little or no reward to the informant for his information.[89] Similarly, given that a third party (the judge) normally has the final word, therein results a familiar problem in bargaining and conflict resolution theory, whereby negotiations by one side (the defendant) are conducted by an authorized party with the power to made final concessions to which he is bound, whereas the other party is not authorized to make a deal but just pass on recommendations, which may or may not be honored.

The government can and should intentionally not provide perfect information about the strength of its case or the sentences that will result from each course of action. It may be in its interest to change the payoffs as the negotiations proceed (*see ibid.*). From the perspective of the defendant, he needs

---

[88] In England, for example, prosecutors are not permitted to serve any purpose in recommending sentences at trial (for reasons such as judicial independence and separation of powers). In the Netherlands, in addition to direct sentencing powers that prosecutors enjoy, the prosecutor directly influences the judge in recommending a sentence (itself a duty), although the judge is not bound to follow the recommendations of this sentence. As we see in section in later discussion on prosecutorial discretion, in the Netherlands there are only approximately 300 public prosecutors. Given that the number is small and repeat dealings between prosecutors and judges so frequent, it should come as no surprise that the opinions of the prosecutors concerning sentencing are taken seriously. Similarly, in Germany prosecutors have a duty to recommend a sentence to the judge, but the judge is not bound to heed this recommendation. The recommendation is often personality based, where the recommendations of more experienced and specialized prosecutors are better received by judges. *See* Fionda (1995); *see* also Chapter VII, Section III.

[89] Furthermore, in the United States, for example, court decisions whether to what extent to mitigate sentence is non-reviewable on appeal (Weinstein 1999:592). There are good reasons why agreements need to be presented to the court to seek approval, otherwise there might be collusion between the prosecution and the defendant or his lawyer, who may be a repeat player in transactions with the prosecution.

to have measures to prevent the government from simply refusing to pay for information, in which case he would still suffer a stigma from cooperation and the threat of retaliation without the benefit. Defendants can seek formal agreements, but these given the bargaining positions of the two sides, will be disproportionately structured according to the governments interests. The government naturally wishes to withhold payment for as long as possible. Governments, therefore, may find it in their best interests to postpone sentencing until after cooperation has occurred, and, similarly, tie leniency to the cooperator's performance (Richman 1995: 95).[90]

There is a rich hoard of bargaining techniques both subtle and not so subtle that the government can employ, some of which may be frowned upon.[91] It is known for example that physical surroundings can be manipulated so as to make someone feel less relaxed and want to rush things (Fischer, Ury and Patton 1991: 136). Another mechanism is that of delay or threatening to delay things. It is a well known result of bargaining theory that those that are more patient (or more accurately can give the impression of being more patient) receive a better deal than if they were less patient.[92] Furthermore, extreme demands may be made to lower expectations. Another tactic in bargaining is escalating demands; once one party thinks that something has been agreed upon, issues are reopened. It can have the affect of making a side wish to close a deal quicker in order to prevent the other party from constantly raising its demands (*ibid.*: 140). Lock-in tactics are another means to achieve a cooperative outcome, where one party commits to a result, leaving the other with little choice but to give in. This is exemplified in the Hawk/Dove game, where one party suggests he is going to be a Hawk irrespective of what the other party does. Other tactics include using the "Hardhearted Partner" routine, frequently exemplified by parents in such sentences as, "I would let you go to the party, but it would upset your mother", and take-it-or-leave-it offers. [93] If the government is interested in using the defendant as an informant and hence developing a long-term relationship, however, these tactics must be used with restraint. A deal is only workable if the defendant is able and willing to perform the deal.

---

[90] In the United States, where the government reneges on an agreement, by urging a position that it has bargained away, the defendant will likely find out about the violation and will be able to seek the withdrawal of his plea or the enforcement of the agreement.

[91] And there are some tactics and tricks, such as false statements, ambiguous authority and misrepresentation of intent frequently invoked in bargaining that the government cannot invoke, for reasons of illegality and practicality (such as the presence of counsel).

[92] For a vivid introduction to this literature, in particular discussion on the concept of brinkmanship, *see* Dixit and Nalebuff (1993). Parties may also be engaged in a war of attrition, trying to tire the other side into surrender.

[93] There are several other tactics that are used in different contexts, such as personal attacks, including attacking status by making them wait, implying ignorance, not making eye contact, and the good-guy/ bad guy routine (Fischer, Ury and Patton 1991:136).

Because there are usually not repeat dealings, the defendant may have scarce means to ensure that the government honors its agreement. One means to overcome this would be to divulge the information on a piece-meal basis, where for every piece of information provided by the defendant, something was given in return. An alternative means to reach a cooperative outcome would be where the defendant could use a lawyer that has specialized in cooperative agreements and is himself involved in repeat dealings. Alternatively, the law could allow for the defendant to withdraw his guilty plea, if the government reneges on its agreement. This does not help him much, however, seeing as he has already divulged the information. Alternatively, the defendant could submit the information to a respected third party (intermediary), who would pass it on to the government after it had submitted the charges to the court, thus fulfilling its agreement.

D. Undercover Agents and Confidential Informants

> "Detection of bribery is difficult, if not impossible, unless either the one who offers or the one who receives the bribe cooperates with law enforcement. Because bribes occur in secret, usually in a "one-on-one" situation, proof of such meetings by electronic recording is essential. In order to detect and successfully prosecute crimes of the type committed here, law enforcement officers must have considerable latitude to infiltrate the activity, to pose as persons willing to pay money for favors, to encourage others to produce corrupt politicians who will accept bribes, to present a misleading appearance by use, for example, of the "sheik" scenario, complete with yacht, airplane, private hotel suites and other trappings of wealth, and to secretly record the resulting bribe transactions."[94]

1. Introduction

With sizable disparities throughout the world, stings and undercover operations have been applied and are commonly applied to uncover many consensual (and less consensual crimes), such as narcotics, prostitution, the exchange of child pornography, the sale of stolen goods (fencing), and particularly the workings of an organized crime family or network. They can be used as a tool turned inward, effectively monitoring the monitors, to unveil corruption. As Marx (1995: 218)notes of the United States, where the practice is particularly pronounced, "it is no longer uncommon to hear of police, legislators and even judges and

---

[94] United States v. Myers, 527 F. Supp.1206, 1236.

prosecutors as the targets of undercover investigations.[95] An important means of curbing corruption is a policy of interjecting honest officials to pose as dishonest officials to increase uncertainty of player type, and therefore the risk of detection. The role of undercover reporting and policing is far more important that this, as it gives us insight into the workings of a corrupt system, the courses of transaction, persons involved etc. In addition, covert policing methods may not be considered merely as tools that are used by law enforcement to monitor the behavior of others and themselves, but are also found in the private sector. For example where airport security tries to get past its own employees; where a distrustful spouse hires a private detective to track down the actions of her partner; or through the use of integrity tests, the classic example being that of leaving a wallet full of money on the ground in someone's office but ranging to far more sophisticated techniques.[96]

To wit, covert policing methods have always been with us. Through history rulers have made extensive use of undercover techniques to guard their political, military and economic interests.[97] Cultural and psychological factors will of course play a large role in the use and acceptance of undercover techniques. Whereas in the Anglo-Saxon tradition, informing is often considered a way of fostering community, in the continental systems, it is perceived often as "a way of destroying rather than sustaining community" (Marx 1995c: 328). Countries in transition may be, or at least should be, particularly reluctant to encourage covert police tactics, given their past experience.[98] In the former U.S.S.R., for example, an ideology that justified control of all aspects of society and legal framework to match justified state intervention in daily life which

---

[95] Undercover work in Germany is not as prolific as in the United States. The Bundeskriminalamt conducted about 70 covert operations a year between 1982 and 1990" (Busch and Funk 1995: 56). Besides the general tendency of police forces to keep undercover operations secret, there may be a simple reason for this. Up till now most German state officials have even denied that we have 'undercover agents' in the American sense of the term. Police officers are supposed to strictly obey the law (Legalitätsprinzip). German criminal procedure does not permit 'covert investigators' to commit crimes in order to infiltrate a targeted group" (*ibid.*). Levi (1995) suggests that there is an apparent paradox in the United Kingdom, which has a liberal law when it comes to undercover work, but outside of the drugs arena and intelligence gathering, it is rarely employed. They are almost never used for white-collar-crime investigations.

[96] Interestingly, the same techniques may be used by a corrupt organization to check the honesty of an official. Where an official takes the bait, he may be locked into the organization and can be blackmailed.

[97] "Authorities in special bureaus opened diplomatic correspondence, recruited informants, and sent spies to learn the secret intentions of their enemies and rivals" (Fijnaut and Marx 1995: 2).

[98] It is, however, disingenuous to assume that human capital that was developed for spying and infiltrating all aspects of citizen and private life has been allowed to dissipate. Its usefulness to organized crime are obvious. This factor has also been assisted by the willingness of enforcement to "cross over" to illegitimate business practices.

permeated all sectors of Soviet life.[99] The line between political and criminal wrongs became obfuscated (Shelley 1995).

In what follows, I highlight some applications and advantages of using undercover tactics and particularly, sting operations to unmask official corruption. Here, more than perhaps any other instrument I have suggested till now, there is, a need to give acute consideration to the varied organizational, juridical and political contexts in which they are used. Covert means can be disclosed or undisclosed, bound or unfettered by the rule of law, publicly accountable or void of culpability, operate restrained or unrestrained by a constitutional-democratic framework that offers protection of civil liberties (a framework subverted by the wishes and exigencies of a ruler). Like other instruments, it is a tactic void of simple conclusions (*see* Monjardet and Lévy 1995). Unrestrained, the dangers are pronounced. As Stiglitz (1999b) submits, "[t]he scourges of secrecy during the past seventy years are well known - in country after country, it is the secret police that has engaged in the most egregious violations of human rights." What in one case appears reasonable, becomes illegitimate or simply dysfunctional in a dissimilar operational setting (Marx 1988: 108). Disquiet as a result of the use of deceit, invasion of privacy, liberty, fear of entrapment, misuse and corruption, the fear of political targeting and the besmearing of the justice system, as a result of its affiliations with criminals and characters of disrepute, are constant features of the discussion that coexist with the use of covert practices.

2. Types of Undercover Activity

In recent years, covert policing methods have become an art form in the United States, a factor that has not gone unnoticed in many other countries throughout the world.[100] Marx (1995a: 215) notes, that "[c]hanges in crime patterns, public attitudes and law enforcement priorities, in conjunction with organizational, legislative, judicial and technical changes, have supported the general expansion of the undercover technique." This was permeated by the Watergate scandal and subsequent revelations which led to an increasing intolerance towards white collar crime. But public policy and understanding are both served by recognizing that there are different kinds and dimensions of undercover activity and that there is a need to closely disassemble it into its particular parts. For a useful, if basic, typology for distinguishing between undercover and conventional policing tactics

---

[99] Ultimate authority rested with the party.

[100] One reason put forward also for this is that police in the United States are more limited in their powers to search, arrest and interrogate than their counterparts in Europe and that police, who have become more fettered by the law particularly after conducting an arrest, apply greater emphasis to the more legally unregulated covert means. In Europe, this is not necessarily the case because the police enjoy greater powers to search, arrest and interrogate and do not require covert means to the same extent (*see* Fijnaut and Marx 1995: 14).

214

I borrow from by Marx (1988). He suggests that we consider the nature of the law enforcement practice according on dimensions: whether the operation is overt (open) or covert and whether it is deceptive or non deceptive.

Overt and nondeceptive police work is common in convention criminal investigations and involves questioning, making arrests etc. It generally involves the police being notified about a crime or police stumbling across an offense. *Overt and deceptive* practices include such factors as faking a long police sentence in order to get someone to confess; telling him his partner has already confessed etc., as often is the case with cooperative defendants. Overt deception is often used by the police to create the impression of police ubiquity. "This so-called "scarecrow" (misinformation) phenomenon" he notes "includes visible surveillance cameras with blinking lights but no film or monitor; signs warning of monitoring through one-way mirrors or electronic devices, and notices that "violators will be towed" or signs stating that traffic laws are strictly enforced when that isn't the case; or highway patrol cars strategically placed along busy roads with a visible radar device and mannequins seated inside" (*ibid.*: 11-12). *Covert and nondeceptive* techniques include surveillance of a suspect, and is generally unobtrusive. *Covert and deceptive* techniques include going undercover, forming a relationship with a suspect or group of suspects, and may proceed "before and during the commission of an offense" (*ibid.*: 12). It generally involves winning a (high) degree of trust and often being part of the preparation or performance of illegal transactions within the group under investigation.) He the problem arises, as Marx notes, given that there is a "deliberate convergence of covertness and deception that makes undercover practices so powerful and sometimes problematic" (*ibid.*: 13).

Marx furthermore distinguishes between intelligence, preventive, and facilitative operations. Intelligence operations use covert and deceptive tactics to gather information about crimes that have already occurred, are or might be planned, or are in progress. Accordingly, the agent's role is inclined to be relatively passive, partaking more in questioning and observation than in any effort to get involved and guide the events. Preventive operations aim to either prevent a crime from transpiring or avert harm if this does not occur. In contrast, facilitative operations seem to be the most controversial as they seek to encourage or invite illicit behavior. In this light, the inquest shifts from, "is someone corrupt?" to "is he corruptible?". The undercover agent may adopt the role of co-consiparator or victim (*ibid.*: 11; Marx 1995b: 317-318). These are common to sting operations.

A successful plan to successfully mitigate corruption 'from the inside' could make use of all the above as part of its anti-corruption strategy. The reforms that resulted following the Commission to Investigate Allegations of Corruption in the City of New York, popularly known as the Knapp Commission (set up as a result of reports in the New York Times of rampant police corruption) provide an illustrative and insightful example of how these techniques can be used. The commission made a host of recommendations that included the establishment of a special prosecutor against corruption within the police department and other criminal justice agencies recommended as a result of the close connection between the district attorney, the police and the judges. As a result of the findings of the Knapp Commission, there were many reforms within the police department that are representative of the measures we are looking at here. The number of officers working within the Internal Affairs Division was doubled. A field unit was established to investigate corruption within each unit of police activity. A field associates program, where hundreds of officers (normally fresh from the academy), delegated to regular duty secretly assented to reporting on corruption-related activities of their colleagues (Anerchiarico and Jacobs 1995: 163; Marx 1995: 221). In addition to this system of internal informants, regular sting operations were also set up and random integrity tests, such as giving an officer a wallet full of money and seeing if it turned up in lost property, were also utililized. These features were all part of the facilitative nature of covert operations. Additionally, members of the police force were informed of such measures, which aimed at deterring police from engaging in corruption in the first place. Beyond these reforms, police commanders were required to submit reports on corruption hazards once or twice yearly (a type of vulnerability test). The Commissioner also introduced an "accountability principle", making commanders responsible for corruption within their precincts. Accordingly, those who failed to tackle corruption were transferred or were passed over for promotion (Anechiarico and Jacobs 1995: 163).

3. Sting Operations

Abscam is conceivably the most famous undercover operation conducted in the United States to date, it began with an FBI informant, who presented himself as a representative of "Abdul Enterprises", an agency backed by two very affluent Arab sheiks that were interested in investing large amounts of cash for business ventures in America.[101] Abscam (derived from the first two letters of Abdul and scam) originated as an investigation into stolen and forged securities and art work, but later shifted its attention to the gambling casinos that were going up in

---

[101] Weinberg the key informant had pleaded guilty to fraud, and in return for a sentence of probation agreed to cooperate with the FBI in setting up and undercover operation similar to an investor's business he had set up before his arrest. He was a known "con man", who had previously worked as an informant for the FBI in the 1960's and 1970's, providing them with information on certain criminal activities for which he received small sums of money. After his arrested and charged for the fraud charges mentioned above, his informant status was revoked only to be reinstated after pleading guilty and agreeing to cooperate with the FBI. *See* discussion of ABSCAM by Judge Pratt in U.S. v. Myers, 527 F.Supp. 1206, 1209 (1981).

Atlantic City. Word spread about the bountiful funds to which the key informant was privy and it wasn't long before a mayor (who was also a senator), came forward and promised "extraordinary influence in obtaining gambling casino licenses, power over the commissioners that issued the licenses, connections with organized crime, ability to deal in narcotics, guns and counterfeit securities, as well as intimate knowledge of which members of the New Jersey legislature could be bought."[102] Following a meeting between the senator, his lawyer, the key informant and an undercover agent, the senator and his lawyer "undertook to produce ... public officials who, in return for money, were willing to use their influence with the government on the sheik's behalf. Meetings were arranged... where the FBI monitored the proceedings with concealed videotape cameras and microphones."[103]

The investigation resulted in the conviction of the aforementioned mayor/senator, a senior senator, six members of Congress, three members of a city council, an inspector for the United States Immigration and Naturalization Service, and associates of public officials. For his role in the investigation, the key informant, received about $150,000 and avoided a three-year prison. After the investigation, he also received another substantive sum. Weinberg [the key informant] it was disclosed had used the government-created business front to operate his own scam, through which he allegedly swindled numerous persons out of at least $150,000 sentence (see Schreiber 2001: 326).

Abscam is one example of a 'successful' sting operation that raised many of the questions legal orders must ask themselves concerning the legality and permissiveness of undercover operations. It used and rewarded a confidential informant, who was a known criminal. It was unusual in the sense that law enforcement had little or no indication at the beginning of corrupt activity, and no proper target, but rather went fishing for corruption. The government had not merely sought out criminal activity, but had created it. It accents the fact that entrapment is one of the cardinal issues that undercover operations must affront.[104] Other troubling features include the fact that the key informant continued to engage in criminal activity during the operation. Additionally, one of the senators that was convicted had refused to reciprocate on two occasions, but

---

[102] Judge Pratt in U.S. v. Myers, 527 F.Supp.1206, 1210 (1981).

[103] Ibid.

[104] For entrapment to be a defense, two factors are normally considered: Did the government induce the defendant's criminal conduct? If so, was the defendant predisposed to commit the crime? Black's law Dictionary considers entrapment as "[a] law-enforcement officer's or government agent's inducement of a person to commit a crime, by means of fraud or undue persuasion, in an attempt to bring a criminal prosecution against that person...To establish entrapment (...), the defendant must show that he or she would not have committed the crime but for the fraud of undue persuasion." Black's Law Dictionary (1999, 7th ed.) p. 553. Interestingly, there is no general defense of entrapment in the United Kingdom (Levi 1995: 196).

finally agreed on the third, after he was led to believe he would not have to take any illicit action. Moreover, two of the councilmen that were convicted were told that if they did not accept the sheik's gifts, then plans to rebuild their city would be closed, raising the issue of how large inducements can actually be.[105]

3.1. Confidential Informants

> "Middlemen are a necessary part of the overall investigative effort, for a corrupt politician would be most unlikely to respond directly to a strangers overtures. More likely, he would prefer to work through a "bag man" or at least through someone in whom he has confidence, generated perhaps by past personal experience in such matters."[106]

From the dawning of law enforcement there has been the confidential informant. The informant like the undercover agent is an indispensable tool in the investigation of victimless or consensual crimes, such as, prostitution, drug dealing and official corruption. Beyond "lending credibility and legitimacy to an undercover agent wishing to infiltrate a criminal enterprise" the confidential informant, as Schreiber (2001: 302) suggests, "may be used as a steady source of reliable information." Confidential informants are often in it for the long run, building up long term relationships with individual law enforcement agents, providing information on an on-going basis.

An illustrative case highlighting the potential for collusion and continued malfeasance indicative of the multifarious issues that may arise is reported in United States v. Salemme.[107] Flemmi and Bulger were two well-known characters in Boston's organized crime scene conducting longstanding business with La Cosa Nostra. They began a thirty-year long relationship with the authorities, where they served as high-level informants to the FBI providing information that furthered the FBI's efforts against the Mafia. Flemmi worked together with an official that promised him confidentiality and protection. Flemmi and Bulger together in exchange for information related to the Mafia, received continued protection. This included protection from threats by both law enforcement officials and others. For example, the FBI agent who instructed Flemmi, warned

---

[105] For a more complete overview, *see* the defenses raised at trial surveyed in United States v. Myers, 527 F. Supp. at 1217-19.

[106] United States v. Myers, 527 F. Supp.1206, 1236 (1981).

[107] United States v. Salemme, 91 F. Supp. 2d. 141, 193, 334 (D.Mass.1999). *See* also review in United States v. Flemmi, 225 F.3d 78, 81-82 and Schreiber (2001: 330-340). Much of the following was revealed by Flemmi, one of the two key FBI informants discussed here, who filed a motion to have multiple charges of *inter alia* racketeering and extortion dropped against him, based on an alleged deal that he would not be prosecuted.

him against possible indictment on murder charges, allowing him to flee and avoid arrest. He returned four years later, after assurance that he would be released on bail and the indictments would thereafter be dismissed, which was actually what happened upon his return. In another instance, they faced imminent indictments on a race-fixing scheme for bribery-related charges, which were dropped by a federal prosecutor upon disclosure of the status of the two as FBI informants.

As noted earlier, dissimilar to cooperating defendants, confidential informants are not fundamentally themselves the aim of an investigation or persons indicted on a particular charge who have agreed to inform in exchange for leniency; some may never speak in a courtroom but rather remain within a long term relationships with law enforcement officials. Such confidential informants are difficult to control, given that when they go unindicted, they can retain their anonymity and maintain a informal relations with agents to whom they are answerable. More importantly perhaps, owing to their sustained anonymity, their actions can remain unsupervised by the courts, government and defense counsel at trial (Schreiber 2001: 303-304). Given their situation, they normally continue in their criminal activity, under the guise of maintaining their anonymity and credibility in the face of those whom the government targets in their operations. Where proper safeguards are not in place to counter the aforementioned, one can easily see how opportunities for corruption would be able to evolve and sustain itself in such a secretive environment, and indeed how corrupt systems would shift their activities to such areas, given the low level of transparency and accompanying vulnerability.

As a result of their continuing criminal activity and the aforementioned secrecy aspects of their activity, confidential informants, whilst often indispensable in curbing victimless or consensual crimes, open up several problems of their own. Abuse by the informant, who frequently enjoys practical (though perhaps not legal) immunity, and the potential for collusion between law enforcement officials and informants are often a real threat. The informant may use his long term "protection" not just to continue in this criminal activities, but to strategically dispose of competition by informing on his rivals.[108] Confidential informants may be assisted in their efforts by colluding with corrupt law enforcement officials, extending the arms of the law to dispense of rivals and avail of a particular market for themselves. The potential symbiotic nature of this collusive relationship is easily identifiable.

---

[108] In the case of Flemmi and Bulger above, for example, they seized an advantage to "hamstring their competitors and simultaneously ingratiate themselves with the authorities." *See* United States v. Flemmi, 225 F.3d 78, 81(1st Cir.2000).

3.2. Controlling Improbity in Operations

Important internal forms of control with regard to controlling undercover operations, should include *inter alia* guidelines, operational procedures and review boards. External forms of control generally include auditors, courts, prosecutors, and legislative oversight (Marx 1988: 181). Courts have an important role to play in controlling improper behavior in such operations. Among the more significant contributions they can make include protections against violations of civil liberties and invasion of privacy, efforts to limiting the use of deceit in faciliative operations, and curbing political targeting as well as self-interested motivations. A statutory obligation to keep parliamentary oversight committees informed may also mitigate malfeasance. An outside audit of intelligence operations is another option as is the option of establishing civil damages for outrageous actions by law enforcement officials. Similarly, necessitating the use of a warrant would also reduce discretion, but could involve the court system too early into the operational phase (*see* Marx 1988: 195).

Realistically, given that a confidential informant wishes to engage in confidence building requirements, to gain the trust of the party that is the target of the investigation, he needs to be afforded a certain amount of leniency and so needs to enjoy de facto immunity from prosecution for these actions. The issue becomes more problematic where the informant oversteps any bona fide intentions and decides to take advantage of his new-found opportunity to make some money of his own as was the case above. One important decision was taken in the United States recently that mitigates somewhat the potential for collusion between the supervising agent and the informant - the court held that FBI agents lacked the expressed or apparent authority necessary to make promises of immunity to confidential informants.[109] Furthermore, given the condition that if they are to work properly as a mechanism to get inside criminal organizations, they must enjoy more secrecy and anonymity than other law enforcement activities, covert actions of the type described above need to be substituted with other safeguards. Indeed, realistically the need for secrecy and anonymity is always going to make the use of informants a likely candidate for self-regulation, and most of the control mechanisms in the day-to-day operations will take place here. Controls such as parliamentary or congressional oversight are generally reactive and in response to public outcry or disclosure of abuse and therefore are inadequate.

There are a series of internal measures that can be taken. The first of which are strong procedural and operational guidelines. To curb corruption, guidelines should be provided by a range of parties, external to the organization.

---

[109] United States v. Flemmi, 225 F.3d 78, 91 (1st Cir.2000) which reversed the decision in United States v. Salemme, 91 F. Supp. 2d. 141, 193,33 (1999).

They should ensure that actions are documented and subject to subsequent review both internally and by external bodies (Marx 1988: 183). Second, since confidential informants are in a trust relationship with a particular agent, similar mechanisms such as those proposed earlier may be useful. One mechanism would be not to permit one agent to work together with a particular informant after some time, a system of mandatory rotation. This, however, should not occur until after sufficient trust has been developed between the officer and his informant. An additional measure would be to randomize the checking of informant-officer relationships, where for example, a certain percentage of relationships are monitored extensively and regularly. This may be more efficient than constantly supervising all relationships for a few reasons: *First*, anonymity of informants may still in most cases be preserved, thus reducing the chances of information leaking out or taking away important discretion and flexibility of agents. *Second*, conducting random monitoring save costs. *Third*, it allows more extensive monitoring of those cases that are selected. Hierarchical review is, however, important as it provides for documentation and limits both the discretionary and monopoly power of officials, who should not be allowed to operate alone.

Randomizing may also be done in a manner where no individual feels he or she is being targeted for investigation- it should, therefore, be done in a lottery-type manner. Note, this suggestion naturally does not suggest diminishing the discretion of the supervising officer from selecting any case he or she considers necessary. It is a proposal that manages to maintain both line-level discretion (important for building up trust relationships with informants) as well as supervisory-level discretion (important for higher ranking officials to use their experience in monitoring individuals).

Unlike in a misconduct complaint process, random review does not rely on the unveiling of practices or policies currently concealed from public view. It enables active investigations to search out bad practices, and, moreover, its random nature, which adds greater uncertainty to illicit exchanges (where parties do not know who will be targeted next) is more likely to discourage nonfeasance, erroneous decisions and malfeasance alike. Of course, an alternative suggestion, but one that should be restricted in use, would be to go undercover and monitor the agents themselves.[110] Such measures may best be conducted by an organization outside of the agent's organization in order to reduce the damage to organizational capital and trust.

A factor which must be taken into consideration is that covert investigations when conducted egregiously can be more costly than other

---

[110] A particular danger of utilizing undercover tactics on employees include the fact that they may lead to excess conformity and risk aversion. As Marx (1995a: 232) suggests, "conformity may increase as candor, spontaneity, innovation, and risk-taking decline." Fears that discussions will be monitored and integrity tests prevalent, may lead to passivity and less reciprocity, generally.

mechanisms, as the course of events depicted in Box 1 vividly illustrates. Surveillance and sting operations must be considered against an array of other mechanisms as part of a process of selecting the appropriate tool. Like all other forms of enforcement, there is an optimal level of enforcement. Estimates of the (marginal) costs and (marginal) benefits of continued operation must be weighed against each other. It highlights the potentials of zealousness that may be particular to sting operations, as well as the dangers accompanying its secrecy.

Box 1: The Costs of Zealousness – A Cautionary Tale

The National Investigation Service responsible for criminal investigations into duty evasion allowed the widespread illegal sale of duty-free spirits from warehouses in England, losing an estimated £2 billion in revenue in the process. Lorries picked up duty-free cargoes that were for export selling them to shops all over Britain.

Instead of tightening checks at the warehouse and prosecuting the offenders, investigators preferred to allow the lackadaisical controls at the warehouse to remain, enabling investigators working at the custom's house to spy on the activities. Furthermore, they prevented other customs officers from continuing routine checks that may have unveiled the criminal activity. News spread concerning the laxity in checks, and it was estimated that the warehouse had 1,500 accounts, a third of which were regarded as dubious. Some customs officials that had been prevented from conducting their own regular checks began surveillance operations for themselves. Officers started spying on investigators. Prosecutions only trickled in and the scam started to take hold in other warehouses around the country.

The National Investigation Service became apparently overwhelmed by the number of persons involved. Surveillance had lasted four years. The few arrests and convictions that had been made are themselves in danger. One individual serving a sentence is claiming abuse of process, suggesting that the information should have been revealed that he and others were only able to engage in the action because customs officers knowingly allowing the illegal operations to continue for years and had ignored their own regulations. Other challenges may ensue.

Source: "The Sting that Cost Pounds 2.000,000,000," *Sunday Times* (London), November 2, 2001.

4. Citizen Strategies to Gather Insider Information

Generally, without an unsettled citizenry unwilling to endure corruption and willing to exert pressure on political leaders, anti-corruption reform initiatives will be modest (*see* Marx 1995: 231). For this reason, parties exogenous to the government must sometimes make use of those very factors I have outlined above to expropriate insider information.

I included at the onset a brief description of a corruption scandal in the defense procurement industry in India exposed by Tehelka.com, a journalist-run website. The exposure eventually led to the dismissal of the chief of the ruling Bharatiya Janata Party, who was caught on camera taking bundles of cash from the journalist, as well the defense minister and six top bureaucrats and generals. Indeed, it nearly caused the Government to topple as two key allies deserted and the opposition Congress Party paralyzed the Parliament for weeks demanding the Prime Ministers resignation.[111]

This serves as an example of how private persons, nonprofit organizations and particularly the media and investigative journalism can use undercover techniques and stings to unveil corruption. Again, it would appear that the United States is the forerunner in investigative journalism.[112] The media conducts copious undercover operations, and regularly reveals the results in both the print media and on television.[113] Whilst many of the considerations that are regularly raised when questioning the use of undercover tactics involving deceit and covert actions can be raised again here, such as invasion of privacy, violation of civil liberties, the use of deceit, entrapment, political targeting, and self-interested motivations etc., there is another concern that may be worrisome related to such tactics. The public can (albeit imperfectly) supervise law enforcement institutions by holding elected and legislative officials responsible, the press on the other hand cannot be held accountable by the same measures (Bell 1999).

It is unwise, however, to exaggerate these problems. The legislature and the courts generally have at their dispense the ability to set limits on the activities of investigative journalists. For example, information that is illegally obtained may be inadmissible in court, as is generally the case in the United States supporting a legal right of privacy. By way of contrast, the United Kingdom does not offer the same protections to the legal right to privacy. They could also, for example, tighten the laws of trespass and control the possible dangers of industrial espionage by increasing civil and criminal penalties for such activities. In short, there are a list of measures that can be taken and the shortcomings of undercover

---

[111] For more on the scandal and its repercussions *see* "PM Trying to Strangle us, says Probing Website Boss," *South China Morning Post*, June 2, 2001.

[112] This type of undercover work involving deceit by journalists is naturally only one form of investigative journalism, which is itself generally very important in uncovering corruption.

[113] Among the range of activities engaged in they have "impersonated patients and employees to report on conditions in nursing home, mental institutions, veterans administration hospitals, and day care facilities. They have represented themselves as ordinary consumers to expose and report on all manner of commercial dishonesty" (Bell 1999: 746).

operations by private sector individuals should not be overstated. Undercover operations by the citizenry and investigative journalists in particular directed against government nonfeasance, malfeasance and ethical laxity is to be encouraged, as they provide insight into areas that may otherwise remain undisclosed, as well as provide the necessary unrest to stir up political will. The desirability of such measures, as with all measures depends on the alternatives, and in particular, is a function of the availability of other sources of information and transparency in government.[114]

Journalists, nonprofit organizations and private persons have developed innovative methods to capture insider information that do not include undercover work and deceit. Although simple in exposition, they may be very effective. I shall now refer to two mechanisms that could very well be exported out of their original environment.

4.1. Method 1 - Private Sector Reward System

In July 1995, an advertisement appeared in the Irish Times offering a £10,000 for information that would lead to the conviction of anyone involved in corruption related to land rezoning. The reward was placed by a firm of solicitors from Northern Ireland, after solicitors in the Republic refused to offer representation, weary of the unorthodoxy of the advertisement and sensitive nature of the subject matter. Within weeks, they had over 30 people offering information. After both police and politicians refused to correspond with the solicitors, the sponsors of the information came forward reading out a five-page statement complaining of "official inertia" and calling for an official enquiry into the allocations of land rezoning corruption. Newspapers were reluctant to print the story because of a restrictive libel law.

After initial inertia the action received a resounding public response. The momentum that was finally developed led to the establishment of a Tribunal (the Flood Tribunal) that called hundreds of witnesses, politicians, county councilors and local authority officials to investigate allegations of corruption that led to ministerial levels in the Irish government.[115]

---

[114] Here, these include the general ability to observe the government decisionmaking process, such freedom of information, government publications and those of external bodies that monitor government etc.

[115] "Crusading Barrister Turning to Politics," *The Irish Times*, July 8, 2000; "Tantalizing Direction for Tribunal," *The Irish Times*, February 15, 2000; "Politicians Reluctant to Shine a Light on Rezoning," *The Irish Times*, October 02, 1997.

Alternatively nonprofit organizations may run advertisements to sequester insider information, as the following Israeli newspaper advertisement illustrates.[116]

Box 2: Offering Consulting Services

Have you found corruption in your work place?

YOU HAVE AN ANCHOR

Turn to us to get **FREE** legal advice and assistance

Join the association and support its activities

The association is approved by the Internal Revenue Service to donation according to §46(a) of the Income Tax Act.

Receiving assistance is not contingent on joining the association.

ANCHOR the association for integrity and combating corruption in Israel

For information and other details: Tel/fax [00972] 03-6702536
POB 2437, 52123 Ramat-Gan [Israel], email: oggen@inter.net.il
w w w . o g g e n . c o . i l

The advantages of such a system are straightforward. First, it serves as an information provider. Second, it provides a coordinating role for activities of those interested in fighting corruption. Third, it raises awareness of the problem. Fourth, it reduces the risks of retaliation for any individual that comes forward, perhaps taking on an intermediary role as described earlier. Such tactics may partially be the luxury of countries where parties do not face substantial risks of retaliation, however. Those that submit the information can generally remain anonymous, but those that place the advertisements or run the nonprofit organizations may have to watch their steps, given the vast array of retaliatory measures at the disposal of government officials targeted or threatened by the information.

The internet provides a tool of great promise in the fight against corruption. On the one hand, it provides a means with which information can quickly be disseminated, gathered and processed. On the other hand, it is a great

---

[116] Advertisement, *Maariv* (Israel), December 2, 2001 (Free Translation).

tool with which to provide information anonymously without fear of retaliation. Those that submit information to the organization, can be virtually guaranteed anonymity (depending of course on how specific the information actually is). There is, however, the familiar problem discussed earlier, that where information can be provided too easily there is not sufficient cost to prevent parties releasing dishonest information.[117] False information can be mixed with good information and we may be left with the familiar problem of adverse selection. An internet company that has developed a reputation may serve as an intermediary, just as journalists who print information sequestered by informants have to vouch for the information, if not legally, then with their own reputation.

E. Concluding Comments

I have suggested generally that there is a need to view corrupt systems from the inside in order to understand the running of the system, the actors involved, acquire prosecutions as well as assess the vulnerabilities of organizations. One problem with some of these mechanisms, as suggested above is that they can trigger a series of ambiguous norms on informing and violations of trust. Trust, like reciprocity, is widely regarded as a value onto itself and is commonly viewed as forming an important basis for social and business transactions alike (Stiglitz 1999a; Fukuyama 1995; Putnam 1993). The fear is that affecting trust levels and encouraging deceit can greatly alter the nature of such relationships, and in societies, particularly those that have emerged from communism, there is strong evidence that the level of trust is already very low.[118] The argument that may be put forward against such mechanisms is they involve deceit and breach of trust which can spill over to other relations. Accordingly, the cost of employing such means is therefore too onerous, as they may affect general levels of trust.[119]

Whilst such criticism may in some instances be valid, it is often a misplaced generalization. First there are broad cultural differences as reported earlier. In the Anglo-Saxon countries reporting improprieties to authority is considered as fostering community, whereas in many countries in continental Europe such measures are seen as community-degenerating. Second, there are huge differences in strategy type and areas of application. Consider, for example, in the terminology provided by Marx (1988) an overt and deceptive tactic such as faking a long police sentence in order to get someone to confess or telling someone his partner has already confessed to a crime. These practices involve

---

[117] *See* further, this chapter, Section II, Subsection C2, related to the virtues and vices of anonymity.

[118] *See* further Chapter V.

[119] The link between general trust levels and trust levels in specific transactions with specific individuals is not clear cut however, and as we shall argue in the following chapter, trust has a strategic undertone to it that make it employable in anti-corruption efforts.

deceit and may even involve trust, but can hardly be considered as practices that should be forgone because they necessarily involve a degree of dishonesty. Similarly, the use of surveillance cameras with blinking lights but no film may be classified as overt deception, necessarily involving deceit, but should it be condemned as a means for deterring crime, merely because it is not 100 percent truthful?

Would we consider forgoing undercover operations because, they involve deceit or trigger some moral ambiguity? As with other instruments there are compromises involved. As referred to in chapter II, the morality argument crept into the original resolution to select a uniformed police force in the United States serving the purpose of "a moral separation of police from criminals and a visual separation of police from everyone else" (Marx 1988: 21). The uniform can offer a deterrent to crime occurring in this whereabouts, but this also serves as a poster board to criminals regarding where to conduct and where not to conduct their activities. To forego such mechanisms would be to forgo an important means of curbing corruption. Recall the suggestion in chapter II that a policy of maintaining honest officials to identify themselves as dishonest officials can increase uncertainty of player type, and, therefore, increase deterrence as well as the risk of detection. But the need for an insider perspective is far more important that this as we have seen; it gives us *inter alia* insight into the workings of a corrupt system, the courses of transaction, persons involved etc.

Cases that seem to raise the level of moral ambiguity include offering rewards to persons who furnish valuable information, particularly those that were involved in the activities themselves. Indeed, realistically it is often the case that those individuals that can provide the information acquired the information as a result of having a trust relationship with a particular persons or group of persons, and in order to acquire this engaged in malfeasance themselves. But to suggest that offering a lesser sentence, for example, as a reward for informing on others raises questions of morality, triggered in particular by violations of trust, is to ignore whose trust was violated in the first place. Violation, for instance, of a group ethic of secrecy owed to a criminal organization or comaradarie inherent within a criminal gang can hardly be considered improper.

Recall, Marx (1988) also distinguished between operations that were intelligence, preventive, and facilitative in nature. Intelligence operations refer to the use covert and deceptive tactics to furnish information about crimes that have already occurred, might be planned, or in progress. Again, one can hardly suggest that the behavior of an individual whose role in this context is generally related to information seeking, questioning and observation is reprehensible. So once again, one can plausibly argue against the position that these activities generally deserve moral reproach. Similarly, preventive operations that seek to prevent a crime from transpiring or ward off harm cannot seriously be perceived as a violation of some preferred moral stance. Facilitative operations seem, however to be more controversial as they engage or encourage illicit or corrupt behavior. They may form a kind of integrity test. It is the active role of the official that makes people more uncomfortable with this phenomenon. But, there are strong arguments to permit such activities that may in many contexts outweigh opposing arguments. In particular, the fact that corruption is secretive and that there is a need to increase the vulnerabilities of corrupt transactions suggest that there is a need to go fishing for it. The question is someone corruptible, as opposed to is there corruption does not make the operation invalid. That there be limitations placed on the temptations that can be made is a different matter entirely. Indeed, temptation should probably be best restricted to a reasonableness test, where enticement should not be beyond what is considered as normal or realistic. Moreover, that the sanctions commonly dished out for corrupt transactions that were facilitative in nature (as a result of enticement) reflect the active role taken by law enforcement is also a valid point. Our point is this; to necessarily wait for malfeasance to occur is foolhardy and given the nature of corruption law enforcement should engage in active searches. Consider, for example, if similar private sector inspections, such as those conducted by airport security, who try to smuggle illegal weapons past their own employees, would only be conducted after violations were reported. This system would be a predictable disaster.

Financial rewards for reporting, as discussed earlier, also have a role to play in collecting insider information but must be used with caution and depend very much on the context of their application. Indeed, of the many costs adumbrated in detail above, particularly the heightened problem of agency costs and the effect on organizational capital must be taken seriously and make this mechanism ill-advisable in a plethora of contexts, particularly in developing countries and those in transition. One other potentially devastating affect of such strategies making them at least temporarily inadvisable in many environments is that they may affect trust in government because private sector individuals and official alike feel targeted. This is a considerable social barrier to reform, which is one of the many issues addressed in the next chapter.

CHAPTER V

SOCIAL BARRIERS AND REQUISITES TO REFORM

I. Introduction

Discussed above, the private sector has a key role to play in fighting corruption. Citizens and members of the private sector assist by supplying information about transgressions and illicit behavior and diagnosing inefficient and corrupt systems. Similarly, they may provide a policing role, which can be supported by either informal or formal sanctions. There are, however, significant social barriers to effective and sustainable anti-corruption reforms. Some of these obstacles are apparent in well-established democracies and less developed countries alike, but these obstacles are especially significant where there has been a long term failure of governments to respect and secure property rights, as well as ensure parties honor contractual obligations. I address here five major obstacles to reform, which are themselves not mutually exclusive. *First*, the willingness to pay or support for reforms is too low to meet the necessary costs of effectively shifting corruption from a high level to a low level equilibrium. *Second*, citizens no longer trust government and reforms in this context are not considered as either credible or feasible so they do not receive widespread support. *Third*, there may be a vacuum of interpersonal or reciprocal trust among citizens, in particular as a result of the continued absence of legal and institutional safeguards to economic transactions. This has the consequence that citizens forgo mutually beneficial legal exchanges making illegal exchanges relatively more profitable. *Fourth*, in order to combat this vacuum societies may have developed interpersonal trust relations with members of their own group, clan etc. which make relations between strangers less likely to evolve. Societies have developed alternative ways of "getting things done" that have led to the establishment of relations which may hinder or sabotage reform efforts. *Fifth*, these divisions can be very large which can make traditional measures aimed at good governance redundant. In this case, public trust in government is not forthcoming as a result of more fundamental cleavages in society.

II. Public Willingness to Pay and the Costs of Supporting Reforms

> "Martyrs and saints are always in short supply, but less altruistic people may be willing to engage in civic activities if the private costs are not too high and the promised social benefits are large" (Rose-Ackerman 2001: 23).

Public support for reforms is fundamental to both their introduction as well as their sustainability. The supply of such support for reforms against corruption is contingent on several factors. As the above comment by Rose-Ackerman suggests, people may be willing to engage in certain activities against corruption if the costs are not too high and the promised benefits are large. There is, however, one other factor not captured by the above statement and that is how much people are willing to pay. In what follows, I suggest looking at support for reforms from two perspectives. First, from the perspective of the willingness to pay, *i.e.*, the amount of support someone has for reforms and the efforts he or she is willing to take upon himself or herself to enforce these measures.[1] Enforcement is informal and can range from general discouragement to reproach or ostracism.[2] Second, I suggest looking at reforms from the perspective of the cost of enforcement, *i.e.*, the cost of distributing the aforementioned informal sanctions. An individual is willing to enforce when the costs of doing so are less than his willingness to pay. Note, there will most likely always be a certain fraction of the population not willing to pay anything, they may free-ride on the efforts of others.

Taking the simple theoretical model developed by Cooter (1996a, 1996b) as a starting point and basis for our discussion, I shall next highlight the importance of both the willingness to pay and the costs of enforcement for anti-corruption reform efforts. I argue that the government should concentrate on strategies to affect both the willingness to pay and the costs of enforcement in order to overcome social barriers to reform.

To simplify the following discussion in this section, I largely take the psychological makeup of the population as given.[3] In other words, a certain

---

[1] Note, here I am looking at informal enforcement. For a discussion on how government can encourage formal enforcement, *see* above, chapter IV, Section II.

[2] Noonan (1984: xxiii) submits: "The commonest sanctions against bribes are moral- the innovation of guilt before God and shame before society, guilt and shame being equally relied on... Sanctions prescribed by the law are more often indirect than direct- not the crime of bribery itself but a related offense is usually punished. Until very recent times, application of direct criminal sanctions to highly placed bribetakers was rare."

[3] The psychological make up as will become clear below is the proportion and propensity of individuals that attach guilt, shame remorse etc. to acts of corruption. It can be the result of several cognitive factors, such as upbringing etc. This can vary strongly from society to society. One suspects, for example, that in the Sicily described by Gambetta (1993) where

fraction of society holds the belief that a particular action, in our case say bribery, is bad and would prefer it did not occur. This fraction is willing to engage in some activity to prevent it from occurring provided it is not too costly to do so. Whether or not these individuals undertake something depends in large part on the costs of doing so, which as with all informal sanctions are affected by the number of others in the population willing to support these measures. We say that these people have internalized the norm against bribery.[4] This does not suggest that they are unwilling to engage in corruption, but rather that internalization attaches a guilt to violating a norm (a social or group obligation on behavior). For terminological purposes consider those that have internalized the norm or rule against bribery to be conformists- they are willing to conform (support the law and enforce it) even where the payoff for those that conform is slightly lower than those that appropriate (continue taking bribes). By way of contrast, those that do not internalize the norm will conform only if the expected objective payoff (in terms of wealth or power) for doing so is greater than not doing so (Cooter 1996a: 14). For example, where the expected sanction for engaging in bribery is higher than the expected losses of not doing so, they will not engage in it.

Considered within an evolutionary game-theoretical framework we can view individuals, such as government officials as pursuing two strategies, choosing to be corrupt or choosing not to be corrupt.[5] In an evolutionary equilibrium, both strategies render the same objective payoff. A result of which as Cooter (1996b: 155) suggests, "there is no strain on commitment." The number of those persons that have internalized the norm is relatively constant, while those that advantageously conform to the norm (of not taking the bribe) will change

---

there is endemic distrust, feelings of remorse, guilt etc. for breaking an agreement with an outsider are not nearly as decisive in the decisionmaking calculus of individuals as they are in say Denmark or Sweden for similar agreements.

[4] For simplification here I use the term bribery to represent corrupt transactions.

[5] The aforementioned is, of course a great oversimplification. Bribery may be seen as a four part phenomenon. A gives B a sum X to perform Y. I may, for instance, have internalized the norm against performing for A, because he is not a close member of my family, which I place higher up on my list of priorities. I do not feel guilty if I do it for my family, but I do if I do it for someone else. Alternatively, I might consider payment of X cash to be inappropriate, but a subtle indication of an offer of friendship without explicitly suggesting that this is a payment in return for performance of a favor, might not elicit the same feelings of guilt or shame. Similarly, I might consider it inappropriate to grant you a contract on the basis of a payment (cash, friendship etc.), but speaking to my superior and suggesting that you are the best man for the job, knowing that this will sway the decisionmaking process in your favor, may not come at any psychological cost whatsoever. Indeed I might feel goods about it, knowing that I didn't explicitly violate the rules, but still helped a 'friend' out. For all of these reasons, the above is largely to be understood in heuristic terms and is more indicative of potentialities for consideration that may differ greatly depending on the identities of the players involved, the type of payment and the nature of the service performed.

depending on the objective payoffs available.[6] Where one player internalizes a norm (and the payoffs are still held constant), an opportunist will immediately move over to violate the norm with the end result that internalization by one player changes the identities of the opportunists but not the number of conformers at equilibrium (Cooter 1996a: 14).[7] Those that have internalized the norm are willing to engage in some activity to prevent it from occurring or sanction those that engage in it, provided the costs of doing so are not too high, by enlisting informal sanctions, such as gossip, ostracism and threats.[8] To reiterate a point stated above, whether or not these persons undertake anything depends in large part on the costs of doing so, which with all informal sanctions is affected by the number of others in the population willing to support their actions.

Figure 1: Willingness to Pay for Enforcement

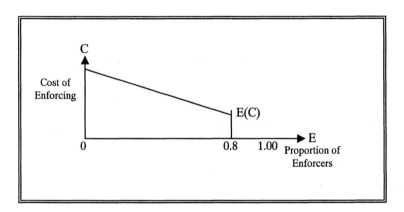

These factors are illustrated in Figure 1. Similar to Cooter (1996a,1996b) I assume that 80 percent of the people have internalized the norm and are conformists, whilst the other 20 percent have externalized it and are willing to pay nothing to enforce it. The curve E(C) depicts the willingness to pay for enforcement. The X

---

[6]   In strict economics, we may consider those that have internalized the norm as being inframarginal players, and those that have not internalized the norm as being marginal players.

[7]   Cooter uses a different example. He discusses an agency game with payoffs as in the prisoner's dilemma, where people can either cooperate, what I have termed conform, or appropriate (not conform).

[8]   The importance of informal sanctions was already recognized by Mill (1848: 135-136) in his renowned book, "Principles of Political Economy" who suggested that "much of the security of person and property in modern nations is the effect of manners and opinions", "the fear of expose" and not "the direct operation of the law and the courts of justice." Internalization of norms promotes the sanctioning of nonconformists by disseminating information about their behavior (Cooter 1996a: 15).

axis depicts the proportion of enforcers in a society and the Y axis the costs of enforcing. It is downward sloping indicating the decline in the proportion of enforcers as the cost of enforcement increases (replicating a demand curve).[9] In this context, many will pay something to enforce the norm and few will pay a lot. It should be noted that the willingness to pay curve ends at .8 or 80% of the population, which suggests that 80% of the population is willing to expand at least some resources to prevent bribery.

Let us now cast our attention to the costs of enforcement. It is easy to see, that the price of enforcing a norm or rule decreases, the more people are willing to enforce it. Consider, for example, the following: In Munich, people frequently admonish others that cross the street when the traffic light is green and the don't walk sign is lit up. They habitually wait for the walk sign to light up even when there is no traffic whatsoever in sight. We may consider these people as having internalized the norm that one shouldn't cross the road when the don't walk sign is lit up, or that they are nonconformist for whom it doesn't pay to breach the rule. By way of contrast, in New York pedestrians frequently run across the street without even the slightest risk of being reproached for such doing so (leaving aside the fact that it is almost a sport among taxicab drivers to come as close to them as possible without hitting anyone). In fact, shouting at someone for crossing when the don't walk sign is shown would probably be considered as a sign of insanity. One clear explanation for this is that the sheer number of people that are willing to violate the rule in enormous and the low number of people that would be willing to support you if you complain is so low, that the costs of enforcing the rule are exorbitant.

Figure 2: Cost of Enforcement

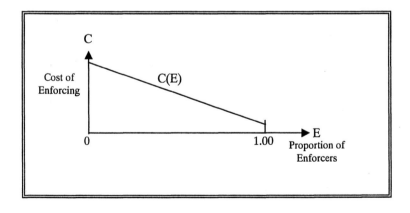

---

[9]   For simplicity, I have assumed that it is constant and downward sloping.

To understand the costs of enforcement, I refer the reader to Figure 2. As in the last illustration, the X axis denotes the proportion of enforcers in a population and the Y axis the costs of enforcing. The curve C(E) depicts the cost of enforcement and is a function of the proportion of enforcers in a society. It is downward sloping, indicating the greater the number of enforcers, the less the cost of enforcement (resembling a supply curve). As suggested above, informal sanctions commonly include ostracism, gossip, criticism and threats. One can easily understand that there are costs involved in administering these punishments, such as the risk of revenge and confrontation. One can also easily see that these costs plausibly fall per person the greater the proportion of other members in a society willing to support an individual's actions. This fact is depicted by the slope of the C(E) curve. We can see from the illustration that as the proportion of enforcers approaches 0, the cost of enforcement is at a maximum, and conversely as the proportion of enforcers approaches a maximum, the cost of enforcement is at a minimum.

Figure 3: Unstable Equilibrium

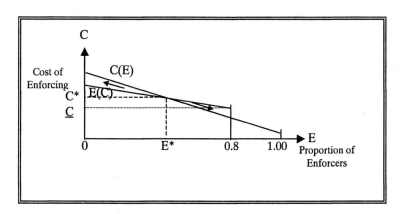

Comparing Figure 1 with Figure 2, we see that Figure 1 indicates how many people are willing to enforce the norm- taking the cost of enforcement as given- whereas Figure 2 indicates what proportion of the population are required to enforce a given cost of enforcement. The intersection of the curves depicted in Figure 1 and Figure 2 denotes an equilibrium in the number of enforcers and the costs of enforcement. There are many different equilibria that may occur. Consider Figure 3, where an equilibrium occurs at the point where the curves C(E) and E(C) intersect, *i.e.* where the willingness to pay is equal to the cost of enforcement. What is particularly interesting about this illustration is the dynamics involved. Where the actual number of enforcers (indicated as a proportion of society) is greater than the number required to sustain the costs of enforcement, the cost of enforcement will fall. The direction that the arrows point in indicates the directional change. By way of contrast, where the actual proportion of enforcers is lower than that required to sustain the norm at a particular point, the cost of enforcement will rise and society will find itself with a lower level of enforcement. We can see in Figure 3 that at a level of enforcement lower that E* society will find itself unable to sustain any enforcement of the norm. On the other hand, once E* is reached, society will be able to enforce the norm up to the point of (0.80, C̲), the point where all that are willing to pay to enforce the norm actually enforce it. The point (E*,C*) is known as a tipping point and is an example of an unstable equilibrium. The system is said to tip in to a high level of enforcement when E >E* (C>C*), or the willingness to pay exceeds the cost of enforcement (for a given proportion of enforcers) (*see* Cooter 1996a: 20; Schelling 1975). A key feature of this figure is that random shocks that change either the cost of enforcement or the willingness of the population to pay for enforcement can have a serious impact on the level of enforcement of a norm and see society move from an equilibrium with high level of enforcement to a low level of enforcement equilibrium.

Figure 4: Stable Equilibrium

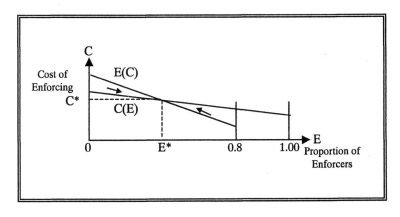

Turning our attention to Figure 4, we once again see that an equilibrium occurs at the point (E*,C*). Here we have an example of a stable equilibrium. If the number of enforcers exceeds the number essential to maintain the cost of enforcement, then the cost of enforcement will fall. Society in this case finds itself propelled towards point (E*,C*). Beyond the point (E*,C*) the actual number essential to maintain the cost of enforcement is too low, so the costs rise and society finds itself back at (E*,C*). These movements are denoted by the direction of the arrows. We see that (E*,C*) is an example of a stable equilibrium.

Figure 5: Zero Level Enforcement

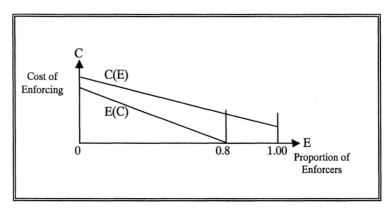

Of course, there need not be any intersection of the two curves. This point is illustrated in Figure 5. This figure indicates that the proportion of the population willing to enforce the norm is always lower than the cost of enforcing the norm (for any given level of enforcement). In other words, there is zero-level enforcement.

Many norms are, of course, reflected in laws on different matters in every legal jurisdication. There are, for instance, an iceberg of laws and regulations against corruption in most legal jurisdictions throughout the world.[10] Lawmakers naturally wish to tap into the informal enforcement of laws in order to increase their credibility and feasibility. There are a plethora of reasons why there may be a low willingness to enforce a law or regulation. A regulation may be considered as overly burdensome or inefficient, which can invite transgression. In the context of corruption, frequently a particular law against certain types of quid pro quo exchanges may be considered as unjust or unfair. Where, for instance, wages are low, certain bribes may be considered as a means of supplementing income (Klitgaard 1988; Klitgaard MacLean-Abaroa and Parris 2000).[11] Under such circumstances, a raise in salary level to what is perceived as a fair wage is necessary is order to procure any support for laws against bribery. Another reason for a low willingness to pay may be that the sanction is perceived to be unjust; or alternatively, there may be a fear that no action will be taken as a result of complaint. I dealt with commonly given reasons for not reporting corruption,

---

[10] *See* below, Chapter VI.

[11] For a discussion thereof, *see* above Chapter III, Section V, Subsection D.

which are also of particular importance here in considering informal sanctions.[12] There is no need here to restate the importance of initiatives at involving the public in anti-corruption reforms; it suffices to say that initiatives involving the citizenry such as those undertaken in Hong Kong against corruption, discussed above, may have an indispensable role to play.[13] These serve, of course, just as examples. The problem may run deeper.

Support may not be available for numerous reasons. Citizens may no longer trust government, and reforms are not considered as either credible or feasible so they do not receive widespread support. A reform-minded government faces the formidable task of credibly signaling that the rules of the game have changed, in order to be trusted by its people and have the requisite support for reforms.

III. Trust in Government as a Prerequisite to Sustainable Anti-Corruption Reforms

The proposition I develop here is simple: if successful and sustainable anti-corruption reforms are conditional upon citizen support as I argued above, but there are low levels of trust in government, reforms cannot be successful without tackling the problem of trust if not prior to serious reform initiatives then accompanying them. The notion of trust has started to receive increasing attention in the literature by such academic luminaries as Putnam (1993, 2000), Fukuyama (1995) and Stiglitz (1999), who commonly have emphasized that economic welfare and performance are widely influenced by the level of trust in a society. This interest has no doubt also been fueled in part because of the spate of still recent events, more that most the overturning of communist systems in Eastern Europe, but also the recent flourish of global democratization movements, which toss up queries of how best to institute trust in a reformed state or government (*see* Levi 2001: 1). Reforming government depends on the development of confidence in a state and distrust can lead to reforms foundering, never getting started, or worse still to ethnic and religious conflict that hinder effective governance. Trust is, therefore, part of a deeper embedded phenomenon, which if ignored, can render reforms untenable.

---

[12] Recall, these included: a belief that the action is not wrong or sufficiently wrong to be reported; fear of retaliation; a belief that effective action would not follow; a belief that evidence was not sufficient to warrant reporting and a belief that the actions do not really have an impact on the observer (Gorta and Forell 1995: 321).

[13] *See* above Chapter IV, Section II.

A. Characteristics of Trust

To crystallize our understanding of the notion of trust, so as not to look at it as merely an abstract concept, it is important that we trace some of its essential characteristics. The essence of trust is that it implies confidence but not certainty, that some person or institution will act in an expected way (Rose-Ackerman 2001: 2). It necessarily evokes a sense of expectations about the actions of another person or institution that impact one's own action choice: an action is taken by person B when he cannot properly be monitored by person A (Dasgupta 1988). When one can perfectly monitor the other party, one need no longer speak of trust.

Another feature of trust is that it is composed of three distinct parts: A trusts B to do X (Hardin 2001; Levi 2001). Accordingly, the act of trust is the knowledge or belief that the trusted will have an incentive to do what she engages to do (Levi 2001: 2). One can, therefore, see that trust is also incentive driven. To wit, according to Hardin (1999, 2001) trust is best understood in self-interest terms, which he calls encapsulated interest.: "I trust you because I think it is in your interest to take my interests seriously in the following sense. You value the continuation of our relationship and you therefore have your own interest in taking my interest into account" (Hardin 2001: 1). In other words, I trust you because I think it in your interests to hold your side of the bargain as it is desirable for you to continue our relationship.

It is an unwieldy prospect to categorize the manifold forms of trust. Rose-Ackerman (2001) recently considered three basic forms. One kind she considered is generalized interpersonal trust, that describes a background or general psychological attitude of tendencies to trust rather than trust in any particular person or institution. It has been used as an indicator of the health of a society (Inglehart 1997,1999). For example, in the World Values Surveys conducted between 1995 -1997, attempting to measure this type of generalized trust, when asked whether "most people can be trusted", only 3 percent of all Brazilians agree, whereas at the other end of the scale 65 percent of Norwegians consider that most can be trusted (Inglehart 1999). The parties "live in fundamentally different social climates" (*ibid*.: 92). One should accept these values with caution. From a reformer's perspective, the problem with these measures of trust is as Rose-Ackerman acknowledges (2001: 4) that they are "very difficult to interpret and to translate into concrete proposals."

The second type of trust identified by Rose-Ackerman (2001) is one-sided trust or reliability. This is typified by the game of trust I depicted earlier, where only player 1 has to trust player 2 to honor an agreement, given that player 1 can never cheat on player 2. The decision of player 1 to enter into an agreement with player 2 depends on the expectations the former has that the latter will honor his covenant. As suggested below, this is typical of many citizen-government relationships. The final category of trust she considered is two-sided reciprocal trust, as exemplified by the prisoner's dilemma, which as proposed in chapter II typifies many forms of economic and social exchange. I extrapolate on the latter two types of trust in greater detail below.

B. Creating Trust

Any discussion on generating trust in government would be incomplete without addressing in some form the contribution of Putnam (1993, 2000) to the debate. According to Putnam, trust can only be created through encouraging people to join civic organizations and clubs that foster interpersonal trust and generate "social capital", which in turn should bring about accountable government. This notion of social capital, which Putnam believes to be fundamental to overcoming cooperation failures refers to "features of social organization, such as trust, norms, and networks, that can improve the efficiency of society by facilitating coordinated norms" (Putnam 1993: 167). Accordingly, spontaneous cooperation can be facilitated by social capital. He cites the following example.

> "A rotating credit union association consists of a group who agree to make regular contributions to a fund which is given, in whole or in part, to each contributor in rotation...A typical rotating credit association, each of twenty members might contribute a monthly sum equivalent to one dollar, and each month a different member would receive that month's pot of twenty dollars to be used as he or she wished (to finance a wedding, a bicycle, a sewing machine, or new inventory for a small shop). That member is ineligible for subsequent distributions, but is expected to make regular contributions until all members have had a turn at receiving the pot. Rotating credit associations vary widely in size, social composition, organization, and procedures for determining the payout. All combine sociability with capital formation" (Putnam 1993: 167-68).[14]

Putnam emphasized that third party enforcement itself is a public good, subject to the same basic dilemma in many respects that it aims to resolve, just one step removed (*see ibid.*: 165). In this context he suggests, for example, that "[h]istory has taught southern Italians the improbability of the Hobbesian solution to dilemmas of collective action" (*ibid.*: 166). Accordingly, where the state has "coercive power", as Hobbes describes it, its actors are willing to pursue only their own interests.

For Putnam essentially those individuals that learn that cooperation pays in horizontal organizations learn to cooperate in other areas in which they have little

---

[14] Footnotes omitted. Putnam suggests that rotating credit associations have been reported in countries as diverse as Nigeria, Scotland, Peru Vietnam, Japan and Egypt and the United States. He also reports that many U.S. savings and loans apparently began as rotating credit association (Putnam 1993: 167).

information. As Levi puts it, "[f]inding themselves in an iterated prisoner's dilemma, they refer to past experiences and choose the "nice" strategy" (Levi 2001: 7). From a policy perspective, a key point of Putnams is worth reiterating, namely that generating generalized interpersonal trust and social capital is a prerequisite to good governance. Reforms accordingly cannot be considered as credible nor the government as trustworthy unless interpersonal trust is generated by persons that have joined horizontal groups, such as civic organizations, that generate interpersonal trust among members and produce "social capital" which in turn helps foster accountable government. The most significant problem with Putnams solution is that there appears to be equally as much support for the non-transmission as for the transmission of trust (Levi 2001: 7; Rose-Ackerman 2001). For example, Mishler and Rose (1998) study empirically the relationship between trust and political institutions. They compare what they call "culturalist" theories, such as that proposed by Putnam (1993), to the institutional perspective, largely representative of our arguments here. According to the "culturalist" theories trust in political institutions is largely politically exogenous. It is "projected onto institutions rather than being a consequence of their character or performance". According to the institutionalist perspective, on the other hand, "the critical determinant of institutional trust is what is done by political leaders and government institutions, not how individual citizens behave within their circle of family, friends, workmates and neighbors" (Mishler and Rose 1998: 3-4). They found that perceptions of political performance exert substantial influence on individual trust levels of government and that institutions that perform well generate additional trust that can lend itself to a spiral of good governance. Those that perform badly on the other hand can have the opposite effect.[15]

Looking at Table 1, we can see that there is a great difference between trust in others and trust in government. Indeed we can see that interpersonal trust is frequently quite high and trust in governmental institutions quite low. In Russia, for example, trust in people scores 3.4 on a scale of 0 to 7, meaning approximately, that as many people believe people can be trusted as not be trusted. On the other hand, the level of trust in private enterprises and trade unions was only 2.6 on both accounts. Trust in the military was 3.7 which was even greater than the level reported for people. Other countries reveal even more dramatic differences in the level of trust. For example in Romania, trust in the church scored 5.6 from a maximum of 7 points, an institution according to Putnam (1993) based on vertical relationships, which are nonconducive to the

---

15 Mishler and Rose use data collected by the fifth New Democracies Barometer (NDBV), the results of extensive interviews (approx. 1000 in each of the seven countries surveyed) conducted between January and May, 1998 in seven Central and Eastern European countries organized by Paul Lazarfeld Society, Vienna, and the seventh New Russian Barometer (NRB VII), which conducted nearly 2000 interviews, organized by the Centre for the Study of Public Policy at the University of Strathclyde.

production of trust. The link between trust in people and trust in particular organizations, according to these figures, is capricious and weak at best.

Table 1

COUNTRY MEANS FOR TRUST IN INSTITUTIONS AND PEOPLE

Trust in:	Bul	Cze	Slk	Hun	Pol	Rom	Rus	Slv	Bel	Ukr	All
Parties	2.7	3.1	3.0	2.9	2.7	2.9	2.2	2.6	2.6	2.4	2.7
Courts	3.0	3.5	3.8	4.0	3.7	3.9	3.4	3.6	3.6	2.7	3.5
Police	3.5	3.6	3.7	3.9	3.8	3.9	3.1	3.9	3.1	2.4	3.5
Parliament	3.1	2.9	3.2	3.4	3.5	3.4	2.7	3.1	3.5	2.3	3.1
President/ Prime Minister	4.1	4.5	3.1	3.7	3.9	4.4	2.6	3.9	4.1	2.5	3.7
Military	4.6	3.8	4.7	4.1	4.6	5.4	3.7	3.9	4.3	3.9	4.3
Churches	3.4	3.6	4.1	3.8	4.4	5.6	3.4	3.1	4.8	4.4	4.1
Trade Unions	2.7	3.7	3.6	2.9	3.6	3.8	2.6	3.5	3.5	2.5	3.2
Television & Radio	3.8	4.4	3.8	4.4	4.3	4.4	3.3	4.1	4.0	3.7	4.0
Press	3.6	4.4	3.9	4.2	4.4	4.2	3.3	4.1	3.9	3.6	4.0
Private Enterprise	3.3	3.9	3.6	3.8	3.4	4.1	2.6	3.5	3.3	2.9	3.4
Average All Institutions	3.5	3.5	3.6	3.7	3.7	4.0	3.0	3.5	3.5	2.7	3.5
Trust in People	4.0	4.7	4.2	4.6	4.7	3.7	3.4	4.5	5.1	5.0	4.4

Note: Trust in institutions on a scale of 1 (great distrust) to 7 (great trust). Standard deviations omitted.
Source: Paul Lazarfeld Society, Vienna, New Democracies Barometer V (1998) and Centre for the Study of Public Policy, New Russia Barometer VII (1998). Reproduced in Mishler and Rose (1998: 33) Appendix A

Indeed, there appears to be a fundamental shortcoming in Putnam's analysis in that it fails to take strategic elements into account. In this context, Rose-Ackerman (2001: 11) notes: "People who express high or low levels of generalized trust may trust others in one strategic context, say involving neighborhood cooperation in a common task, and distrust others in another, say in deciding whether to pay taxes or apply for a scarce public benefit." It fails to take into account that trust is a three-part relationship (A trusts B to do X), as mentioned above (Hardin 2001;

Levi 2001). One can trust ones neighbors but not ones state, or vice-versa depending on the context (Levi 1997). People can trust their government with their property rights but not with the power to transcript soldiers to war as reportedly was the case of the United States prior to World War I (*ibid.*).

1. Generating Trust in Government

In this section, I outline suggestive measures that may be used to increase the level of trust in government. Contrary to the aforementioned position adopted by what may be described as the "culturalists camp", I argue in line with Rose-Ackerman (2001: 2) that the government can generate trust onto itself and that this one-sided trust is fundamental to the "development of legitimate, well-functioning governments and markets".[16] Here I address some forms of resistance that arise between developing this type of trust in government and other patterns of reciprocal trust that are already established, particularly within networks or kin, oftentimes a response themselves to government failures to respect property rights and secure contractual obligations between parties.

Cooperation can result from correct expectations of a person acting in a manner we cannot observe and control, but cooperation may also result because it is clearly in someone's interest to do so, particularly when we can observe their actions. In the first case, there is clearly a greater need for trust than in the second. In all the lamenting about lack of trust, it is easy to see how this clear distinction could be misplaced and easily forgotten. Indeed, our key argument is this: it is those factors that mitigate the need for trust in government that make government actors more accountable in the first place, and citizens confident in government performing in accordance with their broader wishes. So to increase confidence in government, the first step is to reduce the need for trust!

---

[16] Recall that one-sided reliability refers essentially to the structure of the game of trust "where person A decides whether or not to trust another person or institution B, on the basis of information about incentives motives and confidence. The situation is one-sided in the sense that the trusted person is uninterested in whether A is trustworthy. B may, however, be influenced by A's expected reactions to B's actions" (Rose-Ackerman 2001: 6). Rose-Ackerman also distinguished between three different types of one-sided reliability, where there is a strategic element involved, as in the case of Akerlof's car salesman in his famous "market for lemons" example (*see* Akerlof 1970, *see* also Dasgupta 1988). A second type of one-sided trust or reliability is where you need to know, if the material incentives are aligned with your interest as in the above, but also you need knowledge about competence and reputation for unbiased judgment. This is typical of a doctor-patient relationship. A third type of one-sided trust is based on organizational functioning, where one trusts that organizational rules and procedure will be followed in an unbiased manner (ibid.: 6-9).

From this distinction, we can see that it is generally rational for citizens not to trust government, when interests are not aligned.[17] When interests are aligned, we can say that we have minimized the need for trust. The need for trust in our sense is greater, the higher the level of risk involved. Therefore, it is important for government to align the interest of officials and in this case enforcement officials with those of the citizens it represents. Naturally, however, even where interests are perfectly aligned, there may still be a certain amount of uncertainty, given *inter alia* incompetence, the potential for mistakes, malicious decisions etc. Trust itself is, therefore, not good per se. The need to trust in government in the above sense is unfavorable and should be minimized.[18] A government that wishes to signal it is trustworthy needs to minimize the need to have its citizens trust it. Where the costs of aligning interests are too high, then a certain amount of trust is invariably necessary. As a side, I hasten to add that trust should not be confused with altruism, and is born out of reciprocity.[19] This, argument is an extension of David Hume's now famous suggestion found in his work entitled "Essays on the first principals of government" of 1758 where he suggested:

> "In constraining any system of government and fixing the several checks and controls of the constitution, every man ought to be supposed a knave and to have no other end in all his actions than private interest" (Hume 1987, first pub. 1758).

It is equally reflective of the position taken by Madison and the federalists in the development of the US Constitution.[20]

---

[17] For Hardin (1999) trust in an institution is difficult to reconcile with his definition of trust as encapsulated interest described above. Recall that under his definition of trust as encapsulated interest, person A essentially trusts person B, because he believes it is in the interests of person B to act in his own interests. Hardin suggests that there are three means of understanding trust in an institution. First, we could trust every individual in the institution. Second, we could trust the structure of incentives to get officials to act well as our agents. Thirdly, and most plausibly, "we might merely depend on its [the organizations] apparent predictability by induction from its past behavior. Then we merely have an expectations account of the organization's behavior" (*ibid.*: 30).

[18] Ideally until the point where the marginal gains from doing so equal the marginal losses. Given, however, the uncertainty involved this is more a rule of thumb than a rule.

[19] Trust should not be considered as altruistic behavior. As (Binmore 1997: 266) professes: "I agree that altruists are more congenial companions than egoists, but I do not see how one can square the facts of human history with a belief that people need to be altruists to make society work."

[20] In an equally famous suggestion normally attributed to James Madison, he states: "Ambition must be made to counteract ambition...If men were angels, no government would be necessary. If angels were to govern men, neither external nor internal controls on government would be necessary." The Federalist no. 51.

As mentioned, there will always be a certain amount of uncertainty involved, and interests will never be fully aligned. But, to reiterate my argument, it is precisely the need not to have to trust government, that increases citizen confidence in its government in the first place. Information on the alignment of interests is, of course, only gathered inductively by individuals, on the basis of past experience. In this sense, we can speak of trust in government where we have a belief or expectation that government will pursue our interests even in the face of imperfect information.

To design institutions in a manner that mitigates the need for trust is only one important factor in achieving trust. Trust is incremental. Trust in institutions in the face of such uncertainty will be increased by a good record, in the sense that expectations of government truth-telling, promise keeping, fairness etc. have been fulfilled (Offe 1999). As Levi (2001: 15) puts it, "healthy skepticism of citizens is a prerequisite of democracy. Citizen trust of government should be and is conditional." Inglehardt (1999) has reported a decline in trust of government officials, but according to the above, we do not have to consider this as a problem. Margaret Levi, a leading authority on the subject describes the key sources of distrust in government as "promise-breaking, incompetence, and the antagonism of government actors towards those they are supposed to serve" (Levi 2001: 9). She submits:

> "Citizens are likely to trust government only to the extent they believe that it will act in their interests, that its procedures are fair, and that their trust of the state and of others is reciprocated. These are the conditions necessary to produce contingent consent, behavioral compliance with government demands even when an individual's costs somewhat exceed her individual benefits and even in the absence of strong ideological convictions that make costs totally irrelevant. Contingent consent is a citizen's decision to comply or volunteer in response to demands from a government only if she perceives government as trustworthy and she is satisfied other citizens are also engaging in ethical reciprocity [the norm of contributing one's fair share when others are also doing so]" (*ibid.*).

"History matters" (North 1990: vii). And for this reason, inductive reasoning by citizens about the pursuit by government of interests that are harmonious to citizens' interests is so important. According to Putnam (1993: 166), "[h]istory has taught southern Italians the improbability of the Hobbesian solution to dilemmas of collective action (Putnam 1993: 166). History ensures that reform can only be an incremental process. In some sense, reformers are locked-in by past shortcomings. Trust is grounded on reputation which fundamentally has to be obtained through "behavior over time in well understood circumstances" (Dasgupta 1988: 5). Institutions that perform well generate additional trust (Braithwaite and Levi 1998). It should not, therefore, be surprising that in Russia trust in governmental institutions is so low, where for the year 1998 "less than two in five Russians routinely receive[d] the wage or pension to which the are entitled", and wages and pensions "more likely to be paid late to employees of such public sector organizations as the military, education and state enterprises than to employees in the private sector" (Rose 1998: 12). Where the government is perceived as untrustworthy or its policies as illegitimate and unfair, then, before it can successfully recruit the efforts of citizens in reform, it may have to make other more fundamental changes to sell its policies or indeed come up with new ones. Its procedures for making and implementing policy must adhere to perceived standards of fairness, and it should be capable of making credible commitments (Braithwaite and Levi 1998: 88). These considerations extend beyond immediate relations between an individual and the state and include perceptions of how the state treats others.

According to Levi (2001: 10-11), "there are four important and quite distinctive ways in which a state signals its fairness: coercion of those who are not compliant; universalistic policies; establishment of credible courts and other impartial institutions for arbitrating disputes and ensuring that those who lose can sometimes win; and the involvement of the citizens in the actual making of policy." She readily admits, "[s]ome of these are in the tool bag of any government; others are clearly democratic devices." Here, coercion in large part involves getting past free-riding. An important feature of n-person dilemmas or public goods problems, the free-rider is an omnipresent phenomenon that inhibits governance. Taxation provides an excellent example, in particular given that the capacity to collect taxes is the defining characteristic of the state and a good indicator of the level of trust in other citizens and government (Rose 1998). Evidence on tax evasion seems to indicate, for example, that in countries like Sweden where there is a high willingness to pay taxes, the belief that other citizens are also paying their taxes is an important motivating factor (Rothstein 2001). Similarly, in the United States research on tax paying seems to indicate that citizens pay their taxes as part of their obligation to the collective as long as they feel that others are doing their bit to maintain to social contract (Scholtz 1998). One difficulty in interpreting these results, however is that people are poorly informed about the chance of audit (Rose-Ackerman 2001: 11).[21] Universalism, the second means with which a state signals its fairness according to Levi (2001: 11) refers to "universalistic criteria in recruitment of agents and in regulating the institutions of both government and civil society." These are common across-the-board standards. Impartial institutions and courts, the third factor identified, are self-explanatory. A key advantage they provide is that "those

---

[21] In tax evasion, as with corruption, there is a familiar dynamic involved where the number of people that choose to engage in these activities depends on the number of others they expect to engage in them. As the sense of expectations on the number of others participating in these activities increases, so too will the actual number.

who consider a process as fair are far more likely to accept individually unfavorable outcomes *(ibid.)."* Another related consideration here is the fear of tyranny of the majority and the protection of the minority. Where a minority feels that its basic rights are not protected or that it receives unfair treatment, it is less likely to support government in its reform efforts. The fourth category she refers to is participation, the involvement of citizens in policy, where they can affect direction, procedures and perhaps implementation.

Emphasized in chapter II, cooperation may evolve and sustain itself where there are clear strategies and clear signals, i.e. where actions are observable. Moves by a reform-minded government towards the free speech, free assembly, and free press increase access to information allowing citizens to observe the actions of government officials *(see* also Levi 2001: 13). Additionally, when the government provides these measures, it provides the citizenry with information that can be used to sanction government and keep it in line, serving as a commitment device. Precisely for these reasons, of course, government is often reluctant to pursue such strategies There are, however, several self-interested reasons why such a policy may be pursued, particularly because a reform-minded government that pursues such strategies decreases the ability of successive governments to renege on its reforms. It burns its bridges preventing successive governments from retreat.[22] Moreover, movements towards more democratic measures have the potential to fundamentally change the behavior of government actors. As Levi *(ibid.:* 13-14) suggests: "By providing citizens with a variety of effective means for sanctioning government actors, for interacting with them in the creation of policy, and for reducing the costs of citizen monitoring of governance, democratic institutions create a basis of cooperation between government officials and citizens."[23] Open discussion about government actions adds to trustworthiness by providing a check on obfuscation and secret promises (or promise-breaking). Free speech permits a level of public and scientific information-gathering and monitoring (Cooter 2000).

There may even be legitimate temporary reasons to slow down this process. A reform-minded government may, be hesitant to opening up its actions to close public scrutiny particularly where it cannot properly constrain the actions of its own officials. There is a narrow line that can easily be crossed between soliciting public help in reforming the machinery of government, and exposing oneself to new founded public reproach based on previous failures. This clearly acts as a significant deterrent to reform. In this vein, disclosures of nonfeasance, bad policy, corruption, or inconsistency may consume fledgling citizen confidence in government and its actors. The potential for political suicide is,

---

[22] On burning bridges as a commitment device, *see* Dixit and Nalebuff (1993).
[23] Where she considers the "defining aspects of democracy ...[to be] effective enfranchisement, civil liberties, and the right of citizens to influence governmental decision-making through political parties, corporatist arrangements, and other forms of legal pressure *(ibid.)."*

however, a short-term defense at best for the delay in the extensive promulgation of those institutions and devices that increase the transparency of government actions. But given that politicians frequently have only a short time horizon, whereby they discount future gains strongly, one can easily see how reforms fail to get started or get halted on one of the multiple steps along the way.[24]

IV. Overcoming Problems of Interpersonal Trust

Patterns of reciprocal behavior have developed alongside and sometimes because of inefficient government institutions. They have become part of the institutions or the rules of the game in a society or, more formally, part of "the humanly devised constraints that shape human interaction" (North 1990: 3). They are important "not just because we learn from the past, but because the present and the future are connected to the past by the continuity of societies institutions" (*ibid.*: vii). Some of these generate patterns of behavior that actively undermine state functions, the corrupt systems analyzed in chapter II fit this description. On the other hand, these organizations can sometimes be viewed positively depending on how one evaluates the state (Rose-Ackerman 2001: 10). In some cases "close-knit, criminal groups may create networks based on a mixture of empathy threats and shared goals that leave the state powerless." In others, "organizations based on interpersonal solidarity in the face of an illegitimate state can sow the seeds of revolutionary change" (*ibid.*). A significant barrier to reform, however, is that "the development of legitimate and well-functioning markets [that] requires one-sided trust" can be impeded when tensions arise with other reciprocal relations that have developed (ibid.: 2) Formal rules may be subject to overnight change according to political or judicial authority; informal or nonofficial constraints on the other hand that are embedded in traditions, customs and codes of conduct can generally only scarcely be altered by deliberate policies (North 1990: 8).

Arrow suggests: "Virtually every commercial transaction has within itself an element of trust, certainly any transaction conducted over a period of time. It can be plausibly argued that much of the economic backwardness in the world can be explained by the lack of mutual confidence" (Arrow 1972: 357). The aforementioned qualities of formal institutions can play an important role in aligning the interests of both parties to honor their agreements and generating the important mutual confidence Arrow refers to above. Formal institutions can, play a significant role in overcoming cooperation-related problems, and problems associated with interpersonal trust. They can function in the role of a central authority (as discussed in chapter II), where aggrieved parties can bring their complaints. Within these institutions, rules of reciprocity can be outlined and oftentimes shaped by the parties; a system of gradual sanctions can be provided

---

[24] *See* below, Chapter VIII, Section III, Subsection D.

and administered thus providing where the "force of words is too weak... some coercive power, to compel men equally to the performance of their covenants" (Hobbes 1996: 94-95). In the process, formal institutions can utilize numerous economies of scale advantages in several areas such as monitoring, and a platform for resolution and debate of conflicts that arise can be afforded. Generally, formal institutions may play an important role in reducing transaction costs and enabling agents to surmount problems associated with shirking, free-riding and opportunistic behavior, that prevent transactions from happening over time, and limit mutually beneficial transactions (*see* Williamson 1985).

A. Networks

Zucker (1986) in what has already been described as a classic article on the production of trust,[25] identifies three types or modes of trust production: "(1) processed-based, where trust is tied to past or expected exchange such as in reputation or gift exchange; (2) characteristic-based [ascribed], where trust is tied to person, depending on characteristics such as family background or ethnicity; and (3) institutional-based, where trust is tied to formal societal structures, depending on individual or firm-specific attributes (*e.g.*, certification as an accountant) or on intermediary mechanisms (*e.g.*, use of escrow accountants) (Zucker 1986: 60). Whether or not one agrees with this precise taxonomy is not so important. What is important is that it provides a lens under which to assess the potential friction associated between these network-types and the development of well-functioning governmental institutions.

There seem to be a host of networks that are a hybrid form of these characteristics. McMillan and Woodruff (1999) conducted extensive research on business networks in Vietnam and found that they are frequently local and make extensive use of sanctions such as gossip to keep parties in check. To compensate for the failings of the court, firms used repeated-game type incentives, but managers, however, were often reluctant to sanction trading partners, and would often allow them to forgo part of a debt and were reluctant to withdraw business. Because of their unwillingness to sanction as the basic approach of repeated-game incentives would suggest by retracting all future business, sanctioning was weak.[26] To overcome this, they use a rather elaborate system of governance structure to support sanctions. In particular, community sanctions were used, and firms closely scrutinized the reliability of other firms by seeing how they transact with others or family connections. In such an environment, parties are sometimes willing to continue with a supplier that provides a significantly higher price,

---

[25] *See* Warren (1999) and Raiser (2001).
[26] One explanation given for this is based on imperfect monitoring. When firms could not identify whether failure is a result of error, it can be rational to forgive (minor) failings (McMillan and Woodruff 1999: 642).

because of the uncertainties involved in conducting transactions with third parties. Such a system highlights what may be considered as a hybrid between both process- and characteristic-based trust. There is a significant difference between the two. Whereas markets can more easily expand in the former (which replicate market based repeated-exchange relationships), in characteristic based types of networks, trust is ascribed and is "generally very difficult to alter, and hence it is not likely that markets will form" (Zucker 1986: 61).

Once again transition economies provide a significant platform with which to assess the stability of networks. Raiser (2001) suggests that there are three types of institutional links between enterprises in transition economies. The first of which are business networks built on ascribed trust, usually confined to the local economy, "with the potential to expand through selective interaction with outsiders". The second are networks based on nomenclatura - "recombined during the transition to accommodate the reorganisation of the enterprise sector through corporatisation and privatisation, but continued to be built primarily on process built trust." Commonly "many existing business networks in the transition economies, grown out of former bureaucratic bargaining relationships are not sufficiently open and trust is not sufficiently generalized to fully realize economic opportunities" (*ibid.*: 2). The third network, he identifies are links between modern corporations based largely on the allocation of property rights, formal contracts and the integration into global production networks.

In particular, the second structure identified above, has shown itself to be particularly damaging to the entire transition process, to reforming government and to economic development particularly in Russia as illustrated in the following observation by Braguinsky (1999: 519):

"Too many decades under ruthless communist rulers (...) strongly entrenched the pattern of (especially business) behavior in which private trust was held in high esteem while trust in state authority was close to zero. The private enforcement rings, which built on this limited trust and had to act so as to avoid detection by the state authority, were by their nature confined to small insider-oriented segments (enclaves) with the progressively senile planning system... When the planned economy finally collapsed in the former Soviet Union, those private rings and interest groups suddenly became almost all that remained of the institutional infrastructure. The outcome was the locking in of a highly segmented and inefficient market structure and the transition to a specific form of "monopolistic competition" stemming not from increasing returns to scale or consumer's preference for variety, but from high barriers to entry, erected and maintained by each private protection ring. In other words, the Russian economy was not freed from old Soviet-type monopolies; rather, those monopolies were themselves freed to pursue their goals and objectives without restraint and at the expense of the larger society."

In a host of articles in Grabler and Stark (1997), the authors cite many similarities in networks in economies in transition. Networks based on previous bureaucratic ties are a common feature. As we have seen in our analysis of privatization, the stripping of state assets assisted the formation of economic empires that wield strong influence over policy makers. As Raiser (2001: 10) readily points out, "[b]ureaucratic networks transformed themselves into business organizations aiming to secure maximum rents" and "[t]he stifling effects for private sector development are shown in the negative correlation between corruption and private sector development."

Empirical work provides important insight into the social networks that have developed and their potential to hinder government reforms. In another important contribution by Rose (1998) to the literature, he empirically looks at the means Russian citizens use to "get things done" in what he terms as "anti-modern societies", denoted as environments where formal institutions of state and market do not function properly. Rose suggests that citizens challenged by organizational failure have to make a choice between a variety of possibilities. Informal networks can substitute for the failure of modern bureaucratic organizations. Additional tactics include trying to personalize relations with impersonal bureaucrats or using connections or bribery in an attempt to get bureaucrats to violate rules; or fatalistically accepting that nothing can be done" (Rose 1998: 13). He defines the means to "get things done" as "the stock of formal and informal social networks that individuals can use to produce or allocate goods and services" (Rose 1998: 5). In addition to the above typology based on Zucker (1986) and the hybrid forms I suggested exist between them, Rose's work emphasizes that networks are importantly just one means of getting things done, and relatedly that people have many such networks. As he suggests, "[i]n every situation, a variety of networks are applicable- and the Russians differ in their choice. Whatever the situation, some people will rely in the public bureaucracy to deliver goods and services, while others rely on informal do-it-yourself cooperation, personalistic cajoling of bureaucrats or anti-modern bending or breaking of rules, and if the situation makes it feasible, some turn to the market" (Rose 1998: 19).

Importantly, this work propounds that these networks are more in response to the rules of the game on the allocation of goods and services, rather than more underlying features. Russians rely on the logic of redundancy, "maintaining links with more networks than are normally necessary so that if one fails another can be invoked" (*ibid.*: 20). Seen in this manner, multiple networks are instrumental in satisficing, *i.e.*, attempting a number of different ways of procuring a benefit or getting something done until the desired result is produced (*ibid.*: 21). From our perspective, what is specially important is the insight that in such an environment there is strong reason to suggest that the social networks that are established would very often subside should the benefits be provided by the government itself. Indeed, Rose observed that the most frequently used portfolio was quite defensive whereby a person tries a modern organization first and, this failing seeks informal social networks as a surrogate.

Table 2

Strategies of Population in Response to Problems with Public Service
(answers given in percent)

	Anti-modern connections	Personal	Market	Passive
1. *Getting into university without good enough grades*				
Russia	33	6	39	22
Ukraine	31	3	45	21
Czech Republic	7	2	72	18
Korea	3	2	37	57
2. *Actions to get a better flat when not entitled to publicly subsidized housing*				
Russia	45	n.a.	30	25
Ukraine	34	10	28	27
Czech Republic	14	23	48	15
Korea	8	13	64	15
3. *Action if an official delays issuing a government permit*				
Russia	62	18	n.a.	20
Ukraine	61	18	n.a.	21
Czech Republic	35	46	n.a.	19
Korea	21	45	n.a.	34
4. *Getting treatment for a painful disease when hospital says one must wait for months*				
Russia	57	13	11	19
Ukraine	39	12	34	15
Czech Republic	24	31	31	14
Korea	(not applicable; no government health service)			

Anti-modern connections (Corrupt option): Offer Bribe, use connections, make up a story. **Personal (Bureaucratic):** Write a letter of complaint, push officials to act. **Market:** Buy what you want legally; education: pay a tutor. **Passive:** Nothing can be done. Sources: New Korea Barometer 1997 (N:1,117); New Democracies Barometer V 1998 (N:1,017); Russia Social Capital Survey 1998 (N:1,908) (Cited in Rose 1998: 25).

How unique an environment is Russia? Comparing data collected in similar, albeit less extensive, surveys in Ukraine, the Czech Republic and the Republic of Korea provides some interesting results, see Table 2 above. We can see from the data that Russia and the Ukraine bare many similarities. The favorite tactic to get a flat when not entitled to one, acquire a permit where an official delays issuance, or treatment in a hospital is through "anti-modern techniques", such as bribery, using connections or deceit. One third of all Russians and nearly one third of all Ukrainians would try to use "anti-modern methods" for purposes of University admission, compared to only 7 percent of all Czechs. Russians, according to the figures, are three times more likely than Czechs to use these methods to acquire a better flat than they are entitled to it. Koreans on the whole, seem far less likely to resort to "anti-modern methods" to acquire a benefit to which they were not entitled and seem to accept far more easily that nothing can be done about the actions of government officials. Koreans according to Table 2 are far closer to the Czechs in their reluctance to use anti-modern techniques than the Czechs are to the Russians or the Ukrainians, highlighting that Asian countries may not be so distinctive and that there is strong divergence within the countries in transition in Central and Eastern Europe.[27] Mentioned at the initial stages of our discussion in this chapter, networks and systems frequently developed alongside and sometimes because of inefficient or avarice government. Furthermore, I stressed that where formal institutions do not govern economic transactions, there is often a climate of distrust and these transactions either don't take place or rely on ascribed (family, background etc.) or process based trust (reputation etc., informal governance structures). Perhaps, however, one of the most threatening networks that can develop is organized crime, which in such a climate of "endemic distrust" as that described above is provided with multiple opportunities (see Gambetta 1993). It can be particularly deleterious to economic development and can provide a significant barrier to anti-corruption reforms. In lieu of the above discussion, note that organized crime is frequently a hybrid of network types built on ascribed trust and process based trust. Even this distinction is not necessarily accurate, because such networks are often supported by formal institutional factors, particularly when there is a Mafia-dominated or Mafia-influenced state. It is here we turn our attention in the next section.

---

[27] See above, Chapter III, Section VIII.

B. The Problem of Organized Crime: Operating in an Environment of Endemic Distrust

The legal and institutional structure of society is instrumental in shaping the activities of its citizens. Where these structures do not provide expected payoffs for legal activities higher than illegal activities, we can expect a shift from legal to illegal activities until such a point as the expected gains from both approximate one another.[28] Within both environments, there is room for entrepreneurial activity. In an environment dominated by the rule-of-law, entrepreneurs will engage their efforts built upon or alongside the constraints and safeties of formal institutions. In an environment where the rule-of-law is absent, entrepreneurial activity will be shaped by those areas that return the greatest earnings outside or irrespective of those same constraints that would be provided by well-functioning formal institutions. In a similar vein Baumol (1990: 893) hypothesizes that

> "... while the total supply of entrepreneurs varies among societies, the productive contribution of the society's entrepreneurial activities varies much more because of their allocation between productive activities such as innovation and largely unproductive activities such as rent seeking or organized crime. This allocation is heavily influenced by the relative payoffs society offers to such activities. This implies that policy can influence the allocation of entrepreneurship more effectively than it can influence its supply..."

In an environment shaped by endemic interpersonal distrust, where parties do not have the legal means to make agreements enforceable, there are obvious returns to activities that guarantee such commitment. Accordingly, it is not difficult to see how organized crime is furnished with opportunity in such an environment. As Gambetta (1993: 19), one of the foremost scholars on organized crime submits: "Mafia are first and foremost entrepreneurs in one particular commodity-protection- and this is what distinguishes them from simple criminals, simple entrepreneurs, or criminal entrepreneurs."[29]

---

[28] Of course, we may have what the economist refers to as a corner solution, where the returns to one activity are always higher than the other, so the parties all engage in either all legal or all illegal activities.

[29] There is much discussion in the literature as to what actually constitutes organized crime. There seems to be some agreement that organized crime provides some protection of property rights and the enforcement of contracts or agreements. According to Schelling (1971) for example, the main business of organized crime is to *impose* its protection on other legal and illegal firms under a threat of violence. Organized crime strives to acquire a monopolistic supply of violence in the market, given that it faces competition from other groups. Gambetta (1988, 1993) on the other hand considers the main business of organized crime to not be the supply of trust and the provision of a stable business environment particularly for illegal firms.

> "When the butcher comes to me to buy an animal, he knows that I want to cheat him. But I know that he wants to cheat me. Thus we need, say, Peppe [a third party] to make us agree. And we both pay Peppe a percentage of the deal" (Gambetta 1993: 15).

As the above illustrates, a lack of trust among parties that engage in transactions opens up opportunities for those who provide guarantees that agreements will be honored. The players here again find themselves in a familiar prisoner's dilemma type problem (redepicted in Figure 6) as discussed in chapter II and elsewhere, except that in previous discussion transactions were necessarily illegal; here many of the transactions are both legal as well as illegal. In fact it does not make any difference, as in either case the parties are operating outside or despite the law. Here the parties- the butcher and the farmer- forgo mutually beneficial transactions because they cannot be sure that either side will honor their agreement. For convenience I have once again taken numerical examples and have assumed a symmetry in payoffs. A rational player as we know will rank the four possible outcomes: The best scenario is for him to defect on the opposing player and have his opponent cooperate. Next best is for him to cooperate and have the opposing player also cooperate. The third best outcome is for him to defect and the other player also to defect. The worst possible outcome is for him to cooperate and other player to defect. Here given the structure of the payoffs the gains from trade are not necessarily exploited because the dominant strategy for both parties is unconditional defection.[31] The unique equilibrium as we know is defect/defect.

Figure 6: Prisoner's Dilemma

		Farmer	
		Cooperate	Defect
Butcher	Cooperate	2, 2	-2, 4
	Defect	4, -2	0, 0

"Rather than producing cars, beer, nuts and bolts, or books, they produce and sell trust" (Gambetta 1988: 128). Note, we use the term Mafia and organized crime interchangeably.

[30] Title taken from Thomas C. Schelling (1971) in his article of the same name.

[31] Defection by Player 1 strictly dominates cooperation as a strategy, as does defection by Player 2 strictly dominate cooperation.

In such an environment, one can easily see that there are opportunities for a third party that is willing to supervise transactions. There are two distinct types of punishment that a (solicited) central authority may administer. Consider, for example, the scenario where a third party such as Peppe is called into play where one party defects. I cast the readers attention to Figure 7.

Figure 7: Assurance Game

		Farmer	
		Cooperate	Defect
Butcher	Cooperate	2, 2	-2, -2
	Defect	-2, -2	0, 0

Let us assume that Peppe is willing to repossess the gains a defecting party enjoys from not cooperating and administer a beating the equivalent of a payoff of -2. The payoffs for defection are no longer 4, as in the former example, but -2. There are two Nash Equilibrium in the game, Cooperate/Cooperate and Defect/Defect. Each player willingly cooperates if it can be sure that the other one will, hence the name assurance game. It is not difficult for the parties to select an equilibrium as they only have to chose from the two that exist. The cooperative equilibrium is better for the two so it may be easy to sustain as a focal point if expectations can converge.

It is, however, unlikely that a figure such as Peppe in the example above would be willing to take the risk of both parties not converging, as this is potentially very damaging for his reputation. It is more likely that the set of payoffs that will emerge are those that make cooperation the unconditionally preferred strategy.

Figure 8: Third Party Enforcement of all Defection

		Farmer	
		Cooperate	Defect
Butcher	Cooperate	2, 2	-2, -2
	Defect	-2, -2	-2, -2

This is depicted in Figure 8. Peppe is no longer willing to sit back and watch both parties defect, but is willing to administer a beating equal to -2 for their noncooperation. Cooperation is the dominant strategy for each player and a Cooperate/Cooperate is the unique Nash Equilibrium.[32]

There are networks of willing agents and Peppe and his cohorts may be considered as entrepreneurs of trust (Gambetta 1988, 1993). This offers some explanation as to why the Mafia has survived for so long, given the consensual aspect of its operations.

The opportunities for entrepreneurial activities of the type supplied by Peppe are subject to the returns to such activities, which are highest, as suggested, when there is an environment of endemic distrust. Just how damaging such an environment is to economic development is easily understood. But what of the services provided by organized crime in such an environment, and what of the impact on potential reforms. There are some key problems associated with the use of the Mafia to supervise transactions, ensuring cooperative outcomes, which I outline next.

The first problem is clearly the fact that many potential cooperative relationships that the Mafia may supervise are particularly undesirable, and we wish to prevent them from taking place. The Mafia does not respect property rights or legal requisites. The corruption market, because it is illegal by definition, has an abundant supply of "fraudulent salesmen" (Della Porta and Vannucci 1999 :54). These open up opportunities for the supervisory role of the Mafia. For example, in a study conducted by the "Organized Crime Task Force" Report (1989) in New York State, the involvement of organized crime in the allocation of public funds was a result of two discernible features: First, they bribed and coerced public officials and second, coordinated collusive agreements between the firms and the public administration. In legitimate business, organized crime frequently adopts a coordinating role in auction activities with the public administration in such areas as waste disposal, road and building construction. Characteristic of these markets is that there are low barriers to entry and a low level of specific inputs which make cartel agreements particularly unstable (Gambetta and Reuter 1995). In lieu of the above, we can see how in addition to providing a steady flow of bribes to public officials, the Mafia's role as central authority (discussed in chapter II) can make collusive and corrupt deals particularly stable. Defection of members is hampered by coordinating successful collusive arrangements; a platform for dispute settlement is given within the organization, and efforts are made to deter others outside of the organizations protection from entering into the market in order to keep the returns from illegal activities high and the demand for the services, that are contingent on these returns, equally so.

---

[32] In the payoffs, I have not included Peppe rewards for his efforts. This can easily be understood as merely a percentage of the gains from trade that both parties enjoy.

A second account why the use of the Mafia for the supervision of transactions is undesirable is based on the well documented fact that, like a kleptocrat, it has a limited amount of transactions that it is able to supervise and reaches a point where negative returns are accrued to each additional member that requests its services (Gambetta 1993). It therefore has an interest in keeping the number of buyers of its services at a specific level; its optimal level. Furthermore, there is an associated reputation loss where it overextends itself and cannot provide its services, thus offering incentives for its own members to leave and other groups to enter into its market. Consequently, it provides barriers to entry to the "market for protection", and accordingly barriers to competition in the markets in which its protection market operates- these barriers and the associated monopoly rights that come with them make their services from the perspective of the buyer so significant. [33]

Relatedly, organized crime signals that without its assistance transactions could not occur, so it has an interest in selling goods that otherwise a buyer could not consume. In order to keep the demand for its goods high, it has an interest in "regulated injections of distrust"(Gambetta 1993). This has the effect of preventing agents from getting over the trust problem on their own. More discomfitingly, it may inject distrust into transactions through the use of its resources to "persuade" state officials not to make efforts to overcome the trust problem, or to work with them in order to manufacture or maintain the problem of distrust. Formal institutions and legal efforts to overcome the trust problem are effectually hampered.[34]

A third significant problem associated with organized crime is its adverse impact on the development of reputation, a fundamental factor inherent in many market transactions. The existence of the Mafia may not just prevent parties in their efforts to establish dealings among one another based on personal initiative to overcome the problem of distrust, but may actually prevent the desirability for private persons of developing such as reputation for trust in the first place. As we

---

[33] As we have seen in chapter II, the greater the number of participant in illicit activity, frequently the more difficult it is (at least up to a point) for the parties to control each other. Like any other central authority, when the Mafia operates in such a role in order to reduce the possibility of defection it wishes to find out as much information as it can about player type and the probable moves of players (here players refer to (potential) parties under their protection). In order to acquire this information on the "creditworthiness" of players, and to use the possible benefits of alternative information and sanctioning systems (*e.g.*, spying and social sanctions respectively), in addition to insider knowledge on where payoffs are to be had, it is often observed that the Mafia is limited by geographical factors. *See* further Chapter II, Section III, Subsection D and Gambetta (1993).

[34] Here when we refer to the trust problem, we refer to the problem of reciprocal trust as highlighted in the prisoner's dilemma, where one side can trust another side to honor his obligations because it is not in his interests to honor these obligations (*see* Hardin 2001). We could just as easily have referred to it as the problem of mutual defection.

know from the path-breaking work of Akerlof (1970) and numerous other authors that followed, where we have a breakdown in the reputation market, we can quickly see a market for lemons developing. Gambetta (1993: 28-29) puts it as follows:

> "A seller that does not live off occasional (once off) transfers has a rational interest on acquiring a reputation for honesty. Even if he is dishonest he may have a rational interest in securing long term gains. A seller has less incentive to look after his own reputation when he is "protected" unless the other party is "protected" by something more powerful. When he already has a steady patronage he does not suffer the same reputation effects as they know the reasons for his actions. The greater the number or returns from patronage, the less likely he is to behave honestly. This results in lemons being sold in the market where the Mafia itself has no direct interest in the sale. Even without the Mafia trying to increase distrust, the demand for his services will increase. Distrust is self-perpetuating and endogenous and need no longer be considered as a precondition external to the market. This also affects the likelihood of good norms becoming dominant. The reputation factor is therefore absent."

A fourth difficulty is the tax-like characteristic associated with extortionary practices. To suggest, that that organized crime does not enter into extortionary activities would be disingenuous, but there are arguments that can be made as to why it may not be the primary business of organized crime, particularly if we take long-run considerations into account.[35] Where the law is ineffective in fighting organized crime, extortionary practices can become rampant. There may also be an interesting dynamic involved, where the more people that purchase protection, the more concentrated the activities of the Mafia actually become, thus making it more desirable for those that do not have "protection" to actually purchase it.[36] The situation in Russia is extremely alarming. As Black, Kraakman, Tarassova (2000: 1751) note:

---

[35] Gambetta (1988) suggests four reasons for this. *First*, he suggests that there is an information bias, because businessmen that experience extortion are more likely to talk to the police about it than those that voluntarily collude. *Second*, extortion may actually be a punishment for freeriding on those that are actually paying for protection. *Third*, extortion is just one activity in business and is comparable to legal firms that lobby to gain monopoly rights and rents from politicians often by illegitimate means. *Fourth*, the protection that is supplied by organized crime provides rents for the firms under its protection and the latter want organized crime to maintain barriers to entry to preserve their economic rents. They gain protection from competition.

[36] (Gambetta 1993: 30-31) highlights another interesting aspect of purchasing protection. He suggests that where one cannot distinguish between those than have protection and those that don't, then those that have paid the money find it in their interest to get the others to also cough it up. There is, therefore, a kind of a free-rider problem among the parties.

"If there is a street-level retail establishment in a major Russian city that doesn't pay a healthy share of revenue for "protection", we haven't heard of it. Arguing too strongly over how much to pay can reduce one's life expectancy, as can complaining to the police, who are likely to be in the pay of the Mafia. This leaves businesses to try to persuade their protectors to leave them enough profit to stay in business."

Another related troublesome feature of large business in Russia is the use of private sector enforcement and security forces, which can be employed for malicious as well as benevolent reasons, such as "enforcing price- fixing and market-division agreements with competitors or scaring off competitors" (*ibid.*: 1760). A development that is aided by the fact that in Russia there is still no effective protection of property rights. The line between private sector security and private sector protection of the kind discussed above is blurred at best. Black, Kraakman, Tarassova (*ibid.*) consider the choice vector of Russian managers to get parties to honor there debts to be as follows.

"...Russian managers can write off unpaid debts, try to enforce them through ineffective courts, or engage their krysha (Russian for "roof," a slang term for Mafia protection) to collect the bill. They can compete on price and quality or pay the krysha to put competitors out of business. They can pay the bribes demanded by local officials or hire the krysha to negotiate a lower payment. Yet when managers rely on the Mafia for services like these, they strengthen the Mafia, strengthen government-Mafia ties, shorten managers' time horizons (you could be put out of business next), and contribute to a lawless environment."

A fifth predicament associated with organized crime is that when it becomes powerful enough, it can challenge the state for the provision of certain services. Indeed, where it becomes powerful enough, the state may even see itself forced to share its revenue with organized crime. It can hold the state hostage, where it effectively controls inputs, such as labor and other supplies, and the spread of local government officials. This problem may be exasperated where a corrupt ruler decides to share illicit gains with the Mafia, not having to worry about coordinating activities with other groups because it may find itself in a bilateral monopoly situation (Rose-Ackerman 1999: 121-124). In Russia, the extent of criminal impediments in the assessment and collection of taxes, although unavailable is substantial. The tax-like property of the payments that private businessmen make for "protection" interfere with the collection of legitimate governmental taxes, in part because they lower the willingness to pay of the business, and further, because it lowers the ability to make such payments (Tanzi 2001).

A sixth problem related to organized crime from our perspective, is related to its engagement in legal activities. Traditionally, authors considered the sphere of activity of organized crime in legal markets to extend to the investment and management of legitimate business often to exploit economies of scale and scope related to their illegal activities (Anderson 1979). Legitimate income is a means of hiding illegitimate income, and premises such as bars and restaurants are used to cover up other activities such as illegal gambling. Moreover, illegal activities often require infrastructure and general inputs and outputs that can also be used in legitimate business, such as warehouses and transportation and communication facilities. These activities naturally also serve for reasons of money laundering. It has also been argued that legitimate activities can offer some diversification of the investments of the organization (Gambetta and Reuter 1995). As one may further expect, where organized crime can furnish a monopoly hold on inputs, such as labor unions, or can direct its "persuasion" activities to acquiring inputs at low cost, effectively giving itself a competitive advantage, we can expect an infiltration of organized crime into legal activities. Recent work also suggests that organized crime is likely to directly invest in mature industries that enjoy protection from international competition (Fiorentini and Pelzman 1995). But what is particularly disconcerting about recent developments in organized crime, particularly in Russia is the extent of its infiltration in legitimate activities and the scope of the activities that it has been able to infiltrate. Specially true of Russia, organized crime has shown a worrying competence in infiltrating official institutions thus blurring the line between legal and illegal transactions and politics and organized crime per se. As reported by Sakwa (2000: 128):

"According to MVD (Ministry of Internal Affairs, in June 1997 there were some 900 organized criminal groups with some 100,000 members, controlling banks, money exchanges and systematically subverting the state administration and new entrepreneurial activity. At least a quarter of Russia's business people were linked to the mob ...Whereas in eastern Europe a civic culture had developed in the framework of the decaying communist system, in Russia the main counter-culture appeared to be a criminal one."

Whereas previously, organized crime generally either bribed politicians (particularly local politicians) and bureaucrats, or alternatively, as Grossman (1995) pointed out, worked together with them by implementing distributive policies to buy support, contemporary Russia has seen the infiltration of its institutions not by actors willing to work together with organized crime but by organized crime itself. In Russia, the development of markets and the democratization process were intertwined with organized crime. Criminal networks have advanced into the banking sector, telecommunications, large scale corporations and a host of other areas that are not commonly considered the territory of organized crime.

Arising out of these developments, organized crime has set itself up in a manner that enables it to prescribe to Russian industries how to behave in the market and have set up closed syndicates that can penetrate the states institutions (*see* Sakwa 2000: 130). Indeed, one may even speak of a fragmentation of the government, where links to particular parts of the state apparatus and the political elite are shared by several private groups separately, each effectively dictating a certain aspect of government responsible for the provision and allocation of goods and services. This entails huge costs in terms of the organization of corruption as we saw in chapter I (*see* Shleifer and Vishny 1993). Corruption is decentralized which makes it more detrimental than centralized corruption because all of the parties involved try to maximize their own bribe intake irrespective of the behavior of others (*ibid.*; Braguinsky 1999).

A seventh predicament is related to the intrinsic uncertainty in protection markets and the resulting short time horizon shared by organized crime relative to a constitutional state (*see* Braguinsky 1999: 520-21). Short time horizons and accompanying short-term preferences are conducive to directly unproductive or destructive rent-seeking activities, which produce distortions in the allocation of talent and entrepreneurial activity as adumbrated above. (*ibid.*: 521; Baumol 1990). The returns to unproductive rent-seeking activity over productive activity have moved beyond a somple influx of pressure groups that exercising political influence within Kremlin quarters. This is captured by Braguinsky (*ibid.*), who laments: "The edifice thus goes far beyond simple business; oil and gas pipelines, electric power stations, and money from the budget represent the cornerstone of the whole system of national political power in Russia under transition. It can be claimed almost without exaggeration that the state and the government have effectively been privatized."

V. Conclusions

As the above discussion makes clear, recent work shows us that networks are often the result of governmental failures to perform basic functions of government. Indeed, two characteristics shared by many developing countries and countries in transition are that the citizenry frequently has low levels of trust in public institutions and that there is a reliance on inter-personal relations for getting things done (Rose-Ackerman 2001: 1). Where networks and anti-modern practices are widespread, the first step that the government should take is to change the manner in which the country is governed (Rose 1999: 29). To increase citizen confidence in government, the government should take measures that reduce the need for trust. Measures discussed elsewhere in this work that can increase performance and decrease malfeasance are important here, such as revoking inefficient regulations and programs. Moreover, to increase trust governments must concentrate on institutions, which must be both well-designed and well-manned. Another important step is for those that govern to change their behavior, to signal to others that the rules of the game have changed. They need to signal their commitment to reforms, by, for example, enacting laws and policies that limit their own discretionary behavior. More generally, they need to reform government so that the allocation of productive activities relative to unproductive activities is decreased. As North (1990: 8) observes, "[b]oth the formal and informal institutional constraints result in particular exchange organizations that have come into existence because of the incentives embodied in the framework and therefore depend on it for the profitability of the activities they undertake." A reform-minded government should concentrate simultaneously on reducing the profitability of illegal or undesirable activities, whilst increasing the reward for desirable productive undertakings. In this light, in addition to building confidence in government, a significant task for less developed countries and those in transition is to deliver at least a minimal level of rule enforcement, which can increase the payoffs and lower the risk for economic actors of disengaging themselves from existing networks and agreements in search of legitimate undertakings.

VI. A Final Note: The Problem of Divided Societies

Depending on the particular cultural, historical, and political context, certain more traditional measures of engendering trust and confidence may be required. A society may experience powerful "residues of distrust" (Horowitz 1992: xiii). Administrative, civil service and procurement reforms as anti-corruption reforms per se may not be enough to ensure public trust in government, when there are more fundamental cleavages in society. Mindful reformers interested in curbing corruption may be faced with such divisions which stagnate efforts. The character of cleavages oftentimes manifest themselves along tribal, religious, ethnic, racial, linguistic, or cultural lines or some fusion of these factors (*see* Issacharoff, Karlan and Pildes 2001: 1168). Corruption and patronage and the perception thereof may themselves be organized neatly along the same such divisions. It is quite possible that in societies, engulfed by such divisions, government systematically favors one group or groups over others, and corruption has taken on the form of extensive patronage or, worse still, legalized expropriation.

More fundamental shifts are, therefore, necessary to elicit interpersonal trust, and public trust in government and its reforms. The most profound means is naturally to have the relevant groups separated and move outside the confines of the same, single nation-state. Alternatively creative engineering of democratic institutions might enable stability and a sufficient level of cooperation to emerge even in the midst of these kinds of conflicts. Institutional structures may need to be devised in several countries to attempt to sustain democracy in the midst of powerful differences. One such means is based on consociational democracy.

There are at least four common characteristics of such structures: (1) Government by grand coalition of all notable fractions; (2) the use of a mutual veto (particularly on fundamental issues) or concurrent-majority voting rule in significant issues; (3) the use of proportionality as the principle in the allocating of political representation, civil service positions and public funds; (4) substantial autonomy for various fractions of society in the governance of their internal affairs (*ibid.*: 1168-1169; *see* also Lijphart 1977, 1985).

The purpose of grand coalitions is in essence to supplant the structure of a governing majority and an opposition that is seen as fueling this satisfaction and the trust. Where there is endemic distrust, extreme measures such as grand coalitions where a governing majority and opposition take turns in office may be important in order to provide security and protection. This may also entail rotating prime ministership (Lijphart 1985).[37] Consociationalism relies to a large extent on the prospect that elite leaders of the various divided groups can cooperate and compromise, and thus requires wagers on their commitment to democratic, sustainable reforms, and a show of leadership.[38]

Horowitz (1985) provides pioneering work on the feasibility and desirability of extending such a structure to divided societies, with a focus on Africa. He suggests that compared with the group conflicts within modern African states, the ones in the European countries are "less ascriptive in character, less severe in intensity, less exclusive in their command of the loyalty of participants, and less preemptive of other forms of conflict" (ibid.: 572). Thus, he concludes that finding democratic arrangements to stabilize these divisions is both urgent and more onerous. He also provides case studies of consocialitionalism in several other countries including Lebanon, Nigeria, Sri Lanka, and Guyana.

---

[37] Lijphart focused on four European countries in his study that have taken on different forms of consociationalism, namely Austria, Belgium, the Netherlands, and Switzerland. Austria, Belgium and the Netherlands are viewed as the most divided of Western democracies, with Switzerland in the middle of the gamut. Consociationalism was particularly salient in the late 1950s; since then, it declined, perhaps because it wasn't as required. In Switzerland, as Issacharoff, Karlan and Pildses (2001: 1169) document, the federal executive branch was governed by a seven-member body, according to a system where the seats were set aside for the four main parties, 2-2-2-1, which approximated their nationwide support. The seven members also depicted the multipel regions and languages of the country. Post-World War II Austria was governed for over twenty years by a coalition cabinet from the two major parties with balanced representation. In Belgium today, it is a constitutional requirement for any bill affecting the "cultural autonomy" of the country's two principal linguistic groups to receive not only a two thirds majority in each legislative chamber, but also endorsement by a majority of the legislators from each linguistic group (*ibid.*)

[38] For the conditions that make its success more likely, *see* Lijphart (1977).

Broad observations on the manifold dangers of introducing consociational structures are important, but given the shear weight of individual problems one should not be distracted from the inherent complexities of such cases. Particularly worrisome is the fear that such a system may actually entrench interests, at least in the short run. As a measure to overcome divisions and ensure support for government it comes with a series of potentially very significant costs; a prior assessment of the seriousness of the divisions and the desirability of strong measures must be, consequently, carefully looked at. Another potential concern is that it can inject inertia into the reform process and government can become paralyzed or unable to act efficiently. Granting autonomy to specific groups, engenders a focus on inter-group rather than intra-group equality, which can enable officials and groups to exert significant pressure over members.[39]

In such societies, the electoral system is perhaps the most significant trust building instrument. According to Horowitz (1992: 163) it prevails as "the most powerful level of constitutional engineering for accommodation and harmony in severely divided societies, as indeed it is a powerful tool for many other purposes." He proposed electoral systems that rewarded politicians for making broad appeals across these cleavages. To wit, elections can be polarizing and are an important factor in the decline of democracy in many countries in both Asia and Africa (Horowitz 1985, 1992).[40] Such polarization can set off a deleterious chain of events.[41]

There is some strong support in favor of proportional representation electoral systems in divided countries, sometimes framed as part of a consociational constitution (Lijphart 1985). Proportional representation allows for a more accurate picture of the number of votes relative to the number of seats, increasing minority representation, and also "permits the segments to define themselves" (Lijphart 1985: 68-69). Similarly, federalism, so often praised for

---

[39] A further difficulty identified by Horowitz (1985: 570-71) is how to measure success or performance in these societies- according to financial prosperity, absence of violence, stability etc.?

[40] The cost and extent of such elections is long. Horowitz propounds: "Polarizing elections have divided such countries as Nigeria, Uganda, the Sudan, Chad, Congo (Brazzaville). Burkina Fasso (then Upper Volta), Mali, Zambia, Togo, Ghana, Sierra Leone, and, most recently, Zimbabwe. In the first four countries on this list, such elections were the indispensable prelude to civil war, as they were also in Pakistan and Sri Lanka. In the remaining countries, military coups or the institution of a one-party state replaced democratic elections with authoritarian regimes, sometimes more or less benign, more often highly oppressive, almost always ethnically less than fully inclusive." (Horowitz 1992).

[41] "A common initial response to polarized election results of this sort is for Group B- the permanent minority-to engage in violent strategies of resistance. These include riots and, if Group B is well represented in the armed forces officer corps, military coups (Nigeria, January 1966, being merely one example) or, if Group B is territorially concentrated, secessionist movements" (Horowitz 1992: 97).

increasing participatory rights, has substantial accommodating appeal. It can, *inter alia*, devolve power to those groups that would always lose out at the center, proliferate points of power, provide an arena in which politicians are "socialized" to tackle conflict before doing so at the national level and make hegemony for any particular group more difficult to attain (Horowitz 1992: 216-222).[42]

In a similar vein, recent waves of decentralization that have swept over many less developed countries, have sometimes had a taste of conciliatory appeal. In Brazil, decentralization accompanied the transition from military to civilian rule (Burki, Perry and Dillinger 1999: 2). Importantly, for example, in Brazil, through shifting the fiscal and political resources to the municipal level, negotiators were able to mitigate popular discontent with military centralism and permit the military to pull back in good order (*ibid.*). In Guatemala, decentralization was "one of the key tenets of the peace accords (1996) and raised the expectation of greater self-government for indigenous communities (ibid.). Decentralization may, however, also widen regional disparities, and is not per se desirable.[43] Furthermore, decentralization opens up many potentials for corruption of its own as well as room for local level capture.[44]

---

[42] Horowitz (*ibid.*: 224-25) notes that when federal and state powers are not identical, hegemony of one group becomes much more difficult to impose. Under these conditions, it is implausible to claim that when the same party repeatedly to power at the center, the voters specifically desire this party to rule over the country in its entirety, which is a common assertion of "aspiring single-party authoritarians", such as Robert Mugabe, following the Zimbabwe elections of 1990. He suggests that by mitigating the all-or-nothing nature of politics, federalism has the potential to lower the stakes of the game. It has the ability to make elections more than a perceived zero-sum game, where there can only be losers and winners, as where politics is perfectly centralized (*see ibid.*: 222).

[43] See further Chapter. VII, Section I.

[44] The debate on the desirability of political structures in divided societies does not, naturally end here. Also worthy of attention is the on-going discussion on the role of presidentialism in divided societies. Compare for example Horowitz (1992) to Linz (1990). Horowitz argues that a presidential system may be preferable for conflict-ridden societies mainly because it makes intergroup power sharing more likely given that it is more difficult for one group to capture all political institutions, and that it provides a conciliation function because a group that a group has increased avenues to decision-makers, i.e. beyond the parliamentary level. (*see* Horowitz 1992: 205-206). Linz suggests, on the other hand, that many of the woes of Central and Latin America are related to the presidential form of government.

A. Divided Societies, Trust and Oversight

> A government which robs Peter to pay Paul can always
> depend on the support of Paul. (George Bernard Shaw)

A trustworthy government is a necessary condition for what Levi (1997, 2001) terms contingent consent (recall, contingent consent refers to cooperation as long as others are also cooperating). Trust in the state influences its capacity to create interpersonal trust, which in turn affects the state's governance capabilities. Where a state is not perceived by its citizens as trustworthy, citizen tolerance of the regime is diminished as is the degree of compliance with governmental regulations and requests (Levi 2001: 9). Furthermore, where distrust of government is high, antagonism toward governmental policy can be far-reaching and transpire beyond low compliance to include active resistance (*ibid.*). Divided societies are characterized by distrust. What's more, divided societies are characterized by the fact that citizens do not agree on the limits of government and broad division make coordinating such boundaries difficult. The ability of a society to monitor government can in part be viewed as a coordination dilemma among its citizens. Instability and cognitive dissensus plague government in many societies where cleavages are drawn along tribal, religious, ethnic, racial, linguistic or cultural lines, or some composite of these. There is no consensus on the legitimate role of the state, and society can be stuck in an equilibrium where government is composed of one (or more) group(s) systematically expropriate along ascriptive lines. Where trust in government is drawn along ascriptive or group lines, not just is what Levi terms contingent consent low, but there is not an effective means to curb governmental transgressions. In such an environment widespread trust in government cannot evolve.

Some of these features are particularly well demonstrated in the following two basic models, borrowed from Weingast (1997). The first model indicates the importance of citizens coordinating on what constitutes governmental transgressions against it citizens in order to make government accountable. In the second model, the government or sovereign can collude with one group against another which makes coordination between citizens becomes more labile or unpreferable. Violations of the rights of some may benefit others and such transgressions can be stabile.

1. Model I

Consider a simple game with a political official or sovereign, denoted by S and two groups of citizens, A and B. In this economy all players enjoy a share in the social surplus. The sovereign can transgress citizens rights, say by expropriating wealth. These transgressions generate an economic loss. For the sovereign to remain in power, he requires the support of a subset of all citizens. In the model, it is assumed that one group is sufficient for the sovereign to remain in power. The sequence of player moves is as below in Figure 9. The sovereign, S chooses to transgress or not to transgress citizen rights. After S has selected, A and B must move simultaneously (or rather within an "information set", *i.e.*, without the knowledge of what the other player has chosen), whether to challenge the sovereign or not to challenge the sovereign. Challenging is costly, and the success of a challenge is determined by whether or not one challenges alone.

The payoffs for the game are shown in Figure 10. Where the sovereign does not transgress and neither one of the groups challenge, social surplus is maximized. In this case the social surplus carries a value of 18, 2 going to the sovereign, and 8 to both groups respectively. Challenging the sovereign costs 1, irrespective of whether one acts alone or not. Where the sovereign successfully transgresses, he can appropriate a total of 3 from the surplus from both A and B, *i.e.*, a total of 6. A transgression destroys half of the appropriated surplus, costing each victim 6. The game is therefore not merely redistributive.

Figure 9: Sovereign Transgresses Against None or Both Players

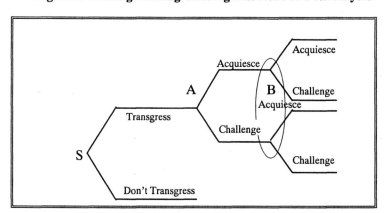

The payoffs for the game are depicted below in Figure 10. Payoffs are determined by the strategy combination chosen by all three players. When S successfully transgresses against both, he acquires a payoff of 8; this occurs when neither party or only one party challenges his transgression. When both challenge, he is desposed and receives a payoff of 0. When S transgresses and B acquiesces, A receives a payoff of 2 when acquiescing, or 1 when challenging. But when S transgresses, B challenges and A decides to challenge, he receives a payoff of 7, one short of what he would have received had S not transgressed and he not had to challenge - recall the costs of challenging are equal to 1, irrespective of success. The payoffs for *B* are symmetric to those of *A*.

Figure 10: Payoffs to Game when Sovereign Transgresses Against None or Both Players

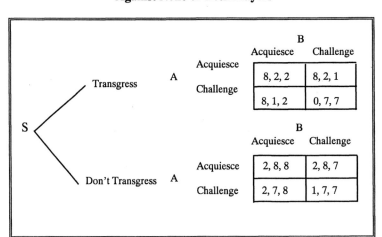

The game induces a problem of coordination. When the citizens act together, they can prevent transgressions. However, if they do not act jointly, the sovereign can transgress and not be deposed. One group of citizens will choose to act according to the actions of the others. Where the first group expects the second to challenge, then it will act similarly, however, if it expects it not to challenge it will acquiesce. There are two equilibrium in the game (that are both Nash and subgame perfect equilibrium).[45]

The first is where both acquiesce and the sovereign transgresses. No party has an incentive to change its behavior given the (expected) actions of the other party. One can see that this is a dissatisfactory position from the perspective of the citizens, but they may find themselves in this equilibrium as a result of the coordination problem. According to the second equilibrium, both challenge whenever the sovereign transgresses.. Given that the sovereign is aware that parties will challenge him (provided they have solved the coordination problem), he has incentives not to transgress in the first place, and parties therefore have incentive not to challenge, maximizing social surplus. To reiterate, the greatest

---

[45] Recall a Nash equilibrium occurs when there is a set of strategies with the property that no player can benefit by changing his strategy while the other players keep their strategies unchanged. A Nash equilibrium (of the entire game) is also a subgame-perfect equilibrium if the players' strategies constitute a Nash equilibrium in every subgame.

quandary in the above is, therefore, whether the members of the society can agree to challenge a sovereign, if he transgresses. Note, as we shall see below, this problem becomes more complex, when the society is divided between what is transgression and what is not, or what are citizen rights and what are not.

2. Model II

In the second model introduced by Weingast (1997), there is again a simple game with a sovereign, *S*, and two groups of citizens *A* and *B*. The economy again produces a social surplus which is maximized when the sovereign does not transgress and neither group challenges. All players receive some of the social surplus, but the quantity and distribution thereof varies. Again, where economic and political rights are transgressed by the sovereign, there is a basic loss in social surplus. In this case, however, the sovereign can choose to transgress and appropriate from just one of the citizens and share or distribute some of the spoils with the other. He need not transgress against both groups simultaneously. Again, he can be deposed of where both groups challenge the sovereign, but challenging is costly. If he is challenged by only one group, again he will stay in power.

The sequence of action is shown in Figure 11. *S* moves first and may choose to transgress against either *A* alone, or *B* alone, against both, or neither. After S moves, both A and B move simultaneously (or rather *B* is not aware of what A has chosen within the "information set"). They can either challenge or acquiesce. When both challenge, then the sovereign fails and is deposed. When only one group challenges then the sovereign escapes with the transgression.

Figure 11: Sovereign Transgresses Against None, One or Both Players

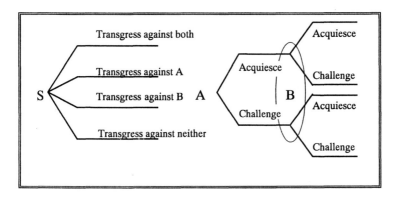

269

The payoffs from the game are depicted in Figure 12. As in the last game, social surplus is maximized when the sovereign does not transgress and neither party challenges yielding 18. The cost of challenging is 1. When the sovereign transgresses against both and both acquiesce, he receives a payoff of 8.

Figure 12: Payoffs to Game when Sovereign Transgresses Against None, One or Both Players

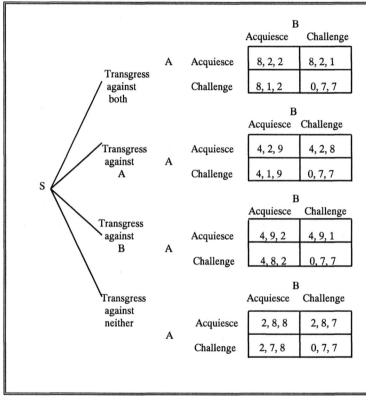

He has appropriated 6 from the players, 3 from each and has destroyed 6 from the social surplus.[46] Where he transgresses against A, A can either challenge or not challenge. Where A challenges at a cost of 1, and B also challenges at a cost of 1, A receives a total of 7, and B receives a total of 7. But where B does not challenge,

---

[46]   6 is the difference between the maximum social surplus that can be attained, where the sovereign doesn't transgress and neither A nor B challenges, yielding a payoff of 18 (2+ 8+ 8), and the surplus when the sovereign challenges and both acquiesce, equal to 12 (8 +2+ 2).

270

he receives a payoff of 9 irrespective of A's strategy choice, so acquiescing is his dominant strategy. It is therefore in B's interest to not challenge when wealth has been appropriated from A and distributed to B. Given, the symmetry in payoffs, we can see that similarly, when S transgresses against B, it is in A's interest to acquiesce, or put differently, it is his dominant strategy to acquiesce, irrespective of whether or not B challenges, given that it will yield a higher payoff.

The one-shot game has three pure strategy (Nash and subgame perfect) equilibrium, none of which maximizes social welfare. The situation where the sovereign transgresses against both and both acquiesce is an equilibrium. Here none of the players have an incentive to deviate given the strategy choices of the other players. The other two equilibria occur at: transgress against A, A acquiesces, B acquiesces, and transgress against B; A acquiesces, B acquiesces. When S transgresses against one group, the other is always better off not challenging. It has, therefore, no incentive to keep the sovereign in check, when the sovereign only challenges the other group. This asymmetry in payoffs between the two citizen groups leaves ample room for collusion and favoritism. Of course, this is a one shot game, and like most games in life, it may be repeated. In repeated games, as we have seen earlier, according to the folk theorem virtually any outcome is possible and can be sustained as an equilibrium (note, each equilibrium of a one-shot game is an equilibrium of a repeated game). Generally speaking, the parties can acquire the socially optimal strategy choices when players decide to punish each other, when they fail to challenge the sovereign for transgressions against them.

B. Insights and Closing Comments

What is particularly insightful about the above models and approach is that as Weingast (1997: 251) notes, alternative "economic positions, beliefs and mental models, as well as information make decentralized coordination difficult... Because the positions and interests of citizens differ, violations of the rights of some may benefit others."[47] When one considers this heterogeneity, citizen perspectives on what constitutes state transgressions, what can be considered the appropriate role of the state and what is a citizens duty in curbing this role are likely to differ (*ibid.*). It is, therefore, easy to see how collusion between the state and one segment of society against another can be relatively stable and how a coordination failure among citizens can transpire as a result of the game. Transgressions by the sovereign are only constrained when citizens hold the limits in high enough esteem that they are willing to punish the sovereign for these transgressions. The black letter rule of the law, specifying behavior on the social

---

[47] In this manner he notes that "expropriating the wealth of specific economic groups, sectors, or other organization as- such as large landowners, laborers, agricultural workers, exporters or the church- provides a source of funds for others" (Weingast 1997: 251).

contract, can only succeed when citizens are willing to defend it. Citizens do not have to agree on what exactly constitutes a transgression, and cannot coordinate exactly according to their ideal limits, but social consensus should agree on a specific set of actions that trigger their reaction (*ibid.*). The behavior of the citizenry can alter elite behavior by forming some social consensus on what actions trigger a certain reaction. When this consensus does not occur, then elites are less constrained in their behavior (*ibid.*: 252). To reiterate, these self-enforcing limits on state officials behavior that result when members of a society resolve their coordination dilemmas about appropriate behavior of the state or state officials are necessary to prevent violation of democratic rights. This coordination dilemma is exasperated in divided societies where no social consensus exists on the appropriate reach of the state, and where one party gains from the systematic appropriations of another group's rights or wealth.

CHAPTER VI

LEGAL BARRIERS AND REQUISITES TO REFORM: CLARIFYING OBLIGATIONS AND CLOSING OFF CONDUITS TO PREVENT SELF-DEALING

> "Bribes are a species of reciprocity. Human life is full of reciprocities. The particular reciprocities that count as bribes in particular cultures are distinguished by intentionality, form, and context. What s a bribe depends on the cultural treatment of the constituent elements" (Noonan 1984: xiii).

I. Introduction

In a comparative survey conducted by the International Business Lawyer in 1996, published in 1997, on the law applicable to bribery of public officials, it was revealed that there was quite some consistency in the approaches to criminal law of domestic officials, but great divergence in the laws concerning international officials. Of the thirteen jurisdictions surveyed, they all had established domestic bribery as a criminal offense of one kind or another, whether the act referred to the offer of a bribe, the actual payment of a bribe and /or acceptance of a bribe (Hepkema and Booysen 1997: 415). Some countries it appears favor an asymmetry in sanctions between the bribe-giver and the bribe-receiver. In Denmark, Japan and the Netherlands, for example, the receipt of a bribe by an official comes with a higher penalty than the offer or payment thereof (*ibid.*). Similarly, there is an asymmetry in sanctions in Israel; a person that gave a bribe is subjected to a penalty only half of that facing an official.[1]

Miller, Grodeland and Koshechkina (1998) who conducted extensive interviews in the Czech Republic, Slovakia, Bulgaria and the Ukraine between November 1997 and February 1998 found that the majority of citizens in all countries surveyed were supportive of the notion that bribe-givers should not be punished as severely as bribe-takers, ranging from 53 percent in the Czech Republic to 80 percent in the Ukraine. But these factors are clearly indicative of the climate in which state officials and private citizens operate, which clearly must be factored into sanctions. There are frequently expectations of payment even for a legal right. Such practices, therefore, resemble extortion. As Miller, Grodeland and Koshechkina (1998: 274) note, "For every bribe-taker there must be a bribe giver, but the relationship is not necessarily an equal one. If citizens take the initiative, pressing their bribes- and their- demands upon reluctant but

---

[1]   Section 291 of the Israeli Penal Law (1977), S.H. 236.

perhaps badly paid officials, then we might describe citizens as the source of corruption."

Citizens may be victims or accomplices. From the perspective of deterrence, it is ambiguous as to the importance of symmetry in sanctioning both bribe giver and bribe receiver. It is clearly dependent, *inter alia*, on bargaining positions, as well as on potential gains from bribery. Although the analysis of asymmetry of fines is complex, and to my knowledge not yet explored in the literature, clearly where a citizen acquires a legal right only in return for a bribe, citizen deterrence can only serve as an ancillary measure to more fundamental reforms. In such an environment a high fine becomes a tool for subjecting citizens to harassment and blackmail, as well as for subjecting citizens to the whims of official and prosecutorial discretion. Indeed, there is currently a draft bill before the parliament in Poland on amending the Criminal Code, to ease the sanctions against bribe-givers as a means of curbing corruption, by giving one side an incentive to confess to bribery. It has, however, been argued that this may be a redundant inducement as officials may still be able to cover up their actions in an official capacity and the bribe-giver who confesses still faces imminent sanction. A prominent judge, who is Deputy Speaker of the Sejm, has argued that common types of bribery resemble extortion and intimidation, and that the only means to curb it is to give immunity to the bribe-giver in these cases.[2] This proposal, however, rests on the assumption that there is an asymmetry, weighed strongly in favor of the official, and that bribery is not a result of active solicitation and temptation by the bribe-giver.

Another approach to sanctioning was that reported for Chile, where only the payment of the bribe is an offense, whereas the receipt is only an offense if followed by further criminal conduct. Additionally, the offer of the bribe is not considered a criminal offense (Hepkema and Booysen 1997: 415). When we consider bribery as composed in essence of the offer by a "donor" and acceptance by a public official of a payment with intent to influence official acts, it may well be enough to dissuade only one party from entering into corrupt transactions. Making nonacceptance of a bribe the unconditionally preferred choice of public officials is, of course, enough to deter bribery in all circumstances- recall the game of trust discussed earlier. However, reliance on punishment of just one party is undesirable for many reasons. Differences in the aforementioned bargaining power of the parties involved, where one party if he does not face a sanction may be able to coerce another to perform. More subtle measures may be at play if one side is able to tempt the other by inundating him with gifts and favors etc. without facing a sanction in order to build up a relationship and create a sense of obligation. In such an environment, we may, given, as we have seen earlier, that corruption is a form of reciprocal behavior, for perceived reasons of fairness or

---

[2] Polish News Bulletin; Jan 30, 2002.

feelings of reciprocation, find officials will "pay back" donors for their gifts. This is particularly likely in societies, that are dominated by IOU's, where patterns of reciprocation are the norm and are embedded in cultural traits. Similar observations have also been submitted for many developed countries. For example, Heymann (1996: 335) reports that prices for public construction in Frankfurt, Germany in the mid-nineties were up to thirty percent higher than in other parts of Germany, allegedly traceable to the corrupting effect of large gifts made over a period of up to five or six years before a favor is asked.

Intent is prerequisite is all jurisdictions in the survey provided by Hepkema and Booysen and knowledge of intent of an intermediary to bribe is necessary to get a bribery conviction against a principal. Knowledge of the intent to bribe is, however, not prerequisite to establishing the offense of receipt of a bribe in all jurisdictions.[3,4]

It appears that there are some inconsistencies or ambiguities in the law of bribery, however, with regard to legislative officials in some western democracies. For example, in Britain, where the standards of conduct in public life are delineated in a diversity of ways, including civil and criminal law, case law statute, and codes of practice, Members of Parliament are currently excused from nearly all of them,[5] relying heavily on the system of parliamentary self-regulation (Oliver 1997: 541).[6] It is unclear whether or not offer and solicitation and acceptance of a bribe is an offense- the law is clear, however, that it is an offense where parliamentarians enjoy a role as government official.[7] The Salmon

---

[3]   In Hepkema and Booysen's (1997) study, they reported that of the thirteen jurisdictions surveyed only five explicitly prohibited bribery of international officials, when the offense was in its territory, and three prohibited international bribes when it was committed outside its territory. This information is, however, today outmoded, since the signing of the OECD Convention on Combating Bribery of Foreign Officials in International Business Transactions in 1997, which has been ratified in numerous countries. For the text of this convention *see* http://www.oecd.org/oecd/pages/home/displaygeneral. For a list of the countries that have ratified the convention, constantly updated, *see* http://www.oecd.org. Furthermore, a number of countries, also participated in the signing of the Inter-American Convention Against Corruption 1996 which had been ratified by 14 countries by the middle of 1998.

[4]   As noted earlier, in all but Japan, a state-owned party has the remedy of nonperformance of a contract, if it were acquired through bribery. In all the jurisdictions, the government, can under civil law seek pecuniary remedies from the bribe giver, and in almost half of the jurisdictions from the bribe receiver (*ibid.*: 416). The losing party has normally a remedy against the bribe giver and in eight jurisdictions against the state-owned party. Remedies include actions for damages, and do not preclude injunctions and annulment of contract and restitution.

[5]   For example, "The Prevention of Corruption Acts" 1889-1916 cover only public bodies and Parliament is not considered a 'public body' for these purposes. Members of Parliament are, thus, under this provision are not deemed as agents (Oliver 1997: 542).

[6]   There is no dispute, however, that for a member of both Houses of Parliament to accept a bribe is in contempt of the House (Bradley 1998: 356).

[7]   Compare Oliver (1997) and Bradley (1998).

Commission on standards of conduct in public life concluded that the statutory offenses related to bribery and corruption do not relate to Members of Parliament.[8] The position is under review, however, due to efforts of the Nolan committee and academics who recommend that the position be clarified.[9] Similarly, it would appear that German law has no penalty directed at bribing deputies, regardless of whether the action is initiated by the donor or the recipient. Again, this is not the case where politicians serve as government officials.[10]

II. Gift or Bribe

> "Although the definition of a bribe depends on the conventions of the culture, so that ceremony and context, form and intention, determine whether an exchange counts as a crime or a virtuous act, ultimately the distinction between bribe and gift has become fundamental. Without this distinction the condemnation of bribes appears arbitrary, and intermediate offering such as a tip or a campaign contribution are indeterminately lumped into a single category which includes all reciprocities" (Noonan 1984: xxi).

Clearly, as Noonan notes above, it behooves a society to adequately distill a bright line between those transactions it considers as gifts or gratuities and those that it considers as bribes. Both are a form of reciprocity- although the former are often considered in the law as acts without consideration, or one-way exchanges- and complex to disentangle; the disencumbering of which is made more complex by the pervasiveness of patterns of reciprocity conditional to a particular practice or society. The defining elements of the constitution of a bribe in discriminate cultures are defined by "intentionality, form, and context" (Noonan 1984: xiii).[11] But, as we shall see, bribery, with its connotation of an illicit quid pro quo, is only at "the black core of a series of concentric circles representing the degrees of impropriety in official behavior" (Lowenstein 1985: 786).[12] It becomes difficult to

---

[8] Cmnd. 6534 (1976), Chapter 17.

[9] See respectively, First Report of the Committee of Standards in Public Life, Cm. 2850-I (1995); Bradley (1998).

[10] See Das Strafgesetzbuch (StGB), vom 15. Mai 1871 (RGBl. S.127), §§ 331 – 358 (Straftaten im Amt).

[11] As Noonan suggests: "In twentieth-century America, payment to a candidate for his vote is a penal offense; a licensed contribution to a campaign committee is lawful. In some instances, there is only verbal camouflage; in some instances, the verbal distinction points to a real difference" (Noonan 1984: xxi).

[12] Furthermore, think of the perverse results a narrowly defined bribery law admonishing all forms of quid pro quo behavior between officials and private persons actually could have. For example, in Brown v. Hartlage, 456 U.S. 45 (1982), the Supreme Court in the United States

separate the black from the gray circles of impropriety which is, as I argue below, a fundamental rational and necessity behind more general laws against official improbity, and a precursor to covering the fitful and concealed nature of bribery transactions.

A gratuity or gift can be considered as the transferal of a good or something of value without receiving consideration for the transfer.[13] A bribe, on the other hand, is given with view to influence the judgment or action of an individual enjoying in a position of trust.[14] Bribery, however, refers to two sides of the relationship including offer, payment and receipt of a thing of value in regard to an official action.[15] The overlap of the two should be apparent from former discussion, which generally leads to the prohibition of many types of gratuities.

American Law highlights some discernible starting points with respect to the difference between illegal gratuities and bribes. In American law at the federal level, the fundamental difference between bribery and an illegal gratuity is the intent element requisite for each. Bribery suggests a quid pro quo, where something of value is given to influence an official to perform a specific act. Illegal gratuities, conversely, do not demand a quid pro quo.[16] In this case, something of value is given to reward actions a public official has already performed or is already committed to conduct. A transfer with a former official, for example, is considered an illegal gratuity, but not a bribe, the official's acts having already been executed.[17]

To uphold a bribery conviction, four conditions need to be satisfied. (i.) A thing of value[18] (ii.) must have been given, offered or promised to (or,

---

was even confronted with the question of whether promises made to voters might be treated as bribery.

[13] See, Black's Law Dictionary (1999, 7th ed.) p. 708.

[14] Ibid., at 186.

[15] Ibid., at 186.

[16] 18 U.S.C. §201.

[17] It has been suggested that many states in the United States have extended the concept of bribery to cover gifts and payments to public officials whether or not there was an intent to corrupt or a verifiable quid pro quo (Anecharico and Jacobs 1996).

[18] The term "thing of value" is broadly interpreted, referring to "the value which the defendant subjectively attache[d] to the items received". When the bribe is not monetary, there can be some confusion as to whether a "thing of value" was transferred (Kaiser and Spiegelhalter 2000: 465).Adumbrated throughout this work, bribery comes in many shapes and size which obfuscate its detection. It is, therefore, important that criminal statutes if these are to serve as a deterrent make no distinction between payments in kind and monetary payments. See, for example, the Israeli Penal law, which makes no distinction "whether it was cash or in kind, a service or any other benefit" (Section 293(1) of the Israeli Penal Law (1977)). Indeed, for parties, there may be connotations associated with a bribe so they wish to pass off bribes as gifts to not just reduce the risk of penal sanction, but also the moral sanction. Della Porta and Vannucci (1999: 50), discuss a conscience plagued supplier to the Milanese Municipal

alternatively, in the case of the official, demanded, sought, received, accepted by or agreed to by) (iii.) a public official[19] (iv.) with intent to influence or induce the performance or nonperformance of an official act.[20] For a gratuities conviction, the government must show that (i.) A thing of value (ii.) was given, offered or promised to (or as in the case of the official demanded, sought, received, accepted by or agreed to by) (iii.) a public official, former public official, or person chosen to become a public official (iv.) "for or because of any official act performed or to be performed by such public official."[21]

In a recent Supreme Court decision, the court upheld the position that in order to get a conviction under 18 U.S.C. § 201(c) for illegal gratuities, there is a need to identify an "official act", for fear of perverse results. Justice Scalia who wrote the opinion suggested that "[i]t would criminalize, for example, token gifts to the President based on his official position and not linked to any identifiable act- such as the replica jerseys given by championship sports teams each year during ceremonial White House visits" and "[s]imilarly, it would criminalize a

---

Transport Company who feeling abashed about going to the company's offices with a wad full of money decided to pay in gold sterling, which offered him psychological relief, now that he considered himself to be offering a gift rather than a payoff.

[19] Clearly, distinguishing between public officials and nonpublic officials is problematic, given the difficulties in identifying the proper province of government, and the intangibility of a concrete public private divide. For the purposes of the federal bribery and gratuities statutes in the US, "public official" is defined as a:

Member of Congress, Delegate, or Resident Commissioner, either before or alter such official has qualified, or an officer or employee or person acting for or on behalf of the United States or any department, agency or branch of Government thereof, including the District of Columbia, in any function, under or by authority of any such department, agent or branch of Government, or a juror"(18 U.S.C. § 201(b)(a)(1) and 18 U.S.C. § 201(c)(a)(1), respectively).

The scope of the definition of "public official" is best left to the courts, given the aforementioned transient province of government. In the United States Courts have found the following to all fall within the scope of federal public official: "[A]n Army private, a building services manager for a Federal Reserve Bank, a District of Columbia corrections officer, a director of a halfway house which had contracted with the Bureau of Prison pursuant to a federal statute to house and supervise federal convicts, a fee appraiser for the Veterans Administration, an "eligibility technician" for a municipal housing authority who administered federal funds, an executive director for a city housing authority who administered both federal and state funds in a federal program, doctors who made referrals for federal health care programs, an employee of a defense contractor who assisted the Air Force in procuring equipment and materials, and postal employees" (Kaiser and Spiegelhalter 2000: 467-68). It is arguably important that no distinction be made between whether the function of the person who received or requested the bribe was permanent or temporary, voluntary or remunerative, elected or appointed, general or specific (See, for example, sections 290-297 of the Israeli Penal Law (1977), S.H. 236).

[20] 18 U.S.C. § 201(b) (1994).

[21] 18 U.S.C. § 201(c) (1994).

high school principal's gift of a school baseball cap to the Secretary of Education, by reason of his office, on the occasion of the latter's visit to the school" (United States v. Sun-diamond Growers).[22] The Supreme court in United States v. Sun-Diamond Growers seemed to be afraid that any gift as a result of the officials position may be enough to incriminate the official.

Under such a distinction we can see that a campaign contribution, would normally also not be considered as either a bribe or an illegal gratuity, when it cannot be tied to any particular event. Furthermore, absent a showing that a payment is made specifically in exchange for a particular promise to perform or not perform a specific official act, a campaign contribution cannot be adjudged to be a bribe (Kaiser and Spiegelhalter 2000: 469).[23] Hence under this statute, a gift that is meant to generate goodwill that might ultimately affect some unspecified act or acts cannot be considered an illegal gratuity (*ibid.*: 470).

For all the distinctions provided the U.S. federal law on gratuities and bribery does, in particular after the recent Supreme Court interpretation in United States v. Sun-Diamond Growers, present the undesirable situation that expensive gifts to a government official can fall outside the federal gratuity statute (*see* Brown 2000: 750-51). In particular the reliance on identifying a particular official action with both a gift and a bribe tends to make the distinction between the two arbitrary and ad hoc. There appears to be a tendency in the United States to leave hard-core conduct such as quid pro quo bribery to the domain of criminal law, and soft-core conduct like gratuities to public officials to the gray area related to noncriminal processes (*ibid.* : 751). It would appear that bribery laws are intentionally not supposed to be "dangerously broad" and to pierce deep into "gray areas" (Lowenstein 1985: 786-87). Therefore, as suggested earlier, other more general laws, against official improbity are required.

---

[22] United States v. Sun Growers, 526 U.S. 398, 407 (1999).
[23] In U.S. v. Tomblin, 46 F.3d 1369, 1379 (1995) for example, the Court of Appeals held: "The solicitation and offer of campaign contributions and the payment of expenses related to campaigns are necessary and permissible forms of political activity and expression. Such conduct is not only well within the law, but unavoidable so long as election campaigns are financed by private contributions and expenditures. Thus the payment of a campaign contribution, the promise of one, or the reimbursement of travel costs related to a campaign do not, in and of themselves constituted bribery...This requires more than some generalized hope of expectation of ultimate benefit. The money must have been offered and paid with the intent and design to influence official action in exchange for the donation- the payment serving as a condition for a specified and bargained action."

III. Immunity: Sword or Shield

> The privileges of the House exist chiefly for the maintenance of the dignity and the independence of the House.[24]

The virtues of parliamentary immunity have long been recognized, and have in one form or another embedded themselves in the constitutional framework of established democracies and fledgling democracies alike the world over.[25] For example, already in Anglo-Saxon times, persons traveling to a gemot (a meeting or assembly) were traveling in the King's peace, enjoying freedom from arrest (Biegon 1996: 683). As of 1541 freedom of speech and as of 1554 freedom from arrest were added to the privileges of the House (*ibid.*: 683). The early expanse in parliamentary privileges culminated in the English Bill of Rights, which codified Parliament's speech and debate privilege. Article Nine of the Bill of Rights of 1689 states: ... "the freedom of speech and debates, or proceedings in Parliament ought not to be impeached or questioned in any court or place out of Parliament." The privileges and the determination of self-regulation arose largely in light of conflicts between Parliament and the monarchy during the fourteenth and fifteenth centuries. They were fashioned to protect the Houses from such external pressures, and in particular the monarch itself (Boylan and Newcombe 1997: 209; Oliver 1997: 542-43).

Despite the fact that parliamentary immunity has shown itself to be an important tool to provide institutional security, it oftentimes does not lend itself favorably to efforts to curb official corruption and malfeasance. Ill- or generously-defined, it can present a shield to well-organized collusive arrangements, within the guise of self-regulation. It is here I turn my thoughts in the next section.

A. Abuses

By virtue of Article I, Section 6 of the US Constitution senators and representatives:

> "[s]hall in all Cases, excepts Treason, Felony and Breach of Peace, be privileged from Arrest during their Attendance at the Session of their respective Houses, and in going to and returning from the same; and for any Speech or Debate in either House, they shall not be questioned in any other Place."

---

[24] 1 Sir William Anson, The Law and Custom of the Constitution 153 (5th ed. 1922).

[25] *See* Flanz (1998).

Similarly, the Supreme Court has also conferred immunity to aides of Members of Congress for the purpose of the speech and debate clause to reduce pressures of the Legislative branch by the Executive.[26]

In the United States, congressional immunity generally covers acts performed in the line of duty. Courts in the U.S. developed a distinction between acts that are political and acts that are purely legislative. Voting, congressional debates, hearings, the formation of committee reports, and conduct within legislative committee hearings are protected. Immunity, however, does not extend itself to those situations when representatives perform tasks for constituents, or bring constituent demands before government agencies nor to investigations of waste in government (Boylan and Newcombe 1997: 215).

Where illicit quid pro quos are in return for an act in a legislative capacity, they are not just particularly difficult to detect, but also to proceed against. The Supreme Court, for example, has ruled that whilst members of Congress can be prosecuted for bribes related to legislative acts,[27] legislative acts cannot be used as evidence by the prosecution, by right of the speech and debate clause.[28] Because of the general inability to solicit information and impunity related to voting, it can be impossible to tie bribery to vote buying. Furthermore, prosecutors may be reluctant to introduce such evidence, because it can represent the produce of an illegal search. In addition, it provides a basis for Members of the House and the Senate to refuse requests for information on matters related to the legislative process, thus obfuscating investigative efforts. The nature of this problem is common to most countries, given that similar protections related to voting and acting in a legislative capacity are generally available. As we shall see below, the U.S. grants relative to other systems very limited immunity, given that they do not enjoy a qualified immunity from arrest for actions outside of their legislative capacity. Next, I address some of the problems associated with a system of double immunity, from the perspective of curbing corruption.

Consider Italy where parliamentarians enjoy absolute immunity for any opinions expressed or votes cast while performing their parliamentary duties.[29] Furthermore, operating under a system of double immunity common to other European countries, members of parliament enjoy more than just substantive immunity, covering acts directly related to their work, but also a procedural immunity, which extends to violations of law unrelated to the performance of

---

[26] Gravel v. United States, 408 U.S. 606 (1972).
[27] Johnson v. United States, 383 U.S. 169 (1964).
[28] United States v. Helstoski, 442 U.S. 477 (1979).
[29] In the House of Commons in the United Kingdom, this refers generally to acts that took place in the parliamentary building.

their work.[30] Under this model, prior authorization has to be given by a chamber of deputies and then the parliament to lift the immunity so criminal prosecutions can proceed. The "clean hands" investigation in Italy brought "the most serious crises in the history of the Italian Republic" (Della Porta and Vannucci 1999: 2). Conducted in the early to mid-nineties, it engulfed more than five hundred former parliamentarians, several former ministers, five previous premiers, thousands of local administrators civil servants, members of the army and customs and even the magistracy. (*ibid.*: 2-3). Prior authorization, that was necessary to initiate criminal proceedings had to be obtained from the Chamber to which suspect members belonged. When allegations spread to Andreotti and the Chamber of Deputies refused to lift immunity for Craxi, both former Prime Ministers, the people took to the streets (Boylan and Newcombe 1997: 223). After some time, the prior authorization by the Chamber of Deputies to initiate criminal proceedings was repealed, however, prior authorization must still be given before a Member of Parliament is detained, arrested, or subjected to a search of his or her person or premises (*ibid.*: 223). The latter is heavily criticized because it limits any pre-trial search (*ibid.*). A similar compromise was reached in France in 1995 after a spate of corruption scandals and general citizen discontent over inequalities of parliamentarians vis-a-vis citizens. A traditional requirement that a prosecutor obtain the authorization of the Bureau of the Assembly to which the MP belongs prior to initiating any sort of criminal process has been eliminated. A member of parliament can be placed *mis en examen* but not arrested or subjected to any actions restricting his liberty without the Bureau's authorization (*ibid.*: 230).[31]

How parliamentary immunity can be abused is best illustrated in the case of Russia. As is common to established democracies, Russian parliamentarians enjoy substantive (absolute) immunity from prosecution for opinions voiced and votes cast in parliament. Similarly, members of parliament enjoy protection from detention, arrests and searches of deputies, except when discovered "*in flagrante delicto*".[32] Operating under a system of double immunity, only the parliament has the discretion to lift a members qualified or procedural immunity.[33] In Russia,

---

[30] This provision, of course, is not unique to Italy. *See* for example, Article 46 of the Bundesgesetzbuch (German Basic Law) which renders it necessary for the permission of the Bundestag for criminal proceedings against a member.

[31] *Mis en examen* refers to "the point in the criminal process at which a suspect is formally notified of evidence allowing a presumption of his participation in acts for which he is being placed under investigation" (Boylan and Newcombe 1997: 230).

[32] *In flagrante delicto* literally while the crime is ablaze, refers to being in the act of committing a crime or other violation (Black's Law Dictionary (1999, 7th ed.) p. 782). The *in flagrante delicto* exception permitting arrest is not particular to Russia. It is common for example to Italy, *see* Article 68 of the Italian Constitution, to Germany, *see* Article 46 of the German Basic Law, and to France, *see* Article 26, Title IV of the French Constitution.

[33] Russia provides a clear illustration of how the same model can be abused in different countries. For example, Israel operates under a system of double immunity, but has rarely, outside of

amazingly parliamentary immunity has even been extended to the local level (*ibid.*: 238). Solidarity within the Houses of the Russian Parliament has rendered the possibility of complete immunity a reality (*ibid.* : 240). Another contrivance suggests candidates for elections can only be held with the authorization of the Supreme Court (*ibid.*: 247).[34] Under the benefactions of current immunity laws, there is *de facto* complete immunity from criminal prosecution for the entire duration of a parliamentarian's electoral stay. This has enticed those trying to hide from the law to the Russian Parliament, who find themselves in a position to pierce the highest ranks of government and governmental decision making. Several investigations had to be dropped after an individual successfully ran for office. Managers of partially state-owned enterprises also delight in de facto immunity, since their prosecution faces numerous legal impediments (Sakwa 2000: 153).

IV. Conflicts of Interest

> For the 'sale' of shares in Norilsk Nickel, a metals combine that generated alone $2 billion a year in exports, the Russian government delegated the authority to accept and evaluate bides to Onekisbank, which as it happened also decided to put a bid to acquire the shares. Not surprisingly, it won. It put in a bid of $170.1 million, $100,000 over the government's minimum bid. A competing bid that was two times its size was rejected.[35]

Whilst the above must be regarded, almost euphemistically, as an extreme example of woeful conflict-of-interest laws, it is indicative of just how neglected these laws and uncommonplace even the most basic safeguards can actually be.[36] Recall, from our discussion on privatization, just how deleterious the long term effects of neglect for fundamental conflict-of-interest safeguards can be for long-term development, where, for example, it is recognized that the fruits of insider

purely political cases, refused to lift immunity. There have been several instances where Knesset Members have had their immunity lifted for bribery and campaign finance fraud including: the recent cases of Shas leader Arye Deri on bribery charges in 1993 and Ehud Olmert on campaign finance fraud in 1996 (*Jerusalem Post*, November 12, 2001). Similarly in Germany, the Bundestag has generally waived the immunity of a member of the Bundestag at the behest of the state prosecutor (members of the Bundesrat do not enjoy immunity), except in purely political cases (Boylan and Newcombe 1997: 226).

[34] In the 1995 parliamentary elections over seventy-nine candidates had criminal records (Boylan and Newcombe 1997: 247).

[35] *See* Bivens and Bernstein, "The Russia you Never Met," first published in Russian in Demokratizatziya (1999) available in English without footnotes at http://www.wayan.net/journal/russia/feb_22.htm.

[36] *See* Chapter III, Section VIII for more examples.

dealing in state assets and the failure to erect any type of public-private divide has left concentrated managerial ownership structures that will hamper these economies for many years (see also Black, Kraakman and Tarassova 2000).[37] Indeed many former socialist economies seem to suffer from a hang-over from earlier days and managers still retain old political ties. If they are faced with impotent shareholders, and a rapacious or ineffective state with ill-designed, stringent tax laws that dampen the overall business climate, the manager may decide it not worth his while to promote shareholder value, and choose the easier option of lobbying friends for assistance, or depending on the ineffectualness of the law strip assets with the collusion and blessing of like-minded supervisory government officials, bankers, fund managers and friends.

The United States again provides a useful illustration of the sheer weight and expanse that conflict-of-interest laws can encompass and is particularly insightful from the perspective of corruption control of the range of legal instruments and measures available and is worthy of inspection by (would-be) reformers. In addition to section 201, that we have seen in our discussion above, federal regulation is supplemented by a host of administrative and criminal regulations that govern not just direct illicit quo pro quo exchanges, but the relationship between government official and private sector parties generally in a effort to mitigate the potential for and appearance of such exchanges.[38] Federal officials are regulated by criminal provisions before, during, and after the duration of their governmental service. Federal employees are prohibited from demanding, seeking, receiving, accepting or agreeing to accept any compensation for representational services in which the United States has a direct interest.[39] They are also forbidden from acting as agent or attorney for any claim against the United States, or receiving any gratuity, or receiving any compensation from such a claim.[40]

There are strong restrictions on post-employment activities of executive officials and other such agencies, including a full prohibition on knowingly making any communication to or appearance before any government body in connection with a matter in which the official was personally and substantially involved, particularly to limit lobbying by persons after they leave government service.[41] Furthermore, there is a two year restriction on working in any area that

---

[37] See further Chapter III, Section VIII.

[38] Indeed, the Supreme Court in the United States ruled that the extent to which Congress could restrict political finance in the United States was within the confines of "corruption and the appearance of corruption spawned by real or imagined coercive influence of large financial contributions on candidate's positions and on their actions if elected to office" (Buckley v. Valeo, 424 U.S. 1 (1976), see Ortiz 1997: 64.

[39] 18 U.S.C. § 203 (1994).

[40] 18 U.S.C. § 205 (1994).

[41] 18 U.S.C. § 207(a)(1) (1994).

was formally under the officials responsibility within a period of one year before terminating his or her service.[42] The Ethics Reform Act of 1989 expanded this section by extending its scope to legislative branch employees, including members of the House. Employees of the legislative branch, including members of Congress are prohibited from knowingly making any communication to or appearance before other Members of Congress and their employees in connection with any matter in which they had an official role.[43,44]

Members of the executive branch and independent agencies are prohibited from knowingly participating personally and substantially in any particular matter in which "he, his spouse, minor child, general partner, organization in which he is serving as officer, director, trustee, general partner or employee, or any person or organization with whom he is negotiating or has any arrangement concerning prospective employment has a financial interest."[45] Members of the executive branch and independent agencies are also forbidden from receiving any additional salary or payment for their services in an official role from any other source than the government.[46] Furthermore, entry into federal service is regulated by prohibitions against the solicitation, payment, or receipt of any thing of value (including campaign contributions) in return for aid in procuring an appointive office or position in the executive.[47] There are also more specifically defined criminal statutes such as a provision in the Internal Revenue Code that prohibits federal employees from accepting a gift for the "compromise, adjustment, or settlement of any charge or complaint" in connection with the revenue laws.[48] And, as Justice Scalia of the Supreme Court recently remarked, "the criminal statutes are merely the tip of the regulatory iceberg".[49]

The Ethics in Government Act and the Ethics Reform Act created a framework governing mandatory financial disclosure requirements, extending to a significant proportion of federal employees, including the President, Vice President, officers and employees of the executive branch, members of Congress, officers and employees of Congress, and judicial officers and employees.[50] Senators and Representatives are obliged to file an extensive annual declaration of

---

[42] 18 U.S.C. § 207(a)(2)(1994).
[43] 18 U.S.C. § 207(e) (1994).
[44] Moreover, in the United States, it is generally not permitted for a legislative official on the side to assume private gains from "the prestige or stature officials may enjoy from their public role" and for a member of the executive, particularly high level official to accrue private gain on the side from "the knowledge or skills they may derive from that role" (Stark 1997: 113).
[45] 18 U.S.C. § 208 (1994).
[46] 18 U.S.C. § 209 (1994).
[47] 18 U.S.C. §§ 210-211 (1994).
[48] 26 U.S.C. § 7214(a)(9) (1994).
[49] United States v. Sun Growers, 526 U.S. 398, 410 (1999).
[50] Pub. L. 95-521, 92 Stat. 1824 (October 26, 1978), Pub. L. 101-194, 103 Stat. 1716 (November 30, 1989), respectively. Codified in 5 U.S.C. app. §§ 101-111 (1994).

their financial holdings, which includes capital gains, rents, interest, dividends and any transactions (including gifts) exceeding $200 or lower if established by another statute in one year.[51] In an effort, perhaps to weed out whether members are beholden to any outside parties, they are also enjoined to declare all liabilities in excess of ten thousand dollars owed to any person other than a relative, excluding mortgages and other secured loans.[52] These provisions cover both senior congressional staff, as well as spouses and dependent children. Disclosure requirements may be perceived as an anti-corruption mechanism one step removed from corruption itself (Anecharico and Jacobs 1996: 47). They are "preventive and prophylactic" and aim not so much to detect and punish wrongful behavior but rather to set up a safeguard against unwanted behavior taking place (*ibid.*).

Furthermore, pursuant to the authorization by Congress, ethical rules have been promulgated by each branch of federal government regulating the acceptance of gratuities.[53] Moreover, these statutes and regulations do not cover all types of malfeasance and misuse of office, and are supported by the right of impeachment permitting by the Constitution, even when there has being no violation of the provision of the criminal code (Beale 2000: 703-704).[54]

If I selected the United States as being indicative of the expansive range of statutes, codes and regulation worthy of consideration in a reformer's tool kit, Britain, serves as a useful contrast instructive for our discussion here in particular with respect to regulation of legislative officials.[55] For much of its history, Members of Parliament in Britain received little or no payment for parliamentary services and were dependent for their livelihood on occupation and income from outside the House Membership in Parliament was considered a public service, not a job and outside employment for MPs was an accepted component of the representative process (Atkinson and Mancuso 1992: 8-9).

It is not uncommon for Members of Parliament to engage in contractual activities outside of their Parliamentary duties, many of which are customarily prohibited in the United States. In recent years, Members of Parliament continued to accept retainers and salary to serve as parliamentary advisors, directors of corporations, PR firms, and interest groups and even established their own parliamentary consultancy firms, where they themselves serve as director or

---

[51] *See* 5 U.S.C. app. § 102.

[52] *ibid.*

[53] For employees and agents within the executive branch, *see* 5 C.F.R. §§ 2635.201 *et seq.* (1999); Rule XXXV of the Standing Rules of the Senate (1997); and Rule XXVI of the Rules of the House of Representative (1999).

[54] According to the U.S. Constitution, Article II, Section 4: "The President, Vice President and all civil officers of the United States, shall be removed from Office on Impeachment for, and Conviction of, Treason, *Bribery*, or other high Crimes and Misdemeanors." (Emphasis added).

[55] This is especially valid before recent modest reforms discussed in brief below.

president, thereby earning additional income by vending their knowledge on how to influence the parliamentary process (*ibid.*: 9). There is, however, a well-established understanding within both Houses that for a Member of Parliament to agree to limit his or her freedom of action in his or her role as a parliamentarian by virtue of contractual agreements with outside bodies is in contempt of Parliament and a violation of privilege (Oliver 1997: 543) For a Member of Parliament to enter into contractual arrangements with outside bodies which do not limit the aforementioned freedom of action is, however, not considered inimical to the law of Parliament. Under recent reforms, however, such contracts must be deposited with the Parliamentary Commissioner for Standards, and, as a further precaution, parliamentarians are enjoined to disclose their interests (*ibid.*: 543).

Similarly instructive is the willingness and ability among parliamentarians in Britain to hire family and kin to positions on their own staff. In the United States, federal law expressly prohibits federal officials, including members of the executive, legislative and judiciary from advancing kin.[56] The reasoning behind the British approach is perhaps as Atkinson and Mancuso (1992: 5) suggest that:

> "MPs are trusted to appoint qualified staff at their own discretion, and a familial relationship in no way disqualifies even candidates who do not meet the formal job requirements. The argument that spouses or other family members often have special knowledge and sensitivity is widely accepted. It is also tacitly recognized that MPs are entitled to keep their staff allowances "within the family," as some recompense for their low official salaries."

These recent reforms within the British House of Commons, run contrary to former practices, where legislative norms and parliamentary standards defined ethical behavior and the "forces of social and cultural evolution" were preferred to codification to further ethical practices (Atkinson and Mancuso 1992: 2). The British system was, and is to a large extent, indicative of a system of self-regulation that relies on the powers of social and cultural forces to engender and craft desired results. It does not provide a template upon which one can measure the viability of two systems, one highly regulated, the other largely unregulated.

---

[56] According to 5 U.S.C. § 3110(b): "A public official may not appoint, employ, promote, advance or advocate for appointment, employment, promotion, or advancement, in or to a civilian position in the agency in which he is serving or over which he exercises jurisdiction or control any individual who is a relative of the public official. An individual may not be appointed, employed, promoted, or advanced in or to a civilian position in an agency if such appointment, employment, promotion or advancement has been advocated by a public official, serving in or exercising jurisdiction or control over the agency, who is a relative of the individual." Note, relative is also defined very broadly to include "father, mother, son, daughter, brother, sister, uncle, aunt, first cousin, nephew, niece, husband, wife, father-in-law, stepdaughter, stepbrother, stepsister, half brother, or half sister." 5 U.S.C. § 3110(a)(D)(3).

The reason, however, the British system could maintain, relative to most other democracies, a high level of ethical behavior was in large part due to the pool of social and evolutionary processes which sustained a high level of general conformity at a low level corruption equilibrium.[57] It would be impractical and haphazard of countries without a similar pool of social norms and constraints to adopt a bottom-up-type approach to the regulation of its legislative officials.

Before closing our discussion, it is important to note that Britain has experienced concrete reforms in recent years pertinent to our discussion of conflicts-of-interest. Members of Parliament, ministers, civil servants, local government officials, National Health Service official, and university employees have all come in for strong criticism in recent years (Oliver 1997: 540). This is in part due to conflicts between public duties and private interests of public bodies and their members, and allegation of patronage by governmental ministers responsible for appointments to public bodies and hybrid governmental bodies, such as non-departmental public organizations, quasi autonomous non-governmental organizations and semi-public organizations (*ibid.*: 540). To answer these concerns, a Commissioner for Public Appointments was appointed in 1996 following concerns expressed in a highly influential report.[58] Furthermore, the same report into standards in public life found that the standards encompassed by Parliament's own law were not well understood, and made many recommendations that were later implemented which significantly tarnished the appearance of Parliaments own self-regulation. It saw the establishment of a new committee entitled, the Select Committee on Standards and Privileges, under whom a Parliamentary Commissioner for Standards functions, whose job is in large part to oversee that Members of Parliament follow tightened requirements for the registration and declaration of interests.[59] As an aside, it should be noted, however, that in England, as in the United States there is a longstanding obligation on a legislative official (today including his employees) to disclose a financial interest that can lead to a conflict of interest in any particular case, and that disclosure law in Britain dates back several centuries.

---

[57] Arguably, a key reason behind recent codification efforts, was derived as a result of the system's failure to guarantee consensus or coordination on accepted standards. *See*, Atkinson and Mancuso (1992) for a discussion on ethical consensus among parliamentarians.

[58] First Report on the Committee of Standards in Public Life, Cm 2850 (1995). *See* also, Second Report of the Committee on Standards in Public Life, Local Public Spending Bodies, Cm 3270 (1996).

[59] The responsibilities of the Parliamentary Commissioner for Standards include, "maintaining the Register of Member's Interests, advising Members on matters related to registration, advising the Committee on Standards and Privileges and individual members on the interpretation of the new code of conduct and on questions of propriety, monitoring the operation of codes and registers, investigating complaints of breach of standards, and making recommendations to the Standards and Privilege Committee" (Oliver 1997: 550).

His supervisory role is, however, not comparable to others in a similar position such as Ombudsman or Comptroller and Auditor General, who are statutory and monitor more than the House of Commons; he is a "*sui generis*" and is part of Parliaments self-regulatory framework (Oliver 1997: 550). Similarly, as a result of the aforementioned report, the practice of paying to ask questions in the House that caused so much controversy has been expressly prohibited in a resolution of the House of Commons.

In many countries, the boundaries between government administration and the economy are themselves blurred, as in China, where government actively encouraged people, including civil servants, in the 1980's and 1990's to go into business (Burns 1993). Officials are in a position where they can use influence to the benefit of those companies in which they have a financial stake (Rose-Ackerman 1999: 75). In such cases, bribery is not necessary, because officials simply pursue their own financial interests (*ibid.*).

Indeed, hybrid forms of organization seem to be more prone to lapses of inefficiency and corruption, not merely because they seem to enjoy soft budget constraints, but because there is no clear delineation between what lies within the public realm of responsibility and what falls within the domain of market forces. To wit, the structure of corporate enterprise in China appear to be conducive to insider dealing and self-service. In China, only one-third of the shares in publicly -listed former Chinese state-owned enterprises can be acquired by individuals; the remaining two-thirds of the shares remain in the hands of the state and domestic (usually financial) institutions- which themselves are unfailingly state-owned (Megginson and Netter 2001: 36-37). A constraint on the reform of this structure and more complete privatization in China is the fact that state-owned enterprises and not the government itself, provide the country's social safety net (*ibid.*: 36-37).[60] Public officials have even found themselves working for the company that they in their official role are supposed to be monitoring (Chow 1997). Similarly, lobbying activities may even involve getting to know and entertaining officials and their families, having dinner at their homes and hiring researchers actively working for ministries.[61]

Where conflict of interest laws are nonexistent, ill-defined or ineffectual, it cannot be considered implausible to find businessmen entering politics to change the laws for themselves as part of a rational utility calculus. The government in Thailand, for example, is impeded by the sheer number of businessmen (normally

---

[60] This is further divided into A -shares which may be acquired and traded only by Chinese citizens, whilst B-shares are listed in Shanghai or Shenzen and may be owned and exchanged by foreigners only. So called H-shares are listed in Hong Kong (H-shares) or New York (N shares), and are also restricted to foreigners only... These government could, however, revoke these ownership limitations by government fiat if it so desired (Megginson and Netter 2001:36-37).

[61] "The Gentle Art of Lobbying in China," *The Economist*, February 17, 2001.

small to mid-sized) in government (Khan 1998). With such an influx of businessmen in government, it is not uncommon for governmental economic policy decisions to be looked upon with great suspicion, given that they almost inevitable help at least some person or group within government.[62]

V. Political Financing as a Conduit to Corruption

Though political systems can differ substantially, and the concept of political party and models of political organization adapt multifarious forms and configurations, how parties and party members acquire political funding and how to restrict unwanted influences, remain a common problem (Williams 2000: 1). The solution to laws governing self-dealing is not to exempt party finance or campaign contributions from the bribery statutes and other regulations but to review the system of campaign and party finance and its propensity to serve as a conduit to undesirable influence and particularly quid pro quo agreements.

As an aside, it should be noted that in the political culture of North America which is largely campaign- and candidate-oriented, political finance primarily denotes campaign finance indicating money transferred in to sway the outcome of an election. In Europe and other less campaign- and candidate-oriented socities, on the other hand, the term political finance can fittingly be substituted as a synonym for party finance (Nassmacher 1989: 237). This is suggestive of the stronger position held in Europe by political parties and the candidate-oriented tradition in American politics (Gunlicks 1993: vii). Closing out this chapter, I shall look at some salient issues in party finance and campaign finance in lieu of previous discussion and analysis with respect to closing off and clarifying avenues to self-dealing.

A. The Problem Defined

Money buys "access, favours, skills goods and services that are essential to party activity" (Williams 2000: 1). As, we have seen governments have to draw the line between legal and illegal gifts and transactions, and permissible and impermissible activities. Given that, as I have argued, undesirable activities and corrupt scenarios are in many conventional settings conducted without explicit quo pro quo agreements and that corrupt behavior may be the result of feelings of reciprocity and obligation, particularly when such norms of reciprocation are pervasive among peers, there is a strong case for anticipatory anti-corruption

---

[62] "With so many businessmen in the government, it can hardly avoid suspicion when its investment policies obviously aid their interests," *Bangkok Post-Thailand*, Feb. 10, 2002. In 1998, remarkably 150 businessmen and bankers in the Ukraine were elected to Parliament, many of whom will legislate their own economic interests (Rose-Ackerman 1999: 137).

reform measures, one step removed from corruption itself. Conflict-of-interest laws are one such prophylactic measure.

In particular, there is a fear, beyond illicit quid pro quo agreements that politicians become beholden to wealthy contributors. In Rose-Ackerman's landmark analysis of corruption published already in 1978, she suggested that we look at our system of allocative choices as a mixed form in which "both market and nonmarket mechanisms clearly have important allocative roles to play" (Rose-Ackerman 1978: 1). It is a fundamental role of government and reformers to decide the preferred system of allocation of particular goods, the (democratic) political system being in particular the preferred mechanism for allocating public goods. The distinction between market and nonmarket is jeopardized because "wealth and market forces can undermine whatever dividing line has been fixed. Thus, political decisions that are made on the basis of majority preferences may be undermined by wide use of an illegal market as the method of allocation" (*ibid.*: 2). Well-organized special interest groups and the "plain" wealthy may infuse market-pervasive inequalities into a democratically selected alternative allocative mechanism (Brown 2000: 752), finding themselves in a better position to offer gifts, gratuities and in extreme cases, bribes outright.[63]

Bribery is, of course, an axiomatic example illustrative of how disparities in wealth and access to officials can infiltrate the political market to influence allocative decisions, designed to take place beyond the reach of market forces. But, as adumbrated above, reciprocities may be generated for several reasons, and wealthy interests seem to have a comparative advantage over other members of society. The electoral process can function as a means to discipline politicians, but the electorate cannot act unless it is privy to reliable information on the behavior of politicians and political parties and the identity of their benefactors (Rose-Ackerman 1999: 133).

The influx of scandals in recent years in democratic states have led citizens to a demand a review of the practices of political figures and parties and the "nature, sources and consequences of their financial sources" (Williams 2000: 1). Though "the contexts vary, the complaints and charges are remarkably similar: a lack of openness and transparency in party finance; ineffective or inadequate government regulation; and undesirable closeness between large financial contributors and the leadership of political parties leading to a subversion of

---

[63] Problematic to the analysis is the fact that being in the position to offer gifts, contributions and bribes is, of course, quite distinct from actually doing so. The position may be a result of bona fide rent seeking activities, but the perception of improbity can manifest itself into pervasive beliefs of corruption. Furthermore, one must ask whether the influence of large interest groups is really a result of money, or is the result of them carrying large numbers of votes which they can utilize quite efficiently Smith (2000: 49) cites the NRA (National Rifle Association) as an example of this. The NRA has 2.8 million members, but donated just $2 million to congressional campaigns through its PAC in 1993-94.

democratic processes; and, more simply, straightforward bribery" (*ibid.*: 2). A particular trend that gives cause for concern manifests itself in the fact that costly campaigns in particular plausibly rouse or are perceived to arouse corruption.

It is instructive for our discussion to take a step back and cast a abridged look at a basic typology of party financing. Beyne (1985) suggests three major forms of party financing which work concurrently in Western democracies. The first type of party finance is internal financing, which at its most basic refers to the funding of political parties through membership fees and affiliated groups as well as investments, party rallies, newspapers and the likes. Prior to reforms in 1988, political parties in France, for example, were officially financed solely from membership dues. There was no direct public funding and donations were proscribed (Drysch 1993: 171). The status of what is considered to be an affiliated group is obviously problematic. In the UK, by way of comparison, the Labour Party was heavily dependent on the contribution by trade unions, which were viewed by rivals as external interest groups trying to gain undesired political influence (Williams 2000: 5). In order to supplement their income parties may also obligate supporters working in the legislative or executive branches of local and national government to give a certain donation or percentage of their income to the party. In Germany members of the assemblies are required to contribute a given fraction of their salary to the party (*ibid.*: 5). Furthermore, political parties can be practically owned by individuals, Berlusconi's *Forzia Italia* being a prime illustration, tending also to own newspapers and other media sources (*ibid.*: 5).

The second type of financing refers to external financing, which as its name suggests refers to the funding of political parties from outside the organization. These types of contribution often attract the most attention. One cannot deduce the motives of those that offer donations, and where there is secrecy involved, there is even greater cause for suspicion of malintent. It is important to note that such funding may be both direct and indirect as in the case of "offers of office space, equipment, fundraising expenses, payments to third parties on behalf of a politician, among other things", all regulated in the U.S. (Potter 1997: 5).

The third form of income for parties is through state or public funding, which is perceived as a means of releasing parties from their need to rely on internal and external funding and the pressures and resulting obligations therefrom. Practiced extensively in western democracies and Eastern Europe, it provides the bulk of party funding in Germany, Austria, Sweden and Italy, but to name a few (Gunlicks 1993: 5,13; Nassmacher 1989: 256-258). It is argued that public subsidies can "contribute to less corruption, more control of lobbying, more equal opportunities in party competition and some control of the cost explosion" (Nassmacher 1989: 238). State funding can also be direct and indirect. Among the more important aspects, this might include tax benefits, free broadcasting, newspaper advertisements, billboards etc. I shall return to this again below.

B. Campaign Contribution and Spending Limits

Noble prize laureate Gary Becker has argued that if political competition among interest groups is unfettered where no pressure group enjoys advantages making it significantly more efficient that the others, there will be an efficient allocation of resources (Becker 1983). In such a competitive system, where voters are well informed, a policy of speedy and complete disclosure may be sufficient, given that the electorate would be able to punish those that violated their preferences in favor of wealthy interest groups. This is largely the position of deregulation camp in the United States who are in favor of complete deregulation and immediate disclosure of all contributions (*see* Anderson 2000). As a system becomes less competitive, where politicians behavior is noisy (less transparent) and voters are poorly informed, it becomes important to look at other means to restrict transactions between politicians and their contributors (Rose-Ackerman 1978: 33-45; Rose-Ackerman 1999: 138-139).

Unrealistic restrictions can be counterproductive and may actually insure that politicians, their employees and contributors transgress the law, which can have the adverse effect in itself of promoting public cynicism, a factor reformers implicitly and explicitly should try to mitigate.[64] Indeed, there seems to be strong evidence in the United States that although corruption is arguably, though by no means certainly, less common today, there is surely more distrust among the citizenry. In respect of this phenomenon, Brown has asked a critical question: "Is it possible that we have become too strict on corruption, that the search for evil has become a self-fulfilling prophesy?" (Brown 2000: 756).[65]

Restrictions should, therefore, not reinforce illegality or be ad hoc, inviting violation or noncompliance or the appearance thereof. But the cries of the deregulation camp in the United States, where political finance is clearly the most complex and regulated in the world, should not become the salvo of reformers in less developed countries and fledgling democracies. Clearly, those measures that befit an established democracy with an affluent, relatively well-informed citizenry, are not a panacea for the ills of all political environments.

---

[64] *See* Robert J. Samuelson Newsweek October 6, 1997 *reprinted in* Anderson (2000: 261-264).

[65] Deeper cognitive and behaviorial factors seem to be at work here. The spotlight that has turned politicians in America into celebrities has also resulted in a greater abundance of information on politicians, clearly putting them under greater scrutiny than at any time past. Laws and reforms seem to have the affect of coordinating long-term scrutiny on a particular subject area, whereas without such laws, a certain amount of coordination (and interest) is lost. Additionally, the constant bombardment of scandal-oriented information by the media, realizable in large part as a result of the establishment of private television companies, has clearly affected how citizens perceive their politicians.

It is difficult in truth to know whether money is given to candidates because they know how candidates may vote, or do legislators honor the wishes or pressures of contributors? Put differently: "Does money follow the votes, or do the votes follow the money?" (Sorauf 2000: 7). For example, in the United States, it is clear that there is a correlation between PAC donations and candidates that vote in their favor, but this does not tell us much about the direction of the causality.[66] Furthermore, in the candidate- and campaign-oriented society of America, it is also relatively clear that the candidate that spends the most money more often wins, but as Smith (2000: 46) emphasizes, this correlation is clearly not indicative of cause and effect, and this correlation may come from reasons cited earlier, such as the desire of contributors to 'back the winning horse', or the popularity of a particular candidate.

Spending and contribution limits are increasingly considered a means to curb undesired influence, as suggested by the number of countries that have included them or are considering introducing them in their system of party (campaign) finance.[67] Contribution limits may be justified as a means to control corruption, but they should not be too strict to affect illegality itself (Rose-Ackerman 1999: 139). In particular, reformers should be clear on the instruments and clear on the goals they wish to attain. To wit, I hasten to add, anti-corruption reforms should not function as a cover to nullify the bona fide efforts of well organized interest groups within the political process, in a blanket attempt at

---

[66] Sorauf (2000) presents an extensive selection of academic studies that suggest that the influence of PACs on legislative voting is greatly overstated, ranging from none to very weak.

[67] Germany currently has no cap on either expenditure or party contribution. At present, there are also no restrictions on the amounts political parties may spend during an election campaign. In Canada, at the Federal level, contributions are not limited in the amount, however the source is regulated. The amount that can legitimately be spent during election is restricted both for parties and candidates. The election expenses constraint for a candidate is based on the amount of names on the preliminary list of electors in his or her electoral district. In the United States, there are limits on contributions by individuals and groups to candidates, party committees and public action committees (PACs. Spending limits in primary or general elections are relevant only for those candidates who select public funding. There is currently no spending limit for Presidential candidates who are not active in the public funding programs or for nominees in Congressional elections. In Australia, no limit exists on the amount which may be transferred to a political party, and there are no limits on election expenditure. In Denmark, there is similarly no limit on how much may be given. There is also no upper limit on spending but state aid obtained by parties and independent candidates must be used up within the financial year. In France, the expenditure of both candidates and their parties are restricted within limits. In India, parliamentary election hopefuls are allowed to spend up to Rs450,000 (£6400). In Italy, there are expenditure limits on both candidates and parties. There are no limitations on the amount which may be given to a political party, but only 23,792,462 lira (£8,200) may be contributed to an individual candidate. Information valid for the year 1998. See, "Fifth Report of the Committee on Standards in Public Life," Chairman: Lord Neill of Bladen, QC. Standards in Public Life: The Funding of Political Parties in the United Kingdom Appendix I: Survey of Foreign Countries. Available at http//www.labourint.org/neill/survey.html.

equalization of the political and electoral process. We should be weary of repackaging the equalization goal.

There are some arguments worthy of consideration by reformers when introducing spending and contribution limits on elections. In particular, the fact that incumbents frequently enjoy an advantage over challengers given their access to nonmonetary resources and their easier recognition and familiarity to the public must be taken into account. In the U.S., there is some evidence suggesting that placing spending limits may actually affect challengers more than incumbents, and that the marginal gains from additional spending by challengers are higher than those of incumbents.[68] It is, therefore, not surprising that limiting spending attracted more support from Democrats than Republicans because they held a majority in Congress for so long deriving the privileges of incumbency, including the aforementioned familiarity and name recognition that that can be cashed in at election time (*see* McSweeney 2000: 56). Similarly, caps on contribution limits may favor the status quo, as incumbents are in a position to use their office and the aforementioned benefits of easier recognition and familiarity to accumulate contributions from a wider range of small contributors. Challengers, probably must rely on donations from a narrower audience, and given the aforementioned tendency that they need to outspend their counterpart in order to win elections and are reliant on larger donations from a narrower spectrum of contributors, would be hit harder by caps on contribution limits (*see* Smith 2000: 57). Moreover, contribution limits may also favor wealthy candidates, when there are no limits on personal expenditure, as they can use their own finances to attain political aspirations (*ibid.*: 62-63).

A very important implication of spending limits is that, as with other laws and regulations they shift the balance in power to other entities. A big winner is the media. This dilemma is noted by Smith (ibid.: 61), who suggests "...although most corporations are limited in what they may contribute to a particular campaign, newspapers, magazines, and television and radio stations can spend unlimited sums to promote the election of favored candidates. Thus Rupert Murdoch has at his disposal the resources of a media empire to promote his views, free from the campaign finance restriction to which other persons are subjected. Donald Graham, publisher of the *Washington Post*, can run editorials and shape news coverage in favor of a preferred candidate seven days a week, as can the publishers of *Time* and *Newsweek*." This has highly relevant implications for countries like Russia where major television stations and newspapers are concentrated wholly or partially in the hands of a few. Similarly, capping contribution limits and spending limits can encourage advertising by private

---

[68] *See* Smith (2000) for a list of those studies.

parties directly for a particular candidate or party, and where this is outlawed on a particular issue.[69]

Although many countries and regions already limit both political contributions and political spending, there is an underlying fundamental issue that is worthy of attention and that is the authority or desirability of democratic governments to interfere in the political preferences of its citizens and the expressions of political support (Rose-Ackerman 1999: 140). Reform can easily get tied up in concerns related to freedom of speech and freedom of expression.[70] A similar question that must be debated for particular circumstances is, how much regulation of party or campaign finance do concerns over corruption actually warrant?

As should be clear to the reader by now, there are multiple reasons for corrupt transactions which are important to take into consideration in any reform proposal. It is often contested that malfeasance or the appearance of malfeasance in electoral systems such as the United States, is a result of financial pressures. In this scenario, parties find themselves caught in a dilemma, a type of arms race no side can stop because it is its unconditionally preferred strategy to seek more funds, irrespective of what the other one does. In such a scenario, it is easy to understand how politicians are forced to allocate their time to activities within their electoral or representational role. Again in the United States, this is especially pronounced. For example, a former Congressman Bob Elgar suggested: "Eighty percent of my time, 80 percent of my staffs time, 80 percent of my events and meetings were fundraisers. Rather than go to a senior center, I would go to a party where I could raise \$3,000 or \$4,000."[71] Where corruption is a result of financial pressure, then there are some important steps that can be considered.

---

[69] In the United States, issue advocacy has been protected by Supreme Court as a form of free speech. Even in countries, where private parties are not entitled to expressly advocate or advertise on behalf of a particular candidate or party, it is difficult and perhaps undesirable to control more indirect forms of advocacy and advertising. In the US, the distinction between express and issue advocacy is a farcical.

[70] In the United States, there were several First Amendment arguments raised both in the literature and more importantly by the Supreme Court with regard to campaign finance regulation. The Supreme Court in the landmark case of *Buckley v. Valeo*, 424 U.S. 1 (1976) seriously limited the extent to which Congress may regulate these funds, given that it may be considered a violation of the First Amendment. The Court held that spending limits fixed for Congressional and House elections as well as independent expenditure limits are unconstitutional (Potter 1997: 33). Apparently, the Court believed that expenditures were a more remote and speculative danger of quid pro quo corruption than contributions (Ortiz 1997: 64). The Court made a basic distinction between expenditures by candidates who sought to advocate their positions and run for office, on the one hand, and contributions by benefactors of these candidates on the other. The Court seemed to present the notion that money is speech when it comes to expenditures, but not when it comes to contributions.

[71] Cited in Stern (1992: 119).

C. Mitigating Financial-Pressure Driven Corruption

Where corruption is related to financial pressures of the type alluded to above, several conceivable measures can be taken.

1. Broadcasting and Advertising

Suggested above, an important feature of campaign regulation is indirect funding. Among the more salient aspects of indirect public funding, include tax benefits, free broadcasting, newspaper advertisements, billboards etc. Favorable treatment is given to broadcasting in most countries. Many countries range in the measure of this favorable treatment, from free broadcasting on the one hand, typical in general of Western Europe to more moderate requirements such as obligating stations to charge candidates the lowest advertising rate charged to their best client.[72] As with other forms of public funding of parties, allocation procedures are complex and there is a danger that allocation procedures can assist the status quo, or they may infringe on the rights of private networks.[73]

2. Direct Public Funding

Can direct public funding mitigate corruption and the types of pressures that politicians and political parties face alluded to above? State funding of parties aims to release parties from internal and external funding and the pressures and resulting obligations therefrom. It is perceived that *inter alia* as a means of furthering equal opportunities among the parties, asserting greater control over lobbying and therewith limiting the need for funding and mitigating the chances of corruption (see Nassmacher 1989: 238). There are, however, several problems associated with public financing, in particular with how it is practiced today in many Western European Democracies. The factors discussed above by Nassmacher, in particular that public funding can limit corruption when it is a result of financial pressures is limited. the reason it is limited follows from the rational I discussed earlier, that parties find themselves in a type of arm's race, scrounging for funds- a type of prisoner's dilemma scenario. *But* even if, parties

---

[72] On this latter proposition, *see* 47 U.S.C. § 315(b), (c)(9). Forcing broadcasting companies to give free air time may stand on weak constitutional footing in the United States given First Amendment interests and the Fifth Amendment "takings clause" (Corrado and Ortiz 1997: 343). A tax incentive based solution may be a viable alternative, as it is not subject to the same constitutional restrictions.

[73] A compromise must be reached between younger and more established parties on criterion. Israel, for example, has developed a formula where every party, including those which were not represented in the previous parliament, is allocated ten minutes of air time and those parties already in the outgoing parliament receive three additional minutes for each parliament member (Law Library of Congress 1991: 4).

receive public funding, it is still the unconditionally preferred strategy to seek additional contributions. Hence, the basic problem seems to have changed very little. This simple rational has been, in my reading of the literature, completely overlooked.[74] This incentive problem could be mitigated if parties were not allowed to receive private funds in addition to public finances, a measure that would open up several problems of its own and is generally not followed in Western Democracies.[75] As noted of Germany in a recent report published in the United Kingdom on alternative systems of party finance: "The system is supposed to lessen the dominance of lobby pressure groups and big business, but a party's donations could add up to substantially more than its entitlement to state funding under the DM230 million (£77 million) cap."[76]

Another important criticism of state funding, however, is that it may lead to parties being "less beholden to their voters, supporters and members, and this may erode ties of loyalty and accountability" (Williams 2000: 7).[77] This factor may foreseeably be worsened as a result of following a system of proportional representation. Moreover, a significant shortcoming of public funding is the potential for self-service. In Germany, it is argued that the established parties seem to be self-serving when it comes to party finance and agree relatively easily on compromises. These grand-coalition type agreements are often made by group leaders, party treasurers and even the party chairmen (von Arnim 1993: 202). Given that they more or less control the nature of and amount of finance themselves, they are granted license to act in their own self- interest and have incentives to decide only in their own self-interest. Von Arnim likens the situation to "a state in which a voter is confronted by a single party or a united block of

---

[74] As one may expect, this scenario of political financing as a type of arms race could easily be overstated, however, as it only captures one aspect of party financing. Public financing, for example, may be able to cover fixed costs necessary to run a campaign, leaving politicians enough discretion to allocate time to other activities important to maximize electoral votes, other than spending. It may also serve other public or ideological goals that are not easily quantifiable.

[75] For example, in Germany and Sweden, the two countries in Western Europe with perhaps the most sophisticated electoral formulas related to state financing of political parties, private donations are still accepted in addition to public funds. In Germany, private funds may even exceed the already generously divided state funds. Preventing private donations altogether may, however, open up new avenues to corruption, particularly when there are weak conflict-of-interest laws, and there is an under-allocation of the requisite state funding to sustain an electoral campaign.

[76] Fifth Report of the Committee on Standards in Public Life, Chairman: Lord Neill of Bladen, QC. Standards in Public Life: The Funding of Political Parties in the United Kingdom Appendix I: Survey of Foreign Countries. Available at http//www.labourint.org/neill/survey.html.

[77] A Law Library of Congress survey of 16 countries indicated that in approximately have direct funding was given to parties or candidates. These countries were Australia, Canada, Germany, Greece, Israel, Italy, Mexico, Sweden, Taiwan, and Turkey (Law Library of Congress 1991).

parties in so far as he has no opportunity to use his vote as a defense against certain developments and abuses" (*ibid.*: 203).[78] The citizen is powerless because he has a lack of options (*ibid.*: 202). For this reason the Federal Constitutional Court has been a fundamental institutional check which instigates parliament to introduce new laws (Saalfeld 2000: 112). Not surprisingly then, in Germany developments in party finance were originally the result of judge-made law, which later was itself adopted by parliament into legislation (von Arnim 1993: 202). Where parties are gatekeepers to their own funds, an adverse effect of over-reliance on government funding, is clearly the risk of an institutionalization of existing party systems, that favor central or established party organizations over new or local ones, thereby stiffening ties among major parties, dominant coalitions or fractions, and externalizing new or emerging parties and agendas, leaving policies that are obsolete or unresponsive to public opinion and welfare.[79]

D. Disclosure

Dona clandestina sunt semper suspiciosa.[80]

Corruption thrives in secrecy. Comprehensive disclosure requirements are a *sine qua non* of anti-corruption reforms. They help lift the veil of secrecy around implicit and explicit quid pro quo agreements. They encourage parties and candidates to be responsive to voter preferences, when voters have the ability to open the books of party funding and sanction those candidates and parties they consider to have made deals with generous supporters. Furthermore, they can reduce the appearance of corruption, where disclosure provides a type of commitment device by politicians and candidates to democratic processes. Moreover, disclosure can help inform voters of the policies favored by parties or candidates when in office, given that supporters will give contributions to those political entities they consider most aligned with their preferences.

Even within established democracies laws on disclosure differ substantially. At the extreme is Britain where parties have not been subject to any compulsion to fully disclose their annual accounts (Johnston and Pattie 1993: 150).[81] Individual donations do not need to be reported, although Labour

---

[78] *See* also von Arnim (1996).

[79] Another reason why public funding may not be so successful is for the obvious reason that corruption may not be as a result of electorally-driven financial pressures, but be premised on other less noble forms of self-interest. Italy for example, clearly one of the most corrupt countries in Western Europe, had until a referendum in 1993 an expansive system of state funding. Similarly, the reliance on state funding has also not assisted Germany in avoiding its fair share of well-publicized corruption scandals in recent years.

[80] Clandestine gifts are always suspicious (Black's Law Dictionary (1999, 7th ed.) p. 1631).

[81] Though currently under review at the time of writing, Britain not just lags behind in its disclosure laws, but its party finance remains formally a relatively unregulated practice.

volunteers the names of those persons that donate a sum above £5000 but not the amount (Fisher 2000: 25-26). The Conservative Party does not disclose either the names of individual or corporate contributors. It has succeeded remarkably in avoiding disclosing such details in its accounts due to the standing of the party as an unincorporated association with no legal status, and as such is circumscribed only by its own internal rules. Interested parties can only acquire information regarding corporate donations, via examining company accounts. (*ibid*.: 26). Long discussed in the public domain, the situation in Britain is likely to change in the near future.[82] Similarly, parties currently in Luxemburg are not obliged to publish party accounts, and donations are normally not divulged.[83] France provides another example of a western democratic country where party funding can only be described as a complete enigma prior to reforms in 1988. Parties were not required to present any information on their income and expenditure, and given that private donations were forbidden, direct public funding not available and membership dues regulated by law, one could only hypothesize where the funding actually came from (Drysch 1993: 155-156).

Just how difficult it can be to properly draw up laws on disclosure and close off conduits to corruption is exemplified by the United States, and should

---

Existing law is limited and applies principally at the local level. The Representation of the People Act placed limits on expenditure on local elections but not on national campaigns, and, furthermore, there are no limits on income (Fisher 2000: 25; Johnston and Pattie 1993: 151). Factors that legitimately or illegitimately awaken anxiety, such as donations from both domestic and foreign corporations are permitted without any cap on limits, as are donations from foreign nationals.

[82] The scandal that captured the most attention in recent years and lead subsequently to the formation of the Neill Committee and the Neill Report (or formally the "Fifth Report of the Committee on Standards in Public Life, Chairman: Lord Neill of Bladen, QC. Standards in Public Life: The Funding of Political Parties in the United Kingdom") was that involving Bernie Ecclestone, the Head of Formula 1, who it was revealed donated 1 million to the Labour Party, which had excluded Formula 1 from the proposed ban on tobacco advertising. The Neill Report would overhaul party finance in the United Kingdom making no less than 100 summary points and recommendations including: The establishment of an election commission with comprehensive executive and investigative powers, which would registration of political parties and to whom an audited accounts shall be regularly submitted; donations to political parties above £5000 nationally are to be publicly declared as are those over £1,000 at a local level; a prohibition on anonymous donations above £50; a limits of £20 million on national campaign expenditure by a political party in a general election, that includes benefits in kind shareholders must be regularly balloted prior to political donations made to companies; the prohibition of foreign donations. It suggests maintaining the current ban on political advertising on the radio and television, as well as free access to radio and television for party political broadcasts.

[83] *See*, Fifth Report of the Committee on Standards in Public Life, Chairman: Lord Neill of Bladen, QC. Standards in Public Life: The Funding of Political Parties in the United Kingdom Appendix I: Survey of Foreign Countries, *available at* http//www.labourint.org/ neill/survey.html.

serve as an awakening to would-be reformers in other countries. Highlighted earlier, the United States is an example of a highly regulated system of party and campaign finance, worthy of analysis by any country considering reform. Indeed, due to the reporting and publicity obligations the Federal Election Commission Act places on candidates, parties, and political action committees, the Federal Election Commission in the United States is privy to the largest data archive of any campaign finance system in the world (Sorauf 2000: 7). The importance, however, of extending disclosure laws to a wide listing of political bodies, committees and sources is clearly exemplified by the influx of soft money contributions in federal electoral politics in the United States. Soft money denotes party funds not covered by federal law. "Soft money" includes contributions to federally regulated campaign committees outside of the aggregate amounts permitted for federal elections by the Federal Election Commission Act. These donations, are legitimate even if directed to national campaign entities, if the money is not used for the purposes of federal elections.[84] Therefore, unlike the hard money that goes to the campaigns, soft money can legally come directly from corporate and union accounts, and in unlimited sums from wealthy persons. Donations are less accountable because they are more onerous to trace and less systematically disclosed (Ornstein, Malbin and Corrado 1997). Just to give an indication of the numbers involved, in the presidential elections in 2000, breaking previous records, parties spent $500 million of soft money.[85]

Similar shortcomings in laws on disclosure are associated with issue ads, which are essentially advertisements that pretend to be about an issue, but in fact are attacking a particular candidate. They are commonly run during elections and formulated in a manner so as not to qualify themselves as spending on federal elections. Sponsoring organizations, therefore, do not have to disclose the sources of their money. National committees themselves are often behind the running of these advertisements, enabling them to spend money they would otherwise not have been able to spend in accordance with federal regulations (*see* Potter 1997: 227). Such loopholes in the law allow important conduits of financial support to go undisclosed. Though contributions may generally look for "a line of last defense", disclosure of funds by organizations that are within a certain "proximity" of political parties and candidates is fundamental.[86]

---

[84] Common Cause v. Federal Election Commission, 692 F. Supp. 1397 (D.D.C. 1988).

[85] "Soft Money, Tough Measures," *The Economist*, February 16, 2002.

[86] Just how difficult it is to close of loopholes is apparent in the following example. The aforementioned issue advocacy groups in the United States, often organize themselves under section 527 of the Internal Revenue Code, which allows them not to be taxed on income obtained by contributions (*see* Recent Legislation - Campaign Finance Reform (2000)). They can procure both a tax exemption and also not be regulated by the Federal Election Commission Act. Congress in 2000 promulgated a law that obligated section 527 organizations to disclose their contributions and expenditures to the IRS (*ibid.*). The aim of this law was to warrant that all political organizations disclose their contributors. These disclosure laws do not

The importance and complexity of closing off undisclosed conduits of party finance were also vividly exemplified in Germany during the 1970s and 1980's in scandals related to "Umwegfinanzierung" (financing in a roundabout manner). At the time, according to the Political Parties Act of 1967, tax deductions were valid only to a limit of 600DM for individuals and legal entities (1200 DM from 1980) (Saalfeld 2000: 100-101). One important mechanism for getting around this restriction was for money to be donated to professional associations or "nonpartisan" bodies which unlike political parties held the status of charitable organizations. These associations were entitled to make donations to political parties often up to 25% of their own dues. The remaining 75% was then transferred to Association B who did likewise (25% of 75%), and passed the buck to Association C etc. (Gunlicks 1988: 37).[87]

Similarly, it is imperative, that disclosure rules go beyond the party at the national level to include candidates, party groups and foundations. Von Arnim (1993) suggests that contributions to individual deputies in Germany are not of trifle sums as they were once thought, and may be as significant as contributions to parties themselves. Direct contributions prior to the Federal Constitutional Courts ruling in 1992 did not have to be publicized and lacked the same regulation and publicity that has been devoted to parties (*ibid.*: 205, 216). Often overlooked is the fact that party groups and foundations should also be subjected to the same disclosure requirements as they are less open to public scrutiny, as should regional organizations and commercial enterprises (*see* Nassmacher 1993: 260).

---

cover nonprofit organizations, who file under section 501(c) of the Internal Revenue Code. Within this section, nonprofit organizations are sub-divided into two groups, namely 501(c)(3) and 501(c)(4) organizations. Section 501(c)(3) organizations are for the greater part prohibited from engaging in political campaigns. Section 501(c)(4) organizations however are permitted to engage in political activities as long as they are not the primary purpose of the organization. There engagements will continue to go unreported as long as they do not engage in express advocacy of a particular candidate, something easily avoided. Similarly, for all extensive purposes, most donations to these nonprofits are also tax deductible; although donations by private persons above $10,000 may be subject to a gift tax, corporate and institutional contributors will not be subject to this tax.[86] Sophisticated organizations can, therefore, easily change their status in order to avoid these disclosure requirements.

[87] Following a scandal known as the Flick affair, money from charitable and religious organizations and party foundations were banned outright. Furthermore, parties received the status of charitable organizations, with more generous tax deductions (Saalfeld 2000:102-3). In the Flick affair a large holding company owned by Friedrick Karl Flick apparently offered donations of up to DM 10 million to a charity operated by Augustine monks of which it saw 8 million returned to itself in cash. Flick profited from a tax deduction of about half of the contribution, thus skimming off 3 million for itself and 2 million for the charity and leaving 8 million untracable. It was reported that he allegedly used some of the money to grant around the board donations to all major political parties in order to receive tax exemptions for the sale of 1.8 billion worth of shares in Daimler-Benz. A representative of the Flick group, and two former ministers were found guilty of tax evasion (*ibid.*).

To increase transparency, general budgetary accounting procedures should be introduced for groups that receive a substantial part of government subsidies. It is also desirable that deliberations on subsidies be discussed in public debates, in order to allow the media to perform some type of monitoring function (*see* von Arnim 1993: 212).

1. A Note on Auditing Procedures

Strong auditing practices and procedures should accompany reforms, in order to mitigate at least the most blatant of abuses. For example, it is estimated that Yeltsin spent $500 million on his campaign in 1996, when the limit was actually $3.2 million per person (Sakwa 2000: 130-131). As we have seen, even in established western democracies, mandatory obligations of political parties to account for expenditures and income are slow to manifest themselves.[88] Moreover, even when there is mandatory submission of income and expenses accounts, there is often not mandatory inspection by the authority in possession of the documents, as is the case in Germany.

The Israeli model on auditing procedures seems to stand up well in comparison to other countries. In Israel, political parties are required to keep accounts containing both income and expenditure as directed by the State Comptroller, and keep the money that is determined for expenses in bank accounts, the numbers of which were reported to the Chairman of the Knesset (Law Library of Congress 1991: 103). Furthermore, the State Comptroller may order a signed declaration from the representatives that the accounts are complete and correct (*ibid.*: 103). Parties have to follow very specific laws and regulations which govern bookkeeping procedures. Following elections, the State Comptroller has to report on whether the organization followed the directives and whether its expenses and income were within specified limits (*ibid.* 103-104). In addition, he is also responsible for inspecting the accounts for running expenses. Detection or suspicion of a criminal violation is reported to the Attorney General and Funds may be recanted if directives were not observed. As an additional safeguard, the State Comptroller reports to the Knesset and not to the government itself (*ibid.*: 103).

An important factor in mitigating collusion and the ethical lethargy that can arise within cosy long-term relationships is, as suggested above, the rotation

---

[88] *See*, for example, our discussion above on disclosure requirements in the United Kingdom. Similarly, even in those countries that have mandated disclosure requirements, this frequently did not develop until relatively recently. For instance, a mandatory obligation to account for both income and expenditures in Germany only took place in 1984 (Law Library of Congress 1991: 60).

of supervisors - in this case the auditors of party accounts.[89] Legislation mandating that party auditors are changed every four years would be beneficial, because it would offer a fresh pair of eyes to look over the books of the organizations. The old auditor would be given incentive to keep the books clean because of his replacement and the new auditor, preferably unconnected to the last, would have a strong incentive to start off on a clean slate, because he is aware than his books in turn will also soon be monitored.

To be successful as a tool to unveil improbity and corruption, auditing bodies require *inter alia* a high degree of independence. This independence can be removed quite blatantly, as reportedly was the case of a General Control Inspectorate in 1992 established by Yeltsin to tackle corruption, the head of which was later removed from his position when he went after Yeltsin's political associates as well as his adversaries (Sakwa 2000: 151). There are, however, far more subtle means of doing this. The Federal Election Commission in the United States provides a remarkably vivid example of mistakes that can (intentionally) be made in oversight mechanisms, and should be in the notebooks of all would-be reformers.

It is widely recognized that the Federal Election Commission (FEC) in the United States has for the greater part been a failure.[90] In fact, it seems to be well accepted that the Federal Election Commission, which was established shortly after the Watergate hearings, was never intended by Congress to be independent and effective, but rather that it would "operate on a tight leash held firmly by its master" (Mann 1997: 277). In one commentators words, "It was born handicapped, then kidnapped" (Jackson 1990: 26). The list of measures taken by Congress to insure its ineffectiveness are astonishing. The Commission was composed of six voting members, three of which are Republican and three Democrat, who serve as chairmen for a one-year rotating basis. In order to take any action, four of the six need to agree to any regulatory efforts (Issacharoff, Karlan and Pildses. 2000: 457). It was given no authority to investigate anonymous complaints and was inhibited by complex procedural requirements (*ibid.*; Mann 1997: 278). Congress had even granted itself a veto over FEC regulations which was later declared unconstitutional by the Supreme Court in

---

[89] An alternative solution would be to take the decision of who audits the parties books entirely out of the hands of the parties themselves and into the hands of an independent auditing body, similar to the SAI (Supreme Audit Institution), but this can deprive auditing of the financial resources and know-how of the private sector.

[90] Among its responsibilities are: the disclosure of both the sources and expenditure of funds used in the federal election process; securing the compliance committees, candidates, and others with federal electoral law, and the provision of information on the aforementioned activities (Mann 1997: 228, Federal Election Commission, "Administering and Enforcing the FECA," Twenty Year Report (April 1995), pp. 10-19, 38). It takes on responsibility in violations within the domain of civil law, whereas the Department of Justice investigates criminal violations (*ibid.*: 20).

1983 (Mann 1997: 277). Congress initially involved itself in the selection process (selecting four of the six commissioners), a clear conflict-of interest, which was later struck down as unconstitutional (*ibid.*: 277-78). Even after it was excluded from the nomination process, it continued to "cajole" presidents into drawing nominees from their own list, which often lead to the long term reappointment of the same voting members (*ibid.*: 278). Indeed, Congress seemed to pull out all the stops, and understood how to sabotage an anti-corruption reform as if it were a homework assignment. It denied the FEC multiyear budgeting authority, unlike other independent agencies and, almost as if with game theoretical insight, prohibited random audits of Congresspersons, installing time consuming procedural prerequisites to any audit. In the meantime it consistently showered the Commission with unrelenting criticism of its legitimacy (*ibid.*: 278).[91]

E. Concluding Comments

A law that is perceived to be poorly enforced or ill-defined, where politicians are perceived to be operating in a structure of de facto immunity or loopholes, has the effect of disenfranchising citizens from their government. Where activities are perceived to be illegitimate but widely practiced, either not illegal or de facto not enforced, there is frequently no cost for an individual politician or party (as the case may be) to continue common practices, enjoying a type of safety in numbers. The willingness of individual persons or individual parties to volunteer additional information above and beyond that required by law or volunteered by others depends realistically on whether it is politically justifiable to do so. Where voters are willing to reward additional voluntary efforts at increasing transparency (that offset the cost of doing so), parties may be willing to go beyond that required by them in the law, or attempt to reform the law itself. The unwillingness of the Conservative Party in the United Kingdom, for example, to disclose its donors was perhaps indicative of public dissensus (or apathy)- the demand for disclosure did not offset the gains associated with doing so for the party. Raising public awareness and feelings about such matters among voters may be facilitated by political entrepreneurs, nonprofit organizations or the media in order to facilitate public demand for transparency and importantly the requisite sanction, in terms of loss of support, for not doing so.

---

[91] It should be noted that the Supreme Court put another nail on the coffin of the Federal Election Commission in Buckley v. Valeo, 424 U.S. 1 (1974) by declaring much of the regulatory system it was supposed to oversee unconstitutional on First Amendment Grounds (relating to freedom of speech and expression).

VI. Corporate Liability

When one wishes to clarify the laws governing self-dealing and bribery, one had necessarily examine the source of the bribes and quid pro quos. Realistically, when one looks at the business or corporate world, much of the bribery and corruption we hear of occurs through the use of agents, subsidiaries and middlemen. Payoffs are frequently used to further the interests of the firm in order to obtain business. Arising therefrom, there appears to be *a priori* sound reasons upon which to employ a broad basis of vicarious liability for agents actions. Indeed, many civil law European countries seem to be moving in the direction towards corporate liability, although notable differences still exist (Coffee 1994: xix). In the British system only those acts by officials of high position within the corporation may be imputed to the corporation (*ibid.*). France changed its own criminal code in 1991 so that criminal liability could be ascribed to organizations, and in the Netherlands, similarly as a result of a recent amendment to its criminal code, corporations can be held criminally liable provided two criteria are fulfilled: First, could the company determine whether an agent did or did not do the criminal act(s) and second, did the corporation tolerate such acts (*ibid.*: xx). In Germany, by way of contrast, corporations are still not subject to criminal liability, but to administrative sanctions (Khanna 1996: 1490).

American law is very far advanced along the road to corporate liability, particularly as a result of the adoption of the Federal Sentencing Guidelines in 1991. U.S. law seems to recognize that that corruption is a form of cooperative behavior involving many parties which may "team together" with the aim of furthering a corporate interest.[92] Under the doctrine of respondeat superior, corporations are generally liable for the criminal acts of agents or employees, in addition to liability under tort, when the agents or employees were acting within the scope of their employment, and at least partially, to further the interests of the business. Even where this behavior was detrimental to the company but was motivated by the intent of benefiting the company, the corporation may be liable. Indeed, a corporation may be held criminally liable for the actions of an agent or employee, when the action was committed within the scope of their authority or course of their employment, whether this authority is actual or apparent,[93] even when these acts were expressly forbidden by the corporation (*see* Propper 2000). The American system, thus, with regard to liability seems to be quite unique when compared with its European counterparts, but on the pragmatic level of fining this

---

[92] Common law in the U.S. has followed the notion that collective action is enough, *i.e.*, aggregation of several employees can equal intent. *See* U.S. v T.I.M.E. - DC., Inc (1974), U.S. v Bank of New England (1987).

[93] Apparent authority refers to the authority an outsider would ordinarily assume an agent to have, arising from his position within the organization and the circumstances and events surrounding his past conduct.

is less so as large fines are commonly withheld for crimes "committed, condoned or tolerated by substantial authority personnel (Coffee 1994: xxi)."[94]

A. Justifications for Corporate Liability

As in cases of decentralized monitoring, for numerous reasons an outside party may find itself in a better position than law enforcement to sanction transgressions. Where a corporation is better positioned to monitor and sanction than government, corporate criminal liability may be justified (Arlen 1994: 835). There have been numerous arguments made for corporate liability of one type or another.

Incentives should be given to organizations to screen employees for honesty and carefulness (Kornhauser 1982: 1349). Similarly, Posner (1998) has suggested that shareholders will hire those managers that are willing to commit crime if they are not held accountable for managerial actions. This latter argument is somewhat refuted by Coffee for two reasons: First, managers often have reasons to resist shareholders preferences and will not be willing to commit crime only for their benefit, and secondly de facto it is often managers that hire other managers. Alternatively, agents do not have adequate funds to cover the extent of the social costs their actions impose, i.e. they are not judgment proof. Social costs in this context are the costs to society resulting from the unlawful behavior of the agent. Put differently, agents may not internalize the damages they induce. This argument is weakened considerably when the agent can be held personally criminally liable for any infringement in addition to the corporation itself. This may be seen as a basic principal of agency law and dual liability and should not be overlooked in the discussion (Kraakman:1984: 858). There may, however, be another undesirable affect when the agent accounts for all the losses personally, as he may have incentive to take more care than is socially desired, a problem further aggravated when he is risk averse. Kraakman (1984) develops this argument. He suggests a system of liability just for agents may result in a shifting of risky activities (contractually or as part of company policy) to the agents by managers, hence waving all company liability (ibid.: 860). He argues that even in the case of dual liability, be it under the doctrine of respondeat superior or alternative doctrines, such as a fiduciary duty of care, the result may also be risk shifting activities by managers, albeit under the additional constraint of corporate

---

[94] As Coffee (1994: xxi) submits, "whether at the doctrinal level in Europe or at the level of pragmatic decisions in the U.S., there is a seeming convergence on a basic point: corporate criminal liability should trigger significant penalties only when persons within a management possessing significant discretion are shown to have authorized, condoned or tolerated the criminal acts or omissions."

liability.[95] Corporate managers seem to be insulated from personal liability except when there was self-dealing or intentional disloyalty to the firm.[96]

The corporation having greater assets may cover these costs and additionally be a position to influence the agents behavior (Khanna 1996). Related to social costs, assignment of liability to one agent may be insufficient as damages may be the result of the actions of many agents actions (Kornhauser 1982). A further reason for holding an organization liable is that there may be inadequate supervision of workers or careless production factors causing risk to third parties (*ibid.*: 1350). An alternative argument related to the disposition of the corporation relative to the individual is that individuals may not respond rationally, whereas the corporation may have greater incentives to do so (Khanna 2000: 1245).

Summing up, the primary justification for corporate liability is probably that by imposing liability on the corporation, it encourages it to monitor the individual when the government cannot do so efficiently. It is a version of the best cost avoider argument (*see* Coffee 1994).

B. Shortcomings and Quandaries

The incentive effects for the corporation cannot be understood without looking at the costs for the corporation in detecting and investigating these crimes, as well as their interest in actually reporting them. In a system such as the United States, corporate criminal liability is governed at a federal level by the doctrine of respondeat superior, according to which a corporation is held criminally liable for the acts committed by its agents or employees within the scope of their authority. The more crime the corporation detects ex ante, the less liability it encounters, but this comes at the price of increasing its enforcement costs (Arlen 1994). There may be an unforeseen cost of such a liability system. Corporations are for all extensive purposes held strictly liable for the actions of their agents, so additional enforcement costs may furthermore increase the firms criminal liability (when acts are discovered ex post), therefore giving it disincentives to engage in monitoring in the first place, and possibly encouraging inattentiveness to managerial or employee transgressions (*ibid.*). This problem is somewhat mitigated in the United States where whistleblower statutes, as seen above, may make it financially worthwhile to do so, or where failure to come forward may increase the corporate fine.[97]

---

[95] "Respondeat superior" is defined in Black's Law Dictionary (1999, 7th ed.) p. 1313, as follows: "[t]he doctrine holding an employer or principal liable for the employee's or agent's wrongful acts committed within the scope of the employment or agency."

[96] Additionally, top corporate officials can and indeed customarily do, procure indemnification or liability insurance for virtually all legal risks incurred on behalf of the firm except those generated by intentional torts or knowingly criminal conduct (Kraakman 1984: 861-2).

[97] *See* above Chapter IV, Section II, Subsection F. *et seq.* for a discussion of this litigation.

The question then arises how best to persuade corporations to put internal mechanisms in place to align agents behavior with socially desirable legal behavior. Coffee (1994: xxvi) suggests that whether or not credit should be given to the corporation for compliance programs is similar to the argument of strict liability versus negligence. The outcome of this discussion is generally that negligence is efficient under certain circumstances, namely when the victim has incentive to take care (*ibid.*). But who are the victims of corporate corruption? Do they really have incentive to take care? Does society have an interest in altering the victims action. Unlike tort law, criminal law generally does not require a victim. It is more interested in risk creation than actual damage (*ibid.*). It is difficult to say with any degree of precision whether from the perspective of corruption, compliance plans are desirable. A negligence rule that determines whether a firm is responsible when it has neglected is own internal enforcement responsibilities is further dependent on the courts' ability to evaluate internal firm behavior, which is a difficult task to accomplish (Rose-Ackerman 1999: 57). Further support against placing too much reliance on compliance plans as a means of curbing general malfeasance is captured by looking at the strong disincentives companies face against undertaking extensive disciplinary action. As Fisse and Braithwaite (1993: 8-9) note, "a disciplinary program may be disruptive, embarrassing for those exercising managerial control, encouraging for whistle-blowers, or hazardous in the event of civil litigation against the company or its officers."[98]

Of course, one should also distinguish within a system of dual responsibility between corporate criminal and corporate civil liability. Khanna (1996: 1492) identifies four major differences between the two. First, corporate criminal liability has stronger procedural protections. Second, it has more powerful enforcement devices; third, there are more severe sanctions, *e.g.*, stigma, and fourth it sends a greater message than corporate civil liability.[99] In practice, systems of dual responsibility (*i.e.*, agent and corporate responsibility) break down and the distinction between criminal and civil penalties may not be so important. Corporations are typically held responsible for the tort damages or criminal fines arising from agency actions (Kraakman 1984: 859).[100] From a

---

[98] *See* above, Chapter III, Section V, Subsection D, where I discuss internal systems of accountability in greater detail.

[99] *See* also Gruner (1994: chp. II).

[100] Of course, this forms part of a larger question of whether corporate criminal liability and criminal penalties are desirable per se. Fischel and Sykes (1996) suggest, for example, that it makes no sense to have a corporation face criminal charges, as corporations cannot be imprisoned so they are therefore forced to pay monetary damages, which may be achieved through civil liability. Criminal proceedings require higher levels of proof than civil proceedings and the ultimate penalty is still a fine in any case. Commentators have argued against the notion of criminal liability for corporations, often along the lines that it is foreign to

reputational perspective, the costs of either criminal or civil cases seems to be very similar (Block 1991).

Indeed, precisely because this system of dual liability breaks down, the deterrence effect against malfeasance at a corporate level may be particularly low. Individual liability is often forgone for corporate liability. There are concrete examples for corruption-related cases, where individual liability has been ignored in favor of corporate liability. The McDonnell Douglas bribery affair concerned with sales to Pakistani Airlines is one such high level case (Fisse and Braithwaite 1993: 3, *see* also Fisse and Braithwaite: chp. 14).[101] In consideration for a guilty plea by the organization to charges of fraud and making false statements, charges of fraud and conspiracy against four leading McDonnell Douglas corporate executives were dropped (*ibid.*: 4).[102]

This position is positively supported by statistical evidence for the U.S. on incidences of corporate crime among large companies in the 1970's highlighting that only 1.5 per cent of all actions resulted in the prosecution of a corporate officer (*ibid.*).[103] Even in countries that use administrative sanctions as opposed to corporate criminal sanctions such as Germany, the common targets of investigations are corporations not individuals (*ibid.*: 6). The effect of which is to reduce the deterrent effect of improbity at the agent level.

C. Alternatives to Monetary Sanctions

The most obvious alternative to corporate fines is to impose large penalties on individuals, but for reasons adumbrated above this may not be desirable. For example, the corporation would not have any incentives to monitor its own agents, except for reputation loss when malfeasance is publicly revealed. Further, the main justification of corporate liability includes the fact that the corporation may be in a better position than the government to monitor malfeasance; removing corporate liability reduces the best cost avoider advantages associated with corporate monitoring. Moreover, agents typically act for the benefit of the corporation, particularly in the case of corruption. Alternatives are, therefore, worth looking at. Indeed, the government should incorporate as wide a portfolio

---

the underlying concepts of the constitution of criminal law (Lederman 1985). This is a key reason behind its slow reception in the United Kingdom.

[101] For a list of other high profile cases where individual responsibility was compromised in favor of liability for a corporate entity, *see* Fisse and Braithwaite 1983, 1993.

[102] Following the settlement conducted between the Assistant Attorney General and company representatives in the absence of the prosecutors in the case, four prosecutors subsequently resigned from the justice department (Fisse and Braithwaite 1993: 4).

[103] Similarly, corporate executive often escape prosecution in Canada, Europe and Australia (Fisse and Braithwaite 1993: 7).

of sanctions as possible in order to accommodate many different potentialities. As Coffee, Gruner and Christopher (1988-89: 79) suggest:

"[P]lacing exclusive reliance on fines to deter serious instances of criminal behavior tends to exaggerate the state of existing knowledge about deterrence. To be sure, in economic theory, deterrence can be achieved by raising the expected penalty so that it exceeds the expected gain from the misbehavior (after discounting both by the probability of detection and conviction). Yet even if one accepts this theory without reservation (and most criminologists do not), it is unlikely that this approach can be reliably implemented today or in the near future, because we lack the ability to estimate accurately the critical variables that this approach depends upon."

It is easy to see how such a critique can even more readily be expanded to less developed countries with fewer resources. Moreover, reliance on a fine based system may give the appearance to the public of corruption and expand the belief that a company can purchase its way out of difficulties (*ibid.* : 82).

Given that corporate bodies cannot be sent to jail, this option is forgone; one possible alternative is corporate probation, as suggested in the US Sentencing Commission's Guidelines for Organizational Defendants, and the American Bar Association's Standards for Criminal Justice (Fisse and Braithwaite 1993: 42). This entails fundamentally a limited, probationary period of judicial monitoring of the activities of an organization that is subject to sanction. The aim of measures such as probation is to assure the corporation takes upon itself procedures to monitor the behavior of their agents. The incentives for them not voluntarily doing so were discussed above. One additional factor that may result from means such as probation is that the reputation loss is now potentially higher. Given that the company is undergoing extended external monitoring, there is always the possibility that noncompliance may lead to yet another scandal.

1. Reputation and Shaming

I have emphasized throughout the importance of secrecy to corrupt transactions and how making transactions more visible is a potentially powerful tool against corruption. Publicity is a particularly useful device in curbing corruption through shaming and affecting reputational losses. Publicity is a strong though imperfect device in achieving deterrence. It is imperfect because, like reputation loss in general, it is difficult to measure and can, therefore, lead to both over- and under-deterrence. But given that corruption scandals come with a particularly high public sanction (reputation loss, ostracism etc.), it is a particularly useful tool in curbing corruption. Of course, precisely because its impact is so difficult to measure and the associated social sanction potentially be so high, this should be taken into account when awarding formal sanctions. Work by Kaploff and Lott

(1993), for example, estimates that on average the loss incurred by a corporation for allegations of fraud against corporate shareholders consisted of only 6.5 percent formal sanctions based on legal fees and penalties. Should shaming, however, be left to the media and the political arena, and is it use in the court unwarranted? The answer for cases of corruption I argue is a resounding no! Shaming can heighten reputation losses, prevent transgressions and serve as an alternative to imprisonment. Shaming more so than fines expresses a type of moral condemnation (Kahan and Posner 1999: 368). It may impose a stigma and shape social norms (*ibid.*). The usefulness of shaming as a tool is furthered where individuals are singled out as opposed to corporations, thus concentrating the intensity of the punishment. It is a potent tool that can be adopted both by government as well as nongovernmental entities. It can be incorporated by media, politicians and nonprofits alike to particular affect mobilizing opinion against corrupt practices and highlighting the potential sanction associated with scandals, which can have repercussions for companies operating at a multinational level. To further encourage the potency of shaming as a tool against corruption, in addition to concentrating on key functionaries, reputational costs can be spread to those that do business with companies engaging in corruption. A further useful tool is to collect and publish information on companies that have engaged in such transgressions. Reputation can function as a type of informal blacklisting of companies.

There are, however, additional costs than the aforementioned of using shaming as a mechanism against corruption. In a corrupt regime, it is a potentially powerful tool in the hands of the authorities. Another possibly unintended affect of shaming echoes the aforementioned problem that because the expected sanction upon exposure is now higher, managers may have added incentives to exert fewer resources in detecting transgressions. Indeed for corruption, where the moral sanction is especially high, the temptation to shirk on monitoring responsibilities is especially significant! Moreover, when this sanction is too high, the willingness to come forward may decrease, because it is a function of the level of the sanctions- this is the familiar argument that the punishment must fit the crime. Another deterrent is related to the fact that there may be a collective reputation loss that affects more that one party leading to a general unwillingness to report. Where there are such collective reputation losses, an informal system of sanctioning whistleblowers is likely to develop.[104] On the other hand it may lead to greater self-monitoring given the fear that the information may leak out.

Reputational sanctions are a particularly useful tool against and deterrent for companies operating at a multinational level, given that the costs of revelations of corrupt payments are disseminated widely to a broad spectrum of actors. Companies suffer embarrassment when payoffs are revealed, which can

---

[104] *See* above, Chapter IV, Section II, Subsection E. *et seq.*

mobilize international public opinion and result in a broader array of sanctions. Where a company enjoys a strong market-based position such as Boeing or IBM, they may be able to refuse to make corrupt payoffs (Rose-Ackerman 1999: 188). Of course, this depends highly on the competitiveness of the market. Where there are few competitors collusive or corrupt agreements are all the more attractive, or where a strong position is enjoyed as a result of certain protections, these companies can be expected to do little to "rock the boat".

Economists frequently propound the use of the market to discipline corporate impropriety. Can market disciplining measures weed out corruption? Consider the following three arguments commonly put forward.[105] First, under ideal conditions, when fine levels are significantly high making corporations internalize the costs they impose on society, corporations would choose activities that are legal. This argument does not, even under the most optimistic of environments hold up, as the optimal fine for corporations is not necessarily the optimal fine level for corporate agents. In other words, agents still have incentive to transgress (Polinsky and Shavell 1993). Second, when firms are sanctioned for illegal behavior, according to a competitive market-type approach, they will try to reduce their compliance costs to a minimum in order to reduce overall costs (compliance costs are similar to the costs of production). In a perfectly competitive market, firms that produce at higher costs will be unable to supply the goods at market competitive prices and will be driven out of the market. But the assumption of perfect market conditions by its very nature does not hold for corruption which prevents perfect market conditions developing in the first place. Moreover, firms that have incentives to lower costs of production also have every incentive to lower monitoring costs. Third, another feature of market discipline put forward is investor discipline. This can have an impact on corruption, but it depends on the nature of the corruption and its impact on future company profits. Indeed, empirical evidence suggests that frauds perpetrated against stakeholders, governmental organizations, and investors can come with sizable market-based penalties (Lott 1999, Block 1991). By way of contrast, empirical work highlights that violations of regulatory restrictions are not accompanied by any serious market-based sanctions when an explicit or implicit contract with shareholders was not violated and actions are perhaps seen as furthering corporate objectives (Lott 1999). Investors are sophisticated. When the offense concerned is something that may not be repeated in the future and is not directly linked to corporate sales, investors are likely forgetful of the offense and little change in stock price is likely to ensue (Gruner 1994: 132). This suggests that investor monitoring of corruption can only be relied upon when the costs substantially affect future earnings.[106] The

---

[105] For a more complete discussion of how the market may discipline corporate managerial offenders, see Gruner (1994: 127-134).

[106] There are several ways an investigation can affect future earning. As Propper (2000: 58) notes: "Once an investigation commences, any number of events and decisions relation to the

truth is, however, that corruption related scandals in large multinational corporations frequently do not necessitate financially any substantial costs as shown in well publicized scandals such as the Lockheed Bribery Scandal and the McDonnell Douglas Scandal.[107]

D. The Importance of Multinational Initiatives

Companies frequently contend that they are in a briber's dilemma when operating in environments where corruption is common place (*see* Della Porta and Vannucci 1999: 205-207).[108] In such an environment, it is argued that parties in order to do business offer bribes or payments in kind, given that others with whom they are in competition are equally willing to do so, despite the fact that all firms are potentially better offer where no firm makes payments. Given the propensity of such an environment to fuel dishonesty and offer rewards to dishonest business as well as the desire to level the playing field, multilateral initiatives have taken an important stage in the anti-corruption campaign, particularly on such platform issues as cross-border bribery and the tax deductability of these bribes, as well as the development of competitive procurement systems (Rose-Ackerman 1999: 185; Galtung and Pope 1999).

The need for an international legal framework to eliminate bribery and corruption of public officials particularly by multinational corporations has led to prominent legal initiatives in recent years.[109] Whilst essentially every country in the world seemed to have some laws outlawing domestic bribery, only the United States had foreign anti-bribery laws until very recently. Enacted largely as a result of public outcry following a voluntary disclosure program of the U.S. Securities and Exchange Commission (SEC) which revealed slush funds and off-book accounts used for the bribery of foreign officials, the U.S. Foreign Corrupt

---

investigation may affect the company's stock price, including whether or not to announce the fact of the investigation. What the company says, or does not say, can lead to shareholder suits and a possible investigation by the Securities and Exchange Commission or other agency."

[107] For a discussion of these scandals, *see* Fisse and Braithwaite (1993) and Fisse and Braithwaite (1983)

[108] For further discussion of the bribers' dilemma, *see* above, Chapter III, Section VII, Subsection D.

[109] There are numerous mentionable multilateral initiatives that I shall not address here, including those by many international, professional and business organizations that have taken anti-corruption efforts into their list of activities. Among the more prominent of these organizations with anti-corruption initiatives include: the International Chamber of Commerce, *see* http://www.iccwbo.org/home/menu_extortion-bribery.asp; the Council of the International Bar Association, *see* http://www.ibanet.org and the International Association of Supreme Audit Institutions located in Vienna, see http://www.intosai.org. Furthermore, the work of Transparency International referred to elsewhere in this work operates at an international level facilitating and coordinating multilateral initiatives, *see* http://www.transparency.org.

Practices Act (FCPA) passed in 1977 criminalized the bribery of foreign officials by U.S. companies operating or wishing to operate overseas.[110] This was not the first initiative taken by the U.S. legislature against bribery, where already in 1958 tax deductions for bribes paid to foreign officials were already made nondeducatable.[111] Given that it was the first such body of laws, it was naturally the tool of reference for international initiatives with similar objectives.

One such important initiative was the Inter-American Convention Against Corruption (IACAC) supported by the members of the Organization of American States (OAS) in March 1996. Broad in scope and unique from the perspective that it incorporated so many low-income and mid-income countries, it sought the criminalization of both domestic and foreign bribery and the enactment of measures to combat the illicit enrichment of government officials. Furthermore, states agreed to consider measures relating to transparency and accountability in government operations, particularly procurement. Moreover, explicitly mentioned was that states need to consider measures aimed at promoting government ethics, including conflict-of-interest statutes and standards of behavior, and that parties consider laws that prevent the tax deduction of expenditures covered by anti-corruption laws.[112] Further explicitly mentioned are the need for book-keeping standards that "reflect the acquisition and disposition of assets, and have sufficient internal accounting controls to enable their officer to detect corrupt acts"[113] as well as the need to take measures to enhance whistleblower protection.[114]

The effectiveness of such agreements remains to be seen and is largely dependent of political and prosecutorial will. In the United States, there is strong enforcement commitment, for example, the FCPA's antibribery provisions are enforced by both the SEC and the Department of Justice. Another notable initiative is the Convention on Combating Bribery of International Officials in International Business Transactions signed in December 1997 by the Council of the Organization for Economic Cooperation and Development (OECD).[115] The fundamental aim of the treaty is as its name suggests to combat bribery of foreign officials as an international business practice. As with the above, it used the FCPA as a basis for the document. It also requires adequate sanctions and like the above emphasizes *inter alia* the setting up of accounting and auditing standards, and

---

[110] Foreign Corrupt Practices Act, 15 U.S.C.§§ 78m, 78dd-1, 78dd-2, 78ff. An important statutory exception to the antibribery provisions is related to so-called "grease payments" or "facilitating payments", paid to government officials performing routine governmental acts, to expedite these acts. See 15 U.S.C. §§78dd-1(b), 78dd-2(b).

[111] Internal Revenue Code, 26 U.S.C.§ 162(c).

[112] See Inter-American Convention Against Corruption, Mar. 29, 1996, 35 I.L.M. 724 (1996) Article III.

[113] Ibid. art. III (10).

[114] Ibid. art. III (8).

[115] For a look at the text of the convention, see http://www.oecd.org/oecd/pages/home/displaygeneral/0,3380,EN-document-88-nodirectorate-no-no-7198-31,00.html

transparency in governmental operations. Moreover, the OECD has recommended a re-examination of tax-deductability laws related to bribery in member countries.[116] Although expressly covered by the FCPA, both the OAS convention and the OECD convention do not make reference to payments to political parties, party officials and candidates for political office. This is quite a substantial drawback, as a fundamental channel for making payoffs has not yet been closed. As with the above it is a step in the right direction, but indications of political and prosecutorial will as well as enforcement will only become manifest with time.[117]

E. Conclusions

Summing up, the willingness of corporations to enlist effective long term monitoring mechanisms depends on the size of sanctions and similarly, the nature of possible sanctions - for example, whether there are long term reputation losses associated with a scandal or whether it may be better for those involved to let things blow over. Another important factor is whether there are other efficiency gains to be acquired by such a mechanism, such as reducing company fraud and increasing overall effectiveness in operations generally. Possible sanction mitigation and recognition for voluntary compliance may be important. When corporate efforts are perceived as an act of good faith in an ongoing investigation they should be rewarded. Also significant from the perspective of deterrence is the extent to which at the investigative level management has the ability to shift blame onto lower level officials or scapegoats. Relatedly, the willingness of the prosecution to settle for corporate penalties as opposed to penalties raised at the individual level are important from the perspective of deterrence and compliance. Internal corporate investigations as a mechanism against corruption and fraud are more likely to succeed when corporations are rewarded for their efforts. More particularly, when curbing malfeasance is correlated with other performance or cost-cutting related measures, efforts to curb corruption are more likely to succeed. This occurs when malfeasance for the corporation as a whole is actually costly, but beneficial for the individual agents involved. These costs can be quite significant. It is reckoned that the costs of criminal or unethical behavior to U.S. industry are about $400 billion a year (Propper 2000). As with mechanisms aimed at curbing corruption in government, there is a significant overlap between those

---

[116] OECD, Meeting of the Council at the Ministerial Level, Paris, May 21-22, 1996, Communique, SG/COM/NEWS(96)53, section 9(x).For an update on the implementation on the OECD recommendation on tax deductability of bribes to foreign officials, see http//:www.oecd.org/pdf/m00018000/m00018527.pdf.

[117] Attention should be furthermore drawn to other international initiatives salient to anti-corruption efforts, such as money laundering and the fight against organized crime. There have been several international initiatives. For a list of these international initiatives with links to individual texts, see http://www1.oecd.org/fatf/Initiatives_en.htm.

mechanisms that decrease shirking and increase performance and efficiency generally. Well-oiled internal monitoring systems may curb theft of company assets and general malfeasance, whilst also eliminating careless and inefficient practices, even helping to reduce insurance premiums (*ibid.*: 22). Realistically, corporate commitment to curbing corruption is a *sine qua non* to effective sustainable reforms. Whether this commitment can result purely because of well-designed structures of corporate and personal liability as well as social sanctions based on reputational losses and market disciplining measures is unclear. The sheer size and influence of multinational corporations compared to the GDP of some nations in which they operate is representative of their importance. Rose-Ackerman (1999: 187) has calculated that for the year 1995 the sales of the twenty largest multinationals ranged from $61.5 billion to $152.5; the smallest of which had sales that surpassed the GDP of ninety-eight of the 138 countries that submitted data to the World Bank. Credible commitment, given corporate size and bargaining power, must come from the corporate elite.[118]

---

[118] In one experiment conducted on business students and middle managers by Rosenburg (1987), over 70 percent of participants were willing to pay a bribe to acquire a sale for their companies. For those test subjects that were willing to pay bribes saw a distinction between honesty in their private and in business lives, where in the latter company goals took priority over morals. *Cited* in Rose-Ackerman (1999: 189).

CHAPTER VII

BARRIERS AND REQUISITES TO EFFECTIVE EXTERNAL OVERSIGHT

I. Introduction

Both experience and logic teach us that elections are not enough to curb high level corruption. Well-designed laws clarifying legal obligations to avoid self-dealing are an important first step, but are similarly not sufficient to mitigate malfeasance in office. Decentralizing government structures is currently in vogue, but as I argue in brief below, this can only at best be of limited impact in curbing corruption. Institutions of external oversight are imperative for the control of corruption, particularly high level corruption. Of course, the *locus classicus* of external or inter-branch oversight is the separation of powers among judicial, legislative and executive bodies; this tripartite division is, however, no longer indicative of the operative demarcations of the state. There are multifarious institutions common to a well-functioning system of governmental and administrative control. At the top of this list, one can expect to find, the processes of the courts and judiciary, auditing bodies including auditing commissions, appeals tribunals, internal complaints procedures, extensive parliamentary committees and perhaps the ombudsman and other inspectorates.[1] The issue of law and accountable government and administration is, however, far broader than that of corruption, though sharing an obvious overlap. I concentrate here on select aspects of those institutions currently salient in the debate on corruption and reform, and, those, in addition, deserved of greater attention and not referred to in earlier parts of my work.

A. The Limits of Federalism and Decentralized Structures of Government in Curbing Corruption

Decentralized government structures such as federalism may provide some ability to constrain high level transgressions, according to which when one body oversteps its boundaries, it may expect to be pulled up.[2] But, their impact is limited and varied and they can raise significant problems of their own which I

---

[1] One could also add to this list, particularly if one looks beyond government in its administrative capacity, electoral commissions and tribunals, constitutional courts, human rights commissions, and central banks.

[2] An advantage of such a structure is as Rose-Ackerman (1999: 149) notes, that "national government can constrain the states, and the states, the localities. Institutions operating internationally may provide a check on national governments."

adumbrate in brief below. Because of the inherent notion of federalism, characterized generally as a hierarchy of governments where each level of government is autonomous in its own sphere of authority and each government's autonomy is guaranteed, the needed watchdog role of central government in corruption-related issues may actually be untenable. It can be inconsistent in many cases with the notion of federalism itself.[3] For example, the compatibility of prosecution of state and local corruption with the principles of federalism is the subject of widespread discussion in the United States (see, e.g., Beale 2000). Moreover, as we learn from experience in the United States, federal regulations aimed at combating corruption, malfeasance and ethical laxity in government, frequently don't have a counterpart at local or state level, that can be used for the prosecution of nonfederal officials. Thus, federalism may even function as a shield that protects against corruption-related prosecution (Beale 2000). Strong federalist concerns can lead to a reduction in the number of successfully unveiled and prosecuted cases of corruption, erecting a barrier to the penetration of local offenses.[4]

Predictably, decentralization of governmental structures potentially brings officials in close contact with citizens which can incite personalism and reduce arms length relationships (Tanzi 1995). Search costs for corruption are reduced given the geographical proximity of functionaries. In a society where "hand on" relations are commonplace and reciprocal obligations and IOU's are a common feature of economic and social life, there is a potential breeding ground for corruption. Factors highlighted in chapter II conducive to cooperation, such as kinship, economic and social embeddedness, and familiarity with local functionaries can also be more active. Similarly, where local authorities can put up both political and economic barriers, competition can be stifled and cartels may be more stable, given the increased ability to monitor the actions of members, and the homogeneity of groups. Where competition can be guaranteed niches may remain within the local market. These problems are exasperated when monitoring by local bodies is underdeveloped and central authorities, who may lose some power if decentralized structures are introduced, have less incentives to monitor and detect corrupt activities. Clearly the desirability of decentralized structures depends on the level of administrative and technical capabilities as well as the degree of local political accountability (Bardhan and Mookherjee 1999; Burki, Perry and Dillinger 1999). The commonly exposed advantage of

---

[3] See Riker (1964) for an authoritative definition and discussion of federalism.

[4] For Rose-Ackerman (1999: 149) there are two justifications in the realm of corruption control for intervention of higher level entities in federalist structures. The first of which occurs when corrupt politicians restrict commerce across state borders. This is done to protect local business from interstate commerce. The second reason is when state and local governments are under the control of local elites who exploit gains associated with corruption where competition between jurisdictions cannot reverse it (ibid.).

decentralized structures that citizens as local stakeholders are better able to monitor local officials than others in central government may not be utilized where citizens are politically unaware or unskilled. Efforts of widespread decentralization in Latin America in the nineties have only produced mixed results at best (Diamond, Hartlyn, Linz and Lipset 1999).

Finally, another suggested advantage of federalism and decentralized structures particularly salient to the issue of corruption, has a long that can be traced back as far as Tiebout (1956). Accordingly, it is argued that in a environment of decentralized structures, "competitive governments will allow for a national regulatory marketplace, in which individuals move among local jurisdictions or states to select the regulatory combination that they most desire" (Inman and Rubinfeld 1999: 669). This suggestion bares semblance to an argument made earlier that competitive forces can push down the returns to corruption, thus making corruption less profitable.[5] Similar to private market forces, when the citizen or buyer is subject to higher prices (as a result of corruption or otherwise), he can go elsewhere. Like a customer in a restaurant, economic actors make decisions based on the menu they are offered by the government; when they do not like the menu, they can leave and go to another location.[6] The threat of exit under federalism may in this light be considered a factor that not just decreases the size of the bribe possible, but also the returns to bribery, because the rents that can be achieved therefrom cover only a geographically small area. Mobility, however, is not necessarily a good thing from the perspective of curbing corruption. For example, successful efforts at reforming law enforcement in jurisdiction A may just lead criminals to move across to jurisdiction B. Money laundering of funds across borders to "financial paradises" provides another example of how competition can be undesirable and make control of malfeasance more and not less difficult (Rose-Ackerman 1999: 150-51).[7] Given the fact that one cannot foretell whether competition will be harmful or beneficial, as well as a plethora of other considerations, particularly those touched upon above, decentralization of government structures is likely to only to be at the most of moderate assistance in quelling corruption (*see* also *ibid.*: 151). Decentralized structures are not a substitute for well-functioning institutions.

---

[5] *See* above, Chapter I, Section IX.

[6] The price and returns on corruption are not the only thing, of course, on the menu. On the menu are such factors as the levels of taxation, security of property rights, social amenities, public goods etc. (*see* Weingast 1995: 5).

[7] There is also support from the game theoretical literature that when a person can choose with whom he can cooperate, the chances are significantly greater that the parties will honor cooperative agreements. *See*, for example, Yamagishi (1992).

II. The Judiciary

Failure to guarantee and enforce legal rights and norms is particularly devastating for development. In many countries, legal inertia and legal adhocary have become a norm and failure to provide a legal safety net has had social, economic and political consequences (Nolte 2000: 70). In Latin America, cases can take up to twelve years to resolve (Buscaglia Dakolias and Ratliff 1995). One of the most fundamental insights of institutional economics and law and economics has been to highlight the importance of the security of property rights and the enforceability of contracts for economic development (*see* North 1990). Where these two factors are not guaranteed, economic development cannot properly ensue. The returns to illegal activity relative to legal activity increase, thus shifting the allocation of talent to nonproductive activities. Hence the role of the judiciary in overcoming corruption is not just within it governmental oversight capacity, but rather also in securing the attractiveness of legitimate over illegitimate activities. To wit, where the judiciary is ill-functioning, firms wishing to do business in countries must frequently operate without the "shadow of the law", thus injecting great uncertainty into transactions, increasing transaction costs and opening up possibilities for opportunism.[8] Below, I briefly examine the specific problems of "creating a legal framework for economic development" and curbing corruption.[9] I discuss reform measures that have been or are being introduced, the successes thereof and, more generally, the significance of the judiciary in overcoming corruption.

A. Legal Institutional Reform

Countries interested in reforming their legal framework, should concentrate on creating law that are well-drafted, clear and accessible.[10] It is cheaper to produce efficient rules for inefficient institutions than to create efficient legal institutions (Hay Schleifer and Vishny 1996) Posner distinguishes between procedurally efficient and substantially efficient laws. Procedurally efficient laws are laws that govern the working of the court at the lowest possible cost. Substantially efficient laws are laws that are good in substance per se, *i.e.*, socially desirable laws (Posner 1998). Whether one should begin by focusing on formulating substantially and procedurally efficient laws before focusing on institutional reforms is unwise or highly moot at best, particularly given past experiences in transition economies, as we have seen in our discussion of privatization. However,

---

[8] *See* above, Chapter V, Section IV on the important role a central authority can play in economic transactions.

[9] Term coined by Posner (1998).

[10] *See* above, Chapter III, Section IV.

it is clear that beyond the immediate short term focus must be given to institutional issues.

The role of institutions in general and legal institutions in particular was already of importance to decision-makers intent on stimulating economic development in the arenas of politics and administration in the eighteenth and nineteenth century (Schäfer 1998: 2).[11] The focus of economic development is once again leaning towards addressing institutional hindrances in developmental processes (*ibid.*). The focal point of development economics and politics has shifted from closing the so called "savings gap" between rich and poor countries, by mere transferal of capital, to economic analysis of the effects of institutions and the role of the law in developmental processes.[12]

Little is known precisely on the importance of judicial reform to economic development, and, moreover, there is widespread disagreement on what measures are necessary to any package of reforms (Messick 1999). However, even those persons hard pressed against the importance of judicial reforms to economic development would scarcely suggest that well-functioning government does not require serviceable legal and judicial institutions to promote long-term private sector development, further the development of other societal institutions, lessen poverty and consolidate democracy (*see* Dakolias 1995: 167). One reason for skepticism was the generally acknowledged failure of the American- sponsored initiative in the 1960's and 1970's that generally sought to transplant American Law to developing countries. Furthermore, skepticism remains as a result of a widespread criticism of an over-emphasis on the applicability of market-like rational to situations were they can not be successfully applied. This is particularly the case when exchanges are based more on customs, morals, trust and reputation and not within an anonymous structure.[13] For example, in Latin America, it is often reported that people are more comfortable relying on informal factors, such as long-standing business relations, or family, when doing business and settling disputes.

From an economic point of view, an unwillingness to enter into anonymous exchange can only lead to a loss in productivity and seriously hinders long-term economic development. The ability of legal rules to shift the behavior of individuals may be, therefore, exaggerated (Schäfer 1998: 2). Yet another criticism rests on the discussion of the emergence or production of norms

---

[11] *See* Schäfer (1998) for historical examples of the aforementioned.

[12] A casual search of the World Bank homepage (www.worldbank.org) shows a vast number of articles published on the subject, and, moreover, an extensive range of policy reforms based on institutional analysis.

[13] A number of studies now examine the role of repeat dealings and informal enforcement mechanisms in insuring reciprocity in business relations, *see* North (1990) and references cited therein. Furthermore, many of these mechanisms can be seen as running both parallel to and instead of the courts to enforce legal obligations.

conducive to economic development. The literature seems to be divided into two camps, namely those that believe in the top down approach, i.e. where law can effectively be imported from one legal system to another or as a result of innovative judicial-making, or those that believe that law must come from the bottom up, i.e. as a result of well established norms within a society being promulgated into law.[14] The latter are, therefore, doubtful about the usefulness of judicial and institutional reform without the safety net of well established norms conducive to these institutions. It appears likely that the truth lies somewhere between the two. From the point of view of reform, this argument is also related to the discussion on whether a broad consensus is necessary to push through reforms, or whether reforms themselves can generate support by their (potential) success.

Nevertheless, it seems pervasive among most scholars and policy reformers today that judicial reform within the larger goal of legal reform warrants sufficient attention. To wit, "[t]here are well over 300 Bank financed projects which deal with, or include components for, legal and judicial reform." (World bank 2002).[15] The Bank's projects are aimed solely at increasing the economic performance of a nation as it is proscribed from interfering in the political affairs of its members (Messick 1999: 119). Judicial reform is part of a greater body of legal reform in developing countries, but refers to reform within the courts and the judicial branch of government (ibid.: 118).[16]

B. Recent Initiatives

The importance of the judiciary in establishing democracy, curbing high level corruption and overseeing the rule of law is easily understood. It has played a key role in anti-corruption investigations and official transgressions in innumerable countries around the world, and has even taken upon itself measures under the veil of judicial activism, where other governmental entities were perceived as slacking.[17]

---

[14] For a lively discussion on legal transplants, see Mattei (1998). For a discussion of the bottom up approach and its importance for economic development, see Cooter (1996).

[15] World Bank. 2002. Initiatives in Legal and Judicial Reform. Legal Vice Presidency, The World Bank, available at http://www4.worldbank.org/legal/publications/initiatives-final.pdf.

[16] As noted by Messick (ibid.: 118): "The broader legal reform movement encompasses everything from writing or revising commercial codes, bankruptcy statutes, and company laws through overhauling regulatory agencies and teaching justice ministry officials how to draft legislation that fosters private investment."

[17] For example, for an illuminating discussion on the role of the magistrates in tackling corruption in Italy, see Della Porta and Vannucci (1999). For a discussion of judicial activism, see McAdams (1997). For an account of judicial activism on the part of the Supreme Court in Israel, see Dotan (1997).

One encouraging sign has been the rise of constitutional tribunals or courts as a meaningful device to foster governmental accountability. Though not without criticism, they have shown some signs of success particularly in Central and Eastern Europe (Schwartz 1999a, 1999b). Constitutional courts with the power of judicial review over the legislative and executive are an important tool against high level executive and legislative corruption. They provide some defense against leaders who avail of their marionette legislature and administrative agencies to bring into existence their desired legislation and regulations. These qualities of constitutional tribunals were recognized by Western European nations that had been subjected to authoritarian regimes such as Germany, Italy, Spain, and Portugal, who all established constitutional courts shortly after becoming nascent democracies (Schwartz 1999b: 195). Indeed, by the year 1989, some provision for judicial review of the constitutionality of legislative and administrative acts was available in practically every Western European country, as was the case in Japan, Latin America, and the emerging nations of Africa (Schwartz 1999a: 149). Subsequently, similar provisions were made for those countries emerging from communism. Such institutions are particularly important where notions of legislative supremacy still prevail as in many Eastern European countries, where they provide a medium for reviewing laws and regulations that may otherwise go uncontested by the remaining judiciary or other bodies (Schwartz 1999b: 210 -211).

Unfortunately the work of the judiciary in many countries is hampered by a plethora of technical and organizational deficiencies including a lack of human capital aggravated by low remuneration, improper or flawed appointment and promotion procedures, administrative inefficiency, inertia and even corruption outright. Moreover, the work of the judiciary is obfuscated by its weak independence from political entities. Latin American countries provide a strong case in point. For decades the governments of Latin America have proclaimed their willingness to reform, a terminology mainly used to describe macroeconomic measures but now shifted to issues of governance (Dakolias 1995: 167). The Latin America judicial system is commonly perceived to be unable to fulfill basic expectations of ordering "social relationships among private and public entities and individuals and to resolve conflicts among these societal actors" (*ibid.*: 168). These factors are aggravated by both political and cultural obstacles to judicial reform in the region, including a tradition of judicial submissiveness and executive encroachment furthered by opposition to change by both judges and presidents alike (Diamond, Hartlyn, Linz and Lipset 1999: 6)

Several initiatives have been undertaken to strengthen the role and capacity of the judiciary, some of which are pertinent to our discussion here. I briefly refer to the following important areas: (1) Reform of judicial administration; (2) alternative dispute resolution; handling times of cases, backlogs and procedural steps; (3) judicial independence and getting the incentives right, i.e. issues related to freedom from political, peer and bureaucratic influence, as well as tenure, job security, prestige, pension, output and performance mechanisms; (4) and the importance of education and human capital among members of the judiciary.

1. Reform of Judicial Administration

I have suggested above that the role of the judiciary in overcoming corruption is not just within its capacity as monitor of governmental and administrative actions, but rather also in securing the attractiveness of legitimate over illegitimate activities. Improving the operation of the courts should be part of a larger goal of securing a legal framework for private market activity, a factor oftentimes hindered not just by malfeasance, but more commonly by maladministration. It is common in judicial systems around the world that the judiciary and particularly the supreme court is responsible for much of its own administration, particularly budgetary decisions, recruitment etc. It is not uncommon that judges spend much of there time on mundane matters such as the day-to-day running of the court, as is the case in Latin America where judges frequently spend up to 65 to 70 percent of their time on administrative duties (Buscaglia, Dakolias and Ratliff 1995: 13). Efforts have been made to decentralize management, handing over administrative responsibilities to the hands of administrative bodies. The aims of these efforts are naturally to give the judge more time to cope with his judicial responsibilities as opposed to administration. Furthermore, it is intended to provide the courts with a more skilled administration and a better division of labor. Caution needs to be given to the fact that a clear separation of the administration from the judiciary may result in a challenge to the independence of the judiciary. Furthermore, as a measure on its own, shifting responsibility for administrative decisions reduces the influence of the judge but increases the role of the personnel. In order to reduce the level of corruption there must be a decrease in the expected payoffs from corrupt transactions.

2. Alternative Complaints Systems

Surveys conducted in Latin America highlight the lack of confidence people have in the judicial system in their respective countries. In Argentina, Brazil, Ecuador, and Peru surveys show that between 55 percent and 75 percent of the public has a very low opinion of the judiciary. Among the complaints is that it is inaccessible. It is even internally commonly perceived that there is a crises within the judiciary (Buscaglia, Dakolias and Ratliff 1995: 5). Not surprisingly people look for alternative methods of settling disputes. Proponents of alternative dispute resolution mechanisms (ADR's) usually site the following as being the positive factors associated therewith. First, where the judiciary is overburdened with cases, alternative dispute resolution mechanisms provide a means to reach an early decision. Second, ADR provides an alternative means to voice complaint. This is especially valuable when the judiciary is not trusted, or when decisions by the judiciary are perceived to be uncertain by the parties. Third, arbitrators usually have specialized knowledge of an area which increases confidence. Fourth, where parties want to continue their relationship, they may prefer to use ADR, or when they do not wish to disclose information to public records (Dakolias 1995: 200). Arbitration is not the only means of ADR, other types include conciliation, mediation and justices of the peace. In some countries such as Brazil, it has become mandatory that judges make conciliatory efforts in the vast majority of cases (Rosenn 1997). Mediation is a process that encourages negotiations among parties to help them reach a settlement. Justices of the peace are sometimes elected by the community, or alternatively by the judicial system. In most cases they may only propose a settlement, but in some cases they are able to impose a sentence, particularly when the dispute is over small sums.

Questions here remain whether or not they should be self-regulated professions; how binding their decisions should be; what ethical standards need to be obeyed; what training is required; for what type of cases are they best suited, and whether their use should be mandatory or voluntarily (Dakolias 1995). Another consideration is that there are possibilities of coordination failures and overlapping with the judiciary, which can add another layer of confusion. Where the ADR is considered binding this may have dramatic effects as it can open up a whole new avenue of corruption, especially exploited by insiders. Another argument voiced by public lawyers is that they don't provide the same institutional safeguards as operating within a traditional judiciary.

3. Handling Times of Cases, Backlogs and Procedural Steps

Naturally much of the focus of judicial reform has concentrated on speeding up the hearings of cases and judicial decisions. Among other things, administration and procedure has become modernized. Where procedures are slow, backlogs are created offering opportunities for officials that can speed up cases. Even where judges are honest, administrative staff can avail of these opportunities. The use of computers has been found to significantly alter the speed of the handling of cases (Buscaglia 1999). Other areas of importance include the maintenance of statistics that allow case related data to be used for "resource allocation, forecasting, case flow management, performance measurement, public information and national trend analysis" (Dakolias 1995: 7). As mentioned this is a mechanism that has increased the processing time of cases as well as the transparency and accountability of the judiciary. Whilst the number of judges is often considered to be a factor that increases the processing of cases, it may not necessarily be the case. Buscaglia (1999) has shown that an increase in the number of judges does not have a significant impact on the processing of cases. Increasing the number of judges in the judiciary and particularly in the supreme court may actually decrease the accountability of the individual judges.[18]

The practice of private meetings between judges and lawyers for individual litigants is common throughout Latin America which may be used to influence both judges and court personnel (Rose-Ackerman 1999: 155). In China, legal officials is has been reported may require parties to lawsuits to even furnish them with "lavish banquets" before litigation commences (*ibid.*). These practices encourage impartiality and corruption outright. I emphasized in chapter II that potential parties to corrupt exchanges need to find a partner with whom they can engage in corruption, hammer out a corrupt deal and find a means of enforcing the agreement. These factors are made significantly easier where parties can operate in secrecy or seclusion, coordinating their efforts. Compare the possibilities for corrupt exchanges in the above scenarios to that of the United States, where a judge who was handling a civil case faces many legal obstacles in signaling to the parties her willingness to accept a bribe without evoking attention and possible investigation. Judges are not allowed to meet with a single party in the absence of another, thus private meetings are impermissible are likely to raise suggestions of improper behavior. This impediment makes secrecy uncertain and difficult to maintain. Long-term relations between the litigants and the judge are also unlikely to develop because they change so frequently, making it riskier for either litigant or judge to initiate the possibility of payoffs. Judges are therefore more likely to deal with lawyers, but they in turn would have to approach their own clients with the proposal which further involves risks (see Heymann 1996: 332-333).

4. Judicial Independence and Judicial Incentives

Judicial independence here refers to a system where politicians, bureaucrats and other extra-judicial figures do not intervene in the running of the courts. Accordingly, an independent judge does not need political support to remain in office, whereas a dependent judge does. Interference by the legislative and executive branches of government is still a common feature in several countries, particularly in Latin America, Eastern Europe and parts of Asia and Africa. Here, the judicial branch is far from achieving the status of equipotent particularly due to historical, political and structural forces. In Argentina and Peru, for example, leaders like Menem and Fujimori frequently pushed through their reforms by

---

[18] Another area that has received attention in civil law countries is the inability of judges, particularly in high courts to select the most important cases they wish to address. This is, however, also common in many developed countries. For example, constitutional courts in Europe are not allowed to choose their dockets (schedule of cases addressed by a court) unlike the Supreme Court in the US. One can, therefore, hardly consider such a factor to be a precursor to a successfully functioning judicial system.

bypassing the legislature accompanied by the emasculation of the judiciary and other independent institutions clearly forgoing common standards of transparency and accountability (Manzetti 1999: 322-326). Not surprisingly, the judiciary commonly failed to investigate serious suspicions of massive improbity, in such areas as privatization, because of heavy government influence (*ibid.*: 327). The effects of encroachment echo through many spheres of economic life, having widespread ramifications for economic development. In Russia, for example, it is reported that shareholders who sue a major company are likely always to lose at the local instance and first-level appeal, owing to judicial corruption, home-court bias, or both. A strong case to have any chance of success, must proceed to the higher instances which can take years and judgments must commonly be enforced by the same impartial or corrupt lower court where the case was initiated (Black, Kraakman and Tarassova 2000: 1755-56). Judges who issue rulings against powerful forces may find themselves beaten for as a reward for their efforts (*ibid.*). Similar tales of political encroachment and unpreserved judicial independence could be told for several other countries.[19]

Realistically, in order to understand the presence or absence of judicial independence, it is necessary, to consider the primary stakeholders of reforms. Unsurprisingly perhaps to political scientists, we must move outside of the judiciary to consider the electoral marketplace. "Why do rational politicians in some countries offer independent courts, while politicians in other democracies do not?" (Ramseyer, 1994: 721, *see* also Landes and Posner 1975). Ramseyer suggests that where political parties have greater chances of retaining control, they face lower risk adjusted costs to dependent judiciaries. When these costs are lower they prefer nonindependent judges and well-monitored judiciaries (*ibid.*). Independence is therefore dependent on political competition; where it is absent, the judiciary is less likely to be independent.

Key to judicial independence is the manner of judicial selection. Factors of selection include recruitment, retention, and tenure of judges. Each one can be manipulated to affect judicial incentive, capacity and independence generally. But judicial independence should not be separated from other institutional arrangements composing the broader incentive framework. Among the broader array of factors that constitute the general incentive framework one must include: provisions, either constitutional or statutory in nature, listing minimum formal qualifications such as age and length of law practice; competitive judicial salaries and benefits (relative to opportunities forgone and conducive to honesty);[20] provisions concerning judicial pension plans; the length of judicial terms and possibly mandatory retirement laws; the accessibility of mechanisms of judicial

---

[19] *See*, for example, Dasgupta and Mookherjee (1998) for a discussion on similar practices in Indonesia.

[20] In developed countries, judges are normally paid high wages even beyond opportunities forgone, which serves as an honesty premium.

discipline, and the working conditions of the courts, including the adequacy of court facilities. Additionally one might add the perception or respectability of the position in the eyes of both the public and peers.

5. Legal Education and Training

Legal education and training is fundamental to a well-running judicial system, and moreover, is a fundamental part of any reform package. In countries that are in the process of committing themselves to free market and democratic reforms, new laws must not just be drafted but human capital is of fundamental importance. Lessons from privatization in Eastern and Central Europe provide strong evidence that legal and institutional safeguards must precede or at least accompany broad reform measures. Countries that are still reforming their ownership structures and evolving their tax and regulatory system, require personnel that can implement these laws. As Karl Popper (1966: 126) observed: "Institutions are like fortresses: they must be properly designed and manned." Continuous training for judges, lawyers and other professionals are aimed at increasing the overall professionalism of the judiciary and raising codes of ethics above norms of low standards that have often managed to manifest themselves. Increasing the number of law schools, in addition to modifying the curriculum and securing adequate resources have been part of this aspect of reform.

Although this aspect of reform is necessary in most contexts, it does bring with it some inherent problems. For one, judges and lawyers that receive training abroad or specialized training often take these skills elsewhere where the returns are higher. For example, judges often leave the bench after training for a more lucrative position in the bar (Buscaglia, Dakolias and Ratliff 1995). Secondly, it is often difficult to measure the returns on such projects, leaving room for discretion and rent seeking. Thirdly, reform is a process, and given that politicians operate within a restricted time period, they are slow in supporting something for which instantaneous gains are not forthcoming. An appropriate selection process needs to be in place ensuring those that are qualified actually receive the training, and that it does not serve as a reward for loyalty or other convictions. As with other areas of judicial reform, one can argue that emphasis purely on legal training and education is too narrowly defined to a technical issue at the expense of more underlying, political problems (Messick 1999: 119). Such improvements are important but a more general overhaul of institutional structures may be necessary, and in any case should be combined with other efforts to assign correct incentives that discourage nonfeasance, malfeasance and maladministration generally.

C. Accountability and the Limits of Judicial Review

Judicial review refers to "the exercise of the court's inherent power to determine whether an action is lawful or not and to award suitable relief" (Wade and Forsyth 1999: 22).[21] Judicial supervision of governmental bodies is an essential feature of any constitutional system based on the rule of law. It takes many forms, but in essence refers to the examination of the actions of branches or levels of government with regard to compliance with the principal of legality, where legality itself is derived through and by the law developed and applied to that particular body. The importance of judicial supervision of executive bodies is heightened, where the legislature transfers implementation to executive entities, commonly voluntarily leaving the development of precise standards to the executive, to be elaborated and refined generally within the confines of procedural requirements (*see* Rose-Ackerman, 1992, 1995). We need not, however, overly concern ourselves here with the debate on the efficiency implications or the economic and political justifications for such delegation.[22]

Judicial supervision, though derived and administered within various constitutional traditions quintessentially determines whether governmental bodies function within the confines afforded to them under the law. As an aside, the reader should note that the Anglo-American system is provided by ordinary courts deciding cases involving the legitimacy of governmental action, and not special, separate administrative courts dealing with administrative cases exclusively as is the case of many parts of Europe, such as France, Germany and Poland,. The main requirement for the court to effectually conduct this role is that it be independent from the organs it so monitors.

There are, however, several shortcomings of judicial review as a means of curbing corruption, and in particular systematic corruption, even within a relatively well-functioning judiciary.

---

[21] According to Black's Law Dictionary, judicial review refers to: "1. A court's power to review the actions of other branches or levels of government; esp. the courts' power to invalidate legislative and executive actions as being unconstitutional. 2. The constitutional doctrine providing for this power. 3. A court's review of a lower court's or an administrative body's factual or legal findings" Black's Law Dictionary (1999, 7th ed.) p. 852.

[22] *See* von Wangenheim (1999) for a survey of the literature on the production of rules by agencies and the bureaucracy. According to Rose-Ackerman (1999: 146) the conventional reason given for this "combines a belief in the expertise of the executive agencies with the claims that legislators should not be wither making individual personnel and procurement choices or deciding enforcement priorities. Thus regulatory writing is delegated because the legislature is not competent to carry out this essentially legislative task, and purely executive or adjudicatory functions are not appropriate for the legislature under separation-of-powers principles."

First, the principal of legality, according to which the wide spectrum of procedures and systems of judicial review suggested is based,[23] depends on such factors as laws defining administrative and executive bodies and their limits, laws prescribing procedures to be followed and laws imposing standards on the manner in which rules and decisions are made. Although the court may initiate some of the above factors, in general, the court is beholden to the legislature which must enact many of these proscriptions in the first place. The legislature, thus generally has ample room to willfully neglect the promulgation of laws, adequately restricting executive bodies in the first place (or, if it so desires to inject the current legislative philosophy of the day into the laws). Whether or not it does so, depends in large part of the level of cohesion and collusion between the executive and legislative organs.

A second limitation of judicial review as a means of curbing malfeasance and corruption is that it normally depends on a narrowly drawn definition of a person of group that is affected adversely by a rule or action to initiate the process, although most systems legal systems also provide for a independent public entity, such as the Attorney General, Prosecutor or Commissaire du Government, to take an action before the courts. The American Procedures Act (APA) provides, for example, that "a person suffering legal wrong because of agency action, or adversely affected by agency action within the meaning of a relevant statute, is entitled to judicial review thereof."[24] Israel, however, serves as a model of a common law system where the Supreme Court is willing to hear a wide range of cases on politically sensitive issues for judicial review and has developed a wide concept of standing. Indeed, the courts have advanced a wide concept of standing which, as one legal commentator remarked, has "in essence created an actio popularis in cases involving allegations of governmental corruption or where fundamental constitutional principles (such as the Rule of Law) are at stake" (Dotan 1997: 521). Israel remains, nevertheless, the exception to the rule and judicial review generally rests upon a narrowly drawn definition of a group wronged or adversely affected by a particular governmental action.

This limitation is somewhat mitigated when citizens and affected groups are awarded process rights observed through the requirement of adherence by the agency to procedural constraints. The American Procedures Act (APA), is valuable from this and other perspectives. The APA also requires, and the courts place great emphasis on the fact, that notice of intent to change a regulation and comment procedures by a broad range of individuals and groups affected by the

---

[23] Indeed, it is perhaps not just the fundamental principle of judicial review, but the fundamental tenet of administrative law. See, for example, Wade and Forsyth (1999: 35) who suggest, "The simple proposition that a public authority may not act outside its powers (ultra vires) might fitly be called the central principle of administrative law".

[24] See 5 U.S.C § 702. On the American Procedures Act generally, see 5 U.S.C. §§ 551-559, 701-706.

regulation are adhered to. Exceptions thereto are kept to a minimum. The courts in the United States also attach great weight to the APA requirement that a production of a statement of reasons for the basis of a regulation and the purpose of the final rule be given.[25] When these procedural requirements are not adhered to, the regulation can be challenged in court. Similarly, if the rule is inconsistent with the underlying statute, it can be challenged in court. For this, the courts can apply the hard look doctrine, which "reviews an administrative-agency decision to ensure that the decision did not result from expediency, pressure or whim."[26] The courts, therefore, tendentiously move beyond the legality of a case or rule and into the merits of a case, influencing policy (Ziamou 1999: 729).

I have just touched on a third limitation of judicial review in that it is generally limited to issues of legality and not to the merits of a case or rule. The general rational behind such a limitation along separation-of-power lines is generally obvious and need not overly concern us here. However, from the perspective of corruption, it does place strict limits on judicial review, because corruption can very plausibly influence issues of policy and not just legality. As mentioned above, in the United States the courts have somewhat encroached on the policy merits of a case or rule, but in other countries, such as Germany, the courts primarily ensure only that the legislative mandate has been adhered to by the administration, and parliament is given the role of overseeing the administration and limiting its discretion in the formation of secondary rules (Ziamou 1999: 736-739; Rose-Ackerman 1995). The German system of executive branch rulemaking has been criticized as less transparent than its American counterpart and in particular that it is oft beholden to special interest groups (Rose-Ackerman 1995; Rose-Ackerman 1999: 147). In this context, bribery is not so much the problem but rather excess influence (Rose-Ackerman 1999: 147).

Appeals bodies that have the authority to look at the substantive merits of an action are, however, customary to many countries. Normally allowed only after internal appeals have been used up, these appeals bodies may also raise questions of law, but they do have the power to look at the facts of a particular case. For example, the French Tribunaux Administrative, which are the first instance of the expansive, specialized system of French administrative courts, may look at the merits as well as the legality of an action in certain cases. The Australian Administrative Appeals Tribunal (AAT) has the power not only to examine the merits of a primary decision, but also addresses anew and can substitute the original decision even if no error was found.

A fourth limitation of judicial review is that some organs are *de facto* or *de jura* immune or partially immune from judicial supervision. These may include the military and other organs related to national security. In the United Kingdom,

---

[25] *See* 5 U.S.C § 553 (c).
[26] Black's Law Dictionary (1999, 7th ed.) p. 721.

for example, according to the law of parliamentary privilege both Houses have sole authority over their own procedures and the courts cannot lack jurisdiction to inquire or question proceedings in Parliament (Oliver 1997: 543).[27] In Israel, however, the Supreme Court has been very active in reviewing the actions of those bodies previously held outside of the realm of judicial review including the military and the General Security Service (Dotan 1997: 521-22). The Supreme Court has expanded the range of supervised organs beyond the executive branch to permit judicial review of the legislator as well and even held that it can by means of judicial review legally bind the different organs of the Knesset to their own procedural rules (*ibid.*).

A fifth limitation of judicial review is that it is time consuming, in particular related to other disciplinary measures. A sixth and related limitation of judicial review from the perspective of curbing corruption is that even pursuant to a successful challenge of an administrative rule or action, only this particular rule or action may be remedied, but there are *de jura* normally no wider implications, bar in rare cases where the ruling provides a general guideline for the law, and de facto only where the case received public of legislative attention. It, therefore, generally does not get to the heart of the problem by affecting underlying incentives and does not facilitate change of the underlying rules of the game.

III. Enforcement and Prosecutorial Discretion

> "Enforcement of law against bribery has nearly always been a function of prosecutorial discretion. Prosecutions for bribery have often depended on motivations distinct from the bribe."
> (Noonan 1984: xxii)

It is unfortunate that enforcement and prosecutorial discretion appears to have wholly escaped the attention of political scientists and economists working on the area of corruption and development. The aforementioned quote taken from Noonan, writer of the most authoritative history of bribery to date, captures the importance of enforcement and prosecutorial discretion to the issue of curbing corruption. The position of the prosecutor in anti-corruption efforts is acute, for she must most actively take upon herself the position that high level officials and power and wealthy actors in society cannot operate willfully according to their own self-interests. Prosecutors enjoy discretion in every legal system, which I adumbrate briefly in a comparative perspective below. The amount of discretion may come as a surprise to the unacquainted reader. The problem is this: the

---

[27] Oliver (1997: 543) notes that effectually "a settlement has been reached between the courts and Parliament that the two will not interfere in each other's spheres, a form of limited separation of powers designed to prevent conflict between the courts and Parliament that could result in questioning by Parliament of the political neutrality of the courts and their authority."

prosecutor herself is often suspected of involvement with the likely targets of investigations, and moreover she can use her position to target rivals or opponents to the status quo. The very politicized nature of high level corruption investigations politicizes the role of the prosecutor and increases suspicion of her motivations. There are, therefore, essentially two types of activities that need to be controlled: *First*, the willful neglect and abuse of discretion to pursue cases of corruption owing to favoritism, bias or worse, and *second*, the abuse of position and discretion afforded to target potential rivals and antagonists of the powerful.[28]

A. Accounting for Low Levels of Prosecution

As any reasonable person will readily admit there are many legitimate reasons for low levels of prosecution when it comes to corruption. There are several reasons commonly behind this, the most salient being perhaps among the following. *First*, corruption by its very nature thrives in secrecy. Where parties have incentive to keep things quite, and keep the number of informed parties to a minimum, information is not forthcoming. *Second*, this factor is assisted by the fact that corruption is frequently, though, as identified earlier, not always a victimless crime, so aggrieved parties are often not there to come forward in the first place, and even when they are there, they may be unaware that corruption was the reason behind their damages. *Third*, as we have also seen,[29] parties that are aware of corruption are frequently either parties to the corrupt system itself, with obvious reasons for not reporting, or alternatively third parties that normally face little or no incentive to come forward, and are additionally burdened by the likelihood of retaliation. *Fourth*, importantly parties to corruption frequently rely on the use of intermediaries and the form of payment can take any manner of means. As Noonan aptly submits:

> "Bribes come openly or covertly, disguised as an interest in a business, as a lawyer's fee, or, very often, as a loan. Bribes come directly, paid into the waiting hands of the bribee or, more commonly, indirectly tot he subordinate or friend performing the nearly indispensable office of bagman. Bribes come in all shapes as sex, commodities, appointments, and most often, cash" (Noonan 1984: xxi).

---

[28] The latter is particularly aggravated where prosecutorial independence is not guaranteed. In Bolivia, for example, only recently was a new penal code introduced that enables the establishment of a prosecution independent, rather than as an extension, of the police. As an aside, other reforms included the complete presumption of innocence until proven guilty, the presentation of oral evidence in open court, and public trial by jury. *See*, "Trial and Error," *The Economist*, June 30, 2001.

[29] *See* Chapter IV, Section II *et seq.*

All of these factors make it difficult to trace the sources of corruption and the means of payment and reciprocity. It makes corrupt exchange less likely to detect and where intermediaries are involved can limit the vulnerabilities associated with finding a corrupt partner for negotiation, striking a deal and ensuring delivery of the agreement. *Fifth*, in order to make an allegation of bribery stick, it may be necessary to show that there was a quid pro quo (Anerchiarico and Jacobs 1996: 92-93).[30] There may is a need to prove causality between payment made and action received, a factor most complex as identified in our discussion of gratuities versus bribes.[31] Because this is understandably difficult, allegations of bribery or corruption, often manifest themselves in alternative accusations such as fraud, breach of conflict-of interest laws, extortion etc. or fail to manifest themselves at all.

Sixth, "corruption cases are expensive and resource-intense" and "are difficult to win at trial and appeal" (*ibid.*: 107). This factor is potentially very important from the perspective of the prosecutor. Corruption and white collar crimes in general are resource-intensive and demand a lot of time. This has the effect of shifting away the time the prosecutor can allocate to other crimes and criminal investigations. Hence, we should not just look at prosecution from the perspective of the time allocated by the prosecution to a particular corruption-related case as being costly, in the sense of high or low effort levels of the prosecutor, but rather that it actually prevents the prosecution from litigating easier cases.

Seventh, the prosecutorial task also becomes notoriously difficult where investigations move up the hierarchy and into the legislative level, where documents and activities may be protected under a speech and debate clause or other statutes providing *de facto* immunity. Senior political figures may hinder investigations in an effort to frustrate the inquiry or make it disappear altogether. Furthermore, they often have the power to punish police or prosecutors that undertake investigation to their displeasure, which can provide "professional, political, and personal disincentives" for furtherance or initiation of investigation (*ibid.*: 94).[32]

That said, there may, however, be more invidious factors at work. For example, where prosecutors are elected or are politically allied to members of the executive or legislature through party membership, it is easy to conjure up multifarious occasions for reciprocity, logrolling and loyalty.[33] Relatedly, where

---

[30] *See* above, Chapter VI, Section II.

[31] *Ibid.*

[32] The list of punishments is numerous including dismissal, cutting off funding, restricting jurisdiction, preventing promotion and more malicious measures such as intimidation and threats of violence.

[33] *See* Anechiarico and Jacobs (1996: 94-106) for a discussion of some of the struggles and strategies of senior officials that have frustrated the work of prosecutors in New York, and

senior judges require a political endorsement as in some states in the United States, they may be particularly hostile to anti-corruption efforts. (*ibid.*). A prosecutor may also use her influence over the police, if not to warn outright against certain investigations (suggesting they are against policy and will not be prosecuted), then to directing policing activities to areas away from corrupt activity (suggesting perhaps because prosecution is so resource-intensive, efforts should not be squandered), hence providing a kind of a coordinating or look-out role for a corrupt system. She may for her part turn a blind eye to certain actions, showing great reluctance to start investigations or to prosecute. Alternatively, she may have alternate motives for prosecution that consist of taking down an economic or political rival, those that trouble the status quo or simply as a means of launching a political career.[34] It is to these more perfidious factors that we turn our attention in the next section, and make some suggestions, relying on the observations of accountability mechanisms of multi-legal orders, that can attenuate the likelihood of willful prosecutorial neglect.

B. Accounting for Prosecutorial Discretion

Generally speaking, there are two common reasons that legal systems offer for nonprosecution. The first is lack of evidence, the second public policy. Whilst the former is open to some interpretation, it must be considered as a prerequisite to prosecution, the latter is a vague standard that can serve the whims of the prosecution.[35] One common explanation for discretionary enforcement (nonenforcement) is legislative "over-criminalization". This corresponds in the rules versus standards debate to the "over-inclusiveness" of a particular rule or body of regulation. As we saw earlier, common explanations are that rules fail to change with societal norms, and that a code of laws is necessarily over-inclusive and efficiency depleting in some circumstances.[36] In these circumstances it may be more efficient for society when enforcement turns a blind eye. Another reason for "over-criminalization" or "over-inclusiveness" of the law, may be that society

---

historical examples where prosecutors themselves were part of the political machinery that drove corruption.

[34] Suspicions of alternative motivations regularly voiced. For an example from the United States, see "Special Prosecutors' Inquiries Have Led to Doubts about Usefulness," *New York Times*, December 1, 1996. For an example from Italy, see "Ciao Time for Italy's Harassed Graft-Buster," *Washington Post*, November 26, 1996. For an example from Columbia, see "Columbia's Chief Is Charged But a Tangled Inquiry Looms," *N.Y. Times*, February 16, 1996.

[35] Prosecution is habitually used to realize the political aims and policy of the executive which in some sense restricts the discretion of the prosecution, but the fact that public policy considerations are taken into account in the first place (in addition to questions of law) suggests that there is ample discretion that must be balanced by due process protections and systematic checks.

[36] *See* above, Chapter III, Section IV.

wants to make laws that are "wholly devoid of loopholes."[37] The latter seems particularly relevant where a certain population are particularly skilled at breaking the law, for example in the case of organized crime

Over-criminalization is particularly common when law makers fail to change the body of laws which make them completely outdated. In such circumstances, where a law has "aged" and no longer expresses the wishes of society, it should be repealed, if not its may only serve for purposes of harassment or extortion. Decriminalization of unpopular, particularly victimless crimes, reduces the opportunities for police corruption, discriminatory enforcement, bias and entrapment and allocates police efforts to more serious crimes.

As outlined above, another common explanation for discretionary enforcement is limited resources. A prosecutor may not have enough resources to handle all the cases available and may have to select those he believes to be more important. Naturally, the prosecutor may also pursue other options, making prosecution in costly cases a last resort.[38] This list is not to be interpreted as exhaustive but indicative of the factors important for our discussion.[39]

C. Controlling Willful Selection and Dismissal of Cases

In the United States it is widely recognized that the state attorney has a broad range of discretion when deciding to prosecute and when to refrain from doing so.[40] Prosecutorial discretion is considered as normal, inevitable, even desirable. Vorenburg (1981: 1324-25) in a widely-cited work suggests: "[T]he core of prosecutors' power is charging, plea bargaining, and, when it is under the

---

[37] 2.A.B.A. Comm'n on Organized Crime, Organized Crime and Law Enforcement 75 (1952) cited in *ibid.*

[38] Where expediency becomes a prerogative, as it explicitly has in the Netherlands, prosecutors may extensively resort to plea bargaining and other such measures.

[39] For example, in the United States, it is also common that a prosecutor will not proceed with a case "[w]hen the victim has expressed a desire that the offender not be prosecuted"..., "When the costs of prosecution may be excessive, considering the nature of the violation"..., "When the mere fact that prosecution would, in the prosecutor's judgment, cause undue harm to the offender"..., When the offender, if not prosecuted, will likely aid in achieving further enforcement goals [informants]"..., When the harm done by the offender can be corrected without prosecution" (LaFave, Wayne R., Jerold H. Israel, and Nancy J. King eds. 2001. *Criminal Procedure*, 2nd ed., vol. 4, §13.2(a).

[40] As the court noted in Pugach v. Klein (193 F.Supp. 630(S.D.N.Y.1961): "The United States Attorney is not a rubber stamp. His problems are not solved by the strict application of an inflexible formula. Rather, their solution calls for the exercise of judgment. Judgment reached primarily by balancing the public interest in effective law enforcement against the growing rights of the accused. There are a number of elements in the equation, and all of them must be carefully considered. Paramount among them is a determination that a prosecution will promote the ends of justice, instill respect for the law, and advance the cause of ordered liberty." *Cited* in LaFave et al., *supra* note 39.

prosecutors control, initiating investigations. Decisions whether to charge, and whether and on what terms to bargain, have been left in the prosecutors' hands with very few limitations."[41] But to suggest that prosecutorial discretion is evident only in common law countries is misleading and inaccurate, as we shall see below. The American Courts have generally interpreted the common law to mean that the prosecutor's wish to dismiss the charge prevails regardless of the position of the judge.[42]

In the Continent, by way of contrast, one can still find a group of scholars in favor of full enforcement operating within the expression of the *Legalitätsprinzip* (legality principle), specifying full enforcement. According to the Legalitätsprinzip, for instance, prosecutors may not engage in deal making with suspects in return for cooperation. The *Opportunitätsprinzip* (expediency principle), on the other hand, permits prosecutors to select their cases to maximize efficiency (*see* Fletcher 1996). Take the case of Germany for instance where as Frase and Weigend (1995: 353) note: "[o]nly in the penal order proceeding can a German prosecutor unilaterally withdraw charges once they have been filed by the court. Felony charges must be filed where there is sufficient evidence. Despite the German rule of "compulsory" prosecution, prosecutors do, however, exercise broad discretion in respect to declination and the level of the charges files". Misdemeanor charges may be declined where there is inadequate evidence or guilt is minor and no public interest would be furthered by the prosecution (*ibid*). For more serious cases, the prosecutor is by law precluded from reducing charge severity or dismissing charges without the consent of the trial court. By way of contrast, Contrarily, American prosecutors commonly reduce or drop charges, often in return for a guilty plea. Plea bargaining is actively encouraged by the Supreme Court, a feature alien to German law (*ibid.*: 340; Misner 1996: 753).[43]

In order to limit the potential abuse of discretion in plea bargaining, it is important that this discretion does not rest with the prosecutor alone. The court may provide a supervisory function, or carry out the function themselves.[44] It is

---

[41] In the U.S. for example at the federal level, "less than one-fourth of the complaints received by U.S. Attorneys appear to result in the filing of formal charges" (LaFave et al. *ibid.*). The proportion of cases that are prosecuted are greatly influenced by whether or not police provide a screening function.

[42] There is, however, authority that the judge can prevent the entry of nolle prosequi, a docket entry indicating that the plaintiff or the prosecution has dropped an action, when the prosecutor's actions are corrupt or when he has acted in bad faith. *See* LaFave et al., supra note 39, at §13.3(c) note 30. On nolle prosequi, *see* Black's Law Dictionary (1999, 7th ed.) p. 1070.

[43] Certain forms of plea bargaining do, however, occur in Germany. In Germany, "the court, with the consent of the prosecutor, indicates that a particular, more lenient sentence will be imposed. In addition, the parties usually promise not to appeal the judgment" (Frase and Weigend 1995: 345).

[44] In England, prosecutors are not authorized to serve any purpose in recommending sentences at trial (for reasoning related to judicial independence and separation of powers). In the

also fundamental for transparency and accountability aims that written reasons be given for the dismissal or non-continuation of a case. In Germany, for example, a prosecutor cannot close a file without specification in a statement of written reasons, which in important cases is subject to review by a superior. This seems to be an important safeguard but reasons themselves must be extensive, case-specific and subject to review. Where reasoning is not case-specific and extensive it cannot be subject to review, and written documentation is ineffectual.[45] Automatization and non-specification of reasoning behind dismissal is clearly insufficient for accountability and transparency purposes.

As noted in earlier discussion, official discretion can be limited by precise drafting of behavior that is considered both desirable and undesirable. For example, guidelines should provide for the effective eradication of commonly nonenforced laws and precision in the substantive criminal law would eliminate many of the cases that are now repeatedly decided by enforcement officials and prosecutors.

Establishing statements of general policies on the exercise of discretion may be formulated solely by the prosecutors office itself or, alternatively, with the assistance of a respected third party. Involvement of a third party may interfere with independence but can mitigate the problem of under-inclusion that emanates from the fact when prosecutorial behavior is subject to supervision, based on policy statements, there are great incentives to formulate guidelines incompletely, in particular to maintain discretion in complex or controversial areas.[46] England and Wales, Germany and the Netherlands all have created sets of guidelines on prosecutorial decisionmaking that fail to avail of the qualities of precise rules discussed earlier.[47] Quite the contrary, these guidelines often sketch out a list of public interest factors that normally do not obligate but can be taken into

---

Netherlands, a civil law country, in addition to the direct sentencing powers that prosecutors enjoy, the prosecutor directly influences the judge in recommending a sentence (which is itself a duty), although the judge is not bound to follow the recommendations of this sentence (*see* Fionda 1995; Vorenberg 1981: 1561).

[45] Fionda (1995: 99) points out that in the Netherlands "written reasons are coded and the prosecutor will often simply write the appropriate code number on the file; the important thing is that the reason is actually stated." She further notes that "neither each individual case, nor a random sample of cases, is routinely checked at any stage, so the practice is unlikely to have any effect in preventing either inconsistent decision-making or decision-making on the basis of irrelevant or improper reasons... (*ibid.*)"

[46] Vorenberg (1981: 1558-59) submits for the United States, "the lack of either a pre-announced set of rules or after-the-fact accountability for exercises of discretionary power is inconsistent with political accountability. Only by signaling what their rules are, what they have done, and why, do prosecutors make their actions visible enough to generate a more coherent public response than the easily manipulated reaction to the occasional newsworthy case."

[47] *See* above, Chapter III, Section IV.

consideration. These factors may even afford the prosecution more discretion.[48] As Fionda (1995: 98) notes of the Netherlands, "a policy waiver allows a prosecutor to drop any case, despite sufficient evidence for its prosecution, where he or she considers it is not in the public interest to prosecute the offender in court." In a list of factors that can be taken into consideration (52 in all), the reasons for dismissing cases are vaguely stated and are unbinding in any case (*ibid.*).[49]

The advantages of precise rules are: accumulated expertise in decisionmaking, the reduction of bias, a greater foothold for supervision, either in the form of judicial, parliamentary or peer review, greater legitimacy, few ad hoc decisions etc.[50] Detailed explanations of decisions outlining reasons for dropping or pursuing a particular case must accompany precise guidelines. There are some considerations, however, that must be balanced and accounted for. First, it may be preferential for deterrence purposes for (potential) violators to be unaware of the policy choices of enforcement officials (Kaplow 1999). Moreover, where sanctions are low, officials may prefer (potential) violators to be unaware of the de facto sanction level (Diver 1983). For example, if I know that the tax authorities will only pursue criminal changes when the level of evasion is X, then I have incentive to evade until X. Second, policy guidelines that emphasize the areas and kinds of offenses that are most vigorously prosecuted can reduce the benefits of randomness that frequently accompany law enforcement and adjudication. Randomness becomes more important as resources become more limited, where enforcement is a scarce resource, uncertainty can provide an effective deterrent. Restated, bluffing is an important part of deterrence! Third, another problem with a proposal of (precise) guidelines is the potential threat of judicial review of prosecutorial actions.[51] I shall present an argument below, however, why this is often desirable.

---

[48] Arguably these guidelines actually increased the amount of discretion enjoyed by prosecutors. In England for example, the number of public interest factors were increased in the newly drafted code in 1994, with one paragraph listing factors that should encourage prosecution and another paragraph indicating factors that should discourage prosecution. It also importantly states that the list of criteria is not exhaustive. In the Netherlands, where criteria number 52, it is widely considered that the prosecutor can legitimately choose between many of the 52. In Germany, where these criteria are unwritten, there is obviously ample discretion (Fionda 1995).

[49] Fionda (ibid.: 1995: 99) suggests that there are ,manifold reasons for non-prosecution. "Some,..., are widely worded and generalized and seek to protect the general legal order of the state. Examples are waiving prosecution in order to preserve national security, or to prevent public disorder and unrest, also waiving prosecution in a case where there is a lack of national interest in its prosecution, where the offender is foreign or the crime was committed abroad..."

[50] See Chapter III, Section IV.

[51] *See* LaFave et al., *supra* note 39, at §13.2(f). A familiar corollary to the above is the fact that, with increasing oversight and the dissemination of information, there is sometimes greater potential for parties to a corrupt agreement to trace the steps of those players in the agreement.

But even in the case that the three aforementioned considerations are considered of vital importance, there are obvious means to mitigate their potentially adverse effects that should not deter from the introduction of prosecutorial guidelines to limit discretion. One means would be to prevent the information from becoming publicly available, making it only available to the courts, parliamentary committees or other supervisory bodies. Another, would be to grant exceptions from judicial review of prosecutorial actions, discussed below, in all but the grievous cases.

Courts frequently show a tendency to refrain from applying the normal standards of judicial review in the case of prosecutorial discretion.[52] It may be advantageous, however, for judicial review to play a greater role in reviewing prosecutorial discretion and is perhaps the institution most suited to doing so, given the fact that parliamentary review is most often *ad hoc* and that the expertise required for judicial review of decisions not to prosecute are most similar to those skills already utilized by the courts. This factor is made even more significant where the prosecution process has become politicized. Israel, in contrast many other countries, provides a leading example where the prosecution is not safe from judicial review. As Justice Barak, now head of the Supreme Court noted:

"It seems to me... that as to the issue of the scope of intervention of this court there is no difference between the Attorney-General and any other public official. Both should exercise their discretion with fairness, honesty, reasonableness, without arbitrariness or discrimination, and by taking into account only relevant considerations. Both are subject to judicial review...

Making prosecutorial actions subject to widespread observance by the judiciary, political committees, peers and the public may have the unfortunate effect of making a cartel more stable. Where the prosecutor strays from his agreements, this can be detected and punished earlier than before. This is, however, more of a theoretical point than a practical possibility and should probably not give cause for concern.

[52] The Supreme Court in the United States has expressed the view that:
"the decision to prosecute is particularly ill-suited to judicial review. Such factors as the strength of the case, the prosecution's general deterrence value, the Government's enforcement priorities, and the case's relationship to the Government's overall enforcement plan are not readily susceptible to the kind of analysis the courts are competent to undertake. Judicial supervision in this area, moreover, entails systematic costs of particular concern. Examining the basis of prosecution delays the criminal proceeding, threatens to chill law enforcement by subjecting the prosecutor's motives and decisionmaking to outside inquiry, and may undermine prosecutorial effectiveness by revealing the Government's enforcement policy. All these are substantial concerns that make the courts properly hesitant to examine the decision whether to prosecute." Wayte v. United States, 470 U.S. 598, 105 S.Ct. 1524, 84 L. Ed.2d 547 (1985) cited in (LaFave et al., *supra* note 39, at §13.2(g)). The courts in England have also shown particular reluctance to apply the normal standards of judicial review (Dotan 1997). This reluctance was reflected in R. v. Humphrys: "A judge must keep out of the arena. He should not have or appear to have any responsibility for the institution of prosecution. The functions of prosecutors and of judges must not be blurred." [1977] 1 A.C. 1 at 26, in Dotan (1997: 515).

there is no special law concerning the scope of review [of the Attorney-General's decisions]."[53]

Furthermore, Israel has effectively granted *locus standi* to almost any member of public in order to guarantee access to court to challenge prosecutorial decisions (Dotan 1997: 526). Results therefrom seem to contradict the familiar floodgate argument normally positioned against such a measure.[54]

The actions that private persons can take in order to force a unwilling prosecutor to take action are often very limited.[55] Providing victims rights to conduct or compel prosecution is a safeguard against particularly reluctant prosecutors to initiate legitimate cases. It is important to provide such a protection in order to increase the legitimacy of the criminal justice system and encourage participation and voluntary compliance with law enforcement. But remedies such as private prosecution of criminal cases are largely symbolic. In addition to legal realities, there are several practical issues related specifically to corruption that must be taken into consideration.[56]

Whilst theoretically entertaining, private prosecution for cases of corruption is a near practical impossibility for several reasons, among the more important are the following. First, corruption is often victimless, therefore no one normally has incentive to take action. Second, standing is often only given to the victim, for whom it is easier to recover via civil law and a suit for damages. Third, at a practical level, the prosecutor normally has and should have the ability to take over proceedings when it is in the public interest to do so. This is an important safeguard against vindictive or malicious suits, but this safeguard disables the usefulness of the device as a means for getting around prosecutorial laxity, which is a key advantage of private prosecution. Fourth, given the secretive nature of corruption, it is highly improbable that an outside party (victim) could reach the evidentiary requirements to attain a conviction. Fifth, there are very high costs associated with litigating corruption cases.

It seems that given these impracticalities, civil law provides a more appropriate instrument with which to mitigate the problems associated with reluctant prosecutiorial enforcers, particularly through expanding the right of

---

[53] H.C. 329/81, Nof v. Gen. Att., 37(4) P.D.326 at 334, in Dotan (1997: 523).

[54] In Germany, a civil law country, by comparison, there is prior judicial review of every charge, with only limited exception for "expedited trials for petty offenses" (Frase and Weigend 1995: 340-341).

[55] For a discussion thereof, *see* Fionda (1995)

[56] For example, the right of private prosecution may be restricted to just the victim of the crime (as in Germany for instance) or may be granted to almost anyone (as in the case of Israel for minor crimes). It may be considered as an inherent right of a victim (as is the case in England and Wales), or as per se undesirable (as in the United States). It may be restricted to minor crimes (as in Israel) or be extendible to a broad range of criminal law. Furthermore, legal orders commonly give the public prosecutor powers to interject and take over the case.

standing and permitting victorious parties to receive a reward for their efforts. Furthermore, there are many incentive-based reasons why private enforcement can also founder as an instrument- such as the familiar free-rider problem-particularly when damages are dispersed, where victim could ride on the backs of others that made efforts to prosecute.

Summing up legal systems frequently have in place some mechanism for sanctioning prosecutors engaging in misconduct or abuse of office.[57] But even in a system as sophisticated as the United States criminal enforcement and public sanctions are rare. In a study conducted by the Chicago Tribune, over a thirty-six year period, it was found that over 381 homicide convictions were overturned because it prosecutors engaged in such misconduct as using false evidence or withholding exculpatory evidence. Amazingly of the 381 cases, not a single prosecutor was ever brought to trial for the misconduct, or received a public sanction from a state lawyer disciplinary agency. Two persons were indicted but the charges were dismissed before trial commenced.[58] If even in an advanced nation such as the United States, sanctions against prosecutors cannot be relied upon to deter improbity, it raises a big question on the control of prosecutorial discretion, particularly in such a charged subject as high level corruption. Independent of the mixture of the principals of full and discretionary enforcement selected by a legal order -and countries in transition to democracy must grapple with this problem- there are several features worthy of consideration as safeguards against improbity, some of which I adumbrated above including the following:

- For whatever reason the prosecutor decides to waive a case in the interests of the public, that reason must be extensively documented on file. There should be a written duty to explain why cases have been dropped.
- Dismissal powers in more serious cases should require the consent of a judge or second party and be subject to review.
- Strengthening supervision by higher ranking officials of the prosecution service.[59]

---

[57] For example, although it varies substantially from state to state in the United States, grounds for removal of a prosecutor from office include malfeasance, incompetency, delinquency in office, misfeasance, nonfeasance, nonadministration in office, or for criminal conviction. *See,* National District Attorneys Ass'n, National Prosecution Standards 16 (1977) cited in (LaFave et al., *supra* note 39, at §13.3(f)).

[58] "The Verdict: Dishonor Series: Trial and Error. How Prosecutors Sacrifice Justice to Win," *Chicago Tribune,* January 10, 1999.

[59] For example, the state Attorney General in the United States theoretically offers a check on local prosecutors where the latter refuse to initiate prosecution. In practice, this rarely transpires and requests to intervene are usually at the behest of the local administrator where he or she feels ill-equipped to handle a case. Only occasionally will the Attorney General interfere where there appears to be a conflict of interest (LaFave et al., *supra* note 39, at §13.3(e)).

- Instituting proper prosecutorial guidelines. The primary purpose of existing guidelines is to disseminate public policy. As we have seen above, existing guidelines are often quite ineffective in preventing biased and improper use of discretion. This is in part due to the vague wording of the guidelines, but also as a result of the increasing usage of public policy factors themselves in decisions to prosecute, which unconditionally afford prosecutor discretion. Providing for fewer public policy defenses (that incidentally, normally defy any form of judicial review) and clearly delineating those cases where policy considerations may be taken into account, would limit discretion.

- Review by senior ranking prosecutors and outsiders, who should check all files to assess decisions not to prosecute, or alternatively decisions to prosecute in cases of corruption. Random samples of dismissed cases should be checked regularly by a respected external authority.[60] The loss in prosecutorial independence must be weighed against the potential for prosecutorial abuse. The make-up of the external body is especially important and may consist of members of the judiciary. If the make-up of this body were political in nature, it would be particularly important that members of the opposition party be adequately represented in order to curb opportunistic behavior, but there would be an unavoidable political shadow over operations. Alternatively, a small body made up of members of the judiciary could report to parliament on its findings.

Clearly a system that credibly screens prosecutors, in particular senior prosecutors (District Attorneys, State Attorneys, Directors of Public Prosecution, Attorney Generals etc.) is imperative to ensure a high level of integrity in office.[61] Furthermore, for cases of corruption, particularly at local level, it would be advantageous to have outside prosecutors handling the cases, as is common in the United States at state and local level. Within a federalist structure, this is of course easier to realize, but this difficulty need not discourage innovative measures of moving discretion in such cases beyond the impressionable comforts of the local level.

---

[60] For example, in 1990 The Home Affairs Committee called on an external monitor to review Crown Prosecution Service (CPS) decisions in individual cases. Shortly after the report, the government established a national inspectorate to monitor the decisions of Crown Prosecutors (Fionda 1995: 60). It should be noted that such an inspectorate is the exception as opposed to the rule.

[61] In the United States at the local level prosecutors independently of whether the office is constitutionally based or statutorily created, are usually elected officials (Misner 1996: 733). A process of screening here is more difficult. Theoretically, they are accountable to the electorate, but in practice other structure need to be in place to ensure against improbity.

IV. Ombudsman

The notion of the ombudsman as an accountability mechanism is, bar in Sweden where it has its roots, a relatively new device. The growth and expanse of the ombudsman is unprecedented and indicative of its success, or alternatively the expectations of its success. Indeed, it would appear that the mechanism has captured a lacuna in many governments, that otherwise may not have been satisfied. In Britain, for example, after having been established for the central government, the concept was expanded to the national health service, the local government and the police (Wade and Forsyth 1999: 110). It is particularly popular in the new democracies of eastern Europe, and there are new extensions of the concept in one form or another perennially to various countries. It has also been incorporated into the private and nongovernment sector, and is seen, for example in Britain in legal services, banking and insurance, prisons and pensions (*ibid.*: 110-111).

The general concept of an ombudsman is an independent statutory or constitutional body whose job is to investigate complaints voiced against the actions of administrative bodies by individuals, groups and other entities. Normally created under a statute or law which stipulates its powers, it is accountable to parliament. His role can be general, with a far-reaching power to investigate all aspects of the administration, or he may be confined to specific areas and specific functions and mandate, as suggested above. For example, Canada, Germany and Israel all have a military ombudsman (*see*, Gregory and Giddings 2000: 5-11).[62]

There are several characteristics that can generally be ascribed to an ombudsman. In general, he follows up on complaints to ascertain whether there are procedural or substantial errors in administrative action, or may initiate his own investigations. Moreover, he generally has within his powers the ability to question officials and obligate them to produce documents. Further, should an investigation disclose error or incorrectness by the administrative body, the ombudsman cannot normally impose a sanction or reverse an administrative action, but can put forward a solution or recommend redress. It is normally then up to the administrative body to repair its error or incorrectness according to the ombudsman's findings, motivated by the wish to avoid unwanted publicity and a confrontation with parliament. The ombudsman, therefore, often provides a conciliatory role, as is often identified by the name of his office. For example, in

---

[62] Indeed, the need for a military ombudsman is perhaps greater than other institutions because of the veil of secrecy that surrounds many military activities. In Latin America, in particular, demand for resistance to a military ombudsman can be great, because of a long history of human rights abuses. *See*, "Fox Pries Open Mexican Army's Door of Secrecy; Rights Abuses may be Targeted," *Washington Post*, November 11, 2001. *See* also, "Freed Mexican Vows to Clear his Name," *Washington Post*, February 9, 2002.

France, he is the Mediator de la République. Within the Anglo-Saxon legal tradition, his conciliatory role is considered as "an alternative to the adversary system for resolving disputes".[63] But, the fact that the ombudsman functions rather informally and cannot hand out a legal sanction may actually be a strength, as formal sanctions are in some conditions not necessarily conducive to compliance (Ayres and Braithwaite 1992). By gaining confidence and cooperation, he can rectify mistakes and errors and increase voluntary compliance, which can be jeopardized by the antagonistic threat of formal legal sanctions.

There is no simple general notion of what the ombudsman represents and what defects an ombudsman investigates or should investigate. The purpose and nature of the ombudsman may be very different depending on what defects he investigates, and there are a few general models.[64] According to the illegality model, an ombudsman investigates complaints based on the alleged illegality of decisions or actions of the administration, where illegality refers to the rules, regulations, statutes, constitution etc. as applied to the administration. An alternative model is the maladministration model, that as its name suggests the ombudsman investigates complaints that are based on maladministration and not just on violations of the law, although most acts of maladminstration are generally illegal. It is, naturally, difficult to accurately define acts of maladministration, but it goes beyond the former model of illegality to include other factors that may or may not fall under the realm of illegality. Common throughout much of the European Union, New Zealand also fits this later model where, for example, the ombudsman is authorized to report any decision which was unreasonable, unjust, based on mistake or simply wrong (Wade and Forsyth 1999: 96). A third model seems to incorporate civic or human rights into the range of defects investigated and protections offered by the ombudsman. For example, in Italy the office is known as the "Defensore Civico", in Quebec as the "Protectuer du Citoyen" and in Costa Rica as the "Defensor de los Derechos Humanos" (Gregory and Giddings 2000: 4-5). This model is especially prevalent in eastern European Democracies and Latin America, reflective of cultural and historical legacies. The desirability of a particular model is dependent in large part on the institutional shortcoming of various systems of administrative accountability.

---

[63] 4 Am. Jur. 2d, Alternative Dispute Resolution § 23 (1995).

[64] This generalization should be taken as rather imprecise. In addition to the ombudsmen that operate strictly within the institutions of the private sector (such as banking and insurance described above), and the three general models of ombudsmen identified here that operate within public sector institutions, there are also private sector organizations that have devoted themselves to those investigations that public sector ombudsmen would normally conduct. In India, this grew out of disappointment at parliaments consistent failure to establish an ombudsman's office.

Where courts, are well-functioning, strong arguments can be made for the administrative model, given that it can fill in the lacuna left by both gaps in and the formalities of the judicial system. Where the courts, are not well established, it would appear that the administrative model may leave the ombudsman reaching beyond his grasp, which could quickly lead to the mechanism suffering the same criticisms as the judiciary, backlogs, time lags etc. In such a circumstance, narrowing down the function or mandate of the ombudsman to issues of illegality is desirable.

There are inherent dangers in the establishment of an ombudsman, related to his functionability as a substitute for other institutions. The ombudsman cannot substitute the courts, and sufficient attention has to be paid to the definition of the ombudsman within the entire balance of the institutional accountability framework related to government and the administration.[65] The office of the ombudsman as we have seen is by its very nature distinct from the courts. Overburdening the ombudsman can cause more than discomfort; it can cause general unfeasibility which can discredit the office and occasion long-term failure.

A. Components for a Successful Ombudsman Office

The ombudsman like other supervisory bodies to operate successfully must be fully independent of the bodies it monitors. It is subject to the same sabotage as other independent organs, and sufficient safeguards need to be made in order to insure this independence is maintained. Among the most important considerations, I adjudge to be the following:

Security of office for the ombudsman. Tenure should be not too short to prevent rash decisions and abuse of office according to the political whims of the day. It should not be too long, so as to become a cushy position, that potentially disassociates the ombudsman from his function and mandate, embedding him gradually with the administrative and political bodies he is supposed to monitor. A clear mandate is important to protect the legitimacy of investigations, and exemptions should be kept to a minimum.[66] Appointment is, of course, crucial. Selection of a person of known integrity is imperative, who would suffer a substantial reputation loss for any transgressions, and can signal this to attain

---

[65] Although the Ombudsman cannot substitute the courts or public prosecutor's office, this does not suggest that, as with judicial activism, there are not cases of "ombudsman activism". For example, in Peru, where the courts did not function well and the district attorney's office, seemed to turn a blind eye to certain transgressions, the ombudsman took on investigations into area, such as vote fraud because no one else would. See, "Ombudsman Rewriting Peru's History Justice: Jorge Santistevan, a 'Defender of the People,' has tackled Human Rights, Electoral Fraud," Los Angeles Times, November 7, 2000.

[66] For example, contractual and commercial transactions both at central and local government are exempt from investigations by the ombudsman in the United Kingdom (Wade and Forsyth 1999: 137). This is also true for similar agencies in Australia (Pearce 2000: 104).

credibility. For example, a retired member of the supreme or high court, with a proven nonpartisan record would make an ideal candidate. Appointment procedures should be transparent and observable by the public. The appointment procedure must be removed, at least partially from the government of the day. The ombudsman should be allowed to investigate anonymous complaints. He should have direct access to the public and complaints should not have to go through any other body or Member of Parliament.[67] He should report to parliament and not to the government. His reports should be detailed but not subject to extensive procedural requirements that are too time consuming and burdensome. His findings should regularly be made public. Clearly the budget is crucial, as are his resources. An ombudsman office with a small budget is a paper tiger. It does not need to become politicized or corrupt, as it is already ineffectual. Furthermore, as with other mechanisms and pronouncements, it can intentionally serve as a mere signaling device of a government that professes to operate against improbity and malfeasance, cashing in on the reputation the ombudsman enjoys, without actually doing much. To operate successfully, it should be granted a multiyear budget to avoid the political vagaries and witch hunts of the day. The ombudsman should be allowed to work on his own initiatives randomly.[68] To increase its investigative powers, the office should be staffed by both lawyers and in particular auditors. Where there is a shortage of qualified staff, it should operate independently but closely with a supreme audit authority, such as the comptroller general.[69] Combined with the latter authority, frequently conducting random audits (subject to the aforementioned conditions), the ombudsman can significantly mitigate corruption and malfeasance in government.

To reiterate, however, the ombudsman is not a substitute for the courts, but this should not necessarily reflect adversely upon him. Given that his formal authority is limited, he is not subject to the same formalities, particularly, the same procedural formalities of the courts and is, therefore, more accessible than the courts. It is this accessibility that is his strength and makes a strong ombudsman a constant threat to corrupt networks. Precisely for this reason,

---

[67] In the United Kingdom, for example, the Parliamentary Commissioner for Administration (Parliamentary Ombudsman) is not entitled to investigate complaints unless they first go through a Member of Parliament (Wade and Forsyth 1999: 90; Gregory and Giddings 2000: 24).

[68] In the United Kindom, for example, this is not the case for the Parliamentary Ombudsman (Gregory and Giddings 2000: 38).

[69] This is the practice, for example, in Israel. *See,* http://www.mevaker.gov.il/english/index.htm. There is a clear overlap in the role of the two supervisory organs. In the United Kingdom, for example, since 1866 the Comptroller and Auditor- General has played the role of a type of financial ombudsman, disclosing maladministration of government finances (Wade and Forsyth 1999: 89).

however, he may be bombarded by unrelenting political criticism and have to fight for the legitimacy of his own actions.[70]

V. An Independent Commission Against Corruption (ICAC): A Cautionary Note

There is no one model against corruption. The creation of an Independent Commission against Corruption is rather like creating a "super agency" against corruption, that can coordinate and conduct many activities normally conducted by numerous agencies, or sub-units within organizations. It is not a replacement for more fundamental reforms of those factors that encourage corruption, such as red tape, excessive regulation, and weak incentive structures within the civil service. The establishment of an Independent Commission against Corruption represents, a fundamental re-shifting in the balance of powers among administrative accountability institutions, and, therefore, is not a decision that can be taken lightly, nor should it be perceived as a panacea to wrestle the woes of misgovernance from a complacent "old" administrative structure to a more dynamic, "newer" form of governance.

The successes of Hong Kong in transforming a society of endemic corruption to a society with low levels of corruption are clearly appetizing for reformers interested in reforming governmental institutions. Hong Kong created an Independent Commission against Corruption in 1974, that incorporated many separate strategies employable in an anti-corruption package under one roof. It was given huge powers and authorization for activities that are normally conducted by numerous agencies, or sub-units within organizations. These included: police-like powers of investigation (within their Operations Department); the development of prevention strategies that would normally be formulated by legal specialists, consultants etc. (within their Corruption Prevention Department), and popular participation that would normally fall within the duties of community relations offices and the local authorities (within their Community Relations Department) (*see* Klitgaard, MacLean-Abaroa and Parris 2000: 20-21, 68-69).[71] Furthermore, the ICAC was also given powers of prosecution (*ibid.*; Rose-Ackerman 1999: 159).

The temptation to adopt or transplant the Hong Kong framework of anti-corruption measures is great given that the success of reforms against corruption

---

[70] Recent polls have shown, for example, that the ombudsman's office in Peru has a superior approval rating than any other institution bar the Roman Catholic Church. *See*, "Ombudsman Rewriting Peru's History Justice: Jorge Santistevan, a 'Defender of the People,' has tackled Human Rights, Electoral Fraud," *Los Angeles Times*, November 7, 2000.

[71] As mentioned earlier, other countries with similar models preceded the Hong Kong model, including the Corrupt Practices Investigation Bureau in Singapore founded in 1952 and the Anti-Corruption Administration of Malaysia established in 1967 (De Speville 1998: 10).

in Hong Kong is legendary.[72] Hong Kong in the 1960's and 1970's was notoriously corrupt. The police were complacent or actively participating in many forms of illegal activity from prostitution rings to drug trafficking (Klitgaard MacLean-Abaroa and Parris 2000: 17-18; de Speville 1998). Corrupt systems were organized as syndicates and complex payment systems were developed ranging of both the bottom-up and top-down model type discussed in chapter I, where high ranking officials commonly turned a blind eye to major violations and distributed corrupt payments to lower ranking officials and members of the private sector. Similarly, low ranking officials extorted money from shop owners, and fixed traffic violations (Klitgaard, MacLean-Abaroa and Parris 2000: 18). Corruption was endemic, and the usual approaches were considered inadequate. Hong Kong's new governor decided to establish an Independent Commission against Corruption (ICAC) (Klitgaard 1988: 98-121; Klitgaard, MacLean-Abaroa and Parris 2000: 17-46; de Speville 1998). Undeniably, the success of Hong Kong's anti-corruption reform hinged on the establishment of an Independent Commission Against Corruption that was able to operate separately from the police.[73] Its three pronged approach mentioned above showed itself to be very successful. It took several measures that emphasized the sincerity of reforms including "frying the big fish", appointing a person of unquestioned integrity as the head of the Commission and incorporating both citizens and business in the overall anti-corruption reform program (Klitgaard 1988; Klitgaard, MacLean-Abaroa and Parris 2000).[74] Furthermore, the sheer financial resources that were given to the Commission served as a commitment device as did other guarantees of independence.

It is clear that the systematic approach and the radical change that resulted therefrom were persuasive in signaling both political will and that the rules of the game had changed, as well as altering citizens perceptions and expectations of the integrity of its government officials. It also emphasized that once perceptions and expectations are altered, low-level corruption can be a self-enforcing equilibrium. But, to return to my initial point, the dangers of reshaping the landscape and balance of administrative accountability mechanisms are great, and the successes of Hong Kong (and also notably Singapore) are subject to several factors, some of which are unique. These include extremely high levels of political will and commitment from the top, substantial human and financial resources, a tight insulated geographical city-state structure, guarantees of commitment backed up

---

[72] In addition to Singapore and Malaysia, other countries such as Malawi and Botwana have similar bodies as has New South Wales in Australia.

[73] *See* de Speville (1998: 21-36) for a comprehensive overview of the authority and structure of the ICAC.

[74] This commitment was later jeopardized when four years after inception, pressure forced the government to declare a partial amnesty in 1977, which nearly led to the demise of the ICAC (de Speville 1998: 22).

by civil service reform and moderate chances of political backlash. The dangers of politicization are great, and a unitary anti-corruption mechanism may be easier for an autocratic ruler or powerful interests to steer against enemies than a series of nonunified entities. Nonunified enforcement bodies increase the coordination costs for a corrupt system and may directly or indirectly keep a watchful eye on one another. Independent agencies can be tempered by an independent judiciary and other watchdogs. As with other independent bodies, there are several means to increase their accountability and independence. These are similar to the list I developed under our discussion of the ombudsman above, including staffing, multiyear budgeting, transparent appointment process for leadership etc.[75]

VI. Secrecy, Information and the Proper Limits of Transparency

> "Publicity is justly commended as a remedy for social and industrial diseases. Sunlight is said to be the best of disinfectants; electric light the most efficient policeman."[76]

Noble prize laureate Amartya Sen remarked over 20 years ago that where there is a free press famines do not occur (Sen 1981, *see* also Sen 1999). Indeed the virtues of a more open society where information is readily available have become the salvo of many different organizations in recent years. Cries for transparency have echoed from manifold quarters, such as banking (Enoch et al. 1997), multilateral development assistance (World Bank 2001), financial markets (Tanzi 1996), accounting and auditing practices (Economist 2002) and, of course, anti-corruption efforts (Transparency International 1998), but to name a few.[77] Informed public opinion and greater openness play an important role in good governance and are a potent deterrent against misgovernance. Forceful arguments for openness are ostensible, including perhaps most persuasively that in any democratic process participation hinges on informed participants. Secrecy diminishes the information available to the citizenry, hampering their ability and entitlement to meaningfully participate in democratic processes (Stiglitz 1999b: 7). Effective democratic oversight, in which citizens restrain the state, seems to compel that the citizenry is informed, which includes knowledge of what actions were taken, what alternative actions were available, and what alternative results could have been (*ibid.*).[78] The advantages of openness and public scrutiny were

---

[75] *See* above, Section IV, Subsection A.

[76] Buckley v. Valeo, 424 U.S. 1, 67 (1976) (per curiam) (quoting L. Brandeies, Other People's Money 62 (National Home Library Found. Ed., 1933).

[77] For additional areas, *see* Fiorini (1999).

[78] Stiglitz (1999b: 7) presents a persuasive normative argument with an economic characteristic in favor of access to government information. He asks, "given that the public has paid for the gathering of government information, who owns the information? Is it the private province of

already expounded by John Stuart Mill in his essay On Liberty (1859) where he suggests that public scrutiny is unconditionally beneficial as it renders the most assured way of classifying good from inferior governments. Free speech fosters beneficial ideas and undermines harmful ideas. The separation of good from bad ideas can only be established where the threat of liability or other sanction does not accompany discussion and particularly the utterance of bad ideas; the threat of liability (accompanied by informal sanctions) serves to prevent false assertions (*see* Cooter 2000: 332). To increase the flow of information libel laws for public officials should not offer public officials more protection than private citizens as is commonly the case but actually less protection (*see* Pope 1996: 129-141). Public figures have voluntarily taken upon themselves positions of public scrutiny and are able to refute allegations publicly before the media.[79] The case for information is, therefore, strong and generally clear as a default rule.

But information is not always uniformly good. We have seen, for example, that one important anti-corruption strategy is to alter the information structure of corrupt actors to break patterns of corruption.[80] For similar reasons, the privacy of the voting booth became a fundamental feature of democratic societies. In the case of the United States, for example, privacy of the voting booth only entered the electoral arena in the nineteenth century. Previously, people could buy and sell their votes, and enforcement was easy because the buyer (truster) could observe the sellers (trustees) behavior. Voting anonymously implied that parties could no longer enforce their agreements, because they could not be sure if the trustee, who moved second, honored the agreement (Ackerman 1993; Ayres and Bulow 1998). Formulating my point concisely; the arguments for transparency generally are strong and persuasive, but are not always as clear cut as their exponents may wish them to be. The rational behind the anonymous voting booth is illustrative of the need to look at exceptions to what I consider to be a general right of access to information.

---

the government official, or does it belong to the public at large?" He argues that information collected at public expense by public officials should be owned by the public, no different to "the chairs and buildings and other physical assets used by government belong to the public" (ibid.).

[79] Examples of poorly structured libel laws include Singapore, where high level officials are active in suing media and other politicians, or the United Kindgom where libel is notoriously easy for politicians to prove, particularly as a result of the fact that politicians are treated no differently to ordinary citizens. In Latin America libel law is often prosecuted under criminal law as opposed to civil law offering a further deterrent to the free flow of information (Rose-Ackerman 1999: 167).

[80] *See* Chapter II, Section III, Subsection D on controlling the parties information structure as a means to curb corruption.

A. Information and Governance

The ability of private parties to monitor government is largely dependent on the information the government makes available. Some of this information may be regularly and constantly disclosed, other information may be available at the request of the citizen or private party. Amid all the cries for transparency, one could easily be forgiven for assuming that all governmental information should be readily available, and, as highlighted above, this is an important default rule. I sketch out below some important considerations to the nonrevelation of information.

Public markets do not provide the same discipline as private markets (Stiglitz 1999b). The importance of exit and voice as instruments of market discipline have been emphasized at least since Hirschman (1970) (*see,* also Stiglitz *ibid.*). For public organizations, who generally enjoy a high degree of monopoly control, exit is generally not a possible course of action, and therefore greater reliance is placed on voice (Stiglitz 1999b: 10-11). There is commonly not a world of decentralized governments and governmental bodies á la Tiebout (1956), according to which individuals can shop like a customer in a restaurant looking for their favorite aperitif. Because of this, information becomes even more important for effective governance and discipline.

There are several costs of secrecy. In addition to the loss in participatory rights referred to above, secrecy provides room for public officials and private parties to collude, and limits the degree of accountability that can officials are held to for their actions given that they can generally hide their mistakes between poorly drawn lines of accountability, as we have seen in chapter II.[81] Stiglitz (1999b) identifies several other costs and adverse effects of secrecy that are pertinent to our discussion including: (1) It limits information and thus creates scarcity which can generate ill-begotten rents; (2) It increases the costs of becoming informed, which given that is a limit on the willingness to pay of citizens for information, increases the costs and decreases the likelihood of private agents monitoring illicit activities; (3) it can lead to inferior internal decisions when outside opinion is not taken into consideration; (4) it results in less timely decisions and less efficient allocations of resources, including private sector decisions (for example, when the government does not disclose macro-economic indicators, such as the level of employment, the rate of inflation etc.); (5) it can

---

[81] There is a vicious circle according to Stiglitz (1999b: 10-11), because when the amount of information that is exposed is limited, that which comes out is considered more important. Hence, there are even greater incentives to prevent information from flowing out in the first place, which reinforces secrecy.

lead to a form of bonding or separation of those that have the information from those that don't share the information.[82]

In addition, related to corruption we could add some of the following characteristics: (6) Secrecy reduces the vulnerabilities of corrupt exchanges and particularly the costs of finding a partner, negotiating a deal and seeing to it that an agreement is delivered and honored; (7) secrecy necessarily demands that the number of individuals privy to information is kept small, so as to increase the ability of maintaining the benefits of secrecy as well as the ability to sanction nonconformists, therefore the extent of exclusion is necessarily high; (8) secrecy increases the sanctioning power of corrupt systems because corrupt superiors can hide sanctions for nonconformists more easily within intransparent laws and codes of behavior; (9) secrecy can bread distrust of those persons outside a group, thereby adversely affecting relationships beyond and outside of the area of secrecy; (10) it can prevent those with moral qualm from engaging in certain behavior, particularly when it is illegal; (11) secrecy increases distrust in government. The arguments against secrecy and for transparency are, therefore, strong and in most cases completely justified.

B. Possible Exceptions to Transparency

There are, however, some strong arguments for controlling information in particular situations that should be given more reflection. Non-transparency is not necessarily a euphemism for corruption or illegality (*see*, Von Furstenberg 2001a: 2). There is a transparency bandwagon, and as we know about other bandwagons, they are not inexorably fortuitous.[83] The following are not necessarily exemptions, but concerns.

1. Consideration 1: Deterrence and Enforcement

1.1. Example I: Randomizing Strategies

It is well known among game theorists that players should avoid patterns of behavior that can easily be exploited (Dixit and Nalebuff 1993). Consider for example a football player who when taking a penalty would always hit the ball to the goalkeeper's left-hand side. A predictable result is, therefore, that the goalkeeper will attain this information and always dive to the left-hand side. This logic runs throughout all aspects of competitive behavior with strategic elements. Concealment and bluffing can be an important part of any "survival" strategy.

---

[82] We have seen this last point already in chapter II, with regard to the Mafia's code of silence known as Omertá, ensuring secrecy, bonding and separation.

[83] As von Furstenburg (2001a: 4) notes: "... the assumption that greater transparency necessarily is used for the greater good of all is insufferably Pollyannish."

Consider for example, a poker player, who always scratched his head when he had a good hand, and did not develop the potential to conceal and bluff his opponents. This logic is especially true for law enforcement, as I alluded to in chapter II. Where "too much" information is available on the pattern of behavior of law enforcement officials, strategic elements can take advantage of this weakness. Predictability can feed opportunism in a strategic setting.

1.2. Example II: Silent Alarms

There are distinct advantages to taking hidden precautions over more visible precautions in preventing crime. The classic deterrent is often considered to be sunlight or electric light. But turning on the electric light in front of your house can result in crime shifting toward your unlit neighbors houses, whilst installing a silent alarm prevents burglars gaining knowledge of which houses are protected and can reduce crime throughout the neighborhood because burglars can be discouraged generally from stealing (Ayres and Levitt 1998). This becomes more effective when we advertise that the area is fitted with such alarms. Bluffing is a similar rational. We have probably all come across residents who advertise, "Beware of Dog", even if they don't have a dog. The fact that some do, however, keeps the threat credible.

1.3. Example III: Vague Policy as Deterrent to Transgressions

Authorities frequently randomize their actions, as we have seen, in order to prevent themselves from becoming predictable, because predictable actions can be easily exploited. But authorities are frequently not permitted to randomize their actions, because of procedural reasons and protections of fairness. In such a case, the authorities may try to withhold their practices or policies in order to prevent them from becoming predictable.[84] One lucid example of this is public prosecutors, who generally follow guidelines set by the state attorney or another central figure. As a recent Israeli case highlights, sometimes they do not want these guidelines to become public knowledge for reasons of deterrence. In this case, the tax authorities did not want to disclose how large a transgression has to be before they will take a party to court or pursue criminal charges. It is clear that when authorities do not disclose this information, there is additional deterrence. If the minimum level to pursue a transgression was set at say $1000, then one could clearly expect citizens to use this information to their advantage. Similarly, if the tax authorities were unwilling to criminally pursue violations under $5,000, we could expect rational tax payers to be far more willing to take their chances on

---

[84] See Harel and Segal (1998) for a discussion of how behavioral factors play an additional role in deterrence pertinent to our discussion here.

being given an administrative fine than criminal sanctions, and would, therefore, be encouraged to engage in more infractions but within the $5,000 limit.[85]

1.4. Example IV: Undercover Work

As discussed elsewhere, undercover agents are more than an important deterrent; they can provide a perspective on the actions of a criminal organization from the "inside".[86] Used in the private sector and public sector alike, there are strong arguments why precise information on activities and the extent of operations should be withheld, including effectiveness, safety etc.

1.5. Example V: Personnel and Function Anonymity as Deterrent

In chapter II, I developed the idea of personnel anonymity and function anonymity as a deterrent to corruption. Recall the basic argument was that many transactions are processed anonymously, *i.e.*, the official is generally aware of the identity of the citizen, but the citizen is not aware of the identity of the official. This is common for many transactions such as tax returns etc., but uncommon in other areas, such as licensing. Re-addressing the number of anonymous services has large potential to decrease the level of corruption. For example, consider an applicant who submits a request for a government scholarship. Is it wise that she will know who will be handling his application? When she is unaware of who processes his application and considers her chances of legitimately receiving a scholarship to be poor, she may make efforts to influence the functionary, through cajoling, persuasion or even corruption, outright. Withholding information related to the identity of officials further implies that the private citizen incurs substantial search costs, before she can influence the functionary.

2. Consideration II: Rivalrous Information

Greater transparency is not a simple public good with non-rival benefits, but is bound by contentious issues of parties jockeying for control. Calls for transparency are, of course, often strategic and should not necessarily be put on the side of virtue (*see* von Furstenberg 2001a: 2).

The most obvious example of rivalrous information occurs in times of war, when information is withheld because it can benefit the enemy. For example, before the Normandy landings, the allies notoriously sent out "noisy signals" in order to frustrate the attempts of the enemy to find out where and when they were

---

[85] In this case, the court held that the public's right to know outweighed the said deterrence effect, which was the argument taken up by the state. C.A. 5539/91 Efrati v. Ostfeld, 46(3) P.D. 501.

[86] *See* Chapter IV.

going to land (Hirschleifer 1995). This example can also be extended to other cases of national security (Stiglitz 1999b: 19). On the other hand, in arms control, information is often voluntarily shared between rivals to assure one another than they will not attack; the same information, however, can be used by enemies to locate attacks (Fiorini 1999: 8). The problem with a broad national security exemption is that it can easily be protracted beyond those cases that directly entail national security, and there may be no means of ascertaining this when the information is kept silent. Much government security indeed draws its boarders beyond national defense infringing on other domains where there should be general access to information (Stiglitz 1999b: 19).

NGO's, firms, international organizations and political adversaries realistically often manipulate information to rebuke government officials for standards they never agreed to fulfill (Fiorini 1999: 7). It is not wise to assume the motives of those requesting greater information are *bona fide*; there is often a strategic element involved, as argued above. Indeed, cries for transparency can be related purely to efforts to better one's bargaining position in the socio-political arena (von Furstenburg 2001b). But to what extent motives should matter is moot. In Canada, for example, the Federal Court has held that the motives behind the request for the information are largely irrelevant, and that there is a general obligation to answer all access to information requests (Banisar 2001: 7). Although calls for transparency can score political points and are not necessarily nonrivalrous public goods, this does by no means suggest, as government officials wishing to protect information may argue, that pure self-interest is not justified as a motive to acquire information.

3. Consideration III: Privacy

Government gathers immense bounties of information concerning individuals, which should not be released for reasons of privacy (Stiglitz 1999b: 18). This, however, begs the question of how issues of privacy should affect knowledge and information of government actors and their actions. As discussed elsewhere,[87] government employees can be subject to extensive disclosure requirements, not just with regard to their financial position but also that of their family and kin. Although there is no bright line that can be drawn here, care must clearly be given to the general right of privacy.

4. Consideration IV: Panic

Stiglitz (1999b) identified occasions that may cause panic to be a possible exception to the release of information. He referred to this as "crying fire in a

---

[87] *See* above Chapter VI, Section IV.

theater" which can cause an outbreak of hysteria. Monetary and central bank policy is often promulgated as an area in which secrecy is important (*see*, von Furstenburg 2001a, 2001b). Stiglitz refutes these claims suggesting that "[n]either theory nor evidence provides much support for the hypothesis that fuller and more timely disclosure and discussion would have adverse effects... With a flow of information, less attention would be paid to any single piece; and there would be smaller revisions in posterior distributions" (Stiglitz 1999b: 20). He submits that the argument is at best only a justification, if at all, concerning both the timing and means of disclosure and cannot be used for the "infinite postponement of public discussion" (*ibid.*). Further, he notes that, "[n]o one would argue that, if one knew that there was a fire in the theater, that the patrons should not be informed in a way that allows an orderly evacuation" (*ibid.*: 20-21). One can, naturally, often find significant overlap between these arguments in arguments related to national security. For example, countries as a result of the recent anthrax scare in the United States, withheld precise information on the size of their anthrax vaccines, whilst at the same time, increasing supplies. The public, naturally, has a right to know the state of its health care system and its supplies, but the disincentives to the government were twofold, ranging from preventing panic to reasons of national security by presenting its weaknesses to hostile entities.

A similar but related argument found in the conflict-resolution literature, is that preferences when revealed can actually fuel conflict that would otherwise remain hidden beneath the surface (Fiorini 1998: 60). In particular, where there are serious divisions within a society, information may be best withheld, where it can cause widespread panic and/or violence. Again, this argument can easily be overdrawn, and may be more in favor not of the non-release of this information, but rather the timing of the release of this information.

5. Consideration V: Cost

Demands for information can be costly. Disclosure of information requires time and effort, and where there are high demands, governmental bodies can be bogged down by requests. There are several means for mitigating this problem. One is denying requests where information is easily accessible elsewhere. Another is charging a nominal fee equal to the marginal processing costs. Information should not be seen as a means of making profits or revenue by governmental agencies. The danger therefrom is that strong incentives are given to governmental bodies to withhold information that is of wide public interest and should, therefore, be published widely and freely on the internet, in order to "cash in" on requests. Where the government follows this approach, it increases the costs of information beyond the willingness to pay of many "would-be" monitors. The cost argument is significantly weakened now that technology, and particularly the internet, is reducing the burden of the provision of information. Furthermore, this information should be provided in a user-friendly manner. It is very easy for an audited body to provide too much information, so as to obfuscate attempts to identify improprieties. This has been termed in the literature the "white noise effect" (Fiorini 1999: 9).

6. Consideration VI: Flexibility & Stalemates

Where discussions and advice are not subject to oversight by third parties, there can frequently be freer speech and a broader discussion of ideas. For example, state attorneys and members of the legal department of government frequently have to give advice to enforcement agencies and public prosecutors on legal matters. This advice can be over the telephone or in written form via letter. Demand for this information is very high. Technically speaking, these may often be considered as directives that affect prosecutorial and enforcement policy. To what extent should all of these communications, which can be vast in number, be published? Clearly, where all communications are published, they would decrease substantially in number creating significant bottlenecks.

Closely related are confidentiality considerations: here information is only forthcoming upon reliance that this information will not be passed on to others (Stiglitz 1999b: 18). Stiglitz (*ibid.*) cites the example of donors that ask the World Bank for assistance to review their banking system. If it were known that errors would be disclosed, then assistance may not be requested in the first place.

7. Consideration VII: Negotiations

Delicate negotiations are a related area where restricting access to information to third parties can encourage the free flow of ideas among the parties crucial to negotiation (Stiglitz 1999: 21-22; von Furstenburg 2001a, 2001b). Von Furstenberg (2001a: 8-9) gives the example of the famous "Green Room" used in WTO meetings, whereby powerful members could deliberate complex issues in private before submitting their proposals to other members. This came in for substantial criticism because of non-transparency, but was a factor in overcoming stalemates. Where there is a deadlock, it can be important for parties at least temporarily to throw ideas on the table. The above scenario referred to limiting the access of third parties in an attempt to increase the chances of a pareto optimal outcome.[88] But parties to negotiations are not necessarily interested in what is pareto optimal, but what is optimal for them. In such scenarios, candor and full disclosure of preferences if practiced by one party can leave it weakened in the distributive features of bargaining (Arrow, Mnookin, Ross, Tversky, and Wilson

---

[88] Pareto optimal outcomes refer to outcomes where at least one party is better off and no party is worse off.

1995: 8-9). In such a scenario, the rational bargainer, if he optimizes his strategy will practice secrecy and maybe outright deceit. By the same logic, governments may be excused for not revealing their true preferences in international trade negotiations (or international conflicts) even to their own people, because doing so would put them at a competitive disadvantage against their rivals.

8. Consideration VIII: Anonymity and Retribution

Anonymity can facilitate communication, in particular by lowering the chances of retribution, as we have seen in cases of whistleblowing discussed above.[89] Similarly, students habitually evaluate their teachers anonymously which fosters feedback, and businesses occasionally provide drop boxes for suggestions and complaints on their services and staff (Levmore 1996: 2193). Government can increase the willingness of persons to inform by guaranteeing them anonymity. Similarly, secrecy can be the shelter of the weak against the strong as in the case of human rights organizations working in repressive countries. As von Furstenberg (2001b: 2) submits: "Making 'me' more transparent gives 'you' more power to abuse, intimidate and exploit me, and to force disclosure of ever more of my information."

9. Summing Up

I have emphasized the many advantages that accompany an open society and the free flow of information, as well as some possible consideration for withholding information, at least temporarily temporarily. Of course, the incentives to maintain secrecy are manifold, as everyone not just the corrupt prefers his or her mistakes to go unnoticed and unsanctioned. The possibilities for evading secrecy are also multifarious. When written material is subject to disclosure, less information will be written down. Where letters are filed and disclosed, people will shift to telephone calls. Where they cannot shift to telephone calls, they may even withhold the information entirely or produce less, because the costs of error are now higher. If formal meetings are open, then there is incentive to hold negotiations in informal meetings. In short, discretion can be pushed underground. In order to curb this commitment is fundamental, as is the need to change the beliefs and expectations of officials towards the position that the public has a general right to know (see Stiglitz 1999b). Information is instrumental as a tool to ensure citizen confidence in government as well as create voluntary compliance and contingent consent, factors conducive to sustainable reform and economic development.

---

[89] See Chapter IV, Section II, Subsection C2.

B. Auditing Bodies

We know from the above discussion that the effectiveness of the public as a check on the actions of government is determined in large part by the nature of the information provided by government. It is incumbent among governments at a minimum to make information on consolidated budgets, legislative proceedings, rules and statutes and revenue collection available (Rose-Ackerman 1999: 163). Indeed, information is an effective tool only when the nature of that information is accurate in its published form. Certain respected reporting requirements and standards should be met. Further, information should not only be published but controlled or audited by independent bodies. Financial information should be monitored by independent authorities. State audit offices, also known as supreme audit institutions (SAIs), play an important role in curbing corruption resulting from their capacity to increase accountability in the use of public funds and detect broader elements of slack and improbity.[90]

Before progressing with our discussion a word en passant on accounting and auditing in general is important. Both accounting and auditing serve essentially two different purposes, one internal and one external. They are used internally within an organization as tools of management, and externally by independent bodies as means to hold an organization and its officials responsible (White and Hollingsworth 1997: 443). The importance of auditing would appear to be growing as recent changes in government, often associated with "new public management" (NPM) entail greater use of audit and auditing as a management device (White and Hollingsworth 1999: 10).[91] The sheer number of new agencies that have cropped up in recent years suggests that there are more organizational parts to be audited, thus expanding the role of auditing bodies. In addition to growing in quantitative importance, in qualitative terms the implications of NPM for public sector audit flow mainly from the introduction of private sector concepts and practices into public sector management.[92] This has led to the widespread use of more commercial style accounts. The British central government for instance has adopted a system of accounting and budgeting known as resource accounting and budgeting common to the private sector (*ibid.*: 10-11).

Supreme audit institutions (SAIs) are national agencies that audit government income and expenditure and serve as a watchdog over the

---

[90] In Columbia, for example, for the year 2000, the national auditor's office reported that officials had skimmed off $27 million from the education budget alone. *See* "Wanted- A Crusade to Purify Public Life," *The Economist*, June 16, 2001.

[91] *See* further Chapter III, Section V, Subsection F1.

[92] As an aside, Roberts (2000) argues that early indications are that changes in government accompanying "New Public Management" reforms have adversely affected the supply of information.

management of public finances. They monitor the quality and credibility of reported financial information by the government, in addition to reporting on agency and department accounts, SAIs in recent years increasingly offer an independent external evaluation to legislature of the value-for-money attained by government.[93] As a general rule, they are not allowed to question the merits of a policy,[94] the reasoning behind which is the separation of powers doctrine.[95] In the United Kingdom, for example, the National Audit Office (NAO) headed by the Comptroller and the Auditor General (C&AG), an officer of the House of Commons, submits periodic reports to the parliament on the accounts given by government bodies and departments (White and Hollingsworth 1999: 3). This is an example of the Westminister model of auditing, adopted by many Commonwealth countries, the characteristics of which include *inter alia* that members of the audit office are professional auditors, they are not members of the civil service (but enjoy a similar status and similar benefits) and the office submits regular reports on government financial statements and operations, without emphasis on legal compliance (Dye and Strapenhurst 1998: 282-283, Stapenhurst and Titsworth 2001: 2).[96]

The GAO (General Accounting Office) is the supreme audit institution in the United States and monitors the financial data of the federal executive branch reporting directly to the House.[97] These bodies are independent of the government

---

[93] "At the same time, vfm is a criterion government increasingly uses to evaluate itself. In particular, the pursuit of vfm has been a driving force behind the 'new public management'" (White and Hollingsworth 1999: 10).

[94] For example, the National Audit Act 1983 of the United Kingdom explicitly prohibits the questioning of policy objectives by auditors when conducting value-for-money audits. *See,* however, Sharkansky (1988) who contends that SAI actually do challenge policy merits. He cites an example of how Israel's State Comptroller explicitly criticized policy and made alternative policy suggestions in their place, as well as more subtle examples of how the General Accounting Office (GAO) in the US, the National Audit Office (NAO) in the UK and the Philippines Commission on audit criticize policy.

[95] As Sharkansky suggests, "The auditor who becomes identified with policy formation may have trouble being viewed as a thorough critic of policy implementation" (Sharkansky 1988: 88).

[96] The supreme audit institution model with the widest authority is perhaps the Napoleonic or Cours des Comptes. "[I]t is an integral part of the judiciary, makes legal judgments on compliance with laws and regulations, and exercises a budget control function to assure that public funds are well used. The French Cours des Comptes is independent of both the legislative and executive branches of government. It audits the accounts of every government body (departments, ministries, and agencies; commercial and industrial entities under the purview of ministries; and social security bodies). Its jurisdiction is derived from primary legislation. The Latin countries of Europe, Turkey and most South American and Francophone African countries use this model (Strapenhurst and Titsworth 2001:1)." For a look at other models, *see* Strapenhurst and Titsworth (2001) and Dye and Strapenhurst (1998).

[97] The GAO has a multiplicity of functions and is not confined to strictly auditing the accounts of federal government. As Rose-Ackerman (1999: 163) notes: "It resolves contracting disputes,

agencies they audit- a necessary condition for credibility. This removes from self-monitoring the temptation that a public agency has of suppressing wrongdoing it discovers that may lead to negative publicity (Rose-Ackerman 1999: 163). The supreme audit institution model with the widest authority is perhaps the Napoleonic or Cours des Comptes. An inherent part of the judiciary, with its jurisdiction obtained via primary legislation and independent of both the executive and legislative branches of government, the French Cours des Comptes in addition to exercising a budget control function to secure that public funds are well used, formulates legal judgments on compliance with laws and regulations. It monitors the accounts of every governmental body, beyond ministries, departments and agencies to social security bodies and commercial and industrial entities falling under the competence of the ministries (Strapenhurst and Titsworth 2001:1). A version of this model can be found in the other parts of Europe sharing the romantic languages, in many states in South America, Francophone Africa and Turkey (ibid.).[98]

SAI auditing would seem to be growing in esteem and importance as a means of producing better governance. As suggested above, they have adopted private sector practices making them more sophisticated and in recent years moved their role beyond the traditional role of "minimizing waste, abuse and fraud and ensuring compliance with financial and administrative laws and regulations to value-for-money assessments" (Dye and Strapenhurst 1998: 5).[99] As an aside, we see once again that those instruments and mechanisms that decrease corruption are commonly those that decrease slack and inefficiency generally. Value-for-money is usually defined as the economy, efficiency and effectiveness of the expenditure (White and Hollingsworth 1999: 4).[100] In Britain for example value-for-money auditing was introduced in 1983 as a result of the National Audit Act, which gave the Comptroller and Auditor General (C &AG) the power to investigate how departments use their resources. It is estimated that the National Audit office (NAO) through performance auditing has identified savings of £270 million , or £7 salvaged on every £1 consumed on an audit (Dye and Strapenhurst 1998: 6).

---

settles the accounts of the United States government, resolves claims for or against the United States, gathers information for Congress, and makes recommendations to it."

[98] For a look at other models, see Strapenhurst and Titsworth (2001) and Dye and Strapenhurst (1998).

[99] "The responsibilities of the SAI's now include, in addition to assuring that the executive complies with the will of Parliament (...), the promotion of ethical behavior, efficiency and cost effectiveness and the encouragement of sound internal financial controls that reduce the opportunities for corruption and increase the likelihood of detection" (Dye and Strapendurst 1998: 5).

[100] "Economy means obtaining resources at the lowest cost; efficiency means finding the best use of the resources; and effectiveness means maximizing the attainment of objectives" (Sheldon and McNamara 1991: 1).

1. Structural Requisites to a Well-Functioning SAI

The status and precise mandates of Supreme Audit Institutions differ greatly.[101] Mandates should be well-defined and embedded in a set of rules and boundaries determined by Parliament (*ibid.*: 7). Legislating a clear set of rules and boundaries can institutionalize independent auditing authorities and insulate the SAI from criticism concerning *inter alia* its access to records, reporting requirements, independence, access to records, scope of audit and budget, and also ensure that it addresses what parliament wishes it to address (*ibid.*).[102]

As with the judiciary and the executive, independence is a prerequisite to a well functioning external auditing body. Essential factors include the following. Insulation from pressure groups either within the executive or the legislative should be guaranteed. There should be a complete separation between the auditing body and the agency it needs to audit, *i.e.*, the auditor and the auditee. An area of concern is perhaps the (quasi-) consultancy role of SAIs. Auditors frequently engage in developing systems of internal control and financial management.[103] Given limited resources that prevent the monitoring of many activities each year, an argument can be made for ensuring adequate systems of self-monitoring are in place (White and Hollingsworth 1999: 110). However, as Pollitt and Summa (1998) warn, when audit bodies assist auditees in increasing their performance, there is potential for an unwanted relationship to develop that jeopardizes independence.

The legislature has an important role to play in controlling the activities of the executive. In the United States, congressional committees, with the support of information provided by independent agencies, such as the GAO, provide a prominent, if responsive, oversight mechanism. In parliamentary systems such as the United Kingdom, Public Accounts Committees (PAC's), generally headed by a leading opposition member of parliament, perform a comparable function (Rose-Ackerman 1999: 163). Rose- Ackerman captures nicely the strengths and weaknesses of such a system. As she suggests: "This is how it should be in a well-functioning democracy, but it is hardly an unbiased way of uncovering malfeasance. If violations of the criminal law are uncovered, there must be an unbiased prosecutorial and judicial system available to pursue the allegations"

---

[101] *See* for example, State Audit in the European Union, a document prepared by the National Audit Office which provides a comprehensive survey of the role of SAI in European Union member states. Available online at http://www.nao.gov.uk/publications/state_audit.htm.

[102] For an up-to-date look at alternative mandates for SAIs, *see* http://www.cagindia.org/mandates/index.htm.

[103] For example, in a response document to the Modernising Government White Paper published in March 1999, the NAO refers to one of the roles of an auditor as "providing advice and encouragement to managers implementing Modernising Government initiatives by drawing on their audit work in this area, seeking to identify and promote good practice so that experience can be shared and risks minimized" (NAO 1999: 3).

(Rose-Ackerman 1999: 164). The problem is naturally that that these bodies may become politicized, jeopardizing independence and preventing their intended mandate causing institutional stalemate and inertia.

Influence can also manifest itself at the recruitment stage. Safeguards should include such factors as secure lengths of tenure, particularly for the Auditor General or head of the organization as well as a transparent non-biased selection process. These factors were covered in previous sections for alternative bodies and need not overly concern us here.[104] Clearly, such factors as budgetary freedoms are fundamental to a well-functioning state audit body. Insufficient funds can reduce an auditing body to a mere token organization, whose only purpose is that of providing corrupt officials with evidence of their apparent good will, a trophy piece that the government can use to legitimize its actions. Imperative is also the autonomy to determine what audits it shall conduct, when it shall conduct these audits as well as the nature of these audits. For example, review by auditing bodies is hampered by permissiveness in the law that allows members of the executive to have secret funds. As Rose-Ackerman (1999: 164) notes: "In the Unites States the budgets of the national security agencies such as the Central Intelligence Agency are not published. Oversight is provided by a special committee of Congress- a level of review that goes beyond many other countries where the executive essentially has unfettered discretion over a secret account. For example, before 1989 the United Kingdom simply refused to formally acknowledge that it had an intelligence service." The auditor general or head of a department should be granted legal status to ensure that bureaucrats have to comply with his wishes. When legitimate legal demands are not met, expeditious legal measures should be made available to the auditing body.

C. Closing Comments

In addition to the structural factors sketched above, I emphasize again (as in earlier discussion on wages and remuneration within the administration) the importance of the overall incentive package facing incumbent and potential employees.[105] Recall for example, that competitive wages have been espoused to foster performance and probity through at least three forces: First, the allocation of talent where there are competitive wages to public service is greater. Second, given competitive wages, there is less need or temptation to engage in malfeasance. Third, a competitive wage increases the status of the authority as perceived both by staff and outside bodies. Moreover, expectations for SAIs should be kept within reasonable limits as they are only part of the overall structure of institutions that should hold government accountable. Moreover, the

---

[104] *See* in particular Section IV and Section II Subsection B4 this chapter.

[105] I refer the reader's attention again to the table presented on packaging incentives in Chapter III, Section V, Subsection D.

auditing body is particularly dependent on the records that it audits,[106] the audience of its reports,[107] and the willingness of other organs, such as the Finance Ministry and the judiciary to follow up on its findings. Moreover, in the case of sophisticated corrupt systems, where accounting rules are not precisely defined, auditing cannot function as a substitute for a more fundamental strategy of redefining the underlying incentives behind corruption.[108]

---

[106] For example, where there are secret funds or where no accounts have been kept, it is ineffectual against improbity.

[107] For example, are the audits made public or are they confined to closed corridors?

[108] Indeed, according to Dye and Strapenhurst (1999: 13-14), "auditors in the private or public sector who have been trained to audit financial statements do not have a history of finding much fraud through their audits. Their main contribution to preventing corruption has been the strong psychological factor of deterrence."

CHAPTER VIII

POLITICAL BARRIERS AND REQUISITES TO REFORM: A NOTE ON POLITICAL FEASIBILITY AND THE INCENTIVES TO ADOPT THE INCENTIVES

I. Introduction

In this work, primary focus has been given to designing and addressing incentive effects in anti-corruption reform measures. But, one should also be mindful of the incentives to adopt the incentives.[1] Though particularly dependent on local conditions, I offer some tentative arguments and observations as well as tendencies. Of course, one of the central problems with measures aimed at mitigating undesirable discretion and high level corruption is that it can appear to wish away the most central problem by assuming high level officials are willing to constrain their own behavior. An adherent to the Madisonian belief of sober mistrust of government can find it difficult to reconcile the notion that leaders would be willing to introduce measures that limit their own powers and must, therefore, be judged as costly to them. Argumentation can appear circular and not consistent with effective reform. But such judgments are rash and premature for numerous reasons, and the circularity argument does not necessarily hold, but depends on socio-political realities and on the nature and particularities of a reform. For example, it is not necessarily the case that reform measures affect those leaders that introduce the reforms adversely, at least beyond a certain level of tolerance. Reforms that are internal to the administration and do not need to be legislated against may come at little political cost. Similarly management enforcement techniques adumbrated elsewhere appear to yield little political agitation. Moreover, reforms may be introduced to tie the hands of subsequent government and shift politically sensitive issues onto other entities.

Institutional inertia and failed reforms are not necessarily the result of low political will or lack of commitment to reform, but rather also a host of other structural factors that affect the costs and the benefits of reform measures. This is not to suggest that structural factors can necessarily account for the scope, timing and type of reforms. History and logic teach us that leadership is fundamental to reform. Without political leadership, there can be no substantial reforms against corruption! However, leadership is ill-positioned when it must operate with an environment where the costs of anti-corruption reform measures are exorbitant.

---

[1] I owe this formulation to Horowitz (1992: 261).

These structural factors affect costs and benefits and shape the incentives to adopt the incentives.

II. The Fallacy of Supporting Reform in Kleptocratic Societies

It is unwise to always consider corruption an effect rather than a cause of bad governance. As suggested, history and logic instruct us that leadership is fundamental to reform and without which there can be no substantial reforms against corruption. Oftentimes, models of corruption reform are expressed in principal-agent or principal-supervisor-agent terminology, offering suggestions on how the principal, normally prescribed as a senior public official or government, can reshape institutions to weed out corruption, given that it is a symptom of poorly designed institutions. Indeed, most of the literature takes the position, that what is needed is better governance in order to lessen the payoffs associated with corruption, particularly among low-level officials. Put differently, corruption is seen as the effect of poorly designed institutions, and what is needed is to redesign or align the incentives of the officials or agents with those of the principal. Whilst this approach is insightful- indeed have even adapted ourselves in previous chapters - because of the assumption inherent in its implementation, it doesn't bring us very far in more serious circumstances where corruption is not a symptom of weak governance but the design the of principal. In this case, corruption is endogenous to the design of governmental institutions; it is a cause and not an effect of poorly designed governmental institutions. In such a scenario corruption is the cause not the effect of poor governance structures.

In political science and economics such states are frequently referred to as kleptocratic states, a term associated with Andreski (1968).[2] As one may suspect, there is no neat dichotomy of such systems. Recent work on kleptocracy is invariably associated with Mancor Olson (1993) in which he developed the concept of the "roving and stationary bandit." Olson puts forward a scenario where roving bandits devastate a country. As a result of competition, one bandit dominates others and expels them from his territory, asserting an exclusive right to exploit the territory for economic gain. The now stationary bandit who wishes to maximize his personal fortune has two means of attaining wealth. He can do

---

[2] Aspects of kleptocracy are also to be found at an institutional level, where corruption has been institutionalized. In these cases, agents and supervisors may not always have the ability to reshape the design of formal structures to maximize their wealth, they may, nevertheless, shape informal structures. Consider for example, corruption in the police force. Where this is institutionalized, payoffs frequently run from the bottom-up, whereby low level agents that come into contact with private persons receive bribes and transfer them up to superior officers. These officers may or may not have the power to restructure the police department or organization so as to maximize payoffs, but they can structure the day-to-day operations so as to maximize bribes. Under such circumstances, it is easy to see how reform measures that tighten supervision of low level officials by superiors may be ineffectual.

this either through expropriation (taking of property) or through taxation. According to Olson, a rational bandit will not choose expropriation and will set taxation at a level equal to that which maximizes his welfare, given that expropriation discourages production and reduces society's future wealth. Unlike the "roving bandit", the "stationary bandit" maximizes his wealth over the long term, so his interests encompass the future revenue of the society. He does not over-fish the commons in search of private gain, as he has appropriated all property rights (*see* Hardin 1968). The insecurity of modern dictators alters their time horizons, so they resemble roving bandits more than stationary bandits. As Olson (1993) suggests, the rational stationary bandit sets the tax rate at the point that maximizes his revenue, whereas a democratic society (should) set the tax rate at a level that maximizes the nations welfare, which is necessarily lower than that set by the former. The more "encompassing" the states interest, the better it maximizes the welfare of a nation. Although the government is itself hampered by special interest groups, it still operates in a means preferable to the stationary bandit from the perspective of social welfare maximization.

The "stationary bandit" who is interested in maximizing his welfare will operate like a monopolist and under-produce output in order to maintain monopolistic rents (Shleifer and Vishny 1993; Rose Ackerman 1999: 114-15).[3] State run enterprises would be designed so as to maximize his monopoly profits and he would spend little time on politics and petty favoritism (Rose-Ackerman 1999: 115). If the kleptocrat shared the characteristics and particularly the security that Olson associates with the stationary bandit, he would also favor recruitment and promotion based on meritocracy as well as good business practices and oppose policies that redistribute benefits widely throughout society that did not allow extraction for himself at the center (*ibid.*: 115).

---

[3] "Rent seeking" is a different concept than corruption but is subject to some fundamental overlap. Corruption is generally considered as the (illegal) abuse of power for private gain and violates legal obligations to principals. Rent seeking is a concept introduced by Tullock (1967; 1971) that refers to the economic concept of rent, earnings in excess of relevant costs, often termed monopoly profits. "Rent seeking is an effort to acquire access to or control over opportunities for earning rents" (Coolidge and Rose-Ackerman 1997: 3). Whilst advertising and public relations may be considered a form of rent-seeking, it is most commonly associated with resources expended by interest groups in order to persuade governments to provide returns greater than they would earn without governmental protection. As a return for investment on rent-seeking outlays, politicians who act as brokers securing fees for themselves distribute these rents (Rowley 2000: 141). Rent seeking under the conditions I am looking at here, is largely of a different type. The kleptocrat has strong controls over the instruments of state, operating outside of the rule-of-law, trying to maximize the amount of wealth he can appropriate for himself and balance this somewhat with his chances of remaining in power. As Rose-Ackerman and Coolidge (1997: 7) note: "It does not matter whether we describe such a ruler as corrupt or a rent seeker. The basic point is that the ruler is in control of the levers of state power and can manipulate them for personal gain."

Clearly, most modern day kleptocrats do not share these far-reaching endowments.[4] Were the kleptocrat to favor recruitment and promotion along meritocratic lines, he would most likely instigate his own downfall. Most kleptocrats need to surround themselves, with institutions filled by their own supporters along the lines of patronage in order to insulate themselves from forces within government that may threaten their existence and, in doing so, forgo some of the additional revenue associated with more efficient officials. Kleptocrats will need to acquiesce a certain number of people around them by allowing them a share in the spoils in order to prevent themselves from being toppled (Grossman 1991). In Somalia for example, President Barre reportedly bequeathed fiefdoms to various political factions in the shape of government ministeries, agencies or departments (Coolidge and Rose-Ackerman 1997: 29). State patronage becomes a tool which kleptocratic rulers can use to insulate themselves from competition. Furthermore, it must be noted that the bureaucracy is the main tool or set of tools with which the kleptocrat can acquire his wealth, therefore, efforts at reform are generally fruitless. They represent merely exercises in public relations. Anti-corruption reform has not failed in such environments, it was never on the agenda in the first place! The ruler doesn't want to bite the hands that feed him.

Whilst the strong kleptocrat, as noted above, can set output in a means to maximize his economic rents in a centralized manner, which is less detrimental to society, a weaker kleptocrat would be unable to rely on a perfectly vertical organizational structure and would have to delegate discretion to others to supervise activities. Similarly, should taxing and other sources of rent be associated with high transaction costs, for example as a result of geographical distance, he might have to delegate power to others to collect the revenue, from whom he in turn would collect (Charap and Harm 1999). There is therefore a principal-agent problem for the kleptocrat (Coolidge and Rose-Ackerman 1997: 21). Most kleptocrats, therefore, face different incentives and are less powerful than the strong kleptocrat presented by Olson (1993). Though they still pursue personal wealth maximization, they have only the use of imperfect tools and operate in an inefficient system characterized by a weak bureaucracy and poor resource base (Rose-Ackerman 1999: 115). Controlling the levers of state power, they control the state but not the whole economy and pursue their self-interest and those of their family and cronies by utilizing their massive discretion *inter alia* for

---

[4]   The list of modern day kleptcrats is unfortunately a long one; examples include President Mobutu in Zaire, President Barre in Somalia, General Alfredo Stroessner in Paraguay, President Marcos in the Philippines, the Duvaliers in Haiti and President Suharto in Indonesia. As an illustration of the numbers involved, President Mobutu of Zaire once boasted on U.S. national television in 1984 that he was the second wealthiest person in the world, professing to have $8, billion dollars stashed away in Switzerland. It is reckoned that for the duration of his rule, sixty percent of the annual budget was passed onto personal accounts of himself, his family and his supporters (*see* Rowley 2000: 154).

the purposes of deleterious state intervention, privatization and striping of public physical assets and infrastructure, awarding procurement contracts, granting licenses permits and subsidies, securing monopoly power for businesses operating in the domestic market, and personally operating or turning a blind eye to criminal and gray and black market activity. Moreover they engage in rent extraction as opposed to rent seeking, virtually blackmailing businesses into giving them money by threatening to have laws and regulations changed in a manner costly to them.[5]

To repeat, kleptocrats are generally of the weaker type described above. To compensate for their inefficient tools at hand, unlike the strong kleptocrat discussed by Olson, they usually run "an intrusive and inefficient state organized to extract bribes from the population and the business community" (ibid.: 119).[6] Indeed, most African kleptocrats learned quite quickly that they did not possess a lengthy time horizon in power accompanied by an impervious monopoly on corruption and theft. In this vein Rowley (2000: 139) notes, "[a]s dictator after dictator succumbed in a rapid sequence of coups d'etat, governance in Africa rapidly began to resemble that of a roving bandit in an environment of anarchy ... By definition, the roving bandit does not exhibit a stable and encompassing interest in the domain over which he rules."

In such an environment, where there is little investment in domestic productivity, it should not come as a surprise, then that foreign aid becomes an attractive alternative for appropriation (ibid.). For example, the most profitable posts in Somalia were those related to control of foreign aid and foreign financed projects (Coolidge and Rose-Ackerman 1999: 29). Already in 1984, "it was common knowledge in Somalia that officials at the Mogadishu Port Authority (MPA) were routinely demanding deposits of $10,000 in foreign bank accounts from shipping lines bringing in food aid before they would be allowed to unload" (ibid.). History teaches us, competition for state rents can become fierce. The fact that the kleptocrat achieves such rents make his position all the more attractive. In

---

5   Note, rent extraction as opposed to rent seeking is apparently more common in advanced economies than is commonly recognized. See McCheseny (1987) for an analysis of this practice in the United States.

6   Naturally, there are other possibilities that may themselves be worse. Lessons from the study of anarchy teach us that any number of possibilities may be possible. For example, no warlord may assert his dominance over a territory and high amounts of resources can be devoted over extensive periods of time to military activities, in preference to productive activities (Hirschleifer 1995). "Unproductive" activities, such as increasing military size and conflict, may increase the human capital skills of those involved in this area, thus making it more profitable for them to concentrate their efforts in conflict relative to productive activities. On the rival's side, the same thing might happen and additionally knowledge that the other side is willing and has higher returns from conflict than productive activities may be taken as a signal of intent. The disability to resolve this problem would also seem to be related to the endowments of the parties, the number of parties involved and cohesion within these groups.

order to fend off attacks, he frequently must insulate himself with members of the military and other elites outside of his line of patronage. Where the kleptocracy becomes more of the roving bandit type, rent-seeking activities of the nature associated with Western democracies, where competing interest groups expend resources to influence government in order to acquire long-term economic rents, become uncommon (Rowley 2000: 142). The ruler is unable to make credible commitments that lower the returns on investment from rent-seeking or bribery, thus making it less attractive as a form of investment (Rose-Ackerman 1999: 118). Indeed, all investment will be hampered because of low investor confidence associated with the short-time horizon of the kleptocrat, the inability to sufficiently sanction him for reneging on any agreements, and more generally the inability to prevent expropriation of investments. Investors will generally avoid putting their money into projects that are capital intensive and only invest where they can be assured quick payoffs (Coolidge and Rose-Ackerman 1997: 23).

Even where a kleptocrat is sufficiently stable to be able to commit to investments, he is limited by the line of loyalty and patronage that are often expected of him. Therefore, he must often necessarily exclude certain sections of the population from rent-seeking activities. As a result of this, outside groups will decide not to waste resources on trying to acquire rents from the kleptocrat, but rather to seize control for themselves through coup d'etat (Rowley 2000: 142). Just as we discussed earlier, civil servants who acquire a job in the bureaucracy through patronage or paying for the post have built up expectations on how much the position is worth and have invested accordingly, thus entertaining a belief in the "right" or legitimacy of continued corruption (Jagannathan 1986, 1988). Members of outside groups that acquire power after a bitter struggle will also have invested in the struggle an amount relative to what they expect in return. Thus the cycle goes on and on. This is of course a very serious deterrent to democratic reform. Past behavior of former rulers, weak or non-existing social and legal constraints, and an absence of guilt, based on the belief of entitlement due to investment and former harms suffered, are all conditions that unfortunately make cycles of kleptocracy a stable long-term equilibrium.

III. Political Feasibility and the Costs and Benefits of Reform Measures

The basic message of the above discussion of kleptocracy was that where political will and political leadership is lacking reform measures are not credible and instruments of reform remain unheeded. Lessons from anti-corruption reforms in developed countries as well as work on the political economy of adjustment - which although primarily concerned with macro-economic reforms provides useful insight on instituting broad-based reforms - in addition to furnishing general models of reform, provide some general observations on the nature of the problems and dilemmas facing politicians and would-be reformers. As we shall see, there are several difficulties commonly (associated with substantial reforms, such as collective action and coordination problems, distributive problems, associated with distribution among the winners and losers of reform), the ability of parties to veto reforms, the political time horizon of reformers, as well as the social climate in which reforms take place.

A. Collective Action and Coordination Problems

Reform frequently has the characteristics of a public good and thereby suffers from collective action problems. Recall that public goods are characterized by the fact that once produced, it is impossible to exclude others from their use. Unlike private goods, there is no link between payment and consumption of the good, which leads to an obvious free-rider problem where each person hopes that another will provide the good so that he or she can enjoy the benefits associated with it. A common result, therefore, is that goods go unproduced. In this vein, Geddes (1991, 1994) has suggested that politicians in Latin America are in a dilemma. Those that propose reforms are burdened with costs imposed by the (potential) losers of reform. The groups that endure the costs of reform, she suggests "include the administrators and politicians who under traditional arrangements have the power to decide who will be hired to fill government posts" (Geddes 1994: 27).[7] The gains associated with reform are dispersed and there is a first-mover disadvantage, which is worsened when the losers of reform can shift their allegiance to other politicians, who capitalize on attempts of other political groups to institute reforms by procuring the allegiance of the potential losers of reform. Reform in this scenario can only occur in two conditions: where there is either a dominant party whose sheer strength ensures that it can incur the costs of reform (and still not be disposed from power); or alternatively, where parties are of equal strength and equally similar in their access to patronage appointments then the gains from reform are symmetric which make cooperation in order to pass reforms more likely. Similarly, Geddes (1994) emphasized the role of voting and party systems which can discipline candidates refusing the chances of defection. It is questionable, however, how many reforms can accurately be characterized as public goods, but the rationale behind it is useful nevertheless.

---

[7] The costs Geddes (1994: 27) suggests may be understood as follows: "These officials have the choice of hiring the people who will contribute most to the officials' welfare (usually members of their own families); hiring the people who will contribute most to consolidating political support for themselves or their parties; or hiring the people who will contribute most to administrative effectiveness (probably the most technically qualified applicants). For the administrator or politician involved, choosing the applicant most likely to contribute to improving the administration often involves a certain and immediate loss of either personal or political benefits....".

B. Veto Power and Political Dissensus

Systems of governance necessitate the allocation of decisionmaking authority among parties. Political scientists and economists sometimes speak of vetoes or so called veto gates, which refer to institutions with the power to block policy initiatives (Haggard and Kaufman 2001: 15; Tsebelis 1995).[8] Veto gates may encompass *inter alia* the government's coalition partners, the legislature, the Constitutional or Supreme Court, or corporatist bargaining schemes depending on the constitutional design (Haggard and Kaufman 2001: 15). The gist of the work in this area is that as the number of vetoes or veto gates rise, the wider the array of interests the government must oblige and the greater the necessity for broad-based political support for reform, which when it becomes excessive or fractured can lead to the dilution of reform, delay and inertia (*ibid.*).

In a pure dictatorship, a single person enjoys the only veto, whereas in a system of unanimous rule, every individual controls a veto (Haggard and McCubbins 2001: 5). Dispersing the number of vetoes among a number of players has the affect of decreasing the chances that any single individual or group will capture all vetoes (*ibid.*). In a system where the effective number of vetoes is large, it is difficult for any one group to deliver on corrupt agreements or capture the process itself. On the downside, however, instituting reforms is more difficult and the status quo is favored. Tendencies for collective action problems increase. The argument that resonated particularly in the 1990s that nondemocratic systems are better at achieving reform, also known as the "Lee Hypothesis", after Lee Kuan Yew, the former president of Singapore, bares similarity to the above logic. It is, however, quite impossible to verify whether or not this hypothesis actually holds. Systematic empirical studies do not provide strong support to the position that between political rights and economic performance there is general discord.[9] Nobel prize laureate Amartya Sen has recently argued that this hypothesis is "based on sporadic empiricism, drawing on very selective and limited information, rather than on any general statistical testing over the wide-ranging data that are available" (Sen 1999: 6). He further notes:

> "A general relation of this kind cannot be established on the basis of very selective evidence. For example, we cannot really take the high economic growth of Singapore or China as "definitive proof" that authoritarianism does better in promoting economic growth, any more than we can draw the opposite conclusion from the fact that Botswana, the country with the best record of economic growth in Africa, indeed with one of the finest records

---

[8] This approach is perhaps most associated with Tsebelis (1995) who essentially addressed how the number of veto gates within a political system and the divergence of interests among persons occupying these positions act upon legislative productivity.

[9] *See* Prezworski (1995) and Barro (1996).

of economic growth in the whole world, has been an oasis of democracy on that continent over the decades" (*ibid.*).

There is another consideration pertinent to our discussion here. Concentrating on the number of veto players represents only a fractured picture of the feasibility of reforms. One must also look at a separation of purpose (Haggard and McCubbins 2001: 5). Where power is divided but purpose is unified, the de facto number of vetoes may be closer to one, given that each institution has similar preferences and strives towards a common ends. On the other hand, where preferences are divergent and payoffs independent of one another, as is the case when electoral fates are separate, the de facto number of vetoes may approximate the maximum possible number of vetoes (*ibid.*).

Electoral structures significantly influence the extent to which politicians must create their own base of electoral support, increasing the likelihood that and necessity for politicians to pursue their own preferences, potentially producing a form of political dissensus. In this light, closed-list systems counterbalance the need and the desirability of politicians to pursue their own electoral agenda and electoral reputations. On the other hand, open-list systems compel the politician to differentiate himself from his party members and establish his or her own electoral reputation and base, given that votes are swayed as a result of the personalization of elections. A system of low level patronage is more forthcoming, and the collective action problem exasperated.[10]

It is easy to comprehend how, in such an environment, politicians face greater incentives to form factions as part of a strategy to distinguish themselves from their intra-party competitors (Cox and McCubbins 2001: 43). Moreover, as the number of parties and factions increase, the more likely it becomes that policy enactment necessitates deals transversing party lines; coordination and negotiation costs increase given that multifaction/multiparty agreements have different electoral repercussions across the members of policy coalitions (*ibid.*: 43-45). Conceivably, the more parties to any particular coalition that are possible, the more difficult it becomes to break the stalemate. Clearly, a party system may emulate the degree of centralization within democratic governments. From the above discussion then, it comes as no surprise that a uniform majority party enjoys more discretion and authority to pass reforms than a set up where the interests of a diverse legislative coalition must be taken into consideration. The need to attract a personal electoral base and reputation, anti-party sentiments and even coalition governments may confound the problem of collection action, as can factional infighting within parties, where there is a separation of purpose. Many of these problems seem to be particularly pronounced in Brazil, which Sartori (1994: 113) considers to be an "antiparty, both in theory and practice". He suggests that

---

[10] For a game-theoretical analysis of the impact of electoral systems on corruption, *see* Myerson (1993).

politicians consider their party to he a "partido de aluguel", as a form of rental. "They freely and frequently change party, vote against the party line, and refuse any kind of party discipline on the ground that their freedom to represent their constituency cannot be interfered with. Thus parties are powerless and volatile entities, and the Brazilian president is left to float over a vacuum, an unruly and eminently atomized parliament" (*ibid.*).

This is not to suggest that reforms cannot be pushed through without a strong centralized government with intraparty discipline. As Haggard and Kaufman (2001: 17) suggest, "[a] more diffuse and consultative decision-making process slows policy making and necessarily expands the scope of interests to be accommodated, but precisely for that reason it makes any decision more stable." Experience tells us, however, that it is improbable. Recent experience in Latin America seems to indicate that the capacity of governments to push through reforms has much to do with the ability to enlist "traditional" politicians to support their efforts.[11] There is an inherent dilemma here for the reformer: If reforms are to be sustainable, they require good performance in order to uphold public support. Performance is hampered, however, by the involvement of persons with ties to the old system; but without their support reforms would not be passed in the first place. Moreover, lessons from the Latin American experience teach us that socioeconomic and state crises in an environment where parties and party systems are ruptured succeeds in concentrating power in the hands of a president who can function outside the realm of accountability without checks on his power (*see* Diamond, Hartlyn and Linz 1999: 30). As an aside, one should also note, that resulting from the ineffectualness of legislatures and their lack of power, legislatures in Latin America often operating within the "shadow of presidential decree" and other constraints are either unwilling or unable to provide a check on executive malfeasance; they have shown themselves to be more capable of obfuscating rather than generating active agendas or reforms (ibid.: 33). Dissensus, combined with a lack of institutional resources (budget etc.) and structural incongruity prevent any significant check and balance on executive power (*ibid.*).[12]

---

[11] "Latin America: The Slow Road to Reform," *The Economist*, December 2, 2000.

[12] The role of presidentialism has recently been the focus of substantial criticism in the literature by highly respected academics, lead by Linz. *See*, for example, Linz (1990). Key criticisms include that presidentialism is a zero sum game, where there is only one winner and there are losers, making the stakes of elections very high and the winner only carries a certain unsatisfactory proportion of the electorate. Fixed terms in office are said to make presidents unresponsive and elections have more to do with candidates than parties or lower-level leaders. It is also argued that presidentialism generates competing claims to legitimacy between the legislature and the president, creating impasses and policy inertia. Moreover, contended is that presidentialism fails to provide an inadequate check on the executive when there are fragmented parties. For a good indication of the broad band of perspectives, compare Mainwaring (1999), Lijphart (1994), Sartori (1994), and Horowitz (1992).

C. Distributive Conflicts

A significant obstacle posed to reform are distributional conflicts. This is a familiar scenario whereby reform is supported by winners and opposed by losers, the outcome of which is generally dependent on the balance of power between the opposing sides (Haggard, Lafay, and Morrisson 1995: 20). Reforms that can reduce the level of corruption commonly face the familiar precarious situation that losers are concentrated and winners are dispersed, or maybe even unknown. Furthermore, there may be problems of redistribution as patronage relationships create property rights which tend to legitimize themselves over time (Khan 1998). Moreover, relationships and institutions may have been founded for ideological and paternalistic reasons which adds legitimacy to the status quo. Interest groups that prevent reform may not be well organized, as is commonly the case in western democracies, but this characteristic can be replaced by loyalty along other lines such as kinship, which because it is based on ascribed trust can be a far more stable form of inertia.

There are significant organizational asymmetries between the concentrated "winners" of the status quo and the potential but dispersed, "winners" of reform. Institutional design may give losers a unsymmetrical weight in policy matters, effectively granting them an effective veto power to block the passage of reforms (Haggard, Lafay and Morrisson 1995: 20-21). This is clearly the case in countries, commonly described as "corporatist" in the political science literature, where specific groups are legally bequeathed with essentially "monopoly lobbying rights," often accompanied by an executive right to administer on diverse consultative and policy-making boards and commissions (Cox and McCubbins 2001: 37 n.15).[13] In many developing countries, where interest groups that represent the potential winners from reforms are not well organized, the necessary demand to create supply is not available. Demand for anti-corruption reform is commonly so low, that although socially beneficial, politicians are not willing and see no need to incur the costs of altering the status quo.[14]

For less developed countries, it can be particularly problematic where a firm or industry is so powerful that it can hold a government hostage. For example, when an industry is concentrated on mining commodities such as oil, it can have specially perverse consequences for the economic, social and political structure of an economy (Diamond, Hartlyn, and Linz 1999: 58). Winners from potential reforms cannot be identified before hand, which can result in a status

---

[13] Pluralist countries on the other hand do not regulate the lobbying process in this manner (Cox and McCubbins 2001: 37 n.15).

[14] Kulick and Wilson (1992: 38) for example identify how corruption in Thailand is considered simply as a way of life commonly accepted as a norm. A poor farmer in northeastern Thailand candidly admits that "a general election is a time for collecting money. Democracy? I must pay off my debts first before thinking about it."

quo bias (Fernandez and Rodrik 1991). In addition to being able to identify winners, there are substantial problems with discounting gains, which may occur only in the long-term. Furthermore, these gains are uncertain which can prevent cooperation from evolving among the winners of potential reforms (Geddes 1994).

D. Political Time Horizon

There are several institutional and political factors that affect a politicians time horizon. Political leaders may will discount future gains steeply, particularly when there is a risk that they will disposed from power, a risk of rioting, forthcoming elections etc. Reforms in certain areas are more sensitive than others. One reason for the persistence of inefficient institutions is that to alter their design would entail substantial political backlash; in developed countries, this can be and is commonly ignored in the analytics of reform proposals, for less developed countries where the threat of political backlash can manifest itself in the form of conflict, a reformer may have to settle for second best (Roe 1998). A specially important factor that distinguished less developed countries from developed countries is commonly the perceived threat of violence that can be associated with reforms (Haggard, Lafay and Morrisson 1995: 13; Roe 1998). One means for politicians to overcome the threat of political backlash is to rank reforms along the lines of sensitivity in a manner as highlighted in Figure 1 in Chapter III. Countries should begin with those reforms that are least sensitive. For example, those policies that are subject only to administrative control and are of a preventative nature are subject to much more rapid implementation than those that require legislation and administrative staff to carry them out. As discussed under downsizing earlier, there are a plethora of considerations that a government can take into account in order to make those measures that are more politically sensitive more politically feasible. For example, having some form of indirect compensation visible for the losers may mitigate the problems associated with reform measure or group of measure, but one should be careful that this does not provide for other rent-seeking opportunities. Compensation may also manifest itself in the form of complementary reforms. As noted in previous discussion, compensation should not appear as a means of buying off the losers, as this can in itself give the impression of improbity.[15] Moreover, compensatory schemes are restricted in use because of limited financial and managerial capacities.

It is clear that some institutions will be slower to reform than others and reformers have greater incentives not to attempt to introduce the same norms of transparency and openness to those bodies that can most endanger reform. In

---

[15] But as Haggard Lafay, and Morrisson (1995: 23) note: "Political feasibility and equity are two different things."

380

many developing countries and particularly in Latin America, the military is an example of an institution that is especially resistant to change. Years of successive interventions in politics and the running of government have significantly altered the perceived role of the armed forces, particularly among the military itself (Diamond, Hartlyn, and Linz 1999: 20).[16] In Latin America "military coups became an institutionalized means for political leaders to alternate in power and keep popular participatory political institutions under control": the military has even infringed upon the political realm of governmental responsibilities in such diverse areas as "rural development, "civic action," forensic intelligence, policing, and participation directly in the cabinet" (*ibid.*: 20, 22-23). Politicians that push through reforms sometimes therefore compromise by providing what Lijphart (1994: 92) terms "reserved domains of undemocratic power."

E. The Role of Scandals and Crisis

"A scandal occurs. For example a municipal councilor may be found guilty of bribe-taking. Or the police may be found to be systematically involved in collusion with criminals. Public works programs may be found to contain inflated costs as the result of fraud and kickbacks. Bidders on municipal projects may be discovered to have formed a collusive ring to restrict competition and inflate prices. As the scandal erupts the public is outraged. The press fulminates. Politicians express dismay and call for decisive action. An inquiry commission is formed. Six months later, the commission's recommendations emerge. They tend to include more layers of oversight, bigger budgets for investigation and enforcement, and a new code of conduct. But in the six months that have passed, the public's outrage has subsided, and so the press and politicians pay little attention to the recommendations. In fairness, this is partly because the recommendations tend to be expensive and to promise little real prevention" (Klitgaard, MacLean-Abaroa and Parris 2000: 12).

The above depiction of a typical course of action after a scandal occurs by Klitgaard and his colleagues captures well both the promise and limitations of scandals in achieving reform. Citizen demand for reforms is a prerequisite to any action being taken! Scandals provide an important, though temporary means, that can cause citizen demand to increase. Indeed given the fact that public demand must accompany or precede any substantial reforms against corruption, it is not surprising that practically all reforms specifically aimed at curbing corruption are a result of a preceding scandal. Moreover, scandals provide an important tool with which the citizenry can receive information and discipline its public servants.

---

[16] The same is true, for example, also of Thailand which experienced nineteen coups alone in the period between 1932 and 1992 (Quah 1999: 249).

Ironically investigators themselves may not wish to make big cases in order to avoid a scandal. This is of particular concern where there is self-regulation, or where the monitors are somehow connected to the monitored.[17] In New York, for example, it was reported that the police department intentionally lessened corruption controls as it became "more concerned about bad publicity that corruption disclosures generate than the devastating consequences of corruption itself" (*see* Anerchiarico and Jacobs 1996: 166).

It is a useful exercise to look at the incentives to bring large corruption cases to public attention from the perspective of the monitors themselves. For the same reasons that corporate criminal liability fails to effectively induce corporations to monitor their employees and report this information to authorities, self-regulation which still governs most day-to-day monitoring against improbity in government is frequently ineffective.[18] *First*, there is an associated reputation loss for the group as a whole. *Second*, the infraction would probably not be discovered by outsiders, so why expose it. *Third*, discovery of transgressions can frequently lead to an investigation of other practices of both the governed and the governing. *Fourth*, the oftentimes rapacious nature of media coverage can act as a deterrent to revealing transgressions, or exerting effort in finding them in the first place because the expected sanction is now considerably higher. *Fifth*, the public perception of corruption scandals unfortunately commonly fails to take into account the fact that because the scandal came to light may well be an indication of a well-functioning monitoring system and not the contrary. Discovery per se is frequently treated as if it were invidious behavior in itself and an indication of former failures to discover.

Scandals are, therefore, frequently the work of investigative journalism and the independent press. When scandals occur, the media legitimately or illegitimately is often accused of personalizing occurrences and ignoring more systematic conditions behind the event (Rose-Ackerman 1999: 209-210). There is always the concern that such scandals may turn into witch hunts, particularly where powerful individuals with their own private agenda pull the strings of reports- a factor made significantly more potent by the globally observed phenomenon of concentration of ownership of mass media entities in fewer hands.[19] Though the media will follow its own agenda and its interests, which are

---

[17] *See* Anerchiarico and Roberts (1995: 164-70)

[18] Indeed, it should be noted that self-regulation is not just confined to the professions but much government activity is generally self-regulated. This is a significant factor that should be recognized. For example in a police force, the office of internal affairs in the United States and similar bodies in other countries are still normally part of the police department. Many other external bodies such as the General Auditing Office rely on the information that is given to them by the very body they are supposed to monitor, making them rather ineffective in controlling corruption.

[19] Moreover, the role of the media may be transcending further into what Sartori (1994) has called "videopolitics," which can actually increase the chances of populist regimes emerging.

not necessarily aligned with social welfare, it is a critical factor in unveiling and airing scandals that frequently may have been completely ignored, particularly in countries with poor judicial systems (*see* Diamond, Hartlyn, and Linz 1999: 57-58). Particularly in weaker democracies, when there is a sentiment that corruption is not being sufficiently addressed, the media function in the role of surrogate courts, which can impose sanctions on those that would otherwise have gone unpunished, but also inevitably leads to others being accused of wrongdoing without any semblance of due process in their defense (O' Donnell 1999: 30). The mass media can significantly contribute to both the evolution and maintenance of democracy under the conditions that it is "autonomous, pluralistic, vigorous, and democratic in editorial orientation" (Diamond, Hartlyn, and Linz 1999: 57-58).

Economic crises are further advanced as an opportunity for advancing anti-corruption related reforms. It is contended that they can have the effect of providing the necessary shock to shift countries out of their normal equilibrium structures, put pressure on politicians to change policies and practices and temporarily destabilize interest groups and other parties that can veto reform (*see* Haggard, Lafay and Morrisson 1995). Furthermore, in times of economic crises distributive conflicts may be temporarily muted. But, this is an unnecessarily unbalanced perspective on the possibilities of (perceived) economic crises initiating reform. Crises, are a potential threat to political stability, and are one of the most common dangers to democratic stability (*see* Diamond, Hartlyn, and Linz 1999: 37). Economic crises frequently occur for reasons other than corruption, but where the public fisc and numerous macro-economic factors are considered to have been influenced by corruption, patronage etc., there is an opportunity for broad-based anti-corruption reforms (Rose-Ackerman 1999: 212). In general crises remain undesirable. It is in those socieities where corruption scandals do not lead to crises that one can say that practices of responsible government are consolidated!

Instead of the media bringing about increased transparency by making politics more visible, what we witness, he argues, under the semblance of visibility, "is largely a display of petty appearances that cover up the substance and leave the issues in greater darkness than ever... [P]opular, direct election of presidents provides no safeguards and no buffers against a disastrous election (mis- election) of the *primus solus*- and this will be ever more the case" (Sartori 1994: 114).

IV. Concluding Comments: The Affects of Recent Ideological Shifts towards Democracy and Globalization

> "In any age and social climate, there are some sweeping beliefs that seem to command respect as a kind of general rule- like a "default" setting in a computer program; they are considered right *unless* their claim is somehow precisely negated. While democracy is not yet universally accepted, in the general climate of world opinion, democratic governance has now achieved the status of being taken to be generally right. The ball is very much in the court of those who want to rubbish democracy to provide justification for that rejection. This is a historic change from not very long ago, when the advocates of democracy for Asia or Africa had to argue for democracy with their backs to the wall" (Sen 1999: 5).

When reflecting on political will and political feasibility, it would be imprudent not to make reference to the unique shift in ideological setting that has swept our recent age and social mood. There has been a significant concurrence in the nature of political and economic institutions fostered by the end of broader ideological cleavages.[20] Systems of democratic governance, whilst still not globally practiced are nevertheless widely regarded to be generally right (Sen 1999). Advanced economies are being closely watched as they further embrace liberal democratic political institutions and market-oriented reforms, opening up their doors to the "global capitalist division of labor" (Fukuyama 1995: 3). The nature and momentum of changes it has been suggested constitutes the "end of history" (Fukuyama 1992).[21]

Indeed, it would be naive to suggest that globalization and pressures associated with "democratic" reforms have not opened up some new opportunities for corruption. For example, open boarders can allow the profits from contraband and organized crime to make their way across international lines, and countries strategically capitalizing on such funds, particularly by providing banking havens, may make criminal activity less risky. But there are some very significant positive

---

[20] Furthermore, with the fall of the last great ideological enemy, accompanied by the realization that the military is incapable of governing in an era of global markets and global integration support for military intervention particularly in Latin America (by both the United States and by key societal actors) has shrunk considerably- witnessing a shrinkage in the role of the military and greater demand for democratic governance (Diamond, Hartlyn and Linz 1999: 22). Moreover, with globalization, countries have to be more aware of investor confidence which serves as an additional check on high level corruption and old-fashioned military coups (*ibid.* : 64-65)

[21] Fukuyama (1992) refers to history in the Marx-Hegelian sense of the word as an evolution of human societies towards a final goal.

factors associated with these developments. Deregulation and opening up markets to outside goods and services potentially reduces corruption, as it dries up the gains that were once enjoyed by firms and industries with monopolistic control of markets, reducing effectively any returns to corruption or rent seeking. As an aside, there are always of course niches to be had, and collusive agreements can still be made, but open markets reduce beyond any doubt the size of the niches available. Another positive factor associated with this trend is the pressure that is imposed by foreign investors and financial institutions to reform judicial and legal systems, particularly to preserve their own property and intellectual property rights as well as contractual agreements. Although there have been mixed results, most notably poor results in Russia and some other Balkan states, and some positive results in Latin America, these pressures remain an important factor that can motivate reforms towards more democratic forms of governance.

Of course introducing institutions of democratic governance is not per se a panacea to solve the cures of endemic corruption as observers of countries that made the shift from authoritarian rule must readily admit. As Diamond, Plattner and Schedler (1999: 1) submit, "now that these polities have reached democratic shores, often after years of intense struggle, they are discovering that they cannot just lean back, relax, and enjoy the democratic sun."

Moreover, with more open economies, come cries for transparency by international investors and domestic actors interested in procuring investor confidence and foreign investment. Blamed for the woes of the Asian crises in the end of the 1990s, increasing transparency and overcoming opaque business practices is seen as the only way forward (*see* Sen 1999). Norms of disclosure have manifested themselves, and in international business and international relations are more taken for granted now than ever before. As Florini (1998: 53) notes, "the world is embracing new standards of conduct, enforced not by surveillance and coercion but by willful disclosure: regulation by revelation." The short-term impact on corruption is difficult to assess and depends on local circumstances, but I would forecast with some confidence that there is great potential in the long-run for such trends to serve as an important factor in mitigating corruption.

CONCLUSIONS

Although some strategies to curb corruption are clearly better than others, given the distinct cultural, historical, political and economic conditions of different societies, there is arguably no list of best or conclusive practices to curb corruption. It would be foolhardy to attempt to restate the extensive list of reform measures and subtleties accompanying each instrument that I have addressed here, or recapitulate the possible costs and benefits accompanying these initiatives. Moreover, reform measures have to be selected according to local conditions. Rather, I shall restate some of the basic messages of this work and take this as an opportunity to put anti-corruption initiatives in the overall context of good governance and economic development.

Corruption is a form of reciprocal, cooperative behavior. The fact that corruption is a form of cooperative behavior is ordinarily overlooked in the literature or mentioned *en passant* and has never been given systematic attention in developing reform proposals. Central factors that potentially increase the likelihood and maintenance of cooperation have never been analyzed in the context of corruption. We have seen that the fact that corruption is a form of cooperative behavior is a mixed blessing. On the one hand, parties need to be able to search for and identify one another, agree on the terms of an agreement and enforce the provisions of the deal without being detected which leaves parties exposed to detection. One can see that in each of these steps, parties must incur substantial risks and there is a significant degree of uncertainty and trust involved. On the other hand, corruption must be understood within the broader perspective of reciprocal rewards and sanctions, often firmly entrenched within regular (legal) social and economic transactions. This factor makes corruption particularly difficult to curb. Reform efforts, for instance, may be seriously distorted when one considers corruption only within the light of explicit agreements. A factor one should not overlook is that corruption may not just be the result of formally agreed upon behavior but actually the result of action as part of reciprocation of patterns of behavior. Employees for example will generally reciprocate the conduct, or codes of behavior of their colleagues, particularly, senior coworkers and no explicit agreement may be necessary. To cope with this I suggested there is a need to think in terms of systems. If one does not think in terms of systems reforms may be ineffective in targeting the source of the problem, or more ominously, reforms may sometimes increase rather than decrease the stability of patterns of corrupt exchanges. Within this web of reciprocities and punishments, there are key conditions that make corruption more likely to manifest itself. For reformers the task is to identify those factors that are most conducive to corruption and to eliminate as many of them as possible, a theme to which must of this work is devoted.

Arising therefrom, it is important for reformers to concentrate on and develop means for removing incentives and opportunities to engage in corruption and turn our attention to potential institutional and structural reforms that shape government activity, and the potential desirability and stability of corrupt exchanges. The changing province of governmental activity in recent years, accompanied by such movements as, for example, decentralization, privatization, contractualization and localization of delivery systems, and further supported by a wave of globalization has shaped the character of governmental institutions and shifted great emphasis to the costs of corruption and the need to rectify governmental malfeasance. But malfeasance is only part of the story. In truth it is difficult to distinguish between poor results induced by either nonfeasance (shirking), malfeasance, ethical laxity or plain erroneous decisions.[1] As a result of this, there are a wide range of instruments aimed at performance generally, that may be used to curb corruption. Addressing corruption may be a pathway to broader public sector reforms, particularly given that maladministration and corruption are frequently heavily intertwined. To wit, as a general principal, what is useful for performance is useful to mitigate corruption. Given, however, that my aim here generally was in developing tools to mitigate corruption and not to increase performance per se, I have only transgressed into those factors I felt were of direct, or substantial importance or relevance for curbing corruption. For some readers, my transgressions may seem excessive, for others I will not have gone far enough.

These factors are part of one larger phenomenon, that must be associated with corruption; its complexity. Corruption does not let itself be neatly entangled from a broader set of variables. Three years ago when I first started to look at the subject, I intended to narrow my analysis down to mechanisms to curb corruption merely within the administration. Any serious study of corruption, however, that confines itself to bureaucratic or administrative mechanisms to curb corruption is seriously limited and flawed in my opinion in its ability to give broader policy advice. For example, it can plausibly be argued that factors such as rules, guidelines and mechanisms to fight corruption are themselves inherently political. Moreover, the fact that so many administrative bodies today display aspects of all three forms of government (legislative, executive and administrative) is a clear indication of how flawed and misplaced separating reforms can be.

---

[1] For example, there is increasing support for the proposition that poor countries perform badly relative to rich countries and fail to catch up as a result of both poor policies and poorly designed institutions (Olson 1996). Adumbrated above, it is sometimes difficult to tell the two reasons apart.

To remove incentives and opportunities for corruption effectively, there is a need to understand how corrupt systems operate. It is important, for instance, to recognize that where there is systematic corruption, the areas of governmental activity may provide a type of coordinating role for parties in corrupt exchanges, as well as commitment devices. For example, a police officer who regularly patrols one area is likely to collect payments from persons during his patrol. Parties interested in procuring favorable treatment know where to find him (solving the coordination problem) and the fact that he will be back again regularly is a form of commitment device. Similar examples, could be given for any area of corruption. The point is this, organizational structures and guidelines provide the loci of payoffs, and that where corruption is systematic, it is not implausible to expect that in some instances legal procedures are used as disciplinary device to supplement informal devices to insure that parties fulfill their side of the bargain. Arising from this, the suggestion I make is that there is a need to get inside a corrupt organization in order to understand the inner-workings of the systems, including the patterns of payoffs, the mechanisms of exchange-including the ability of the parties to sanction- as well as the role and identity of the various actors involved. To receive this information, we need to recruit the assistance of parties with knowledge of corruption. There is a need for an insider view. To reiterate a former point, only by understanding the pattern of illicit reciprocal exchanges and obligations that have developed (within the over picture of legal and illegal reciprocities) can the reformer accurately identify those measures most pertinent to curbing corruption in a given environment.

In order to curb corruption, there may be a need to address social barriers to reform. Some of these obstacles are apparent in well-established democracies and less developed countries alike. Shared problems include a low willingness to pay or support for reforms or laws making them effectively obsolete, and the high cost of enforcing norms against corruption because of the fear of retaliation, but also because of the low number of other persons willing to follow suit. In a similar vein, there may be a collective action problem, where efforts made by one party "to change things" may be subject to the familiar problem of free-riding, or general apathy. These obstacles are especially significant where there has been a long term failure of governments to respect and secure property rights as well as ensure parties honor contractual obligations. These problems are further aggravated where citizens no longer trust government thereby depriving reforms of widespread support. Similarly, in the continued absence of legal and institutional safeguards, there may be a vacuum of interpersonal or reciprocal trust among citizens, with the consequence that citizens forgo mutually beneficial legal exchanges making illegal exchanges relatively more profitable. Societies may have developed alternative ways of "getting things done" that have led to the establishment of relations which may hinder or sabotage reform efforts particularly where loyalties are to members of ones own group, clan etc. Where divisions are very large traditional measures aimed at good governance may become redundant, and public trust in government may not forthcoming as a result of more fundamental cleavages in society.

Similarly, reformers must address legal barriers to reform and particularly the need to clarify duties and close off conduits to curb self-dealing. Despite cultural differences and preferences, there is a need to delineate clear lines of conduct important to check undesirable self-interested behavior. At the forefront of the discussion, reformers in there own specific environment must necessarily address complex questions. One such quandary is related to the distinction between what may be determined as a gift to a public official and what as a bribe. Should all gifts as well as bribes be forbidden? Both are after all a form of reciprocity with only subtle distinctions that may be used to foster good will and favoritism. If a gratuity or gift can be considered as the transferal of a good or something of value without receiving consideration for the transfer, then how can we check for consideration? If all gifts should not be forbidden then where should we draw the demarcation. Should bribery law be intentionally defined broadly, or should one leave more ambiguous types of reciprocity outside of the domain of criminal law, to be regulated by other codes and regulations? It would appear that bribery laws are intentionally not supposed to be "dangerously broad" and to pierce deep into "gray areas" Similarly, are immunity laws in there present composition more a sword or a shield against corruption? The virtues of parliamentary immunity have long been recognized, and have in one form or another embedded themselves in the constitutional framework of established democracies and fledgling democracies alike the world over, but are they subject to abuse by corrupt high level officials? If so, is the cost of this abuse less than the benefit of maintaining the status quo? Ill- or generously-defined, it can present a shield to well-organized collusive arrangements, within the guise of self-regulation. Conflict of interest laws may need to be reexamined.

Well-defined conflict of interest laws are imperative to curbing not just directly undesirable quo pro quo exchanges, but in shaping the relationship between government officials and private sector parties generally, in a effort to mitigate the potential for and appearance of such exchanges. In some form or another, provisions relating to the nature of a public official's relationship with the private sector must extend not just to the period of employment, but to the period before and for some duration thereafter. Moreover, reformers may consider possible distinctions between employment activities of executive officials (and other such agencies) and those of legislative officials. It is imperative that at a minimum certain boundaries between governmental activity and the economy must be delineated. Moreover, the solution to laws governing self-dealing is not to exempt party finance or campaign contributions from the bribery statutes and other regulations but to review the system of campaign and party finance and its propensity to serve as a conduit to undesirable influence and particularly quid pro quo agreements. Restrictions, however, should not reinforce illegality or be ad hoc, inviting violation or noncompliance or the appearance thereof. Well-designed laws clarifying legal obligations to avoid self-dealing are an important first step, but are not sufficient to mitigate malfeasance in office. Decentralizing government structures is currently in vogue, but can only at best be of limited importance in curbing corruption. Institutions of external oversight are essential for the control of corruption, specially high level corruption. There are multiple institutions common to a well-functioning system of governmental control. At the top of this list, one can expect to find the processes of the courts and judiciary, auditing bodies including auditing commissions, appeals tribunals, internal complaints procedures, extensive parliamentary committees and perhaps the ombudsman and other inspectorates. The locus classicus of external or inter-branch oversight based upon the separation of powers among judicial, legislative and executive bodies is, however, no longer indicative of the operative boundaries of state actors, where many organs display more than one of these functions. Supervisory bodies to operate successfully must be fully independent of the bodies they monitor. Certain safeguards need to be made in order to insure independence and functionability is maintained. In particular, judicial officials and officials in independent bodies need to enjoy a certain amount of security in office. For independent organs, tenure should be not too short to prevent rash decisions and abuse of office according to the political whims of the day. It should not be too long, so as to become a cozy nest, that potentially disassociates independent investigators from their function and mandate, embedding them gradually with the administrative and political bodies they is supposed to monitor. Moreover, a clear mandate is important to protect the legitimacy of investigations, and exemptions should be kept to a minimum. Appointment is crucial and selection of persons of proven integrity, who would suffer a substantial reputation loss for any transgressions, is imperative and can signal the credibility of an office. Appointment procedures should be transparent and observable by the public. For independent bodies to function properly, they must be allowed to investigate anonymous complaints. Furthermore, auditing bodies, inspectorates etc. need to be able to operate randomly at their own initiative in order to successfully deter malfeasance. Budget is crucial for the judiciary and independent bodies. An ombudsman's office or independent auditing body, for example, with a small budget is a paper tiger. It does not need to become politicized or corrupt, as it is already ineffectual. Furthermore, as with other mechanisms and pronouncements, such bodies can intentionally serve as a mere signaling device for a government that professes to operate against improbity and malfeasance, cashing in on the appearances such offices present, without actually doing much. To operate successfully, they should be granted multiyear budgets to avoid the political vagaries and witch hunts of the day. Informal institutions such as the office of the ombudsman are no substitution for the courts, but formal and informal institutions together have an important role to play in mitigating malfeasance in office. For example, in the case of the ombudsman given that his formal authority is limited, he is not subject to the same formalities, particularly the same procedural formalities of the courts. It is this accessibility that is his strength and makes a strong ombudsman a significant threat to corrupt networks. Precisely for this reason, however, he may be bombarded by unrelenting political criticism and have to fight for the legitimacy of his own actions.

To understand successful anti-corruption reform initiatives, one should not just be cognizant of the design and structure of such initiatives but one should also be mindful of the incentives of high level official in public office to adopt the incentives. One of the central problems with measures developed to mitigate undesirable discretion and high level corruption is that they can appear to wish away the most central problem by assuming high level officials are willing to constrain their own behavior. Here I transgress into political barriers to reform. At its most basic one must distinguish between political feasability and political will. History teaches us that leadership is fundamental to reform. However, leadership is ill-positioned when it must operate within an environment where the costs of anti-corruption reform measures are exorbitant. History should also teach us that it is wise to sometimes consider corruption a cause rather than an effect of poor governance.

This brings me to a further point I wish to make which refers to the common framework used in developing anti-corruption policy proposals. As a general rule, much analysis of corruption, particularly conducted by economists but also increasingly by political scientists and others, assumes a principal-agent (or principal-supervisor-agent) framework. Even that which does not work within a principal-agent framework often at least implicitly assumes a principal ready to act bona fide; a watchful character that monitors his supervisors and agents and worries about the general nonalignment of their interests for the common good. I hesitate not to suggest that this assumption may be legitimate, and the volume of literature that has developed is testament to the belief in the usefulness of the approach. After all, to whom are these reforms addressed if not to a principal? This assumption is frequently a serious limitation, however, and can lead to erroneous policy proposals and erroneous inferences, particularly in an environment of institutionalized or endemic corruption. Although, clearly many principals are not malevolent and do strive to acquire the technical know-how (forming, indeed, part of the target audience of this work), there are many instances where assuming a principal acting bona fide for the greater good is fanciful. For observers, it is of course a complex exercise to recognize the intent of "would be" reformers, because it is difficult to distinguish between political will and political feasibility.

Further complicating matters is the potential for abuse of each instrument against corruption. This provides a breeding ground for public opinion to manifest the belief that little can be done against perceived high levels of corruption and a platform for cynics to point at the futility of reforms. Reforms that are successful in one country may fail in another because of different political, legal, economic and social conditions, and particularly as a result of the different systems of corruption that have managed to evolve and the resources at their disposal. As with crime in general, the optimal level of corruption in a society is not zero. It is inadvisable for any society to try to eliminate all corruption, because doing so utilizes scarce resources. To wit, it is inefficient to try to reduce the level of corruption beyond the point where the marginal gains from doing so are less than the marginal costs. Some measures however are clearly more effective than others and must, as suggested above, be adapted to local conditions. Given that corruption generally is secretive, often victimless -where parties with information about the activities have incentives to remain silent- commonly involves intermediaries and operates in an ambiguous legal environment within a broader web of legal and illegal reciprocities, it comes as no surprise that enforcement strategies against corruption are especially costly, as are corruption cases expensive and resource-intensive to prosecute. Therefore, more substantial reforms may be necessary that fundamentally reshape the nature, scope and range of governmental activity to tackle the underlying causes of payoffs, as well as institutional reforms to initiate proper systems of checks and balances.

The impact of international aid for the purposes of curbing corruption in poorer countries is ambiguous at best. Shoveling money into environments where corruption is endemic is not conducive to economic development and can assist in financing corrupt actors, making their organization more efficient in plundering from their own population and increasing the aid burden of poorer countries. Aid should not be transferred to assist an existing, ill-functioning system to survive a little longer by replacing lost revenues and providing fodder for corrupt officials. The irony exists, however, that those countries that need international assistance the most are frequently the most corrupt. Even so, lessons learned clearly teach us that political will is imperative for reform. A government that does not signal promise by credibly committing to socially-advantageous reforms by, for example, enforcing basic rules and commitments, going after some corrupt officials and frying some "big fish" is hardly trustworthy. Generally, useful steps with such leadership are scarce. This, however, does not suggest that pockets of political will and support for reforming specific governmental institutions and practices should not be supported. Reform in some areas, such as legal institutions may be more beneficial than others, creating a climate in which the returns to legal, directly productive activities increase. Similarly, fostering human capital and skills necessary for a well-run market economy may bring important returns in the long run to economic development and foster a climate which increases public demands to curb corruption and increase governmental accountability.

Moreover, an important lesson, as our discussion on privatization made clear, is that a weak government cannot expect to curb self-dealing and or support a complex market economy. Initial conditions are important and institutions of governance should precede complex reforms. Another general lesson of privatization was that far from letting bargaining-like forces lead to the development of proficient institutions, those that gain from reforms, as one would rationally expect, commonly aim to prevent institutions from developing if they are incongruous to their own self-interest with staggering long-term effects for economic development.

Another clear link is the relationship between corruption and a market-hostile environment. Opportunities for corruption manifest themselves in a market-unfriendly environment. There are several important regulatory obstacles to earning an honest wage particularly common to poorer countries: these commonly include *inter alia* inefficient laws and regulations governing business operations; an ill-designed, poorly functioning, complex and avarice tax system, and a restrictive, time-consuming system for the acquisition of licenses and permits. The repercussions are costly and numerous. When arbitrary and punitive regulatory obligations are not eliminated, not only are much needed finances denied to a state as in the case of taxes, but business and entrepreneurial activity is conducted off the books and in the black and gray sectors of society, affecting not just relations between business and government but internally fueling agency problems, where many transactions occur out-of-sight from stakeholders and affected parties. Moreover, in a highly market-unfriendly environment opportunities are created for organized crime and others operating in an environment of "endemic distrust". This is crippling for economic development. After making multiple payoffs to government officials, payoffs must then commonly be made to organized crime by businesses in order to continue operations, further taxing productive activities. This is one more example of how anti-corruption efforts need to be seen in lieu of and coordinated with larger reforms, in this case the fight against organized crime.

A long-term goal of reforming a society where corruption is endemic is to achieve a certain amount of compliance with the law, rules and regulations, without ever having to apply them. Voluntary compliance and contingent consent can only be achieved where the government respects its own rules. In a country where the government, for example, does not pay what it owes to businesses that provided it with services, or frequently does not pay the wages it owes to its employees, it should come as no surprise that these companies and persons have little incentive to pay their own taxes and a climate conducive to high levels of probity is not forthcoming. Put succinctly, successful anti-corruption reforms require credible commitment to good government.

Ackerman, Bruce. 1993. "Crediting the Voters: A New Beginning for Campaign Finance," *The American Prospect* 13:71-80.

Ades, Alberto., and Rafael Di Tella. 1995. "Competition and Corruption," *Applied Economics Discussion Paper*, vol. 169, Oxford: Oxford University Press.

Ades, Alberto., and Rafael Di Tella. 1996. "The Causes and Consequences of Corruption: A Review of Recent Empirical Contributions," in Barbara Harris-White and Gordon White eds., *Liberalization and the New Corruption*, IDS Bulletin Vol. 27(2), pp. 6-11.

Akerlof, George. 1970. "The Market for Lemons: Quality Uncertainty and the Market Mechanism," *Quarterly Journal of Economics* 84:488-500.

Akerlof, George A. 1980. "Theory of Social Custom of which Unemployment may be One Consequence," *Quarterly Journal of Economics* 94:749-795.

Alderman, Harold, Sudharshan Canagarajah, and Stephen D. Younger. 1994. "Consequences of Permanent Layoff from the Civil Service: Results from a Survey of Retrenched Workers in Ghana," in David L. Lindauer, and Barbara Nunberg, eds. *Rehabilitating Government – Pay and Employment Reform if Africa*, Washington D.C.: The World Bank, pp. 211-237.

Aman, Alfred C., and William T. Mayton. 1993. *Administrative Law*, St. Paul, Minn: West Publishing Company.

American Bar Association, Final Report on Collateral Consequences of Convictions of Organizations, Feb. 1991.

Anderson, Annelise. 2000. *Political Money: Deregulating American Politics: Selected Writings on Campaign Finance Reform*, Stanford: Hoover Institution Press.

Andreski, Stainslav. 1968. *The African Predicament: A Study in the Pathology of Modernisation*, NY: Atherton.

Andvig, Jens C. 1991. "The Economics of Corruption: A Survey," *Studi Economici* 43:57-94.

Andvig, Jens C. 2001. "Issues of Corruption: A Policy Oriented Survey of Research," Paper Prepared for the Workshop on Honesty and Trust in Post-Socialist Societies at Collegium Budapest, May 25-26, 2001, *available at* http://www.colbud.ho/honesty-trust/andvig/pub01.htm.

Andvig, Jens C., and Karl Ove Moene. 1990. "How Corruption May Corrupt?," *Journal of Economic Behavior and Organization* 13:63-76.

Anechiarico, Frank, and James B. Jacobs. 1996. *The Pursuit of Absolute Integrity*, Chicago and London: The University of Chicago Press.

Arlen, Jennifer. 1994. "The Potentially Perverse Effects of Corporate Criminal Liability," *Journal of Legal Studies* 23:833-867.

Arrow, Kenneth J, Robert H. Mnookin, Lee Ross, Amos Tversky, and Robert Wilson eds. 1995. *Barriers to Conflict Resolution*, NY: W. W. Norton & Company.

Atkinson, Michael M., and Maureen Mancuso. 1992. "Edicts and Etiquette: Regulating Conflict of Interest in Congress and the House of Commons," *Corruption and Reform* 7(1):1-18.

Axelrod, Robert. 1984. *The Evolution of Cooperation*, NY: Basic Books.

Axelrod, Robert. 1986. "An Evolutionary Approach to Norms," *American Political Science Review* 80(4):1095-1111, *reprinted in* Robert Axelrod ed, *The Complexity of Cooperation*, Princeton, New Jersey: Princeton University Press. pp. 45-68.

Ayres, Ian, and John Braithwaite. 1992. *Responsive Regulation – Transcending the Deregulation Debate*, NY: Oxford University Press.

Ayres, Ian, and Jeremy Bulow. 1998. "The Donation Booth: Mandating Donor Anonymity to Disrupt the Market for Political Influence," *Stanford Law Review* 50:837-891.

Ayres, Ian, and Steven D. Levitt. 1998. "Measuring the Positive Externalities from Unobservable Victim Precaution: An Empirical Look at Lojack" *Quarterly Journal of Economics* 113:43-77.

Bac, Mehmet. 1996a. "Corruption and Supervision Costs in Hierarchies," *Journal of Comparative Economics* 22:99-118.

Bac, Mehmet. 1996b. "Corruption, Supervision and the Structure of Hierarchies," *Journal of Law, Economics and Organization* 12:277-298.

Bac, Mehmet. 1998. "The Scope, Timing, and Type of Corruption," *International Review of Law and Economics* 18:101-120.

Baldwin, Robert. 1995. *Rules and Government*, Oxford: Clarendon Press.

Bale, Malcolm, and Tony Dale. 1998. "Public Sector Reform in New Zealand and Its Relavannce to Developing Countries," *The World Bank Research Observer* 13(1):103-21.

Banfield, Edward C. 1975. "Corruption as a Feature of Government Organization," Journal of Law and Economics 18(3):587-605.

Banisar, David. 2001. "Freedom of Information and Access to Government Records Around the World," *available at* http://www.privacyinternational.org/issues/foia.

Bardhan, Pranab. 1997. "Corruption and Development: A Review of the Issues," *Journal of Economic Literature* 35:1320-46.

Bardhan, Pranab, and Dillip Mookherjee. 1999. "Relative Capture of Local and Central Govenments," First Draft, Nov. 1999, *available at* http://globetrotter. berkeley.edu/macarthur/inequality/papers/cap31.pdf.

Barro, Robert J. 1991. "Economic Growth in a Cross-Section of Countries," *Quarterly Journal of Economics* 106:407-44.

Barro, Robert J.. 1996. *Getting it Right: Markets and Choices in a Free Society*, Cambridge, Massachusetts.: MIT Press.

Barzelay, Michael. 2000. New Public Management: A Bibliographical Essay. *International Public Management Journal* 3:229-265.

Basu, Kaushik, Sudipto Bhattacharya, and Ajit Mishra. 1992. "Notes on Bribery and the Control of Corruption," *Journal of Public Economics* 48:349-359.

Baumol, William J. 1990. "Entrepreneurship: Productive, Unproductive and Destructive," *Journal of Political Economy* 98:893-921.

Beale, Sara Sun. 2000. "Comparing the Scope of the Federal Governments Authority to Prosecute Federal Corruption and State and Local Corruption: Some Surprising Conclusions and a Proposal," *Hastings Law Journal* 51:699-722.

Beck, J. Randy. 2000. "The False Claims Act and the English Eradication of Qui Tam Legislation," *North Carolina Law Review* 78:539-642.

Becker, Gary S. 1968. "Crime and Punishment: An Economic Approach," *Journal of Political Economy* 76:169-217.

Becker, Gary S. 1981. "Altruism in the Family and Selfishness in the Market Place," *Economica* 48:1-15.

Becker, Gary S. 1983. "A Theory of Competition among Pressure Groups for Political Influence," *Quarterly Journal of Economics* 98:371-400.

Becker, Gary, and George .J. Stigler. 1974. "Law Enforcement, Malfeasance and the Compensation of Enforcers," *Journal of Legal Studies* 3:1-19.

Bekke, Hans A.G.M, James L. Perry, and Theo A.J. Toonen eds. 1996. *Civil Service Systems in Comparative Perspective*, Bloomington & Indianapolis: Indiana University Press.

Bhagwati, J. 1982. "Directly Unproductive Profit-Seeking (DUP) Activities," *Journal of Political Economy* 90:988-1002.

Biegon, Brandford E. 1996. "Presidential Immunity in Civil Actions: An Analysis based upon Text, History and Blackstone's," *Virginia Law Review* 82:677-719.

Binmore, Ken. 1997. *Just Playing – Game Theory and the Social Contract II*, Cambridge, Massachusetts: The MIT Press.

Bivens, Matt and Jonas Bernstein. 1999. "The Russia you Never Met first published in Russian in Demokratizatziya," *available at* http://www.wayan.net/journal/russia/feb_22.htm.

Black, Bernard S. 2001. "The Legal and Institutional Preconditions for Strong Securities Markets," *UCLA Law Review* 48:781-849.

Black, Bernard S., and Reinier Kraakman. 1996. "A Self-Enforcing Model of Corporate Law," *Harvard Law Review* 109:1911-1981.

Black, Bernard S., Reinier Kraakman, and Anna Tarassova. 2000. "Russian Privatization and Corporate Governance: What Went Wrong?," *Stanford Law Review* 52:1731-1804.

Blomquist, Robert F. 1988. "Rethinking the Citizen as Prosecutor Model of Environmental Enforcement Under the Clean Water Act: Some Overlooked Problems of Outcome-Independent Values," *Georgia Law Review* 22:337-423.

Bös, Dieter. 1993. Privatization in Europe: A Comparison of Approaches," *Oxford Review of Economic Policy* 9(1):95-111.

Bolton, G. and R. Zwick. 1995. Anonymity Versus Punishment in Ultimatum Bargaining. "*Games and Economic Behavior*," 10:95-121.

Bouckaert, Boudewijn. 1997. "Political Corruption," Mimeo. University of Ghent.

Bowles, Roger. 1999. "Corruption," in Boudewijn Bouckaert and Gerrit De Geest, Gerrit eds., *Encyclopedia of Law and Economics, Volume V, The Economics of Crime and Litigation*, No. 8500, Cheltenham: Edward Elgar, pp. 460-491, *available at* http://allserv.rug.ac.be/~gdegeest/8500book.pdf.

Boycko, Maxim, Andrei Shleifer and Robert W. Vishny. 1994. "Voucher Privatization," *Journal of Financial Economics* 35:249-266.

Boylan, Scott P., and Catherine L. Newcombe. 1997. "Parliamentary Immunity: A Comparison Between Established Democracies and Russiaa Crisis of Democratic Legitimacy for Russia," *Journal of International Legal Studies* 3:205-252.

Brada, Josef C. 1996. "Privatization is Transition – Or is it?," *Journal of Economic Perspectives* 10:67-87.

Bradley, A.W. 1998."Parliamentary Privilege and the common law of corruption: *R v. Greenway and Others*," *Public Law* (Autumn) 356-363.

Braguinsky, Serguey. 1999. "Enforcement of Property Rights During the Russian Transition: Problems and Some Approaches to a New Liberal Solution," Journal of Legal Studies 28:515-544.

Braithwaite, Valerie, and Margaret Levi eds. 1998. *Trust and Governance,* New York: Russel Sage.

Breton, Albert. 1995. "Organizational Hierarchies and bureaucracies: An Integrative Essay," *European Journal of Political Economy* 11:411-440.

Brown, George D. 2000. "Putting Watergate Behind Us – Salinas, Sun-Diamond, and Two Views of the Anticorruption Model," *Tulane Law Review* 47:747-813.

Brunetti, Aymo Gregory Kisunko and Beatrice. Weder. 1997. "Institutional Obstacles to Doing Business: Region by Region Results from a Worldwide Survey of the Private Sector Survey." World Bank *available at* http://worldbank.home.by/wbi/governance/ pdf/wps1759.pdf.

Burki, Shahid Javed, Guillermo E. Perry, and William R. Dillinger. 1999. Beyond the Center: Decentralizing the State, Prepublication Conference Edition, Washington, D.C.: The World Bank.

Busch, Heiner and Albrecht Funk. 1995. "Undercover Tactics as an Element of Preventive Crime Fighting in the Federal Republic of Germany," in Fijnaut, Cyrille and Marx, Gary T. ed., *Undercover – Police Surveillance in Comparative Perspective*, The Hague: Kluwer Law International, pp. 55-70.

Burns, John P. 1993. "China's Administrative Reforms for a Market Economy," *Public Administration and Development* 13:345-360.

Buscaglia, Edgardo. 1999. *Judicial Corruption in Developing Countries: Its Causes and Economic Consequences.* Hoover Institution. Essays in Public Policy. Stanford.

Buscaglia, Edgardo. 2001. Paper presented at Workshop in Law and Economics, Hamburg University February 2001.

Buscaglia Edgardo Jr., Maria Dakolias and William Ratliff. 1995. *Judicial Reform in Latin America: A Framework for National Development*, Hoover Institution on War, Stanford University.

Cadot, Oliver. 1987. "Corruption as a Gamble," *Journal of Public Economics* 33:223-244.

Calvo, Guillermo A. 1987. "The Economics of Supervision," in Haig R. Nalbantian ed., *Incentives Cooperation and Risk Sharing – Economic and Psychological Perspectives on Employment Contracts*, Rowman & Littlefield Publishers, pp. 87-103.

Cameron, Samuel. 1988. "The Economics of Crime Deterrence: A Survey of Theory and evidence," *Kyklos* 41:301-23.

Carmichael, H. Lorne, and W. Bentley MacLeod. 1997. "Gift Giving and the Evolution of Cooperation," *International Economic Review* 38(3):485-509.

Carter, Neill and Patricia Greer. "Evaluating Agencies: Next Steps and Performance Indicators," *Public Administration* 71:407-416.

Charap, Joshua and Christian Harm.1999. Institutionalized Corruption and the Kleptocratic State. *IMF Working Paper* WP/99/91.

Chow, Daniel C.K. 1997. "An Analysis of the Political Economy of China's Enterprise Conglomerates: A Study of the Electric Power Industry in China," Law & Policy in International Business 28:383-433.

Chu, C.Y.C. 1990. "Income Tax Evasion with Venal Tax Officials – the Case of Developing Countries," *Public Finance* 45: 392-408.

Cleary, Edward W. ed. 1984. *McCormick on Evidence*, Paul, Minn.: West Publishing Co.

Coase, Ronald H. 1937. "The Nature of the Firm," Economica S.N, pp. 386-405.

Coffee, John C. Jr. 1994. "Introduction," in Gruner, Richard S. 1994. *Corporate Crime and Sentencing*, Charlottesvill, Va, Michie.

Coffee, John C. Jr., Richard Gruner, and Christopher D. 1988/9. "Stone Standards for Organizational Probation: A Proposal to the United States Sentencing Commission" *Whittier Law Review* 10:77-102.

Colazingari, Silvia, and Susan Rose-Ackerman. 1998. "Corruption in a Paternalistic Democracy: Lessons from Italy for Latin America," *Political Science Quarterly* 113(3): 447-479.

Coleman, James S. 1990. *Foundations of Social Theory*. The Belknap Press of Harvard University Press.

Collins, Paul. 1993. "Civil service reform and retraining in transitional economies: strategic issues and options," *Public Administration and Development* 13(4): 323-344.

Cook, Paul, Colin Kirkpatrick and Frederick Nixson (eds.). 1998. *Privatization, Enterprise Development and Economic Reform: Experiences of Developing and Transition Economies*, Cheltenham, UK: Edward Elgar Publishing.

Coolidge, Jacqueline, and Susan Rose-Ackerman. 1997. "High-Level Seeking and Corruption in African Regimes: Theory and Cases," Policy Research Working Paper No. 1780, World Bank, Washington DC *available at* http://www.worldbank.org/wbi/governance/pdf/wps1780.pdf.

Cooter, Robert D. 1996a. "The Rule-of-State Law Versus the Rule-of-Law State: Economic Analysis of the Legal Foundations of Development," Paper Prepared for the World Bank's *Annual Bank Conference on Development Economics* (ABCDE), Washington D.C, April 25 and 26, 1996.

Cooter, Robert D. 1996b. "The Theory of Market Modernization of Law," *International Review of Law and Economics* 16: 141-172.

Cooter, Robert D. 2000. *The Strategic Constitution*, Princeton, NY: Princeton University Press.

Cooter, Robert, and Nuno Garoupa. 2000. "The Virtuous Cycle of Distrust: A Mechanism to Deter Bribes and Other Cooperative Crimes," Berkeley Olin Program in Law & Economics, Working Paper Series Paper 32.

Cooter, Robert, and Tom Ulen. 1999. *Law and Economics*. Reading, Massachusetts. Addison Wesley Longman Publishing.

Corrado, Anthony, and Daniel R. Ortiz. 1997. "Recent Innovations," in Anthony Corrado, Thomas E. Mann, Daniel R. Ortiz, Trevor Potter, and Frank J. Sarauf eds. *Campaign Finance: A Sourcebook*, Washington, FC: Brooking Institutions Press.

Corrado, Anthony Thomas E. Mann, Daniel R. Ortiz, Trevor Potter, and Frank J. Sarauf eds. *Campaign Finance: A Sourcebook*, Washington, FC: Brooking Institutions Press. *Available at* http://www.brook.edu/gs/newcfr/ reform.htm.

Cox, W. Gray. And Mathew McCubbins. 2001. "The Institutional Determinants of Economic Policy Outcomes," in Stephan Haggard and Mathew D. McCubbins eds. *Presidents, Parliaments, and Policy*, Cambridge: Cambridge University Press, Pp. 21-63.

Dakolias, Maria. 1995. "Strategy for Judicial Reform: The Experience of Latin America," *Virginia Journal of International Law* 35:167-231.

Dasgupta, Partha. 1988. "Trust as a Commodity," in Diego Gambetta ed., *Trust: Making and Breaking Cooperative Relations*, NY & Oxford: Basil Blackwell Ltd, pp. 49-72.

Davis, Angela J. 2001. "The American Prosecutor: Independence, Power, and the Threat of Tyranny," *Iowa Law Review* 86:393-465.

Davis, Kenneth C. 1969. *Discretionary Justice: A Preliminary Inquiry*, Urbana: University of Illinois Press.

Davis, Kenneth Culp and Richard J. Pierce .1994. *Administrative Law Treatise*, 3rd ed., Boston: Little Brown.

de Speville, Bertrand. 1997. *Hong Kong Policy Initiatives Against Corruption*, Development Centre of the Organization for Economic Co-Operation and Development.

Della Porta, Donatella, and Alberto Vannucci. 1999. *Corrupt Exchanges: Actors, Resources, and Mechanisms of Political Corruption*, NY: Aldine de Gruyter.

Dia, Mamadou. 1993. "A Governance Approach to Civil Service Reform in Sub-saharan Africa," World Bank Technical Paper No. 225, Washington D.C.

Dia, Mamadou. 1996. *Africa's Management in the 1990s and Beyond – Reconciling Indigenous and Transplanted Institutions*, Washington D.C.: The World Bank.

Diamond, Larry, Marc F. Plattner, and Andreas Schedler. 1999. "Introduction," in Andreas Schedler, Larry Diamond, and Marc F. Plattner eds., *The Self-Restraining State: Power and Accountability in New Democracies*, London: Lynne Rienner Publishers, pp. 1-10.

Diamond, Larry, Jonathan Hartlyn, and Juan J. Linz. 1999. "Introduction: Politics, Society, and Democracy in Latin America," in Larry Diamond, Jonathan Hartlyn, Juan J. Linz, and Seymour Martin Lipset eds., *Democracy in Developing Countries – Latin America*, London: Lynne Rienner Publishers, pp. 1-70.

Diver, Colin S. 1983. "The Optimal Precision of Administrative Rules," Yale Law Journal 93:65-109.

Dixit, Avinash K., and Barry J. Nalebuff . 1993. *Thinking Strategically: The Competitive Edge in Business, Politics and Everyday Life*, NY: Norton.

Dotan, Yoav. 1997. "Should Prosecutorial Discretion Enjoy Special Treatment in Judicial Review? A Comparative Analysis of the Law in England and Israel," *Public Law* (Autumn) 513-531.

Drysch, Thomas. 1993. "The New French System of Political Finance," in Arthur B Gunlicks ed., *Campaign and Party Finance in North America and Western Europe*, Boulder, Colo.: Westview Press, pp. 123-155.

Dubois, Philip L. 1986. "Accountability, Independence, and the Selection of State Judges: The Role of Popular Judicial Elections," *Southwestern Law Journal* 40:31-51.

400

Dye, Kenneth M., and Rick Strapenhurst. 1998. "Pillars of Integrity: The Importance of Supreme Audit Institutions in Curbing Corruption," EDI/World Bank Institute Working Papers.

Ehrlich, Isaac, and Richard A. Posner. 1974. "An Economic Analysis of Legal Rulemaking," *The Journal of Legal Studies* 3:257-280.

Enoch, Charles, Stella, Peter and May Khamis. 1997. "Transparency and Ambiguity in Central Bank Safety Net Operations,"International Monetary Fund Working Paper WP/97/1338-EAWP/97/138.

Evans, P. and J. Rauch. 2000. "Bureaucratic Structure and Bureaucratic Performance in Less Developed Countries," *Journal of Public Economics* 75:49-71.

Federal Election Commission. April 1995. "Administering and Enforcing the FECA," Twenty Year Report in Corrado, Anthony Thomas E. Mann, Daniel R. Ortiz, Trevor Potter, and Frank J. Sarauf eds. *Campaign Finance: A Sourcebook*, Washington, FC: Brooking Institutions Press. *Available at* http://www.brook.edu/gs/newcfr/ reform.htm.

Fehr, Ernst, and Simon Gächter. 1998. "Reciprocity and Economics: The Economic Implications of *Homo Reciprocans*," *European Economic Review* 42:845-859.

Fernandez, Raquel, and Dani Rodrik. 1991. "Resistance to Reform: Status Quo Bias in the Presence of Individual Specific Uncertainty," *American Economic Review* 81: 1146-1155.

Fifth Report of the Committee on Standards in Public Life, Chairman: Lord Neill of Bladen, QC. Standards in Public Life: The Funding of Political Parties in the United Kingdom Appendix I: Survey of Foreign Countries, *available at* http//www.labourint.org/neill/survey.html.

Fijnaut, Cyrille and Gary T. Marx. 1995. *Undercover – Police Surveillance in Comparative Perspective*, The Hague: Kluwer Law International.

Fijnaut, Cryille, and Gary T. Marx. 1995. "Introduction: The Normalization of Undercover Policing in the West; Historical and Contemporary Perspectives," in Fijnaut, Cyrille and Marx, Gary T. ed., *Undercover – Police Surveillance in Comparative Perspective*, The Hague: Kluwer Law International, pp. 1-27.

Fionda, Julia. 1995. *Public Prosecutors and Discretion – A Comparative Study*, Oxford: Clarendon Press.

Fiorentini, G., and S. Peltzman eds. 1995. The Economics of Organized Crime, Cambridge: Cambridge University Press.

Fiorini, Ann M. 1999. "Does the Invisible Hand need a Transparent Glove? The Politics of Transparency," Paper prepared for the Annual World Bank Conference on Development Economics, Washington D.C. April 28-30.

Fischel, Daniel and Alan O. Sykes. 1996. "Corporate Crime," *Journal of Legal Studies* 25:319-350.

Fischer Roger, William Ury with Bruce Patton. 1991. *Getting to Yes*, 2nd Edition, New York: Penguin Books

Fisher, Justin. 2000. Party Finance and Corruption: Britain in *Party Finance and Political Corruption*, St. Martins Press: NY pp. 15-36.

Fisman, Raymond, and Tarun Khanna. 1999. "Is Trust a Historical Residue? Information Flows and Trust Levels," *Journal of Economic Behavior & Organization* 38:79-92.

Fisse, Brent, and John Braithwaite. 1983. *The Impact of Publicity on Corporate Offenders*, Albany: State University of NY Press.

Fisse, Brent, and John Braithwaite. 1993. *Corporations, Crime and Accountability*, Cambridge: Cambridge University Press.

Flanz, Gisbert H. ed. 1998. *Constitutions of the Countries of the World*, New York: Oceana Publications.

Fletcher, George P. 1996. *Basic Concepts of Legal Thought*, New York: Oxford University Press.

Florini, Ann M. 1999. "Does the Invisible Hand Need a Transparent Glove? The Politics of Transparency," Paper Prepared for the Annual World Bank Conference on Development Economics, Washington D.C., April 28-30, 1999.

Fox, Merritt B., and Michael A Heller. 2000. "Corporate Governance Lessons from Russian Enterprise Fiascoes," *New York University Law Review* 75:1720-1780.

Frase, Richard S., and Thomas Weigend. 1995. "German Criminal Justice as a Guide to American Law Reform: Similar Problems, Better Solutions?," *Boston College International and Comparative Law Review* 18:317-360.

Frey, Bruno S. 1992 "Teritum Datur: Pricing, Regulating and Intrinsic Motivation," *Kyklos* 45:161-184.

Frydman, Roman, Cheryl W. Gray, Marek Hessel, and Andrzej Rapaczynski. 1999. "When Does Privatization Work? The Impact of Private Ownership on Corporate Performance In Transition Economies," *Quarterly Journal of Economics* 114:1153-1191.

Fudenberg, Drew , and Jean Tirole. 1996. *Game Theory*, the MIT Press.

Fukuyama, Francis. 1992. *The End of History and the Last Man*, NY: Free Press.

Fukuyama, Francis. 1995. *Trust: The Social Virtues and the Creation of Prosperity*, NY & London: Free Press.

Gächter, Simon, and Ernst Fehr. 1999. "Collective Action as a Social Exchange," *Journal of Economic Behavior & Organization* 39:341-369.

Galtung, Fredrick. 1998. "Criteria for Sustainable Corruption Control," in Mark Robinson ed., *Corruption and Development*, London: Frank Cass, pp. 105-128.

Galtung, Fredrik, and Jeremy Pope. 1999. "The Global Coalition Against Corruption: Evaluating Transparency International," in Andreas Schedler, Larry Diamond, and Marc F. Plattner eds., *The Self-Restraining State: Power and Accountability in New Democracies*, London: Lynne Rienner Publishers, pp. 257-283.

Gambetta, Diego ed. 1988. *Trust: Making and Breaking Cooperative Relations*, NY & Oxford: Basil Blackwell Ltd.

Gambetta, Diego. 1988. "Fragments of an Economic Theory of the Mafia," *Archives Europ'ennes de Sociologie*, XXX (1): 127-45.

Gambetta, Diego. 1993. *The Sicilian Mafia: The Business of Private Protection*, Cambridge, MA: Harvard University Press.

Gambetta, Diego, and Peter Reuter. 1995. "Conspiracy Among the Many: The Mafia in Legitimate Industries," in Gianluca Fiorentini, and Sam Peltzman eds., *The Economics of Organized Crime*, Cambridge: Cambridge University Press, pp. 116-139.

Garret, Geoffrey. 1998. *Partisan Politics in the Global Economy*, Cambridge: Cambridge University Press.

Garoupa, Nuno. 1997. "The Theory of Optimal Law Enforcement," *Journal of Economic Survey* 11:267-295.

Geddes, Barbara. 1991. "A Game-Theoretic Model of Reform in Latin American Democracies," *American Political Science Review* 85(2):371-392.

Geddes, Barbara. 1994. *Politician's Dilemma: Building State Capacity in Latin America*, Berkeley: University of California Press.

Gorta, Angela, and Suzie Forell. 1995. "Layers of Decision: Linking Social Definitions of Corruption and Willingness to Take Action," *Crime, Law & Social Changes* 23:315-343.

Gregory, Peter. 1994. "Dealing with Redundancies in Government Employment in Ghana," in David L. Lindauer, and Barbara Nunberg, eds. *Rehabilitating Government – Pay and Employment Reform if Africa*, Washington D.C.: The World Bank, pp. 195-210.

Gregory, Roy, and Philip Giddings eds. 2000. *International Institue of Administrative Sciences Monographs – Righting Wrongs – The Ombudsman in Six Continents*, Vol. 13, Amsterdam: IOS Press.

Grossman, Herschel. 1991. "A General equilibrium Model of Insurrections," *American Economic Review* 81(4):912-21.

Gruner, Richard S. 1994. *Corporate Crime and Sentencing*, Charlottesvill, Va, Michie.

Güth, Werner, Peter Ockenfels, and Markus Wendel. 1997. "Cooperation Based on Trust – An Experimental Investigation," *Journal of Economic Psychology* 18:15-43.

Güth Werner, Rolf Schmittberger, and Bernd Schwarze. 1982. "An Experimental Analysis of Ultimatum Bargaining," *Journal of Economic Behavior and Organization* 3:367-388.

Gunlicks, Arthur B. ed. 1993. *Campaign and Party Finance in North America and Western Europe*, Boulder, Colo.: Westview Press.

Haggard, Stephan, and Robert R. Kaufman. 2001. "Introduction," in Janos Kornai, Stephan Haggard, and Robert R. Kaufman eds., *Reforming the State – Fiscal and Welfare Reform in Post-Socialist Countries*, Cambridge: Cambridge University Press, pp. 1-22.

Haggard, Stephan, and Mathew D. McCubbins. 2001. "Introduction: Political Institutions and the Determinants of Public Policy," in Stephan Haggard and Mathew D. McCubbins eds. *Presidents, Parliaments, and Policy*, Cambridge: Cambridge University Press, Pp. 1-17.

Haggard, Stephan, Jean-Dominique Lafay, and Christian Morrisson. 1995. "The Political Feasibility of Adjustment in Developing Countries," in Christian Morrisson ed., *Political Feasibility of Adjustment*, Development Centre of the Organisaton for Economic Co-Operation and Development.

Haggard, Stephan, and Steven B. Webb eds. 1994. *Voting for Reform – Democracy, Political Liberalization, and Economic Adjustment*, Oxford: Oxford University Press.

Hansmann, Henry. 1996. *The Ownership of Enterprise*, Cambridge, Mass: The Belknap Press of Harvard University Press.

Harden, Ian. 1992. *The Contracting State*, Buckingham, U.K.: Open University Press.

Hardin, Garrett. 1968. "The Tragedy of the Commons," *Science* 162:1243-1248.

Hardin, Russel. 1999. "Do We Want Trust in Government," in Mark E Warren ed., *Democracy and Trust*, Cambridge: Cambridge University Press, pp. 22-41.

Hardin, Russell. 2001. "Trust," Paper Prepared for the Workshop on Honesty and Trust in Post-Socialist Societies at Collegium Budapest, May 25-26, 2001, *available at* http://www.colbud.ho/honesty-trust/hardin/pub01.htm.

Harsanyi, John. 1969. "Rational choice models of behaviour versus functionalist and conformist theories," *World Politics* 22:513-538.

Harel, Alon, and Uzi Segal. 1998. "Criminal Law and Behavioral Law and Economics: Observations on the Neglected Role of Uncertainty in Deterring Crime," *available at* http://www.law.berkeley.edu/institutes/law_econ/workingpapers/PDFpapers/olinwp99_13.PDF.

Hatry, Harry. 1999. *Performance Measurement: Getting Results*, Washington, DC: Urban Institute Press.

Hauge, Arlid. 2001. Strengthening Capacity for Monitoring and Evaluation in Uganda: A Results Based Management Perspective," ECD Working Paper Series No. 8, January 2001, Washington D.C.: The World Bank.

Hay, Jonathan R., Andrei Shleifer, and Robert Vishny. 1996. "Privatization in Transition Economies: Towards a Theory of Legal Reform," *European Economic Review* 40:559-65.

Heady, Ferrel. 1996. "Configurations and Civil Service Systems," in Bekke, Hans A.G.M, James L. Perry, and Theo A.J. Toonen eds. 1996. *Civil Service Systems in Comparative Perspective*, Bloomington & Indianapolis: Indiana University Press, pp. 207-226.

Hellman, Joel S., Geraint Jones, and Daniel Kaufmann, *Seize the State, Seize the Day: An Empirical Analysis of State Capture and Corruption in Transition*, World Bank Policy Research Paper 2444, September 2000, Washington D.C.: World Bank.

Hendricks, Kenneth, and Robert H. Porter. 1989. Collusion in Auctions," *Annales D'Economie et de Statistique* 15/16: 218-230.

Hepkema, Sietze, and Willem Booysen. 1997. "Bribery and Public Officials: An IBA Survey," *International Business Lawyer*, October 1997, pp. 415-422.

Heymann, Philip B. 1996. "Democracy and Corruption," *Fordham International Law Journal* 20:323-346.

Heymann, Philip B. 2000. "The New Policing," *Fordham Urban Law Journal* 28:407-456.

Hirschleifer, Jack..1982. „Evolutionay Models in Economics and Law: Cooperation Versus Conflict Strategies," *Research in Law and Economics* 4:1-60.

Hirschleifer, Jack. 1995. "Theorizing about Conflict," Working Paper No. 727, Department of Economics, UCLA, February 1995.

Hirschleifer, Jack..1998. "There are Many Evolutionary Pathways to Cooperation," Working Paper No. 778, Department of Economics, UCLA, May 1998.

Hirschleifer, Jack. 2000. "Game-Theoretic Interpretations of Commitment," Working paper No. 799, Department of Economics, University of California, LA.

Hirschman, Albert O. 1970. *Exit, Voice and Loyalty: Responses to Decline in Firms, Organizations and States*, Cambridge, Massachusetts: Harvard University Press.

Hirschman, Albert O. 1992. *Rival Views of Market Society and Other Recent Essays*, Cambridge, MA: Harvard University Press.

Holler, Manfred J. 1993. "Fighting Pollution when Decisions are Strategic," *Public Choice* 76:347-356.

Hood, Christopher .1996. "Exploring Variations in Public Reform of the 1980s,". in Hans AGM Bekke, James L. Perry and Theo A. J. Toonen, eds., *Civil Service Reform in Comparative Perspective*, Bloomingtom Indiana Univ. Press, pp. 268-287.

Horowitz, Donald L. 1985. *Ethnic Groups in Conflict*, Berkeley and Los Angeles: University of California Press.

Horowitz, Donald L. 1992. *A Democratic South Africa: Constitutional Engineering in a Divided Society*, Berkeley: University of California Press.

Huber, Peter. 1984. "Competition, Conglomerates, and the Evolution of Cooperation," *The Yale Law Journal* 93:1147-1172.

Hume, David. 1758. *Essays, Moral, Political and Literary*, republished with a foreword from Eugene F. Miller (Ed.). 1987, Indianapolis, Ind.: Library Fund.

Huntington, Samuel P. 1968. *Political Order in Changing Societies*, New Haven: Yale University Press.

IFAC Public Sector Committee, International Public Sector Guideline 1, "Financial Reporting by Government Business Enterprises," July 1989, *available* at: http://www.ifac.org

IFAC Public Sector Accounting Studies, Study 7, "Performance Reporting by Government Business," January 1996, *available* at: http://www.ifac.org

IFAC Public Sector Accounting Studies, Study 11, "Government Financial Reporting," May 2000, *available* at: http://www.ifac.org

Inglehart, Ronald. 1997. *Modernization and Postmodernization: Cultural, Economic and Political Change in 41 Societies*, Princeton: Princeton University Press.

Inglehart, Ronald. 1999. "Trust, Well-Being and Democracy," in Mark E Warren ed., *Democracy and Trust*, Cambridge: Cambridge University Press, pp. 88-120.

Inman, Robert P., and Daniel L. Rubinfeld. 1999. "Federalism," in Boudewijn Bouckaert and Gerrit De Geest, Gerrit eds., *Encyclopedia of Law and Economics, Volume V, The Economics of Crime and Litigation*, No. 9700, Cheltenham: Edward Elgar, pp. 661-691, *available at* http://allserv.rug.ac.be/~gdegeest/9700book.pdf.

Issacharoff, Samuel, Pamela S. Karlan, and Richard H. Pildses. 2001. *The Law of Democracy – Legal Structure of the Political Process*, Westbury, NY: The Foundation Press.

Jackson, Brooks. 1988. *Honest Graft: Big Money and the American Political Process*, New York : Knopf (Distributed by Random House).

Jagannathan, N. Vijay. 1986. "Corruption, Delivery Systems and Property Rights: Rejoinder," *World Development* 14:127-32.

Jagannathan, N. Vijay. 1988. "Corruption Delivery Systems and Property Rights: Rejoinder," *World Development* 16:1393-1394.

Johnson, Simon, John McMillan, and Christopher Woodruff. 2001. "Courts and Relational Contracts," Paper Prepared for the Workshop on Honesty and Trust in Post-Socialist Societies at Collegium Budapest, May 25-26, 2001, *available at* http://www.colbud.ho/honesty-trust/woodruf/pub01.pdf.

Johnston, Michael. 1996. "The Search for Definitions: The Vitality of Politics and the Issue of Corruption," *International Social Science Journal* 149:321-35.

Johnston, Michael. 1999. "A Brief History of Anticorruption Agencies," in Andreas Schedler, Larry Diamond, and Marc F. Plattner eds., *The Self-Restraining State: Power and Accountability in New Democracies*, London: Lynne Rienner Publishers, pp. 217-226.

Johnston, R.J., and C.J. Pattie. 1993. "Great Britain: Twentieth Century Parties Operating Under Nineteenth Century Regulations," in Arthur B Gunlicks ed., *Campaign and Party Finance in North America and Western Europe*, Boulder, Colo.: Westview Press.

Kahan, Dan M. and Eric A. Posner. 1999. "Shaming White Collar Criminals: A Proposal For Reform of the Federal Sentencing Guidelines," *Journal of Law, Economics and Organization* 42: 365-391.

Kaiser, Bridgette, and Stephen J. Spiegelhalter. 2000. "Federal Criminal Conflict of Interest," *American Criminal Law Review* 37:461-.492.

Kaplow, Louis. 1992. "Rules versus Standards: AM Economic Analysis," *Duke Law Journal* 42:557-623.

Kaplow, Louis. 1999. "General Characteristics of Rules," in Boudewijn Bouckaert and Gerrit De Geest, Gerrit eds., *Encyclopedia of Law and Economics, Volume V, The Economics of Crime and Litigation*, No. 9000, Cheltenham: Edward Elgar, pp. 502-528, *available at* http://allserv.rug.ac.be/~gdegeest/9000book.pdf.

Karpoff, Jonathan M. and Lott, J.R., Jr. 1993. "The Reputational Penalty Firms Bear from Committing Criminal Fraud," Journal of Law and Economics 36(2):757-802.

Kaufman, Daniel. 1998a. Research on Corruption: Critical Empirical Issues in Jain, Arvind K. *The Economics of Corruption*, Mass: Kluwer Academic Publishers, pp. 129-175.

Kaufman, Daniel. 1998b. "Revisiting Anti-Corruption Strategies: Tilt Towards Incentive-Driven Approaches?," in *Corruption and Integrity Improvement Initiatives in Developing Countries*, Chapter 4, United Nations Development Programme/OECD Development Centre, pp. 63-82.

Kaufman, Daniel, A. Kraay and P. Zoido-Lobaton. 1999. "Aggregating Governance Indicators," World Bank Policy Research Working Paper No. 2195, Washingron D.C., The World Bank.

Kaul, Mohan. 1997. "The New Public Administration: Management Innovations in Government," *Public Administration and Development* 17:13-26.

Kelman , Steven. 1990. *Procurement and Public Management: The Fear of Discretion and the Quality of Government Performance*, Washington DC: AEI Press.

Kelman, Steven. 1994. "Deregulating Federal Procurement: Noting to Fear but Discretion Itself?," in John J. DiIulio ed., Deregulating the Public Service: Can Governance Be Improved?, Washington DC: The Brookings Institution, pp. 102-128.

Khan, Mushtaq H. 1998. "Patron-Client Networks and the Economic Effects of Corruption in Asia," in Mark Robinson ed., *Corruption and Development*, London: Frank Cass, pp. 15-49.

Khanna V.S. 1996. "Corporate Criminal Liability: What Purpose does it Serve?," *Harvard Law Review* 109(7):1477-1534.

Khanna V. S. 2000. "Corporate Liability Standards: When Should Corporations be held Criminally Liable," *American Criminal Law Review* 37:1239-1283.

Klemperer, Paul. 1999. "Auction Theory: A Guide to the Literature," *Journal of Economic Surveys* 13(3):227-286.

Klitgaard, Robert. 1988. *Controlling Corruption*, Berkeley, CA: University of California Press.

Klitgaard, Robert. 1996. "National and International Strategies for Reducing Corruption," in OECD Symposium on Good Governance, OECD Working Papers No. 78, OECD: Paris, pp. 37-54.

Klitgaard, Robert, Ronald MacLean-Abaroa, and H. Lindsey Parris. 2000. *Corrupt Cities: A Practical Guide to Cure and Prevention*, Oakland: ICS Press.

Kornhauser, Lewis A. 1982. "An Economic Analysis of the Choice Between Enterprise and Personal Liability for Accidents," *California Law Review* 70:1345-1392.

Kornhauser, Lewis A. 1998. "Fair Division of Settlements: A Comment on Silver and Baker," *Virginia Law Review* 84:1561-1580.

Kovacic, William E. 1996. "Whistleblower Bounty Lawsuits as Monitoring Devices in Government Contracting," Loyola of Las Angeles Law Review 29:1799-1857.

Kovacic, William E. 1998a. "Law, Economics, and the Reinvention of Public Administration: Using Relational Agreements to Reduce the Cost of Procurement Regulation and other Forms of Government Intervention in the Economy," *Administrative Law Review* (Winter) 50:141-156.

Kovacic, William E. 1998b. "The Civil False Claims Act as a Deterrent to Participation in Government Procurement Markets," *Supreme Court Economic Review* 6:201-239.

Kraakman, Reiner H. 1984. "Corporate Liability Strategies and the Costs of Legal Controls," *The Yale Law Journal* 93:857-898.

Kreps, David M. 1990. *A Course in Microeconomic Theory*, Princeton, NY: Princeton University Press.

Kreps, David M. 1997. "The Interaction Between Norms and Economic Incentives: Intrinsic Motivation and Extrinsic Incentives," *American Economic Review Papers and Proceedings* 87:359-364.

Kreps, David M., Paul Milgrom, John Roberts, and Robert Wilson. 1982. "Rational Cooperation in the Finitely Repeated Prisoner's Dilemma," *Journal of Economic Theory* 27:245-252.

Kreps, David M., and Robert. Wilson. 1982. "Sequential Equilibria," *Econometrica* 50(4):863-894.

Kreuger, A. O. 1974. "The Political Economy of the Rent-Seeking Society," *American Economic Review* 64:291-303.

Kulick, Elliot, and Dick Wilson. 1992. *Thailand' Turn: Profile of a New Dragon*, New York: St. Martin's Press.

LaFave, Wayne R., Jerold H. Israel, and Nancy J. King eds. 2001. *Criminal Procedure*, 2nd ed., vol. 4, §13.2-3.

Laffont, Jean-Jacques, and J. Tirole. 1993. *A Theory of Incentives in Procurement and Regulation*, Cambridge: Cambridge Massachusetts: MIT Press.

Lambsdorff, Johann Graf. 2001. "How Precise are Perceived Levels of Corruption," Background Paper to the 2001 Corruption Perceptions Index, Transperancy International (TI) & Göttingen University.

Landes, William M., and Richard A. Posner. 1972. "The Private Enforcement of Law," *Journal of Legal Studies* 4:1-46.

Landes, William M., and Richard A. Posner. 1975. "The Independent Judiciary in an Interest-Group Perspective," *Journal of Law and Economics* 18:875-901.

Langseth, Petter. 1995. "Civil Service Reform in Uganda; Lessons learned from Uganda," *EDI Staff Working Paper*. Washington: EDI, No 95-05

Law Library of Congress. 1991. *Campaign Financing of National Elections in Foreign Countries*, Washington DC: Law Library of Congress.

Lawler, Edward J., Shane R. Thye, and Jeongkoo Yoon. 2000. "Emotion and Group Cohesion in Productive Exchange," *American Journal of Sociology* 106(3):616-657.

Lawyer's Committee for Human Rights (2000) *Building on Quicksand: The Collapse of the World Bank's Judicial Reform Project in Peru*. New York: Lawyers Committee for Human Rights.

Lederman, Eliezer. 1985. "Criminal Law, Perpetrator and Corporation: Rethinking a Complex Triangle," *The Journal of Criminal Law and Criminology* 76(2):285-340.

Leff, Nathaniel H. 1964. "Economic Development through Bureaucratic Corruption," *American Behavioral Scientist*, 8(3):8-14.

Levi, Margaret. 1997. *Consent, Dissent, and Patriotism*, Cambridge UK: Cambridge University Press.

Levi, Margaret. 2001. "A State of Trust," Paper Prepared for the Workshop on Honesty and Trust in Post-Socialist Societies at Collegium Budapest, May 25-26, 2001, *available at* http://www.colbud.ho/honesty-trust/levi/pub01.htm.

Levi, Michael. 1995. "Cover Policing and the Investigation of 'Organized Fraud': The English Experience in International Context," in Marx, Gary T. ed., *Undercover – Police Surveillance in Comparative Perspective*, The Hague: Kluwer Law International, pp. 195-212.

Levin, Mark and Georgy Satarov. 2000. "Corruption and Institutions in Russia," *European Journal of Political Economy* 16:113-132.

Levmore, Saul. 1996. "The Anonymity Tool," *University of Pennsylvania Law Review* 44:2191-2236.

Lieberman, Ira W., and Rogi Veimetra. 1996. "The Rush for State Shares in the "Klondyke" of Wild East Capitalism: Loans-for-Shares Transactions in Russia," *George Washington Journal of International Law and Economics* 29:737-767.

Lijphart, Arend. 1977. *Democracy in Plural Societies – A Comparative Exploration*, New Haven: Yale University Press.

Lijphart, Arend. 1985. Power-Sharing in South Africa University of California Institute of International Studies: Berkeley.

Lijphart, Arend. 1994. "Presidentialism and Majoritarian Democracy: Theoretical Observations," in Juan J. Linz and Arturo Valenzuela eds., *The Failure of Presidential Democracy*, Baltimore and London: The John Hopkins University Press, pp. 91-105.

Lindauer, David L. 1994. "Government Pay and Employment Policies and Economic Performance," in David L. Lindauer, and Barbara Nunberg, eds. *Rehabilitating Government – Pay and Employment Reform if Africa*, Washington D.C.: The World Bank, pp. 17-32.

Lindauer, David L., and Barbara Nunberg, eds. 1994. *Rehabilitating Government – Pay and Employment Reform if Africa*, Washington D.C.: The World Bank.

Linz, Juan J. 1990. "The Perils of Presidentialism," *Journal of Democracy* 1:51-69.

Litwack, John M. 1991. "Legality and Market Reform in Soviet-Type Economies," *Journal of Economic Perspectives* 5(4):77-89.

Livingston, Debra. 1997. "Police Discretion And The Quality Of Life In Public Places: Courts, Communities, And The New Policing" *Columbia Law Review* 97:551-672.

Loveman, Mara. 1998. "High Risk Collective Action: Defending Human Rights in Chile, Uruguay, and Argentina," American Journal of Sociology 104:476-525.

Lowenstein, D.H. 1985. "Political Bribery and the Intermediate Theory of Politics," *UCLA Law Review* 32:784-851.

Lui, Francis T. 1986. "A Dynamic Model of Corruption Deterrence," *Journal of Public Economics* 31:215-236.

MacGregor, John, Stephen Peterson and Claudio Schuftan. 1998. "Downsizing the Civil Service in Developing Countries: The Golden Handshake Option Revisited," *Public Administration and Development* 18:61-76.

MacMullen, R. 1988. *Corruption and the Decline of Rome*, New Haven: Yale University Press.

Mainwaring, Scott. 1999. "The Surprising Resilience of Elected Governments," *The Journal of Democracy* 10(3):101-114.

Mancuso, Maureen. 1993. "The Ethical Attitudes of British MP's: A Typology," *Parliamentary Affairs* 46(2):179-191.

Manion, Melanie.1996. "Corruption by Design: Bribery in Chines Enterprise Licensing," *The Journal of Law, Economics & Organization* 12(1):167-195.

Mann, Thomas E. 1997. The Federal Election Commission: Implementing and Enforcing Federal Campaign Finance Law," in Anthony Corrado, Thomas E. Mann, Daniel R. Ortiz, Trevor Potter, and Frank J. Sarauf eds. *Campaign Finance*, Washington, FC: Brooking Institutions Press.

Manzetti, Luigi. 1999. *Privatization South American Style*, Oxford: Oxford University Press.

Marjit, Sugata, Meenakshi Rajeev, and Diganta Mukherjee. 1997. "Incomplete Information as a Deterrent to Corruption," Discussion Paper No. A-555, Rheinische Friedrich-Wilhelms-Universität Bonn.

Marx, Gary T. 1988. *Undercover – Police Surveillance in American*, Berkeley: University of California Press.

Marx , Gary T. 1995a. "When the Guards Guard Themselves: Undercover Tactics Turned Inward," in Marx, Gary T. ed., *Undercover – Police Surveillance in Comparative Perspective*, The Hague: Kluwer Law International, pp. 213-233.

Marx , Gary T. 1995b. "Undercover: Some Implications for Policy," in Marx, Gary T. ed., *Undercover – Police Surveillance in Comparative Perspective*, The Hague: Kluwer Law International, pp. 313-321.

Marx , Gary T. 1995c. "Undercover in Comparative Perspective: Some Implications for Knowledge and Social Research," in Marx, Gary T. ed., *Undercover – Police Surveillance in Comparative Perspective*, The Hague: Kluwer Law International, pp. 323-337.

Mattei, Ugo. 1998. *Comparative Law and Economics*, Michigan. The University of Michigan Press.

Mauro, Paolo. 1995. "Corruption and Growth," *Quarterly Journal of Economics* 110: 681-712.

Mbaku John M. 1997. Institutions and Reform in Africa - The Public Choice Perspective, Praeger.

McAdams, A. James ed. 1997. *Transitional Justice and the Rule of Law in New Democracies,* Notre Dame, IN: Notre Dame Press.

McAfee, R. Preston, and John McMillan. 1987. "Binding Rings," *The American Economic Review* 82(3):579-599.

McCheseny, F.S. 1987. "Rent Extraction and Rent Regulation in the Economic Theory of Regulation," Journal of Legal Studies 16:101-18.

McKinney, Jerome B, and Lawrence C. Howard. 1998. *Public Administration – Balancing Power and Accountability,* Westport, Connecticut: Praeger.

McMillan, John, and Christopher Woodruff. 1999. "Dispute Resolution without Courts in Vietnam," *Journal of Law, Economics and Organization* 15:637-658.

McSweeney, Dean. 2000. Parties, Corruption and Campaign Finance in America *Party Finance and Political Corruption,* St. Martins Press: NY pp. 37-60.

Megginson, William L., and Jeffry M. Netter. 2001. "From State to Market: A Survey of Empirical Studies on Privatization," *available at* http://papers.ssrn. com/paper.taf?abstract_id=158313.

Messick, Richard E.. 1999. "Judicial Reform and Economic Development: A Survey of the Issues," *The World Bank Research Observer* 14:117-36.

Milgrom, Paul R. 1985. "The Economics of Competitive Bidding: A Selective Survey," in L. Hurwicz, D. Schmeidler, and H. Sonnenschein, eds., *Social Goals and Social Organization: Essays in Memory of Elisha Pazner,* Cambridge: Cambridge University Press.

Milgrom, Paul R. 1987. "Auction Theory," in T. F. Bewley ed., *Advances in Economic Theory: Fifth World Congress,* Cambridge: Cambridge University Press.

Milgrom, Paul R. 1989. "Auctions and Bidding: A Primer," *Journal of Economic Perspectives* 3:3-22.

Milgrom, Paul, and John Roberts. 1992. *Economics, Organization and Management,* Englewood Cliffs, NJ: Prentice Hall.

Miller, William L, Ase B. Grodeland, and Tatyana Y. Koshechkina. 1998. "Are the People Victims or Accomplices?," *Crime, Law & Social Changes* 29:273-310.

Mishler, William, and Richard Rose. 1998. "Trust in Untrustworthy Institutions: Culture and Institutional Performance in Post-Communist Societies," Glasgow: University of Strathclyde Studies in Public Policy No. 310.

Misner, Robert L. 1996. "Recasting Prosecutorial Discretion," *Journal of Criminal Law and Criminology* 86:717-777.

Monjardet, Dominique and Rene Lévy. 1995. "Undercover Policing in France: Elements for Description and Analysis," in Fijnaut, Cyrille and Marx, Gary T. ed., *Undercover – Police Surveillance in Comparative Perspective,* The Hague: Kluwer Law International.

Morris, Gillian S. 1999. "Fragmenting the State: Implications for Accountability for Employment Practices in Public Services," *Public Law* (Spring) 64-83.

Mountfield, Robin. 1997. "Organizational Reform within Government: Accountability and Policy Management," *Public Administration and Development* 17:71-76.

Mueller, Dennis. 1979. *Public Choice,* Cambridge: Cambridge University Press.

Murphy, Kevin M., Andre Shleifer, and Robert W. Vishny. 1991. "The Allocation of Talent: Implications for Growth," *Quarterly Journal of Economics* 15:503-30.

410

Murphy, Kevin M., Andre Shleifer, and Robert W. Vishny. 1993. "Why is Rent Seeking so Costly to Growth?," *American Economic Review Papers and Proceedings* 83:409-420.

Myerson, Roger B. 1993. "Effectiveness of Electoral Systems for Reducing Corruption: A Game-Theoretic Analysis," *Games and Economic Behavior* 5: 118-132.

National Audit Office (NAO). 1999. "Modernising Government", June 1999.

Nassmacher, Karl-Heinz. 1989. "Structure and Impact of public subsidies to political parties in Europe: the examples of Austria, Italy, Sweden and West Germany," Herbert E. Alexander and Joel Friedman eds., *Comparative Political Finance in the 1980s*, Cambridge University Press, pp. 236-263.

Nellis, John. 1999. "Time to Rethink Privatization in Transition Economics," in *International Finance Corporation* (IFC) Discussion Paper No. 38.

Newell, James. 2000. Party Finance and Corruption: Italy *Party Finance and Political Corruption*, St. Martins Press: NY pp. 61-88.

Nolan Committee. 1995. First Report on the Standards of the Committee on Standards in Public Life, Cm 2850.

Nolte, Detlef. 2000. "Ursachen und Folgen mangelnder Rechtssicherheit und hoher Kriminalitätsraten in Latinamerika," *Brennpunkt Latinamerika*, 27 April 2000, 8:70-80.

Noonan, John T. 1984. *Bribes*, Berkeley, CA: University of California Press.

North, Douglas C. 1981. *Structure and Change in Economic History*, NY: Norton.

North, Douglas C. 1990. *Institutions, Institutional Change, and Economic Performance.* Cambridge. U.K: Cambridge University Press.

Nunberg, Barbara. 1994. "Experience with Civil Service Pay and Employment Reform: An Overview," in David L. Lindauer, and Barbara Nunberg, eds. *Rehabilitating Government – Pay and Employment Reform if Africa*, Washington D.C.: The World Bank, pp. 119-159.

Nunberg, Barbara. 1995. "Managing the Civil Service – Reform Lessons from Advanced Industrialized Countries," World Bank Discussion Paper No. 204, Washington D.C., World Bank.

Nunberg, Barbara. 1999. "Rethinking Civil Service Reform," *Prem Notes* 31 (October).

Nunberg, Barbara, and John Nellis. 1995. "Civil Service Reform in the World Bank," World Bank Discussion Paper No. 161, Washington D.C., World Bank.

O' Donnell, Guillermo. 1999. "Horizontal Accountability in New Democracies," in Andreas Schedler, Larry Diamond, and Marc F. Plattner eds., *The Self-Restraining State: Power and Accountability in New Democracies*, London: Lynne Rienner Publishers, pp. 29-51.

Ochs, Jack. 1995. "Coordination Problems," Roth, Alvin E. 1995. "Bargaining Experiments," in John Kagel and Alvin E. Roth eds., *Handbook of Experimental Economics*, Princeton, New Jersey: Princeton University Press, pp.195-251.

Ockenfels, Axel. 1999. *Fairness, Reziprozität und Eigennutz - Ökonomische Theorie und Expermentelle Evidenz*, Mohr:Siebeck.

Offe, Claus. 1999. "How Can We Trust Our Fellow Citizens?," in Mark E Warren ed., *Democracy and Trust*, Cambridge: Cambridge University Press, pp. 42-87.

Oliver, Dawn. 1997. "Regulating the Conduct of MPs. The British Experience of Combating Corruption," *Political Studies* XLV:539-558.

411

Olson, Mancur. 1993. "Dictatorship, Democracy, and Development," *American Political Science Review* 87:567-576.

Olson, Mancur.1996. "Big Bills Left on the Sidewalk: Why Some Nations Are Rich and Others Poor," *Journal of Economic Literature* 10:3-24.

Opp, Karl-Dieter. 1989. "The Economics of Crime and the Sociology of Deviant Behaviour: A Theoretical Confrontation of Basic Propositionsm" *Kyklos* 42:405-430.

Organisation for Economic Co-Operation and Development (OECD). 1999. *Public Sector Corruption – An International Survey of Prevention Measures*, Paris.

Ornstein, Mann, Taylor, Malbin and Corrado, "Reforming Campaign Finance" in Anthony Corrado, Thomas E. Mann, Daniel R. Ortiz, Trevor Potter, and Frank J. Sarauf eds. *Campaign Finance Reform: A Sourcebook*, pp. 379-384, *available at* http://www.brook.edu/gs/newcfr/ reform.htm.

Ortiz, Daniel R. 1997. "The Reform Debate: Politics and the First Amendment", in Anthony Corrado, Thomas E. Mann, Daniel R. Ortiz, Trevor Potter, and Frank J. Sarauf eds. *Campaign Finance*, Washington, FC: Brooking Institutions Press. *Available at* http://www.brook.edu/gs/newcfr/ reform.htm.

Osterfeld D. 1992. *Prosperity Versus Planning - How Government Stifles Economic Growth*. N.Y, Oxford.

Ostrom, Elinor. 1998. "A Behavioral Approach to the Rational Choice Theory of Collective Action Presidential Address, *American Political Science Association 1997*," *American Political Science Review* 92(1):1-22.

Ott, Claus and Hans-Bernd Schäfer. 1993. "Emergence and Construction of Efficient Rules in Legal System of German Civil Law," *International Review of Law and Economics* 13:285-302.

Panther, Stephan M. 1995. "The Economics of Crime and Criminal Law: An Antithesis to Sociological Theories?," Journal of Law and Economics 2:365-378.

Philp, Mark. 1997. "Defining Political Corruption," *Political Studies*, XLV (3), Special Issue:417-35.

Pearce, Dennis. 2000. "Ombudsman in Australia," in Philip Giddings and Roy Gregory eds., *International Institue of Administrative Sciences Monographs – Righting Wrongs – The Ombudsman in Six Continents*, Vol. 13, Amsterdam: IOS Press.

Polinsky, A. Mitchell., and Steven Shavell. 1993. "Should employees be subject to fines and imprisonment given the Existence of Corporate Liability," *International Review of Law and Economics* 13(3): 239-257.

Polinsky, A. Mitchell, and Steven Shavell. 1999. "Corruption and Optimal Law Enforcement," National Bureau of Economic Research (NBER) Working Paper No. 6945, *available at* http://www.nber.org/papers/w6945.

Pollitt, Christopher, and Hilkka Summa. 1997. "Comparative and International Administration – Reflexive Watchdogs? How Supreme Audit Insitutions Account for Themselves," *Public Administration* 75:313-336.

Pope, Jeremy, ed. 1996. *National Integrity Systems: The TI Source Book*, Berlin: Transparency International.

Popper, Karl Raimund. 1966. *The Open Society and its Enemies,* Princeton N.J.: Princeton University Press.

Porter, Robert H., and J. Douglas Zona. 1993. "Detection of Bid Rigging in Procurement Auctions," *Journal of Political Economy* 101(3):518-538.

412

Posner, Eric A. 2000. *Law and Social Norms*, Cambridge, Mass: Harvard University Press.

Posner, Richard. 1975. "The Social Costs of Monopoly and Regulations," *Journal of Political Economy* 83:807-827.

Posner, Richard. 1998. "Creating a Legal Framework for Economic Development," *The World Bank Research Observer* 13:1-13.

Posner, Richard A., and Eric B. Rasmusen. 1999. "Creating and Enforcing Norms, with Special Reference to Sanctions," *International Review of Law and Economics* 19:369-382.

Potter, Trevor. 1997. "Where Are We Now? The Current State of Campaign Finance Law," in Anthony Corrado, Thomas E. Mann, Daniel R. Ortiz, Trevor Potter, and Frank J. Sarauf eds. *Campaign Finance: A Sourcebook*, Washington, FC: Brooking Institutions Press, pp. 5-24, *available at* http://www.brook.edu/gs/newcfr/ reform.htm.

Premchand, A. 1993. Public Expenditure Management, Washington DC: International Monetary Fund.

Prezworski, Adam. 1995. *Sustainable Democracy*, Cambridge: Cambridge University Press.

Pritzl, R.F.J and Schneider F. 1996. "*Korruption,*" Working Paper (Arbeitspapier): 9703. University of Bonn.

Propper, Eugene M. 2000. *Corporate Fraud Investigations and Compliance Programs.* Ocean Publications: NY.

Putnam, Robert. 1993. *Making Democracy Work*, Princeton, NJ: Princeton University Press.

Putnam, Robert. 2000. *Bowling Alone: The Collapse and Revival of American Community*, NY: Simon and Schuster.

Quah, Jon S.T. 1999. "Combating Corruption in South Korea and Thailand" in Andreas Schedler, Larry Diamond, and Marc F. Plattner eds., *The Self-Restraining State: Power and Accountability in New Democracies*, London: Lynne Rienner Publishers, pp. 245-256.

Raiser, Martin. 2001. "Trust and Business Networks in Transition," Paper Prepared for the Workshop on Honesty and Trust in Post-Socialist Societies at Collegium Budapest, May 25-26, 2001.

Ramseyer, J. Mark.1994. "The Puzzling Independence of the Courts: A Comparative Approach," *Journal of Legal Studies* 23:721-747.

Rasmusen, Eric, and J. Mark Ramseyer. 1994. "Cheap Bribes and the Corruption Ban: A Coordination Game among Rational Legislators," *Public Choice* 78:305-27.

Richman, Daniel C. 1995. "Cooperating Clients," *Ohio State Law Journal* 56:69-151.

Ridgeway, Cecilia L., and Kristan Glasgow Erickson. 2000. "Creating the Spreading Status Beliefs," *American Journal of Sociology* 106(3):579-615.

Riker, William. 1964. *Federalism: Origins, Operation, Significance*, Boston: Little Brown & Co.

Roberts, Alasdair S. 2000. "Less Government, More Secrecy: Reinvention and the Weakening of Freedom of Information Law," *Public Administration Review* 60(4):308-320.

Robinson, Mark. 1998. "Corruption and Development: An Introduction," in Mark Robinson ed., *Corruption and Development*, London: Frank Cass, pp. 1-14.

413

Roe, Mark J. 1998. "Backlash," *Columbia Law School* 98:217-241.

Rose, Richard. 1998. *Getting Things Done in an Anti-Modern Society*, Glasgow: University of Strathclyde.

Rose-Ackerman, Susan. 1975. "The Economics of Corruption," *Journal of Public Economics* 4:187-203.

Rose-Ackerman, Susan. 1978. *Corruption: A Study in Political Economy*, NY: Academic Press.

Rose-Ackerman, Susan. 1986. "Reforming Public Bureaucracy through Economic Incentives?," *Journal of Law, Economics, and Organization* 2:131-161.

Rose-Ackerman, Susan. 1992. *Rethinking the Progressive Agenda – The Reform of the American Regulatory State*, NY: The Free Press.

Rose-Ackerman, Susan. 1995. Controlling Environmental Policy: The Limits of Public Law in the United States and Germany, New Haven: Yale University Press.

Rose-Ackerman, Susan. 1999. *Corruption and Government – Causes, Consequences, and Reform*, Cambridge: Cambridge University Press.

Rose-Ackerman, Susan. 2001. "Trust, Honesty and Corruption: Theories and Survey Evidence from Post-Socialist Societies," Prepared for the Workshop on Honesty and Trust in Post-Socialist Societies at Collegium Budapest, May 25-26, 2001. Draft of April 24, 2001, *available at* http://www.colbud.ho/honesty-trust/rose/pub01.htm.

Rosenn, Keith S. 1997. Judicial Reform in Brazil. *NAFTA: Law and Business Review of the Americas.*

Ross, Lee. 1995. "Reactive Devaluation in Negotiation and Conflict Resolution," in Kenneth J. Arrow et al. eds., *Barriers to Conflict Resolution*, NY: W. W. Norton & Company, pp. 27-42.

Roth, Alvin E. 1995. "Introduction to Experimental Economics," in Roth, Alvin E. 1995. "Bargaining Experiments," in John Kagel and Alvin E. Roth eds., *Handbook of Experimental Economics*, Princeton, New Jersey: Princeton University Press, pp. 3-109.

Roth, Alvin E. 1995. "Bargaining Experiments," in John Kagel and Alvin E. Roth eds., *Handbook of Experimental Economics*, Princeton, New Jersey: Princeton University Press.

Rothstein, Bo. 2001. "Trust, Social Dilemmas and Collective Memories," Paper Prepared for the Workshop on Honesty and Trust in Post-Socialist Societies at Collegium Budapest, May 25-26, 2001, *available at* http://www.colbud.hu/honesty-trust/rothstein/pub01.htm.

Rowley, Charles K. 2000. "Political Culture and Economic Performance in Sub-Saharan Africa," *European Journal of Political Economy* 16:133-158.

Rubinfeld, Daniel L. 1997. "On Federalism and Economic Development," *Virginia Law Review* 83:1581-1592.

Rubinfeld, Daniel L. and Jonathan B. Baker. 1999. "Empirical Methods in Antitrust: Review and Critique," *American Law and Economics Review*, Fall, 386-435.

Saalfeld, Thomas. 2000. Courts and Parties: Evolution and Problems of Political Funding in Germany *Party Finance and Political Corruption*, St. Martins Press: NY pp. 89-122.

Sachs, Jeffrey D. 1992. "Accelerating Privatization in Eastern Europe: The Case of Poland," *New Europe Law Review* 1:71-88.

414

Sah, Raaj K. 1991. "Social Osmosis and Patterns of Crime," *Journal of Political Economy* 99:1272-1295.

Sakwa, Richard. 2000. Russia: from a Corrupt System to a System with Corruption? *Party Finance and Political Corruption*, St. Martins Press: NY pp. 123-162.

Sappington, David E. M. and Joseph E. Stiglitz. 1987. "Privatization, Information and Incentives," *Journal of Policy Analysis and Management* 6:567-582.

Sartori, Giovanni. 1994. "Neither Presidentialism nor Parliamentarism," in Juan J. Linz and Arturo Valenzuela eds., *The Failure of Presidential Democracy*, Baltimore and London: The John Hopkins University Press, pp. 106-118.

Scalia, Antonin. 1983. "The Doctrine of Standing as an Essential Element of the Separation of Powers," *Suffolk University Law Review* 17:881-914.

Schäfer, Hans-Bernd. 1998. "The Significance of a Well-Functioning Civil Law in the Development Process," Paper Presented at the Latin American Law and Economics Association in Quito (Ecuador), June 15th to June 17th 1998.

Schäfer, Hans-Bernd. 2000. "Enforcement of Contracts," Deutsche Stifung für internationale Entwicklung, Villa Borsig Workshop Series: The Institutional Foundations of a Market Economy *available at* http://www.dse.de/ ef/instn/schaefer.htm.

Schäfer, Hans-Bernd and Claus Ott. 2000. *Lehrbuch der ökonomischen Analyse des Zivilrechts*, Springer Verlag.

Schelling, Thomas C. 1971. "What is the Business of Organized Crime?," *Journal of Public Law* 20:71-84.

Schelling, Thomas C. 1975. "A Process of Residential Segregation: Neighborhood Tipping," in Bruce A. Ackerman ed., Economic Foundations of Property Law, Boston: Little, Brown and Company.

Schick, Allen. "Why most Developing Countries should not try New Zealand Reforms," *The World Bank Research Observer* 13(1):123-31.

Scholtz, John T. 1998. "Trust, Taxes, and Compliance," in Valerie Braithwaite and Margaret Levi eds., *Trust and Governance*, New York: Russel Sage, pp. 135-166.

Schreiber, Amanda J. 2001. "Dealing with the Devil: An Examination of the FBI's Troubled Relationship with its Confidential Information," *Columbia Journal of Law and Social Problems* 34:301-368.

Schwartz, Herman. 1999a. "A Brief History of Judicial Review," in Andreas Schedler, Larry Diamond, and Marc F. Plattner eds., *The Self-Restraining State: Power and Accountability in New Democracies*, London: Lynne Rienner Publishers, pp. 145-150.

Schwartz, Herman. 1999b. "Surprising Success: The New Eastern European Constitutional Courts," in Andreas Schedler, Larry Diamond, and Marc F. Plattner eds., *The Self-Restraining State: Power and Accountability in New Democracies*, London: Lynne Rienner Publishers, pp. 195-215.

Second Report of the Committee on Standards in Public Life, Local Public Spending Bodies. 1996. Cm. 3270.

Selten, Reinard and Rolf Stöcker. 1989. "End Behavior in Sequences of Finite Prisoner's Dilemma Supergames: A Learning Theory Approach," *Journal of Economic Behavior and Organization* 7:47-70.

Sen, Amartya. 1981. "Ingredients of Famine Analysis: Availability and Entitlements," *Quarterly Journal of Economics* 96(3):433-64.

Sen, Amartya. 1999. "Democracy as a Universal Value," *Journal of Democracy* 10(3): 3-17.

Sharkansky, Ira. 1988. "Israeli's Auditor as Policy-Maker," *Public Administration* 66:77-89.

Sheldon, D.R., and E.F. McNamara. 1991. *Value-For-Money Auditing in the Public Sector – Strategies for Accountability in the 1990s*, Altamonte Springs, Florida: The Institute of Internal Auditors Research Foundation.

Shelley, Louise. 1995. "Soviet Undercover Work," in Fijnaut, Cyrille and Marx, Gary T. ed., *Undercover – Police Surveillance in Comparative Perspective*, The Hague: Kluwer Law International, pp. 155-174.

Shleifer, Andrei., and Robert W. Vishny. 1993. "Corruption," *Quarterly Journal of Economics* 108(3):599-617.

Shleifer, Andrei., and Robert W. Vishny. 1998. *The Grabbing Hand: Government Pathologies and Their Cures*, Cambridge, Mass: Harvard University Press.

Sorauf, Frank J. 2000. "If It's Not Broken ... Or Is It," in Anderson, Annelise. 2000. *Political Money: Deregulating American Politics: Selected Writings on Campaign Finance Reform*, Stanford: Hoover Institution Press, pp. 3-35.

Spence, David B. 2001. "The Shadow of the Rational Polluter: Rethinking the Role of Rational Actor Models in Environmental Law," *California Law Journal* 89:917-998.

Stark, Andrew. 1997. "Beyond Quid Pro Quo: What's Wrong with Private Gain from Public Office," *American Political Science Review* 91(1):108-120.

Stigler, George. 1970. "The Optimum Enforcement of Laws," *Journal of Political Economy* 78:526-536.

Stiglitz, Joseph E. 1999a. "Whither Reform," prepared for the Annual Bank Conference on Development Economics, Washington, D.C., April 28-30, 1999.

Stiglitz, Joseph E. 1999b. *On Liberty, the Right to Know, and Public Discourse: The Role of Transparency in Public Life*, Oxford, UK: Oxford Amnesty Lecture.

Stapenhurst, Rick and Jack Titsworth. 2001. "Features and Functions of Supreme Audit Institutions," *PREM Notes* – Public Section No. 59, *available at* http://www.worldbank.org/wbi/governance/pdf/premnotes59.pdf.

Sunstein, Cass R. 1992. "What's Standing After Lujan? Of Citizen Suits, "Injuries," and Article III," *Michigan Law Review* 91:163-236.

Sunstein, Cass R. 1995. "Problems with Rules," *California Law Review* 83:953-1023.

Susman, Susan D. 1994. "Distant Voices in the Courts of India. Transformation of Standing in Public Interest Litigation," *Wisconsin International Law Journal* Fall 1994:57-103.

Tanzi, Vito. 1995. "Corruption, Government Activities and Markets," in Fiorentini, G., and S. Peltzman eds. 1995. *The Economics of Organized Crime*, Cambridge: Cambridge University Press, pp. 161-180.

Tanzi, Vito. 1996. "Money Laundering and the International Financial System," IMF Working Paper 96/55. Washington, DC: International Monetary Fund.

Tanzi, Vito. 1998. Corruption and the Budget: Problems and Solutions in Jain, Arvind K. *The Economics of Corruption*, Mass: Kluwer Academic Publishers, pp.111-128.

Tanzi, Vito. 2000. "The Role of the State and the Quality of the Public Sector," IMF Working Paper 00/36. Washington, DC: International Monetary Fund.

Tanzi, Vito. 2001. "Creating Effective Tax Administrations: The Experience of Russia and Georgia," in Janos Kornai, Stephan Haggard, and Robert R. Kaufman eds., *Reforming the State – Fiscal and Welfare Reform in Post-Socialist Countries,* Cambridge: Cambridge University Press, pp. 53-74.

Thompson, Barton H. 2000. "The Continuing Innovation of Citizen Enforcement," *University of Illinois Law Review* pp. 185-236.

Tiebout, Charles. 1956. "A Pure Theory of Local Expenditures," *Journal of Political Economy* 64:416-424.

Tirole, Jean. 1986. "Hierarchies and Bureaucracies: On the Role of Collusion in Organizations," *Journal of Law, Economics, and Organization* 2:181-214.

Tirole, Jean. 1988. *The Theory of Industrial Organization,* Cambridge, Massachusetts: MIT Press.

Tirole, Jean. 1992. "Collusion and the Theory of Organizations," in Jean-Jacques. Laffont ed., *Advances in Economic Theory: Sixths World Congress,* Vol. II, Econometric \Society Monographs, No. 21, Cambridge: Cambridge University Press, pp. 151-206.

Tirole, Jean. 1994. "The Internal Organization of Government," *Oxford Economic Papers* 46: 1-29.

Transparency International. 1998. *Combating Corruption: Are Lasting Solutions Emerging?,* Berling: TI Annual Report.

Tsebelis, George. 1990. "Penalty has No Impact on Crime: A Game-Theoretic Analysis" *Rationality and Society* 2(3)255-286.

Tsebelis, George. 1993. "Penalty and Crime: Further Theoretical Considerations and Empirical Evidence," *Journal of Theoretical Politics* 5(3):349-374.

Tsebelis, George. 1995. "Decision Making in Political Systems: Veto Players in Presidentialism, Parliamentarism, Multicameralism and Multipartyism," *British Journal of Political Science* 25:289-325.

Tullock, Gordon. 1999. "Non-Prisoner's Dilemma," *Journal of Economic Behavior & Organization* 39:455-458.

van Lange, Paul A. M., Wim B. G. Liebrand, David M. Messick, and Henk A. M. Wilke. 1992. "Introduction and Literature Review," in Wim B. G. Liebrand, David M. Messick, and Henk A. M. Wilke eds., *Social Dilemmas: Theoretical Issues and Research Findings,* GB: BPCC Wheatons Ltd, pp. 3-28.

van Rijkeghem, C., and B. Weder 1997. "Corruption and the Rate of Temptation: Do Low Wages in the Civil Service Cause Corruption?," IMF Discussion Paper No. 97/93.

Vaughn, Robert G. 1993. "Proposals for Judicial Reform in Chile," *Fordham International Law Journal* 16:577-607.

Verheijen, Tony. 1998. "Public Management Reform in New Zealand and Australia," in Tony Verheijen, and David Coombes eds., *Innovations in Public Management – Perspectives from East and West Europe,* Cheltenham, UK: Edward Elgar, pp. 255-281.

Verkuil, Paul R. 1988. "The Purposes and Limits of Independent Agencies," *Duke Law Journal* April/June 1988, pp. 257-279.

Vincent-Jones, Peter. The Regulation of Quasi-markets for Public Services. 1999. *Public Law* (Summer) 304-327.

von Arnim, Hans Herbert. 1993. "Campaign and Party Finance in Germany," translated by Arthur B. Gunlicks in Arthur B. Gunlicks ed., *Campaign and Party Finance in North America and Western Europe* Boulder, Colo.: Westview Press.

von Arnim, Hans Herbert. 1996. *Die Partei, der Abgeordnete und das Geld – Parteienfinanzierung in Deutschland*, München: Knaur.

von Beyne, Karl. 1985. *Political Parties in Western Democracies*, Aldershot: Gower.

von Furstenberg, George M. 2001a. "Hopes and Delusions of Transparency," *North American Journal of Economics and Finance* 12:105-120, *available at* http://www.bnet.fordham.edu/public/finance/vonfurstenberg/busmag3.pdf.

von Furstenberg, George M. 2001b. "Transparentising the Global Money Business: Glasnost or Just Another Wild Card at Play?," Mimeo, *available at* http://www.php.indiana.edu/~vonfurst/6vfo111.pdf

von Wangenheim, Georg. "Production of Legal Rules by Agencies and Bureaucracies," in Boudewijn Bouckaert and Gerrit De Geest, Gerrit eds., *Encyclopedia of Law and Economics, Volume V, The Economics of Crime and Litigation*, No. 9300, Cheltenham: Edward Elgar, pp. 559-586, *available at* http://allserv.rug.ac.be/~gdegeest/9300book.pdf.

Vorenberg, James. 1981. "Decent Restraint of Prosecutorial Power," *Harvard Law Review* 94:1521-1573.

Wade, Robert. 1985. "The Market for Public Office: Why the Indian State is not Better at Development," *World Development* 13(4):467-497.

Wade, William and Christopher Forsyth. 1999. *Administrative Law*, Oxford: Oxford University Press.

Warren, Kenneth F. 1996. *Administrative law in the political system*, 3rd ed. NJ: Prentice Hall.

Warren, Mark E ed. 1999. *Democracy and Trust*, Cambridge: Cambridge University Press.

Wei, Shang-Jin. 1997. "How Taxing is Corruption on International Investors?," National Bureau of Economic Research Working Paper 6030, Cambridge MA, May.

Weingast, Barry R.. 1995. "The Economic Role of Political Institutions: Market-Preserving Federalism and Economic Development," *Journal of Law, Economics, and Organization* 11:1-28.

Weingast, Barry R. 1997. "The Political Foundations of Democracy and the Rule of Law," *American Political Science Review* 91(2):245-263.

Weinstein, Ian. 1999. "Regulating the Market for Snitches," Buffalo Law Review 47:563-632.

Weiss, Andrew and Georgiy Nikitin. 1998. "Effects of Ownership by Investment Funds on the Performance of Czeck Firms," Working Paper, Boston: Boston University.

White, Fidelma, and Kathryn Hollingsworth. 1999. *Audit, Accountability and Government*, Oxford: Clarendon Press.

Williams, Lesley E. 1999. "The Civil Regulation of Prosecutors," *Fordham Law Review* 67:3441-3480.

Williams, Robert J. 1976. "The Problem of Corruption: A Conceptual and Comparative Analysis," *PAC Bulletin* 22:41-53.

Williams, Robert ed. 2000. *Party Finance and Political Corruption*, St. Martins Press: NY.

Williamson, Oliver E. 1985. *The Economic Institutions of Capitalism*, NY: Free Press.

World Bank. 2001. World Development Report (WDR) 2000/2001: Attacking Poverty. International Bank for Reconstruction and Development and Oxford University Press.

World Bank. 2002. Initiatives in Legal and Judicial Reform. Legal Vice Presidency, The World Bank, *available at* http://www4.worldbank.org/legal/publications /initiatives -final.pdf

World Bank. Administrative & Civil Service Reform *available at* http://www1. worldbank.org/publicsector/civilservice/index.html.

World Development Report. 1997. The State in a Changing World, Oxford University Press.

Worthington, Margaret M., and Louis P. Goldsman. 1998. *Contracting with the Federal Government*, NY: John Wiley & Sons, Inc.

Yamagishi, Toshio. 1992. "Group Size and the Provision of a Sanctioning System in a Social Dilemma," in Wim B. G. Liebrand, David M. Messick, and Henk A. M. Wilke eds., *Social Dilemmas: Theoretical Issues and Research Findings*, GB: BPCC Wheatons Ltd, pp. 267-287.

Yamagishi, Toshio. 2001. "Trust as a Form of Social Intelligence," in Karen Cook, eds., Trust in Society, New York: Russel Sage pp. 121-147.

Ziamou, Theodora. 1999. "New Process Rights for Citizens? The American Tradition and the German Legal Perspective in Procedural Review of Rulemaking," *Public Law* (Winter) pp. 726-742.

Zucker. Lynne G. 1986. "Production of Trust: Institutional Sources of Economic Structure, 1840-1920," *Research in Organizational Behavior* 8:53-111.

Luis Gerardo González Morales

The Economics of Corruption and Bureaucratic Inefficiency in Weak States

Theory and Evidence

Frankfurt/M., Berlin, Bern, Bruxelles, New York, Oxford, Wien, 2003.
134 pp., 5 fig., 4 tab.
Kollektive Entscheidungen, Wirtschaftspolitik und öffentliche Finanzen.
Edited by Cay Folkers. Vol.12
ISBN 3-631-51136-1 / US-ISBN 0-8204-6455-4 · pb. € 25.10*

This monograph surveys recent developments in the political economy literature addressing the incentive problems of political decision making, and helps to understand the causes of corruption and bureaucratic inefficiency in countries that lack a constitutional order. Using a principal-agent theoretical framework, the author shows how corruption and patronage may reduce political instability, thus enabling governments in weak states to provide public goods which would otherwise be missing, even though such an institutional arrangement is usually self-defeating in the long run. The theoretical results are used to offer a stylized interpretation of the political history of the Mexican state.

Contents: Economics and the theory of the state · Political stability and corruption in weak states · Constitutional order and bureaucratic efficency · Dynamic aspects of reelection incentives · A theory of Mexico's political history

Frankfurt/M · Berlin · Bern · Bruxelles · New York · Oxford · Wien
Distribution: Verlag Peter Lang AG
Moosstr. 1, CH-2542 Pieterlen
Telefax 00 41 (0) 32 / 376 17 27

*The €-price includes German tax rate
Prices are subject to change without notice
Homepage http://www.peterlang.de